A Treatise on Dynamics

With examples and exercises

Andrew Gray,

James Gordon Gray

Alpha Editions

This edition published in 2019

ISBN : 9789353976941

Design and Setting By
Alpha Editions
email - alphaedis@gmail.com

As per information held with us this book is in Public Domain.
This book is a reproduction of an important historical work.
Alpha Editions uses the best technology to reproduce historical
work in the same manner it was first published to preserve its
original nature. Any marks or number seen are left intentionally
to preserve its true form.

A TREATISE

ON

DYNAMICS

WITH EXAMPLES AND EXERCISES

BY

ANDREW GRAY, LL.D., F.R.S.
PROFESSOR OF NATURAL PHILOSOPHY IN THE UNIVERSITY OF GLASGOW

AND

JAMES GORDON GRAY, D.Sc.
LECTURER ON PHYSICS IN THE UNIVERSITY OF GLASGOW

MACMILLAN AND CO., LIMITED
ST. MARTIN'S STREET, LONDON

1911

PREFACE.

THIS book has been written to provide a discussion of higher dynamics suitable for students of engineering, physics, or astronomy. To a large extent the examples and exercises have been drawn from practical affairs, and have been chosen more for the sake of illustration of physical principles than for their mathematical interest. With hardly an exception, the exercises given at the end of each chapter have been carefully verified, and it is hoped that but few of them are in error. A large number of examples have been worked out in the various chapters, where practical illustration seemed to be required.

A considerable space is devoted to gyrostats and gyrostatic action, and we have used throughout this chapter, and elsewhere, the method set forth in § 9 of calculating rates of change of directed quantities for a moving system. This method of proceeding occurred to one of us about fifteen years ago [see Gray's *Physics*, Vol. I.], and we have found it very useful in our teaching, as enabling solutions of difficult problems of rotational motion to be readily built up from first principles. The advantage of the method is most apparent in Chapter IX., which is an expansion of an article on Gyrostats and Gyrostatic Action in Machinery communicated to the Institution of Engineers and Shipbuilders in Scotland in 1905. Some elementary accounts of gyrostatic action have appeared during the last two or three years, and it is right to say that we are not indebted to these for our method of treatment.

We have derived assistance from various works, but, as was to be expected, our obligations to Sir George Greenhill's writings are especially great. Besides making additions of the most practical and valuable kind to the science of dynamics, Sir George Greenhill has long advocated the use of units of the sort employed by men to whom a comparison with the force of gravity on a given piece of matter is the most ready means of estimating a force, and protested against the common dynamical limitation of the word *weight*. There can be no doubt that the ordinary use of the word in connection with the buying and selling of commodities "weighed" by a balance can never be got over, and that the connotation of the word in that connection is more frequently that of quantity of matter than that of gravity force. And it is better to take advantage of a common connotation than to do something which may tend to confuse it. Hence we have often used the so-called practical units, but without any sacrifice, for none was required, of the real advantages of the absolute system.

We are under obligations also to Jacobi's *Vorlesungen über Dynamik*, Routh's two treatises, Appell's *Mécanique Rationelle*, Despeyrous' *Mécanique*, and Herr Föppl's *Technische Mechanik*. The aim of the last-named work is similar to our own, and the student will find in it, *e.g.* with regard to compound vibrators of different kinds, some interesting developments of matters which have been treated—though generally in a somewhat different manner —in the present volume.

PREFACE.

The proofs of the first two-thirds of the book have been read with great care by our colleague, Dr. R. A. Houstoun, and Dr. Pinkerton, of Edinburgh, has kindly read the chapter on Gyrostats. We offer our thanks to these gentlemen, and also to the officials and workmen of the Glasgow University Press for their care and attention throughout the printing of the book.

ANDREW GRAY.
JAMES G. GRAY.

CONTENTS.

CHAPTER I.

KINEMATICS OF A MOVING POINT.

Section 1. Speed and Velocity. 2. Varying Motion. 3. Illustrations of Varying Speed. Curve of Speed. 4. Distance traversed at Varying Speed. 5. Uniformly Varying Speed. 6. Graphical Representation of Directed Quantities. Composition and Resolution of Velocities. Relative Velocity. 7. Curve of Velocities—Hodograph. 8. Acceleration. 9. Angular Velocity. Directed Quantities referred to Moving Axes. Rate of Growth of Directed Quantity. 10. Examples of Acceleration. 11. Curvilinear Motion. Radial and Transverse Components. 12. Polar Coordinates in Three Dimensional Space. 13. Radial and Transverse Components of Acceleration. 14. Uniplanar Motion of a Point. Revolving Axes. Components of Velocity and Acceleration. 15. Three-Dimensional Motion. Revolving Axes. 16. Curvilinear Motion in Space of Three Dimensions. Normal and Tangential Accelerations. 17. Curvature of a Path in Space of Three Dimensions. 18. Examples. Motion of Point along a Moving Guide. 19. Tangential Acceleration with Space as Independent Variable. 20. Equation of Hodograph. Case of Falling Body. 21. Motion of Projectile in Uniform Field of Force. 22. Properties of Path. 23. Horizontal Range. Range with Path through Fixed Point. 24. Envelope of all Coplanar Paths with given Speed of Projection. 25. Examples of Parabolic Motion. 26. Motion under Acceleration varying inversely as Square of Distance from Fixed Point. 27. First Integral of Equations of Motion. Equation of Hodograph. 28. Equation of Path. 29. Speed at Different Points of Path. 30. Resolution of Velocity into Two Parts of Constant Amount. Path Deduced from Hodograph. 31. Polar Coordinates: Differential Equation of Path of Particle under Central Acceleration. 32. Simple Harmonic Motion. 33. S.H.M. Velocity and Acceleration. Integral Equation. 34. S.H.M. Amplitude, Period and Phase. 35. A Uniform Circular Motion the Resultant of Two S.H.M.s. 36. Composition of Equal and Opposite Circular Motions gives S.H.M. 37. Composition of Two S.H.M.s in Same Line. 38. Composition of any Number of S.H.M.s in Parallel Lines. Tide-Predicter. 39. Composition of S.H.M.s in One Line but of Different Periods. 40. Composition of S.H.M.s in Perpendicular Lines and of Different Periods. 41. Composition of S.H.Ms.

x					CONTENTS.

in Different Lines but of Equal Period. 42. S.H.M.s in Perpendicular Lines but not of the Same Period. 43. Resisted S.H.M. defined by Equiangular Spiral. 44. Differential Equations of Exponential Motion and S.H.M. Exponential Motion repesented Graphically. [Exercises]
pp. 1-82

CHAPTER II.

DYNAMICAL PRINCIPLES.

Section 45. The Laws of Motion. Momentum and Rate of Change of Momentum (R.C.M.). 46. Effect of Change of Mass on R.C.M. 47. R.C.M. in Curvilinear Motion. Force. 48. Kinetic Energy. R.C.M. as Space-Rate of Variation of K.E. 49. Potential Energy. Equation of Motion for Particle under Central Force derived from Energy. 50. Discussion of First Law of Motion. 51. Second Law of Motion. Example. 52. Meaning of Equations of Motion. 53. Non-Rotational Motion of Extended Body. Systems of Varying Mass. 54. Units of Force. Dimensions. 55. Gravities of Bodies Proportional to their Inertias or Masses. 56. Third Law of Motion. Discussion. 57. Action and Reaction across a Surface of Contact or across an Interface. 58. Action and Reaction between Bodies at a Distance apart. 59. Centre of Mass (or Centroid) of a Body or System. 60. Properties of Centroid. External and Internal Forces. 61. Newton's Law of Equal and Opposite Activities. 62. Theory of Work. Units of Work. 63. Active and Inactive Forces. 64. Constant and Varying Constraints. 65. General Variational Equation of Work. Theory of Energy. 66. Forces as Derivatives of Potential Energy. 67. Work spent in overcoming Friction. Dissipative Forces. 68. Meaning of Solution of a Dynamical Problem. 69. Angular Momentum. Rotational Motion. 70. Components of Angular Momentum (A.M.). 71. Angular Momenta about Parallel Axes. 72. Rate of Change of A.M. 73. Rate of Change of A.M. when Effective Inertia different in Different Directions. 74. Rate of Change of A.M. when Body Gains or Loses Mass. 75. Rates of Change of A.M. equal to Moments of Forces. Independence of Motions of Translation and Rotation. 76. Rigid Body, Rolling Motion of. 77. Examples on A.M. of Bodies of Varying Mass. Energy-Changes. 78. Kinetic Energies of Motions of Translation and Rotation. 79. Couples. Equivalence of Couples. 80. Effective Inertia different in Different Directions. Case of a Ship. 81. Why a Ship carries a Weather Helm. [Exercises]		pp. 83-143

CHAPTER III.

DYNAMICS OF A PARTICLE.

Section 82. Rectilinear Motion of a Particle in Resisting Medium. 83. Limiting Speed in Resisting Medium. 84. Resistance varying as n^{th} Power of Speed. Discussion. 85. Motion under Resistance varying as v. 86. Resistance varying as v^2. 87. Resistance varying as v^3. 88. Examples on Resisted Motion in a Vertical Line. 89. Examples

CONTENTS.   xi

of Rectilinear Motion under Gravity. 90. S.H.M. Motion of a
Simple Pendulum. 91. Motion of a Simple Pendulum in a Finite Arc.
Elliptic Integrals. 92. Motion of a Particle in a Vertical Circle.
Elliptic Functions. 93. Revolution of Particle in Vertical Circle.
94. Examples of Motion in a Vertical Circle. 95. Equilibrium of a
Plummet under Gravity. Apparent and Real Gravity. 96. Plummet
in Railway Carriage. Apparent Gravity. 97. Cycloidal Motion.
Cycloidal Pendulum. 98. Tautochronous Motion. 99. Brachisto-
chrones. 100. Brachistochrone in Conservative Field of Force. Euler's
Theorem. 101. Variational Method for Brachistochrone under Gravity.
102. Variational Method for Brachistochrone in Conservative Field of
Copianar Forces. 103. Brachistochrone in any Field of Force. 104.
Conical Pendulum. 105. Double Pendulum. 106. Double Pendulum.
107. Double Pendulum. Discussion of Cases. 108. Physical Ana-
logues of Double Pendulum. 109. Two Connected Spiral Springs in
Same Vertical. 110. Three or more Connected Springs with Attached
Masses. [Exercises]   pp. 144-205

CHAPTER IV.

RESISTED MOTION OF A PARTICLE IN A UNIFORM
FIELD OF FORCE.

Section 111. Uniform Field. Resistance kv. 112. Resistance kv. Trajec-
tory. 113. Construction of Trajectory. 114. Resisted Motion. Tan-
gential and Normal Resolution. 115. Resistance $= kv^n$. 116. Particular
Cases. Hodograph. Intrinsic Equation of Path. 117. Intrinsic
Equation of Path for Resistance kv^2. 118. Flat Trajectory when
Resistance $= kv^2$. 119. Experimental Laws of Resistance to Shot.
[Exercises]   pp. 206-219

CHAPTER V.

FREE MOTION OF A PARTICLE UNDER A FORCE
DIRECTED TO A FIXED POINT.

Section 120. Path lies in a Plane. Differential Equation. 121. Effect of
Force transverse to Radius vector. 122. Speed from Infinity.
Exhaustion of Potential Energy. 123. Concavity or Convexity of
Orbit towards Centre of Force. 124. Force varying directly as
Distance. 125. Examples of Force in Different Cases. 126. Solution of Differential Equation in Various Cases. Energy Relations.
127. Discrimination of Orbit. 128. Period of Particle in Orbit.
129. Determination of Orbit from Distance and Velocity, etc. 130.
Newton's Revolving Orbit. 131. Examples. 132. Acceleration in
terms of Tangential and Radial Forces. 133. Hodograph of Particle describing Orbit. 134. Velocity resolable into Two Components of Constant Amounts. 135. Deduction of Law of Force from
Form of Orbit and Uniform Description of Area. 136. Kepler's Laws.
Verification. 137. Newton's Dynamical Deductions from Kepler's

xii   CONTENTS.

Laws. 138. Effect of Mass of Planet. 139. Correction of Kepler's Third Law by Theory of Gravitation. 140. Weighing the Planets. 141. Newton's Theory of Universal Gravitation. 142. Does Newtonian Gravitation extend to the Fixed Stars? 143. Experimental Illustration of Gravitational Attraction. 144. Elements of an Orbit. 145. Time in an Elliptic Orbit. 146. Time of Describing any Arc. Lambert's and Euler's Theorems. 147. Disturbed Orbits. (1) Tangential Impulse. 148. Disturbed Orbit. (2) Normal Impulse. 149. Disturbed Orbit. (3) Change of Intensity of Central Force. 150. Examples of Disturbed Orbits. 151. Orbit slightly disturbed from Circular Form. 152. Theory of Apsides. 153. Centre attracting according to Inverse Cube of Distance. 154. Force varying as Inverse n^{th} Power of Distance. 155. Different Centres for Same Orbit. Newton's Theorem. 156. Hamilton's Theorem. 157. Second Statement of Hamilton's Theorem. 158. Orbit a Conic touching Two Straight Lines drawn from C.F. 159. Particle acted on by Forces from Several Centres. Bonnet's Theorem. 160. Theorem of Curtis. 161. Examples of Multiple Centres of Force. 162. Earth-Moon System disturbed by Action of Sun. 163. Stability of Earth-Moon System. Hill's Theorem. [Exercises] - - pp. 220-306

CHAPTER VI.

MOTION OF A RIGID BODY.

Section 164. Angular Momentum (A.M.) of a Rigid Body. 165. Moments of Inertia about Parallel Axes. 166. Calculation of Moments of Inertia. Momental Ellipsoid. 167. Principal Axes of Momental Ellipsoid. 168. Meaning of a Product of Inertia. 169. Reactions of an Unsymmetrical Rotating Body on its Bearings. Free Axis of Rotation. 170. A.M. about any Axis. Equations of Rotational Motion. 171. Moments of Inertia in Different Cases. 172. M.I. of a Lamina. 173. M.I. of Triangular Plate. 174. M.I. about Axes at any Point parallel to Principal Axes at Centroid. 175. Examples of M.I. 176. Condition that an Ellipsoid may be a Momental Ellipsoid. 177. Foci of Inertia. 178. Ellipsoid of Gyration. 179. Equimomental Cone. Theorem of Binet. [Exercises] - pp. 307-337

CHAPTER VII.

APPLICATIONS OF DYNAMICAL PRINCIPLES.

Section 180. Practical Applications. 181. Acceleration in the Direction of Motion. 182. Motion of a Railway Train. Time lost in Stoppages. 183. Work done on Trains. Tractive Force. 184. Effect of Nature of Road Surfaces on Vehicular Traffic. 185. Efficiency of Brakes. 186. Time of Train from Station to Station. 187. Dynamics of Self-Propelled Vehicle on Straight Road. 188. Dynamics of a Vehicle on a Curve. 189. Bicycle on Curve on Banked Track. 190. Locomotive on Curve with Super-elevated Rail. 191. Variation of Speed of Rifle Bullet in Air. 192. Effect of Small Periodic Variation

CONTENTS. xiii

of Uniform Speed : (1) Time-Periodic, (2) Space-Periodic. 193. Small Periodic Variations of Speed of Ship. Effect of Relative Motion of Parts of Ship. 194. Activity with periodically Varying Speed. 195. Work done in the Passage of a Carriage over an Obstacle. Extra Work on a Causeway. Effect of Springs. 196. Condition that a Vehicle on Wheels may surmount an Obstacle. 197. Proper Height of Buffers, or of a Line of Draught. Rotary Inertia. 198. Effective Inertia of Wheeled Vehicle or of Train of Wheelwork. 199. Motion of a Wheeled Vehicle on an Inclined Plane. 200. Rolling of a Solid of Revolution on an Inclined Plane under Gravity. 201. Sliding Motion of a Body along an Inclined Plane with Friction. 202. Railway Carriage at Rest on Incline : Front or Back Wheels Braked. 203. Railway Carriage in Motion on Incline. One Set of Wheels Braked. 204. Solid of Revolution Rolling and Sliding on Horizontal Plane. 205. Compound Pendulum. 206. Theory of Compound Pendulum (C.P.). Equivalent Simple Pendulum. 207. Suspension Axes and Oscillation Axes. Interchangeability. 208. Experimental C.P. 209. Buoyancy and Air-Drag of C.P. 210. Examples on the Compound Pendulum. 211. Reactions due to Accelerations. Case of C.P. 212. Theory of Impulsive Forces. Impulse. 213. Collision of Inelastic Bodies. Theory of Pile-Driver. 214. Energy-Change in Inelastic Impact. Advantage of Heavy or Light Hammer. 215. Duration of Impact. How far a Pile should be Driven. 216. Equations of Motion of System under Impulses. 217. Impulse applied to Compound Pendulum. 218. Impulse applied to Rod on Smooth Table. Impulse on Pivot. 219. Double Compound Pendulum. 220. Small Vibrations of Double Pendulum. 221. Double Compound Pendulum under Special Conditions. Bell and Clapper. 222. Driving and Driven Pendulums. Forced Vibrations. 223. Theory of Seismographs. 224. Bell and Clapper. 225. Forced Vibrations. 226. Simple Pendulum with Vibrating Support. 227. Agreement of Natural Period with Forced Period : Resonance. 228. Examples of Resonance. 229. Examples of Forced Vibration. 230. Examples of Mutually Influencing Vibrations. Ex. 1. Oscillations of Balance and Case of a Watch. 231. Ex. 2. Watch hung by Bifilar Suspension. Theory of Bifilar. 232. Dependence of Steadiness of a Vehicle on Period of Vibration. 233. Pendulum with Point of Support in Vertical Vibration. 234. Pendulum Motion retarded by Friction. 235. Resonance modified by Friction. Tidal Example. 236. Ballistic Pendulum. [Exercises] pp. 338-437

CHAPTER VIII.

ROTATIONAL MOTION.

Section 237. Motion of a Rigid Body about a Fixed Point. 238. Every Rigid Body Displacement parallel to Fixed Plane is equivalent to a Rotation. 239. Any Rigid Body Displacement is equivalent to that of a Nut on a Certain Screw. 240. Motion of a Rigid Body parallel to a Given Plane. Space and Body Centrodes. 241. Velocity and Acceleration of Body-Point. 242. Curvature of Path of Body-Point. 243. Signs of Angular Displacements. 244. Composition of Angular Displacements. 245. Turning about any Axis expressed by Component

xiv   CONTENTS.

Turnings about Three Rectangular Axes. 246. Component Linear Velocities of Point in Turning Body. 247. Central Axis. 248. Examples on Central Axis and Rotation. 249. Accelerations of Point in Rotating Body. Equations of Motion. 250. Angular Momenta. 251. Representation of A.M. as a Vector. Rates of Change of A.M. about Moving Axes. 252. Body with One Point fixed. Deductions from Euler's Equations. 253. Body with One Point fixed. Relation of Axis of Resultant A.M. and Instantaneous Axis. 254. Motion of a Rigid Body under No Forces. 255. Invariable Plane and Invariable Line. Rolling of M.E. on Invariable Plane. 256. Polhode and Herpolhode. 257. Stability of Motion of Rigid Body under No Forces. 258. Projections of the Polhodes. 259. Form of the Herpolhode. 260. Examples on Motion of Rigid Body. [Exercises]   pp. 438-474

CHAPTER IX.

TOPS AND GYROSTATS. GYROSTATIC ACTION IN MACHINERY.

Section 261. Symmetrical Top moving about Fixed Point. Equations of Motion. 262. "Spherical" Top. 263. Rise and Fall of Top. 264. Path of Point on Axis of Top. 265. Top started with Rapid Rotation and Zero Precession. 266. Approximate Solution for Rapidly Rotating Top. 267. Reaction of Top on Support. 268. Top on Perfectly Smooth Plane. 269. Examples on the Motion of a Top. 270. Steady Motion of Top Rapidly Rotating about a Fixed Point. Stability of Steady Motion. 271. Graphical Representation of Condition of Stability of Steady Motion. 272. Additional Couple about OD. Effect of forcing Precession above Free Value. 273. Reaction of Ring-Guide or Space-Cone on Top. 274. Explanation of Clinging of Axle of Top to Curved Guide. 275. Astronomical Precession. 276. Rolling of Body-Cone on Space-Cone. 277. Motion of a Top deduced from Euler's Equations. 278. Gyrostats. Motion of a Gyrostat. 279. Gyrostatic Stability. 280. Experiments with Gyrostats. Rising and Falling of Ordinary Top. 281. Equations of Motion of Gyrostat. 282. Steady Motion of Gyrostat. Period of Oscillation about Steady Motion. 283. Gyrostat with Axis Vertical, Stable or Unstable accord, ing to Direction of Azimuthal Motion. 284. Gyrostat on Gimbals. Gyrostatic Pendulum : Analogy of Motion of Electron in Magnetic Field. 285. Gyrostatic Action of Rotating Bodies on their Bearings. 286. Virtual Increase of Moment of Inertia of Vibrating Body produced by Gyrostat. 287. Complete Theory of Vibrator containing Gyrostat. 288. Gyrostatic Controller of Rolling of Ship: Schlick's Apparatus. 289. Foucault's Apparatus to show Earth's Rotation. Gilbert's Barygyroscope. 290. The Brennan Monorail Car. 291. Gyrostatic Action of Turbines in Steamers. 292. Gyrostatic Couple on a Locomotive or Carriage. 293. Drift of a Projectile. 294. Stability of Rotating Projectile in Air. 295. Rolling of a Solid of Revolution on Horizontal Plane. 296. Rising and Falling of Top Spinning on Rounded Peg. 297. Disk or Hoop on Horizontal Plane, Oscillations about Steady Motion. 298. Condition that a Disk or Hoop may Roll Upright in Straight Line. [Exercises]   pp. 475-549

CONTENTS. xv

CHAPTER X.

GENERAL DYNAMICAL METHODS.

Section 299. Dynamics of a Connected System of Particles. Work due to Constraints. 300. Reduction to Independent Coordinates. 301. Generalised Coordinates. 302. Holonomous and Not Holonomous Systems. Derivation of Lagrange's Equations. 303. K.E. in terms of Generalised Coordinates. 304. Generalised Components of Momentum. 305. Equations for Holonomous System. Modified Equations for Not Holonomous System. 306. The Lagrangian Function or Kinetic Potential. 307. Examples on the Lagrangian Equations. 308. Appell's Dynamical Equations. 309. Hamilton's Transformation of Lagrange's Equations. 310. Variation of H with the Time. 311. Hamilton's Equations found by Variation of Lagrangian Function. 312. Ignoration of Coordinates. 313. Meaning of Integration of Equations of Motion. Hamilton's Differential Equation. 314. Jacobi's Theorem. 315. Case in which H does not contain t. 316. Examples on Jacobi's Theorem. 317. Lagrange's Equations for Impulsive Forces. 318. Reciprocal Relation between Two States of Motion. 319. Motion Started from Rest by Impulses. Theorems of Bertrand and Lord Kelvin. [Exercises] pp. 550-586

CHAPTER XI.

STATICS.

Section 320. Equilibrium of a Particle. 321. Particle in Equilibrium in a Smooth Tube. 322. Flexible String in Equilibrium. 323. Horizontal Projections of Sides of Funicular Polygon equal. 324. Chain of Suspension Bridge. 325. Catenary. 326. Geometrical Properties of Catenary. 327. Flexible Chain under Great Stretching Force. 328. Transmission of Power by Belt. 329. Equations of Equilibrium of Flexible Unstretchable String in Field of Force. 330. Application of General Equations to Catenary. 331. Equation of Catenary of Uniform Strength. 332. Rigid Body acted upon by Forces. 333. Resultant of Two Parallel Forces. 334. Centre of System of Parallel Forces. 335. Centre of Gravity of Body. 336. Graphical Method for Parallel Forces. 337. Application to Loaded Bridge. 338. Theory of Couples. 339. Graphical Representation of a Couple. 340. Composition and Resolution of Couples. 341. Reduction of System of Forces to Force and Couple. 342. Conditions of Equilibrium. 343. Poinsot's Central Axis, Wrench. [Exercises]
pp. 587-619

INDEX pp. 620-626

The student is recommended to read first the following more elementary parts of the book:
Chap. I., Sections 1-40. Chap. II. Chap. III., Sections 80-90, 94-97. Chap. V., Sections 120-143 Chap. VI., Sections 164-175. Chap. VII., Sections 180-220, 236. Chap. VIII., Sections 237-246. Chap. IX., Sections 261-263, 270, 271, 275, 276, 278-282, 285, 290, 291, 292. Chap. XI.

ERRATA.

Page 244, lines 14 and 18 from top, *for* $\frac{1}{2}v^2$ *read* $\frac{1}{2}(v^2 - v_0^2)$.

CHAPTER I.

KINEMATICS OF A MOVING POINT.*

1. Speed and Velocity. We suppose that the direction of motion of a point nowhere undergoes absolutely sudden change. The point, materialised as a *particle* of matter so small in every dimension that it only serves to mark position in space, therefore moves in a curve in space the direction of the tangent to which is everywhere perfectly definite.

The displacements of the point are in all cases with reference to some system of marks in space which are taken as at rest. Such a system of marks is called a *reference-frame*. It may be a curve fixed in space along which the point is constrained to move, or it may be *axes of coordinates*, for example Ox, Oy, Oz drawn from a point O, in three different directions which are not in one plane. Most frequently they are taken mutually at right angles, and are supposed either to be at rest, or to be in motion in some specified way, with reference to other coordinates which are taken as at rest. The motion of the point along the given curve may be defined by the variation of its distance measured along the curve from a specified fixed point in it, or it may be by the rate of change of the quantities which specify the position of the point with reference to the axes chosen. The relativity of motion will be found discussed in more detail in our elementary treatise.

The curve may in some extreme cases appear to be such

---

* The kinematics of the motion of a rigid body will be considered in direct connection with problems regarding such motion.

as to contradict the condition here stated. For example, a particle ascends under the retarding action of gravity until it is brought to rest and begins to descend. At every instant except that at which it has come to rest, the direction of motion is perfectly definite. The particle does not change the direction of motion suddenly: its speed has been gradually diminished, and it is at rest at the *instant* of reaching the highest point; it does not remain at rest for an *interval* of time however short, but still continues to gain downward velocity, and the instant of rest is the *point in time* which separates the interval during which the particle ascends from that during which it descends. Again, when a marble is dropped on a stone floor and rebounds, or a cricket-ball is struck by the bat, the direction of motion is changed suddenly, as suddenness is usually understood with respect to ordinary phenomena. But in reality the change of direction of motion occupies an *interval* of time, that of the duration of collision, though, as reckoned with respect to the time required for ordinary changes which can be followed by the eye, the interval is short.

It must be understood from the outset that in dynamics an *instant* is not what in ordinary affairs it is often supposed to be, an interval of time of indefinite length: it is not an interval of time at all. It is the final terminus of one interval of time, and the initial terminus of the interval which immediately succeeds. Two planes meet in a line which is not part of either plane, not being a surface in any sense, but is only a dividing mark or common boundary to be crossed by a moving point passing from one plane to the other. A point again is the dividing mark where one part of a line or curve ends and another portion begins: it is not, however it may be indicated by a spot of chalk on a blackboard or a spot of ink on paper, other than merely a mark of position in space. So with an *instant* in time the distinction between it and an *interval* of time, must be clearly understood. A pendulum bob *at* a certain instant is at the extremity of its swing in one direction; but the bob does not remain at rest for any interval of time however short; the swing

§ 1]   SPEED AND VELOCITY.   3

in the opposite direction begins just when that in the first direction terminates.

The distinction between an instant and an interval of time is the key to the solution of many of the puzzles regarding motion which perplexed the old philosophers. They held that a body could not move from one position to another without occupying in succession a continuous series of intermediate positions, and then came to the conclusion that if that were so motion was impossible, because it was tacitly assumed that occupation of a position implied rest in that position. Each position is occupied *at* an instant in time, but not *during* an interval: the true idea in no way negatives the possibility of motion, and the contradiction had no real existence.

At the instant which marks the beginning of an interval of time the moving point or particle is at P_1, at the instant which marks the end of the interval and the beginning of a succeeding interval it is at P_2. P_1, P_2 are points on the curve along which the moving point is displaced, and are at a definite distance apart, measured along the curve. We form the ratio s/t, that is the ratio of the numerical value of the distance to that of the time in which it is traversed, and call it the *average speed* of the moving point during the time t. The unit of speed is thus the speed in which unit of distance is described *per* unit of time. Speed is thus expressed in feet per second, centimetres per second, miles per hour, or according to any other choice of the units of length and time.

In many cases it would merely cumber our equations to indicate at every symbol or group of symbols the units employed; but when it is necessary, in the statement of results or elsewhere, to specify units we shall do so by adopting for feet per second the symbol f/s, or ft/sec, for centimetres per second cm/s, and so on.

The meaning of the word *per* is to be observed. The point does not necessarily move for an hour or even for a second. But it traverses the distance s, which may be miles, or only a fraction of an inch in length, at such and such an average rate or speed. For example, the statement that the speed is 60 miles per hour means that if this average speed were maintained constant for an hour the distance traversed would be 60 miles: the actual duration of the motion from P_1 to P_2 may be only a small fraction of a second. The distance traversed in a given time is equal to the average rate of displacement multiplied by the number of units of time, just as the amount of a workman's earnings for a given time is equal to the product of the rate of wages into the numerical measure of the time. The speed, or rate of displacement, is no more distance traversed than a rate of wages is a sum of money, and must always be expressed as *distance per unit of time*.

The idea of *uniform* speed presents no difficulty to anyone. Speed, whether the direction of motion remains constant or not, is constant when equal distances along the path are described in equal intervals of time, *however small these intervals are taken*. The proviso contained in the words italicised is necessary: a train, for example, might run 30 miles in each of successive hours, or $7\frac{1}{2}$ miles in each of successive quarter-hours, even though it stopped at stations: a test by a sufficiently short interval of time would reveal the true variability of the motion.

2. Varying Motion. We now consider the varying motion of a point a little more particularly. We suppose that the motion is continuous as regards speed as well as regards direction. By this we mean that the distance s_2 described in any small interval of time τ_2 which follows immediately an equal interval τ_1, differs from that described in the interval τ_1 by an amount $s_2 - s_1$, the ratio of which to s_1 tends towards zero as τ_1 and τ_2 are diminished without limit.

In passing from P_1 to P_2 along the curve, the point occupies in succession every position P between P_1 and P_2. But it does not remain in one position P for any interval of time, however short. Its position is P at an instant or point of time.

At P the motion is along the tangent to the curve at that point. The point does not move along that tangent through any finite distance, for immediately, as it advances, it finds itself moving along a new tangent, and so on. We may indeed regard the motion as one always along a straight line, which continually turns round so as to touch the curve at each successive position of the moving point, and thus at each instant the point has a definite direction of motion. The speed is also definite for each position P of the point. The average speed is s/t for the displacement from P_1 to P_2. Now suppose P_1, P_2, while always having the position P between them, to be brought closer and closer together. The distance traversed is continually diminished, and so also is the time t. In all cases that are here considered the ratio s/t retains a finite value, however much s is decreased in length, and as P_1 and P_2 are brought closer and closer together without limit of closeness, approaches more and more nearly to a limiting value, which we define as the speed of the point at P.

The direction of the motion at P, and the speed thus defined, constitute the complex idea of the *velocity* at P.

3. Illustrations of Varying Speed. Curve of Speed.

That a continuously varying speed has a definite value at each instant may be illustrated in the following manner. Two trains are running side by side, one at uniform speed v, the other with varying, let it be supposed increasing, speed. A passenger on the latter train, regarding the carriages of the other, sees them at first moving ahead; but they do so more and more slowly as time passes, until at last they appear to be falling behind. There is an instant at which the uniformly moving train seems to the passenger in the other to be standing still, and just then the speed of his train is v, the speed of the uniformly moving train. It does not however remain v for any interval of time, however short, but merely passes through that value.

Another illustration is obtained from Atwood's machine, (see p. 139, and Chap. VI.). Two equal weights are attached to the ends of a fine string passed over a vertical pulley, as there described. A small additional weight is placed on one, and the system at once begins to have a varying motion. At a certain instant the additional weight is removed without disturbing the system, and the variation of the motion is thereby annulled. The motion thereafter is as nearly uniform as the slight frictional resistances which act on the system permit: the varying motion which existed at the instant has been, so to speak, stereotyped by the removal of the additional weight.

The existence of a definite value of the varying speed at each instant is recognised in the methods used by practical men for its measurement. For example, Bashforth's chronograph for measuring the speed of a bullet determines the interval of time taken by the bullet to travel from one screen to another in its path. The bullet pierces the screens, and an electrical registering arrangement marks the time by a line drawn on a moving surface by a pencil. The distance between the screens is known, the interval of time in which the bullet traverses it is got from the length of the line drawn and the rate of motion of the pencil, and the speed is calculated.

Now it is important to know as nearly as possible the speed of the bullet when it leaves the muzzle of the rifle. Hence one screen is placed close to the muzzle, and the other as near the former as is consistent with accuracy of the time measurement. The speed found is the average speed of the bullet for the interval, and it is evident that the closer the screens are together the more nearly is this average speed the speed at the first screen.

It is usual to denote the limiting value of the ratio s/t, when t is made small without limit, by the notation $\frac{ds}{dt}$, or, as we shall write it in the text, ds/dt. Here dt may be taken as denoting any interval of time whatever, small or large, provided ds is the corresponding displacement which makes ds/dt have the limiting value of s/t, defined above as the speed at P. Thus, for example, at P the speed may be 88 feet per second, so that the numerical value of ds/dt will be given by assigning to dt any numerical value n, provided we assign at the same time to ds the value $n \times 88$. Or if we denote the value of ds/dt by v, then ds is the distance, $v\,dt$, described in any time dt when the rate of motion is v. The Newtonian or fluxional notation will also be used in what follows for time-rates of change of quantities. Thus, instead of ds/dt we shall often use $\dot{s}$, instead of dv/dt, $\dot{v}$ or $\ddot{s}$, and so on.

4. Distance traversed at Varying Speed. The distance s described in the interval between $t=t_0$ and $t=t_1$, when the value of v varies from instant to instant, is given by the equation

$$s = \int_{t_0}^{t_1} v\, dt, \quad \ldots\ldots\ldots\ldots\ldots\ldots\ldots(1)$$

where the expression on the right has the following signification. Let the interval of time from t_0 to t_1 be divided into a succession of n short intervals $\tau_1, \tau_2, \ldots \tau_n$, and let the value of v at the middle of τ_1 be v_1, at the middle of τ_2 be $v_2, \ldots$, and so on. Then the whole distance which would be travelled along the path in the interval $t_1 - t_0$, if the speed *during each* interval were what it actually is at the middle of that interval, would be the sum

$$s_1 = v_1\tau_1 + v_2\tau_2 + \ldots + v_n\tau_n. \quad \ldots\ldots\ldots\ldots\ldots(2)$$

Clearly in the case of continuously varying motion this approximates more and more closely without limit to the

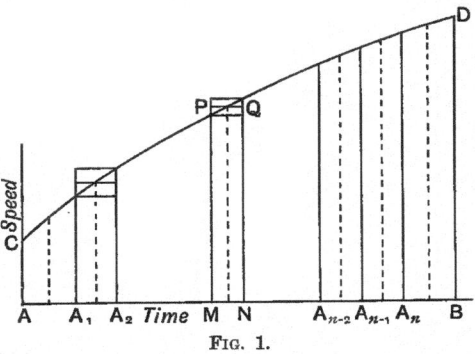

Fig. 1.

true value of the distance traversed in the time $t_1 - t_0$, as the intervals $\tau_1, \tau_2, \ldots \tau_n$ are made shorter and shorter, and their number n increased without limit. The limiting value s of s_1 when this is done is the meaning of the right-hand side of (1).

This is illustrated by the diagrams (Fig. 1 and Fig. 2). The interval of time $t_1 - t_0$ is represented by the straight line AB, and $AA_1, A_1A_2, \ldots, A_nB$, the segments into which

AB is divided, represent the shorter intervals $\tau_1, \tau_2, \ldots, \tau_n$, which make up the interval $t-t_0$. For any instant, represented by M on the line AB, the true value of v is the length of the ordinate MP, drawn from M to meet the curve CPD, which is drawn so as to represent the mode of variation of v. The successive ordinates dotted in midway between A and A_1, A_1 and A_2, A_2 and A_3, and so on, represent the speeds $v_1, v_2, v_3, \ldots$ at the instants represented by the mid-points of the intervals AA_1, A_1A_2, A_2A_3, and

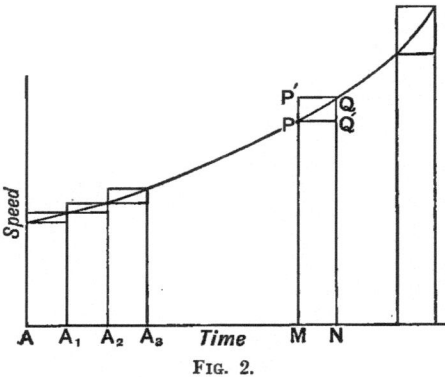

FIG. 2.

so on, of AB. Thus the sum of the areas of the rectangles standing on $AA_1, A_1A_2, A_2A_3, \ldots$ is $v_1\tau_1 + v_2\tau_2 + v_3\tau_3 + \ldots$, or s, that is the distance which would be traversed on the supposition stated above.

But we might have proceeded on either of other two suppositions, (1) that the speed throughout each interval is the actual speed at the beginning of that interval, (2) that the speed throughout each interval is the actual speed at the end of that interval. Calling the speeds according to (1) $v_1', v_2', \ldots v_n'$, we get a distance travelled in time $t_1 - t_0$,

$$s' = v_1'\tau_1 + v_2'\tau_2 + \ldots + v_n'\tau_n.$$

Again, calling the speeds according to (2) $v_1'', v_2'', \ldots, v_n''$, we obtain for the distance traversed,

$$s'' = v_1''\tau_1 + v_2''\tau_2 + \ldots + v_n''\tau_n.$$

VARYING MOTION. 9

Here s' is the area contained between AB, the end ordinates of the curve and the lower steps which form the tops of the rectangles on AA_1, A_1A_2, ... A_nB (see Fig. 2), while s'' is the area bounded by AB, the end ordinates of the curve and the uppermost steps which form the tops of the rectangles. If now, as is always possible, the intervals AA_1, A_1A_2, ..., A_nB, that is τ_1, τ_2, ... τ_n, be so taken that the curve lies everywhere above a lower step and below an upper step, the true area between AB, the end ordinates and the curve will lie between s' and s''. Moreover, the values of S lie between these, for clearly $s' < s < s''$.

If, now, each of the intervals AA_1, A_1A_2, ..., A_nB be diminished without limit and their number n be increased without limit, so that always

$$AB = AA_1 + A_1A_2 + \ldots + A_nB,$$

the difference $s'' - s'$ will diminish without limit, and both s' and s'', with s, which lies between them, will approximate without limit of closeness to the area contained between AB, the end ordinates, and the curve, that is to s, the true distance traversed in the time $t_1 - t_0$. This is the meaning of equation (1) § 4.

The connection of the extremities of the ordinates representing the speeds at successive instants by a definite curve is the graphical representation of the law of dependence of the speed on the time. In other words, the speed is some function of the time, or as it is usually written, $v = f(t)$. We have then for (1) § 4,

$$s = \int_{t_0}^{t_1} f(t) dt. \quad \ldots\ldots\ldots\ldots\ldots\ldots\ldots(1)$$

The body of rules for the evaluation of s when $f(t)$ is known constitutes that part of the Integral Calculus which deals with what are called definite integrals.

A speed-curve drawn with speeds laid down as ordinates against *distances travelled* as abscissae, is convenient for some purposes. It enables, as we shall see, accelerations in the direction of motion to be easily represented graphically.

5. Uniformly Varying Speed. The curve connecting the upper extremities of the ordinate in Fig. 2 is in this case a straight line, and the end ordinates are v_0, $v_0 + \alpha(t_1 - t_0)$. The area contained between AB, the end ordinates, and the curve is now the product of the length of base AB and the length of the mean ordinate, which is

$$\tfrac{1}{2}\{v_0 + v_0 + \alpha(t_1 - t_0)\} \quad \text{or} \quad v_0 + \tfrac{1}{2}\alpha(t_1 - t_0).$$

But $AB = t_1 - t_0$, and therefore, since s, the distance traversed in time $t_1 - t_0$, is numerically equal to this area, we have
$$s = (t_1 - t_0)\{v_0 + \tfrac{1}{2}\alpha(t_1 - t_0)\} \quad \ldots\ldots\ldots\ldots\ldots\ldots(1)$$
or
$$s = v_0(t_1 - t_0) + \tfrac{1}{2}\alpha(t_1 - t_0)^2. \quad \ldots\ldots\ldots\ldots\ldots\ldots(2)$$

If the time be reckoned from the instant represented by A, we have $t_0 = 0$, and the interval is simply t_1. Then

$$s = v_0 t_1 + \tfrac{1}{2}\alpha t_1^2. \quad \ldots\ldots\ldots\ldots\ldots\ldots\ldots\ldots\ldots(3)$$

This is the case of a speed which increases uniformly with the time, and has an initial value v_0, which may be either positive or negative; that is, the initial speed may be either in the direction of the part $\alpha(t - t_0)$ added in time $t - t_0$, or in the direction opposed to that. A body moving vertically under gravity fulfils very approximately these equations.

Ex. 1. Let $f(t) = v_0 + \alpha t$, which is the case of motion of a point which has uniform acceleration α in the line of motion.

We have
$$s = v_0(t_1 - t_0) + \tfrac{1}{2}\alpha(t_1 - t_0)^2;$$
that is, $\alpha s = \tfrac{1}{2}[\{v_0 + \alpha(t_1 - t_0)\}^2 - v_0^2] = \tfrac{1}{2}v_1^2 - \tfrac{1}{2}v_0^2$,

where v_1, v_0 are the final and initial speeds.

Ex. 2. If a body moves under uniform retardation r, and starts with speed v_0, it travels in time $t_1 - t_0$ a distance
$$s = v_0(t_1 - t_0) - \tfrac{1}{2}r(t_1 - t_0)^2.$$
Here the speed at time t is $v_0 - r(t - t_0)$, and therefore
$$s = \int_{t_0}^{t_1}\{v_0 - r(t - t_0)\}dt = v_0(t_1 - t_0) - \tfrac{1}{2}r(t_1 - t_0)^2.$$

If the body is just brought to rest at time $t = t_1$, we have $r(t_1 - t_0) = v_0$, and s becomes $\tfrac{1}{2}r(t_1 - t_0)^2$.

Ex. 3. A train starts from a station A, and after 4 minutes stops at another station B, 2 miles distant. During the first minute the train is uniformly accelerated, during the next $2\tfrac{1}{2}$ minutes it runs

§§ 5, 6] COMPOSITION AND RESOLUTION OF VELOCITIES.   11

uniformly, and during the remaining $\frac{1}{2}$ minute is uniformly retarded. Find the acceleration, the uniform speed and the retardation.

If a, r be the acceleration and retardation, v the uniform speed, and t_1, t_2, t_3 the intervals, we have

$$s = \tfrac{1}{2}at_1^2 + vt_2 + \tfrac{1}{2}rt_3^2,$$

by the last example. But clearly $r = 2a$, and $v = at_1 = rt_3$, so that

$$s = v(\tfrac{1}{2}t_1 + t_2 + \tfrac{1}{2}t_3).$$

Now the distance is 10560 feet, and so taking foot-second units, we get
$$v = 10560/(30 + 150 + 15) = 54\cdot 15.$$
and therefore $\quad a = \cdot 902, \quad r = 1\cdot 805.$

Thus, indicating the units in the manner explained in § 1, we have
$$v = 54\cdot 15 f/s, \quad a = \cdot 902 f/s^2, \quad r = 1\cdot 805 f/s^2.$$

Ex. 4. A bullet from a service rifle has a speed at the muzzle of $2500 f/s$. If it is shot vertically upwards, find, on the supposition of zero resistance, how far the bullet will ascend, its speed when at half that height from the point of projection, and the interval of time after which it will just have returned to that point.

Ex. 5. It is recorded of Hiawatha that

"He could shoot ten arrows upwards,
Shoot them with such strength and quickness
That the tenth had left the bowstring
Ere the first to earth had fallen."

Supposing that he shot off an arrow every four seconds, find the initial speed of the first arrow, and the height to which it ascended.

6. Graphical Representation of Directed Quantities. Composition and Resolution of Velocities. Relative Velocity. Any directed quantity can be represented by a straight line drawn in the specified direction, and made as many units in length as there are units in the numerical measure of the quantity. Hence we may represent a velocity in this manner by a straight line so drawn from any convenient point O.

Let, then, OA (Fig. 3) represent a displacement in direction and magnitude, and OB, OC be adjacent sides of a parallelogram of which OA is the diagonal passing through O. If we consider a point displaced along the line OA, it is easy to see that the step OA is not merely equivalent in result to the two steps OB, BA, or the two OB, OC, or the

12   A TREATISE ON DYNAMICS.   [CH. I.

two OC, CA, taken in succession; but that when it is taken any one of these pairs may be regarded as effected simultaneously. For let the point move along the line OC, and at the same time let the paper with this line upon it be carried in the direction OB in such a manner that the

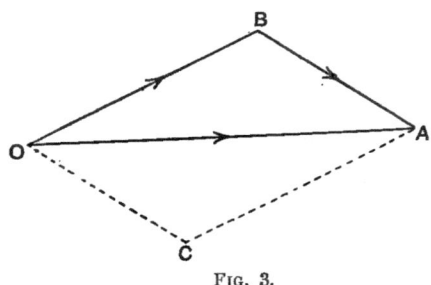

Fig. 3.

motion of the point is along the line OA in space. The displacements effected are OC and CA, where CA is the displacement relative to the point moving along OC. Similarly, BA is the displacement relative to the point moving along OB. [See *Relative Motion* in our *Elementary Dynamics*.]

Similarly, if OA represent a velocity, that is the displacement per unit of time in that direction, OB and BA, or OB and OC, or OC and CA, represent three pairs of velocities made simultaneous or coexistent in the same way, and each pair is equivalent to the single velocity OA. Let α be the angle AOB, and let the other angle OAB, β say, be also given. To find OB and OA, we have

$$OB = CA = OA \frac{\sin \beta}{\sin(\alpha+\beta)}, \quad OC = BA = OA \frac{\sin \alpha}{\sin(\alpha+\beta)}$$

since $OBA = \pi - (\alpha+\beta)$.

If the second condition assigned be not the angle β, but the length of OB, we have

$$OC = BA = \sqrt{OA^2 + OB^2 - 2OA \cdot OB \cos \alpha}$$

with $$\sin \beta = \frac{OB}{OC} \sin \alpha.$$

§ 6] COMPOSITION AND RESOLUTION OF VELOCITIES.

If for OA we write v, for OB, or CA, v_1, and for OC, or BA, v_2, we put these equations in the more compact form

$$v_1 = v \frac{\sin \beta}{\sin(\alpha+\beta)}, \quad v_2 = v \frac{\sin \alpha}{\sin(\alpha+\beta)}, \quad \ldots\ldots\ldots(1)$$

and
$$v_2 = \sqrt{v^2 + v_1^2 - 2vv_1 \cos \alpha}, \quad \ldots\ldots\ldots\ldots(2)$$

$$\sin \beta = \frac{v_1}{v_2} \sin \alpha. \quad \ldots\ldots\ldots\ldots\ldots\ldots(3)$$

Most frequently the resolution is rectangular, that is OB, OC are taken at right angles. Then the equations are simply
$$v_1 = v \cos \alpha, \quad v_2 = v \sin \alpha. \quad \ldots\ldots\ldots\ldots(4)$$

It is clear that in the case of rectangular resolution the problem is definite if one angle α, or one component OB, is given, but that in the more general case, either both angles α and β, or one angle and one component, must be given. In both cases the plane of resolution must also be specified, as the resolution may be made in any plane containing OA.

Further, a given velocity in any direction OA may be resolved into components along three directions not all in one plane. It is usual to consider only three directions

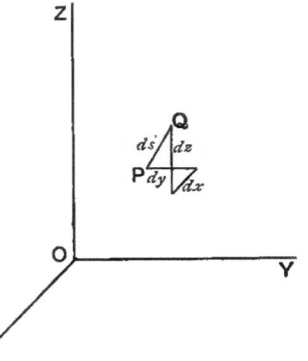

FIG. 4.

which are mutually at right angles, OX, OY, OZ, say. The components v_x, v_y, v_z of v are given by

$$v_x = v \cos \alpha, \quad v_y = v \cos \beta, \quad v_z = v \cos \gamma, \quad \ldots\ldots\ldots(5)$$

where α, β, γ are the angles which the direction of v makes with OX, OY, OZ respectively.

These give
$$v^2 = v_x^2 + v_y^2 + v_z^2, \quad \ldots\ldots\ldots\ldots\ldots\ldots(6)$$
since the condition
$$\cos^2 \alpha + \cos^2 \beta + \cos^2 \gamma = 1 \quad \ldots\ldots\ldots\ldots(7)$$

is fulfilled for the three angles α, β, γ, which three rectangular axes make with any direction in space. The cosines of α, β, γ are called the *direction cosines* of OA.

The three components v_x, v_y, v_z are, when taken together, equivalent to the single velocity of speed v. Now it is a proposition in geometry of space, easily proved, that the projection of any line OA (of length v say) upon any other line OB, inclined at an angle θ to OA, is equal to the sum of the projections upon OB of the components (v_x, v_y, v_z) of OA parallel to the axes OX, OY, OZ. We have thus, if α', β', γ' be the angles which OB makes with these axes,

$$v \cos \theta = v_x \cos \alpha' + v_y \cos \beta' + v_z \cos \gamma', \quad \ldots\ldots\ldots(8)$$

or, by the values of v_x, v_y, v_z found above,

$$\cos \theta = \cos \alpha \cos \alpha' + \cos \beta \cos \beta' + \cos \gamma \cos \gamma', \ldots\ldots(9)$$

a value of $\cos \theta$ which will be frequently of service in what follows. The notation l, m, n for $\cos \alpha$, $\cos \beta$, $\cos \gamma$ is commonly used for brevity. Then (9) is written

$$\cos \theta = ll' + mm' + nn'. \quad \ldots\ldots\ldots\ldots\ldots\ldots(9')$$

Any number of coexisting velocities can be compounded so as to give an equivalent system of velocities. Thus the two velocities of speeds v_1, v_2, discussed above, are equivalent to the single velocity of speed v given by equation

$$v = \sqrt{v_1^2 + v_2^2 - 2v_1 v_2 \cos \theta}, \quad \ldots\ldots\ldots\ldots\ldots(10)$$

where θ is the angle of inclination of the direction of v_2 to that of v_1. The single velocity found is the *resultant* of the two given velocities. Its direction is in the plane of the given velocities and inclined to the direction of v_1 at an angle α given by

$$\cos \alpha = \frac{v_1 + v_2 \cos \theta}{v}. \quad \ldots\ldots\ldots\ldots\ldots(11)$$

Now take the more general case of a number n of coexisting velocities of speeds $v_1, v_2, v_3, \ldots v_n$. Take three axes at right angles to one another, OX, OY, OZ, and let these axes make with the direction of v_1 angles $\alpha_1, \beta_1, \gamma_1$, with the direction of v_2 angles $\alpha_2, \beta_2, \gamma_2$, and so on. Then

§§ 6, 7]   HODOGRAPH.   15

taking the sum of the components of all along OX, of all along OY, and of all along OZ, we get

$$\left.\begin{aligned}v_x &= v_1\cos\alpha_1 + v_2\cos\alpha_2 + \ldots + v_n\cos\alpha_n\\v_y &= v_1\cos\beta_1 + v_2\cos\beta_2 + \ldots + v_n\cos\beta_n\\v_z &= v_1\cos\gamma_1 + v_2\cos\gamma_2 + \ldots + v_n\cos\gamma_n\end{aligned}\right\}\ldots\ldots(12)$$

Thus we get three coexisting velocities of speeds v_x, v_y, v_z which are equivalent to the given system. These have a resultant of speed v given by

$$v = \sqrt{v_x^2 + v_y^2 + v_z^2}.\ldots\ldots\ldots\ldots(13)$$

The direction of v makes with the axes angles the cosines of which are
$$\frac{v_x}{v},\ \frac{v_y}{v},\ \frac{v_z}{v}.$$

These results apply also to other directed quantities which are capable of being resolved and compounded in the same manner.

If the speeds of two particles A, B with reference to chosen axes be v, v', in specified directions, then the velocity of A relatively to B is obtained by compounding with the velocity of A, a velocity equal and opposite to that of B. Thus, for example, the component velocities of the motion of A with respect to B have the speeds, $v_x - v'_x$, $v_y - v'_y$, $v_z - v'_z$. Similarly the components of the velocity of B relative to A have the speeds $v'_x - v_x$, $v'_y - v_y$, $v'_z - v_z$.

7. Curve of Velocities—Hodograph. Fig. 2 is a diagram of speeds, that is the ordinates of the curve $v = f(t)$ represent successive numerical values of the velocities, which may be in different directions; and the area, taken as specified, gives the distance traversed between any limits of time proper to the motion. But now let us suppose that a point is moving in a curve, and let tangents be drawn to the curve at successive positions P, Q, R, ... of the moving point. The directions of motion at these positions are shown by the arrow heads on the tangents. Now, from a point O, let lines Op, Oq, Or, ... be drawn parallel to the tangents at P, Q, R, ... and in the directions of the arrows, and let each line be made as many units in length as there are units in the velocity which it represents. By taking the points $P, Q, R, \ldots$ sufficiently close together we can determine, as nearly as may be desired, a curve $pqr \ldots$ which might be called with more propriety than the former a *curve of velocities*. It is usually called the *hodograph* of the motion of the point.

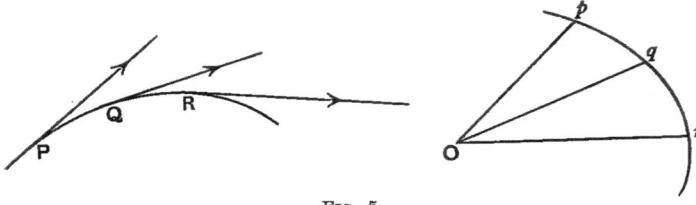

Fig. 5.

The hodograph gives to the eye a picture of the mode of variation of the velocity both in direction and magnitude, and its chief use is in the determination of the rate of this variation. In the general case of the motion of a point along any curve in space of three dimensions it is itself a three-dimensional curve; but for many of the motions considered in elementary dynamics its form is simple. For example, in undisturbed planetary motion, the hodograph of the planet is a circle in a plane parallel to the orbit, with an eccentric point within the circle as the origin O from which the lines $Op, Oq, Or, \ldots$, representing the velocities at different points in the orbit, are drawn. Other cases will be discussed later when the subject of acceleration has been dealt with.

8. Acceleration. At a given instant the velocity of a point is represented by Op, and at a subsequent instant it is represented by Oq (Fig. 5). By the principle of composition of velocities, explained above, the velocity represented by Oq is equivalent to the two coexisting velocities represented by Op, pq. It is reasonable to take as the change of velocity (not change of speed) that has occurred in the interval, τ say, between the two instants, the velocity pq, which, coexisting with the initial velocity, gives the final.

§§ 7, 8]   EXAMPLES.   17

We now define the average *acceleration* during the interval τ as the ratio, (*velocity pq*)/τ. It will be observed that the average acceleration for the interval τ, as thus defined, has direction (that of the chord *pq* of the hodograph) as well as magnitude. It is also clear that as τ is made smaller and smaller without limit, the direction of the chord *pq* approaches more and more, without limit of closeness, to that of the tangent to the hodograph at *p*. Now the limiting value of the ratio *pq*/τ, as *q* is brought more and more nearly into coincidence with *p*, is defined to be the acceleration at the position *P* of the point in its path, that is the acceleration when the velocity is represented by *Op*. Hence the acceleration of the moving point at the instant when it is at *P* is in the direction of the tangent to the hodograph at the corresponding point *p*.

Now suppose a second point to move in the hodograph, so that as the first point moves in the path the second is, at every instant, at the extremity of the line representing the velocity for that instant. The rate at which the second point moves along the hodograph is then, at each instant, both in magnitude and direction the acceleration of the particle; or, as it is sometimes, though not quite properly, put, the velocity in the hodograph is the acceleration in the path.

We insert here some examples of rectilinear motion and acceleration.

Ex. 1. A crank *OA* turns with uniform angular speed ω about *O*, and a connecting rod *AB* pivoted at *A* communicates rectilinear motion in the fixed direction to a cross-head *B* : to find the speed of *B* at any instant.

Let *x* denote the distance *OB*, *a* the length of the crank *OA*, *l* the length *AB* of the connecting rod, θ the angle *AOB*, and ϕ the angle *ABO*. We have

$$x = a\cos\theta + l\cos\phi, \quad a\sin\theta = l\sin\phi,$$

and therefore $\dot{x} = -a\sin\theta \cdot \dot{\theta} - l\sin\phi \cdot \dot{\phi},$

which, since $a\cos\theta \cdot \dot{\theta} = l\cos\phi \cdot \dot{\phi}$, becomes

$$\dot{x} = -x\tan\phi \cdot \dot{\theta} = -\omega x\tan\phi.$$

This simple expression for the speed of the cross-head suggests the following construction, for which the student should draw his own figure. Produce *BA* to meet in *C* a perpendicular to *BO* drawn from *O*. Then, if *OA* be taken to represent the speed of *A*, that is

18   A TREATISE ON DYNAMICS.   [CH. I.

$a\dot{\theta}$ at right angles to OA, OC will represent the speed of B, which is at right angles to OC, from B towards O, or O towards B, according to the position and direction of motion of the crank. Or if a distance $OD = OC$ be laid off from O along the crank, the speed of B is numerically equal to the speed of the point D. According as B is moving towards O or in the opposite direction, OD may be laid off from O towards A or in the opposite direction. At the "dead-points," where ϕ is zero, OD is of zero length. When the crank is at right angles to the line of motion of B, $\dot{x}$ has a maximum numerical value, for then $x \tan \phi = a$. The angle ϕ has then the value $\sin^{-1}(a/l)$, and oscillates from $\sin^{-1}(a/l)$ to $-\sin^{-1}(a/l)$ and back again in each revolution of the crank.

Ex. 2. To find the acceleration of the cross-head B in last example.

From the equation $\dot{x} = -\omega x \tan \phi$ we obtain

$$\ddot{x} = -\omega \{\dot{x} \tan \phi + x(1 + \tan^2 \phi)\dot{\phi}\}$$
$$= -\omega^2 x \left\{ (1 + \tan^2 \phi)\frac{\tan \phi}{\tan \theta} - \tan^2 \phi \right\}$$
$$= -\omega^2 x \left(1 - \frac{\tan \theta - \tan \phi}{\tan \theta} \sec^2 \phi \right)$$
$$= -\omega^2 x \left(1 - \frac{l \cos \phi - a \cos \theta}{l} \sec^3 \phi \right),$$

since $\sin \theta / \sin \phi = l/a$. But

$$(l \cos \phi - a \cos \theta)/l = (xl \cos \phi - xa \cos \theta)/xl = (l^2 - a^2)/xl,$$

since $x = a \cos \theta + l \cos \phi$, and $l^2 \sin^2 \phi = a^2 \sin^2 \theta$. Thus we have

$$-\ddot{x} = \omega^2 \left(x - \frac{l^2 - a^2}{l} \sec^3 \phi \right).$$

This expression for $\ddot{x}$ suggests the following construction. Along BA produced, and backward along AB, lay off AE and AF each equal to OA. Then $BE = l + a$, $BF = l - a$. Along BO lay off $BG = l$ and $BF'' = BF = l - a$. Join EG, and through F'' draw $F''H$ parallel to GE. Then we have $BH/BE = BF''/BG$, that is $BH/(l+a) = (l-a)/l$. Hence $BH = (l^2 - a^2)/l$. It may be noticed that H is the point at which the connecting rod is met by a perpendicular let fall from O to the rod when OA is at right angles to BO.

Now draw HI, IK, KL, perpendiculars to BH, BI, BK, respectively, so that K is on BA, and I, L are on BO. Then $BI = BH \sec \phi$, $BK = BI \sec \phi$, and $BL = BK \sec \phi$, so that

$$BL = BH \sec^3 \phi = (l^2 - a^2) \sec^3 \phi / l.$$

Hence $LO = x - (l^2 - a^2) \sec^3 \phi / l$ and $-\ddot{x} = \omega^2 . LO$.

Thus, on the scale on which $AO(=a)$ represents the acceleration of the point A in the circular motion, LO represents the acceleration of the cross-head B.

Ex. 3. A steamer sails at a speed of 30 feet per second in the direction from North to South, and a wind blows from West to East with a speed of 12 miles per hour. If the particles of smoke are supposed to come to rest relatively to the air just above the funnel mouth, find the speed of a particle of smoke relative to the steamer.

The relative speed is 12 miles per hour or 17·6 feet per second from West to East, and 30 feet per second from South to North, that is a speed of 34·78 feet per second in a direction to the North of East, inclined to the Easterly direction at the angle $\tan^{-1}(30/17\cdot 6)$. This is the direction of the stream of smoke with reference to the steamer.

Ex. 4. To find the motion of the cross-head B in Ex. 1 relative to the crank-pin A.

The cross-head has speed $\omega x \tan \phi$ in the direction from B towards O. The motion of the crank-pin at right angles to OA gives a component $\omega a \sin \theta$ in the direction from B towards O and a component $\omega a \cos \theta$ in the direction of the perpendicular drawn through A from the line OB. Thus we have for the motion of B relative to A the components $\omega x \tan \phi - \omega a \sin \theta$ from B towards O and $\omega a \cos \theta$ along the perpendicular from A on the line of stroke.

The resultant is $\omega (x^2 \tan^2 \phi - 2ax \tan \phi \sin \theta + a^2)^{\frac{1}{2}}$ and makes the angle $\tan^{-1}\{a \cos \theta/(x \tan \phi - a \sin \theta)\}$ with the line of stroke, on the opposite side of that line from A.

It will be noticed that this relative motion is transverse to the line of stroke at the dead points and zero when the crank is at right angles to that line.

Ex. 5. To find the acceleration of the cross-head B relative to the crank-pin A.

The acceleration of B is $\omega^2\{x - (l^2 - a^2)\sec^3 \phi/l\}$ in the direction from B towards O. The acceleration of A is $\omega^2 a$ from A towards O. Applying to B an acceleration equal and opposite to that of A, we have for the components of relative acceleration of B,

$$\omega^2\{x - (l^2 - a^2)\sec^3 \phi/l\} - \omega^2 a \cos \theta$$

in the direction from B towards O, and $\omega^2 \sin \theta$ in the direction from OB towards A along the perpendicular let fall from A on OB. The resultant relative acceleration is therefore

$$\omega^2\{(x - \frac{l^2 - a^2}{l}\sec^3 \phi)^2 + a^2 - 2a(x - \frac{l^2 - a^2}{l}\sec^3 \phi)\cos \theta\}^{\frac{1}{2}},$$

and is inclined to the line of stroke at the angle

$$\tan^{-1}\{a \sin \theta/[x - (l^2 - a^2)\sec^3 \phi/l - a \cos \theta]\}$$

on the side of that line towards A.

9. Angular Velocity. Directed Quantities referred to Moving Axes. Rate of Growth of Directed Quantity.

If a straight line be turning about one extremity, the angular speed of the line is measured by the speed of the point at unit distance from the fixed end. The specification of the plane and direction of turning is required to complete the idea of angular velocity.

The following simple theorem, which is easily proved, will be of great service in what follows. If any directed quantity (of amount L say), characteristic of the motion of a body, be associated with a line or axis Ol (Fig. 6), which is changing in direction, it causes a rate of production of amount ωL of the same quantity for a line or axis, Om, at right angles to Ol, towards which Ol is turning with angular speed ω. If M be the amount of the same quantity already associated with this latter line or axis, the total rate of growth of the quantity in that direction is $\dot{M} + \omega L$.

To prove this, let Ol have turned towards Om, in the short interval of time dt, through an angle $d\theta$, from the position at right angles to Om.

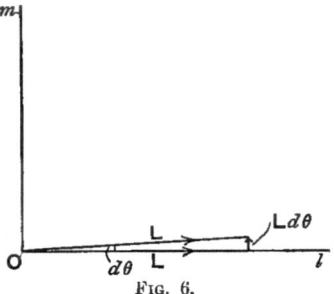
Fig. 6.

The extremity of the vector L has moved a distance $L\,d\theta$ parallel to Om. There is now a component of L along Om of amount $L \sin d\theta$, or simply $L\,d\theta$, since $d\theta$ is small. This is produced in time dt, and therefore the rate of production is $L\,d\theta/dt$, or $L\omega$, if ω denote the angular speed $d\theta/dt$, or $\dot{\theta}$, as we shall usually write it. To $L\omega$ falls to be added $\dot{M}$, the rate of growth of M, the amount of the quantity already associated with Om. The student may easily convince himself that the rate of variation $\dot{L}$ of L contributes nothing to the rate of growth of the quantity along Om.

It will be observed by the student that L is the amount of the directed quantity for the position of Ol at the instant under consideration, and M that for Om in its position at the instant, since Om may also be a line of reference for the motion of the body, and be itself in motion. In short, L and M are the amounts of the directed quantity for fixed axes coinciding with the instantaneous positions of Ol and Om, and the rate $\dot{M}+L\omega$ is associated with the *fixed* axis with which Om at the instant coincides.

It is to be remembered that $L+\dot{L}\,dt$, $M+\dot{M}\,dt$ are components of the directed quantity for the axes Ol, Om, in the new positions which they occupy *after the lapse of the short interval of time dt*, from the instant considered. $\dot{M}+L\omega$ is the rate of growth of the quantity for the direction which Om occupies at that instant.

The same process may be applied to other vectors of the same kind turning during dt towards Om, and the total rate of growth of the quantity obtained for Om by addition.

The theorem just stated is, as we shall see in the discussion of the motion of tops and gyrostats, sufficient to deal with complicated cases of motion;* but it may be regarded as a particular case of the following theorem regarding a system of three moving axes Ox, Oy, Oz (Fig. 7).

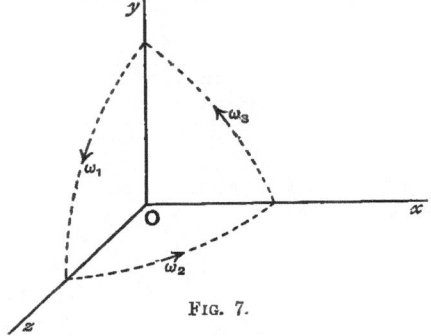

FIG. 7.

Let these make at time t angles α, β, γ with a fixed axis Ok, and be in motion about the fixed point O, so that α, β, γ are changing at the time-rates $\dot{\alpha}$, $\dot{\beta}$, $\dot{\gamma}$. Then the component K of the quantity associated with Ok is given by

$$K = L\cos\alpha + M\cos\beta + N\cos\gamma, \quad\ldots\ldots\ldots\ldots(1)$$

*See a paper by A. Gray in the *Transactions of the Institution of Engineers and Shipbuilders in Scotland* for 1905.

so that

$$\dot{K} = \dot{L}\cos\alpha + \dot{M}\cos\beta + \dot{N}\cos\gamma$$
$$- L\dot{\alpha}\sin\alpha - M\dot{\beta}\sin\beta - N\dot{\gamma}\sin\gamma. \quad\ldots\ldots(2)$$

If now we suppose that Oy coincides at the instant considered with Ok, then $\beta = 0$, $\alpha = \gamma = \pi/2$, and we have

$$\dot{K} = \dot{M} - L\dot{\alpha} - N\dot{\gamma}. \quad\ldots\ldots\ldots\ldots\ldots\ldots(3)$$

But, clearly, if the system of axes be turning, as shown in the diagram, with the angular speeds indicated, namely ω_1 about Ox, ω_2 about Oy, and ω_3 about Oz, Ox is turning towards Ok with angular speed ω_3, and so $\omega_3 = -\dot{\alpha}$; similarly Oz is turning away from Ok with angular speed ω_1, and so $\omega_1 = \dot{\gamma}_1$. Thus we have

$$\dot{K} = \dot{M} + L\omega_3 - N\omega_1. \quad\ldots\ldots\ldots\ldots\ldots\ldots(4)$$

The motion of the system of axes causes growth of the component associated with the fixed axis Ok, with which Oy coincides at the instant, at rate $L\omega_3 - N\omega_1$, of which the part $L\omega_3$ arises from the rate of approach of Ox to Ok, and $-N\omega_1$ from the rate of recession of Oz from Ok. [See further with regard to moving axes, § 15.]

10. Examples of Acceleration. As examples of this theorem we may take the following. The line Ol, of length r say, is turning about O with angular speed $\dot{\theta}$ in a given plane, say that of the paper. The rate at which the point l is moving parallel to Om, that is the rate of growth of the distance of l from any straight line drawn parallel to Ol in the plane of the paper, and to the right of Ol in the diagram, is $r\dot{\theta}$. This result has already been found in § 9, if we take L there as representing the length r of Ol.

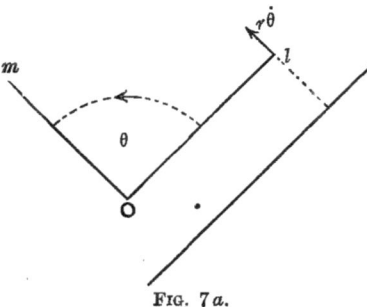

Fig. 7 a.

Again, let us consider a point moving in a given curve, and endeavour to determine its acceleration. If P be the position of the point at the instant, and the speed be v, the component of acceleration along the curve at P is $\dot{v}$. But since the path is curved at P this is not the only component of acceleration. Let PC (Fig. 8) of length R be the radius of curvature of the path at P, that is let C be the centre of the circle passing through P and two points P_0, P_1 infinitely close to P, and situated one on the left, the other on the right of P, as in the diagram. By the theorem stated above the rate of growth of velocity in the direction from P towards C is $v\dot{\phi}$, where $\dot{\phi}$ is the angular speed with which the tangent at P is turning round towards the direction PC. But clearly $\dot{\phi} = v/R$, and therefore velocity of the point in the direction PC is growing up at rate v^2/R.

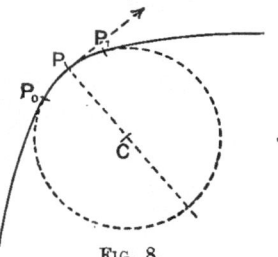

Fig. 8.

The two components, $\dot{v}$ along the curve and v^2/R towards the centre of curvature, thus found are the total components for these directions, and therefore when compounded give the resultant acceleration. This result holds whether the curve lies in a plane or in space of three dimensions.

The result may also be derived from the hodograph. The resultant acceleration, α say, in the path is represented by the velocity of the imaginary particle (Fig. 5, §7) in the hodograph. Resolving α into two components, one perpendicular, the other parallel to Op, we see that the amount of the former is the speed perpendicular to Op, of the imaginary particle. This is clearly $v\dot{\phi}$, that is v^2/R, since $\dot{\phi}$, the angular speed of the radius to the imaginary particle, is that with which the tangent at P is turning. The other component, that parallel to Op, is obviously $\dot{v}$.

Ex. 1. A particle moves in a plane curve with varying speed v, and a second particle moves so as always to be at the centre of curvature of the path for the position of the first. Find the accelerations of the second particle parallel to the tangent and normal of the path.

The speed of the second particle along the normal is $d\rho/dt$ or $v\,d\rho/ds$, where ρ is the radius of curvature, and the speed at right angles to this is zero. But the tangent to the path turns round in time dt through the angle $d\theta = ds/\rho$, and the tangent to the evolute, the radius of curvature of the path, turns in the same time through the same angle, while the point of contact moves a distance $d\rho$. The curvature of the evolute is therefore $(ds/d\rho)/\rho$. The acceleration of the second particle towards the centre of curvature of the evolute, that is parallel to the tangent to the path, is therefore $(d\rho/dt)^2(ds/d\rho)/\rho$ or $(v^2 d\rho/ds)/\rho$, and is clearly in the direction opposed to the motion of the first particle.

Again, the acceleration along the evolute is

$$v'dv'/d\rho, \quad \text{where} \quad v' = v\,d\rho/ds.$$

But $dv'/d\rho = (dv'/ds)ds/d\rho$, so that we obtain $v'dv'/d\rho = vd(v\,d\rho/ds)/ds$.

Ex. 2. A particle moves in a cycloid in such a manner that its resultant acceleration is always perpendicular to the base. Prove that the acceleration is inversely proportional to the fourth power of the radius of curvature at each point.

Refer to Fig. 41. Resolving the acceleration normally and tangentially, and calling the component perpendicular to the base α, we get

$$\alpha = -\frac{v^2}{\rho}\sin\phi + v\frac{dv}{ds}\cos\phi,$$

and also, because the component parallel to the base is zero,

$$\frac{v^2}{\rho}\cos\phi + v\frac{dv}{ds}\sin\phi = 0,$$

But $\rho = 4a\sin\phi$ and $v = 4a\sin\phi \cdot \dot\phi$, and the last equation can be written

$$\frac{\cos\phi}{\sin\phi}\dot\phi + \frac{1}{v}\frac{dv}{dt} = 0,$$

which gives, by integration, $v\sin\phi = \text{const.}$

But the second equation gives $-v\,dv/ds = (v^2/\rho)\cos\phi/\sin\phi$, and so the equation for α becomes

$$\alpha = -\frac{4av^2}{\rho^2} = -\frac{64a^3}{\rho^4}(\text{const.})^2$$

by the relations $v\sin\phi = \text{const.}$ and $\rho = 4a\sin\phi$.

Ex. 3. A particle moves in a catenary of which the intrinsic equation is $s = c\tan\phi$ [Gibson's *Calculus*, § 142]; the direction of its acceleration at any point makes equal angles with the tangent and normal to the path at that point. If the speed at the vertex be u, find the speed and the acceleration at any other point.

The normal and tangential accelerations must have equal values, that is $\ddot{s} = \dot{s}^2/\rho$. But by the equation of the path, we have

$$\rho = ds/d\phi = (c^2 + s^2)/c,$$

§§ 10, 11]   ACCELERATION.   25

so that we get
$$\frac{\ddot{s}}{\dot{s}} = \frac{\dfrac{\dot{s}}{c}}{1+\dfrac{\dot{s}^2}{c^2}}.$$

Integrating, we obtain
$$\log \dot{s} = \tan^{-1}\frac{\dot{s}}{c} + C = \phi + C,$$

where C is a constant. Now let $\phi=0$ at the vertex, where $\dot{s}=u$, and we have $\log(\dot{s}/u)=\phi$, that is
$$\dot{s}=ue^\phi.$$

The whole acceleration is $\sqrt{2}\ddot{s}$, and therefore its value is
$$\sqrt{2}\frac{\dot{s}^2}{\rho} = \frac{\sqrt{2}}{c}u^2 e^{2\phi}\cos^2\phi.$$

Ex. 4. The speed of a particle moving in a parabola is v at distance r from the focus; prove that the acceleration of the particle is the resultant of a component $a=\frac{1}{4}\{d(v^2r)/dr\}/r$ parallel to the axis and a component $a_r=\frac{1}{4}r\{d(v^2/r)/dr\}$ outwards along the radius-vector.

Let ϕ be the angle between the radius-vector and the tangent at the position P of the particle at time t, p the perpendicular from the focus on the tangent, and ρ the radius of curvature. Resolving normally and tangentially, we get

$$\frac{v^2}{\rho} = (a-a_r)\sin\phi, \qquad v\frac{dv}{ds} = (a+a_r)\cos\phi.$$

But $1/\rho=(dp/dr)/r$, $\sin\phi=p/r$, $\cos\phi=dr/ds$. Also, in the parabola, if α be the distance of the focus from the vertex, $p^2=\alpha r$. Hence the equations just written become

Thus we get
$$v^2\frac{1}{p}\frac{dp}{dr} = a-a_r, \qquad v\frac{dv}{dr} = a+a_r.$$

$$2a = v^2\frac{1}{p}\frac{dp}{dr} + v\frac{dv}{dr}, \qquad 2a_r = v\frac{dv}{dr} - v^2\frac{1}{p}\frac{dp}{dr}.$$

But the relation $p^2=\alpha r$ gives $(dp/dr)/p = 1/2r$, and therefore

$$2a = \frac{v^2}{2r} + v\frac{dv}{dr} = \frac{1}{2r}\frac{d}{dr}(v^2r),$$

$$2a_r = v\frac{dv}{dr} - \frac{v^2}{2r} = \frac{1}{2}r\frac{d}{dr}\left(\frac{v^2}{r}\right),$$

which prove the proposition.

11. Curvilinear Motion. Radial and Transverse Components. As another example we find the components of acceleration in two directions chosen as follows: a line OP drawn from any origin O to the position P of the moving point, and a line PT drawn at right angles to OP in the plane determined by OP and the direction of motion at P. Denoting the length of OP by r, and resolving v into two components, one along OP and the other along the transverse PT, at right angles to OP, as in the diagram (Fig. 9), we get for the former $\dot{r}$ and for the latter $r\omega$, if P, as we may suppose it to do, accompanies the point in its motion and ω is the angular velocity with which OP then turns. We have thus

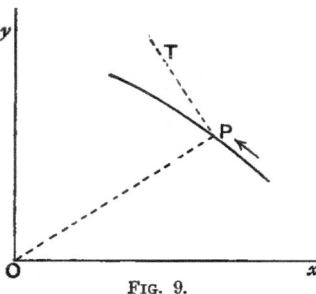

Fig. 9.

$$v = (\dot{r}^2 + \omega^2 r^2)^{\frac{1}{2}}. \quad \ldots\ldots\ldots\ldots\ldots\ldots(1)$$

If the motion is in one plane, ω may be expressed as the rate of growth $\dot{\theta}$ of the angle θ which OP makes at the instant under consideration with some fixed line, Ox say, in the plane of motion. We have then

$$v = (\dot{r}^2 + r^2\dot{\theta}^2)^{\frac{1}{2}}. \quad \ldots\ldots\ldots\ldots\ldots\ldots(2)$$

The reciprocal $1/r$, that is the *shortness* of r, is frequently employed in such expressions as these for the speed in the path. Putting $u = 1/r$, we have

$$v^2 = \frac{1}{u^4}(\dot{u}^2 + u^2\dot{\theta}^2). \quad \ldots\ldots\ldots\ldots\ldots\ldots(3)$$

If, as is the case in a class of motions which we shall have to consider later, $\dot{\theta} = hu^2$, where h is a constant,

$$u^2\dot{\theta}^2 = h^2 u^6, \quad \dot{u}^2 = \left(\frac{du}{d\theta}\dot{\theta}\right)^2 = h^2 u^4 \left(\frac{du}{d\theta}\right)^2, \ldots\ldots(4)$$

so that
$$v^2 = h^2 \left\{\left(\frac{du}{d\theta}\right)^2 + u^2\right\}, \quad \ldots\ldots\ldots\ldots(5)$$

a form which will be of great service in the discussion of the class of motions referred to.

If p be the length of the perpendicular let fall from the origin on the tangent to the path at P, then it is clear that $h = vp$. This value of h substituted in (5) gives

$$\frac{1}{p^2} = \left(\frac{du}{d\theta}\right)^2 + u^2, \qquad \ldots\ldots\ldots\ldots\ldots(6)$$

a geometrical relation which is also of much service in the discussion of orbital motion.

12. Polar Coordinates in Three Dimensional Space. Lastly, in the case of three dimensional motion, the speed of the moving point can be expressed as follows. Take coordinates (Fig. 10) according to the following specification: (*a*) the distance, $OP = r$, from the origin to the moving point, (*b*) the angle θ which OP makes with a fixed plane through O, and (*c*) the angle ϕ which the projection OM of OP on this latter plane makes with a fixed line OX in the same plane. For example, the position of a point on the earth's surface is fixed by the distance r of the point from the centre O, the geocentric latitude θ, that is the inclination of OP to the plane of the equator, and the longitude ϕ, that

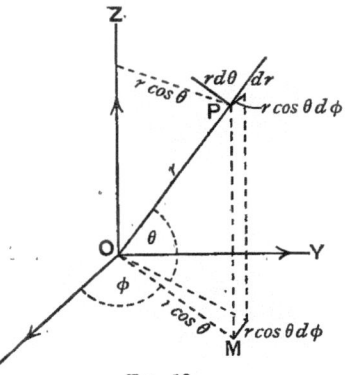

FIG. 10.

is the angle which the meridian plane of the point—a plane through the poles and the point—makes with the meridian plane of some specified place, *e.g.* a certain point in the Greenwich Observatory.

If, then, r, θ, ϕ be the coordinates, as thus defined, of the first extremity of the element of path ds described in the element of time dt, $r + dr$, $\theta + d\theta$, $\phi + d\phi$ will be the co-ordinates of the other extremity. The length of ds is, as the diagram shows,

$$\{(dr)^2 + (r\,d\theta)^2 + (r\cos\theta\,.\,d\phi)^2\}^{\frac{1}{2}}.$$

28   A TREATISE ON DYNAMICS.   [CH. I.

Hence $\quad v = \{\dot{r}^2 + r^2\dot{\theta}^2 + r^2\cos^2\theta \cdot \dot{\phi}^2\}^{\frac{1}{2}}.\quad\ldots\ldots\ldots\ldots(1)$

The change from these coordinates to coordinates x, y, z with reference to rectangular axes OX, OY, OZ, is to be made by the relations, which are obvious from the diagram,

$$\left.\begin{array}{l}x = OM\cos\phi = r\cos\theta\cos\phi\\ y = OM\sin\phi = r\cos\theta\sin\phi\\ z = r\sin\theta\end{array}\right\}\ldots\ldots\ldots\ldots(2)$$

Sometimes the angle which OP makes with a line OZ, perpendicular to the plane in which ϕ is measured—that is the co-latitude in the terrestrial reference—is taken as the second coordinate θ. The expression for v requires only the substitution of $\sin^2\theta$ for $\cos^2\theta$ on the right when this is done; but the relations (2) become

$$x = r\sin\theta\cos\phi,\quad y = r\sin\theta\sin\phi,\quad z = r\cos\theta.\ldots\ldots(3)$$

13. Radial and Transverse Components of Acceleration. We can now find expressions for the component accelerations along and at right angles to the radius-vector for a point moving in any path. Referring again to Fig. 9, we see that PT is turning round with angular speed ω towards the instantaneous position of PO, and that the production of OP outwards, that is PS, is turning, also with speed ω, towards the instantaneous position of PT. We have from the former turning $r\omega \cdot \omega$, or $\omega^2 r$, for the rate of production of speed along PO, or $-\omega^2 r$ along OP, and from the latter turning a rate $\dot{r}\omega$ of growth of speed along PT. But the speed $\dot{r}$, along OP, gives a rate of growth of speed $\ddot{r}$ in the same direction; and the speed ωr along PT gives a rate of growth of speed $\dot{\omega}r + \dot{r}\omega$ in that direction. The total acceleration along OP is thus

$$\ddot{r} - \omega^2 r,$$

and the total acceleration along PT is

$$2\dot{r}\omega + \dot{\omega}r = \frac{1}{r}\frac{d}{dt}(\omega r^2).$$

As before, in the case of motion in one plane, if we call

the angle POx in that plane θ, we have $\omega = \dot\theta$, and the radial acceleration becomes
$$\ddot r - r\dot\theta^2,$$
while that along PT is
$$(2\dot r\dot\theta + r\ddot\theta) = \frac{1}{r}\frac{d}{dt}(r^2\dot\theta).$$

The following method of obtaining these accelerations is also instructive. In time dt the radius-vector has turned forward through the angle $\omega\, dt$, and r has grown to $r + dr$. In order to find the acceleration we have to resolve the velocities, which exist along and at right angles to the radius-vector in its position after the lapse of dt, along and at right angles to the positions of OP and PT at the beginning of the interval dt. The difference in each case between the result of the resolution and the previously existing component in the direction in question gives the change effected in the time dt, and from that, dividing by dt, and proceeding to the limit when dt is infinitely small, we get the acceleration required.

At the end of dt, r has grown to $r + dr$, $\dot r$ to $\dot r + d\dot r$, and ω to $\omega + d\omega$, for the new position of the radius-vector. The speed along the new direction of PT is $(\omega + d\omega)(r + dr)$. Resolving now $\dot r + d\dot r$ and $(\omega + d\omega)(r + dr)$ along the former position of OP, and subtracting $\dot r$, we get the change of speed in that direction. It is

$$(\dot r + d\dot r)\cos(\omega\, dt) - (\omega + d\omega)(r + dr)\sin(\omega\, dt).$$

Now in the limit when dt is made infinitely small, so that all terms of a higher order of smallness than the first, e.g. than $d\dot r$ or $\omega r\, dt$, may be neglected,
$$\cos(\omega\, dt) = 1, \quad \sin(\omega\, dt) = \omega\, dt,$$
and we get for the change specified the value $d\dot r - \omega^2 r\, dt$. Hence the rate of growth of radial speed required is
$$\ddot r - \omega^2 r,$$
as before.

In the same way we resolve $\dot r + d\dot r$ and $(\omega + d\omega)(r + dr)$ along the position PT had at the beginning of dt, and obtain
$$(\dot r + d\dot r)\sin(\omega\, dt) + (\omega + d\omega)(r + dr)\cos(\omega\, dt) - \omega r$$

for the change of speed in this direction which has grown up in dt. Hence in the limit we get for the rate of growth

$$2\dot{r}\omega + r\dot{\omega} = \frac{1}{r}\frac{d}{dt}(\omega r^2),$$

as before.

The results may also be obtained by writing $x = r\cos\theta$, $y = r\sin\theta$, calculating $\ddot{x}$, $\ddot{y}$, and resolving these components along OP and PT (Fig. 9). This process the student may go through for himself.

The results obtained in §12 and the present section are of great importance in the theory of central orbits, where, however, the motion considered is, so far as we shall deal with it, confined to one plane. The expressions for the accelerations are, however, those also for a curve in space.

14. Uniplanar Motion of a Point. Revolving Axes. Components of Velocity and Acceleration. As another example, let the motion of a point P in one plane be referred to two rectangular axes OX, OY, which are revolving in their own plane about O, with angular speed ω. Let the coordinates of the point P, with reference to these axes, at the instant considered, be x, y. Now the axis OY is turning away from the instantaneous position of OX, and the coordinate of P in the direction given by that position is changing in consequence at rate $-\omega y$. The already existing value of x is growing at rate $\dot{x}$. Hence speed of P resolved parallel to the instantaneous position of OX is $\dot{x} - \omega y$.

Again the axis OX is turning towards the instantaneous position of OY, and the rate at which the y-coordinate of P is growing in consequence is ωx. But y is growing at rate $\dot{y}$: hence the speed of the point P parallel to the instantaneous position of OY is $\dot{y} + \omega x$.

Calling these speeds u, v, we have the equations

$$u = \dot{x} - \omega y, \quad v = \dot{y} + \omega x, \quad \dots\dots\dots\dots\dots(1)$$

which we shall have occasion to refer to in the solution of various problems of the motion of a point.

If now we take lines equal in length to u, v, as the x, y coordinates of another point, with reference to the same moving axes, the motion of this point will give the component acceleration of the first point in the directions of the instantaneous positions of OX and OY. Calling the values of these accelerations U, V, we obtain by the same process as before

$$\left.\begin{array}{l}U = \dot{u} - \omega v = \ddot{x} - 2\omega\dot{y} - \omega^2 x - \dot{\omega}y \\ V = \dot{v} + \omega u = \ddot{y} + 2\omega\dot{x} - \omega^2 y + \dot{\omega}x\end{array}\right\}. \quad \ldots\ldots\ldots\ldots(2)$$

The terms $-\dot{\omega}y$, $\dot{\omega}x$ vanish if the angular speed ω is constant.

If U, V be each zero, and ω be constant, the equations become $\ddot{x} - 2\omega\dot{y} - \omega^2 x = 0$, $\ddot{y} + 2\omega\dot{x} - \omega^2 y = 0$, which are the equations of motion, referred to uniformly revolving axes, of a particle moving in the plane of the axes under no forces. The particle therefore, as we shall see later, moves in a fixed straight line; and hence, if we turn the whole diagram of axes and moving particle round in its own plane, with angular speed $-\omega$, the axes will be brought to rest, and the particle will describe a spiral of Archimedes. We infer that the component accelerations $\ddot{x}$, $\ddot{y}$ of the particle referred to the fixed axes are given by the equations
$$\ddot{x} = 2\omega\dot{y} + \omega^2 x, \quad \ddot{y} = -2\omega\dot{x} + \omega^2 y. \quad \ldots\ldots\ldots\ldots(3)$$

Ex. 1. If the spiral of Archimedes, $r = a\theta$, where $\theta = \omega t$, be described by turning the radius-vector in the positive direction, it follows from the result just obtained that the equations of motion are

$$\ddot{x} = -2\omega\dot{y} + \omega^2 x, \quad \ddot{y} = 2\omega\dot{x} + \omega^2 y.$$

This can easily be verified directly by differentiation of

$$x = \omega t \cos \omega t, \quad y = \omega t \sin \omega t.$$

[See Ex. 5, p. 78.]

Ex. 2. A particle in motion on a horizontal table receives (in consequence of friction) acceleration of amount μg in the direction opposed to that of the relative motion. The table rotates with angular speed ω about a vertical axis; show that if u, v be rectangular components of the particle's motion with reference to axes, drawn on the table from the intersection of the axis with its surface, and therefore turning with angular speed ω, the equations of motion are satisfied by the values

$$u = (V - \mu g t)\sin\{\omega(t - t_0)\}, \quad v = (V - \mu g t)\cos\{\omega(t - t_0)\},$$

where V and t_0 are constants depending on the initial circumstances.

[R.N.C.]

32   A TREATISE ON DYNAMICS.   [CH. I.

The components of acceleration with reference to fixed axes, with which the rotating axes coincide at time t, are $\dot{u}-\omega v$, $\dot{v}+\omega u$. The speed-components of the particle are $u-\omega y$, $v+\omega x$ with reference to the same axes. Hence the components of the relative motion are u, v. The direction of the acceleration is therefore opposed to the direction of which the cosines are $u/\sqrt{u^2+v^2}$, $v/\sqrt{u^2+v^2}$. Thus the equations of motion are

$$\dot{u}-\omega v = -\mu g \frac{u}{\sqrt{u^2+v^2}}, \quad \dot{v}+\omega u = -\mu g \frac{v}{\sqrt{u^2+v^2}}.$$

These give at once the two relations

$$v\dot{u}-u\dot{v} = \omega(u^2+v^2), \quad u\dot{u}+v\dot{v} = -\mu g \sqrt{u^2+v^2}.$$

Differentiating now the values of u, v suggested above, and substituting in the equations, we get

$$v\dot{u}-u\dot{v} = \omega(V-\mu gt)^2, \quad u\dot{u}+v\dot{v} = -\mu g(V-\mu gt).$$

But $(V-\mu gt)^2 = u^2+v^2$, and $V-\mu gt = \sqrt{u^2+v^2}$, so that the equations are satisfied.

Ex. 3. The motion of a particle P in a plane is referred to axes Ox, Oy, inclined at an angle α, and rotating in the plane with angular speed ω: to find the component velocities with reference to fixed axes with which Ox, Oy coincide at the instant.

Let the speeds to be found be u, v. Also let the coordinates of the particle with reference to Ox, Oy be x, y, and with reference to two rectangular axes, of which one coincides with Ox be ξ, η, and let these axes also rotate with angular speed ω. We have then

$$\xi = x+y\cos\alpha, \quad \eta = y\sin\alpha,$$

so that $\quad \dot{\xi} = \dot{x}+\dot{y}\cos\alpha, \quad \dot{\eta} = \dot{y}\sin\alpha.$

The speeds with reference to fixed axes coinciding with the rectangular axes at the instant are $\dot{\xi}-\omega\eta$, $\dot{\eta}+\omega\xi$. The speeds u, v must give these components as follows:

$$\dot{\xi}-\omega\eta = \dot{x}+\dot{y}\cos\alpha - \omega y\sin\alpha = u+v\cos\alpha,$$
$$\dot{\eta}+\omega\xi = \dot{y}\sin\alpha + \omega x + \omega y\cos\alpha = v\sin\alpha.$$

Solving for u, v, we get

$$u = \dot{x} - \omega x \cot\alpha - \omega y \operatorname{cosec}\alpha,$$
$$v = \dot{y} + \omega y \cot\alpha + \omega x \operatorname{cosec}\alpha.$$

The same results may be obtained by the reader by subtracting from $\dot{x}\,dt$, $\dot{y}\,dt$ (the displacements in dt along the moving axes) the displacements due to the turning of the axes.

Ex. 4. The position P of the particle in last example is given by the lengths p, q of the perpendiculars let fall from P on the revolving axes Ox, Oy: to find the component speeds u, v along fixed directions with which these perpendiculars coincide at the instant.

We take the components u, v, the first from Ox to P and the second from Oy to P. We get then $\xi = p\cot\alpha + q\cosec\alpha$, $\eta = p$, and

$$\dot\xi - \omega\eta = v\sin\alpha, \quad \dot\eta + \omega\xi = u - v\cos\alpha.$$

Hence, substituting for $\dot\xi$, $\dot\eta$, ξ, η, we obtain

$$v\sin\alpha = \dot p\cot\alpha + \dot q\cosec\alpha - \omega p,$$
$$u - v\cos\alpha = \dot p + \omega(q\cosec\alpha + p\cot\alpha).$$

Solving for u and v, we get

$$u = \dot p(1 + \cot^2\alpha) + \dot q\cosec\alpha\cot\alpha + \omega q\cosec\alpha,$$
$$v = \dot p\cot\alpha\cosec\alpha + \dot q\cosec^2\alpha - \omega p\cosec\alpha.$$

15. Three-Dimensional Motion. Revolving Axes. Equations similar to (1) and (2) can be obtained for any other directed quantities characteristic of the motion, and associated with the axes Ox, Oy. To complete the subject here, we may take three rectangular axes Ox, Oy, Oz, which are in motion as follows: the axes Oy, Oz revolve about Ox with angular speed ω_1, Oz, Ox revolve about Oy with angular speed ω_2, and Ox, Oy revolve about Oz with angular speed ω_3, in the directions shown in Fig. 7. By this motion the mutual rectangularity of the axes is not interfered with.

Now let F, G, H be the components of any directed quantity with reference to these axes in the positions which they occupy at time t. Consider the rate of growth of the component associated with the instantaneous position of Ox. The turning about Oy is bringing the axis Oz round toward the instantaneous position of Ox, and the turning about Oz is carrying the axis Oy away from that position. From the former results a rate of growth $\omega_2 H$, and from the latter a rate of growth $-\omega_3 G$, of the component associated with a fixed axis coinciding with the instantaneous position of Ox. Hence the total rate of growth is $\dot F - \omega_3 G + \omega_2 H$. Similarly we obtain for fixed axes coinciding with the instantaneous positions of Oy, Oz, rates of growth of the components associated with them,

$$\dot G - \omega_1 H + \omega_3 F, \quad \dot H - \omega_2 F + \omega_1 G.$$

If we call these three rates L, M, N, we have the equations

$$\left.\begin{array}{l} L = \dot F - \omega_3 G + \omega_2 H \\ M = \dot G - \omega_1 H + \omega_3 F \\ N = \dot H - \omega_2 F + \omega_1 G \end{array}\right\} \quad\ldots\ldots\ldots\ldots\ldots\ldots(1)$$

In precisely the same way as before (§ 14) we get for the time-rates of variation of the components of the quantity (L, M, N) for fixed axes coinciding with Ox, Oy, Oz,

$$\left.\begin{array}{l} U = \dot L - \omega_3 M + \omega_2 N \\ V = \dot M - \omega_1 N + \omega_3 L \\ W = \dot N - \omega_2 L + \omega_1 M \end{array}\right\}, \quad\ldots\ldots\ldots\ldots\ldots\ldots(2)$$

in which the values of L, M, N are to be inserted from (1).

34   A TREATISE ON DYNAMICS.   [CH. I.

The resultant of L, M, N or U, V, W is the rate of displacement of the outer extremity of the vector representing F, G, H or L, M, N, as the case may be.

If for example $F, G, H = \dot{x}, \dot{y}, \dot{z}$, the speeds of a particle with reference to the moving axes, and u, v, w be the components with reference to fixed axes coinciding with the moving axes at the instant,

$$\left.\begin{array}{l} u = \dot{x} - \omega_3 y + \omega_2 z, \\ v = \dot{y} - \omega_1 z + \omega_3 x, \\ w = \dot{z} - \omega_2 x + \omega_1 y. \end{array}\right\} \quad \ldots\ldots\ldots\ldots\ldots\ldots\ldots\ldots (3)$$

Example. To find the components of velocity and acceleration along the radius-vector, the tangent to the meridian, and the tangent to the parallel of latitude, for the instantaneous position of the point of Fig. 10.

These directions are to be regarded as *fixed axes*, with which the moving OP and the tangents carried with it coincide at the instant considered.

The speed-components are $\dot{r}, r\dot{\theta}, r\cos\theta.\dot{\phi}$, if θ is taken as shown in Fig. 10, and $\dot{r}, r\dot{\theta}, r\sin\theta.\dot{\phi}$ if the angle POZ, the colatitude, is taken as θ. In the latter case $r\dot{\theta}$ is in the opposite direction to $r\dot{\theta}$ in the former.

Now take the acceleration-component along the instantaneous position of OP. We have first the part $\ddot{r}$ of this component. Next we observe that as P makes in dt the step $r\,d\theta$ in the plane POZ that transverse step turns through the angle $d\theta$ away from the fixed outward direction OP, and therefore, by § 9, furnishes $-r\dot{\theta}\,d\theta$, increase of speed along OP, that is a rate $-r\dot{\theta}^2$ of growth of speed along OP is caused by the turning.

Again, as P moves in dt through $r\cos\theta.\,d\phi$ along the parallel, the direction of the parallel turns towards the first perpendicular from P on OZ, and a rate $r\cos\theta.\dot{\phi}^2$ of growth of speed along that perpendicular is the result. This has components $r\cos^2\theta.\dot{\phi}^2$ along the fixed direction PO, and $r\sin\theta\cos\theta.\dot{\phi}^2$ in the direction of the transverse $r\,d\theta$. The total acceleration along the fixed direction OP is therefore
$$\ddot{r} - r\dot{\theta}^2 - r\cos^2\theta.\dot{\phi}^2 = \ddot{r} + (\dot{r}^2 - v^2)/r.$$

The acceleration along the meridian at P is found in the same way to be
$$\frac{d}{dt}(r\dot{\theta}) + \dot{r}\dot{\theta} + r\cos\theta.\dot{\phi}^2\sin\theta,$$
that is
$$\frac{1}{r}\frac{d}{dt}(r^2\dot{\theta}) + r\sin\theta\cos\theta.\dot{\phi}^2.$$

If the colatitude is taken as θ, this must be changed to
$$\frac{1}{r}\frac{d}{dt}(r^2\dot{\theta}) - r\sin\theta\cos\theta.\dot{\phi}^2,$$
and the direction is opposed to the former direction.

§§ 15, 16] NORMAL AND TANGENTIAL ACCELERATIONS. 35

Along the parallel of latitude we have (1) the part $d(r\cos\theta\cdot\dot{\phi})/dt$ of the total component of acceleration, (2) the part due to the moving OP along which the speed is $\dot{r}$, (3) the part due to the moving transverse to OP in the plane POZ, along which the speed is $r\dot{\theta}$. Now, with respect to (2), we observe that $\dot{r}$ along OP resolves into $\dot{r}\sin\theta$ along OZ and $\dot{r}\cos\theta$ along OM, of which the latter only changes direction with respect to the fixed position of the parallel at P. The result is acceleration $r\cos\theta\cdot\dot{\phi}$ along that fixed direction. Again, for (3), $r\dot{\theta}$ resolves into $r\dot{\theta}\cos\theta$ along OZ and $-r\dot{\theta}\sin\theta$ along OM. The latter gives acceleration $-r\dot{\theta}\dot{\phi}\sin\theta$ along the parallel, the former gives nothing. The total acceleration along the parallel is therefore $d(r\cos\theta\cdot\dot{\phi})/dt + \dot{r}\cos\theta\dot{\phi} - r\dot{\theta}\dot{\phi}\sin\theta$, that is

$$\frac{1}{r\cos\theta}\frac{d}{dt}(r^2\cos^2\theta\cdot\dot{\phi}),$$

or, if the colatitude is taken for θ,

$$\frac{1}{r\sin\theta}\frac{d}{dt}(r^2\sin^2\theta\cdot\dot{\phi}).$$

16. Curvilinear Motion in Space of Three Dimensions. Normal and Tangential Accelerations. From the result in §10 we obtain some geometrical results of interest. The components of acceleration of a point moving in a curve in space of three dimensions are v^2/R towards the centre of curvature, and $\dot{v}$, or $\ddot{s}$, along the curve in the direction of motion. Hence the resultant acceleration is $(v^4/R^2 + \dot{v}^2)^{\frac{1}{2}}$, which is inclined to the direction of motion at the angle $\cos^{-1}\{\dot{v}/(v^4/R^2 + \dot{v}^2)^{\frac{1}{2}}\}$ in the osculating plane at the point, that is the plane containing two consecutive tangents at the position of the point, or one tangent there and the radius of curvature.

But the components of velocity along any system of fixed axes Ox, Oy, Oz are $\dot{x}$, $\dot{y}$, $\dot{z}$ (which are such that $v^2 = \dot{x}^2 + \dot{y}^2 + \dot{z}^2$), and the accelerations along these axes are therefore $\ddot{x}$, $\ddot{y}$, $\ddot{z}$. Hence the resultant acceleration is $(\ddot{x}^2 + \ddot{y}^2 + \ddot{z}^2)^{\frac{1}{2}}$. Thus we have the equation

$$\left.\begin{array}{c}\dfrac{v^4}{R^2} + \dot{v}^2 = \ddot{x}^2 + \ddot{y}^2 + \ddot{z}^2 \\[6pt] \dfrac{\dot{s}^4}{R^2} + \ddot{s}^2 = \ddot{x}^2 + \ddot{y}^2 + \ddot{z}^2\end{array}\right\} \quad\ldots\ldots\ldots\ldots\ldots\ldots(1)$$

or

in complete fluxional notation. In the notation of the differential calculus it is

$$\frac{\left(\frac{ds}{dt}\right)^4}{R^2}+\left(\frac{d^2s}{dt^2}\right)^2=\left(\frac{d^2x}{dt^2}\right)^2+\left(\frac{d^2y}{dt^2}\right)^2+\left(\frac{d^2z}{dt^2}\right)^2. \quad\ldots\ldots(2)$$

From the discussion above it will be seen that the acceleration $\ddot{s}$ along the curve coincides with the resultant acceleration only when $R = \infty$. It is not unusual for students to assume that $\ddot{s}$ is the resultant acceleration, chiefly because too frequently the only cases considered in elementary dynamics are those in which there is no acceleration except in the line of motion. The resultant acceleration is the square root of the right-hand side of (2), while

$$\ddot{s}=\frac{dx}{ds}\ddot{x}+\frac{dy}{ds}\ddot{y}+\frac{dz}{ds}\ddot{z}. \quad\ldots\ldots\ldots\ldots\ldots\ldots(3)$$

Equation (1) can be transformed as follows. If, as we have already supposed, ds be an infinitesimal step along the curve, taken by the moving point in the correspondingly small interval of time dt, we have $\dot{x} = \dot{s}\, dx/ds$.

Hence $$\ddot{x}=\dot{s}^2\frac{d^2x}{ds^2}+\ddot{s}\frac{dx}{ds}=\frac{\dot{s}^2}{R}R\frac{d^2x}{ds^2}+\ddot{s}\frac{dx}{ds}, \quad\ldots\ldots\ldots\ldots(4)$$

and similar results are derived in the same way from $\ddot{y}$, $\ddot{z}$. These substituted in (1) give the transformation in question [(3), § 17].

17. Curvature of a Path in Space of Three Dimensions. We infer from (4) of last section that $R d^2x/ds^2$ is the x-direction-cosine of the radius of curvature. For $\ddot{x}$ is the acceleration parallel to the axis of x; this must be equal to the sum of the two rectangular components $\dot{s}^2/R$, $\ddot{s}$, each multiplied by the cosine of the angle which its direction makes with the axis of x. Hence the direction-cosines of the radius of curvature are
$$R\left(\frac{d^2x}{ds^2},\ \frac{d^2y}{ds^2},\ \frac{d^2z}{ds^2}\right).$$

Again dx/ds, dy/ds, dz/ds are the direction-cosines of the tangent to the curve at the element ds, and

$$\left(\frac{dx}{ds}\right)^2+\left(\frac{dy}{ds}\right)^2+\left(\frac{dz}{ds}\right)^2=1, \quad\ldots\ldots\ldots\ldots\ldots(1)$$

$$\frac{dx}{ds}\frac{d^2x}{ds^2}+\frac{dy}{ds}\frac{d^2y}{ds^2}+\frac{dz}{ds}\frac{d^2z}{ds^2}=0. \quad\ldots\ldots\ldots\ldots\ldots(2)$$

CURVATURE OF PATH IN SPACE.

The expression on the left of the last equation should not be confused with the similar in appearance but quite different expression on the right of (3), § 16.

From (1) and (4), § 16, we see that if both sides of (4) be squared, and also both sides of the two similar equations for d^2y/dt^2, d^2z/dt^2, we get by addition

$$\ddot{x}^2 + \ddot{y}^2 + \ddot{z}^2 = v^4 \left\{ \left(\frac{d^2x}{ds^2}\right)^2 + \left(\frac{d^2y}{ds^2}\right)^2 + \left(\frac{d^2z}{ds^2}\right)^2 \right\} + \left(\frac{d^2s}{dt^2}\right)^2. \quad \ldots\ldots(3)$$

Hence, substituting in (1), we obtain

$$\frac{1}{R^2} = \left(\frac{d^2x}{ds^2}\right)^2 + \left(\frac{d^2y}{ds^2}\right)^2 + \left(\frac{d^2z}{ds^2}\right)^2, \quad \ldots\ldots\ldots\ldots(4)$$

a purely geometrical equation for the curvature of the path at the element ds.

This result may also be obtained as follows without the introduction of the idea of motion. If the direction-cosines of the tangent, at a point P in the curve, be $dx/ds, \ldots$, those of the tangent at a point distant ds from the former are

$$dx/ds + d^2x/ds^2 . ds, \ldots.$$

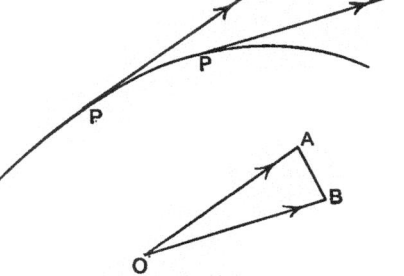

Fig. 11.

Hence if we lay off from an origin O two lines OA, OB, each of unit length, in the directions of the two tangents, the coordinates of A and B will be simply the direction-cosines in each case. This gives for the distance AB the expression

$$\left\{ \left(\frac{d^2x}{ds^2}\right)^2 + \left(\frac{d^2y}{ds^2}\right)^2 + \left(\frac{d^2z}{ds^2}\right)^2 \right\}^{\frac{1}{2}} ds,$$

which, since $OA = OB = 1$, is also the measure of the small angle AOB. But since OA, OB are parallel to the tangents at the extremities of ds, this angle has also the measure ds/R. Thus we obtain

$$\frac{1}{R} = \left\{ \left(\frac{d^2x}{ds^2}\right)^2 + \left(\frac{d^2y}{ds^2}\right)^2 + \left(\frac{d^2z}{ds^2}\right)^2 \right\}^{\frac{1}{2}} = \left\{ \left(\frac{dl}{ds}\right)^2 + \left(\frac{dm}{ds}\right)^2 + \left(\frac{dn}{ds}\right)^2 \right\}^{\frac{1}{2}}, \ldots(5)$$

the same equation as before, with l, m, n put for dx/ds, dy/ds, dz/ds.

If l, m, n thus denote the direction-cosines of OA, and $l+dl$, $m+dm$, $n+dn$ those of OB, we see from what precedes that the angle AOB has the measure

$$\{(dl)^2 + (dm)^2 + (dn)^2\}^{\frac{1}{2}} \text{ or } \{(dl/ds)^2 + (dm/ds)^2 + (dn/ds)^2\}^{\frac{1}{2}} ds,$$

and the cosines of AB have the values $R\,dl/ds$, $R\,dm/ds$, $R\,dn/ds$. Further, as the point moves along the path its direction of motion turns in the plane of the consecutive tangents at the point with angular speed ω given by

$$\omega = (\dot{l}^2 + \dot{m}^2 + \dot{n}^2)^{\frac{1}{2}}. \qquad (6)$$

The same discussion shows that $(\dot{l}^2 + \dot{m}^2 + \dot{n}^2)^{\frac{1}{2}}$ is the angular speed of change of any direction to which direction-cosines l, m, n, which vary with the time, apply, whether successive directions of motion of a moving point or successive directions of an "axis" with which some directed quantity is associated. If we call this angular speed ω, and take two lines OA, OB as above, then the direction-cosines of AB are $\dot{l}/\omega$, $\dot{m}/\omega$, $\dot{n}/\omega$, for $R\,dl/ds = \dot{l}/\omega$, and so for the other direction-cosines found above for AB.

The discussion above has proceeded on the assumption that there is no acceleration perpendicular to the osculating plane, that is the plane of the radius of curvature and the tangent, or the plane of two successive tangents, say that of the tangent at P and the tangent at a close point P_0. This assumption is confirmed by the agreement of the results of the kinematical and geometrical processes, and justified by the geometrical conditions fulfilled by the osculating plane. Consider three close points on the curve, which in order of position are P_0, P, P_1. The osculating plane through P_0 and P contains the tangents at P_0 and P, and the osculating plane through P and P_1 contains the tangents at P and P_1. The latter plane may be regarded as the former turned through a small angle about the tangent at P. The fact that the tangent at P is common to the two positions of the plane renders the acceleration perpendicular to the osculating plane zero.

The reader may, as an exercise, frame a formal proof of this result, by showing that the cosines of the normal to the plane containing the direction of motion and the resultant acceleration are identical with those of the normal to the osculating plane at the position of the moving point.

18. Examples. Motion of Point along a Moving Guide. A point is in motion along a smooth guiding curve or tube, which is itself in motion and undergoing deformation in any given manner; to find the acceleration of the point.

The velocity of the point for any position P would be $\dot{s}$ if the guide were at rest, and the acceleration in the direction of motion would then be $\ddot{s}$. But the tangent is changing direction as the point moves, and this change is in part due to the motion of the guide. Let the plane of the direction PB, of motion, at the instant considered, and of the radius of curvature (length R) of the element of path, be the plane of the paper. If at P the component velocity of the guide towards the centre of curvature O be ξ, and the component along an axis PC drawn upwards at P be η, the components along the corresponding directions at the farther extremity P' of ds will be

$$\xi + d\xi/ds \cdot ds, \quad \eta + d\eta/ds \cdot ds.$$

The element ds is therefore turning round towards the instantaneous

§§ 17, 18]   MOTION ON A MOVING GUIDE.   39

position of PO with angular speed $d\xi/ds$, and towards the axis PC with angular speed $d\eta/ds$. These are therefore the angular speeds with which PO and PC are turning away from the instantaneous position of ds in the planes BPO, BPC; and there are rates of gain of velocity along the instantaneous position of ds from this cause of amounts $-\xi d\xi/ds, -\eta d\eta/ds$.

Again, if the element of the guide were at rest there would, with the displacement along ds, be a change of direction of motion of amount ds/R, that is the rate of turning of the tangent would be $\dot{s}/R$. This would also be the rate of turning of PO away from the instantaneous position PB of the tangent at P. The speed $\dot{\xi}$ along PO gives, on account of this turning, a rate of growth of speed along PB, amounting to $-\xi \dot{s}/R$. Hence if S denote the total acceleration along PB, we have

$$\ddot{s} - \xi \frac{\dot{s}}{R} - \xi \frac{d\xi}{ds} - \eta \frac{d\eta}{ds} = S$$

or

$$\ddot{s} = S + \xi \frac{\dot{s}}{R} + \xi \frac{d\xi}{ds} + \eta \frac{d\eta}{ds}. \quad\quad\quad\quad\quad\quad (1)$$

This theorem is of importance in fluid motion; it is given in Lord Kelvin's Memoir on Vortex Motion (*Collected Papers*, vol. iv.). Lord Kelvin's proof proceeds as follows, and affords an example of some of the results obtained above. Let l, m, n denote the direction-cosines of PB (as specified above) with reference to any chosen system of fixed rectangular axes. Then the component velocities of the point carried as it is with, while moving along, the guide, are $\dot{x}, \dot{y}, \dot{z}$, and its component accelerations are $\ddot{x}, \ddot{y}, \ddot{z}$. Hence

$$s = l\dot{x} + m\dot{y} + n\dot{z}, \quad S = l\ddot{x} + m\ddot{y} + n\ddot{z}. \quad\quad\quad\quad (2)$$

Also $\quad \ddot{s} = l\ddot{x} + m\ddot{y} + n\ddot{z} + \dot{l}\dot{x} + \dot{m}\dot{y} + \dot{n}\dot{z} = S + \dot{l}\dot{x} + \dot{m}\dot{y} + \dot{n}\dot{z}. \quad\quad (3)$

But it has been shown (§ 17) that $\omega = (\dot{l}^2 + \dot{m}^2 + \dot{n}^2)^{\frac{1}{2}}$, is the time-rate at which the direction of motion is changing as the point moves along the guide, and here includes the angular turning which would exist if the guide were fixed, together with that due to the motion of the guide. It has also been shown that $\dot{l}/\omega, \dot{m}/\omega, \dot{n}/\omega$ are the direction-cosines of the line perpendicular to PB in the plane of turning at the instant, towards which PB is turning, and $\dot{l}\dot{x} + \dot{m}\dot{y} + \dot{n}\dot{z}$ is the component, u say, of velocity parallel to that line. Hence we have

$$\ddot{s} - \omega u = S, \quad\quad\quad\quad\quad\quad\quad\quad\quad\quad (4)$$

a result which might have been written down at once by the principle set forth in § 9. But if the guide had been fixed we should have had $\omega = \dot{s}/R$, and we have here also the angular speed $d\xi/ds$, in the same plane as $\dot{s}/R$, that is BPO; and also the angular speed $d\eta/ds$ in the plane BPC. Hence, clearly, $\omega u = \xi(\dot{s}/R + d\xi/ds) + \eta \, d\eta/ds$, so that

$$\ddot{s} = S + \xi\left(\frac{\dot{s}}{R} + \frac{d\xi}{ds}\right) + \eta \frac{d\eta}{ds}, \quad\quad\quad\quad\quad (5)$$

as before.

40   A TREATISE ON DYNAMICS.   [CH. I.

19. Tangential Acceleration with Space as Independent Variable. The tangential acceleration $\ddot{s}$ of a particle which moves along a fixed curve may be written in a special form which is sometimes useful. The distance s traversed from any chosen point P_0, on the curve, at which the particle is situated when $t=0$, is a function of the interval of time t, which has elapsed since it was at P_0, so that if t is known s can be calculated. But, conversely, the interval of time is a function of s, so that the march of time may be traced by the displacement of the particle along the curve. In other words, we may take s as the independent and t as the dependent variable. We have then in the first place $ds/dt = 1/dt/ds$, and therefore

$$\ddot{s} = \frac{d\dot{s}}{ds}\dot{s} = \dot{s}\frac{d}{ds}\frac{1}{\frac{dt}{ds}} = -\dot{s}^3\frac{d^2t}{ds^2}. \qquad \dots\dots\dots\dots(1)$$

For example, in the testing of gun-powder, a bullet fired from a rifle pierces a succession of screens, and the instant of piercing is registered in each case by a chronograph. It is found that the relation between the interval of time, from the instant of discharge, and the distance s traversed, is given by
$$t = a + bs + cs^2, \qquad \dots\dots\dots\dots\dots\dots(2)$$
where a, b, c are constants determined by determining the time for different positions of the screen. This equation gives $dt/ds = b + 2cs$, $d^2t/ds^2 = 2c$, and therefore

$$\ddot{s} = -\frac{2c}{(b + 2cs)^3}. \qquad \dots\dots\dots\dots\dots(3)$$

The bullet is thus subject to a retardation proportional to $\dot{s}^3$, which diminishes as the distance s increases.

20. Equation of Hodograph. Case of Falling Body. The hodograph may be determined in any given case of the motion of a point by substituting in the equations of motion (that is the equations which in that case connect the components of acceleration $\ddot{x}$, $\ddot{y}$, $\ddot{z}$ with certain known quantities, which are in general functions of the coordinates) ξ, η, ζ for $\dot{x}$, $\dot{y}$, $\dot{z}$ and determining a relation between constants and ξ, η, ζ, which are now the coordinates of a point on the hodograph. This is always possible, theoretically at least, since by its definition the hodograph exists in every definite case of motion. But it may frequently be determined without analysis. For example, take the case of an unresisted projectile under an acceleration g, constant in magnitude and in direction. Strictly, however, the acceleration produced by gravity varies in amount with the height of the particle above the earth's surface, and in direction with the horizontal displacement. We here disregard these variations, and refer to the direction of the acceleration as *vertical*, and to any direction perpendicular to that as *horizontal*. The application of the results to any other case of uniform acceleration than that approximately given by gravity, can be made at once by transferring the direction indicated by the adjective *vertical* to the acceleration in the case to be considered. Clearly, then, in this case the hodograph is a vertical straight line. For the change of velocity in every interval of time is vertically downward, and therefore the extremities of the lines Op, Oq, Or, ..., representing the velocity at different positions of the point in its path, must lie in a vertical line.

Each velocity Op, Oq, ... in the diagram (Fig. 12) has the same projection Oa on the horizontal. This expresses the constancy of the horizontal component of velocity, and, as we shall see presently, corresponds to a property of the path, which is a parabola with its axis vertical, as shown in Fig. 13.

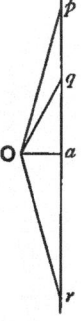

Fig. 12.

To deal with this case analytically, we proceed as follows. The equations of motion are

$$\ddot{x} = 0, \quad \ddot{y} = -g, \quad \ldots \ldots \ldots \ldots \ldots (1)$$

referred to an axis of x drawn horizontally and an axis of y drawn vertically upward. Putting ξ, η for $\dot{x}$, $\dot{y}$, we get

$$\xi = a, \quad \eta = b - gt, \quad \ldots \ldots \ldots \ldots (2)$$

where a and b are constants. The equations just found are those of a vertical straight line.

21. Motion of Projectile in Uniform Field of Force. We consider the motion of a particle projected initially in any direction, and thereafter subjected to acceleration constant in magnitude and direction, which we have seen is approximately the case of an unresisted projectile under gravity.

Let θ_0 be the inclination of the line of projection to the horizontal and V the initial speed; then the vertical and horizontal components of V are $V \sin \theta_0$, $V \cos \theta_0$. The latter remains unaltered during the motion; the vertical component has become $V \sin \theta - gt$, at time t after the instant of projection. Then the horizontal and vertical distances of the particle from the point of projection, x and y say, are (§ 5) given by

$$x = Vt \cos \theta_0, \quad y = Vt \sin \theta_0 - \tfrac{1}{2} gt^2, \quad \ldots\ldots\ldots\ldots(1)$$

which, by elimination of t, give

$$y = x \tan \theta_0 - \frac{1}{2} \frac{g}{V^2 \cos^2 \theta_0} x^2, \quad \ldots\ldots\ldots\ldots(2)$$

a relation connecting x and y, the coordinates of any point on the path, or, as we call it, the equation of the path, from which all the facts of the motion can be derived.

Here y is measured upward from the point of projection. Clearly its maximum value has been reached when $dy/dx = 0$.

Now
$$\frac{dy}{dx} = \tan \theta_0 - \frac{g}{V^2 \cos^2 \theta_0} x, \quad \ldots\ldots\ldots\ldots(3)$$

which vanishes when $x = V^2 \sin \theta_0 \cos \theta_0 / g$, and therefore when $y = V^2 \sin^2 \theta_0 / 2g$. Denoting these special values of x, y by a, b, we see that at the point a, b the direction of motion, the tangent to the path at the point, is horizontal. It is convenient to transfer the origin of coordinates to the point a, b, and to measure y downwards from the new origin. These changes are made by writing $x + a$ for x, and $b - y$ for y, in (2). The equation becomes

$$y = \frac{g}{2 V^2 \cos^2 \theta} x^2 \quad \ldots\ldots\ldots\ldots\ldots\ldots(4)$$

or, as we shall write it, $\quad x^2 = 4\alpha y, \quad \ldots\ldots\ldots\ldots\ldots\ldots(5)$

where $\alpha = V^2 \cos^2 \theta_0 / 2g$.

This is the equation of a parabola of latus rectum, 4α in length, LFM in Fig. 13. The new origin O is the vertex of the curve, and a vertical through O is called the axis, from the fact that for every value of y there are two values of x, viz. $\pm 2\sqrt{\alpha y}$, which are numerically equal and opposite in sign, so that the curve lies symmetrically on the two sides of the axis. The coordinates of F are $y = \alpha$, $x = 0$, and so $LF = FM = 2\alpha$. The distance of F from the point of projection is $\{a^2 + (b-\alpha)^2\}^{\frac{1}{2}}$, that is $V^2/2g$, and the coordinates of F from that point as origin are $V^2 \sin 2\theta/2g$, $V^2 \cos 2\theta/2g$.

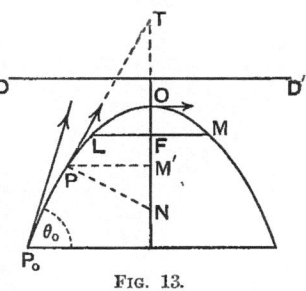

Fig. 13.

22. Properties of Path. If a horizontal line DD' be drawn in the plane of the curve at a height α above the origin, it can be shown that the distance of any point of the curve from the line is equal to the distance of the point from F, which is therefore called the *focus* of the curve. For the former distance is $\alpha + y$, and the latter is $\{(y-\alpha)^2 + x^2\}^{\frac{1}{2}} = \alpha + y$, since $x^2 = 4\alpha y$. The line drawn as specified is called the *directrix* of the curve. The distance H of the point of projection from the directrix, being equal to the distance of that point from the focus, is $V^2/2g$, that is we have $V^2 = 2gH$. The speed of projection is therefore equal to that which a particle would acquire in falling to P_0 from rest at the directrix, and therefore H is called the "head" for the speed V. The distance H of P_0 from the directrix, it will be seen, is independent of the angle of elevation θ_0. H may of course be the distance of *any* point P on the curve at which the speed is v, and we have then $v^2 = 2gH$; H is then the "head" for the speed v.

If P be any point on the curve, the tangent of the inclination of PF to the vertical is $x/(y-\alpha) = 4\alpha x/(x^2 - 4\alpha^2)$, by the value of y. The tangent of the inclination of the tangent to the curve at P to the vertical is $dx/dy = 2\alpha/x$. Now $2(2\alpha/x)/\{1 - (2\alpha/x)^2\} = 4\alpha x/(x^2 - 4\alpha^2)$, and therefore the tangent at P bisects the angle between PF and the vertical, a well-known property of the parabola.

Again, take any two points on the curve, say P_0, which may be taken as the point of projection, and P, which may be regarded as the point which the moving particle has reached after the lapse of an interval of time t. Draw a tangent to the curve at P_0 and let it meet the vertical through P in Q; then Q is the point which the

44   A TREATISE ON DYNAMICS.   [CH. I.

particle would have reached in time t if there had been no acceleration, that is $P_0Q^2 = V^2t^2$. But it is clear that $QP = \frac{1}{2}gt^2$, so that $P_0Q^2 = 2(V^2/g) \cdot QP$.
Hence
$$P_0Q^2 = 4P_0F \cdot QP, \quad \ldots\ldots\ldots\ldots\ldots\ldots\ldots(1)$$
since, as has been proved above, $P_0F = V^2/2g$.

At any point P on the curve (Fig. 13) draw a tangent PT, a normal PN, and a line $l'M'$ at right angles to the axis, and let these lines intersect the axis in T, N, M'. The distance $M'N$ is called the subnormal, and has a constant length. For its length is $x\,dx/dy$, and this by the equation of the curve is 2α. This is a characteristic geometrical property of the parabola.

Again, by the diagram, if ds be a step along the curve from P, and $-dy$, since y is measured downward, be its projection on the axis of the curve, we have $\sin\theta = -dy/ds$. But also $\sin\theta = x/PN$. Hence

$$PN = -x\frac{ds}{dy} = -x\frac{\dot{s}}{\dot{y}} = -2\alpha\frac{\dot{s}}{\dot{x}}. \quad \ldots\ldots\ldots\ldots\ldots(2)$$

But $\dot{x}$ is constant, and therefore PN may be taken as representing the speed $\dot{s}$ of the particle in the path, with direction turned through a right angle. The subnormal represents on the same scale, and with the same change of direction, the constant horizontal speed.

It may be noticed that two paths coplanar with that here discussed, having the same point P_0, and speed V, of projection, but inclinations $\theta_0 + \alpha$, $\theta_0 - \alpha$, where α is very small, will intersect the path for inclination θ_0, at the point where the direction of projection is perpendicular to that of motion. This follows from the fact, which the student may easily verify, that if two particles be projected from the same point at the same instant in any two directions, the line joining the particles remains perpendicular to the line bisecting the angle between the two directions. Thus the two particles in the case supposed must cross together the trajectory for θ_0, as stated above.

23. Horizontal Range. Range with Path through Fixed Point. Denoting the range on the horizontal plane through the point of projection by R, and the latus rectum, or *parameter*, of the curve, that is $2V^2\cos^2\theta_0/g$, by p, and putting $y = 0$ in (2) of § 21, we have
$$x = 0 \text{ and } x = R,$$
where
$$R = \frac{V^2}{g}\sin 2\theta_0 = p\tan\theta_0. \quad \ldots\ldots\ldots\ldots\ldots\ldots(1)$$

Thus we may write the equation (2), § 21, of the curve in the forms

$$y = x\tan\theta_0 - \frac{x^2}{p} = \left(x - \frac{x^2}{R}\right)\tan\theta_0, \quad \tan\theta_0 = \frac{y}{x} + \frac{y}{R-x}. \quad \ldots\ldots(2)$$

The last form is important. Here y is any ordinate of the curve and y/x, $y/(R-x)$ are the tangents of the angles ϕ, ϕ' which the ordinate subtends at P_0, the beginning of the range R, and P_0', the end of the range. Thus we can write the last equation as

$$\tan\theta_0 = \tan\phi + \tan\phi', \quad\quad\quad\quad\quad\quad (3)$$

which gives the "elevation" required to enable the projectile just to clear a wall of height y at distance x from the firing point, and reach an object at a distance $R-x$ beyond.

The head H of the speed V and the range R may be employed to give the equation of the path in a form which is sometimes useful. We have seen that if the point of coordinates x, y—the top of the wall in the last article—lie on the path, $\tan\theta_0 = y\{1/x + 1/(R-x)\}$. Substituting in (2), § 21, and reducing, we obtain

$$(R-x)^2 - 4\frac{y}{x}H(R-x) + \frac{y^2}{x^2}R^2 = 0, \quad\quad\quad\quad (4)$$

the form referred to. Here it is to be understood that if x, y are fixed, R varies with H according to this relation; but if R and H are assigned, that is if the speed V of projection and the angle of elevation θ_0 are given, then x, y are the coordinates of *any* point which lies on the path.

It is easy to show that for a given value of H and a given point x, y on the path (the top of the wall, say, just referred to) there are two values of $R-x$ at which the shot will reach the horizontal through the point of projection. That this must be true is evident from the fact that for the given initial speed there are in general two elevations which will enable the shot to reach a given point, if the point can be reached at all with the given speed of projection. Writing D for $R-x$ in (4), we get, after reduction,

$$(x^2+y^2)D^2 - 2xy(2H-y)D + x^2y^2 = 0, \quad\quad\quad\quad (5)$$

from which we obtain

$$D = \frac{xy}{x^2+y^2}\{2H - y \pm \sqrt{(2H-y)^2 - (x^2+y^2)}\}, \quad\quad\quad (6)$$

There is thus a value below which H cannot be taken if the point x, y is to be reached at all by the shot, that is

$$H = \tfrac{1}{2}\{\sqrt{x^2+y^2} + y\}. \quad\quad\quad\quad\quad\quad (7)$$

For any value of H above this there are two values of D, given by (6), at which the shot will strike the horizontal plane, and there are two corresponding values of R. A point inside the smaller of these distances is in no danger of being struck by the shot.

The foregoing problem may be discussed geometrically as follows. It has been noticed that the head $H(= V^2/2g)$, that is the distance of P_0 from the directrix, is independent of θ_0, so that all paths from P_0, with speed V of projection, are parabolas which have the same directrix. Their foci

46   A TREATISE ON DYNAMICS.   [CH. I.

are all at the same distance $V^2/2g$ from P_0, and therefore lie on a circle described from P_0 as centre with $V^2/2g$ as radius. This construction, made in Fig. 14, enables the path to be found which passes through a given point P, the problem just considered analytically. With the distance of P from the directrix as radius and P as centre, describe a circle. If P can be reached at all by the projectile, with the given speed of projection, this circle will intersect the former circle in two points, or at least touch it. Either of the points of intersection F_1, F_2 is the focus of a path by which the projectile will pass through P, and thus in general there are, as we have seen above, two possible paths for a given V. As P is carried further off towards the right in the diagram, the two points F_1, F_2 come closer and closer together until at last they coincide; if P be carried further off there is no path on which it lies.

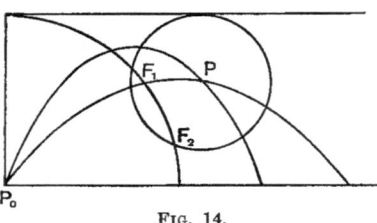

Fig. 14.

24. Envelope of all Coplanar Paths with given Speed of Projection. Consider the position of P (Fig. 15) for which the circles just touch in a point R. Draw the line PM perpendicular to the directrix and produce it to N, so that $PN = OP$, where O is the point of projection. Thus P lies on the parabola of focus O and directrix NL. This parabola is the envelope of all the paths which correspond to different inclinations, all in one plane, of the direction of projection with velocity V from O. To prove this take O as origin. The equation of a path is

$$y = x \tan \theta_0 - \tfrac{1}{2} \frac{g}{V^2 \cos^2 \theta_0} x^2 \quad \dots\dots\dots\dots(1)$$

or, as we can write this equation,

$$\tan^2 \theta_0 - \frac{2V^2}{gx} \tan \theta_0 = -\left(1 + \frac{2y V^2}{gx^2}\right),$$

where we take x, y as the coordinates of the point P_1. The roots of this equation in $\tan \theta_0$ are equal when

$$y = \frac{V^2}{2g} - \frac{g}{2V^2}x^2. \qquad \qquad (2)$$

Thus the point x, y lies on the parabola of which (2) is the equation.

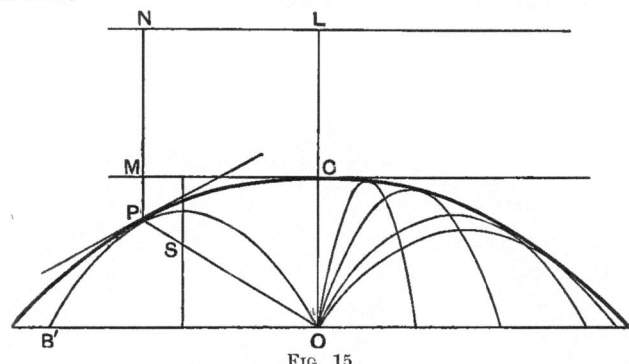

Fig. 15.

The value of dy/dx is zero when $x=0$, and therefore O lies on the axis. When $x=0$, $y = V^2/2g$, hence the point of coordinates 0, $V^2/2g$ is the vertex, and lies on the directrix of the family of parabolas which are the paths for O as point of projection and V as speed of projection. If this point be made the origin, and y be measured downward, the equation of the path becomes

$$x^2 = 4\beta y, \qquad \qquad (3)$$

where $\beta = V^2/2g$. Thus the distance of the focus from the vertex is $V^2/2g$, that is O is the focus. The directrix of this parabola is at a distance $V^2/2g$ above the former directrix, which agrees with the construction stated above.

That this parabola is the envelope of all the paths may be seen at once by differentiating the right-hand side of (1) with respect to θ_0, equating the result to zero, and then eliminating θ_0 between the equation so obtained and (1). [See Gibson's *Calculus*, § 145.] The result is (2), and the proposition is proved.

25. Examples on Parabolic Motion.

Ex. 1. The speeds at the extremities of a focal chord of the path of a projectile are v, v', and u is the horizontal speed: prove that
$$1/v^2 + 1/v'^2 = 1/u^2.$$
By the hodograph, if θ be the inclination of the tangent at one extremity of the focal chord to the horizontal, $v = u/\cos\theta$, $v' = u/\sin\theta$. Thus
$$\frac{1}{v^2} + \frac{1}{v'^2} = \frac{1}{u^2}(\sin^2\theta + \cos^2\theta) = \frac{1}{u^2}.$$

Ex. 2. At three points P, Q, R on the path of a projectile the inclinations of the tangents to the horizontal are $\alpha+\beta$, α, $\alpha-\beta$, and the speeds are v, v', v''. If the time from P to Q be t and from Q to R be t', prove that $v''t = vt'$, and that $1/v + 1/v'' = 2\cos\beta/v'$.

If u be the horizontal speed, we have, by the hodograph (Fig. 12), $v = u/\cos(\alpha+\beta)$, $v' = u/\cos\alpha$, $v'' = u/\cos(\alpha-\beta)$, while the vertical components are $u\tan(\alpha+\beta)$, $u\tan\alpha$, $u\tan(\alpha-\beta)$. Hence
$$gt = u\{\tan(\alpha+\beta) - \tan\alpha\}, \quad gt' = u\{\tan\alpha - \tan(\alpha-\beta)\},$$
and we obtain
$$v''^2 t^2 = \frac{u^4}{g^2}\{\tan(\alpha+\beta) - \tan\alpha\}^2\{1 + \tan^2(\alpha-\beta)\}$$
and
$$v^2 t'^2 = \frac{u^4}{g^2}\{\tan\alpha - \tan(\alpha-\beta)\}^2\{1 + \tan^2(\alpha+\beta)\}.$$

But $\{\tan(\alpha+\beta) - \tan\alpha\}^2 = (1+\tan^2\alpha)^2\tan^2\beta/(1 - \tan\alpha\tan\beta)^2$, and similarly
$$\{\tan\alpha - \tan(\alpha-\beta)\}^2 = (1+\tan^2\alpha)^2\tan^2\beta/(1+\tan\alpha\tan\beta)^2,$$
while
$$1 + \tan^2(\alpha\mp\beta) = (1+\tan^2\alpha+\tan^2\beta+\tan^2\alpha\tan^2\beta)/(1\pm\tan\alpha\tan\beta)^2.$$

Hence, substituting, we get identically $v''^2 t^2 = v^2 t'^2$.

Moreover, we have
$$\frac{1}{v} + \frac{1}{v''} = \frac{1}{u}\{\cos(\alpha+\beta) + \cos(\alpha-\beta)\} = 2\frac{\cos\alpha}{u}\cos\beta = 2\frac{\cos\beta}{v'}.$$

Ex. 3. An unresisted projectile moving under gravity is seen from the point of projection P_0 against a vertical screen at right angles to the plane of projection and at distance D; prove that the projectile appears to descend along the screen with constant speed.

Let the projectile at time t after projection be at a point P, then the line $P_0 P$ is inclined to the horizontal at the angle
$$\alpha = \tan^{-1}\{(Vt\sin\theta_0 - \tfrac{1}{2}gt^2)/Vt\cos\theta_0\}.$$
To continue to move along the line $P_0 P$ the projectile would require a constant vertical speed equal to $V\cos\theta_0\tan\alpha$ or $V\sin\theta_0 - \tfrac{1}{2}gt$. But

the vertical speed at P is $V\sin\theta_0 - gt$, and therefore the projectile has then a vertical speed relatively to the line P_0P of $\frac{1}{2}gt$. It will therefore seem to descend along the screen in time dt a distance $\frac{1}{2}gt\,dt \cdot D/Vt\cos\theta_0 = \frac{1}{2}gD\,dt/V\cos\theta_0$. The rate of falling appears therefore to be $\frac{1}{2}gD/V\cos\theta_0$, which is constant.

Otherwise thus: the apparent height h of the projectile on the screen is given by
$$h = D\,\frac{V\sin\theta_0 - \frac{1}{2}gt}{V\cos\theta_0},$$
and therefore
$$\frac{dh}{dt} = -\frac{1}{2}\frac{gD}{V\cos\theta_0},$$
so that h appears to diminish at rate $\frac{1}{2}gD/V\cos\theta_0$, as before.

Ex. 4. A particle is projected from P_0 so as to pass through a point P at distance l from P_0 on a plane through P_0 inclined at an angle θ to the vertical; find the least speed of projection, and show that the highest point of the path is at a height $l\cos^4\frac{1}{2}\theta$ above P_0.

Taking P_0 as the origin, we obtain, by (2) of §21, since here $x = l\sin\theta$, $y = l\cos\theta$, for the equation of the path,

$$\tan^2\theta_0 - 2\,\frac{V^2}{gl\sin\theta}\tan\theta_0 + 2\,\frac{V^2}{gl\sin^2\theta}\cos\theta + 1 = 0,$$

which gives the speed of projection for a range l on a plane through P_0 inclined at an angle $\pi/2 - \theta$ to the horizontal, when the elevation is θ_0, and the two values of θ_0 when V is given. The roots of this equation in $\tan\theta_0$ must be real, and this imposes the condition

$$\frac{V^4}{g^2l^2\sin^2\theta} > \frac{2V^2}{g}\frac{\cos\theta}{l\sin^2\theta} + 1.$$

The least value of V^2 is therefore given by
$$V^2 = gl(1+\cos\theta) = 2gl\cos^2\tfrac{1}{2}\theta$$
or
$$V = \sqrt{2gl}\cos\tfrac{1}{2}\theta.$$

[This is given at once, by (7) of §23, by writing $l\cos\theta = y$, $l\sin\theta = x$.]

This value of V used in the equation of the path written above leads to $\tan\theta_0 = \cot\frac{1}{2}\theta$, so that $\theta_0 = \frac{1}{2}\pi - \frac{1}{2}\theta$. The greatest height attained is then $y = \frac{1}{2}V^2\sin^2\theta_0/g = \frac{1}{2}V^2\cos^2\frac{1}{2}\theta/g = l\cos^4\frac{1}{2}\theta$.

Ex. 5. To find the time of flight from the point of projection to any point P of the path (oblique range).

Let the line drawn from the point of projection to the point P have inclination α to the horizontal. The speed perpendicular to this line is $(V\sin\theta - gt)\cos\alpha - V\cos\theta\sin\alpha = V\sin(\theta-\alpha) - gt\cos\alpha$. The distance of the projectile from the line at time t is therefore

$$Vt\sin(\theta-\alpha) - \tfrac{1}{2}gt^2\cos\alpha,$$

50   A TREATISE ON DYNAMICS.   [CH. I.

which vanishes when $t=0$, and when
$$t = \frac{2V}{g}\frac{\sin(\theta-\alpha)}{\cos\alpha}.$$

Thus $2V\sin(\theta-\alpha)/g\cos\alpha$ is the time of flight for an oblique range.

If the projection be upwards, α is to be taken positive; if the projection is downwards, α is to be taken negative. Taking α positive in the formula in both cases, we have
$$t = \frac{2V}{g}\frac{\sin(\theta\mp\alpha)}{\cos\alpha},$$
according as the projection is upwards or downwards.

Thus, the time of flight is the same for both upward and downward projection, if the direction of projection is equally inclined in both cases to the line along which the range is taken.

Ex. 6. Prove that the times of flight t, t' corresponding to the two directions of projection for which the horizontal range has the same value R are connected with the elevations θ, θ' by the relation
$$\frac{t^2-t'^2}{t^2+t'^2} = \frac{\sin(\theta-\theta')}{\sin(\theta+\theta')}.$$

We have $t = 2V\sin\theta/g = R/V\cos\theta$, $t' = 2V\sin\theta'/g = R/V\cos\theta'$, and therefore $t/t' = \sin\theta/\sin\theta' = \cos\theta'/\cos\theta$. Hence
$$t^2/t'^2 = \sin\theta\cos\theta'/\sin\theta'\cos\theta,$$
and therefore
$$\frac{t^2-t'^2}{t^2+t'^2} = \frac{\sin(\theta-\theta')}{\sin(\theta+\theta')}.$$

Ex. 7. Find the corresponding relation when the range is inclined at an angle α to the horizontal.

We have seen (Ex. 5) that the times of flight are
$$t = 2V\sin(\theta-\alpha)/g\cos\alpha, \quad t' = 2V\sin(\theta'-\alpha)/g\cos\alpha.$$

But since the horizontal distance travelled is $r\cos\alpha$ (where r is the oblique range), we have also $t = r\cos\alpha/V\cos\theta$, $t' = r\cos\alpha/V\cos\theta'$. Hence we get $t/t' = \sin(\theta-\alpha)/\sin(\theta'-\alpha) = \cos\theta'/\cos\theta$, and therefore $t^2/t'^2 = \sin(\theta-\alpha)\cos\theta'/\sin(\theta'-\alpha)\cos\theta$. Thus we obtain
$$\frac{t^2-t'^2}{t^2+t'^2} = \frac{\sin(\theta-\theta')\cos\alpha}{\sin(\theta+\theta')\cos\alpha - 2\cos\theta\cos\theta'\sin\alpha}.$$

Ex. 8. Prove that the oblique range up a plane inclined at the angle α to the horizontal is $2V^2\sin(\theta-\alpha)\cos\theta/g\cos^2\alpha$.

We have seen that the time of flight is $2V\sin(\theta-\alpha)/g\cos\alpha$. The horizontal distance travelled in that time is $2V^2\sin(\theta-\alpha)\cos\theta/g\cos\alpha$, and this corresponds to a distance $2V^2\sin(\theta-\alpha)\cos\theta/g\cos^2\alpha$ on the slope.

§25]   EXAMPLES OF PARABOLIC MOTION.   51

Ex. 9. Two particles are projected at the same instant from the same point P_0 and in the same plane with different speeds V, V' and different elevations θ, θ': to find the interval of time between the transits of the particles through the point P of intersection of the paths.

If α be the inclination of the line $P_0 P$ to the horizontal, the times of flight are $t = 2V\sin(\theta - \alpha)/g\cos\alpha$, $t' = 2V'\sin(\theta' - \alpha)/g\cos\alpha$, so that we have

$$t - t' = \frac{2}{g}\{V\sin\theta - V'\sin\theta' - (V\cos\theta - V'\cos\theta')\tan\alpha\}.$$

But the last example gives two expressions for the distance of the point of intersection of the paths from the point of projection, from which we at once obtain

$$\tan\alpha = \frac{V^2\sin\theta\cos\theta - V'^2\sin\theta'\cos\theta'}{V^2\cos^2\theta - V'^2\cos^2\theta'}.$$

Substituting this in the expression just obtained for $t - t'$, we get

$$t - t' = \frac{2}{g}\frac{VV'\sin(\theta - \theta')}{V\cos\theta + V'\cos\theta'},$$

which of course may be either positive or negative according to the values of V, V', θ, θ'.

Ex. 10. If t, t' be the times of flight for the two directions θ, θ' of projection by which a particle shot off from P with initial speed V can reach a given point P, and τ, τ' be the times in which the particle in the two cases reaches the highest point of its path; show that

$$(t\tau + t'\tau')/(\tan\theta + \tan\theta')$$

depends only on the distance $P_0 P$ and on the inclination of the line $P_0 P$ to the horizontal. [*Math. Trip.* 1876. The statement has been altered.]

By the previous example,

$$t = \frac{2V}{g}\frac{\sin(\theta - \alpha)}{\cos\alpha}, \quad t' = \frac{2V}{g}\frac{\sin(\theta' - \alpha)}{\cos\alpha}.$$

Also

$$\tau = \frac{V}{g}\sin\theta, \quad \tau' = \frac{V}{g}\sin\theta',$$

so that we obtain

$$t\tau + t'\tau' = \frac{2V^2}{g^2\cos\alpha}\{\sin(\theta - \alpha)\sin\theta + \sin(\theta' - \alpha)\sin\theta'\}.$$

But if R be the horizontal range for the elevation θ, we have, §23,

$$R = r\cos\alpha\tan\theta/(\tan\theta - \tan\alpha) = r\cos^2\alpha\sin\theta/\sin(\theta - \alpha)$$

or $\sin(\theta - \alpha) = r\cos^2\alpha\sin\theta/R = gr\cos^2\alpha\sin\theta/V^2\sin 2\theta.$

Hence $\sin(\theta - \alpha)\sin\theta = \dfrac{gr}{V^2}\dfrac{\cos^2\alpha\sin^2\theta}{\sin 2\theta}.$

Similarly, we obtain
$$\sin(\theta'-\alpha)\sin\theta' = \frac{gr}{V^2}\cos^2\alpha\,\frac{\sin^2\theta'}{\sin 2\theta'}.$$

Hence we have $\quad t\tau+t'\tau' = \dfrac{r}{g}\cos\alpha(\tan\theta+\tan\theta').$

Thus $\sqrt{2}/\sqrt{t\tau+t'\tau'}/(\tan\theta+\tan\theta')$ is the time in which a body falls freely from rest under gravity g through a distance $r\cos\alpha$.

Ex. 11. To find the maximum range of an unresisted projectile on a slope inclined at an angle α to the horizontal.

Let x, y be the coordinates of a point P on the path for elevation θ, and R be the horizontal range, then it is easy to prove (see § 23) that
$$\tan\theta = \frac{y}{x}+\frac{y}{R-x}.$$

If then P be the point on which the shot meets the slope after projection, and r be the range on the slope, we have
$$\tan\theta = \tan\alpha + \frac{r\sin\alpha}{R-r\cos\alpha},$$
and therefore $\quad r = R\,\dfrac{\tan\theta-\tan\alpha}{\cos\alpha\,\tan\theta}.$

Now $R = (V^2\sin 2\theta)/g$, and therefore
$$r = \frac{V^2}{g\cos\alpha}(\sin 2\theta - 2\cos^2\theta\tan\alpha),$$
from which we find for a maximum value of r,
$$\frac{dr}{d\theta} = \frac{V^2}{g\cos\alpha}(2\cos 2\theta + 2\sin 2\theta\tan\alpha) = 0.$$
Thus $\tan 2\theta = -1/\tan\alpha = -\cot\alpha$ or
$$2\theta = \alpha + \frac{\pi}{2}.$$

In this result regard must be had to the sign of α, which is to be taken positive if the shot is fired up the slope, and negative if the shot is fired down. If $\alpha = 0$, we get $2\theta = \frac{1}{2}\pi$ or $\theta = \frac{1}{4}\pi$, which is obvious from the value of R.

Ex. 12. A gun is placed on a plane hillside: prove that the area commanded on the slope by the gun is bounded by an ellipse of which the position of the gun is a focus, the major-axis is along the line of greatest slope, the eccentricity is the sine of the angle of greatest slope, and the semi-latus rectum is of length equal to twice the greatest distance to which the gun can send a shot vertically upwards.

§ 25]   EXAMPLES OF PARABOLIC MOTION.   53

Let β be the angle of greatest slope, then the angle of slope of a line on the hillside, inclined to the line of greatest slope at an angle ϕ, is $\sin^{-1}(\sin\beta \cos\phi)$. Now, by last example,

$$r = \frac{V^2}{g\cos\alpha}(\sin 2\theta - 2\cos^2\theta \tan\alpha).$$

But, since for the maximum range $2\theta = \alpha + \tfrac{1}{2}\pi$, we have

$$\sin 2\theta = \cos\alpha, \quad \cos^2\theta = \tfrac{1}{2}(1 - \sin\alpha).$$

Hence, after reduction, the last equation becomes

$$r = \frac{V^2}{g\cos^2\alpha}(1 - \sin\alpha) = \frac{V^2}{g}\frac{1}{1 + \sin\beta\cos\phi},$$

which is the polar equation of an ellipse of eccentricity $\sin\beta$ and semi-latus rectum V^2/g, as stated above. The major axis is plainly along the line of greatest slope ($\phi = 0$), and the range in the horizontal direction ($\phi = \tfrac{1}{2}\pi$) is V^2/g, the maximum horizontal range R, as it evidently ought to be.

The range along the line of greatest slope is thus $V^2/(1+\sin\beta)g$, upwards, and $V^2/(1-\sin\beta)g$, downwards. The total length of the major axis is thus $2V^2/(1-\sin^2\beta)g$.

Ex. 13. The curve $r = f(\theta)$ is in a vertical plane, and particles slide from the curve to the origin along radii-vectores, and then pursue free paths under gravity with the velocities so acquired as velocities of projection : to find the locus of the foci of the paths.

We suppose the angle θ measured from the horizontal through the origin. The speed of projection is then given for a particle by the equation $V^2 = 2gr\sin\theta = 2g\sin\theta f(\theta)$. The coordinates of the focus of the path are, taken positive, $x = V^2\sin 2\theta/2g$, $y = V^2\cos 2\theta/2g$. The radius-vector to the focus has length $V^2/2g$, and the angle which it makes with the axis of x is 2θ. Calling this ϕ, we have for the equation of the locus, $\rho = V^2/2g = \sin\theta f(\theta)$, that is

$$\rho = \sin\frac{\phi}{2} f\left(\frac{\phi}{2}\right).$$

Ex. 14. Find the locus in Ex. 13 if the curve is a circle and the radii-vectores be chords drawn to the lowest point.

The equation of the circle is $r = 2a\sin\theta$ if a be the radius. Hence the locus of the foci of the path is

$$\rho = 2a\sin^2\frac{\phi}{2} = a(1 - \cos\phi),$$

that is a cardioid.

Ex. 15. A tennis ball is projected from a point A with speed V at elevation θ, and rebounds from a vertical wall B at horizontal distance a, then from a floor at distance h below B. If the normal component of speed of rebound from the wall be e times that of approach, find the time of reaching the floor and the time of return to the vertical through A. [The ball is supposed to have no rotation.]

Before the ball impinges on B its horizontal speed is $V\cos\theta$. Hence the time from projection to the first impact is $a/V\cos\theta$.

After the rebound the horizontal speed is $-eV\cos\theta$, and as this is not affected by the impact with the floor the time of returning to the vertical through A is $a/eV\cos\theta$, and hence the whole time from projection is $a(1+e)/eV\cos\theta$.

The time, t_2 say, from the instant of projection to that of reaching the floor is (since the impact on B does not affect the vertical speed) given by $V\sin\theta \cdot t_2 - \tfrac{1}{2}gt_2^2 = -h$, that is by

$$t_2 = \frac{V\sin\theta}{g} + \frac{1}{g}\sqrt{V^2\sin^2\theta + 2gh},$$

for the negative root given by the solution of the quadratic refers to the case of the ball arriving with *upward* vertical speed $V\sin\theta$ at A from the floor, and gives the *previous* instant at which the ball was at the floor.

Ex. 16. It is required to find the condition that the ball in the last example may return to A, on the supposition that the vertical component of the speed of rebound is e' times that of the speed of approach.

The vertical speed of the ball after leaving the floor is

$$e'(V\sin\theta - gt_2) = e'\sqrt{V^2\sin^2\theta + 2gh},$$

and the horizontal speed is $eV\cos\theta$. The time, t_3 say, required to rise from the floor to the height h is therefore given by

$$e't_3\sqrt{V^2\sin^2\theta + 2gh} - \tfrac{1}{2}gt_3^2 = h,$$

that is $\quad t_3 = \dfrac{1}{g}\{e'\sqrt{V^2\sin^2\theta + 2gh} \pm \sqrt{e'^2(V^2\sin^2\theta + 2gh) - 2gh}\}.$

This interval of time added to t_2 must just make up the whole time of flight. Hence the required condition is

$$g\frac{a(1+e)}{eV\cos\theta} = V\sin\theta + (1+e')\sqrt{V^2\sin^2\theta + 2gh} \pm \sqrt{e'^2(V^2\sin^2\theta + 2gh) - 2gh}.$$

26. Motion under Acceleration varying inversely as Square of Distance from Fixed Point. If the equations of acceleration, or, as we say, of motion, are

$$\ddot{x} = -\frac{\mu x}{r^3}, \quad \ddot{y} = -\frac{\mu y}{r^3}, \quad \ldots\ldots\ldots\ldots\ldots\ldots(1)$$

where μ is a constant, we have the case of a point moving under an acceleration μ/r^2 directed towards the origin O of coordinates, and varying inversely as the second power of the distance, r, of the moving particle from the origin. For if we denote the angle between the line OP and the axis of x by θ, we have $\cos\theta = x/r$, $\sin\theta = y/r$, and therefore the components are as stated in (1). It is supposed that $\dot{z}=0$, so that the motion is in the plane of x, y. If we multiply the first equation by y, the second by x, and subtract the first product from the second, we obtain

$$x\ddot{y} - y\ddot{x} = 0,$$

which gives by integration

$$x\dot{y} - y\dot{x} = h, \dots\dots\dots\dots\dots\dots(2)$$

where h is a constant. This last equation expresses the so-called "law of conservation of areas," that is the fact that the radius-vector (of length $r = \sqrt{x^2 + y^2}$), drawn from the origin to the moving point, sweeps over equal areas in equal times in the plane of motion. For if θ be the angle which the radius-vector makes with a fixed straight line in the plane of the path, the equation may be written

$$r^2\dot{\theta} = h, \dots\dots\dots\dots\dots\dots\dots(3)$$

which renders it obvious that h is twice the rate of description of area. It is interesting to notice that the angular speed $\dot{\theta}$ with which the radius-vector is turning varies inversely as r^2, is, in fact, h/r^2.

We shall see later that the equation expresses the dynamical fact that the angular momentum, about the origin, of a particle moving in the path remains constant throughout the motion.

27. First Integral of Equations of Motion. Equation of Hodograph. Now by means of (2), the equations of motion (1) of last section can be transformed to

$$\ddot{x} = -\frac{\mu}{h}\frac{d}{dt}\left(\frac{y}{r}\right), \quad \ddot{y} = +\frac{\mu}{h}\frac{d}{dt}\left(\frac{x}{r}\right) \dots\dots\dots(1)$$

or, as we may write them, if the axis of x be taken along the fixed line from which θ is measured,

$$\ddot{x} = -\frac{\mu}{h}\frac{d}{dt}(\sin\theta), \quad \ddot{y} = \frac{\mu}{h}\frac{d}{dt}(\cos\theta). \dots\dots\dots(2)$$

For equation (3) gives $1/r^2 = \dot{\theta}/h$. This value of $1/r^2$ substituted in equations (2) transforms them to

$$\ddot{x} = -\frac{\mu}{h}\frac{x}{r}\dot{\theta} = -\frac{\mu}{h}\cos\theta \cdot \dot{\theta}$$

or
$$\ddot{x} = -\frac{\mu}{h}\frac{d}{dt}(\sin\theta) = -\frac{\mu}{h}\frac{d}{dt}\left(\frac{y}{r}\right). \quad\quad\quad (3)$$

Similarly, we obtain

$$\ddot{y} = \frac{\mu}{h}\frac{d}{dt}(\cos\theta) = \frac{\mu}{h}\frac{d}{dt}\left(\frac{x}{r}\right). \quad\quad\quad (4)$$

From the relation $1/r^2 = \dot{\theta}/h$, we see also that the resultant acceleration μ/r^2, which by the equations of motion is along

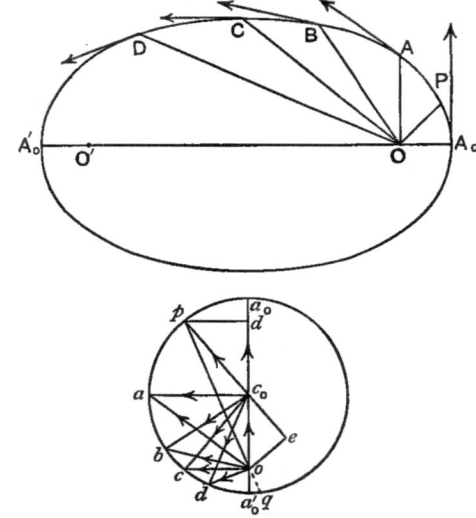

Fig. 16.

the radius-vector towards the origin, is $\mu\dot{\theta}/h$, and is therefore proportional to the angular speed of the radius-vector.

Integrating (3) and (4) and putting ξ, η for $\dot{x}$, $\dot{y}$, we obtain

$$\xi = -\frac{\mu}{h}\frac{y}{r} + a, \quad \eta = \frac{\mu}{h}\frac{x}{r} + b, \quad\quad\quad (5)$$

and therefore $(\xi-a)^2+(\eta-b)^2=\dfrac{\mu^2}{h^2}.$ ....(6)

But ξ, η are the coordinates of a point on the hodograph, and the equation (6) just found is that of a circle of radius μ/h, and coordinates of centre a, b. The hodograph is therefore a circle (see Fig. 16, where an elliptic orbit and the corresponding hodograph are shown separately). That the velocities of an undisturbed planet at the different points in its orbit are represented in magnitude and direction by lines drawn from a chosen fixed point to a circle, is a very remarkable and interesting result, and an elementary geometrical proof of it will be given later, in Chapter V.

28. Equation of Path. From equations (3) and (4) of last section, we can easily find the path and the relation to it of the hodograph. For (5), derived from them, can be written in the form

$$\dot{x}=-\frac{\mu}{h}\sin\theta+a', \quad \dot{y}=\frac{\mu}{h}\cos\theta+b' \quad\ldots\ldots\ldots\ldots(1)$$

(where a', b' are put for a, b to avoid confusion in what follows): multiplying the first by $y=r\sin\theta$, the second by $x=r\cos\theta$, and subtracting the first product from the second, we obtain

$$h=\frac{\mu}{h}r-(a'\sin\theta-b'\sin\theta)r,$$

that is $\quad\dfrac{\mu}{h^2}-\dfrac{1}{r}=\dfrac{1}{h}(a'\sin\theta-b'\cos\theta),$ ....(2)

the polar equation of a curve of the second degree, or a conic section, as it is commonly called.

If we write $b'=A\cos\alpha$, $-a'=A\sin\alpha$, we get

$$r=\dfrac{1}{\dfrac{\mu}{h^2}+\dfrac{A}{h}\cos(\theta-\alpha)}\cdot\quad\ldots\ldots\ldots\ldots\ldots(3)$$

For $\theta-\alpha=0,\quad r=h^2/(\mu+Ah),$
and for $\theta-\alpha=\pi,\quad r=h^2/(\mu-Ah).$

Calling the first of these $a(1-e)$, and the second $a(1+e)$, where a and e are constants, we find
$$\mu/h^2 = 1/a(1-e^2), \quad A/h = e/a(1-e^2).$$
Hence the equation of the path can be written in the form
$$r = \frac{a(1-e^2)}{1+e\cos(\theta-\alpha)}, \quad \ldots\ldots\ldots\ldots\ldots\ldots(4)$$
which is the equation of a conic section of parameter $2a(1-e^2)$, of length of major axis $2a$, and of eccentricity e. For $e<1$ the curve is an ellipse. For $e>1$ the curve is a hyperbola, and we then change the sign of a and write the equation as
$$r = \frac{a(e^2-1)}{1+e\cos(\theta-\alpha)}. \quad \ldots\ldots\ldots\ldots\ldots(4')$$
For the limiting intermediate case $e=1$, the curve is a parabola.

29. Speed at Different Points of Path. The hodographic origin has so far been taken coincident with the origin for the path, but this is not necessary, and it is more convenient to give a separate diagram of the hodograph as in Fig. 16, where also an elliptic orbit is shown for comparison of directions. Now by (1) of last section, we obtain
$$\dot{x}\,d\dot{x} + \dot{y}\,d\dot{y} = -\frac{\mu}{h}(a'\cos\theta + b'\sin\theta)d\theta, \quad \ldots\ldots\ldots\ldots(1)$$
and this vanishes when the speed $\sqrt{\dot{x}^2+\dot{y}^2}$ in the path is a maximum or a minimum. Hence, when this is the case, $\sin\theta/\cos\theta = -a'/b'$, and two values of θ differing by π, for one of which $\sin\theta$ is negative and $\cos\theta$ positive, and for the other $\sin\theta$ is positive and $\cos\theta$ negative, satisfy this condition. A second differentiation shows that in the former case the speed is a maximum, in the latter a minimum.

But (2) of last section gives
$$\frac{1}{r^2}\,dr = \frac{1}{h}(a'\cos\theta + b'\sin\theta)d\theta, \quad \ldots\ldots\ldots\ldots\ldots\ldots(2)$$
and we have the same condition, $\sin\theta/\cos\theta = -a'/b'$, as before, but in this case for a maximum or minimum of r. But the sign on the right of (2) is different in this case; and we see that the speed is a maximum when the length of the radius-vector is a minimum, and *vice versa*.

Now let us measure θ from the minimum radius-vector (OA_0 in Fig. 15). If we do this we have initially $\dot{x} = \dot{r} = 0$, and so we must put $a' = 0$. Thus we have
$$\dot{x} = -\frac{\mu}{h}\sin\theta, \quad \dot{y} = \frac{\mu}{h}\cos\theta + b', \quad \ldots\ldots\ldots\ldots\ldots(3)$$
which, if ξ, η be put for $\dot{x}$, $\dot{y}$ and θ be eliminated, give again the hodograph (6), § 27, but with $a=0$, $b=b'$.

30. Resolution of Velocity into Two Parts of Constant Amount. Path Deduced from Hodograph.

Equations (3), § 29, show that the velocity of which the components are $\dot{x}$, $\dot{y}-b'$ is perpendicular to the radius-vector, the direction of which is defined by the angle θ. Thus when $\theta=0$, the speed for this is $\mu/h+b'$. The velocity thus consists of the constant part b' in the direction of the y-axis, and a part of constant amount μ/h, always at right angles to the radius-vector. This is shown in Fig. 16, where oc_0 represents b', and c_0a, c_0b, etc., each the velocity of amount μ/h, according to the position of the point in the path.

Multiplying in (3), § 29, $\dot{x}$ by x and $\dot{y}$ by y, and adding, we get

$$x\dot{x}+y\dot{y}=r\dot{r}=b'r\sin\theta=-b'\frac{h}{\mu}r\dot{x}. \quad\quad\quad\quad (1)$$

Therefore
$$r=c-b'\frac{h}{\mu}x$$

or
$$r=b'\frac{h}{\mu}\left(\frac{\mu}{hb'}c-x\right). \quad\quad\quad\quad (2)$$

Thus the distance r of any point on the path from the origin is equal to the distance $c\mu/hb'-x$ of the point from a fixed straight line parallel to the y-axis, multiplied by hb'/μ. This is the focus and directrix condition fulfilled by the conic sections, and hence again we see that the path is one of these curves.

The same thing is obvious from (1), for $\dot{r}$, the rate of growth of r, bears a constant ratio to $\dot{x}$, the rate of increase of the distance of the point on the curve from a fixed line perpendicular to the axis of x. This can be seen also from the hodograph. Draw a line from o perpendicular to any of the lines c_0a, c_0b, etc., say c_0p, produced backward from c_0, and let the lines meet in e. Then oe is that component of the velocity op which is at right angles to c_0p, that is parallel to the tangent at p, and therefore parallel to the resultant acceleration at P in the path, that is parallel to r. It therefore represents $\dot{r}$. Again, the perpendicular pd let fall from p on the axis of y in the hodograph represents $\dot{x}$. Now, since the triangles oec_0, pc_0d are similar, we have $oe/pd=oc_0/c_0p$, a constant ratio.

The nature of the path may also be deduced from the circular hodograph thus: Let op produced backward from o meet the circle again in q. Then $qo\cdot op$ is constant, since o is fixed and p, q lie on a circle. Now if p be the length of the perpendicular let fall from the origin O of the path (the point to which the acceleration is directed) on the tangent drawn to the path at the point P, where the speed is v, we have $vp=h$. But $qo\cdot op=v\cdot qo$, and thus $v\cdot qo$ also is constant. Hence qo is proportional in length to p. The locus therefore of the feet of the perpendiculars let fall from the origin O on tangents drawn to the path at different points is a circle. This is a geometrical property of the conic sections, and of no other class of curves. Hence again we see that the path is a conic section.

31. Polar Coordinates: Differential Equation of Path of Particle under Central Acceleration. The equations of motion in polar coordinates may be written down at once from the values of the accelerations along and at right angles to the radius-vector found in § 13 above. They are

$$\ddot{r} - r\dot{\theta}^2 = -\frac{\mu}{r^2}, \\ r^2\dot{\theta} = h, \quad\quad\quad\quad\quad\quad\quad\quad\quad (1)$$

since the second of these equations is equivalent to the equation $2\dot{r}\omega + \dot{\omega}r = 0$, which must hold in the present case since there is no acceleration transverse to the radius-vector. The first of these may, by the second, be written

$$\ddot{r} - \frac{h^2}{r^3} = -\frac{\mu}{r^2}. \quad\quad\quad\quad\quad\quad\quad\quad (2)$$

It is convenient to eliminate the time from this equation. This can be done by remembering that since r and θ vary together, r is a function of θ, and that $\dot{\theta} = h/r^2$. We have

$$\dot{r} = \frac{dr}{d\theta}\dot{\theta} = \frac{h}{r^2}\frac{dr}{d\theta}.$$

Hence
$$\ddot{r} = \frac{h}{r^2}\frac{d^2r}{d\theta^2}\dot{\theta} - \frac{2h}{r^3}\left(\frac{dr}{d\theta}\right)^2 \dot{\theta}$$
$$= \frac{h^2}{r^4}\frac{d^2r}{d\theta^2} - \frac{2h^2}{r^5}\left(\frac{dr}{d\theta}\right)^2.$$

Thus we obtain, instead of (2),

$$h^2\left\{\frac{d^2r}{d\theta^2} - \frac{2}{r}\left(\frac{dr}{d\theta}\right)^2 - r\right\} = -\mu r^2. \quad\quad\quad\quad (3)$$

It is convenient to write $1/u$ instead of r. When this substitution is made the equation becomes, as the reader may verify,

$$\frac{d^2u}{d\theta^2} + u = \frac{\mu}{h^2}. \quad\quad\quad\quad\quad\quad\quad\quad (4)$$

This only holds in the case of acceleration $= \mu/r^2$; but in the general case in which the acceleration is along the radius-vector and has value R, the equation is

$$\frac{d^2u}{d\theta^2} + u = \frac{R}{h^2u^2}. \quad\quad\quad\quad\quad\quad\quad\quad (5)$$

Here R is taken as positive when towards the origin: the outward acceleration is $-R$.

This equation will be established in a totally different manner in Chapter V., where many examples will be found.

Ex. A particle moves in a plane so that the components of its acceleration along and at right angles to the radius-vector drawn to the particle from a fixed point in the plane are respectively $f(r)$ and μr^2, where r is the length of the radius-vector. Prove that if the particle move once round a closed curve, the square of its speed is increased by 4μ times the area of the curve.

We are here given $\ddot{r} - r\dot{\theta}^2 = f(r)$, $d(r^2\dot{\theta})/dt = \mu r^2$ (see § 13). The square of the speed at any point is $\dot{r}^2 + r^2\dot{\theta}^2$. Now we have, since $r^2\dot{\theta} = h$,

$$\ddot{r} = \frac{d\dot{r}}{d\theta}\dot{\theta} = \frac{h}{r^2}\frac{d\dot{r}}{d\theta} \quad \text{and} \quad \ddot{r} - r\dot{\theta}^2 = \frac{h}{r^2}\frac{d\dot{r}}{d\theta} - \frac{h^2}{r^3} = f(r).$$

Thus we obtain, since $\dot{r} = (h/r^2)dr/d\theta$, and $d\dot{r}/d\theta = f(r)r^2/h + h/r$,

$$\frac{d}{d\theta}(\dot{r}^2) = 2f(r)\frac{dr}{d\theta} + 2\frac{h^2}{r^3}\frac{dr}{d\theta}.$$

Again, by the problem, $d(r^2\dot{\theta})/dt = \mu r^2$, that is

$$\frac{h}{r^2}\frac{dh}{d\theta} = \mu r^2 \quad \text{or} \quad \frac{dh}{d\theta} = \mu\frac{r^4}{h}.$$

But $\qquad d(r^2\dot{\theta}^2)/d\theta = \dot{\theta}\,dh/d\theta + h\,d(h/r^2)/d\theta.$

This gives, with the result already obtained for $d(\dot{r}^2)/d\theta$,

$$\frac{d}{d\theta}(\dot{r}^2 + r^2\dot{\theta}^2) = 2f(r)\frac{dr}{d\theta} + \dot{\theta}\frac{dh}{d\theta} + \frac{h}{r^2}\frac{dh}{d\theta}$$

$$= 2f(r)\frac{dr}{d\theta} + 2\mu r^2.$$

Integrating this expression round the closed curve, we get zero for the first term of the integral, and for the second $2\mu \int r^2 d\theta = 4\mu A$, where A is the area swept over by the radius-vector. Thus v^2 increases by $4\mu A$.

32. Simple Harmonic Motion.

We now pass to the consideration of simple harmonic motion of a particle, that is to the kinematical study of vibrations, a species of motion of which we have examples in all parts of physics.

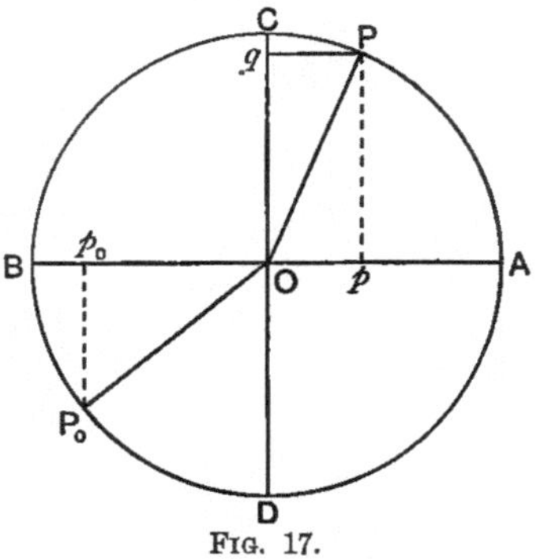

To define the motion let a particle describe the circle $ACBD$ (radius r) of Fig. 17, with uniform speed v. We call this circle the auxiliary circle. Then, by § 10, the particle has no acceleration in

FIG. 17.

62   A TREATISE ON DYNAMICS.   [CH. I.

the direction of motion at any point, but has everywhere acceleration v^2/r toward the centre. The time T, in which the particle describes the circle once, is $2\pi r/v$. Hence also

$$\frac{v^2}{r} = \frac{4\pi^2}{T^2} r. \qquad \qquad \ldots(1)$$

But $2\pi/T$ is the uniform angular speed, n say, with which the radius drawn from the centre of the circle to the particle turns round as the particle moves, and therefore we have also

$$\frac{v^2}{r} = n^2 r \ldots \ldots \ldots \ldots \ldots (2)$$

Now let P_0 be the position of the particle at the zero of reckoning of time, and P its position after the lapse of an interval t. Let fall a perpendicular from each position of the particle to the diameter AB, and let p_0, p be the feet of these perpendiculars for the positions P_0, P. As the particle moves round the circle the perpendicular p moves to and fro along the diameter AB. The motion of p is called simple harmonic.

33. S. H. M. Velocity and Acceleration. Integral Equation. The velocity and acceleration of p are the components, along the line of motion of p, of the velocity and acceleration of the particle in the circular motion. Now taking the position of P in the diagram, and denoting the displacement of p from the centre by x, we have, by the diagram, for the displacement, velocity, and acceleration of p,

$$x = r \cos POA, \quad \dot{x} = -v \sin POA, \quad \ddot{x} = -\frac{v^2}{r} \cos POA. \ldots(1)$$

The values of $\dot{x}$, $\ddot{x}$ can of course be got from that of x by differentiation. If further we denote the angle $P_0 OA$ by e, we get $POA = nt - e$, and therefore

$$\dot{x} = -v \sin(nt - e),$$

$$\ddot{x} = -\frac{v^2}{r} \cos(nt - e) = -n^2 r \cos(nt - e). \ldots \ldots (2)$$

Thus we have $\qquad \ddot{x} + n^2 x = 0. \ldots \ldots \ldots \ldots \ldots (3)$

The last equation shows that the acceleration of p is

directed toward the centre O of the range of motion, and is proportional to the distance Op from that point. It is to be noted that $n^2 = 4\pi^2/T^2$.

Now, for $\dot{x}$ itself we have

$$x = r \cos(nt - e) \quad\quad\quad\quad\quad\quad\quad\quad (4)$$

or, as we may write it if we put $A = r\cos e$, $B = r\sin e$,

$$x = A\cos nt + B\sin nt, \quad\quad\quad\quad\quad (5)$$

and this is the complete integral equation corresponding to the differential equation (3).

The two constants r and e in (2) or A and B in (5) are called *arbitrary* constants, for the reason that their values are immaterial so far as the satisfaction of the differential equation is concerned. They must be determined to suit the circumstances of any given case of motion. For example, the displacement x_0 and speed v_0 of p, when $t = 0$, may be given, and from these we can determine A and B. When $t = 0$, (5) gives $x = A$; therefore $A = x_0$. Again,

$$\dot{x} = -nA\sin nt + nB\cos nt, \quad\quad\quad\quad (6)$$

and therefore $v_0 = nB$ or $B = v_0/n$. Hence (5) becomes

$$x = x_0 \cos nt + \frac{v_0}{n} \sin nt. \quad\quad\quad\quad\quad (7)$$

Thus the value of x at time t is made up of two parts, one depending on the initial displacement, the other on the initial speed of the point. This analysis of the motion at time t is of importance in the theory of waves.

34. S.H.M. Amplitude, Period and Phase. The two constants r and e of (4) of § 33 are called respectively the *amplitude* and the *epoch* of the simple harmonic motion. The epoch is sometimes referred to as the time in the circular motion from P_0 to A; it is then e/n. This is also the time in the S.H.M. from p_0 to A. The period T of revolution of the particle in the auxiliary circle is also called the *period* of the motion.

The *phase* of a simple harmonic motion at any instant is the fraction of the period T which has elapsed since the last passage of the moving point through the middle of its

64   A TREATISE ON DYNAMICS.   [CH. I.

range of motion in the direction regarded as positive. For example, in the motion along AB the phase at time t is

$$t/T - (e - \pi/2)/2\pi \quad \text{or} \quad t/T + \tfrac{1}{4} - e/2\pi.$$

For this is the ratio of the angle DOP to 2π, and therefore also the ratio to T of the time taken by the radius of the auxiliary circle to turn through that angle. The difference of phase of two motions of epochs e_1, e_2 is $(e_2 - e_1)/2\pi$.

It is convenient to remember that $-\ddot{x}/x = 4\pi^2/T^2$, which brings out the fact that the ratio of the positive value, $-\ddot{x}$, of the acceleration, to the displacement x, has always, in a simple harmonic motion, the value $4\pi^2/T^2$. This enables the period to be readily calculated in experimental work.

The reader should notice that when the displacement has its greatest value $+r$ or $-r$ the speed of p is zero, and the acceleration is $v^2/r = n^2 r = 4\pi^2 r/T^2$, towards O, and is thus a maximum. When the point p is at the centre O the speed of p is v and the acceleration is zero.

35. A Uniform Circular Motion the Resultant of Two S.H.M.s. Now let fall a perpendicular from P on the diameter CD, and let q be its foot. Then the point moving in the circle may be regarded as having at P the two displacements Op, Oq at the same instant. As it moves round the circle from P towards C, its displacement Op diminishes and the other Oq increases, and clearly the motion of q is also simple harmonic with the same period and the same maximum and minimum magnitudes of velocities and accelerations as for p. We take as the epoch for the motion of q the angle P_0OC, which we denote by f. Obviously we have here $e = f - \pi/2$. Denoting Oq by y, we get

$$y = r \cos \angle COP = r \cos\left(nt - e - \frac{\pi}{2}\right) = r \sin(nt - e). \quad \ldots (1)$$

Hence $\dot{y} = nr \cos(nt - e) = v \cos(nt - e),$

$$\ddot{y} = -\frac{v^2}{r} \sin(nt - e) = -n^2 r \sin(nt - e) \right\} \quad \ldots\ldots(2)$$

or $\quad \ddot{y} + n^2 y = 0,$

where, as before, $n^2 = 4\pi^2/T^2$.

HARMONIC MOTION.

These results show that a uniform circular motion is the resultant of two simple harmonic motions of the same period, in lines at right angles to one another, and of epochs differing by $\pi/2$. The difference of phase is 1/4. This proposition, that two equal simple harmonic motions, of the same period, and differing in phase by 1/4, give by composition uniform circular motion, has many applications in the theories of sound and light.

If the diagram (Fig. 16) be projected by lines perpendicular to its plane on a second plane inclined to the former at any angle between zero and $\pi/2$, the projection of the circle will be an ellipse and the projections of the lines of the two simple harmonic motions will be two conjugate diameters of the ellipse. The projections of the motions are clearly also simple harmonic motions. Thus we get the important theorem that two simple harmonic motions, in two lines inclined to one another at any angle and differing in phase by 1/4, give by composition an elliptic motion.

Ex. A particle moves in a plane curve, with speeds
$$\omega y(a^2-b^2)/(a^2+b^2), \quad \omega x(a^2-b^2)/(a^2+b^2),$$
along axes Ox, Oy, at right angles to one another and turning with uniform angular speed ω: to find the path relative to the axes.

Here we have
$$\dot{x}-\omega y=\omega y\frac{a^2-b^2}{a^2+b^2}, \quad \dot{y}+\omega x=\omega x\frac{a^2-b^2}{a^2+b^2},$$
and therefore
$$\dot{x}=2\omega y\frac{a^2}{a^2+b^2}, \quad \dot{y}=-2\omega x\frac{b^2}{a^2+b^2},$$
so that
$$\frac{dy}{dx}=-\frac{x}{y}\frac{b^2}{a^2}.$$
Thus, integrating, we get
$$y^2=-x^2\frac{b^2}{a^2}+c^2,$$
where c is a constant. Hence the equation of the relative path is
$$b^2x^2+a^2y^2=a^2c^2,$$
that is an ellipse.

In reality we have here relative to the revolving axes two simple-harmonic motions parallel to these axes. For differentiating $\dot{x}$, $\dot{y}$ again, we find
$$\ddot{x}+4\omega^2\frac{a^2b^2}{(a^2+b^2)^2}x=0, \quad \ddot{y}+4\omega^2\frac{a^2b^2}{(a^2+b^2)^2}y=0.$$

The periods of these simple-harmonic motions have the same value $\pi(a^2+b^2)/\omega ab$. They differ in phase by a quarter of a period, for $\dot{x}$ vanishes with y and $\dot{y}$ with x.

36. Composition of Equal and Opposite Circular Motions gives S.H.M.
Again, consider two uniform circular motions in equal circles (radius a) (Fig. 18) and in the same period but in opposite directions. Let a point move with the sum of the displacements of the points p_1, p_2 and q_1, q_2 along the diameters in the two circles. Its displacement x is the sum of the displacements x_1, x_2 of the p's, and its displacement y (taken downward in Fig. 18 as it is drawn) is the sum of the displacements y_1, y_2 of the q's. The line of motion is obviously equally inclined to the radii drawn from the centre of the circles to the positions of the points in the circular motions at any time. The motion of the point in this line is simple harmonic, and its amplitude is twice the radius of either circle.

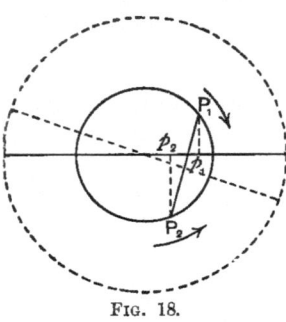

Fig. 18.

The result is obvious at once by analysis. One circular motion is equivalent to the two co-existing simple harmonic motions

$$x_1 = a\cos(nt - e), \quad y_1 = a\cos\left(nt - e + \frac{\pi}{2}\right)$$

or $\quad x_1 = a\cos(nt-e), \quad y_1 = -a\sin(nt-e)$. ....(1)

The other circular motion has components which can be obtained from this by changing the sign of n. They are

$$x_2 = a\cos(nt+e), \quad y_2 = a\sin(nt+e). \quad \ldots\ldots\ldots(2)$$

Hence we have

$$\left.\begin{aligned} x &= a\{\cos(nt-e) + \cos(nt+e)\}, \\ y &= a\{-\sin(nt-e) + \sin(nt+e)\} \end{aligned}\right\} \quad \ldots\ldots\ldots\ldots(3)$$

or $\quad x = 2a\cos e\cos nt, \quad y = 2a\sin e\cos nt,\ \ldots\ldots(4)$

and the resultant displacement $\sqrt{x^2 + y^2}$ is given by

$$\sqrt{x^2 + y^2} = 2a\cos nt, \quad\ldots\ldots\ldots\ldots\ldots\ldots(5)$$

the inclination of which to the axis of x is e. But we see from (1) that at time t the radius to the particle in the first circular motion is inclined to the axis of x at an angle $e-nt$, and from (2) that the radius to the particle in the second motion is inclined to the axis of x at an angle $nt+e$. The line bisecting the angle between these directions is inclined to the axis of x at an angle e. It is shown dotted in Fig. 17, and is perpendicular to P_1P_2. The amplitude of the motion compounded of the two circular motions is thus $2a$, and it has the direction specified. This result is of importance in the theory of polarised light. It shows that what is called plane polarisation may be regarded as produced by two equal and opposite circular polarisations.

It is to be noticed that we have proved incidentally that the two motions

$$x = \alpha \cos nt = 2a\cos e\cos nt, \quad y = \beta\cos nt = 2a\sin e\cos nt, \ldots (6)$$

that is two simple harmonic motions at right angles to one another, and of different amplitudes, but of the same phase, compound into a single harmonic motion in a line inclined to that of the former at the angle $\tan^{-1}\beta/\alpha$.

37. Composition of Two S.H.M.s in Same Line. We now consider some other cases. First let a point move so that it has the sum of the displacements from the middle position of two points describing simple harmonic motions in the same line and in the same period, but with different amplitudes and phases.

Draw the auxiliary circles for the two motions from the same centre O, and let the points P_1, P_2 be in the positions shown in the diagram (Fig. 19) at time t. Describe on OP_1, OP_2 as adjacent sides a parallelogram, and draw the diagonal OQ. Then p_1, p_2 are the positions of the harmonically moving points at the same instant. As P_1, P_2 describe their circles, with uniform speed, the point Q also describes a circle with uniform

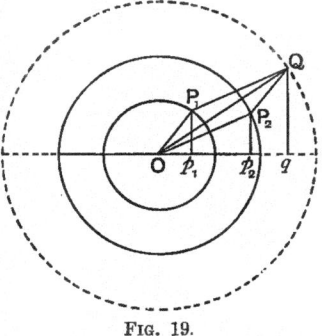

Fig. 19.

speed, that is the auxiliary circle for q, which clearly has displacement equal to the sum of the displacements of P_1 and P_2. The motion of q is thus simple harmonic, of amplitude equal to OQ, in the line AB coinciding with A_1B_1 and A_2B_2 in direction and position. The period is clearly that of the component motions.

The result of the composition of the two motions is clear from the construction in the diagram, but the analytical solution may be stated. We write

$$x = a_1\cos(nt-e_1) + a_2\cos(nt-e_2), \quad \ldots\ldots\ldots(1)$$

where on the right we have the two simple harmonic displacements. We can write this

$$x = A\cos(nt-e), \quad \ldots\ldots\ldots\ldots\ldots\ldots\ldots\ldots(2)$$

if
$$\left.\begin{array}{l} A = \{a_1^2 + a_2^2 + 2a_1a_2\cos(e_1-e_2)\}^{\frac{1}{2}}, \\[4pt] \tan e = \dfrac{a_1\sin e_1 + a_2\sin e_2}{a_1\cos e_1 + a_2\cos e_2}. \end{array}\right\} \ldots\ldots(3)$$

It will be seen from the diagram that the value of A as given by (2) is OQ, and that $nt-e$ is the angle QOq.

38. Composition of any Number of S.H.M.s in Parallel Lines. Tide-Predicter. From this it follows that if we have any number of simple harmonic motions in parallel lines, of any amplitudes and phases, but of the same period, and a point p be made to move in a straight line in such a way that its displacement from a fixed point is the sum of the displacements in the different motions from the middle points of the different ranges, the motion of p is itself simple harmonic. The values of A and e given in (3), §37, may be easily generalised for this case.

A simple mechanism, the elements of which are shown in the diagram (Fig. 20) is used to impart to the writing style of Lord Kelvin's Tide-Predicting Machine, a vertical displacement equal at each instant to the sum of the displacements of a number of points describing simple harmonic motions in parallel lines. Each of the slotted T-pieces shown in the diagram is moved up and down by a pin at the outer end of an arm which revolves about a pivot at the other end. The pin works in the slot, and lateral motion of any part of the T-piece is prevented by guides properly placed. Each T-piece carries a pulley at the upper end, and over these pulleys passes a thin chain, which is fixed at one end and carries the marking pen at the other. It is clear that the rise or fall of the pen in any time is twice the sum of the vertical displacements of all the T-pieces in that time.

This mode of adding together displacements is applicable to any system of simple harmonic motions whether of the same period or not. The various revolving arms may be geared together so as to have any required relation of periods. As a matter of fact it is applied to the Tide-Predicter to add together the displacements in a large number of tidal motions which are of widely different periods not all connected by any simple relationship.

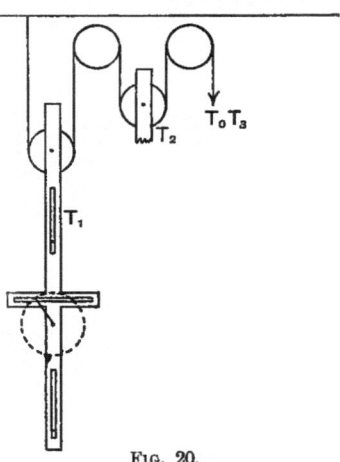

Fig. 20.

The use of the pulleys and chain, or cord, for this summation was suggested to Lord Kelvin by Mr. Beauchamp Tower; but the arrangement seems to have been previously used for purposes of integration.

39. Composition of S.H.M.s in One Line but of Different Periods. If the two motions in the same line which are to be compounded are not of the same period, we can write their resultant

$$x = a_1 \cos(nt - e_1) + a_2 \cos\{(n+\nu)t - e_2\} \quad \ldots\ldots\ldots\ldots(1)$$

in the same form as before; but now the amplitude A and the epoch e vary with the time. The periods are here $2\pi/n$ and $2\pi/(n+\nu)$. The frequencies are $n/2\pi$ and $(n+\nu)/2\pi$, so that the difference of frequency is $\nu/2\pi$.

By (2) and (3) of § 37, we have

$$x = A \cos(nt - e), \quad \ldots\ldots\ldots\ldots\ldots\ldots\ldots\ldots(2)$$

where now
$$A = \{a_1^2 + a_2^2 + 2a_1 a_2 \cos(\nu t - e_2 + e_1)\}^{\frac{1}{2}},$$
$$\tan e = \frac{a_1 \sin e_1 - a_2 \sin(\nu t - e_2)}{a_1 \cos e_1 + a_2 \cos(\nu t - e_2)}.$$
.................(3)

Thus the amplitude oscillates in the period $2\pi/\nu$ from the value $a_1 + a_2$ (at an instant when $\nu t - e_2 + e_1 = 2m\pi$, where m is any integer) to the value $a_1 - a_2$ (at the instant when $\nu t - e_2 + e_1 = (2m+1)\pi$). At each of these instants $\tan e = \tan e_1$.

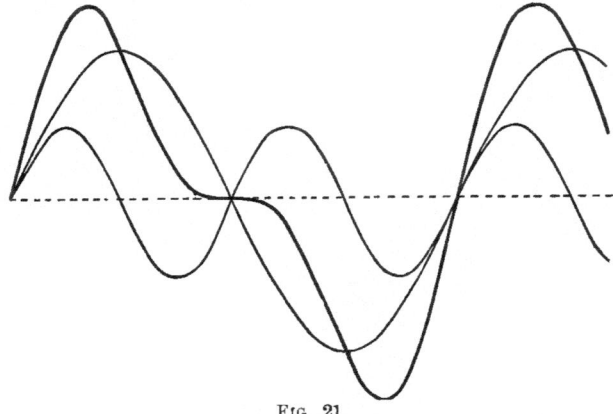

FIG. 21.

An excellent example of this is afforded by the solar and lunar tides at any place. The amplitude of the lunar equilibrium tide is about 2·1 times that of the solar. Thus (on the "equilibrium theory") spring tides are about 3·1, neap tides about 1·1, times the solar tide.

Again, when two musical notes which differ slightly in frequency are sounded together the ear perceives an alternate swelling out and dying away of the sound: the notes are said to *beat*. If the frequency of either note is known, the frequency of the other can be inferred by counting the beats in a given time. The slower the beats the more nearly the notes are in unison.

Fig. 21 shows S.H.M.s (ordinates = displacements, abscissae = times, periods in the ratio 1 : 2, $e_1 - e_2 = 0$) compounded.

40. Composition of S.H.M.s in Perpendicular Lines and of Different Periods. The composition of motions of different periods in lines at right angles to one another can be worked out easily in the case in which the relation of the periods is simple. For example, let the displacements at time t be

$$x = a\cos(2nt - e), \quad y = b\cos nt, \quad \ldots\ldots\ldots\ldots\ldots\ldots(1)$$

so that the ratio of periods is 1 : 2, and an arbitrary difference of phase

$e/2\pi$ exists between the motions. Substituting y/b for $\cos nt$ and $\sqrt{1-y^2/b^2}$ for $\sin nt$ in the expression for x expanded, we get

$$x = a\left(2\frac{y^2}{b^2} - 1\right)\cos e + 2\frac{a}{b}y\sqrt{1 - \frac{y^2}{b^2}}\sin e. \quad\ldots\ldots\ldots\ldots(2)$$

If now $\cos e = 0$, so that $e = \pm \pi/2$, we get

$$x = \pm 2\frac{a}{b}y\sqrt{1 - \frac{y^2}{b^2}}, \quad\ldots\ldots\ldots\ldots\ldots\ldots\ldots(3)$$

or for either sign

$$x^2 = 4\frac{a^2}{b^2}y^2\left(1 - \frac{y^2}{b^2}\right). \quad\ldots\ldots\ldots\ldots\ldots\ldots\ldots(4)$$

Clearly this curve is represented at the origin by the two straight lines $y = \pm x \cdot b/2a$, that is it has there the form of a St. Andrew Cross of vertical angle $\tan^{-1}\{4ab/(b^2 - 4a^2)\}$. Any line parallel to the axis of y on either side of the origin at a less distance than a cuts it in four points, and the pairs of lines $y = \pm b$ and $x = \pm a$ are tangents.

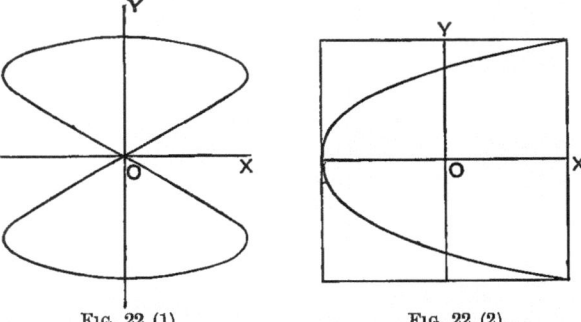

FIG. 22 (1).   FIG. 22 (2).

Each of the latter lines touches the curve at two points for which the values of y are equal but of opposite sign. The curve is thus a "figure of eight," as shown in the diagram [Fig. 22 (1)].

Again, if $\sin e = 0$, so that $e = \pm \pi$, we obtain

$$x = \pm\left(2\frac{a}{b^2}y^2 - a\right), \quad\ldots\ldots\ldots\ldots\ldots\ldots\ldots(5)$$

which represents a parabola with its axis in the direction of x and its vertex to the left or the right of the origin, according as the plus or the minus sign is taken [Fig. 22 (2)].

If the periods are not exactly in the ratio $1 : 2$, that is, if we have

$$x = a\cos\{2(n+\nu)t - e\}, \quad y = b\cos nt, \quad\ldots\ldots\ldots\ldots(6)$$

where ν is small compared with n, we may take as the epoch in the expression for x, $e - 2\nu t$, and we see that the difference gradually alters with the time and the resultant curve passes through all the varieties of form shown in Fig. 23, and back again, in the reverse order, with reversal also of the direction of motion in the intermediate curves.

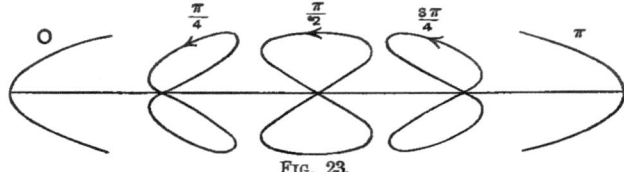

FIG. 23.

Other cases, say the case of periods in the ratio 2 : 3 or 1 : 3, may be worked out and considered by the student. The resultant curves are shown in works on *Acoustics*.

41. Composition of S.H.M.s in Different Lines but of Equal Period. We can find a motion that combines displacements for any number of simple harmonic motions of any amplitudes and epochs in different lines if they are all of the same period. Let l_1, m_1, n_1, l_2, m_2, n_2, ... be the direction cosines of the different lines of motion, and the displacements in these lines be

$$r_1 = a_1 \cos(nt - e_1), \quad r_2 = a_2 \cos(nt - e_2), \ldots ; \quad \ldots\ldots\ldots\ldots (1)$$

then resolving along rectangular axes of x, y, z, we get

$$\left.\begin{array}{l} x = A \cos nt + A' \sin nt, \\ y = B \cos nt + B' \sin nt, \\ z = C \cos nt + C' \sin nt, \end{array}\right\} \ldots\ldots\ldots\ldots (2)$$

where $\quad A = \Sigma(al \cos e), \quad A' = \Sigma(al \sin e), \quad B = \Sigma(am \cos e), \ldots, \ldots\ldots (3)$

and the summations are taken for all the motions. Then taking the first terms on the right of these equations we obtain a simple harmonic motion,

$$\xi = \sqrt{A^2 + B^2 + C^2} \cdot \cos nt. \quad \ldots\ldots\ldots\ldots (4)$$

The second terms on the right give in the same way a simple harmonic motion,

$$\eta = \sqrt{A'^2 + B'^2 + C'^2} \cdot \sin nt. \quad \ldots\ldots\ldots\ldots (5)$$

The displacement ξ has the direction-cosines $(A, B, C)/\sqrt{A^2 + B^2 + C^2}$, and the displacement η has the cosines $(A', B', C')/\sqrt{A'^2 + B'^2 + C'^2}$.

These two harmonic motions are equivalent to the original system in the sense that they give the same sum of component displacements in any direction as the system gives. They differ in epoch by $\pi/2$, and their lines are inclined at the angle

$$\cos^{-1}\{(AA' + BB' + CC')/\sqrt{(A^2 + B^2 + C^2)(A'^2 + B'^2 + C'^2)}\}.$$

A point, therefore, which in its motion combines their displacements moves in an ellipse with the period $2\pi/n$. Since, as we have seen, this

HARMONIC MOTION.

motion can be obtained by the projection of a uniform circular motion, the radius-vector drawn from the centre to the moving point describes equal areas in equal times. According to the elastic medium theory of light this is the motion of a particle of the medium in a beam of elliptically polarised light.

The two displacements ξ, η, the directions of which have been found, are, as we see at once by the projection of the circular motion, parallel to conjugate axes of the ellipse, and the lengths of these axes are the amplitudes of ξ, η. Denoting these by a, b, the angle between them by ϕ, and referring to rectangular axes, taking for simplicity the line of η as the axis of y, we get

$$x = a \sin\phi \cos nt, \quad y = b \sin nt + a \cos\phi \cos nt. \quad \ldots\ldots\ldots(6)$$

Solving for $\sin nt$, $\cos nt$, squaring and adding, we get for the equation of the ellipse

$$x^2\left(\frac{\cos^2\phi}{b^2} + \frac{1}{a^2}\right) + y^2\frac{\sin^2\phi}{b^2} - 2xy\frac{\sin\phi\cos\phi}{b^2} = \sin^2\phi. \quad \ldots\ldots(7)$$

It will be observed that, if in this equation we put $\pm a\cos\phi$ for y, it reduces to
$$(x \mp a\sin\phi)^2 = 0; \quad \ldots\ldots\ldots\ldots\ldots\ldots\ldots\ldots(8)$$
and that, if we put $\pm a^2 \sin\phi \cos\phi/\sqrt{b^2 + a^2\cos^2\phi}$ for x, it reduces to

$$y = \pm\sqrt{b^2 + a^2\cos^2\phi}. \quad \ldots\ldots\ldots\ldots\ldots\ldots\ldots\ldots(9)$$

Thus the ellipse touches each of the lines $x = a\sin\phi$, $x = -a\sin\phi$, and also each of the lines $y = \sqrt{b^2 + a^2\cos^2\phi}$, $y = -\sqrt{b^2 + a^2\cos^2\phi}$, so that it is circumscribed by the rectangle formed by the two pairs of lines.

To find the axes of the curve we notice that if α, β be the lengths of the semi-axes
$$a^2 + b^2 = \alpha^2 + \beta^2, \quad ab\sin\phi = \alpha\beta,$$
so that
$$\alpha \pm \beta = \sqrt{a^2 + b^2 \pm 2ab\sin\phi}, \quad \ldots\ldots\ldots\ldots\ldots(10)$$
from which α and β can be found.

Again, if θ be the angle which either of the rectangular axes used in (6) makes with a principal axis of the curve, say that between the two axes of x,
$$\tan 2\theta = -\frac{a^2\sin 2\phi}{a^2\cos 2\phi + b^2}. \quad \ldots\ldots\ldots\ldots\ldots\ldots(11)$$

Thus the axes may be regarded as determined.

42. S.H.M.s in Perpendicular Lines, but not of the Same Period. Now consider shortly the case in which two given simple harmonic motions parallel to x and y are not of the same period. We may take as their equations

$$x = a\cos nt, \quad y = b\cos\{(n+\nu)t - e\}. \quad \ldots\ldots\ldots\ldots(1)$$

The part $b\cos(\nu t - e)\cos nt$ of y, compounded with x, gives the simple harmonic motion

$$u = \{a^2 + b^2\cos^2(\nu t - e)\}^{\frac{1}{2}}\cos nt. \quad \ldots\ldots\ldots\ldots\ldots(2)$$

74   A TREATISE ON DYNAMICS.   [CH. I.

This motion combined with the second part of y, $-b\sin(\nu t-e)\sin nt$, gives, *for the instant t*, an elliptic motion, of which the directions of the components and their amplitudes, namely, $\{a^2+b^2\cos^2(\nu t-e)\}^{\frac{1}{2}}$ and $b\sin(\nu t-e)$, are the directions and lengths of a pair of conjugate axes; and the angle between the axes is

$$\pi/2+\sin^{-1}\{b\cos(\nu t-e)\}/\{a^2+b^2\cos^2(\nu t-e)\}^{\frac{1}{2}}.$$

Since the difference of phase $\nu t-e$ varies with the time, the ellipse continually changes in form and position.

The axes of the ellipse, and their position at time t, can be found easily. Solving equations (1) for $\cos nt$, $\sin nt$, squaring and adding, we get

$$\frac{\{xb\cos(\nu t-e)-ya\}^2}{a^2b^2\sin^2(\nu t-e)}+\frac{x^2}{a^2}=1. \quad\quad\quad\quad\quad\quad(3)$$

The curve evidently touches the lines

$$x=\pm a, \quad y=\pm b,$$

and is therefore circumscribed by the rectangle formed by these lines.

The coefficient of x^2 in (3) is $1/a^2\sin^2(\nu t-e)$, that of y^2 is $1/b^2\sin^2(\nu t-e)$, and that of xy is $-2\cos(\nu t-e)/\{ab\sin^2(\nu t-e)\}$. Hence, as in § 41, if θ be the angle which the axis of x as here taken makes with the principal axis taken as that of x, we have as before, by the properties of conjugate axes,

$$\tan 2\theta=\frac{2ab}{a^2-b^2}\cos(\nu t-e). \quad\quad\quad\quad\quad\quad(4)$$

This gives $$\frac{1}{\cos^2 2\theta}\frac{d\theta}{dt}=-\frac{2ab\nu}{a^2-b^2}\sin(\nu t-e), \quad\quad\quad\quad\quad\quad(5)$$

so that $d\theta/dt$ vanishes and changes sign when $\nu t-e=m\pi$, where m is any integer. Thus, as $\nu t-e$ increases continually, θ oscillates between values corresponding to $\tan 2\theta=\pm 2ab/(a^2-b^2)$, that is from $\theta=\tan^{-1}b/a$ to $\theta=-\tan^{-1}b/a$, and back again.

To determine the lengths α, β of the semi-axes, we have

$$\sqrt{a^2+b^2\cos^2(\nu t-e)}\,b\sin(\nu t-e)\cos\left\{\sin^{-1}\frac{b\cos(\nu t-e)}{\sqrt{a^2+b^2\cos^2(\nu t-e)}}\right\}=\alpha\beta$$

or $$ab\sin(\nu t-e)=\alpha\beta; \quad\quad\quad\quad\quad\quad(6)$$
and $$a^2+b^2\cos^2(\nu t-e)+b^2\sin^2(\nu t-e)=\alpha^2+\beta^2$$
or $$a^2+b^2=\alpha^2+\beta^2. \quad\quad\quad\quad\quad\quad(7)$$

Thus we obtain

$$\left.\begin{array}{l}2\alpha=\{a^2+b^2+2ab\sin(\nu t-e)\}^{\frac{1}{2}}+\{a^2+b^2-2ab\sin(\nu t-e)\}^{\frac{1}{2}},\\ 2\beta=\{a^2+b^2+2ab\sin(\nu t-e)\}^{\frac{1}{2}}-\{a^2+b^2-2ab\sin(\nu t-e)\}^{\frac{1}{2}}.\end{array}\right\}\quad(8)$$

When $\nu t-e=m\pi$, that is at the turning points of θ,

$$\alpha=\sqrt{a^2+b^2}, \quad \beta=0. \quad\quad\quad\quad\quad\quad(9)$$

These results are easily verified by means of a Blackburn double pendulum [Gray's *Treatise on Physics*, § 88]. The two periods are made nearly equal, and a and b widely different, when it is found

HARMONIC MOTION.

that a slowly varying but always narrow ellipse is described. The major axis oscillates in direction from $\theta = \tan^{-1} b/a$ to $\theta = -\tan^{-1} b/a$, as stated above.

43. Resisted S.H.M. defined by Equiangular Spiral. Another very important case of vibrational motion is that of a point the motion of which is defined by a radius revolving about the pole of a logarithmic (or equiangular) spiral with uniform angular speed, just as ordinary simple harmonic motion is defined by a radius revolving uniformly about the centre of a circle. The latter motion may be regarded as a particular case of the former, inasmuch as a logarithmic spiral is at every point inclined at the same angle to a radius drawn from the pole to the point, and a circle may be regarded as a logarithmic spiral for which this angle is $\pi/2$. Let the radius OP (length r) revolve with constant angular velocity $\dot\theta$ in the direction of r diminishing, and consider the motion along the line AO of the foot p of the perpendicular let fall from P on that line. Then

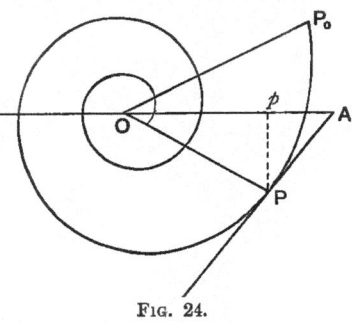

Fig. 24.

if $x = Op$, $y = pP$, $r = R$ initially, $\theta(=\dot\theta t)$ be the angle turned through, from the initial position OP_0 of the turning line to the position OP at time t, and α be the epoch, that is the angle P_0OA, we have

$$r = Ra^{-\theta t}, \quad x = r\cos(\dot\theta t - \alpha), \quad y = r\sin(\dot\theta t - \alpha). \quad \ldots(1)$$

Hence, by differentiation, denoting $\log_e a$ by λ, we get

$$\dot x = -(\lambda x + y)\dot\theta \quad \text{or} \quad -y\dot\theta = \dot x + \lambda x \dot\theta. \quad \ldots\ldots(2)$$

Also $\dot y = -(\lambda y - x)\dot\theta, \quad \dot y \dot\theta = -(\lambda y - x)\dot\theta^2$
$$= +(\lambda^2 + 1)\dot\theta^2 x + \lambda\dot\theta\dot x. \quad \ldots\ldots(3)$$

But differentiating (2) again with respect to t, we get

$$\ddot x = -\lambda \dot x \dot\theta - \dot y \dot\theta$$

or, by (3), $\quad \ddot x + 2\lambda\dot\theta\dot x + (\lambda^2 + 1)\dot\theta^2 x = 0. \quad \ldots\ldots\ldots\ldots(4)$

If we write $k = \lambda\dot{\theta}$ and $n^2 = (\lambda^2+1)\dot{\theta}^2$, the last equation becomes
$$\ddot{x} + 2k\dot{x} + n^2 x = 0. \quad\ldots\ldots\ldots\ldots\ldots\ldots(5)$$
Similarly we obtain
$$\ddot{y} + 2k\dot{y} + n^2 y = 0. \quad\ldots\ldots\ldots\ldots\ldots\ldots(6)$$

Now we have $a = e^\lambda$, $k = \lambda\dot{\theta}$, $n^2 - k^2 = \dot{\theta}^2$, and therefore the values of x and y in (1) are

$$\left.\begin{array}{l}x = Re^{-kt}\cos(\sqrt{n^2-k^2}\,.\,t-\alpha), \\ y = Re^{-kt}\sin(\sqrt{n^2-k^2}\,.\,t-\alpha),\end{array}\right\} \ldots\ldots\ldots(7)$$

and the motions compounded of the motions specified by these equations is that of the point P in the spiral. Equations (7) are the complete integrals of (5) and (6), which they will be found to satisfy on trial. The two necessary arbitrary constants, that is constants the values of which are immaterial as regards the satisfaction of (5) and (6), are R and α.

It will be noticed that for every half-turn of the revolving radius about the pole, the amplitude is diminished in the ratio of $e^{-\lambda\pi}$ to unity. The quantity $\lambda\pi$ is sometimes called the *logarithmic decrement* of the motion. It is the difference of the logarithms of successive maxima of displacement for intervals of time each equal to $\pi/\sqrt{n^2-k^2}$.

The motion here discussed is, as we shall see later, harmonic motion as modified by resistance in the direction of motion proportional to the speed. The bob of a pendulum is thus resisted by the air, if the pendulum moves but slowly. The period is increased beyond its value for $k=0$, in the ratio $1 + \tfrac{1}{2}k^2/n^2$ to 1, if k/n be small. As we shall see in the discussion of resisted motion, if the value of k were great enough, the pendulum, if deflected to any angle from the middle position and then left to itself, would only arrive at the middle position again after an infinite time. In the case considered above, in which the pendulum swings past that position, it will be instructive for the student to consider how it happens that while the direct action of the resistance is obviously to delay arrival at the middle position, and to stop the pendulum sooner after it passes that position, the pendulum takes nevertheless the same time in each swing from one end of the range to the other.

Ex. 1. By supposing $t=0$ when $x=0$, and $t=t_1$ when next $\dot{x}=0$, prove that t_1 is equal to the smallest positive root of the equation

$$\tan(\sqrt{n^2-k^2}\cdot t) - \frac{\sqrt{n^2-k^2}}{k} = 0.$$

Ex. 2. Show that the time t_2, from a turning point to the next zero of x, is (taking the smallest positive root of the equation in Ex. 1) given by

$$t_2 = \frac{1}{\sqrt{n^2-k^2}}\left(\pi - \tan^{-1}\frac{\sqrt{n^2-k^2}}{k}\right).$$

44. Differential Equations of Exponential Motion and S.H.M. Exponential Motion represented Graphically. In the foregoing §§ 32-42, the subject of simple harmonic motion has been discussed, and all contained in these sections may be regarded as illustrative of the properties of the complete integral of the differential equation of the form
$$\ddot{x} + n^2 x = 0. \quad\quad\quad\quad\quad\quad\quad\quad\quad\quad\quad\quad (1)$$
The other differential equation which we obtain when the acceleration $\ddot{x}$ is in the direction of x increasing,
$$\ddot{x} - n^2 x = 0, \quad\quad\quad\quad\quad\quad\quad\quad\quad\quad (2)$$
has as its complete integral
$$x = A e^{nt} + B e^{-nt}, \quad\quad\quad\quad\quad\quad\quad\quad (3)$$
where A and B are constants, the value of which, so far as the differential equation is concerned, may be chosen at pleasure. Take for example the first term and write $x = A e^{nt}$. If, as we suppose, n be positive, the motion may be supposed produced in the following manner. Consider an equiangular spiral of which the equation is, for n positive,
$$r = A e^{nt}. \quad\quad\quad\quad\quad\quad\quad\quad\quad\quad (4)$$
Here nt is the angle which the radius-vector r makes with a fixed line in the plane of the curve, and n is the cotangent of the angle which the curve makes at each point with the radius-vector. Now suppose the axis of x to coincide with this radius-vector, and to remain fixed in space while the spiral revolves with constant angular speed n about the pole. If the spiral turns so that the point of intersection of the curve with the axis of x moves outward, we have x varying exactly as expressed in (4). The (outward) speed of the point of intersection is
$$\dot{x} = nAe^{nt} = nx,$$
and the acceleration, also outward—the distance between two successive convolutions of the spiral increases with distance from the pole—is
$$\ddot{x} = n^2 A e^{nt} = n^2 x.$$

In order to represent the motion expressed by
$$x = B e^{-nt}, \quad\quad\quad\quad\quad\quad\quad\quad\quad\quad (5)$$

78   A TREATISE ON DYNAMICS.   [CH. I.

where n is positive, we must suppose a spiral drawn with $x=B$ for $t=0$ and $x=0$ for $t=\infty$, in fact a spiral the radii-vectores of which are the reciprocals of those of the curve $x=e^{nt}/B$. Then, if we suppose the axis of x to coincide with the initial direction of the radius-vector, and imagine the spiral to revolve with angular speed n in its own plane about the pole, in the direction to cause the point of intersection to move in towards the pole, the speed will be

$$\dot{x} = -nBe^{-nt},$$

and the acceleration, which must be positive, will have the value

$$\ddot{x} = n^2 B e^{-nt} = n^2 x.$$

The sum of these two motions is that represented by the equation (3).

Examples of Exponential and Vibratory Motions.

1. Prove that the hodograph of the motion of the point P (Fig. 24) is a logarithmic spiral of the same angle as the path, and that, if ϕ denote the constant angle between the radius-vector and the tangent to the curve, the acceleration along OA is $+r\dot{\theta}^2 \cos(2\phi - \theta)/\sin^2\phi$. Derive the differential equation (5), § 43. [Here r diminishes as θ increases.]

2. Prove that if $x = e^{-kt}\xi$, the differential equation

$$\ddot{x} + 2k\dot{x} + n^2 x = 0$$

reduces to

$$\ddot{\xi} + (n^2 - k^2)\xi = 0,$$

and show that

$$x = e^{-kt}(A \cos\sqrt{n^2 - k^2} \cdot t + B \sin\sqrt{n^2 - k^2} \cdot t),$$
$$x = e^{-kt}(A e^{\sqrt{k^2 - n^2} \cdot t} + B e^{-\sqrt{k^2 - n^2} \cdot t}),$$

according as n^2 is greater or less than k^2.

3. Prove that if the equation of a logarithmic spiral be written $r = Ra^\theta$, and the radius turn in the direction of r increasing, $\cot \phi = \log_e a$, [Ex. 1] and that the curvature at any point P, to which the radius is r, is $\sin \phi / r$. Prove also that the components of acceleration towards the centre of curvature and along the tangent are respectively $\dot{\theta}^2 r/\sin \phi$ and $r\dot{\theta}^2 \cos \phi / \sin^2 \phi$.

4. From Ex. 3 find the accelerations along and at right angles to OA (Fig. 24), and also those along and at right angles to OP. Prove that these are equivalent to a component $r\dot{\theta}^2/\sin^2\phi$ along PO and a component $2r\dot{\theta}^2 \cos \phi/\sin^2\phi$ in the direction of motion.

5. A radius revolves about one extremity O, with constant angular speed n, and alters in length while revolving, so that the other extremity traces out the spiral of Archimedes, $r = a\theta$, where $\theta = nt$. Prove that the displacements from O, taken along and at right angles to the initial position of the turning radius, satisfy the differential equations $\ddot{x} + 2n\dot{y} - n^2 x = 0, \quad \ddot{y} - 2n\dot{x} - n^2 y = 0.$

EXERCISES I.

1. A boat on a river is distant 300 feet from the shore and 400 feet from a water-fall directly down-stream. If the speed of the stream be 4 miles an hour, find the least velocity with which the boat must be propelled in order to avoid the fall. Show also how to find the direction in which the boat will have the least distance to travel to reach the bank, supposing its speed sufficiently greater than this minimum.

2. A railway passenger seated in one corner of a carriage looks out of the windows on the far side and observes that a star near the horizon is traversing these windows in the direction of the train's motion, and that it is obscured by the partition between the corner window at his end of the carriage and the middle window while the train is moving through the seventh part of a mile. Prove that the train is on a curve, the concavity of which is directed towards the star, and which, if it be circular, has a radius of nearly 3 miles, the breadth of the carriage being 7 feet and the breadth of the partition 4 ins.

3. Two points describe concentric circles uniformly, the time of describing the outer being m times that taken to describe the inner. If v is the speed in the former circle and u that in the latter, show that if the angular velocity of the one point relatively to the other is zero, the actual velocity of the one relatively to the other is

$$\sqrt{\frac{m-1}{m+1}(u^2 - v^2)}.$$

4. In one of Bashforth's experiments three screens, equally spaced apart at a distance of 150 feet, were penetrated by a projectile 0·5569, 0·634 and 0·7069 seconds respectively after projection. Assuming that the motion of the shot may be represented by the equation

$$t = 0·6314 + as + bs^2,$$

where s is the distance of the shot from the middle screen at time t, prove that the resistance to the motion at the middle screen is about eleven times the weight of the shot.

5. In certain experiments on the resistance of the air to the motion of cannon balls it was found that the number s of feet travelled by the shot in t seconds was given by the equation $t = as + bs^2$, where a and b are constants. Find the relation between the velocity and the tangential retardation.

6. A crank OA rotates uniformly about an axis through O; the end A is pivoted to a rigid rod which slides in an oscillating cylinder. The axis about which the cylinder turns passes through its centre O' and is parallel to the axis of the crank. Show that the angular speed of the rod and cylinder is given by

$$\omega = -\omega r (r - d\cos\theta)/(r^2 + d^2 - 2rd\cos\theta),$$

where ω is the angular speed of the crank, r the length of the crank, d the distance between the two fixed axes, and θ the angle between the crank and the line OO'.

7. A crank OP of length a rotates with uniform angular velocity ω about an axle through a fixed point O; a connecting rod of length b joins P to the end D of a crosshead which is constrained to move in a straight line through O at right angles to the axle. If b is so large compared with a that all powers of a^2/b above the first may be neglected, show that the acceleration of D when the angle DOP is equal to θ is $-a\omega^2 \cos\theta - a^2\omega^2 \cos 2\theta/b$.

8. A particle describes the circle $r = 2a\cos\theta$, the component of acceleration towards the origin being always zero. Show that the transversal component varies as $\operatorname{cosec}^5\theta$.

9. A is a fixed point on a plane curve, B is the position at time t of a point which is moving along the curve, and on the tangent at B a point C is taken. If the arc $AB = s$, $BC = r$, and θ be the angle through which the tangent revolves as the point passes from A to B, show that the accelerations of C in the direction BC and in the direction perpendicular to BC (in the sense in which θ increases) are respectively

$$\ddot{s} + \ddot{r} - r\dot\theta^2, \quad \frac{1}{r}\frac{d}{dt}(r^2\dot\theta) + \dot s\dot\theta.$$

10. Prove that in the case of a particle moving in a groove which is made to rotate in its own plane about a fixed point in the plane, the motion of the particle relative to the groove can be obtained by superposing on the external forces on the particle the following system: $m\omega^2 r$ along the radius-vector outwards, $-mr\dot\omega$ perpendicular to the radius-vector, and $2mv'\omega$ perpendicular to the groove, where v' is the velocity of the particle relative to the groove. Indicate by a figure the directions of the forces. [If r be the radius-vector from the origin to the particle, $\dot\theta$ the angular speed of r with reference to a given point of the groove, ϕ the angle between the forward tangent and r, and R the inward normal reaction of the tube, the equations of motion are

$$m\{\ddot r - r(\dot\theta + \omega)^2\} = -R\sin\phi, \quad \frac{m}{r}\frac{d}{dt}\{r^2(\dot\theta + \omega)\} = R\cos\phi.$$

Along the tangent and normal these give

$$v\frac{dv}{ds} = \omega^2 r \cos\phi, \quad \frac{v^2}{\rho} = -\omega^2 r \sin\phi + \frac{R}{m} - 2\omega\dot s.]$$

A groove in the form of a parabola (latus rectum $4a$) is initially at rest with a particle at the vertex. It is suddenly made to rotate about the focus with constant angular velocity ω; prove that the reaction between the particle and the groove when the particle reaches the extremity of the latus rectum is $ma\omega^2(3/\sqrt{2} - 4)$. [There is no force on the particle except that applied by the groove.]

11. A smooth conical cup, whose semi-vertical angle is α, revolves with angular velocity ω about a vertical axis parallel to the axis of the cone and at a distance c from it; show that if a particle be moving on the surface of the cup, the component of its acceleration along the generating line is $\ddot{r} - r\sin^2\alpha(\dot{\phi}+\omega)^2 + c\omega^2\cos\phi\sin\alpha$, where r is the distance of the particle from the vertex and ϕ the angle between a plane through the two axes and a plane through the particle and the axis of the cone.

12. If the position of a point moving in a plane be determined by the coordinates r and ϕ, where r is measured from a fixed circle (radius a) along a tangent which has revolved through an angle ϕ from a fixed tangent, show that if α and β are the accelerations along and perpendicular to r respectively,
$$\alpha = \ddot{r} - r\dot{\phi}^2 + a\ddot{\phi}, \quad \beta = \frac{1}{r}\frac{d}{dt}(r^2\dot{\phi}) + a\dot{\phi}^2.$$

13. Show that, in the case of three dimensional motion (p. 34), if v be the velocity of the moving particle, the radial acceleration is given by $\ddot{r} + (\dot{r}^2 - v^2)/r$.

14. A circle rolls without slipping along a horizontal straight line with angular velocity ω and angular acceleration $\dot{\omega}$. Derive expressions for the horizontal and vertical components of acceleration for any point on the circumference of the circle. (See p. 128.)

Supposing the velocity of the centre of the circle to be v and its acceleration α, find the horizontal and vertical components of velocity and acceleration for the highest and lowest points of the circle.

15. A heavy particle is projected with velocity u so as to reach a point on the same horizontal plane at a distance $2h$. Show that the angle α which the direction of projection makes with the horizontal must satisfy the relation
$$u^2\sin\alpha\cos\alpha = gh.$$

16. A smooth tube ACB, fixed in a vertical plane, is a portion of a circular tube of radius a from which the upper part, subtending an angle $2\alpha(<\pi)$ at the centre, has been removed. The line AB joining the open ends of the tube is horizontal. Prove that a particle will perform complete revolutions in a vertical plane if its speed v at the lowest point satisfies the relation
$$v^2 = ag\left(\sec\alpha + 4\cos^2\frac{\alpha}{2}\right).$$

17. A particle is to be projected so as just to pass through three equal rings, of diameter d, placed in parallel vertical planes at distances a apart, with their highest points in a horizontal straight line at a height h above the point of projection. Prove that the elevation must be $\tan^{-1}(2\sqrt{hd}/a)$.

82   A TREATISE ON DYNAMICS.   [CH. I.

18. Show that the least velocity V with which a stone must be projected so as to clear a wall of height h at distance d from the point of projection is $\{g(h+\sqrt{h^2+d^2})\}^{\frac{1}{2}}$ [Ex. 4, p. 49]. Prove that if the stone be always projected with this same velocity V, the area of the wall that can be struck is bounded by a parabola of latus rectum $2V^2/g$.

19. A man travelling at speed v in a circular path of radius a throws a ball from his hand at a height h from the ground with a relative velocity V, so that it alights at the centre of the circle. Prove that the least possible value of V is given by
$$V^2 = v^2 + g(\sqrt{a^2+h^2} - h).$$

20. The speed v of a point P is given by the relation $v^2 = a - bx^2$, where x is the distance of P from a fixed point on the path, and a and b are constants. Show that the motion of P is simple-harmonic, and determine the amplitude and period in terms of a and b.

21. A simple pendulum of length l is drawn aside from the vertical through an angle α and is then let go. Show that when the thread makes an angle θ with the vertical, the velocity v of the bob is given by
$$v = 4gl\left(\sin^2\frac{\alpha}{2} - \sin^2\frac{\theta}{2}\right).$$
Hence show that for small oscillations the motion is simple-harmonic in period $2\pi\sqrt{l/g}$.

22. A particle of mass M rests on a smooth horizontal plane and is attached to one end of a light elastic string, the other end of which is fastened to the plane. The unstretched length of the string being l, show that if the particle be moved along the plane until its distance from the point of attachment is l' ($l' > l$), and is then let go, it will pass the point of attachment after a time given by
$$t = \sqrt{\frac{M}{\lambda}}\left(\frac{\pi}{2} + \frac{l}{l'-l}\right),$$
if λ be the force required to produce unit extension of the string, and force vary as extension.

23. Describe the rectilinear motion of a particle whose distance from a fixed point in its line of motion is given by $x = a + b\cos\omega t$.

A and B are two points at a distance d apart. A particle moves in the line AB, its speed at time t being given by $(c\sin\omega t)/d$, c and ω being constants. Prove that if the particle start from A it will never reach B if d is greater than $\sqrt{2c/\omega}$.

24. Prove that in the conical pendulum the period is given by $2\pi\sqrt{h/g}$, where h is the vertical projection of the suspending thread. Hence show that if n be the frequency of the pendulum, hn^2 is constant and dh/dn varies inversely as n^3.

Explain how this result shows that the sensitiveness of the pendulum, used as a governor, increases with diminishing speed and *vice versa*.

CHAPTER II.

DYNAMICAL PRINCIPLES.

45. The Laws of Motion. Momentum and Rate of Change of Momentum (R.C.M.). The laws of motion and the comparison of masses and forces will be found treated in detail in our book on Elementary Dynamics, to which also we refer for a short discussion of relativity of motion.* We here repeat, however, some definitions and restate in mathematical language some observations on the laws of motion.

First, a *particle* is a portion of matter which contains so large a number of molecules (or ultimate particles) that the molecular motions, which, taken over a large aggregate of molecules, are equally distributed over all directions, give no momentum to the particle in any direction, and which is yet so small that in indicating its position by coordinates we may regard it as a point.

For a particle, therefore, we consider only motion of translation. Hence its momentum in any direction is the product of its mass m and its component velocity in that direction. Thus, if v be the resultant velocity of the particle its momentum is mv, and if $\dot{x}, \dot{y}, \dot{z}$ be its component velocities parallel to rectangular axes Ox, Oy, Oz drawn from an origin O, the momenta of the particle in these directions are $m\dot{x}, m\dot{y}, m\dot{z}$.

If instead of a particle we have an extended body, that is an aggregate of particles (of mass or weight M),* and the body have no motion of rotation, that is if, at the instant under consideration, no straight line of particles in the body

---

* See also Gray's *Treatise on Physics*, vol. i. chap. iii.

is changing its direction (relatively to any chosen system of axes assumed to be at rest), then at the instant the velocity of each particle is the same. If v be this velocity and $\dot{x}, \dot{y}, \dot{z}$ its components, the body has a resultant momentum Mv at the instant, and its components of momentum are $M\dot{x}, M\dot{y}, M\dot{z}$. If ρ be the density at any point of the body, and $d\varpi$ be a small element of volume there, we have

$$M = \int \rho\, d\varpi,$$

where the integral is taken throughout the whole space occupied by the body.

The rate of change of momentum of a particle under acceleration α in any direction is $m\alpha$ in that direction, if the mass remains unchanged. For example, if in Fig. 5 p, q were close points on the hodograph of a particle, such that the velocity changed from op to oq in time dt, α would be the limiting value of the ratio $\overline{pq}/dt$, where dt was made infinitely small, and the direction of $\overline{pq}$ would be that of the tangent to the hodograph at p. The rate of change of momentum $m\alpha$ would be also along the tangent at p.

If $\ddot{x}, \ddot{y}, \ddot{z}$ be the components of α parallel to the axes, the components of rate of change of momentum are $m\ddot{x}, m\ddot{y}, m\ddot{z}$. The resultant is $m(\ddot{x}^2 + \ddot{y}^2 + \ddot{z}^2)^{\frac{1}{2}}$ or $m\alpha$, and has the direction of α, as already stated.

For a particle we may substitute a body, or any collection of particles, every one of which has the same acceleration—the same, that is, both in direction and magnitude. This condition is fulfilled by a body, or a collection of discrete particles, the velocities of which are at *every* instant the same, for then the rate of change must be the same for all at every instant. The rate of change of momentum of the system is then $M\alpha$, and, though it cannot now be localised along a particular line, as in the case of a particle, its direction is that of α. The components parallel to the axes are $M\ddot{x}, M\ddot{y}, M\ddot{z}$.

46. Effect of Change of Mass on R.C.M. If the mass of the system of particles be changing at rate $\dot{M}$, a rate of change of momentum $\dot{M}v$ exists in the direction of v, along with the rate of change of momentum $M\alpha$ in the direction of α. Hence if ϕ be the angle between the directions of v and α, we may say that we have now a component of rate of change of momentum $\dot{M}v\cos\phi + M\alpha$ in the direction of α, together with a component $\dot{M}v\sin\phi$ at right angles to v in the plane of v and α, or a component $\dot{M}v + M\alpha\cos\phi$ in the direction v and a component $M\alpha\sin\phi$ at right angles to α in the plane of v and α. The resultant rate of change of momentum R is

$$(\dot{M}^2v^2 + M^2\alpha^2 + 2M\dot{M}v\alpha\cos\phi)^{\frac{1}{2}},$$

and makes an angle the cosine of which is $(\dot{M}v + M\alpha\cos\phi)/R$ with the direction of v.

These results are easily verified by means of the components parallel to the axes of x, y, z, which are

$$M\ddot{x} + \dot{M}\dot{x},\quad M\ddot{y} + \dot{M}\dot{y},\quad M\ddot{z} + \dot{M}\dot{z}.$$

Thus the resultant rate of change of momentum is

$$\{(M\ddot{x} + \dot{M}\dot{x})^2 + (M\ddot{y} + \dot{M}\dot{y})^2 + (M\ddot{z} + \dot{M}\dot{z})^2\}^{\frac{1}{2}},$$

which expanded gives at once

$$(\dot{M}^2v^2 + M^2\alpha^2 + 2M\dot{M}v\alpha\cos\phi)^{\frac{1}{2}}.$$

The loss or gain of momentum, through loss or gain of mass, is an important consideration in various cases of motion; and care must be exercised in taking it into account. For example, the rapid burning away of the powder charge of a rocket propels the rocket forward and upward. Again, a tank on wheels may lose mass in a jet of water from a hole in one end of the tank, and a reaction will be exerted on the tank by the jet, either aiding or hindering the motion of the former. But the tank may lose matter by a jet through a hole in the bottom, in which case only a vertical reaction exists. [See § 52 below.]

47. R.C.M. in Curvilinear Motion. Force. From the results stated in §§ 8–11 above for accelerations, we see that a moving particle of constant mass has, at each instant, rate of change of momentum mv^2/R towards the centre of curvature of its path, and $m\dot{s}$ in the direction of motion. We notice that if the curvature of the path at any point be very great, that is if the radius R be very small, the rate of change of momentum mv^2/R is very great. In fact a particle cannot be made to turn a perfectly sharp corner in its motion.

Again, the rate of change of momentum may be resolved along the radius-vector drawn from a chosen origin, and at right angles to the radius-vector in the plane of motion. In the general case the components are

$$m(\ddot{r} - \omega^2 r), \quad m(2\omega \dot{r} + \dot{\omega} r);$$

in the case of motion in a plane curve they are

$$m(\ddot{r} - \dot{\theta}^2 r), \quad m(2\dot{r}\dot{\theta} + \ddot{\theta} r).$$

For brevity we shall now call the rate of change of momentum in any direction the *force* in that direction, in the case for the most part in which the mass is not subject to change. Each more general case will be considered as it arises.

48. Kinetic Energy. R.C.M. as Space-Rate of Variation of K.E. For a particle moving with a velocity v, the product $\tfrac{1}{2}mv^2$ is called the *kinetic energy* of the particle. For an aggregate of particles (of total mass M), all of which have the same velocity v, the product $\tfrac{1}{2}Mv^2$, where M is the total mass, is called the kinetic energy.

In the case of a system of particles, of masses $m_1, m_2, \ldots$, the speeds of which are $v_1, v_2, \ldots$ in different directions, the kinetic energy is defined to be the sum

$$\tfrac{1}{2}(m_1 v_1^2 + m_2 v_2^2 + \ldots),$$

usually written $\tfrac{1}{2}\Sigma(mv^2)$, of the products obtained by multiplying half the mass of each particle by the square of its speed. This case will be considered later.

It will be seen that the rate of change of momentum of a particle in the direction of motion may be written in the form $mv\, dv/ds$, for this is simply $m\ddot{s}$. But it is also the rate of variation of the kinetic energy $\tfrac{1}{2}mv^2$ in the direction of motion. Thus the time-rate of change of momentum, or force, in the direction of motion is equal to the space-rate of change of the kinetic energy in the same direction.

It is convenient when a space integration is required to write $v\,dv/ds$ for dv/dt or $\ddot{s}$, and use $\dot{v}$ when a time integration is convenient. For example, take the case of a shot which is resisted according to the cube of its speed, so that $\dot{v} = v\,dv/ds = -kv^3$. We can at once integrate over a time or a space as may be required.

49. Potential Energy. Equation of Motion for Particle under Central Force derived from Energy. For a material system in motion, each part of which is acted on only by other parts of the system, and is not affected in its motion by frictional resistances, we have

$$\tfrac{1}{2}\Sigma(mv^2) + V = \text{const.}, \quad\ldots\ldots\ldots\ldots\ldots\ldots(1)$$

where V is a single-valued function of the masses and the coordinates of the parts of the system. Thus if we put T for the kinetic energy $\tfrac{1}{2}\Sigma(mv^2)$, we have

$$T + V = \text{const.} \quad\ldots\ldots\ldots\ldots\ldots\ldots\ldots(2)$$

V is what is called the *potential energy* of the system, and it is such that the total rate of change of momentum of the system in any direction, that of x say, is $-\partial V/\partial x$; that is the total force on the system, in the direction of x, is the space-rate of diminution of the potential energy in that direction. But by (2), if the vs are supposed to be expressed as functions of the coordinates,

$$\frac{\partial T}{\partial x} = -\frac{\partial V}{\partial x}, \quad\ldots\ldots\ldots\ldots\ldots\ldots(3)$$

and so the force in the direction of x is the space-rate of increase of the kinetic energy in that direction. [See also § 66.]

As an example, take the equation for v^2 in the case of a particle under a central acceleration (§ 11 above). V is here a function of the distance of the particle from the centre O, towards which the acceleration is directed. Assuming that in this case the equation (2) holds, and taking the mass of the particle as unity, we have

$$T = \tfrac{1}{2}v^2 = \tfrac{1}{2}h^2\left\{\left(\frac{du}{d\theta}\right)^2 + u^2\right\} \quad\ldots\ldots\ldots(4)$$

and

$$\frac{\partial T}{\partial r} = -u^2\frac{\partial T}{\partial u} = -h^2u^2\left(\frac{d^2u}{d\theta^2} + u\right), \quad\ldots\ldots\ldots(5)$$

since $d(du/d\theta)/du = d^2u/d\theta^2 \cdot d\theta/du$, so that T, like V, is treated as a function of u only. Now, by (3), $\partial T/\partial r$ is the outward force along r. If, as in §31 above, R denote the inward acceleration (here the force $\partial V/\partial r$) along r, we have again the result

$$\frac{d^2u}{d\theta^2} + u = \frac{R}{h^2 u^2}. \qquad\qquad (6)$$

We shall return to the subject of energy in Chapter VII.

50. Discussion of First Law of Motion. The first law of motion—*Every body continues in its state of rest or of uniform motion in a straight line, except in so far as it is compelled to change that state by forces impressed upon it*—affirms (1) that no body has its momentum changed except by the action of other bodies, and (2) that every particle in a non-rotating body unacted on by other matter continues to move uniformly in a straight line. Thus if such a body can be found, and its motion be traced by means of a reference system, the times in which each of its particles describes equal times are equal. [We shall see later that in a rotating body a point can be found in it, which, if the body be unacted on by other matter, moves uniformly in a straight line.] Moreover, different bodies, moving in this way, used for the measurement of time will give consistent results.

In strictness, no such body can be found; but it is possible, by considering the changes of configuration of a system such as the sun, moon, and earth, which is affected by other bodies only to a slight extent capable of being approximately allowed for, to test the going of our terrestrial time-keeper, the rotating earth. This we suppose to turn through equal angles in equal times; and there is no doubt that the actions which tend to change the earth's rotation—and there are such actions—are such as to produce no perceptible effect in any ordinary interval of time, such as an interval of several years. But having observed the relative positions of the members of this system of three bodies at different epochs of past time, we can form tables of the positions of the moon for future time, on the supposition that external action is allowed for, and then compare these lunar tables with the observed positions of the moon at times given by the terrestrial timekeeper. If a discrepancy is found to disclose itself after a long interval, then either the original observations, the theory or mode of calculation, or the terrestrial timekeeper must be at fault; and from various considerations it may be possible to ascribe the discrepancy to the last mentioned cause. Thus the "apparent acceleration of the moon's motion" has led to the conclusion that the earth, in consequence of tidal friction, rotates slower and slower as time advances, to such an extent that in a hundred years it falls about 22 seconds behind a true dynamical time-keeper with whose going the rotation of the earth agreed at the beginning of that interval.

51. Second Law of Motion. Example. The second law of motion—*Change of motion is proportional to the moving force impressed, and takes place in the direction in which that force acts*—is sometimes alleged to amount only to a statement that force is proportional to rate of change of momentum. And, apparently, if force be defined, as above, to mean rate of change of momentum, the proportionality is involved in the definition, and the law seems to be completely unnecessary. But, as Newton explained, the law means much more: when a body is placed under different actions each has its full effect in producing rate of change of momentum, just as if the other actions did not exist, so that the effects are to be simply added together, with their proper signs, if they are in the same line, or compounded, that is geometrically added, if they are in lines inclined to one another.

For example, a mass hung by a spiral spring is acted on by the downward pull due to the earth's attraction, and if the mass is in equilibrium, is pulled upward equally by the spring, so that there is no rate of change of momentum produced by this system of two opposite actions. Now we are here to imagine each action as producing the rate of change of momentum which it would produce if it acted alone on the suspended body, as we see at once if we consider the case in which equilibrium does not exist. Let the spring be extended beyond the equilibrium length, and assume, what can be verified by loading the spring to equilibrium with different weights and measuring the elongations, that the upward action exerted by the spring is proportional to its elongation. Denote now the mass of the body suspended by m, and let the whole extension be $s+x$, where s denotes the equilibrium extension. If g be the downward acceleration of a body falling freely, the downward rate of change of momentum due to gravity—the *force* of gravity on the body—is mg. The upward rate of change of momentum due to the spring—the *force* due to the spring—is $mg(s+x)/s$. Thus there is an upward rate of change of momentum mgx/s, which we denote by $-m\ddot{x}$. The equation of motion is therefore

$$\ddot{x} + \frac{g}{s}x = 0,$$

and the mass moves up and down in simple harmonic motion in the period $2\pi\sqrt{s/g}$.

52. Meaning of Equations of Motion. The second law of motion enables us to write for each moving particle what are called equations of motion. Thus if $\ddot{s}$ be the acceleration of any particle of mass m, we have

$$m\ddot{s} = S, \quad\quad\quad\quad\quad\quad\quad\quad\quad (1)$$

where S is the *force* acting on the particle in the direction of s. Or, more usually, we have three equations of motion, one for each rectangular coordinate of the particle, namely

$$m\ddot{x} = X, \quad m\ddot{y} = Y, \quad m\ddot{z} = Z. \quad\quad\quad\quad (2)$$

These are more than mere statements that the rates of change of momentum $m\ddot{s}$, $m\ddot{x}$, ... are denoted by S, X, ... They mean that the various actions on the particle, arising from the circumstances in which it is placed, are by means of our knowledge and experience to be evaluated, and the forms of S, X, ..., as depending on the coordinates of the particle or other known conditions controlling the actions, are to be made explicit in the solution of the problem to determine the motion. When this has been done, the differential equations may, if our mathematical processes are adequate, be integrated, and the solution obtained as a relation, or relations, from which each coordinate can be expressed as a function of the time and the initial coordinates and velocities.

The equations of motion of systems of particles will be discussed later.

53. Non-Rotational Motion of Extended Body. Systems of Varying Mass. An extended body may be regarded as a particle, and have equations of the form (2), § 52, if at each instant the acceleration of each particle of the body is the same in direction and magnitude. This will be the case if the body move without rotation, that is, if at each instant all the particles have the same velocity, that is, are moving in the same direction with the same speed. This, of course, does not mean that the body does not *revolve*, but it means that the body does not *rotate*. Thus the side-rods of a locomotive connecting the cranks attached to the driving wheels with parallel cranks on other wheels, to increase the weight giving "bite" on the rails, revolve but do not rotate. Every point of the rod moves in a path which is compounded of a circular and a rectilineal motion, but if the locomotive is running on a straight road, every straight line of particles in the rod remains throughout in the same direction. The crank-pins, however, to which the rod is attached, revolve, and at the same time rotate with the wheels which carry them, so as to turn always the same side of the pin towards the centre about which the crank turns.

We may therefore apply (1), as in the following examples, to such diverse arrangements of particles as a rain-drop, a tank of water, or a falling chain. The problems are selected so as to illustrate various points, and at the same time guide the student at the outset to deal correctly with the motion of bodies of varying mass.

The equations of motion for such bodies are found as follows. If $M\dot{x}$, $M\dot{y}$, $M\dot{z}$ be the components of momentum, $M\ddot{x}+\dot{M}\dot{x}$, $M\ddot{y}+\dot{M}\dot{y}$, $M\ddot{z}+\dot{M}\dot{z}$ are the components of R.C.M.

92   A TREATISE ON DYNAMICS.   [CH. II.

To each of these we must equate the force in the direction of the component, increased by a component of R.C.M. denoted by R_x, R_y, R_z, due to, as the case may be, *flow of matter to or from the body*, or to any reaction exerted at the same time on the body in consequence of that flow. Thus the equations are

$$\left.\begin{array}{l}M\ddot{x}+\dot{M}\dot{x}=X+R_x,\\ M\ddot{y}+\dot{M}\dot{y}=Y+R_y,\\ M\ddot{z}+\dot{M}\dot{z}=Z+R_z.\end{array}\right\} \quad \ldots\ldots\ldots\ldots\ldots(1)$$

If, for example, matter be deposited on the body, as cosmic dust deposited on the earth may be supposed to be, without bringing with it any momentum, we have

$$R_x = R_y = R_z = 0,$$

and the equations are

$$M\ddot{x}+\dot{M}\dot{x}=X. \quad \ldots\ldots\ldots\ldots\ldots(2)$$

On the other hand, if the withdrawal of matter be accompanied by withdrawal of a corresponding amount of momentum, and there be no reaction in the direction of the component of momentum concerned, the equation for the component is of the form

$$M\ddot{x}=X \quad \ldots\ldots\ldots\ldots\ldots\ldots(3)$$

simply, since $\dot{M}x=R_x$.

The following examples will serve to illustrate the application of equations (1).

Ex. 1. A rain-drop falls through an atmosphere of aqueous vapour, which condenses on the surface so that the radius, initially a, increases at uniform rate c. Show that after time t, when the radius is r, the drop is falling at speed

$$v=\frac{1}{4}gt\left(1+\frac{a}{r}+\frac{a^2}{r^2}+\frac{a^3}{r^3}\right).$$

[Stokes, Smith's Prize Examination, 1853.]

Here the moisture deposited brings no momentum and exerts no reaction, except that which arises in consequence of the starting of each infinitely thin layer deposited at the speed with which the drop is then moving. This must be overcome by the gravity due to the weight of the drop, which, besides, gives the downward acceleration, clearly in this case less than g.

§ 53]   EXAMPLES.   93

The momentum of the drop at time t is $\frac{4}{3}\pi\rho r^3 v$, and therefore the rate of change of momentum is $4\pi\rho r^2 \dot{r} v + \frac{4}{3}\pi\rho r^3 \dot{v}$. The first of these terms is the force required in consequence of the addition, at rate $4\pi\rho r^2 \dot{r}$, of matter which must be made to take up the speed v, while the second term is the force required to give acceleration $\dot{v}$ to the drop as it exists at the instant. These two forces must equal $\frac{4}{3}\pi\rho r^3 g$, since no momentum is brought with the water deposited. Hence

$$\dot{v} + \frac{3\dot{r}v}{r} = g$$

is the equation of motion, which can be written also in the form

$$\frac{dv}{dr} + 3\frac{v}{r} = \frac{g}{c},$$

since $c = \dot{r}$.

Multiplying this equation by $e^{3\log r}$, and integrating, we get

$$r^3 v = \frac{1}{4}\frac{g}{c}(r^4 - a^4) = \frac{1}{4}gt(r+a)(r^2+a^2),$$

since $r - a = ct$. Division by r^3 gives

$$v = \frac{1}{4}gt\left(1 + \frac{a}{r} + \frac{a^2}{r^2} + \frac{a^3}{r^3}\right).$$

Ex. 2. A tank is mounted on a truck and water issues horizontally from an orifice in one end. If the truck be moving with speed v in one direction and the water leave the truck, from an orifice in the hinder end, with speed v' in the opposite direction, and the effective inertia of the truck be M, find the equation of motion.

The jet exerts a reaction on the truck. Since the momentum of the truck and its contents is Mv, the R.C.M. is $\dot{M}v + M\dot{v}$, where, if m be the mass of water which issues per second, $-\dot{M} = m$. Momentum is given to the jet by the truck at rate $m(v+v')$, and the reaction due to the jet has this value. The R.C.M. $\dot{M}v + M\dot{v}$ is due to the net forward horizontal tractive force F applied from without, the reaction of the jet, and the rate of flow of momentum, conjointly. Hence we get

$$\dot{M}v + M\dot{v} = F + m(v+v') - mv,$$

or, since $\dot{M} = -m$,

$$M\dot{v} = F + m(v+v').$$

Ex. 3. A light open carriage runs on horizontal rails. A heavy uniform vertical rain falls, and water is received by the truck on a horizontal area A: find the effect of the deposition of water on the motion.

Let the mass of water which comes down per unit area per second be m, then the rate of gain of mass by the carriage is mA, whatever the speed may be. If the total mass at time t be M and the speed v, the R.C.M. is $\dot{M}v + M\dot{v} = Amv + M\dot{v}$. The rain exerts no horizontal action, but a forward force Amv is required in order that each small addition of mass may take up the speed v. Thus, if F be the balance of tractive force over resistances, we have

$$M\dot{v} + Amv = F.$$

If water at the same time flows out through an orifice in the bottom at rate μ, the R.C.M. is $M\dot{v} + Amv - \mu v$, and this is due to the force F and the flow of momentum conjointly, that is,

$$M\dot{v} + Amv - \mu v = F - \mu v$$

or
$$M\dot{v} + Amv = F,$$

so that the equation of motion is not affected. This is of course on the supposition that all the water which enters takes up the motion.

If $F=0$, we get $\dot{v}/v = -Am/M$, and M is a function of t. If we take this case, we have $M = M_0 + (Am - \mu)t$, if μ be constant, so that

$$\frac{\dot{v}}{v} = -\frac{Am}{M_0 + (Am - \mu)t} = -\frac{Am}{Am - \mu} \frac{Am - \mu}{M_0 + (Am - \mu)t}.$$

Integrating, we find

$$\log v = -\frac{Am}{Am - \mu} \log\{M_0 + (Am - \mu)t\} + C.$$

But when $t = 0$, $v = v_0$, and therefore

$$\log \frac{v_0}{v} = \frac{Am}{Am - \mu} \log \frac{M_0 + (Am - \mu)t}{M_0}.$$

If μ be zero, that is, if the case be the first stated above,

$$\log \frac{v_0}{v} = \log \frac{M_0 + Amt}{M_0},$$

that is,
$$M_0 v_0 = (M_0 + Amt)v,$$

as of course could have been stated at once, since the total momentum at time t must be equal to the initial momentum.

Ex. 4. A thin uniform flexible chain of small links is hung vertically from its two ends. One of the ends is then let go: to find the tensile force at the bight where the chain passes over from the free side to the stationary side.

In the first place, there is no tensile force in the chain on the side that is let go, for every portion is at each instant falling freely under gravity, and has therefore the same downward speed and acceleration. In time t the free end has descended a distance $\frac{1}{2}gt^2$, and acquired a speed $v(=gt)$, which is also the speed of each part of the chain between the free end and the bight. If $2l$ be the whole length of the chain, the falling side has length $l - \frac{1}{2}s$, while the part on the other side, which is stationary, has length $l + \frac{1}{2}s$, and is therefore increasing in length at rate $\frac{1}{2}v$.

§ 53]   EXAMPLES.   95

Thus mass is passing across from the falling to the stationary side at rate $\frac{1}{2}\sigma v$, where σ is the mass of the chain per unit length, and each element as it passes across has its downward speed destroyed. To effect this upward R.C.M., an upward pull must be exerted by the lower end of the fixed part of the chain of amount $\frac{1}{2}\sigma v^2$, since this is the momentum produced per second. Thus (see § 57) *on the fixed side* the tensile force at the bight is

$$\tfrac{1}{2}\sigma v^2 = \tfrac{1}{2}\sigma g^2 t^2.$$

The downward pull P of the chain on the support of the fixed end is $\frac{1}{2}\sigma g^2 t^2 + g\sigma(l + \frac{1}{2}s) = g\sigma l + \frac{3}{4}\sigma g^2 t^2$, which goes on increasing with t until the whole chain has been transferred to the stationary side. Just before this transference has been completed, s is very nearly equal to $2l$, and $t^2 = 4l/g$, so that P is now almost $4g\sigma l$. The tensile force at the bight is now $2g\sigma l$, and becomes suddenly zero as the last element passes across, when P at the same instant suddenly sinks to $2g\sigma l$.

Certain energy changes take place, but these we shall discuss later.

Ex. 5. A chain of the sort described in Ex. 4 is piled in a small heap close to the edge of a table. One end is carried vertically up from the table over a smooth horizontal rod at a distance a, and down again until the free end hangs slightly below the edge of the table: to find the motion and the tensile force in the chain at the rod.

Let the lower end be at a distance x below the edge of the table at time t, the rate $\dot{x}$ of descent of the end is the speed downward of all the chain on that side of the rod. The momentum is therefore $\sigma(a+x)\dot{x}$, and the R.C.M. is $\sigma(a+x)\ddot{x} + \sigma\dot{x}^2$. The first of these terms is the R.C.M. for the part of the chain *already on that side*, the second term $\sigma\dot{x}^2$ is the R.C.M. which arises from the addition of mass which is continually taking place in that part in consequence of passage of the chain from the upward to the downward moving side.

The vertical part on the other side B of the rod remains of length a, for, as successive elements pass the rod, equal lengths are taken from the heap and set it into upward motion of speed numerically equal to $\dot{x}$; for the chain being inextensible must have the same speed upward on one side that it has downward on the other. Hence the lower end of the part B where it joins the heap is (§ 57) under tensile force $\sigma\dot{x}^2$.

Now let T_1, T_2 be the tensile force at the upper ends of A, B respectively. Then the part A is pulled upward at the upper *end* by T_1 and downward by the weight $g\sigma(a+x)$. Momentum is added to A at rate $\sigma\dot{x}^2$ because of the addition, at rate $\sigma\dot{x}$, of matter moving downwards at speed $\dot{x}$. The upward motion of each element at the upper end of B is changed to downward motion at the same speed by the combined downward action of T_1 and T_2, and the upward reaction of the peg, on the element as it passes. Any difference between T_1 and T_2 depends in the absence of friction, as will be shown later in a short discussion of the motion of chains, on the existence of acceleration of the tangential motions of the parts of the chain on the peg. If these motions are the same, or if the mass between be infinitesimal, and there be no friction, T_1 and T_2 are very nearly equal. The equation of motion of A is

$$\frac{d}{dt}\{\sigma(a+x)\dot{x}\} = g\sigma(a+x) - T_1 + \sigma\dot{x}^2,$$

or
$$\sigma(a+x)\ddot{x} = g\sigma(a+x) - T_1.$$

The equation of motion of B is

$$\sigma a\ddot{x} = T_2 - \sigma\dot{x}^2 - g\sigma a.$$

Now, as has been stated, if the length of chain on the rod be very short and there be no friction, T_1 may be taken as equal to T_2, and then we get by addition of the two equations

$$\sigma(2a+x)\ddot{x} + \sigma\dot{x}^2 = g\sigma x.$$

The left-hand side is the time-rate of change of $\sigma(2a+x)\dot{x}$. If then we multiply both sides by $(2a+x)\dot{x}$, and drop the common factor σ, we get by integration

$$\tfrac{1}{2}(2a+x)^2\dot{x}^2 = \tfrac{1}{3}g\{x^2(3a+x) - x_0^2(3a+x_0)\},$$

where x_0 is the initial value of x.

54. Units of Force. Dimensions. In what follows, various units of force will be employed when numerical results are to be obtained. The definitions of these will be assumed to be known to the student. If necessary, he may consult Chapter I. of our *Elementary Dynamics*. In numerical work, $gm.\ cm./sec^2$ placed after a number will mean that the number expresses a force, which has been evaluated in the course of the work, in dynes; $lb.\ ft./sec^2$ similarly will mean that the number after which it is placed expresses a force in poundals. The number expressing the force can then be converted into that for any other system of units by multiplication by the ratio obtained by substituting in this expression the numerical value of each old unit in terms of the corresponding new unit. Or, putting L, M, T for the units of length, mass, and time, whatever these may be, we may write the force as $N \cdot LM/T^2$. LM/T^2 is called the dimensional formula of force. Thus, to transform from dynes to poundals we write for $cm.$, $ft./30\cdot48$; for $gm.$, $lb./453\cdot6$; and obtain, if N be the number of dynes, $N \times \cdot00007233$ for the number of poundals; and finally express the force as $N \times \cdot00007233 \times lb.\ ft./sec^2$.

55. Gravities of Bodies Proportional to their Inertias or Masses. The fact that bodies, except so far as they are resisted by the air, fall with the same acceleration, proves that the forces of attraction at a given place on different bodies are proportional to the masses of the bodies. For if g be the common acceleration, m_1, m_2, ... the masses of the bodies, and F_1, F_2, ... the forces of gravity upon them, we have
$$g = \frac{F_1}{m_1} = \frac{F_2}{m_2} = \frac{F_3}{m_3} = \ldots$$
The same thing is proved by Newton's pendulum experiment, in which bobs of different masses, supported side by side by threads of the same length, keep pace with one another when vibrating as simple pendulums. [See *Elementary Dynamics*.]

56. Third Law of Motion. Discussion. The third law of motion states that: *To every action there is an equal and contrary reaction, or the mutual actions of two bodies are equal and opposite.*

To this law Newton added an explanatory statement, a translation of which will be found in our *Elementary Dynamics*; but in spite of this statement, which is quite clear and definite, the law has been often misunderstood. What the law asserts is, that between any two bodies A and B, which act on one another, there exists a stress, as it has been called, which has two aspects, one of which is a force on A, the other which is an equal and opposite force on B. In other words, if a body B produce a rate of change of momentum of A, there is at the same time an equal but *opposite* production of momentum of B due to A.

The common mistake has been to suppose that because the reaction is equal and opposite to the reaction, one should cancel the other. This they would do if they were forces applied to the same thing, but they are not. The force applied to A produces its effect without interference from the equal and opposite force which exists along with it, and is applied—not to A—but to B. *For a system including both A and B*, the rate of change of momentum of A is balanced by that of B when the effect on the system *as a whole* is considered; but that does not prevent the momentum of A from being increased and that of B diminished by equal amounts. Money passes from one person to another in a community, a person A receives money from a person B, let us say. There is a transaction which affects every two persons between whom money passes, and that transaction has two aspects—one receives, the other parts with money. These aspects are equal and opposite, but for neither A nor B is the transaction cancelled by the fact that one hands over and the other receives. On the other hand, when the community is considered *as a whole*, and whether or not there be transactions of a financial kind between the community considered and another, the totality of the entirely internal transactions is zero, since there must be for them within the system exactly as much handing over as there is of receiving.

This is an exact parallel to the actions of the different bodies of a material system upon one another. The momenta of some bodies are increased, those of other bodies are diminished, and for the individual bodies these changes are perfectly real, though the total momentum, $\Sigma(m\dot{x})$ say, of the system in any direction remains unaffected. To change that, there must be action exerted on the bodies of the system by those of some other system, and there again there is equality of action and reaction, and the momentum of a system including *both* these systems is not affected by their mutual actions.

57. Action and Reaction across a Surface of Contact or across an Interface. Action and reaction are best considered as exerted across a surface in which the two bodies are in contact, as for example the surface of contact of two adjacent links in a stretched chain. One link is pulled towards one end of the chain, the *other* is pulled towards the other end, as is clearly shown by the mode of rupture when a link gives way.

Again, consider a cross-section in a carriage-coupling or trace, or in that member of a structure called a *tie*, which is under stretch. Let AB (Fig. 25 (1)) be the section.

ACTION AND REACTION.

The portion C of the trace or tie is drawn by D in the direction shown by the arrows on the C side of AB, the portion D is drawn by C as shown by the arrows on the D side of AB. The pulls are equal and opposite, but they do not cancel out, since one acts on the matter C, the other on the matter D, which are on opposite sides of AB. Similarly, at the cross-section EF a similar pair of sets of pulls exist, which are equal and opposite. Thus the portion of matter D, between AB and EF, is pulled at its ends and is under stretch.

A pillar, or that member of a structure which is called a strut, is under thrust, and the forces at the cross-sections are as shown in Fig. 25 (2). At AB, for example, D is pushed by C, as shown by the arrows on the D side of AB, and C is pushed by D, as shown by the arrows on the C side of AB. Similarly, thrust of equal and opposite amount is exerted across EF, and thus the matter between AB and EF is under compressing forces applied at its ends.

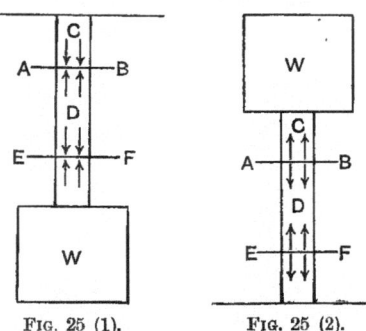

Fig. 25 (1).   Fig. 25 (2).

If the force on D, in either case, is greater at one end than at the other, motion of the matter D will take place unless the difference is balanced by external forces, those due to gravity for example. Equality of action and reaction does not provide that the force on D at one cross-section shall be the same as that on D at the other; it makes certain, however, that the two aspects of the stress at each cross-section shall be equal and opposite. The forces at different cross-sections are all equal, if the matter between is unacted on by external forces and does not suffer change of motion.

The agreement of the results which flow from the third law of motion with those of experience over a wide range of physical phenomena, is the best proof of the validity of the law.

58. Action and Reaction between Bodies at a Distance apart. In the case of bodies which cannot be regarded as being in contact, such for example as the sun and the earth, to say that the pull exerted by the sun on the earth is equal to the pull exerted by the earth on the sun is the only way of expressing the law; and the validity of the law is here again to be regarded as established by the agreement of theoretical results with observation and experience. That the force on the earth and the equal and opposite force on the sun are here referred to as *pulls* is not material; the earth may, in consequence of the presence of the sun in the gravitational field (whatever may be the cause of gravitation), be *pushed* toward the sun, and in the same way the sun pushed toward the earth. The material fact, which is beyond cavil, is that each body experiences a force toward the other, and that these forces are equal and opposite, and that fact remains whatever mode of speech is adopted regarding it.

59. Centre of Mass (or Centroid) of a Body or System. It will be convenient to define here the *centre of inertia* or *centre of mass* (or shortly, the *centroid*) of a system of particles, and deduce some of its properties. Let the positions of the particles be referred to rectangular coordinates, and denote the coordinates of the first, of mass m_1, by x_1, y_1, z_1, of the second, of mass m_2, by x_2, y_2, z_2, and so on. Then the centroid of the system is the point whose coordinates are given by the equations

$$\bar{x} = \frac{m_1 x_1 + m_2 x_2 + \ldots}{m_1 + m_2 + \ldots} = \frac{\Sigma(mx)}{\Sigma m}, \quad \ldots\ldots\ldots\ldots(1)$$

$$\bar{y} = \frac{m_1 y_1 + m_2 y_2 + \ldots}{m_1 + m_2 + \ldots} = \frac{\Sigma(my)}{\Sigma(m)}, \quad \ldots\ldots\ldots\ldots(2)$$

$$\bar{z} = \frac{m_1 z_1 + m_2 z_2 + \ldots}{m_1 + m_2 + \ldots} = \frac{\Sigma(mz)}{\Sigma m}, \quad \ldots\ldots\ldots\ldots(3)$$

that is the x-coordinate is equal to the sum of the products $m_1 x_1$, $m_2 x_2$, ..., obtained by multiplying each mass by its distance from the plane of yz, divided by the sum of the masses, and similarly for the y- and z-coordinates. Thus

§§ 58, 59, 60] DYNAMICAL PROPERTIES OF CENTROID.   101

each coordinate is the mean, when account is taken of the masses, of the corresponding coordinates of the particles.

The student may easily satisfy himself, by changing the origin and turning the axes of coordinates round through any angle, that the centroid as thus determined is a definite point in space, the position of which depends only on the positions of the particles and not at all on the choice of axes. The equations therefore enable us to define the centroid as that point the distance of which from any plane whatever fixed in space is the average distance of the particles from that plane.

We do not here devote space to the calculation of the positions of centroids for different bodies: such calculations form properly a chapter of the Integral Calculus. The student is referred to Gibson's *Calculus*, § 137, and to Ex. 7, Exercises XXX., of the same work.

60. Properties of Centroid. External and Internal Forces. Differentiating the equations (1), (2), (3) of last section, by which $\bar{x}$, $\bar{y}$, $\bar{z}$ are defined, we get, using the abridged notation there indicated,

$$\dot{\bar{x}} = \frac{\Sigma(m\dot{x})}{\Sigma m}, \quad \dot{\bar{y}} = \frac{\Sigma(m\dot{y})}{\Sigma m}, \quad \dot{\bar{z}} = \frac{\Sigma(m\dot{z})}{\Sigma m}; \quad \ldots\ldots(1)$$

and putting M for Σm,

$$M\dot{\bar{x}} = \Sigma(m\dot{x}), \quad M\dot{\bar{y}} = \Sigma(m\dot{y}), \quad M\dot{\bar{z}} = \Sigma(m\dot{z}). \quad \ldots\ldots(2)$$

Now, on the right in each case we have the total momentum of the system of particles in the direction of the axis referred to, and on the left the momentum in that direction which a particle of mass equal to the total mass of the system would have if it moved with the centroid. Hence, if the momentum of the system in any direction is zero, the centroid has no motion in that direction.

Again differentiating, we obtain

$$M\ddot{\bar{x}} = \Sigma(m\ddot{x}), \quad M\ddot{\bar{y}} = \Sigma(m\ddot{y}), \quad M\ddot{\bar{z}} = \Sigma(m\ddot{z}), \quad \ldots\ldots(3)$$

which asserts that the rate of change of momentum of the particle just referred to as moving with the centre of mass, is for every direction equal to the total rate of change of momentum of the system. Now, going back to the equations of motion of a particle (§ 53), and writing for X, Y, Z in the equations of any particle X_e+X_i, Y_e+Y_i, Z_e+Z_i, where X_e denotes the force on the particle, in the direction of x, produced by matter external to the system, and X_i the corresponding force on the same particle produced by the other particles of the system, we have for the equations of motion,

$$m\ddot{x} = X_e + X_i, \quad m\ddot{y} = Y_e + Y_i, \quad m\ddot{z} = Z_e + Z_i. \quad \ldots\ldots(4)$$

Writing the equations for all the particles in this way and equating the sum of the left-hand sides of the x-equations to the sum of the right-hand sides, and doing the same for the other axes, we get

$$\Sigma(m\ddot{x}) = \Sigma X_e, \quad \Sigma(m\ddot{y}) = \Sigma Y_e, \quad \Sigma(m\ddot{z}) = \Sigma Z_e, \ldots\ldots(5)$$

for the sums ΣX_i, ΣY_i, ΣZ_i must each vanish, since the contribution to each of the forces X_i, Y_i, Z_i, on the particle considered, made by any other particle, is accompanied by an equal and opposite force on the latter, which comes into the account when the equations of motion are added.

Hence we have the very important result that if no forces from without act on the particles of the system, that is if $\Sigma X_e = 0$, $\Sigma Y_e = 0$, $\Sigma Z_e = 0$, we have

$$\ddot{\bar{x}} = 0, \quad \ddot{\bar{y}} = 0, \quad \ddot{\bar{z}} = 0 ; \quad \ldots\ldots\ldots\ldots\ldots(6)$$

and therefore we get by integration

$$\bar{x} = at + e, \quad \bar{y} = bt + f, \quad \bar{z} = ct + g, \quad \ldots\ldots\ldots\ldots(7)$$

where a, b, c, e, f, g are constants; that is the centroid moves with constant component velocities a, b, c in a straight line.

We see moreover that if external forces *do* act on the system of particles, the internal forces cannot affect the motion of the centroid. Thus if, for example, a shell bursts in the air, the motion of the centroid is sensibly the same just after the explosion as before, except so far as the gas into which the powder is changed has been affected by the resistance of the air. The motion of the centroid of the solid casing which contained the powder sustains little or no change in its motion, since the increased action of the air on the matter now in fragments is practically negligible. We shall find many other examples in what follows.

61. Newton's Law of Equal and Opposite Activities. In a *scholium* appended to the third law of motion Newton gives another view of action and reaction. To understand this it is necessary to go back to the forces exerted in opposite directions across a cross-section of a tie or strut (§ 57). Let F denote the force exerted by the matter C, which is on one side of the section AB, on the matter D on the other side; then $-F$ is the force exerted by D on C across the same section Let now the cross-section be in motion with speed v in the direction of a line drawn from C to D. Then we may call the product Fv the action of C on D. The reaction of D on C is now $-Fv$, and is equal and opposite to Fv. The product Fv is what we shall call in future a *rate of working*, or an *activity*; it is the rate at which work is being done by C. On the other hand, while C advances at the section AB, D there recedes, and work Fv is done on D, that is D *does* work $-Fv$ on C.

In the same way, when a piece of matter is acted on by force the matter reacts on the agent. The reaction may be due only to the inertia of the body; and the reaction on the agent, when the acceleration produced is what it is agreed shall be the unit of acceleration, and there are no resistances such as friction to be overcome, is the proper measure of the inertia of the body. It may therefore be, as it is sometimes, called the *inertia-resistance* of the body.

And everywhere, when matter has force applied to it, there is an equal and opposite force applied to the agent; and therefore, if we regard the acting forces on any system as one group, and the reacting forces as another group, these two groups of forces if applied together to the same body or system would give zero rate of change of momentum in any direction, that is the two groups would, as it is usually put, form a system of forces in equilibrium.

104   A TREATISE ON DYNAMICS.   [CH. II.

This statement may be taken as an expression of the principle known as that of D'Alembert. In the case of the attraction of the earth by the sun (or the *vis a tergo*, exerted on the earth in consequence of the existence of the sun in the gravitational field, or whatever the cause of the action may be) there is work done on the earth when the earth moves in the direction of the attraction; the attraction then does positive work; the earth, by the resistance which its inertia offers, and which is overcome, does negative work. The two rates of working, that by the force and that by the resistance, are equal and opposite. And so for any complex of forces applied to a material system.

62. Theory of Work. Units of Work. The work done by a force in any displacement of a body acted on, or as we may put it, in any displacement of the point or place of application of a force to a body (generally some particle or part of the system), is measured by the product of the force into the component of the displacement in the direction of the force. Thus, if the displacement is from A to B, and the force, supposed of constant amount during the displacement, act in the direction AC, the work done by the force in the displacement is $F \cdot AB \cos \angle BAC = Fs \cos \theta$, if $s = AB$ and $\theta = \angle BAC$. In any finite displacement, under a variable force, the work done is $\int F \cos \theta \, ds$, where θ is the angle between the directions of ds and F when the step of displacement ds is being taken, and the integral is taken along the whole displacement. It is not necessary that these directions should remain the same throughout the displacement. Thus the work done in a displacement along any curve, along which the force acts at each step, is $\int F \, ds$.

If l, m, n be the direction-cosines, and X, Y, Z the components of F, and l', m', n' the direction-cosines, and dx, dy, dz the components of ds, then (see § 6)

$$F \cos \theta \cdot ds = F(ll' + mm' + nn') \, ds = X \, dx + Y \, dy + Z \, dz.$$

WORK AND ACTIVITY.

Hence $$\int F\cos\theta\, ds = \int (X\, dx + Y\, dy + Z\, dz), \quad \ldots\ldots\ldots(1)$$

where the integrals are taken for the whole finite displacement.

When the chosen unit of force acts over a displacement of unit distance in its own direction unit of work is done. Thus a force of 1 dyne in a displacement of 1 centimetre does the C.G.S. unit of work, the *erg*. A force equal to that of gravity on a pound of matter does work of amount 1 foot-pound in a displacement of 1 foot; and so on for other units. [For further particulars as to units of work see *Elementary Dynamics*.]

Again, if $\dot{s}$ be the rate of displacement at any instant, the product $F\dot{s}\cos\theta$ is the time-rate of working, or, as it is often called, the *activity*. For this we may write also $X\dot{x} + Y\dot{y} + Z\dot{z}$. The whole work done in any interval of time t is, if A be the activity,

$$\int A\, dt = \int (X\dot{x} + Y\dot{y} + Z\dot{z})\, dt, \quad \ldots\ldots\ldots\ldots(2)$$

where the integral is taken over the interval of time t.

The unit of activity is that rate of working in which unit of work is done per unit of time, *e.g.* one erg per second is the C.G.S. unit of activity. Another is one foot-pound per second (f.p.s.), still another is 550 foot-pounds per second, or, which is the same, 33,000 foot-pounds per minute. This last unit is called a *horse-power*, and is based on estimates made by James Watt for use in deciding the power of steam-engines required for different practical purposes.

The dimensional formula for work and energy is that of force × displacement, or ML^2T^{-2}. The dimensional formula for activity is that of work/time, or ML^2T^{-3}. The mode of using such formulae for change of units has been explained in § 54.

63. Active and Inactive Forces. Now consider any system of forces acting on a material system; the forces are partly internal forces between the different parts of the system, and partly forces exerted on its parts by matter outside the system. For the system as a whole the former forces constitute what has sometimes been called, not quite properly, an equilibrating system: they produce no change of the total momentum in any direction, but they produce relative displacements of the parts. Hence, in estimating the effects of the forces in changing the momentum of the system, we may disregard the whole group of internal forces. Not so, however, when we consider the *work* done by the different individual forces. The works done by the equal and opposite forces between a pair of particles do not necessarily give a zero sum. For example, consider two particles united by a stretched band of indiarubber. Neglecting any force necessary to set the matter of the band in motion, or to change its motion, we see that there are equal and opposite forces applied by the band to the particles, on which act also in general other forces. Let each particle be displaced towards the other, one particle, A, a distance a, and the other, B, a distance b. If F be the force on A, $-F$ is the force on B. The displacement a is in the direction of F, the other, b, in the opposite direction, and therefore ought to be reckoned a negative displacement. Whatever the other forces do, F does work Fa, $-F$ does work $(-F)\times(-b)=Fb$, and the whole work done by these two forces is $F(a+b)$; and so, even if the displacements were equal, which they are not necessarily, the work of these forces would not be zero, but $2Fa$. Or, to take an example from the dynamics of extended bodies, two carriages of a train are in contact by their buffers. If one carriage is urged against the other, as for example in stopping the train, the buffer springs are compressed in opposite directions, but the work done in compressing one spring has the same sign as the work done in compressing the other, and the two quantities of work must be added together.

If, however, instead of an elastic band between two particles, we had a connection of invariable length, then whatever small displacement parallel to the length of the link one end sustained. would have to be accompanied by an equal displacement of the other end in the same direction. Hence, if equal and opposite forces were applied by the link along its length to the particles, work would be done on the particle at one end by the bar, and by the particle at the other end on the bar, and these works, having opposite signs and the same numerical value, would cancel one another.

We have therefore to distinguish in considering work done, not between internal and external forces, but between forces which do work and those which do none—between *active forces* and *inactive forces*. Denoting the components, parallel to the axes, of the force F acting on a particle of the system by X, Y, Z, and supposing the particle to sustain any small displacement of components δx, δy, δz parallel to the axes, then the work done by F in the displacement is $X \delta x + Y \delta y + Z \delta z$. If, similarly, all the particles are displaced, the work δW done is the sum of all such expressions as that just found, that is

$$\delta W = \Sigma (X \delta x + Y \delta y + Z \delta z).$$

In the sum on the right no component of the inactive forces appears, since each of these must appear twice in equal and opposite contributions to δW.

64. Constant and Varying Constraints. The displacement (δx, δy, δz) of the specimen must be such a displacement as the conditions of the system, *as they exist at time t*, permit. With this restriction it may be any displacement that can be imagined. It is therefore called an *arbitrary displacement*. In their motions the particles may fulfil conditions of constraint, which may or may not be expressed by equations. For example, the particles may constitute what is called a *rigid body*, that is they may fulfil the condition of invariability of their relative positions and distances, however the body which they compose may be displaced or turned. This condition is not directly expressed by equations, but only, as we shall see later, gives a certain form to the equations of motion.

It is to be noticed that the system may be under *varying* conditions of constraint, so that at the time $t + dt$, the conditions may have changed from those which held at time t. Thus the *arbitrary* displacement δx, δy, δz, though possible under the conditions which hold at the instant t, may be a displacement which the system cannot actually sustain in its motion.

Whatever the conditions of constraint may be, their fulfilment involves the application to each particle of forces of constraint, over and above the forces which are applied by external bodies, or by particles of the system so distant from any particle considered as not to have any influence on its constraint. We shall return to this point in the chapter on *General Dynamics*.

65. General Variational Equation of Work. Theory of Energy.

The equations of motion of a particle give

$$\Sigma\{m(\ddot{x}\,\delta x+\ddot{y}\,\delta y+\ddot{z}\,\delta z)\} = \Sigma(X\,\delta x+ Y\delta y+ Z\,\delta z).\ldots\ldots(1)$$

This is not a mere identity, for it is to be observed that the components of acceleration of every particle appear on the left, while all the corresponding forces for each particle do not appear on the right. The inactive forces have disappeared, those applied from the outside, *each by itself*, on account of its zero amount of work, and those mutual actions within the system which do no work, in pairs. But it is not to be forgotten that when we have to find the motion of a particular particle, all the force on that particle, whether of external origin or arising from the constraints to which the system is subjected, must be taken account of.

So far we have considered only an arbitrary displacement (δx, δy, δz); now let the displacement considered be the actual displacement sustained in the interval dt by the specimen particle in the motion. Thus, instead of δx, δy, δz, we have components of displacement, which we shall usually denote by dx, dy, dz (reserving the symbol δ for arbitrary changes) and which have the values $\dot{x}\,dt$, $\dot{y}\,dt$, $\dot{z}\,dt$ respectively. Then (1) becomes, if we denote active forces by X_a, etc.,

$$\Sigma\{m(\dot{x}\ddot{x}+\dot{y}\ddot{y}+\dot{z}\ddot{z})\} = \Sigma(X_a\dot{x}+ Y_a\dot{y}+ Z_a\dot{z})$$

or $\quad\dfrac{1}{2}\dfrac{d}{dt}\Sigma\{m(\dot{x}^2+\dot{y}^2+\dot{z}^2)\} = \Sigma(X_a\dot{x}+ Y_a\dot{y}+ Z_a\dot{z}).\ \ldots\ldots(2)$

The expression $\quad \tfrac{1}{2}\Sigma\{m(\dot{x}^2+\dot{y}^2+\dot{z}^2)\},$

of which we have the time-rate of variation on the left-hand side of the last equation, is called the kinetic energy of the system. We shall usually denote it by T. In consequence of possessing kinetic energy, the system can do work on other bodies, losing, in whole or in part, its motion in doing so, and the work so done will, as can be seen by (2), be equal to the work done on the system in building up the kinetic energy; so that the kinetic energy is a real and useful equivalent of the work done in creating it.

In a considerable number of cases, indeed in almost all those with which we have to deal in nature, the expression on the right of (2) is derivable from a function V of the coordinates of the particles in the following manner. Let V be such a function, if one exists, that

$$-dV = \Sigma(X_a dx + Y_a dy + Z_a dx). \quad \ldots\ldots\ldots\ldots(3)$$

Here $-dV$ is understood to be a *perfect differential* of a single-valued function of the coordinates of the particles, or of a sufficient number of them for the specification of the work done in the displacements considered. The meaning of a perfect differential is explained in Gibson's *Calculus*, §§ 94, 165; but it is important to remark that, for all displacements for which V thus exists, the work done by the forces X_a, Y_a, Z_a, in the transference of the system from one given configuration to another, is independent of the paths followed by the particles in the passage, that is *the excess of the initial value of V above the final value depends only on the initial and final coordinates.*

From (3) we obtain

$$-\frac{dV}{dt} = \Sigma(X_a \dot{x} + Y_a \dot{y} + Z_a \dot{z}), \quad \ldots\ldots\ldots\ldots(4)$$

so that (2) becomes, when T is written for the kinetic energy,

$$\left.\begin{array}{c}\frac{d}{dt}(T+V)=0 \\ T+V=h\end{array}\right\} \quad \ldots\ldots\ldots\ldots\ldots\ldots(5)$$

or

where h is a constant.

V is usually called the potential energy of the system and $T + V$ its total energy. Here the system is supposed

110   A TREATISE ON DYNAMICS.   [CH. II.

to be taken large enough to include all the bodies effectively acting, so that the forces concerned are only internal forces; the kinetic energy is also in strictness that of all the bodies of the system. In some cases, for example that of a stone falling to the earth or a planet moving under the sun's attraction, the changes of motion of the larger body—the earth in the former case, the sun in the latter—are so small that the corresponding variations of the kinetic energy is left out of account, and we refer to the kinetic and potential energies as of the stone or the planet; but this reference to only one of the bodies is not quite just, and the results, though accurate in a high degree, are not absolutely correct.

If the system is not uninfluenced by other systems, and also if all the forces are not related to the potential energy, we may be able to refer *part* of the sum on the right of (4) to the potential energy of the system under consideration, while leaving the remainder under the sign of summation as above. Thus we may write

$$\Sigma(X_a dx + Y_a dy + Z_a dz) = -dV + \Sigma(X' dx + Y' dy + Z' dz)$$
$$+ \Sigma(X_e dx + Y_e dy + Z_e dz), \ldots (6)$$

where X', Y', Z' are the components of an active force which exists within the system, but has no relation to the potential energy, and X_e, Y_e, Z_e are components of force on a specimen particle exerted by matter outside the system. We obtain

$$\frac{d}{dt}(T+V) = \Sigma(X'\dot{x} + Y'\dot{y} + Z'\dot{z}) + \Sigma(X_e\dot{x} + Y_e\dot{y} + Z_e\dot{z}), \quad (7)$$

where T and V on the left refer to the limited system under consideration. Thus we see that the rate of increase of the energy of the system is equal to the rate at which work is done on the system by the forces which arise from matter outside the system, by *external forces* as we call them, and by the forces, if such there be, which exist within the system and are unrelated to any energy-function. As a rule, no forces of the latter kind, except frictional forces (§ 67), at present excluded, have to be taken account of. A system on which external forces do not act we shall call a *self-contained* system.

THEORY OF ENERGY.

It is here assumed that no frictional forces exist: they will be found dealt with in § 67 below. They always resist the relative motions of the parts of the system, and so diminish the energy.

66. Forces as Derivatives of Potential Energy. The expression for V as a rule will not contain the coordinates of all the particles of the system, but as usually known will suffice only to enable the forces on certain parts, into which the system is divided, to be found. For such parts of the system the forces which are derivable from the function V will be found by the relations

$$X = -\frac{\partial V}{\partial x}, \quad Y = -\frac{\partial V}{\partial x}, \quad Z = -\frac{\partial V}{\partial z}; \quad \ldots\ldots\ldots\ldots(1)$$

and in the most general case we shall have

$$\left. \begin{aligned} X_a &= -\frac{\partial V}{\partial x} + X' + X_e, \quad Y_a = -\frac{\partial V}{\partial y} + Y' + Y_e, \\ Z_a &= -\frac{\partial V}{\partial z} + Z' + Z_e. \end{aligned} \right\} \ldots(2)$$

This is to be regarded as a specimen set of forces acting at a point x, y, z. A similar set is to be regarded as existing for each part of the body, and the coordinates in each case are those of the point at which the forces are regarded as applied—the *point of application* of the force.

The differential coefficients $-\partial V/\partial x$, ... are *partial*, that is the differentiations are carried out in each case with reference to the variable (x, say) indicated, supposed appearing in the expression for V either explicitly or through given functions of the coordinates, while the other variables (y and z) are kept unvaried. If he has any difficulty, the student should here read §§ 89–91 of Gibson's *Calculus*.

It will be noticed that if we write T in the form $\frac{1}{2}\Sigma(mv^2)$ we have for any coordinates x, y, z, when there are no external forces and none underivable from V,

$$\Sigma\left(mv\frac{\partial v}{\partial x}\right) = -\frac{\partial V}{\partial x}, \quad \Sigma\left(mv\frac{\partial v}{\partial y}\right) = -\frac{\partial V}{\partial y}, \quad \Sigma\left(mv\frac{\partial v}{\partial z}\right) = -\frac{\partial V}{\partial z}. \quad (3)$$

Here the v of each part of the equation is regarded as a

112   A TREATISE ON DYNAMICS.   [CH. II.

function of the coordinates of some or all of the parts, in which, if the variables were made explicit, we should have T equal to the function $-V$ of the coordinates together with the constant h. It is to be remembered that the forces thus obtained are those only of the field of force in which the part considered is placed, and have nothing to do with the reactions of fixed guides or with other inactive forces.

The following are examples of partial differentiation:

Ex. 1. $V = \mu/\sqrt{x^2+y^2+z^2}$. This is the case of a repulsive force directed from the origin towards the point x, y, z, and varying inversely as the square of the distance $r = \sqrt{x^2+y^2+z^2}$. We have

$$-\frac{\partial V}{\partial x} = \frac{\mu x}{r^3} = V\frac{x}{r^2}, \quad -\frac{\partial V}{\partial y} = \frac{\mu y}{r^3} = V\frac{y}{r^2}, \quad -\frac{\partial V}{\partial z} = \frac{\mu z}{r^3} = V\frac{z}{r^2},$$

so that
$$x\frac{\partial V}{\partial x} + y\frac{\partial V}{\partial y} + z\frac{\partial V}{\partial z} = -V,$$

as might have been written down at once from Euler's theorem [Gibson's *Calculus*, § 158, 2].

Again, $-\dfrac{\partial^2 V}{\partial x^2} = \mu\dfrac{r^2-3x^2}{r^5}, \quad -\dfrac{\partial^2 V}{\partial y^2} = \mu\dfrac{r^2-3y^2}{r^5}, \quad -\dfrac{\partial^2 V}{\partial z^2} = \mu\dfrac{r^2-3z^2}{r^5};$

so that
$$\frac{\partial^2 V}{\partial x^2} + \frac{\partial^2 V}{\partial y^2} + \frac{\partial^2 V}{\partial z^2} = 0.$$

Ex. 2. $T = \frac{1}{2}m(\dot{r}^2 + r^2\dot{\theta}^2)$. This is the kinetic energy of a planet of mass m, when at a point in its orbit for which the radius-vector is r and the vectorial angle θ. The speed along the radius-vector is $\dot{r}$, and the speed at right angles to the radius-vector is $r\dot{\theta}$ (see § 11 above). We have

$$\frac{\partial T}{\partial r} = mr\dot{\theta}^2, \quad \frac{\partial T}{\partial \dot{r}} = m\dot{r}, \quad \frac{\partial T}{\partial \dot{\theta}} = mr^2\dot{\theta}.$$

The coordinate θ is in this case absent from the expression for the kinetic energy, but if it had been present the fact that r for every point of the path is a function of θ would not have affected the differentiation with respect to r.

The student should notice that here

$$\frac{d}{dt}\frac{\partial T}{\partial \dot{r}} - \frac{\partial T}{\partial r} = m(\ddot{r} - r\dot{\theta}^2),$$

that is the rate of change of momentum in the direction outwards along the radius-vector. The expression on the left belongs to a theory which we shall explain and illustrate later. Again, to illus-

§§ 66, 67]   DISSIPATIVE FORCES.   113

trate the distinction between partial and total differentiation, take $d(mr^2\dot\theta)/dt$. We have
$$\frac{d}{dt}(mr^2\dot\theta) = 2mr\dot r\dot\theta + mr^2\ddot\theta.$$

This is the rate of change of angular momentum of the planet about the origin, which must vanish if no force transverse to the radius-vector act upon the body.

67. Work spent in overcoming Friction. Dissipative Forces.

So far we have supposed that frictional resistances to the motion of the system do not exist; and the theory of energy explained above is not applicable without correction to systems in which friction is present—*dissipative systems* as they are often called. For a long time it was supposed that work done against friction—unlike that done against inertia-resistance—was without equivalent; but the experiments of Joule have shown that when work is so done an amount of heat proportional to the work expended is generated; and the dynamical theory of heat, which was worked out mainly during the latter half of the nineteenth century, proves that under certain ideal conditions the heat so generated can be made to do an amount of work equal to that expended. Thus the heat generated is the energy-equivalent of the work done in overcoming friction. The laws of friction are stated in § 201.

The equations written above can be modified so as to include frictional or dissipative forces. Let, as before, X_a, Y_a, Z_a be the component forces actually applied to the particle chosen for consideration, and X_f, Y_f, Z_f be the frictional or dissipative parts of these, and so for other particles. Then, for the system, we have

$$\Sigma\{m(\ddot x\,\delta x + \ddot y\,\delta y + \ddot z\,\delta z)\} = \Sigma(X_a\,\delta x + Y_a\,\delta y + Z_a\,\delta z)$$
$$- \Sigma(X_f\delta x + Y_f\delta y + Z_f\delta z), \dots(1)$$

where only the active non-frictional forces are included in the first expression on the right. If, now, we can write, as before,

$$\Sigma(X_a dx + Y_a dy + Z_a dz) = -dV + \Sigma(X_e dx + Y_e dy + Z_e dz),$$

where dx, dy, dz are the components of the actual displacement of the system in the element of time dt, and $-dV$ is

G.D.   H

a perfect differential of a function of the coordinates, we have

$$\frac{d}{dt}(T+V) = \Sigma(X_e\dot{x} + Y_e\dot{y} + Z_e\dot{z}) - \Sigma(X_f\dot{x} + Y_f\dot{y} + Z_f\dot{z}). \ldots(2)$$

On the right we have first the rate at which the energy of the system is being increased by the action of external systems, and in the second line the rate at which the sum of the kinetic and potential energies of the system is being diminished by the dissipative forces. If forces of the sort referred to in §65, and denoted there by accented letters, exist, a term must be included, as there explained, to represent their activity. The differentiation on the left with respect to t is *total*, that is it includes the rate of change of the quantity differentiated, arising through the rates of change of the coordinates, as well as the rate of change (if such there be) due to the explicit appearance of t in the expression of the quantity.

68. Meaning of Solution of a Dynamical Problem. It is to be remembered that the solution of a dynamical problem consists in expressing the coordinates which determine the configuration of the system at any time as explicit functions of the time and of the initial coordinates and the initial velocities. The simple result expressed in (7), §60, is an example in point.

The function V has been assumed to be an explicit function of the coordinates only; but it may also be an explicit function of the time t, as well as of the coordinates for that time. This more general case will be dealt with later. (See Chapter XI., where the integration of the equations of motion of a material system is more fully considered.)

69. Angular Momentum. Rotational Motion. It is convenient to consider here another application of the laws of motion, namely to the motions of the particles of a system about a straight line, or *axis* as we shall call it, given in position. In the first place, let a single particle P of mass m be moving at the instant considered along the line PQ in the plane of the paper with speed v, and let O be the point in

ANGULAR MOMENTUM.

which an axis at right angles to that plane intersects it. If p be the length of the perpendicular let fall from O on PQ, the product mvp is called the *moment of momentum* or the *angular momentum* of the particle about the axis. Taking first the speed v and the perpendicular p as both positive, we attach the positive or negative sign to the product according as the radius-vector OP appears to an observer, regarding the motion as here shown to be turning as in the diagram (Fig. 26) with the motion of P in the direction in which the hands of a watch appear to turn, or in the contrary direction.

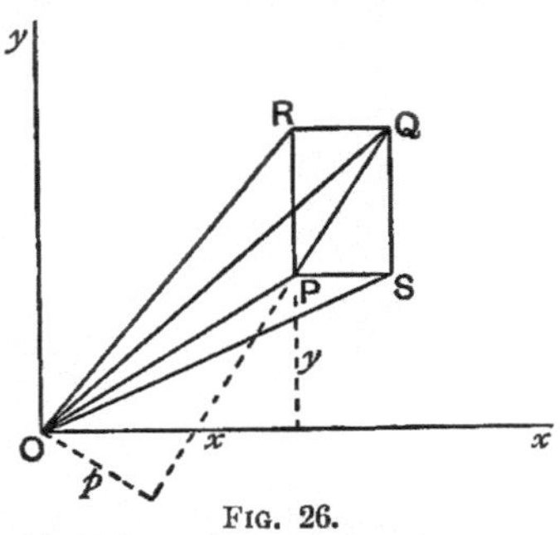

The product mvp is twice the rate of description of area by the radius-vector just referred to multiplied by m. For let the particle go from P to Q in time dt, then the radius-vector sweeps over the area of the small triangle POQ, which is clearly $\frac{1}{2}pv\,dt$ by the diagram. Hence vp is twice the rate of description of area.

Fig. 26.

Now at P resolve the velocity into two components in the plane of the paper—we suppose for the present that there is no component perpendicular to the paper. Let the x-component be $\dot{x}$, the y-component $\dot{y}$. The student can easily convince himself from the diagram that by the construction there given,

$$\text{area } POR - \text{area } POS = \text{area } POQ,$$

that is that $\quad m(\dot{y}x - \dot{x}y) = mvp.$

Now $m\dot{y}x$ is the angular momentum about the axis through O at right angles to the plane xOy and due to the component velocity $\dot{y}$, while $m\dot{x}y$ is that due to the component $\dot{x}$, and the signs are chosen according to the convention stated above.

If the axis be not, as it is taken here, at right angles to the direction of motion, we resolve the momentum into two components in a plane containing the line of motion

116   A TREATISE ON DYNAMICS.   [CH. II.

at the instant and parallel to the given axis, taking one component parallel to the axis, the other perpendicular to it. The angular momentum of the particle about the axis is now defined as the product of the latter component of momentum into the distance of the axis from the plane just defined.

70. Components of Angular Momentum (A.M.). Let a, b, c be the direction-cosines of the axis, which we suppose as above to pass through the origin, and $\dot{x}, \dot{y}, \dot{z}$ be the components of v parallel to the axes Ox, Oy, Oz. Then the direction-cosines of a normal to the plane parallel to the axis and containing the line of motion at the instant are
$$(c\dot{y} - b\dot{z}, \; a\dot{z} - c\dot{x}, \; b\dot{x} - a\dot{y})/v \sin \theta,$$
where θ is the angle between the directions of the axis and the line of motion. If x, y, z denote the coordinates of P (or indeed of any point in the plane just referred to), the distance of the origin from the plane is
$$\{(c\dot{y} - b\dot{z})x + (a\dot{z} - c\dot{x})y + (b\dot{x} - a\dot{y})z\}/v \sin \theta.$$

But the component of momentum at right angles to the axis is $mv \sin \theta$, and hence the angular momentum, as defined above,
$$m\{(c\dot{y} - b\dot{z})x + (a\dot{z} - c\dot{x})y + (b\dot{x} - a\dot{y})z\},$$
which may be written as
$$a\{m(\dot{z}y - \dot{y}z)\} + b\{m(\dot{x}z - \dot{z}x)\} + c\{m(\dot{y}x - \dot{x}y)\}.$$
Clearly this may be regarded as the result of resolving along the given axis (direction-cosines a, b, c) three components, $m(\dot{z}y - \dot{y}z), \ldots$, of angular momentum associated with the axes Ox, Oy, Oz respectively. In point of fact they are, as the student will see from § 69, the angular momenta of the particle about these axes. We shall denote them by F, G, H.

If we measure, from O along Ox, Oy, Oz, distances representing F, G, H, and project these upon the given axis through O, we obtain a distance along it which represents the angular momentum about it. The distance for each component is drawn in the positive or negative direction from the origin, according as to an observer, looking towards the origin from a point on the positively drawn axis, the turning of the radius OP, drawn from the origin to the projection P_1 of P on the plane at right angles to the axis considered (in the diagram the axis Ox), is against or with the turning of the hands of a watch held in the plane with its face towards the observer. Thus we obtain a vector through O representing the angular momentum about the given axis by its direction and its length.

The resultant angular momentum of the particle is $(F^2+G^2+H^2)^{\frac{1}{2}}$, and the direction-cosines of the axis are $(F, G, H)/(F^2+G^2+H^2)^{\frac{1}{2}}$. The axis of resultant angular momentum, K say, for the chosen origin, passes of course through the origin, and the angle it makes with the given axis is

$$\phi = \cos^{-1}\{(aF+bG+cH)/(F^2+G^2+H^2)^{\frac{1}{2}}\} = \cos^{-1}K'/K, \quad (1)$$

if K' denote $aF+bG+cH$, the angular momentum about the given axis. Thus
$$K' = K\cos\phi. \quad \dots\dots\dots\dots\dots\dots\dots(2)$$

71. Angular Momenta about Parallel Axes. Now consider how K and K' are affected by a change of origin to a fixed point O' of coordinates h, k, l. The old x, y, z are to be replaced by their values in terms of the new, namely $x+h, y+k, z+l$, while $\dot{x}, \dot{y}, \dot{z}$ remain unchanged. We have now for the given axis through the old origin,

$$K' = a\{m(\dot{z}y-\dot{y}z)\} + b\{m(\dot{x}z-\dot{z}x)\} + c\{m(\dot{y}x-\dot{x}y)\}$$
$$+ a\{m(\dot{z}k-\dot{y}l)\} + b\{m(\dot{x}l-\dot{z}h)\} + c\{m(\dot{y}h-\dot{x}k)\}.\dots(1)$$

The expression in the first line is the angular momentum about a parallel axis through the new origin, the expression in the second line is the angular momentum about the old axis of a particle of mass m situated at the new origin and having components $m\dot{x}, m\dot{y}, m\dot{z}$ of momenta. A similar conclusion holds for the resultant angular momentum K. This theorem has important applications in the case of a system of particles, as we shall see later.

118   A TREATISE ON DYNAMICS.   [CH. II.

The student can easily prove that if O' lie on the given axis the expression in the second line identically vanishes. For any system of particles in motion in any manner the angular momentum is obtained by summing for all the particles of the system expressions of the form just obtained for a single particle. We have, simply,

$$F = \Sigma\{m(\dot{z}y - \dot{y}z)\}, \quad G = \Sigma\{m(\dot{x}z - \dot{z}x)\},$$
$$H = \Sigma\{m(\dot{y}x - \dot{x}y)\}, \quad\quad\quad\quad\ldots\ldots\ldots\ldots\ldots\ldots(2)$$

with [see (2), § 70]

$$K = (F^2 + G^2 + H^2)^{\frac{1}{2}}, \quad K' = aF + bG + cH. \quad\ldots\ldots(3)$$

Equation (1) shows that if, instead of the axes drawn from the fixed origin O, we take parallel axes drawn from another fixed origin O', the coordinates of which are h, k, l, and x, y, z now denote the coordinates of a representative particle with reference to the new axes,

$$K' = a[\Sigma\{m(\dot{z}y - \dot{y}z)\}] + b[\Sigma\{m(\dot{x}z - \dot{z}x)\}]$$
$$+ c[\Sigma\{m(\dot{y}x - \dot{x}y)\}]$$
$$+ a\{k\Sigma(m\dot{z}) - l\Sigma(m\dot{y})\} + b\{l\Sigma(m\dot{x}) - h\Sigma(m\dot{z})\}$$
$$+ c\{h\Sigma(m\dot{y}) - k\Sigma(m\dot{x})\}. \ldots(4)$$

The first part on the right is the angular momentum of the system about a parallel axis through the new origin O', the second part represents the angular momentum which the system would have about the given axis through O, if all the particles could be, and were, transferred without alteration of their component velocities to the new origin O'; or, which is equivalent, it is the angular momentum, about the given axis, of a single particle situated at O', and moving so that its component momenta are equal to $\Sigma(m\dot{x}), \Sigma(m\dot{y}), \Sigma(m\dot{z})$.

If $\bar{\dot{x}}, \bar{\dot{y}}, \bar{\dot{z}}$ be the component velocities of the centroid and M denote the total mass of the system, we have (§ 60) $M\bar{\dot{x}} = \Sigma(m\dot{x}), M\bar{\dot{y}} = \Sigma(m\dot{y}), M\bar{\dot{z}} = \Sigma(m\dot{z})$. Hence, whatever point O' may be, if we suppose placed there a single particle of mass equal to the total mass of the system, and

§§ 71, 72]   ANGULAR MOMENTUM.   119

having the component velocities of the centroid, the angular momentum of this particle about the given axis added to that of the system about the parallel axis through O', makes up the angular momentum of the system about the given axis.

The point O' here considered is, like O, at rest; if it is in motion, then h, k, l are variable as well as x, y, z, and the component speeds for a particle are no longer $\dot{x}$, $\dot{y}$, $\dot{z}$, but $\dot{x}+\dot{h}$, $\dot{y}+\dot{k}$, $\dot{z}+\dot{l}$. Equations (1) and (4) must then have terms added depending on $\dot{h}$, $\dot{k}$, $\dot{l}$. These are

$$a\{\dot{l}\Sigma(my) - \dot{k}\Sigma(mz) + M(\dot{l}k - \dot{k}l)\} + \ldots.$$

If O' coincide then with the centroid, $\Sigma(m\dot{x})$, $\Sigma(m\dot{y})$, $\Sigma(m\dot{z})$ are now the momenta relative to axes through the centroid, and vanish by § 60; so that all the terms in the second line of (4) disappear, and the angular momentum is represented by the first line and the additional terms just indicated. Hence, since $\dot{h}$, $\dot{k}$, $\dot{l}$ are then $\dot{\bar{x}}$, $\dot{\bar{y}}$, $\dot{\bar{z}}$, and

$$\Sigma(mx) = \Sigma(my) = \Sigma(mz) = 0,$$

we get for an origin at and moving with the centroid,

$$K' = a\Sigma\{m(\dot{z}y - \dot{y}z)\} + \ldots + aM(\dot{\bar{z}}\bar{y} - \dot{\bar{y}}\bar{z}) + \ldots \quad \ldots(5)$$

and $\quad K^2 = [\Sigma\{m(\dot{z}y - \dot{y}z)\} + M(\dot{\bar{z}}\bar{y} - \dot{\bar{y}}\bar{z})]^2 + \ldots \quad \ldots\ldots(6)$

72. Rate of Change of A.M. Since, when there is no alteration of the mass of the system,

$$\frac{d}{dt}\Sigma\{m(\dot{z}y - \dot{y}z)\} = \Sigma\{m(\ddot{z}y - \ddot{y}z)\}, \quad \ldots\ldots\ldots\ldots(1)$$

we have for the rates of change of angular momentum relatively to the axes with fixed origin O,

$$\frac{dF}{dt} = \Sigma\{m(\ddot{z}y - \ddot{y}z)\}, \quad \frac{dG}{dt} = \Sigma\{m(\ddot{x}z - \ddot{z}x)\},$$

$$\frac{dH}{dt} = \Sigma\{m(\ddot{y}x - \ddot{x}y)\}. \quad \ldots\ldots\ldots\ldots\ldots(2)$$

If we transfer to another *fixed* origin O', as before, we get for the old axes, if x, y, z be now the coordinates of a representative particle, relative to the new axes,

$$\frac{dF}{dt} = \Sigma\{m(\ddot{z}y - \ddot{y}z)\} + k\Sigma(m\ddot{z}) - l\Sigma(m\ddot{y}),$$
$$\frac{dG}{dt} = \Sigma\{m(\ddot{x}z + \ddot{z}x)\} + l\Sigma(m\ddot{x}) - h\Sigma(m\ddot{z}), \quad \ldots\ldots\ldots(3)$$
$$\frac{dH}{dt} = \Sigma\{m(\ddot{y}x - \ddot{x}y)\} + h\Sigma(m\ddot{y}) - k\Sigma(m\ddot{x});$$

and finally, when the origin O' is the centroid and moves with it, the values of the components of angular momentum about axes at O, which has now the coordinates

$$(h, k, l) = (\bar{x}, \bar{y}, \bar{z})$$

relatively to the centroid, are,

$$\frac{dF}{dt} = \Sigma\{m(\ddot{z}y - \ddot{y}z)\} + M(\ddot{\bar{z}}\bar{y} - \ddot{\bar{y}}\bar{z}),$$
$$\frac{dG}{dt} = \Sigma\{m(\ddot{x}z - \ddot{z}x)\} + M(\ddot{\bar{x}}\bar{z} - \ddot{\bar{z}}\bar{x}), \quad \ldots\ldots\ldots\ldots\ldots(4)$$
$$\frac{dH}{dt} = \Sigma\{m(\ddot{y}x - \ddot{x}y)\} + M(\ddot{\bar{y}}\bar{x} - \ddot{\bar{x}}\bar{y}),$$

since the terms in $\dot{h}, \dot{k}, \dot{l}$, arising from the motion of the centroid, are identically zero by the property of that point.

73. Rate of Change of A.M. when Effective Inertia different in Different Directions. The cancelling in dF/dt of the term $(\Sigma m\dot{z}\dot{y})$ by the term $\Sigma(m\dot{y}\dot{z})$ in the differentiation of $\Sigma\{m\dot{z})y - \dot{y}z)\}$ is worthy of a little attention. $\Sigma(m\dot{z}y)$ is the angular momentum of the system about the axis Ox, arising from the motions of the particles parallel to the axis Oz, and $\Sigma(m\dot{z}\dot{y})$ is the rate of growth of this angular momentum arising from the rates of change of the y-coordinates. Similarly, $-\Sigma(m\dot{y}z)$ is the angular momentum about Ox, arising from the motions of the particles parallel to Oy, and $-\Sigma(m\dot{y}\dot{z})$ is the rate of growth of this arising from the rates of change of the z-coordinates.

In ordinary circumstances these two rates of growth cancel one another, but there are cases of motion in which it is convenient to ascribe different inertias in different directions to the body, or bodies, composing the system. The motion of a medium in which a body is immersed resulting from the displacement of the body may thus be taken account of. For example, we may, in explaining certain effects of the motion of the water, conveniently consider a ship as having a larger inertia for displacements at right angles to its length than it has for displacements along the fore and aft direction. An example of this kind is considered in detail in § 91 below. Thus, if the system consist of a single body moving without rotation in a medium, with component speeds $\dot{x}$, $\dot{y}$, $\dot{z}$, it may be convenient to regard it as having momenta $M_1\dot{x}$, $M_2\dot{y}$, $M_3\dot{z}$, parallel to O_x, O_y, O_z. In this case we should have for the rate of growth of angular momentum about Ox,

$$M_3\ddot{z}y - M_2\ddot{y}z + (M_3 - M_2)\dot{z}\dot{y},$$

with similar expressions for the other two axes.

74. Rate of Change of A.M. when Body Gains or Loses Mass. It may be that the system is gaining or losing mass. Thus the earth is constantly receiving meteoric matter from space, and (if we distinguish here between the earth and the atmosphere) gaining matter also by condensation of water-vapour from the atmosphere, and losing matter by evaporation from the surface of the sea, lakes, and rivers as well as from the surface of the land. Thus, if dm/dt be the rate of growth of mass at any point, and if the mass gained there takes up speeds $\dot{x}$, $\dot{y}$, $\dot{z}$, the total rates of gain of angular momentum from this cause are

$$\Sigma\left\{\frac{dm}{dt}(\dot{z}y - \dot{y}z)\right\}, \quad \Sigma\left\{\frac{dm}{dt}(\dot{x}z - \dot{z}x)\right\}, \quad \Sigma\left\{\frac{dm}{dt}(\dot{y}x - \dot{x}y)\right\},$$

where of course dm/dt may be either positive or negative, or positive at some places, negative at others. Taking these into account, we have

$$\frac{dF}{dt} = \Sigma\{m(\ddot{z}y - \ddot{y}z)\} + \Sigma\left\{\frac{dm}{dt}(\dot{z}y - \dot{y}z)\right\} \quad \ldots\ldots\ldots(1)$$

with similar expressions for dG/dt, dH/dt.

A case in point is that of a chain wound on a horizontal cylinder, or windlass, which is turning so as to unwind the chain. Let the free end be attached to a fixed point close to the windlass so that the chain which is not on the barrel hangs down in two vertical parts connected by a short bight at the lowest point. Every element of the vertical part attached to the barrel is moving downward with speed v, and if we suppose all the *moving* chain on the barrel and attached to it to be at distance r from the axis, M to be its mass, and $\dot{\theta}$ the angular speed of the barrel at any instant, the angular momentum of the chain about the axis is at that instant $Mr^2\dot{\theta}$. But chain is continually being unwound and successive elements pass from the side attached to the barrel to that attached to the fixed point, and as each element passes across the bight from the moving side to the other, it is brought to rest. The rate of transfer of mass is half the rate at which it is unwound from the barrel, namely $\tfrac{1}{2}mr\dot{\theta}$, if m be the mass of the chain per unit length. Hence the rate of loss of angular momentum from the moving chain, in consequence of the transfer, is $\tfrac{1}{2}mr^3\dot{\theta}^2$, being the rate of loss of mass $\tfrac{1}{2}mr\dot{\theta}$ multiplied by $r^2\dot{\theta}$, the moment about the axis of the speed $r\dot{\theta}$ of the chain. This problem will be found fully solved in § 77 below.

If the matter added to the system brings with it angular momentum, or if matter on being added or removed acts on the system (as, for example, does a jet thrown from a reaction turbine or from a hose or fire-engine), the rate of addition of angular momentum brought with the matter, and the moments of the reactions, must where necessary be entered on the other side of the account, that on which the actions producing rate of angular momentum appear. These we now go on to consider.

75. Rates of Change of A.M. equal to Moments of Forces. Independence of Motions of Translation and Rotation. Going back to the equations of motion of a specimen particle referred to any rectangular axes, say those through O,

$$m\ddot{x} = X_e + X_i, \ldots, \quad \ldots\ldots\ldots\ldots\ldots\ldots\ldots(1)$$

where the suffixes distinguish, as before, the internal forces of the system from the external forces on the particles, we

ANGULAR MOMENTUM.

multiply the z-equation by y and the y-equation by z, and subtract the second equation from the first. We get
$$m(\ddot{z}y - \ddot{y}z) = Z_e y - Y_e z + Z_i y - Y_i z. \quad \ldots\ldots\ldots(2)$$
Doing this for all the particles and adding, we obtain
$$\Sigma\{m(\ddot{z}y - \ddot{y}z)\} = \Sigma(Z_e y - Y_e z) + \Sigma(Z_i y - Y_i z). \quad \ldots(3)$$

The products on the right are *moments of forces* about the axis of x. We suppose now that the equal and opposite internal forces between the two particles of every distinct pair in the system act along the line joining the particles. Then the pair of forces obtained by the projection of such a line, with the forces acting along it, on any plane, must obviously be a pair of equal and opposite forces. Thus, projecting all the pairs of forces on the coordinate plane yOz, we see that $\Sigma(Z_i y - Y_i z) = 0$. For the Y_i and Z_i obtained at the particle at one extremity of such a line have, taken together, the same moment about the axis of x as the force F, of which they are components, along the line, and in the same sense the forces $-Y_i$, $-Z_i$ at the other end are equivalent to the force $-F$ in the same line which acts on the other particle. Hence, extending this process to all three coordinate planes, we obtain

$$\left.\begin{array}{l}\Sigma\{m(\ddot{z}y - \ddot{y}z)\} = \Sigma(Zy - Yz), \\ \Sigma\{m(\ddot{x}z - \ddot{z}x)\} = \Sigma(Xz - Zx), \\ \Sigma\{m(\ddot{y}x - \ddot{x}y)\} = \Sigma(Yx - Xy),\end{array}\right\} \quad \ldots\ldots\ldots\ldots(4)$$

where the suffixes are dropped on the right on the understanding that only external forces are there included. With these are the equations of motion of the centroid
$$M\ddot{\bar{x}} = \Sigma X, \quad M\ddot{\bar{y}} = \Sigma Y, \quad M\ddot{\bar{z}} = \Sigma Z. \quad \ldots\ldots\ldots\ldots(5)$$

Now (§ 60) it has been seen that
$$\Sigma(m\ddot{x}) = M\ddot{\bar{x}} = \Sigma X, \quad \Sigma(m\ddot{y}) = M\ddot{\bar{y}} = \Sigma Y, \quad \Sigma(m\ddot{z}) = M\ddot{\bar{z}} = \Sigma Z.$$
Hence, $\qquad M(\ddot{\bar{z}}\bar{y} - \ddot{\bar{y}}\bar{z}) = \bar{y}\Sigma Z - \bar{z}\Sigma Y, \quad \ldots\ldots\ldots\ldots\ldots(6)$

with two other similar equations for the axes of y and z. These show that the moments about any axis of $M\ddot{\bar{x}}$, $M\ddot{\bar{y}}$, $M\ddot{\bar{z}}$, or the sums $\Sigma(m\ddot{x})$, $\Sigma(m\ddot{y})$, $\Sigma(m\ddot{z})$ transferred without change to the centroid, of what are often called the *effective forces*, taken parallel to the axes, is equal to the sum of the moments about the same axis of the externally applied forces, supposed all similarly transferred to the same point.

In (4) x, y, z denote the coordinates of a specimen particle relative to axes drawn from any fixed origin O. If parallel axes be set up from the centroid as origin, and x', y', z' denote the coordinates of a particle relative to these axes, we have $x = \bar{x}+x'$, $y = \bar{y}+y'$, $z = \bar{z}+z'$, and the left-hand sides of (4) reduce to

$$\Sigma\{m(\ddot{z}'y' - \ddot{y}'z')\} + M(\ddot{\bar{z}}\bar{y} - \ddot{\bar{y}}\bar{z}), \ldots;$$

for all terms of the form $\Sigma(m\ddot{z}'\bar{y})$, $\Sigma(m\ddot{\bar{z}}y'), \ldots$ are zero, since $\Sigma(m\ddot{z}') = 0$, $\Sigma(my') = 0, \ldots$. Thus, by (6) we get, dropping accents *on the understanding that the axes are at the centroid, equations of precisely the same form as* (4), where, however, x, y, z now stand for x', y', z'.

On the left in these are the sums of moments, relative to axes through the centroid and carried with it, of the rates of change of momentum of the particles of the system relative to these axes, and on the right are the sums of moments about the same axes, of the external forces, taken exactly as they are applied. These equations are of great importance, as they enable the rotations of bodies, or systems of bodies, about axes through the centroid of the body or system, *to be dealt with as if the centroid were at rest*. This property is peculiar to the centroid because of the vanishing of $\Sigma(mx)$, $\Sigma(m\dot{x})$, $\Sigma(m\ddot{x}), \ldots$ when x, y, z refer to the centroid as origin.

Again, equations (5) are the equations of motion of a particle, the mass of which is equal to the total mass of the system, to which are applied all the external forces without change of magnitude and direction. The motion of the centroid is thus reduced to that of a single particle, and may be discussed without reference to the relative motions.

The two properties, stated in the last two paragraphs, are sometimes referred to as the principle of the independence of the motions of translation and rotation.

To take account of the change of mass of the system

§§ 75, 76]   ANGULAR MOMENTUM.   125

we must use (4) for the given axes (at the chosen origin let us suppose), with the modifications referred to above: that is, we should write

$$\Sigma\{m(\ddot{z}y - \ddot{y}z)\} + \Sigma\left\{\frac{dm}{dt}(\dot{z}y - \dot{y}z)\right\} = \Sigma(Zy - Yz) + DF, \quad \dots(7)$$

with two similar equations. Here DF, DG, DH denote the rate of change of angular momentum produced in each case by the matter added or removed.

76. Rigid Body, Rolling Motion of. A rigid body is defined at the beginning of Chapter VI., to which the student may refer. It is an aggregate of particles so connected that the line joining any two remains unaltered in length, and the angle between every pair of such lines remains unchanged as the body moves. But this definition is violated continually by bodies which we class as rigid: they expand and shrink with heat and cold; in some cases they gain and lose mass, and so we obtain the idea of a body which moves at a given *instant* as a rigid body, but which is changing in some respect or other as time passes.

For many problems regarding such bodies it is convenient to express equations of the form (7), § 75, in another way, that in fact shown in (4) below. Thus, let the body be turning about the axis of x, for example, and θ be the angle which a line fixed in the body, through the centroid, for example, and at the instant parallel to the plane of yz, makes with the axis of y. All the perpendiculars from the points of the body to the axis of x turn at the same angular speed $\dot{\theta}$ at the same instant in the same direction about that axis. If θ_1 be the angle which the perpendicular, of length r_1, from a particle m, the coordinates of which are x, y, z, makes with the axis of y, we have

$$y = r_1 \cos\theta_1, \quad z = r_1 \sin\theta_1, \quad \dots\dots\dots\dots\dots(1)$$

and therefore $\quad \dot{z}y - \dot{y}z = r_1^2\dot{\theta}_1 = r_1^2\dot{\theta}.$

Therefore, for the whole body,

$$\Sigma\{m(\dot{z}y - \dot{y}z)\} = \dot{\theta}\Sigma(mr^2). \quad \dots\dots\dots\dots\dots(2)$$

The quantity $\Sigma(mr^2)$ is called the *moment of inertia* of the body about the axis of x. The properties of moments of inertia and their calculation are discussed in Chapter VI.; the values of $\Sigma(mr^2)$ for the bodies referred to in the examples will be stated. They will be expressed in the form Mk^2, where M is the whole mass, and k^2 is such a quantity that $\Sigma(mr^2) = Mk^2$.

The kinetic energy T of the motion of rotation about Ox is $\tfrac{1}{2}\Sigma\{m(\dot{y}^2+\dot{z}^2)\}$, and by (1) can therefore be expressed by the equation
$$T = \tfrac{1}{2}\dot{\theta}^2 \Sigma(mr^2). \qquad\qquad\qquad (3)$$

Now, in calculating the rate of change of A.M. about a given axis, we have, as a general rule, cases to consider in which $\Sigma(mr^2)$ is constant, so that the A.M. only varies through $\dot{\theta}$, and not at all through variations of mass or its distribution. But in the general case we have, for the rate of change of A.M.,
$$\frac{d}{dt}\{\dot{\theta}\Sigma(mr^2)\} = \ddot{\theta}\Sigma(mr^2) + \dot{\theta}\frac{d}{dt}\{\Sigma(mr^2)\}.$$

This we have to equate to the sum of the moments of the external forces about the axis, together with any rate of increase (or diminution) of A.M. directly due to action between the body and external matter, such as the interchange of mass bringing or carrying with it A.M. We get, for the moment of the forces, $\Sigma(Zy - Yz) = \Sigma(Pp)$, where P is the resultant of Y, Z, and p is the perpendicular distance from its line of action to the axis of x. Hence we have
$$\frac{d}{dt}\{\dot{\theta}\Sigma(mr^2)\} = \Sigma(Pp) + DF. \qquad\qquad (4)$$

Similar equations hold for the other two axes.

As examples of the value of DF in different cases, we may take the following: (1) a cylinder rolling on a horizontal or inclined plane, and expanding or contracting without variation of mass, so that $DF = 0$; (2) a cylinder of ribbon (Exs. 3 and 4, § 77) rolling along a horizontal or down an inclined plane.

The "rolling motion" referred to in some of the following examples is that combination of turning and translatory motion which enables a wheel to move along a rail without any slipping at the contact. When the axle of a wheel

§§ 76, 77]   EXAMPLES OF ANGULAR MOMENTUM.   127

is at rest, the top of the wheel moves forward, and the bottom backward with the same speed v. If now the axle be carried forward with speed v as the wheel turns, the forward speed of the part which is the top at the instant in space will be $2v$, while the speed of the part which is at the bottom at the instant will be zero. This is the motion of the wheel in space when it rolls without slipping along the rail. If the radius of the wheel be r, the centre moves forward a distance $r\theta$, when the wheel turns through an angle θ, and the forward speed v is $r\dot{\theta}$.

77. Examples on A.M. of Bodies of Varying Mass. Energy-Changes.

Ex. 1. If the radius of the earth is diminishing as time advances, find the effect of the contraction on the length of the day.

The radius at time t will be $r_0(1-at)$, if we assume that the contraction is proportional to the time. Hence, since the A.M. then must be equal to the A.M. at time $t=0$, we have

$$M\tfrac{2}{5}r_0^2(1-at)^2\omega = M\tfrac{2}{5}r_0^2\omega_0.*$$

Hence, if a be small, we have

$$\omega = \frac{\omega_0}{1-2at} = \omega_0(1+2at)$$

nearly. The day is therefore shortened in the ratio of 1 to $1+2at$.

Ex. 2. A layer of cosmic dust of thickness h, small compared with a, the radius is deposited on the earth's surface; show that if the dust brings with it no A.M. about the earth's axis, the change in the length of the day is nearly $5h\rho/aD$ of a day, where ρ and D are the densities of the dust and the earth respectively.

Here we must have, since there is no moment of forces changing the earth's A.M., exerted by the dust, and no A.M. brought with it,

$$(\tfrac{4}{3}\pi a^3 D \tfrac{2}{5}a^2 + 4\pi a^2 h\rho \tfrac{2}{3}a^2)\omega = \tfrac{4}{3}\pi a^3 D \tfrac{2}{5}a^2\omega_0,*$$

since the moments of inertia of a uniform sphere of mass M, and a uniform spherical shell of mass m are $M\tfrac{2}{5}a^2$ and $m\tfrac{2}{3}a^2$ (§ 175, Ex. 6). This is equivalent to $d(Mk^2\omega)/dt = DF = 0$, and gives

$$\left(1+5\frac{h}{a}\frac{\rho}{D}\right)\omega = \omega_0.$$

Thus the angular speed of the earth is diminished, and the day is lengthened in the ratio $1+5h\rho/aD$ to 1.

---

* It is here assumed, what is far from being exact, that the moment of inertia can be calculated by assuming the density uniform throughout and equal to the mean density.

Ex. 3. A roll of cloth of small thickness h, lying at rest on a horizontal table with the edge of the cloth along the line of contact, is propelled with initial angular speed Ω, so that the cloth unrolls. If friction brings the cloth to rest as it comes into contact with the table, show, on the supposition that no work is done by the rolling cloth against friction, or against cohesion of the folds or stiffness of the cloth, that the radius of the roll will diminish from a to r in the time

$$\frac{2\pi}{h}\sqrt{\frac{1}{3g}}\{(c^3-r^3)^{\frac{1}{2}}-(c^3-a^3)^{\frac{1}{2}}\},$$

where $4(c^3-a^3)g = 3\Omega^2 a^4$. [Math. Tripos, 1878.]

If we take the roll as of unit breadth and unit density, as we may do without loss of generality, and as very approximately a circular cylinder (undeformed as it rests on the table under its own weight) of radius r, its A.M. about the line of contact at time t is $\tfrac{3}{2}\pi r^4 \omega$. Hence the rate of change of A.M. is $\tfrac{3}{2}\pi r^4 \dot\omega + 6\pi r^3 \dot r \omega$. This is the expression on the left of (7), § 75. But in consequence of loss of matter from the roll, we have $DF = \tfrac{3}{2}\pi\omega\, d(r^4)/dt = 6\pi r^3 \dot r \omega$, and since, as will be shown below, the centroid of the roll is at a distance $3h/2\pi$ in front of the line of contact with the table, gravity forces have a moment $\pi r^2 g 3h/2\pi$ about that line.

We find next the acceleration of the centroid G of the roll regarded as an unchanging body. Take a section S perpendicular to the length of the roll through G and consider any point P of S. Take a point H of the section at the same distance r from the table as G, but on the normal to the table through the line of contact. Let $HP = \rho$, and make an angle θ with the upward vertical. P has coordinates ξ, η with reference to a fixed origin on the table in the plane of S at distance x behind the line of contact, given by $\xi = x + \rho \sin\theta$, $\eta = r + \rho\cos\theta$. Hence $\ddot\xi = \ddot x + \rho\dot\omega\cos\theta - \rho\omega^2\sin\theta$, $\ddot\eta = -\rho\dot\omega\sin\theta - \rho\omega^2\cos\theta$, since $\dot\theta = \omega$. But $\ddot x = r\dot\omega$, and if P be coincident with G, $\rho = 3h/2\pi$, $\theta = \pi/2$. But, as will be seen presently, $h = -2\pi\dot r/\omega$, and therefore for G $\ddot\xi = r\dot\omega + 3\dot r\omega$, $\ddot\eta = -3h\dot\omega/2\pi$. The R.C.A.M. is therefore

$$\tfrac{1}{2}\pi r^4 \dot\omega + \pi r^2(r\dot\omega + 3\dot r\omega)r = \tfrac{3}{2}\pi r^4 \dot\omega + 3\pi r^3 \dot r\omega,$$

since $\ddot\eta$ has moment $-9h^2\dot\omega/4\pi^2$, which may be neglected. The equation of motion (7) of § 75 is therefore

$$\tfrac{3}{2}\pi r^4\dot\omega + 3\pi r^3 \dot r\omega = \tfrac{3}{2}r^2 gh,$$

which can be written

$$\tfrac{3}{2}\pi r^2\omega\,\frac{d}{dt}(r^2\omega) = \tfrac{3}{2}ghr^2\omega = -3\pi g r^2 \dot r,$$

since $-2\pi\dot r/h = \omega$. Integrating and assigning the constant of integration to suit the initial circumstances, we get

$$\tfrac{3}{4}\pi r^4\omega^2 = \tfrac{3}{4}\pi a^4\Omega^2 + \pi g(a^3 - r^3).$$

We can verify this equation by the method of energy, which, on the supposition made above, is here applicable. The potential energy of the roll relatively to the table is $\pi g a^3$ initially and $\pi g r^3$ at time t.

EXAMPLES OF ANGULAR MOMENTUM.

The kinetic energy is $\frac{3}{4}\pi a^4 \Omega^2$ at starting and $\frac{3}{4}\pi r^4 \omega^2$ at time t. Hence, equating the gain of kinetic energy to the loss of potential, we get
$$\tfrac{3}{4}\pi r^4 \omega^2 = \tfrac{3}{4}\pi a^4 \Omega^2 + \pi g(a^3 - r^3),$$
the equation to be verified.

Now, if s be the length unrolled at time t, we have $\dot{s} = -2\pi \dot{r}/h = \omega$. Thus the equation found above becomes
$$12\frac{\pi^2}{h^2} r^4 \dot{r}^2 = 3a^4 \Omega^2 + 4g(a^3 - r^3),$$
and therefore
$$4\frac{\pi^2}{h^2}\left\{\frac{d}{dt}(r^3)\right\}^2 = 9a^4\Omega^2 + 12g(a^3 - r^3) = 12g(c^3 - r^3),$$
if $4(c^3 - a^3)g = 3\Omega^2 a^4$. Hence, since $\dot{r}$ is negative,
$$\pi\, dr^3/dt = -h\sqrt{3g(c^3 - r^3)},$$
which gives by integration the result to be established,
$$t\sqrt{3g} = \frac{2\pi}{h}(\sqrt{c^3 - r^3} - \sqrt{c^3 - a^3}).$$

To prove the statement made above as to the position of the centroid of the roll, we observe first that the cross-section of the spires of cloth is an equiangular spiral of angle α very nearly $\pi/2$. Hence, as the distance of the normal at any point to which the radius-vector from the pole is of length r is $r\cos\alpha$, and the radius increases by $\frac{1}{2}h$ in each half turn, we have by the equation of the spiral, $(r = ae^{\theta \cot\alpha})$, $\frac{1}{2}h = \pi r\cot\alpha$, that is $h/2\pi = r\cos\alpha$, nearly.

Again, if the roll were kept at rest and the cloth unwound from it, each half turn, at radius r, would shift the centroid a distance $2h/\pi$, since the distance of the centroid of a semicircle of radius r from its centre is $2r/\pi$. Hence the centroid would oscillate from a distance h/π from the pole on one side to an equal distance on the other side. Therefore the centroid of the bale of cloth when the radius is r is at a distance h/π in front of the pole of the spiral, and, as shown above, the line of contact with the table is at a distance $h/2\pi$, on the other side. The gravity $\pi r^2 g$ of the cloth has therefore a moment
$$\pi r^2 g(h/\pi + h/2\pi) = 3\pi r^2 gh/2\pi,$$
as stated above.

It is noteworthy that the solution by the method of energy would enable the position of the centroid of the spiral to be inferred from a comparison of the equation of motion with that obtained by differentiating the equation of energy.

If the roll is allowed to run completely out, a question arises as to what becomes of the energy. The potential energy has been exhausted, and there is no kinetic energy. The last part of the roll running very fast will bring the free end round on the table like a whip, and there will be commotion of the cloth which will dissipate the energy.

G.D.

Ex. 4. A ribbon of very small uniform thickness h is coiled up tightly in a cylindrical form, and placed with its curved surface in contact with a plane inclined to the horizon at an angle α. The axis of the cylinder is parallel to the intersection of the plane with the horizon, and the outer end of the ribbon is along the line of contact. Find the time in which the cylinder will unroll from radius a to radius r, comparable with a.* The ribbon is prevented by friction from sliding on the plane.

The equation of motion is, by the last example,
$$\tfrac{3}{2}\pi r^2 \omega \frac{d}{dt}(r^2\omega) = \pi r^2 g\left(r\sin\alpha + \frac{3h}{2\pi}\cos\alpha\right),$$
since it will be seen, partly from the last example, that the moment of forces, about the line of contact of the roll with the plane, has the value $\pi r^2 g(r\sin\alpha + 3h\cos\alpha/2\pi)$. The equation can be written
$$3\pi(r^2\dot\omega + 2\omega r\dot r) = 2\pi g\left(r\sin\alpha + \frac{3h}{2\pi}\cos\alpha\right),$$
that is, multiplying by $r^2\omega$,
$$3\pi r^2\omega\frac{d}{dt}(r^2\omega) = 2\pi g r^2\omega\left(r\sin\alpha + \frac{3h}{2\pi}\cos\alpha\right).$$
From this we get, by integration (first substituting $-2\pi\dot r/h$ for ω),
$$\tfrac{3}{2}\pi r^4\omega^2 = -\frac{4\pi^2}{h}g\left(\tfrac{1}{4}r^4\sin\alpha + \frac{h}{2\pi}r^3\cos\alpha\right) + C.$$
But when $t=0$, $\omega=0$, $r=a$, and therefore we obtain
$$\tfrac{3}{2}\pi r^4\omega^2 = \pi^2\frac{g}{h}(a^4 - r^4)\sin\alpha + 2\pi g(a^3 - r^3)\cos\alpha.$$
This divided by 2 is the equation of energy.

We can verify the solution of the problem, so far as it has been carried, by calculating the energy at time t directly. The potential energy, relative to the point of contact at time t, is
$$\pi a^2 g(s\sin\alpha + a\cos\alpha) - \pi r^2 g r\cos\alpha - \tfrac{1}{2}\pi(a^2 - r^2)gs\sin\alpha,$$
where $s = \pi(a^2 - r^2)/h$ is the length of ribbon unrolled along the plane. This expression for the potential energy can be written
$$\tfrac{1}{2}\pi^2\frac{g}{h}(a^4 - r^4)\sin\alpha + \pi g(a^3 - r^3)\cos\alpha.$$
The equation of energy is therefore
$$\tfrac{3}{4}\pi r^4\omega^2 = \tfrac{1}{2}\pi^2\frac{g}{h}(a^4 - r^4)\sin\alpha + \pi g(a^3 - r^3)\cos\alpha,$$
as found above.

* This is a modified statement of a problem set in the Mathematical Tripos of 1860, in which it was required to prove that the time in which the *whole* would be unrolled was $\tfrac{1}{3}\pi\sqrt{6d^2/gh\sin\alpha}$, where d is the diameter of the original coil. The solution given in the *Collection of Problems* for that year is different from that given above.

§ 77] EXAMPLES OF ANGULAR MOMENTUM. 131

Substituting now for ω^2 its value $4\pi^2 \dot{r}^2/h^2$, we obtain

$$9\frac{\pi^2}{h^2} r^4 \dot{r}^2 = \frac{1}{2}\left\{3\pi\frac{g}{h}(a^4 - r^4)\sin\alpha + 6g(a^3 - r^3)\cos\alpha\right\},$$

that is, $\quad \dfrac{\pi}{h}\dfrac{d}{dt}(r^3) = \sqrt{\dfrac{1}{2}\left\{3\pi\dfrac{g}{h}(a^4 - r^4)\sin\alpha + 6g(a^3 - r^3)\cos\alpha\right\}},$

that is, $\quad t = \dfrac{\pi}{h}\displaystyle\int_a^r \dfrac{3r^2 dr}{\sqrt{\dfrac{1}{2}\left\{3\pi\dfrac{g}{h}(a^4 - r^4)\sin\alpha + 6g(a^3 - r^3)\cos\alpha\right\}}},$

which gives the time in which the roll diminishes in radius from a to r. If we put $\sin\alpha = 0$, $\cos\alpha = 1$, we fall back on the solution of the problem of Ex. 3.

Ex. 5. The problem of the windlass referred to in § 74. Chain is wound on a windlass, in a single layer, and has the free end attached to a fixed point near the windlass and on a level with its axis, so that the chain hangs down in two nearly vertical parts. Find the motion.

Let the moment of inertia of the windlass without the chain be Mk^2. If $2l$ be the length of the chain, x the length of each of the vertical parts, σ the mass of the chain per unit length, and r the radius of the layer in which the chain is wound, the moment of inertia of the chain is $\sigma(2l - x)r^2$. The equation of motion is therefore

$$\frac{d}{dt}[\{Mk^2 + \sigma(2l - x)r^2\}\omega] = Pr + r^2\omega\frac{d}{dt}\{\sigma(2l - x)\},$$

where Pr is the moment of applied force on the barrel and chain attached to it. Now, the whole of the chain with the exception of the stationary part is included in the length $2l - x$, and the force applied is therefore $g\sigma r$. The equation of motion can therefore be written

$$\{Mk^2 + \sigma(2l - x)r^2\}\dot{\omega} = g\sigma xr.$$

But $\omega = 2\dot{x}/r$, and therefore $\dot{\omega} = 2\ddot{x}/r$. Substituting in the equation of motion, then multiplying by $2\dot{x}$ and integrating, we get

$$2\{Mk^2 + \sigma(2l - x)r^2\}\frac{\dot{x}^2}{r^2} = g\sigma(x^2 - x_0^2) - 2\int_0^t \sigma\dot{x}^3 dt,$$

which, since $\dot{x}^2/r^2 = \omega^2/4$, is the equation of energy. On the left is the expression of the kinetic energy; on the right $g\sigma(x^2 - x_0^2)$ is the loss of potential energy; and the term remaining, $2\int_0^t \sigma\dot{x}^3 dt$, which is subtracted, is the energy dissipated at the bight. For the tensile force at the bight, on the side of the stationary part of the chain, brings an element of length $\dot{x}\,dt$ to rest in time dt, thus annulling momentum $\sigma\dot{x}\,dt \cdot 2\dot{x}$. The tensile force is therefore $2\sigma\dot{x}^2$, and it works at rate $2\sigma\dot{x}^3$. The kinetic energy is thus equal to the excess of the potential energy lost over the energy dissipated, which verifies the equation of motion.

The equation is of the form

$$(A - Bx)\ddot{x} - Cx = 0,$$

or, if multiplied by $\dot{x}$ and rearranged,

$$\dot{x}\ddot{x} = -\frac{C}{B}\dot{x} + \frac{CA}{B}\frac{\dot{x}}{A - Bx}.$$

This gives, by integration,

$$\tfrac{1}{2}\dot{x}^2 = -\frac{C}{B}(x - x_0) + \frac{CA}{B^2}\log\frac{A - Bx_0}{A - Bx};$$

and therefore

$$t = \int_{x_0}^{x} \frac{dx}{\sqrt{2\dfrac{C}{B}\left\{\dfrac{A}{B}\log\dfrac{A - Bx_0}{A - Bx} - x + x_0\right\}}}$$

is the time of motion.

Ex. 6. To examine the energy changes in Ex. 4, § 53. It is there shown that on the stationary side the tensile force at the bight is $\tfrac{1}{2}\sigma v^2 = \tfrac{1}{2}\sigma g^2 t^2$. The work done by it in time dt is $\tfrac{1}{2}\sigma g^2 t^2 . gt = \tfrac{1}{2}\sigma g^3 t^3$. For an element of length $\tfrac{1}{2}v\,dt$, moving with speed v, and therefore having kinetic energy $\tfrac{1}{4}\sigma v\,dt . v^2$, is reduced to rest in that time.

The whole time of motion is $\sqrt{4l/g}$, as shown in the example. The whole energy dissipated at the bight is therefore

$$\tfrac{1}{4}\sigma g^3 \int_0^{\sqrt{4l/g}} t^3\,dt = \tfrac{1}{16}\sigma g^3 t^4 = \sigma g l^2.$$

The change of potential energy consists in the transference of a length l of the chain through a difference of level l. The exhaustion of potential energy is therefore $\sigma g l^2$, the amount of kinetic energy destroyed at the bight. Since the chain is left finally at rest, the energy is completely accounted for. The energy dissipated is converted into heat.

Ex. 7. Examine in a similar manner the energy changes involved in the motion described in Ex. 5, § 53.

78. Kinetic Energies of Motions of Translation and Rotation. The kinetic energy of a system can be separated into two parts, (1) the kinetic energy of a particle equal in mass to the system moving with the velocity of the centroid, and (2) the kinetic energy of the motion of the system with respect to axes drawn from the centroid and moving with it. Denoting as usual the kinetic energy by T, we have

$$T = \tfrac{1}{2}\Sigma[m\{(\dot{\bar{x}} + \dot{x})^2 + (\dot{\bar{y}} + \dot{y})^2 + (\dot{\bar{z}} + \dot{z})^2\}], \quad\ldots\ldots(1)$$

ENERGIES OF TRANSLATION AND ROTATION.

where $\dot{\bar{x}}, \dot{\bar{y}}, \dot{\bar{z}}$ are as usual the component speeds of the centroid parallel to fixed axes through a chosen origin O, and $\dot{x}, \dot{y}, \dot{z}$ are the component speeds of a specimen particle relative to parallel axes drawn from the centroid as origin. Thus we have

$$T = \tfrac{1}{2}\Sigma\{m(\dot{\bar{x}}^2+\dot{\bar{y}}^2+\dot{\bar{z}}^2)\} + \tfrac{1}{2}\Sigma\{m(\dot{x}^2+\dot{y}^2+\dot{z}^2)\}$$
$$+ \dot{\bar{x}}\Sigma(m\dot{x}) + \dot{\bar{y}}\Sigma(m\dot{y}) + \dot{\bar{z}}\Sigma(m\dot{z}). \quad\quad\quad(2)$$

But since x, y, z are the coordinates of a particle relative to the centroid $\Sigma(m\dot{x}) = \Sigma(m\dot{y}) = \Sigma(m\dot{z}) = 0$, and we have

$$T = \tfrac{1}{2}\Sigma\{m(\dot{\bar{x}}^2+\dot{\bar{y}}^2+\dot{\bar{z}}^2)\} + \tfrac{1}{2}\Sigma\{m(\dot{x}^2+\dot{y}^2+\dot{z}^2)\}, \quad\quad(3)$$

the theorem stated above.

In §15 we have dealt with the motion of a particle with reference to axes revolving as there specified. Let the axes be $Oxyz$ and be fixed in a rigid body, turning about the fixed point O. Then the angular speeds about the axes $Oxyz$ are $\omega_1, \omega_2, \omega_3$, and $\dot{x}, \dot{y}, \dot{z}$ are zero, since there is no motion of the body relative to the axes. We have for the speeds relative to fixed axes coinciding with the moving axes at the instant

$$u = \omega_2 z - \omega_3 y, \quad v = \omega_3 x - \omega_1 z, \quad w = \omega_1 y - \omega_2 x.$$

The kinetic energy is $\tfrac{1}{2}\Sigma\{m(u^2+v^2+w^2)\}$; and

$$\tfrac{1}{2}\Sigma\{m(u^2+v^2+w^2)\}$$
$$= \tfrac{1}{2}[\omega_1^2\Sigma\{m(y^2+z^2)\} + \omega_2^2\Sigma\{m(z^2+x^2)\} + \omega_3^2\Sigma\{m(x^2+y^2)\}$$
$$- 2\omega_2\omega_3\Sigma(myz) - 2\omega_3\omega_1\Sigma(mzx) - 2\omega_1\omega_2\Sigma(mxy)]. \ldots(4)$$

For axes that are called *principal axes* (see Chapter IV.), $\Sigma(myz) = \Sigma(mzx) = \Sigma(mxy) = 0$; and therefore writing

$$r_1^2 = y^2+z^2, \quad r_2^2 = z^2+x^2, \quad r_3^2 = x^2+y^2,$$

we have

$$\tfrac{1}{2}\Sigma\{m(u^2+v^2+w^2)\} = \tfrac{1}{2}\{\omega_1^2\Sigma(mr_1^2) + \omega_2^2\Sigma(mr_2^2) + \omega_3^2\Sigma(mr_3^2)\}. \ (5)$$

If the origin O be in motion with the body with speeds u_0, v_0, w_0 along the fixed axes, we have to increase the values of u, v, w given above by u_0, v_0, w_0 respectively. The student will easily make out what the kinetic energy becomes, and verify that if O be the centroid of the body, we have simply to add to the right-hand side of (4) the quantity $\frac{1}{2}M(u_0^2+v_0^2+w_0^2)$, the kinetic energy of a particle of mass equal to that of the body and moving with the centroid. This is the kinetic energy of the motion of translation. Equation (4) gives the kinetic energy of rotation.

79. Couples. Equivalence of Couples. The subject of Couples will be fully considered in the chapter on Statics. But it is necessary to introduce the notion here. If two forces be equal in amount but opposite in direction, the system is called a *couple*. It possesses the property of producing about any specified axis a moment which depends on the direction of the axis, but not on its position in space. A couple has no effect on the acceleration of the centroid of a body on which it acts; it has no single force resultant, and can only be equilibrated by the action of an equal and opposite couple, as we shall now prove. Consider axes of x, y, z through the centroid. Let x, y, z be the coordinates of a point A on the line of action of the force P of the couple which is in the direction given by the cosines α, β, γ, and x', y', z' be a point B on the line of action of the other force. The moment of the couple about the axis of x is

$$P(\gamma y - \beta z) - P(\gamma y' - \beta z'),$$

that is $\quad P\{\gamma(y-y') - \beta(z-z')\}.$

Hence, only the difference of coordinates $y-y'$, $z-z'$ are involved, not their absolute values. Similar expressions hold for the other two axes, so that we have the three component moments

$$P\{\gamma(y-y')-\beta(z-z'),\ \alpha(z-z')-\gamma(x-x'),\ \beta(x-x')-\alpha(y-y')\}.$$

These are equivalent to the single moment

$$P[\{\gamma(y-y')-\beta(z-z')\}^2 + \{\alpha(z-z')-\gamma(x-x')\}^2 + \{\beta(x-x')-\alpha(y-y')\}^2]^{\frac{1}{2}}$$

about an axis the direction-cosines of which are proportional to the component moments just written, that is about an axis at right angles to the plane containing the forces. The multiplier of P in this expression for the resultant moment is simply the distance between the lines in which the forces act. For it can be written

$$[(x-x')^2+(y-y')^2+(z-z')^2 \\ -\{\alpha(x-x')+\beta(y-y')+\gamma(z-z')\}^2]^{\frac{1}{2}},$$

where the first term in the brackets is the square of the distance AB (Fig. 27), and the second is the square of Bb. The component moments are the moments of the couples obtained by projecting the two forces in succession on the coordinate planes of yz, zx, xy.

We may therefore regard a couple as a vector defined by its moment Pp, the product of either force into the distance p between the lines of action, (2) its "axis," that is any line at right angles to the plane of the forces, and drawn towards that side of the plane on which an eye must be situated to see the direction of turning positive, that is counter clockwise. It thus indicates the aspect or orientation of the plane in which the forces are situated. When the axis taken in this direction is made as many units in length as there are units of moment Pp, it represents the

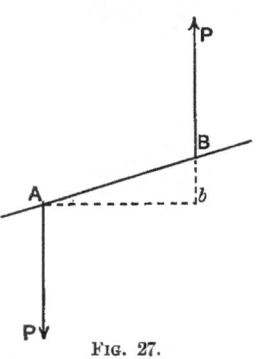

FIG. 27.

moment as well as the orientation and direction of turning, and thus represents the couple in all respects.

The moment of a couple about any axis, as already noticed, is independent of the actual plane in which the forces act; it is also independent of the magnitude of the forces, and of their direction, provided the orientation of the plane in which they act is given and the moment. Thus a couple can be changed from any plane to a parallel plane without change of its moment about any axis.

The rule for finding the resultant of two parallel forces gives for a couple a zero resultant, but at the same time prescribes for it a line of action at an infinite distance from either of the forces. The interpretation of this is the fact, already noticed, that a couple cannot be balanced except by the action of a couple of equal and opposite moment in the same or in a parallel plane. In fact couples represented by their axes can be compounded like forces, as the analysis just given indicates.

This rule can be experimentally illustrated by a floating stand, on which act couples in different planes, applied by strings passing over pulleys and supporting weights.

80. Effective Inertia different in Different Directions. Case of a Ship. Consider a rigid body of mass M moving without rotation parallel to a fixed plane. Take axes Ox, Oy from any origin in that plane, and let $\dot{x}$, $\dot{y}$ be the speeds of the body parallel to these axes. The momenta of the body in these directions are $M\dot{x}$, $M\dot{y}$, and the body has angular momentum $M(\dot{y}\bar{x} - \dot{x}\bar{y})$ about an axis of z through the origin, since we may regard the body as replaced by a particle of mass M situated at the centroid (coordinates $\bar{x}$, $\bar{y}$) and moving with the velocity $(\dot{x}, \dot{y})$. The time rate of change of this angular momentum is $M(\ddot{y}\bar{x} - \ddot{x}\bar{y})$, which for the present we shall suppose to be zero, through the vanishing of $\ddot{x}$, $\ddot{y}$.

Now let there be matter set in motion by the body, so that the total momentum in the direction of Ox is $M_1\dot{x}$, and that in the direction of Oy is $M_2\dot{y}$. Then if we associate these components of momentum with the body, we regard it as having inertia M_1, in the direction of Ox, and a different inertia M_2 in the direction of Oy. The angular momentum about the origin is now $M_2\dot{y}\xi - M_1\dot{x}\eta$, where ξ, η are the coordinates of a point, moving with the body, the position of which it is not necessary for our present purpose to specify. The rate of change of this angular momentum (since $\ddot{x} = \ddot{y} = 0$) is $M_2\dot{y}\dot{\xi} - M_1\dot{x}\dot{\eta} = (M_2 - M_1)\dot{x}\dot{y}$, since $\dot{\xi} = \dot{x}$, $\dot{\eta} = \dot{y}$, and therefore does not depend on ξ, η.

Or, to put the matter in another way, consider a point A of space with which a point B of the body, or moving with the body, coincides at time t. By the displacement $\dot{x}\,dt$ of the body, in an interval of time dt, B is carried this distance parallel to Ox from A, and angular momentum $M\dot{y}\dot{x}\,dt$ is produced. Similarly angular momentum $-M\dot{x}\dot{y}\,dt$ about A is produced by the displacement $\dot{y}\,dt$ of the body. Thus zero angular momentum is produced on the whole. But if the momentum associated with the body be $M_1\dot{x}$ parallel to Ox, and $M_2\dot{y}$ parallel to Oy, the former gain of angular momentum is $M_2\dot{y}\dot{x}\,dt$ and the latter $M_1\dot{x}\dot{y}\,dt$, and there is a gain of angular momentum in dt of amount $(M_2 - M_1)\dot{x}\dot{y}\,dt$, that is angular momentum about A is being gained at rate $(M_2 - M_1)\dot{x}\dot{y}$. This is independent of the position of A, that is it is the same for all points.

This rate of gain of angular momentum about every point is wholly due to the matter set in motion by the body, and is effected by the action of a couple exerted by the body on that matter (the action of a ship, for example, on the water), which therefore exerts an equal and opposite couple on the body.

This is the couple that tends to turn a ship at right angles to its course, and that must be counteracted by the rudder, and that actually sets a ship or plank athwart a stream in which it is allowed to drift. A ship set on a course and left with its helm lashed would be unstable; the helmsman has continually to prevent the ship from falling off its course, and good steering consists in correcting each infinitesimal deviation as it arises. For considering an elongated body immersed in a medium indefinitely extended in each of the directions of motion (so that we are not concerned with reactions from the boundaries), let the speed $\dot{x}$ be that of the body in the direction of its length, and $\dot{y}$ be that in a direction at right angles to the length. Let $M_2 - M_1$ be positive. If either $\dot{x}$ or $\dot{y}$ be zero the couple $(M_2 - M_1)\dot{x}\dot{y}$ is zero. Let, for example, $\dot{y}$ be zero. Then if the length be allowed to swerve through the angle ϕ from the direction GB (Fig. 28) in which the body is moving, there will now exist a speed $\dot{x}$ in the direction of the length, and a speed $\dot{y}$ in the perpendicular direction, as shown by the arrows, and a couple $(M_2 - M_1)\dot{x}\dot{y}$ in the direction of the curved arrow will be exerted on the matter outside the body but in motion with it. An equal and opposite couple acts on the body and tends to turn it so to *increase* the angle ϕ, that is so as to set its length perpendicular to the course. When the length is athwart the course the couple is again zero, but that called into play by a deviation of the body from that position is now such as to send the body back to it. The body's position relatively to the direction of motion is therefore one of instability in the first case and of stability in the second.

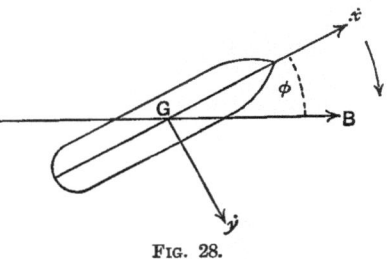

Fig. 28.

A flat dish or plate, if let fall in water, or a card let fall in still air, with its plane horizontal, moves down, in stable equilibrium; if it is let fall with its plane vertical, the equilibrium of position in falling is unstable. In this case we must associate M_1 with the axial direction, and M_2 with a perpendicular direction, and we see that $M_2 - M_1$ is negative, and there is stability in consequence in the first case.

The origin of the couple may be seen in a general way as follows. Consider a ship advancing with speed $\dot{x}$ in the direction of its length, and making leeway $\dot{y}$, say to starboard. The bow is continually advancing with speed $\dot{x}$ into undisturbed water, which on the starboard side, at the ship, is given speed $\dot{y}$ to starboard. There is thus a reaction thrust on the bow of the vessel in the direction to port.

81. Why a Ship carries a Weather Helm. We have here the explanation of the fact that a ship generally carries a "weather helm," that is that the rudder must be held turned to leeward to keep the vessel on her course when a wind blows across it. For, as stated above, she makes leeway, that is has a speed $\dot{y}$ to leeward, along with the speed $\dot{x}$ in the direction of her length. Hence, by what has been stated above, the couple $(M_2 - M_1)\dot{x}\dot{y}$, *on the water*, is in the direction of the arrow A, in Fig. 29, and therefore the reaction-couple, which is of equal moment, tends to turn the ship's head in the direction of the arrow A', that is to windward, and this tendency (to "gripe" as it is called) must be counteracted by a couple applied to the ship by means of the rudder. The tendency of a ship to "fall off" her course (and thereby convert her forward motion into a component $\dot{x}$ along her length, and another $\dot{y}$ at right angles to her length), which, as explained above, always exists, is therefore augmented by the action of wind, and the difficulty of steering is increased. This effect of the wind is consider-

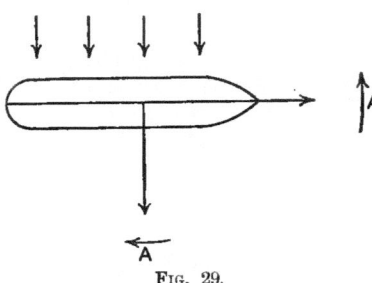

Fig. 29.

able when the ship is driven by sails, and a steamer using sails as an auxiliary sometimes gripes so badly, especially with canvas on the after masts, as to make it almost impossible to steer. Thus sails on steamers used to be almost entirely confined to the foremast, and are now in large vessels completely discarded.

The action here illustrated is of considerable importance as regards the equilibrium of submarine vessels, of æroplanes, and of projectiles thrown from rifled guns. We shall return to it in connection with some of these practical problems, when we shall consider also the effect of rotation of the body.

EXERCISES II.

1. Two particles of mass m, m' are attached to the ends of a uniform inextensible cord of length $2l$ and mass σ per unit length. The cord is passed over a horizontal peg so that parts of the string of lengths x_0, $2l - x_0$, carrying m, m' respectively, hang vertically side by side, when the arrangement is left to itself. If there is no friction of the cord on the peg and no air-resistance, find the motion.

At time t let the lengths of the two parts of the cord be x and $2l - x$. Hence show that the equations of motion of the two parts are

$$\frac{d}{dt}\{(m + \sigma x)\dot{x}\} = (m + \sigma x)g - T_1 + \sigma \dot{x}^2,$$

$$\frac{d}{dt}[\{m' + \sigma(2l - x)\}\dot{x}] = T_2 - \{m' + \sigma(2l - x)\}g - \sigma \dot{x}^2,$$

where T_1, T_2 are the tensile forces (very nearly equal) in the cord at the peg on the two sides.

Add, multiply by $\dot{x}$ and integrate, obtaining
$$\tfrac{1}{2}(m+m'+2\sigma l)\dot{x}^2 = g(x-x_0)\{m-m'+\sigma(x+x_0-2l)\}.$$

Verify that the expression on the right is the loss of potential energy undergone by the system in the descent of m and ascent of m' through the distance $x-x_0$, so that the gain of kinetic energy is equal to the loss of potential energy. There is no dissipation of energy in this case in the passage of cord from one side to the other.

If σ be so small as to be negligible, we get the equation of motion of the masses in an Atwood's machine, simplified by the substitution of a smooth horizontal peg for the pulley over which the cord passes. The equation is
$$\ddot{x} = \frac{m-m'}{m+m'}g,$$
which leads to $\quad \dot{x}^2 = 2\dfrac{m-m'}{m+m'}gx, \quad x = \dfrac{1}{2}\dfrac{m-m'}{m+m'}gt^2.$

A more complete account of the theory of Atwood's machine will be found on p. 436.

2. Two particles A and B of masses m and m' are connected by an elastic string of negligible mass and of unstretched length l, which exerts a pull on a particle at either extremity which is proportional to its elongation. The particles are placed on a horizontal plane at a distance d apart, and the particle A then receives a blow in the direction BA, so that it starts off with initial speed V. Determine the motion on the supposition that there is no friction.

Clearly, the centroid of the system moves in the direction BA with uniform speed v, where $v = mV/(m+m')$. When at a distance $l+x$ apart, the particles have speeds $v + m'\dot{x}/(m+m')$ and $v - m\dot{x}/(m+m')$, so that the kinetic energy is $\tfrac{1}{2}(m+m')v^2 + \tfrac{1}{2}\{mm'/(m+m')\}\dot{x}^2$ (§ 48). If the force required to produce unit extension of the string be k, the potential energy stored in the stretched string is $\tfrac{1}{2}kx^2$. The energy equation is
$$\tfrac{1}{2}(m+m')v^2 + \tfrac{1}{2}\frac{mm'}{m+m'}\dot{x}^2 + \tfrac{1}{2}kx^2 = \text{const.}$$

Show that the equation of motion in x is
$$\frac{mm'}{m+m'}\ddot{x} + kx = 0,$$
representing simple harmonic motion of period $2\pi\sqrt{mm'/k(m+m')}$, combined with uniform motion of the centroid at speed v.

3. A horizontal turn-table in the form of a uniform disk is mounted on a vertical axis at its centre. The weight of the table is 280 lbs. Two men, each of weight 140 lbs., stand at the opposite ends of a diameter. Initially the system is at rest. If, now, the men move round the edge of the table in the same direction at the same speed, show that when they have gone once round the table, they have turned in space through an angle $\tfrac{2}{3}\pi$.

140   A TREATISE ON DYNAMICS.   [CH.

4. A turn-table of mass M rotates smoothly on a vertical axis at its centre, and a man of mass m walks on it at a uniform rate u along a radius, starting from the centre. Show that if ω_0 is the initial angular velocity of the turn-table, and k is its radius of gyration about the axis, the angular displacement after time t is $\omega_0 p \tan^{-1}(t/p)$, where $p^2 = Mk^2/(mu^2)$.

5. A man weighing m pounds stands on a plane lamina weighing M pounds; the lamina rests on a smooth horizontal plane. The man walks on the lamina so as to describe a closed curve in space enclosing an area of A sq. feet: prove that the lamina turns through an angle $2m(M+m)A/MI$ radians, where I is the moment of inertia in lb. ft. units of the lamina about a vertical axis through its centroid.

6. A uniform rod OA of mass m, turning about a fixed horizontal pivot at one end, falls from the horizontal position. Show that if R and S are the forces applied by the axis to the rod along and at right angles to its length at an instant at which the rod is inclined at an angle θ to the vertical (R inward, and S in direction of increasing θ),
$$R = \tfrac{5}{2} mg \cos \theta \; ; \quad S = -\tfrac{1}{4} mg \sin \theta.$$
If the rod starts from the upright position, prove that
$$R = mg(\tfrac{3}{2} + \tfrac{5}{2} \cos \theta) \; ; \quad S = -\tfrac{1}{4} mg \sin \theta.$$
[The equations of motion are, if the length of the rod be $2l$,
$$-ml\ddot{\theta} = S + mg \sin \theta, \quad ml\dot{\theta}^2 = R - mg \cos \theta, \quad -\tfrac{4}{3} ml^2 \ddot{\theta} = mgl \sin \theta.]$$

7. A particle moves with uniform angular speed about a fixed point under the action of forces whose resultant is always at right angles to the radius-vector from the point; show that the equation to the path is of the form $\quad r = ae^\theta + be^{-\theta}$, and find an expression for the force at any point.

8. A particle is acted on by a force always parallel to the axis of y, and proportional to the square of the radius of curvature of the path at the point; show that if the particle move parallel to the x axis at $(0, b)$, the equation of the path is of the form
$$y - b = a \log \left(\sec \frac{x}{a} \right).$$

9. A circular disk of radius a is fixed on a smooth horizontal table and a heavy particle resting on the table is attached by a string to a fixed point on the circumference of the disk. Initially the string is straight and lies along a radius of the disk produced. Its length is half the circumference. The particle is projected with velocity V in a direction perpendicular to the string. Show that the string will just have been all wrapped round the disk when a time $\pi^2 a/V$ has elapsed.

10. A heavy uniform chain of length l and weight W is held vertically with one end in contact with a horizontal table, and is then let go. Show that the force exerted upon the table increases from

0 to $3W$ while the chain is being piled up, and then suddenly sinks to W.

11. A uniform chain lies in a heap close to the edge of a horizontal table. One end of the chain is gently pushed over the edge, and the chain is then left to itself. Show that when the last portion of the chain has just left the table the speed is $\sqrt{\tfrac{2}{3}gl}$, where l is the length of the chain.

12. A flexible chain of mass σ per unit length falls vertically and strikes a horizontal plane. Show that the initial force exerted on the plane is σv^2, where v is the velocity of the chain at the instant of striking.

13. The cable of a ship is coiled on the deck and the free end passes through a hawse-hole in the ship's side at a vertical height h above the coiled cable. An anchor of mass equal to that of a length l of the chain is hung at the free end. If the anchor be released, show (neglecting the large resistances at the hawse-hole, etc.), that after falling a distance x in air it will acquire a speed v given by

$$v^2(l+h+x)^2 = \int 2g\{(l+x)^2 - h^2\}dx.$$

Hence show that if $l=2h$ the anchor falls with uniform acceleration $g/3$.

14. A length k of a uniform chain of length $l+k$ and mass per unit length m is coiled at the edge of a smooth table, and the length l hangs over the edge. Show that the energy dissipated by the time the chain leaves the table is $\tfrac{1}{6}mgk^2(3l+k)/(l+k)$.

15. A smooth circular cylinder is fixed with its axis horizontal and vertically over the edge of a table, on which a length a of a uniform chain, of length l and mass ml, is coiled; the chain passes over the cylinder and has its free end on a level with the table. Prove that if this end be slightly displaced downwards, the amount of energy dissipated by the time the chain leaves the table is $\tfrac{1}{6}mga^3/l$.

16. A uniform chain of length l and weight W is placed on a line of greatest slope of a smooth plane of inclination α to the horizontal so that it just reaches the bottom of the plane, where there is a small smooth peg over which it can run off. Show that when a length x has run off, the stretching force at the bottom of the plane is

$$W(1-\sin\alpha).x(l-x)/l^2.$$

17. A uniform chain AB is held stretched in a vertical plane. If the end A is released, and at the instant at which it passes B the end B is released, prove that the chain becomes straight after an interval equal to three-quarters of the time in which A fell to B.

18. Two scale-pans, each of mass m, are supported by a thread of negligible mass passing over a smooth pulley, and a uniform chain of mass $2m$ and length l is held, by its upper end, above one of the scale-pans, so that it just reaches the pan. If the upper end of the chain is released, show that the whole chain piles up upon the pan in time $\sqrt{(3l/g)}$.

19. A massless string is coiled round a rough uniform solid cylinder whose axis is horizontal; the cylinder has mass M and radius a, and can turn freely about its axis. To the free end of the string is attached a uniform chain of mass m and length l. If the chain is gathered up close and then let go, prove that the angle θ turned through by the cylinder in a time t before the chain is fully stretched satisfies the equation $Mla\theta = m(\tfrac{1}{2}gt^2 - a\theta)^2$. [The moment of inertia of the cylinder about its axis is $\tfrac{1}{2}Ma^2$.]

20. A jet of liquid of density d issues horizontally from a tank which can slide on a horizontal surface. If the velocity of the issuing liquid in space is h, and that of the tank in the opposite direction is k, and A is the area of cross-section of the jet, show that the force applied by the jet to the tank is $Ad(h+k)^2$. [Ex. 2, p. 93.]

21. A horizontal water wheel rotates on a vertical axis; it is fed by water which enters the wheel after descending a distance h from rest and escapes tangentially to the perimeter at outlets symmetrically arranged round it. Show that if v is the speed of the escaping water, the ratio of the energy expended in useful work to the total energy expended is $1 - v^2/(2gh)$.

Prove also that if u is the speed of the perimeter of the wheel,
$$v^2 + 2vu + 2u^2 = 2gh.$$

22. A cylindrical jet of liquid, A square feet in cross-section, issues from an orifice in a vessel. If the pressure of the water within the vessel at the level of the orifice exceeds that of the atmosphere by P pounds per square foot, and the density be ρ lbs. per cubic foot, show that

(1) the flow in lbs. per second $= A\sqrt{2P g\rho}$;
(2) the momentum which issues in t seconds $= 2gAPt$ lb. f/s.

Supposing the liquid to be water, and the jet to have a cross-sectional area of 3 square inches, and the pressure to be 50 pounds per square inch, find the horizontal force acting upon the vessel.

23. A uniform rod, of length $2a$ and weight w, is held at an angle α to the vertical with its lower end in contact with a smooth horizontal plane, and is then let go.

Prove that when the rod makes an angle θ with the vertical,

(1) $$\dot{\theta}^2 = \frac{6g(\cos\alpha - \cos\theta)}{a(1 + 3\sin^2\theta)};$$

(2) the reaction on the plane is
$$\frac{w(4 + 3\cos^2\theta - 6\cos\theta\cos\alpha)}{(1 + 3\sin^2\theta)^2}.$$

[Moment of inertia of the rod about an axis through its centre at right angles to its length $= \tfrac{1}{3}wa^2$, and about a parallel axis through one end $= 4wa^2/3$.]

24. Two particles of mass m and m' are connected by an inelastic string of negligible mass and length a. The particle of mass m is placed in a smooth horizontal groove, and when the string is straightened out along the groove, the second particle is projected at right angles to the string and groove along a smooth horizontal table with velocity V. Show that the particle m oscillates through a space $2am'/(m+m')$, and that if m be large compared with m' the periodic time is $2\pi a(1 - m'/4m)/V$.

25. The potential energy of a particle of unit mass is given by the equation $2V = \mu(x^2 + 4y^2)$. If $x = a$, $\dot{x} = 0$, $y = 0$, $\dot{y} = u$ when $t = 0$, show that the path of the particle is given by $u^2 x^2(x^2 - a^2) + \mu a^4 y^2 = 0$.

26. A heavy uniform rod, OA, rotates in a vertical plane about the end O. It is required to find at what point of the rod the tendency to break is greatest.

Let $OA = 2a$, $AP = 2b$, and T, S denote the components of the resultant force at P along and at right angles to the rod, and L the couple tending to break the rod at the point P (Fig. 30). If C, C' be centroids of OA, PA respectively, we have

$$OC' = 2a - b.$$

Resolving along and perpendicular to the rod, we obtain

$$T = m\frac{b}{a}\{g\cos\theta + (2a - b)\dot{\theta}^2\},$$

$$S = m\frac{b}{a}\{g\sin\theta + (2a - b)\ddot{\theta}\},$$

and taking moments about C', we find

$$L = Sb + \frac{1}{3}m\frac{b}{a}b^2\ddot{\theta}.$$

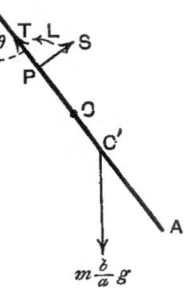

Fig. 30.

Now, $\frac{4}{3}ma^2\ddot{\theta} = -mga\sin\theta$, and therefore $\dot{\theta}^2 = \frac{3}{2}g(\cos\theta - \cos\alpha)/a$, where α is the value of θ when $\dot{\theta} = 0$. Substituting for $\ddot{\theta}$ and $\dot{\theta}^2$ in the equations for L, S, T, we find

$$T = mg\frac{b}{a}\{\cos\theta + \frac{3}{2}\frac{2a - b}{a}(\cos\theta - \cos\alpha)\},$$

$$S = \frac{1}{4}mg\frac{b}{a}\frac{3b - 2a}{a}\sin\theta,$$

$$L = \frac{1}{2}mg\frac{b^2}{a^2}(b - a)\sin\theta.$$

It will be observed that S and L are independent of α, and hence do not depend on the initial conditions.

Where L is a maximum, we have $dL/db = 0$, that is $3b^2 - 2ab = 0$, that is $b = \frac{2}{3}a$.

CHAPTER III.

DYNAMICS OF A PARTICLE.

82. Rectilinear Motion of a Particle in Resisting Medium.
We now proceed to work out some of the more simple of the soluble problems of dynamics, and take first the case of a single particle moving under various simple conditions. A separate chapter will be devoted to the motion of a particle under force directed to a fixed centre.

Hardly anything can be added here to what is said in §§ 21–24 above regarding unresisted motion under gravitational force constant in amount and direction, or in §§ 32–40 regarding simple harmonic motion. We shall, however, on account of its practical importance, consider somewhat fully the motion of a particle under a force constant in amount and direction, and a resistance in the line of motion, exerted by the medium in which the particle moves and depending on the speed. It will be convenient as fixing the ideas to take as the field of force that of uniformly directed gravity, but it is to be understood that the results obtained hold for other fields of force, and not merely for particles but for bodies of considerable extension in space. In the first place we shall deal with motion restricted to a single vertical, and here it will be understood that the motion considered is only an analogue of many others that occur in practice. For example, as we shall see, a body let fall under gravity in a resisting medium, undergoes acceleration until a certain limiting speed is attained, at which the accelerating action of gravity is balanced by the resistance of the medium. So a ship moving through the water, or a railway train moving through the air along a level road, attains a limiting speed, at which the propelling action of sails or engine is just balanced by the resistance experienced, and the speed is uniform. Again, when the engines of a ship, which is moving forward at any speed, are stopped and reversed, we have an analogue of the case in which a body is projected upward with given speed, and so is subjected while its upward motion endures to the combined retarding action of gravity and resistance. Both the action of the propeller and the resistance tend to stop the vessel, and it is brought more quickly to rest than if either acted alone. The passage from the particular gravitational cases which we consider to their analogues will be immediate; it will be necessary only to substitute for the value of g in the equations given below the acceleration which the propelling action would produce in the unresisted body.

83. Limiting Speed in Resisting Medium. It is found in practice that at a given speed bodies of the same shape, and oriented in the same way with respect to the direction of motion, experience resistance proportional to the squares of their corresponding dimensions, if they are completely immersed in the medium. This leads to the conclusion that the resistance of the medium is proportional to the superficial area of the body. For projectiles this conclusion is founded on many experiments: those of Newton, who, in 1687, let fall spherical shells of glass filled with different materials and of different diameters from the dome of St. Paul's Cathedral; those made by Hutton, in 1775, with a Robins ballistic pendulum large enough to receive cannon balls of different diameters; and those of Bashforth, made in 1865-70 and 1878-79, on projectiles from rifled ordnance, with an accurate chronograph which enabled the instants at which screens placed across the range of the projectile were pierced to be determined.

It is found, however, that no simple law connects resistance with speed. At low speeds the resistance may be taken as simply proportional to the speed; that this is the case is proved by the fact that the range of motion of a simple pendulum falls off by the same fraction of its amount in each swing, that is that the logarithmic decrement has a definite value. But at high speeds the resistance increases more rapidly with the speed, and may require a formula like $av + bv^2 + cv^3$, with different values of a, b, c in different cases, and even at different parts of the course of the same projectile, to completely express it.

If the resistance offered to motion is proportional to some power n of the speed, that is, is expressed by kv^n per unit mass of the body, so that kv^n is the retardation produced, the limiting speed is $(g/k)^{\frac{1}{n}}$, where k is a coefficient depending on the shape and size of the body, and g is the acceleration which the propelling force acting alone would give the body. For we have $g - kv^n = 0$ at the limiting speed, and denoting this value of v by L, we have

$$L = \left(\frac{g}{k}\right)^{\frac{1}{n}}, \quad \dots\dots\dots\dots\dots\dots\dots(1)$$

as stated.

If the law of resistance is a mixed one, for example if the retardation is $k_1 v + k_2 v^2$ at speed v, the expression for the limiting speed is more complicated. We have then

$$k_2 L^2 + k_1 L = g, \quad \dots\dots\dots\dots\dots\dots\dots(2)$$

a quadratic equation for L. One root is positive, the other negative; and only the positive root is applicable. It is

$$L = -\frac{k_1}{2k_2} + \sqrt{\frac{g}{k_2} + \frac{k_1^2}{4k_2^2}}, \quad \dots\dots\dots\dots\dots(3)$$

which reduces to $\sqrt{g/k_2}$ when $k_1 = 0$, and approximates more and more closely without limit to g/k_1 as k_2 is diminished towards zero.

We can easily prove that for a body of given shape and density, L is less the smaller the body's dimensions. For the resisting force varies as the surface of the body, and the retardation it produces inversely as the mass of the body. If, then, l be a representative dimension and ρ the density of the body, we see that we may write for a given medium, retardation $= v^n \cdot al^2/\rho l^3$, where a is a coefficient. If L be the value of the speed for which this is equal to a given acceleration g, we have

$$\frac{al^2}{\rho l^3}L^n = g \quad \text{or} \quad L^n = g\frac{\rho}{a}l, \quad \ldots\ldots\ldots\ldots\ldots(4)$$

that is the smaller l the smaller is L. If a given force act on the body, the unresisted acceleration g will be inversely as ρl^3, and so L^n will be proportional to l^2. If the force, as in the case of bodies falling under gravity, is so proportioned as to give for all bodies when unresisted by the medium the same acceleration g, then the circumstances are as in (4), and the limiting speed is smaller the smaller the density of a body of given size, and the smaller the dimensions of a body of given density. For $n = 2$, and bodies of the same material, L varies as $\sqrt{l}$, which is Froude's law of the limiting speeds of vessels of different dimensions moving through water.

We have examples of this limiting speed in the fall of rain-drops of different sizes (small shot let fall from an equal height would reach the ground with a much greater speed), in the almost imperceptible descent of the minute drops of water in a mist, or of minute particles mixed up in a turbid liquid. In this also we have the explanation of the persistence of the gorgeous sunsets, due to the existence of very fine dust in the atmosphere, which were seen for a long time after the Krakatao eruption in 1883.

The law that the limiting speed for similar bodies of different dimensions varies as the square roots of the corresponding linear dimensions, when the resistance is proportional to the square of the speed, is applicable to the motion of vessels whether completely or partially immersed. For it is proved by experiment that the chief part of the resistance to the motion is in that case due to friction exerted on the wetted surface of the vessel, and varying according to the law stated.

Taking, then, different vessels of similar design moving at their limiting speeds when the forces applied are, according to equation (4), such as to give them when unresisted the same acceleration (denoted by g above), that is the forces are proportional to the displacement tonnage, and therefore the coal burned per ton-mile is the same for all. But the tonnage is proportional to the cube of a chosen linear dimension, and therefore, reasoning from a model to a full-sized vessel of given tonnage or of given speed, we find first the limiting speed or the tonnage, as the case may be, from that for the model; then we see that since the tonnage is in proportion to the sixth power of the speed, the power provided will have to be increased in proportion to the tonnage and the speed conjointly, that is to the seventh power of the speed. The H.P. per ton for any other speed will then be proportional to that speed.

Ex. 1. Apply this rule to the calculation of the proper tonnage and power of a 25-knot steamer from the data (given by Sir George Greenhill, *Notes on Dynamics*, § 29) afforded by a steamer 500 feet length, 12000 tons displacement, and 15000 H.P. for a speed of 20 knots.

Increasing the tonnage in proportion to the sixth power and the H.P. in proportion to the seventh power of the speed gives

Tonnage $= 12000(\frac{5}{4})^6 = 45777$, Horse-power $= 15000(\frac{5}{4})^7 = 71500$.

The actual tonnage of the *Lusitania* is 42000 and the H.P. 72000.

Ex. 2. What speed, assuming the same proportions, ought to have been attained by the *Great Eastern*, the length of which was 680 feet (tonnage 32160) and H.P. 11000.

If the *Great Eastern* and the vessel here taken as a standard were on the same model, the tonnage of the former would be 30000. The speed of the *Great Eastern* with H.P. corresponding to this tonnage would be $20\sqrt{680/500} = 23\cdot 34$, in knots, and the H.P. would be about 44000. For 11000 H.P. therefore the speed of the *Great Eastern* should be given in knots by $\sqrt[3]{11000/44000} \cdot 23\cdot 34 = 14\cdot 7$, nearly. For the resistances are proportional to the squares of the speeds, and the rates of working, therefore, to the cubes of the speeds. It is matter of history that the vessel made from 14 to 15 knots under full power.

Ex. 3. If the expenditure of coal on a steamer carrying troops vary as the cube of the speed, show that the most economical voyage is that which makes the coal bill equal to half the amount of the other running expenses. Discuss also the case of a freight and passenger steamer.

Let E denote the total expenses of a voyage, D the whole distance from port to port, v the distance run per day; then the cost of coal per day is Cv^3, where C is a constant, and the total coal bill is CDv^2, since the run takes D/v days. If the rest of the running expenses be R per day, we have $E = CDv^2 + RD/v$.

Hence
$$\frac{dE}{dv} = 2CDv - R\frac{D}{v^2},$$

and this vanishes, that is E is a minimum, when $Cv^3 = R/2$.

If the cost of coal per day were Cv^2, we should have for greatest economy $Cv^2 = R$.

For a steamer carrying freight and passengers, the question of economy is a somewhat different one. As a rule, liners have their fixed times of sailing, so that a certain interval must elapse between the beginning of one trip and the beginning of the next, and a certain part of that interval is required for discharging cargo and reloading. If then the arrangement is possible within the time allowed, the expenses *of the voyage* will be a minimum if the coal bill is made equal to half the amount of the other expenses.

Ex. 4. The following interesting comparison is suggested by Sir George Greenhill (*Notes on Dynamics*). Determine the longest non-losing voyage of a steamer—the *Sirius* of 1838—of 700 tons capacity for coal and cargo when freight is 0·1*d.*/ton-mile, supposing the steamer to go at 8 knots on 20 tons/day of coal, costing 12*s.* per ton, and allowing £20 a day for wages, repairs, depreciation, etc. Compare this with a modern steamer of 5600 tons, going at 12 knots on 50 tons/day of coal.

The steamer travels 192 nautical miles per day, and therefore, if the length of the voyage be D nautical miles, the voyage lasts $D/192$ days. The coal bill is $5D/4$, in shillings, and the remainder of the expenses amounts to $400D/192$, also in shillings. Hence, we have

$$\left(700 - 20\frac{D}{192}\right)\frac{D}{120} = \frac{5}{4}D + 400\frac{D}{192},$$

if the voyage is to be as long as possible without loss. Hence

$$D = \frac{300 \times 192}{20} = 2880,$$

about the distance from England to America. The time taken is 15 days.

For the modern cargo steamer, if we take the coal at 18*s.* per ton, and the daily expenses as eight times the former amount, we get

$$\left(5600 - 50\frac{D}{288}\right)\frac{D}{120} = \frac{50 \times 18}{288}D + \frac{3200}{288}D,$$

and therefore $$D = \frac{112080}{50} = 22416.$$

The voyage occupies 77·8 days, and is nearly equal in length to the earth's circumference. The coal put on board is taken at 3890 tons, and the vessel carries 1710 tons of cargo. Of course a reserve of coal must be carried in any actual case, and the vessel can coal at stations. The comparison is, however, very remarkable.

84. Resistance varying as n^{th} Power of Speed. Discussion.

In the following discussion it will be sufficient, in view of what has been stated above as to the analogy of other cases, to consider the motion of a body in a resisting medium and under the action of uniformly directed gravity. In the first place, we shall suppose the motion restricted to a vertical line.

Let z denote distance upward from a point at which the particle is projected with upward speed V; then if v be the upward speed at time t,

$$\frac{dv}{dt} = v\frac{dv}{dz} = -g - R, \quad \dots\dots\dots\dots\dots(1)$$

where R is the resistance per unit mass of the medium. We suppose that R is of the form kv^n, where n is a positive integer. In that case,

$$\frac{dv}{dt} = -(g + kv^n). \quad \dots\dots\dots\dots\dots\dots(2)$$

The distance dz travelled upward in the interval of time dt is $v\,dt$. Hence, we have the differential equation—the same, in fact, as that just written:

$$v\frac{dv}{dz} = -(g + kv^n). \quad \dots\dots\dots\dots\dots\dots(3)$$

We shall generally, in what follows, write u for v/L, where L is the limiting speed (§ 83), so that the equations of upward motion (2) and (3) can now be written,

$$-\frac{g}{L}dt = \frac{du}{1+u^n}, \quad -\frac{g}{L^2}dz = \frac{u\,du}{1+u^n}. \quad \dots\dots\dots(4)$$

To find the time and distance of ascent from the instant of projection with speed $aL = V$, to that at which the speed has been diminished to bL, we have to find the integrals of (4) between the limits b and a. Thus, if t and z be the time and distance specified, we have

$$t = \frac{L}{g}\int_b^a \frac{du}{1+u^n}, \quad z = \frac{L^2}{g}\int_b^a \frac{u\,du}{1+u^n}. \quad \dots\dots\dots(5)$$

If $v < L$ throughout the motion (which is here supposed for the present to be only upward), the integrals may be obtained by expansion of $1/(1+u^n)$ in powers of u^n. If during part of the motion $v > L$, the integrand must be changed for that part by the substitution $w = 1/u$.

§84] RESISTED RECTILINEAR MOTION. 151

For the time T and distance H to the turning point, we have
$$T = \frac{L}{g}\int_0^a \frac{du}{1+u^n}, \quad H = \frac{L^2}{g}\int_0^a \frac{u\,du}{1+u^n}. \quad \ldots\ldots\ldots(6)$$

It is interesting to take the case of infinite upward speed of projection. Then
$$T = \frac{L}{g}\int_0^\infty \frac{du}{1+u^n}, \quad H = \frac{L^2}{g}\int_0^\infty \frac{u\,du}{1+u^n}.$$

Now, it can be proved (see Gibson's *Calculus*, §175) that
$$\int_0^\infty \frac{x^{p-1}dx}{1+x} = \frac{\pi}{\sin p\pi}, \text{ if } 0 < p < 1.$$

On the left write u^n for x and take $p = 1/n$, so that if $n > 1$ the condition as to p is fulfilled, and we have
$$\int_0^\infty \frac{du}{1+u^n} = \frac{1}{n}\int_0^\infty \frac{x^{p-1}}{1+x}dx.$$

Again, if we take $p = 2/n$, the condition as to the value of p is satisfied if $n > 2$, and we obtain
$$\int_0^\infty \frac{u\,du}{1+u^n} = \frac{1}{n}\int_0^\infty \frac{x^{p-1}dx}{1+x} = \frac{\pi}{n \sin p\pi}.$$

Thus we obtain for infinite speed of upward projection on the conditions stated as to the value of n,
$$T = \frac{L}{g}\frac{\pi}{n\sin\frac{\pi}{n}}, \quad H = \frac{L^2}{g}\frac{\pi}{n\sin\frac{2\pi}{n}}. \quad \ldots\ldots\ldots(7)$$

If n be very great, we have
$$(\pi/n)/\sin(\pi/n) = 1, \quad \pi/n \sin(2\pi/n) = \tfrac{1}{2},$$

and then $gT = L$, $2gH = L^2$, that is T is the time in which a body let fall in an unresisting medium from rest would gain the limiting speed L, and H is the distance which the body would fall in the same time.

The student may imagine that the *finite* values of T and H obtained here for the annulment of an infinite speed of upward projection are paradoxical; but it is to be remembered that when the speed is very great the resistance is correspondingly great, and so the particle is brought to rest in a finite time and space.

It is to be observed that if n be even, the sign of the expression kv^n will not change with that of v, and hence that we cannot find an integral in any such case that will apply without alteration to both upward and downward motion. For, in the ascending motion, both g and kv^n tend to retard the particle. On the other hand, when the particle is descending, g acts to increase the downward speed, while kv^n acts to diminish it. The downward acceleration is then $g - kv^n$. Thus if kv^n changes sign with v, the equation of motion, as written in (2) or (3), will apply to both upward and downward motion, so that the limits a and b of u may be anywhere on the whole course of the motion. When, however, n is even, we must integrate for the ascending motion up to the turning point, and then integrate separately for the downward motion, after reversing the sign of kv^n.

So far we have mainly considered the motion as upward. If it is downward, and n is even, we write, taking for convenience now v as positive downward,

$$dt = \frac{L}{g}\frac{du}{1-u^n}, \quad dz = \frac{L^2}{g}\frac{u\,du}{1-u^n}, \quad \ldots\ldots\ldots\ldots(8)$$

so that integrating from $V/L = a$ to $v/L = b$, we get

$$t = \frac{L}{g}\int_a^b \frac{du}{1-u^n}, \quad z = \frac{L^2}{g}\int_a^b \frac{u\,du}{1-u^n}. \quad \ldots\ldots\ldots(9)$$

If $V = 0$ initially, and finally $v = L$, these give

$$T = \frac{L}{g}\int_0^1 \frac{du}{1-u^n}, \quad H = \frac{L^2}{g}\int_0^1 \frac{u\,du}{1-u^n}, \quad \ldots\ldots\ldots(10)$$

where T and H denote the time and distance travelled downward from rest until the limiting speed L is acquired.

85. Motion under Resistance varying as v. We now consider, very shortly, the special cases of $n = 1$, $n = 2$ and $n = 3$.

When $n = 1$ we have, by (5) of § 84, the equation

$$\frac{g}{L}t = \int_b^a \frac{du}{1+u} = \log\frac{1+a}{1+b}, \quad \ldots\ldots\ldots\ldots\ldots\ldots\ldots(1)$$

for the time t from the instant of projection upward with speed $V = aL$ to that at which the speed has become bL. The displacement

z of the particle from the point of projection in the interval t is given also by (5) of § 84, that is

$$\frac{g}{L^2}z = \int_b^a \frac{u\,du}{1+u} = a - b - \log\frac{1+a}{1+b} = a - b - \frac{g}{L}t. \quad\ldots\ldots\ldots\ldots(2)$$

In the present case, since n is odd, the differential equations apply to both the upward and the downward motion, so that we may suppose the motion to have been changed in the interval from the upward to the downward direction, or to have been wholly downward, that is we may suppose bL negative, or both bL and aL negative. If a is positive and b negative, that is if the initial speed is upward and the final speed downward, z is not the whole distance travelled; to find that we have to calculate the upward distance and the downward distance separately and add their numerical values together.

The time of ascent T to the turning point is got by making $b=0$, in (1).

$$T = \frac{L}{g}\log(1+a) = \frac{L}{g}\log\frac{L+V}{L}. \quad\ldots\ldots\ldots\ldots(3)$$

The distance from the point of projection to the highest point is

$$H = \frac{L^2}{g}\{a - \log(1+a)\} = \frac{L^2}{g}\left(\frac{V}{L} - \log\frac{L+V}{L}\right). \quad\ldots\ldots\ldots\ldots(4)$$

If the initial upward speed be L, the equations become

$$T = \frac{L}{g}\log_e 2, \quad H = \frac{L^2}{g}(1 - \log_e 2). \quad\ldots\ldots\ldots\ldots(5)$$

Equation (2) shows that if $z=0$, so that aL is the upward speed, V say, and bL the downward speed V' of return, at a given point, then the time occupied in the motion is given by

$$t = \frac{V+V'}{g}, \quad\ldots\ldots\ldots\ldots(6)$$

that is it is equal to the time in which gravity would produce in a body falling from rest in a non-resisting medium the speed $V+V'$. Of course if k were zero, the value of t would be $2V/g$ for the same speed of upward projection. The speeds V and V' are by (1), (2) and (6) in the relation

$$\frac{V+V'}{L} = \log\frac{L+V}{L-V'}.$$

86. Resistance varying as v^2. Now let $n=2$. Here we have to deal with the upward and downward motions separately. For the upward motion, we have

$$-dt = \frac{L}{g}\frac{du}{1+u^2}, \quad -dz = \frac{L^2}{g}\frac{u\,du}{1+u^2}, \quad\ldots\ldots\ldots\ldots(1)$$

so that

$$t = \frac{L}{g}(\tan^{-1}a - \tan^{-1}b), \quad z = \frac{L^2}{2g}\log\frac{1+a^2}{1+b^2}, \quad\ldots\ldots\ldots\ldots(2)$$

for initial speed aL and final speed bL.

154   A TREATISE ON DYNAMICS.   [CH. III.

The time of ascent and distance to the highest point are thus

$$T = \frac{L}{g}\tan^{-1}\frac{V}{L}, \quad H = \frac{L^2}{2g}\log\frac{L^2+V^2}{L^2}. \quad \ldots\ldots(3)$$

For the downward motion we take v as positive downward and obtain

$$dt = \frac{L}{g}\frac{du}{1-u^2} = \frac{L}{2g}\left(\frac{du}{1+u} + \frac{du}{1-u}\right), \quad \ldots\ldots(4)$$

$$dz = \frac{L^2}{g}\frac{u\,du}{1-u^2} = -\frac{L^2}{2g}\frac{d}{du}\{\log(1-u^2)\}. \quad \ldots\ldots(5)$$

Hence, integrating from the limit a for the initial point to limit b for the final point, we get

$$t = \frac{L}{2g}\log\frac{(1+b)(1-a)}{(1-b)(1+a)}, \quad z = \frac{L^2}{2g}\log\frac{1-a^2}{1-b^2}. \quad \ldots(6)$$

If the initial speed be zero and the final be bL, these equations give

$$t = \frac{L}{2g}\log\frac{1+b}{1-b}, \quad z = \frac{L^2}{2g}\log\frac{1}{1-b^2}. \quad \ldots\ldots(7)$$

Hence, if the terminal speed L be the final speed, that is if $b=1$, the values of t and z are both infinite.

87. Resistance varying as v^3. Finally, we take the case of resistance kv^3. Here the downward motion need not be separated from the upward. Taking v and z positive upward, with $L^3=g/k$, so that L is the limiting speed,

$$dt = -\frac{L}{g}\frac{du}{1+u^3}, \quad dz = -\frac{L^2}{g}\frac{u\,du}{1+u^3}. \quad \ldots\ldots(1)$$

Hence, if a be the initial and b the final value of u,

$$t = \frac{L}{g}\int_b^a \frac{du}{1+u^3}, \quad z = \frac{L^2}{g}\int_b^a \frac{u\,du}{1+u^3}. \quad \ldots\ldots(2)$$

Now, by splitting $1/(1+u^3)$ into partial fractions, it may be verified that the integrands break up into differentials as follows:

$$\frac{du}{1+u^3} = \frac{1}{3}\frac{du}{1+u} - \frac{1}{6}\frac{2u-1}{u^2-u+1}du + \frac{1}{\sqrt{3}}\frac{\frac{2}{\sqrt{3}}du}{\frac{4}{3}\left(u-\frac{1}{2}\right)^2+1}, \quad \ldots\ldots(3)$$

$$\frac{u\,du}{1+u^3} = -\frac{1}{3}\frac{du}{1+u} + \frac{1}{6}\frac{2u-1}{u^2-u+1}du + \frac{1}{\sqrt{3}}\frac{\frac{2}{\sqrt{3}}du}{\frac{4}{3}\left(u-\frac{1}{2}\right)^2+1}. \quad \ldots\ldots(4)$$

Hence,
$$t = \frac{L}{g}\left[\frac{1}{6}\log\frac{(1+a)^2(b^2-b+1)}{(1+b)^2(a^2-a+1)}\right.$$
$$\left. + \frac{1}{\sqrt{3}}\left\{\tan^{-1}\frac{2}{\sqrt{3}}\left(a-\frac{1}{2}\right) - \tan^{-1}\frac{2}{\sqrt{3}}\left(b-\frac{1}{2}\right)\right\}\right], \quad\ldots\ldots(5)$$

$$z = \frac{L^2}{g}\left[\frac{1}{6}\log\frac{(1+b)^2(a^2-a+1)}{(1+a)^2(b^2-b+1)}\right.$$
$$\left. + \frac{1}{\sqrt{3}}\left\{\tan^{-1}\frac{2}{\sqrt{3}}\left(a-\frac{1}{2}\right) - \tan^{-1}\frac{2}{\sqrt{3}}\left(b-\frac{1}{2}\right)\right\}\right]. \quad\ldots\ldots(6)$$

The reader may work out the different special cases. Some results will be found in the examples.

88. Examples on Resisted Motion in a Vertical Line.

1. If $n=1$, prove that if the upward speed of projection be the limiting speed L, the distance travelled from the instant of projection until the downward speed is V is $L(T_2 - T_1)$, where T_1 is the time occupied in this passage, and T_2 is the time in which gravity would change the speed of an unresisted falling body from V upwards to L downwards.

2. Verify by expansion of the logs in (1) and (2), § 85, that these equations give the ordinary equations of unresisted motion when $k=0$.

3. Show that if $n=2$, and L be the speed of projection upward, the time of ascent to the highest point is $\frac{1}{4}\pi L/g$.

4. Show that if $n=2$, and a particle be projected upward with any given initial speed, the speeds V and V' of the particle when at the same point in its ascent and descent fulfil the equation
$$\frac{1}{V'^2} - \frac{1}{V^2} = \frac{1}{L^2}.$$

5. Show that if the earth were a sphere of uniform density, and did not rotate, a particle dropped at the surface into a tunnel extending right through the earth along a diameter, would, if unresisted, move with simple harmonic motion in the period of a simple pendulum vibrating with bob at the surface and of length equal to the earth's radius. [It is to be understood that the particle would be attracted towards the centre in each position with a force proportional to the whole mass contained in the sphere, concentric with the earth, on which the particle is situated, and inversely proportional to the square of the radius of that sphere.]

Show that this is also the period of revolution of an unresisted small satellite which moves round a great circle and just grazes the surface, and that if the satellite and particle leave the mouth of the tunnel together, they will thereafter be found always in a plane perpendicular to the tunnel.

6. Prove that, if k be such that the limiting speed L (given by $kL^2 = g$) of a particle let fall under gravity g, in a medium resisting with a force kv^2, is the speed of the satellite in last question, the time of ascent of the particle to the highest point when it is thrown up with the limiting speed, is half the time that the satellite would take to describe a quadrant of the earth's circumference.

7. Prove that in the case of resistance kv^3, the time T and distance H to the highest point when the speed of projection is L, are respectively

$$\frac{1}{3}\frac{L}{g}\left(\frac{\pi}{\sqrt{3}} + \log 2\right), \quad \frac{1}{3}\frac{L^2}{g}\left(\frac{\pi}{\sqrt{3}} - \log 2\right),$$

and that therefore $\qquad H + LT = \dfrac{2\pi}{3\sqrt{3}}\dfrac{L^2}{g}.$

8. Show that the time from a given point of projection to the highest point and back again is, for resistance kv^3,

$$\frac{L}{g}\frac{2}{\sqrt{3}}\left\{\tan^{-1}\frac{2}{\sqrt{3}}\left(a - \frac{1}{2}\right) - \tan^{-1}\frac{2}{\sqrt{3}}\left(b - \frac{1}{2}\right)\right\} = \frac{L}{g}\frac{1}{3}\log\frac{(1+a)^2(b^2 - b + 1)}{(1+b)^2(a^2 - a + 1)}.$$

89. Examples of Rectilinear Motion under Gravity.

Ex. 1. A particle slides down an inclined plane along the line of greatest slope, and is resisted by friction; to find the motion.

Let θ be the inclination of the line of motion to the horizontal, $\mu = \tan \alpha$ the coefficient of friction, s the distance travelled at any time from a chosen origin O within the range of the particle's motion. The equation of motion is

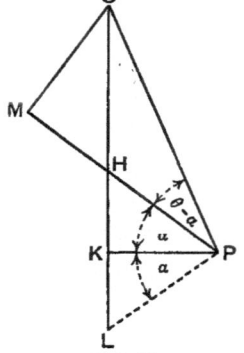

Fig. 31.

$$\frac{d^2s}{dt^2} = g(\sin \theta - \mu \cos \theta)$$
$$= g \sec \alpha \sin(\theta - \alpha). \quad \ldots\ldots\ldots\ldots(1)$$

But $d^2s/dt^2 = v\, dv/ds$, and therefore

$$v\frac{dv}{ds} = g \sec \alpha \sin(\theta - \alpha).$$

Integrating, we get

$$\tfrac{1}{2}v^2 - \tfrac{1}{2}v_0^2 = gs \sec \alpha \sin(\theta - \alpha), \quad \ldots\ldots(2)$$

which, if the particle start from rest at O, becomes $\quad \tfrac{1}{2}v^2 = gs \sec \alpha \sin(\theta - \alpha). \quad \ldots\ldots\ldots(3)$

In Fig. 31, OP is s, OM is in the vertical plane of OP, and inclined at the angle α to the vertical OHK, $\angle HPK$ is also α, so that $\angle HPO$ is $\theta - \alpha$. Hence, $OM = s \sin(\theta - \alpha)$ and $OH = s \sec \alpha \sin(\theta - \alpha)$. Thus equations (2) and (3) become respectively

$$v^2 - v_0^2 = 2g \cdot OH, \quad v^2 = 2g \cdot OH. \quad \ldots\ldots\ldots\ldots\ldots(4)$$

§§ 88, 89]   RESISTED RECTILINEAR MOTION.   157

Thus, whatever the inclination $\theta(>\alpha)$ may be, the value of $v^2 - v_0^2$, for descent from O to a point on the line MN, has the same value $2g \cdot OH$. But for friction, this would evidently have been $2g \cdot OK$, so that $2g \cdot HK$ represents loss of v^2 due to friction. The gain of kinetic energy is $\tfrac{1}{2}mv^2 - \tfrac{1}{2}mv_0^2 = mg \cdot OH$. The loss of kinetic energy due to friction is $mg \cdot HK$, and is greater the farther P is from H.

Ex. 2. Show that if the figure in last example be made to turn about OK, so that HP traces out a right circular cone of semi-vertical angle $\tfrac{1}{2}\pi - \alpha$, the gain of kinetic energy is the same by whatever straight line the particle descends from O to the surface of the cone.

Ex. 3. A piece of machinery, e.g. a clock, is driven by a weight sliding down an inclined plane OP. Show that the efficiency of the arrangement (the ratio of the energy yielded for useful work by the weight, in one descent, to the energy spent in raising it from P to O) is OH/OL (Fig. 31).

Ex. 4. From the equation of motion in Ex. 1 show that

$v = v_0 + gt \sec\alpha \sin(\theta - \alpha),$

$s = v_0 t + \tfrac{1}{2} gt^2 \sec\alpha \sin(\theta - \alpha).$

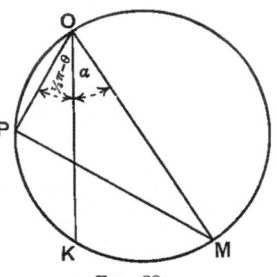

Fig. 32.

Show that if in the circle OPM (Fig. 32), of which OM is the diameter, the lines OK, OP be drawn inclined at the angles α and $\tfrac{1}{2}\pi - \theta$ respectively to the vertical OK, and OK be taken to represent $\tfrac{1}{2}gt^2$, OM will represent $\tfrac{1}{2}gt^2 \sec\alpha$, and OP, $\tfrac{1}{2}gt^2 \sec\alpha \sin(\theta - \alpha)$; and that therefore the time of descent, from rest at O, along any chord OP of the circle on the side of OK remote from the centre, is the same as that along the vertical chord OK.

Ex. 5. If the particle sliding along the chord is resisted also by the air directly as the speed, show that the equation of motion is

$\ddot{s} = g \sec\alpha \sin(\theta - \alpha) - k\dot{s},$

where k is a constant, and that, therefore, if the particle start from rest

$\dot{s} = gt \sec\alpha \sin(\theta - \alpha) - ks,$

and $\qquad s = \dfrac{g}{k^2} \sec\alpha \sin(\theta - \alpha)(kt + e^{-kt} - 1);$

so that, for a constant value of t, this value of s is represented by the lengths of the chords of the circle in Fig. 32, drawn from O on the side of OK remote from the centre.

Ex. 6. Prove that for $k = 0$, the equation for s in the last example reduces to $\qquad s = \tfrac{1}{2}gt^2 \sec\alpha \sin(\theta - \alpha).$

Ex. 7. Show that if a particle slide down a chord PO of a vertical circle (Fig. 33), where KO is a vertical chord, drawn to the lower end of a diameter inclined to the vertical at the angle of friction α, the time of descent is the same for all chords on the same side of KO as PO, and equal to that for KO.

Ex. 8. A particle slides down an inclined plane, under a resistance kv^2 per unit mass; prove that if the particle start from rest the distance s described and the speed v acquired in time t satisfy the equations

$$v = \frac{u}{\sqrt{k}}\sqrt{\frac{e^{ks}-e^{-ks}}{e^{ks}}} = \frac{u}{\sqrt{k}}\frac{e^{\sqrt{k}ut}-e^{-\sqrt{k}ut}}{e^{\sqrt{k}ut}+e^{-\sqrt{k}ut}},$$

and that therefore

$$e^{ks} = \tfrac{1}{2}(e^{\sqrt{k}ut}+e^{-\sqrt{k}ut}),$$

where $u^2 = g\sin\theta$.

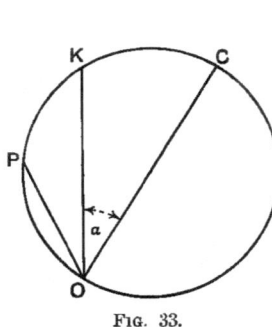
Fig. 33.

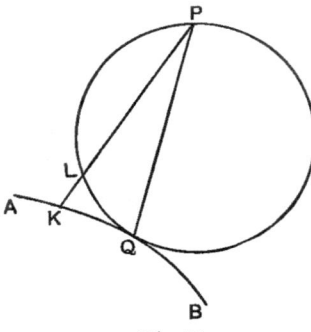
Fig. 34.

Ex. 9. To find the straight line of quickest descent in a vertical plane from a given point P to a given curve in the plane, a circle is drawn so that P is the highest point of the circle, and the circle touches the given curve in a point Q. Prove that the chord PQ is a line of quickest descent if the circle has external contact with the curve, and a line of slowest descent if the contact is internal (Fig. 34).

Ex. 10. Show that the chord PQ of the circle in Ex. 9 bisects the angle between the normal to the curve at Q and the vertical.

Ex. 11. Show that if the particle have its motion resisted by friction, the construction in Ex. 9 is to be modified by drawing the circle to touch a line through P inclined to the horizontal at the angle of friction, and to touch the given curve. The chord PQ is then the required line of descent.

90. S.H.M. Motion of a Simple Pendulum.

The equation of motion of a vibrating particle is easily established. If its mass be m and its displacement along a straight line from the position of equilibrium be x, a force of amount $-mn^2x$ is applied to the particle by the spring or other agent, which tends to restore the particle to the equilibrium position. Thus we have, since $m\ddot{x}$ is the rate of growth of the particle's momentum,

$$m\ddot{x} = -mn^2x$$

or
$$\ddot{x} + n^2x = 0 \quad \ldots\ldots\ldots\ldots\ldots\ldots\ldots\ldots(1)$$

the equation dealt with in § 33 above.

For motion of the same kind, but resisted by a force $mk\dot{x}$ proportional to the speed of motion, the equation is

$$m\ddot{x} = -mk\dot{x} - mn^2x$$

or
$$\ddot{x} + k\dot{x} + n^2x = 0. \quad \ldots\ldots\ldots\ldots\ldots\ldots(2)$$

The complete solutions of equations (1) and (2) have been found in §§ 33, 43 above, and the value of x exhibited in equations (7) of these sections as a function of the interval of time t from a chosen epoch of reckoning, and the displacement and speed at that epoch.

The vibratory motion of a spiral spring has been considered in § 51. We take here as another example the motion of a simple pendulum, that is a pendulum composed of a massive particle called the bob, and suspended from a fixed point by a thin unstretchable string, the mass of which may be neglected. Let m denote the mass of the bob and t the length of the string, and let the motion be in one vertical plane. If θ be the deflection of the thread from the vertical at time t, it is clear from Fig. 35 that the component force along the arc in which the bob moves is $mg \sin \theta$, directed *inward* towards the middle position; if the arc be very small, this force is $mg\theta$. The speed *outward* along the arc is $l\dot{\theta}$ and the acceleration $l\ddot{\theta}$. Thus we have the equation of motion,

$$\ddot{\theta} + \frac{g}{l}\sin\theta = 0. \quad \ldots\ldots\ldots\ldots\ldots\ldots(3)$$

Fig. 35.

If θ be small, this becomes
$$\ddot{\theta}+\frac{g}{l}\theta=0, \quad\dots\dots\dots\dots\dots\dots\dots\dots(4)$$
which is immediately integrable in the form
$$\theta = A\cos\left(\sqrt{\frac{g}{l}}t+\alpha\right), \quad\dots\dots\dots\dots\dots(5)$$
where A and α are constants. Or we may write it
$$\theta=\theta_0\cos\sqrt{\frac{g}{l}}t+\frac{\dot{\theta}_0}{\sqrt{\frac{g}{l}}}\sin\sqrt{\frac{g}{l}}t, \quad\dots\dots\dots(6)$$
where θ_0, $\dot{\theta}_0$ are the angular deflection from the middle position and angular speed of the pendulum, at time $t=0$. Thus θ changes simple-harmonically in period T, given by
$$T=2\pi\sqrt{\frac{l}{g}}. \quad\dots\dots\dots\dots\dots\dots\dots\dots(7)$$

If the more exact equation (3) be considered, it will be obvious at once that while the motion is oscillatory, it is not simple-harmonic; for the factor θ of the second term in (4) is replaced by $\sin\theta$. Since $\sin\theta<\theta$, it is clear that the acceleration falls short for each value of θ of that required for simple-harmonic motion, and that therefore the period of an oscillation for a finite amplitude is greater than that of an oscillation of small amplitude.

91. Motion of a Simple Pendulum in a Finite Arc. Elliptic Integrals. The problem of a simple pendulum vibrating in a circular arc is essentially that of a particle moving without friction on a concave circular ring with its plane vertical, or along the interior of a guide tube bent into a vertical circle. For if l denote the radius of the circular path, and θ the angular deflection of the radius from the lowest position, the equation of motion in both cases is (3) above. We find the period in this case by calculating the time, τ say, taken by the particle to move along the circle from the lowest position to rest at any extreme angular displacement θ_0. The whole period is then 4τ.

Multiplying the equation by $\dot{\theta}$ and integrating, we get
$$\tfrac{1}{2}\dot{\theta}^2 = -\int\frac{g}{l}\sin\theta\,d\theta = \frac{g}{l}\cos\theta+C, \quad\dots\dots\dots\dots\dots(1)$$
where C is constant. Now, when $\theta=\theta_0$, $\dot{\theta}=0$, so that $C=-g\cos\theta_0/l$.

§§ 90, 91, 92] MOTION OF PARTICLE IN VERTICAL CIRCLE. 161

Hence
$$l^2\dot{\theta}^2 = v^2 = 2gl(\cos\theta - \cos\theta_0) \quad \ldots\ldots\ldots\ldots(2)$$

and
$$\frac{dt}{d\theta} = \sqrt{\frac{l}{g}} \frac{1}{\sqrt{2(\cos\theta - \cos\theta_0)}}, \quad \ldots\ldots\ldots\ldots(3)$$

and therefore
$$\tau = \sqrt{\frac{l}{g}} \int_0^{\theta_0} \frac{d\theta}{\sqrt{2(\cos\theta - \cos\theta_0)}}. \quad \ldots\ldots\ldots(4)$$

Writing now
$$\sin\tfrac{1}{2}\theta = \sin\tfrac{1}{2}\theta_0 \sin\phi, \quad \ldots\ldots\ldots\ldots(5)$$

we have $d\theta = 2\sin\tfrac{1}{2}\theta_0 \cos\phi\, d\phi / \sqrt{1 - k^2\sin^2\phi}$, ($k = \sin\tfrac{1}{2}\theta_0$), and when $\theta = 0$, $\phi = 0$, ; when $\theta = \theta_0$, $\phi = \pi/2$. Also the substitution just used gives $1/\sqrt{2(\cos\theta - \cos\theta_0)} = 1/(2\sin\tfrac{1}{2}\theta_0 \cos\phi)$, so that we have, writing n for $\sqrt{g/l}$, $n/\dot{\theta} = 1/2\sin\tfrac{1}{2}\theta_0\cos\phi$, or

$$\dot{\theta} = 2n\sin\tfrac{1}{2}\theta_0\cos\phi. \quad \ldots\ldots\ldots\ldots(6)$$

But by (5), $\cos\tfrac{1}{2}\theta \cdot \dot{\theta} = 2\sin\tfrac{1}{2}\theta_0\cos\phi \cdot \dot{\phi}$, and therefore by (6) we get

$$\dot{\phi} = n\cos\tfrac{1}{2}\theta. \quad \ldots\ldots\ldots\ldots(7)$$

Also, we obtain instead of (2) and (3),

$$n\frac{dt}{d\phi} = \frac{1}{\sqrt{1 - k^2\sin^2\phi}} \quad \ldots\ldots\ldots\ldots(8)$$

and
$$n\tau = \int_0^{\frac{\pi}{2}} \frac{d\phi}{\sqrt{1 - k^2\sin^2\phi}} = K, \quad \ldots\ldots\ldots\ldots(9)$$

The integral K is called *the complete elliptic integral of the first kind*; k is called its modulus and $\pi/2$ its *amplitude*. The time t from the lowest position of the pendulum to that for any deflection θ is given in the same way by

$$nt = \int_0^{\phi} \frac{d\phi}{\sqrt{1 - k^2\sin^2\phi}} = F(k, \phi), \quad \ldots\ldots\ldots(10)$$

where $F(k, \phi)$ is called an elliptic integral of the first kind, of *modulus* k and *amplitude* ϕ. The time for any arc from $\phi = \phi_1$ to $\phi = \phi_2$, say, is thus given by

$$n(t_2 - t_1) = F(k, \phi_2) - F(k, \phi_1). \quad \ldots\ldots\ldots(11)$$

It is clear from (8) that if k (that is $\sin\tfrac{1}{2}\theta_0$) is very small, we have $\tau = \tfrac{1}{2}\pi\sqrt{l/g}$ and $T = 2\pi\sqrt{l/g}$, the result already obtained in § 90.

92. Motion of a Particle in a Vertical Circle. Elliptic Functions. If the pendulum start from rest from a position making an angle θ_0 with the downward vertical, the force toward the centre applied by the cord is at any time thereafter, when the deflection from the downward vertical is θ, $ml\dot{\theta}^2 + mg\cos\theta$, or by (2) of § 91, $mg(3\cos\theta - 2\cos\theta_0)$. At the end of a swing $\theta = \theta_0$, and the pull is then $mg\cos\theta_0$, which is negative if $\theta_0 > \pi/2$. But if instead of a bob suspended by a string we have a particle moving in a guiding tube, bent into a circle, in a vertical plane and of radius l, the amplitude

G.D. L

may have any value from 0 up to π. If there be no friction between the tube and the particle, the equations of § 91 apply to the motion, and the force P applied by the guide to the particle is given by

$$P = mg(3\cos\theta - 2\cos\theta_0). \qquad (1)$$

If the particle start with speed v_0 from the position at distance $l\theta_0$ along the circle from the lowest point, then at deflection θ the speed v is given by $v^2 - v_0^2 = 2gl(\cos\theta - \cos\theta_0)$, and P is then given by the equation

$$P = mg(3\cos\theta - 2\cos\theta_0) + m\frac{v_0^2}{l}. \qquad (2)$$

Hence, if the particle goes completely round the circle, we have when $\theta = \pi$, $P = mg(-3 - 2\cos\theta_0) + mv_0^2/l$, and therefore *if the value of P is not to change sign*, we must have $v_0^2 > gl(3 + 2\cos\theta_0)$, and so if $\theta_0 = \pi$, $v_0^2/l > g$. If this condition be fulfilled, the particle may be suspended by a string.

The reaction on the support is equal and opposite to the force P on the particle.

The amplitude ϕ is the angle DCQ in Fig. 36, where P represents the position of the particle at time t. The circle APB is drawn with radius l, P_0 is the initial position of the particle, CP_0 is horizontal, C is the highest point of the smaller circle, which has diameter BC. DP is drawn through P horizontally and intersects the smaller circle in Q. Then $\angle DCQ$ is ϕ, as we shall prove. For join AP, OP. Then

$$\angle BOP = \theta, \quad \angle BAP = \tfrac{1}{2}\theta,$$
$$\angle OAP_0 = \tfrac{1}{2}\theta_0.$$

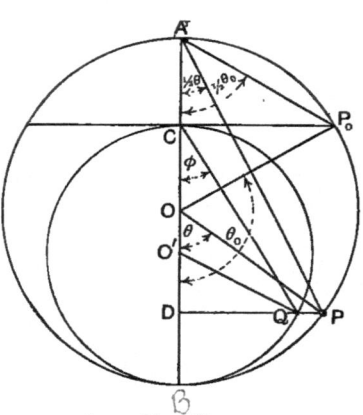

Fig. 36.

By the diagram, $CB = 2l\sin^2\tfrac{1}{2}\theta_0$, and therefore $CD = 2l\sin^2\tfrac{1}{2}\theta_0 \cos^2\angle BCQ$. But also

$$CD = l - AC + OD = l - 2l\cos^2\tfrac{1}{2}\theta_0 + l\cos\theta = 2l(\cos^2\tfrac{1}{2}\theta - \cos^2\tfrac{1}{2}\theta_0).$$

Equating these two values of CD and reducing, we obtain

$$\sin\tfrac{1}{2}\theta_0 \sin\angle BCQ = \sin\tfrac{1}{2}\theta.$$

Hence $\angle BCQ = \phi$.

Also $k = \sin\tfrac{1}{2}\theta_0 = CP_0/AP_0$. If we write $k^2 + k'^2 = 1$, k' is called the *co-modulus*, and is therefore represented by AC/AP_0.

The construction in Fig. 36 replaces the turning of OP, with angular speed $\dot\theta$, by the turning of CQ with angular speed $\dot\phi$ [see equations (5) and (6), § 91] and the motion of P by that of Q. Q

§ 92] MOTION OF PARTICLE IN VERTICAL CIRCLE. 163

starts from C when P starts from P_0, and coincides with P at B. If the particle just goes completely round in the guiding tube, that is if P_0 is infinitely near to A, the smaller and larger circles coincide, and $\phi = \frac{1}{2}\theta$, $\theta = \pi$, so that $k=1$.

Thus t is a function of ϕ given by (9), § 91, or nt is the function $F(k, \phi)$ of k and ϕ. Conversely, ϕ is a function of nt and k, called, as has been stated, the amplitude of nt. If then we write u for nt, we have $\phi = \operatorname{am} u$ to modulus k, and $\sin \phi = \sin \operatorname{am} u$, or, as it is usual now to write, $\sin \phi = \operatorname{sn} u$. We also write $\cos \phi = \operatorname{cn} u$.

We have $d\phi/du = d \operatorname{am} u/du = \sqrt{1 - k^2 \sin^2 \phi}$, and write this $\operatorname{dn} u$.
Thus
$$\left. \begin{array}{l} \dfrac{d\operatorname{sn} u}{du} = \operatorname{cn} u \operatorname{dn} u, \quad \dfrac{d \operatorname{cn} u}{du} = -\operatorname{sn} u \operatorname{dn} u, \\[6pt] \dfrac{d \operatorname{dn} u}{du} = -\dfrac{k^2 \sin\phi \cos\phi}{\sqrt{1-k^2\sin^2\phi}} \dfrac{d\phi}{du} = -k^2 \operatorname{sn} u \operatorname{cn} u. \end{array} \right\} \quad \ldots\ldots\ldots\ldots(3)$$

The functions $\operatorname{sn} u$, $\operatorname{cn} u$, $\operatorname{dn} u$, are called the *elliptic functions* of u. They are usually approached from the point of view of functions of a complex variable. But the dynamical introduction is instructive. [Cf. Greenhill's *Elliptic Functions*.]

In the pendulum motion we have $\sin \frac{1}{2}\theta = k \operatorname{sn} u$, $\cos \frac{1}{2}\theta = \operatorname{dn} u$,

$$DP = AB \sin \tfrac{1}{2}\theta \cos \tfrac{1}{2}\theta = 2lk \operatorname{sn} u \operatorname{dn} u = BP_0 \operatorname{sn} u \operatorname{cn} u.$$

Also $\qquad DQ = BC \sin\phi \cos\phi = BC \operatorname{sn} u \operatorname{cn} u.$

But $BC = 2l \sin^2 \tfrac{1}{2}\theta_0 = 2lk^2$, so that also $DQ = 2lk^2 \operatorname{sn} u \operatorname{cn} u$.

Thus $\qquad DQ/DP = BC/BP_0 = k \operatorname{cn} u / \operatorname{dn} u.$

When the amplitude of oscillation is very small we may take k as zero, and we have then $u = F(k, \phi) = \phi$, that is $\operatorname{sn} u = \sin u$, $\operatorname{cn} u = \cos u$: the elliptic function becomes the ordinary circular function. At the other extreme, when the particle just goes completely round the circle, $k = 1$, and

$$nt = \int_0^\phi \frac{d\phi}{\cos\phi} = \log \frac{1 + \tan\tfrac{1}{2}\phi}{1 - \tan\tfrac{1}{2}\phi} = \cosh^{-1}(\sec\phi), \quad \ldots\ldots\ldots\ldots(4)$$

and so, for $\phi = \pi/2$, t is infinite.

The integrals K and F can be calculated easily by expanding $(1 - k^2 \sin^2 \phi)^{-\frac{1}{2}}$ by the binomial theorem, and integrating term by term. This proceeding is legitimate (since $k < 1$ and the series are convergent), and yields for τ the equation

$$\tau = \frac{\pi}{2} \sqrt{\frac{l}{g}} \left\{ 1 + \left(\frac{1}{2}\right)^2 k^2 + \left(\frac{1\cdot 3}{2\cdot 4}\right)^2 k^4 + \left(\frac{1\cdot 3\cdot 5}{2\cdot 4\cdot 6}\right)^2 k^6 + \ldots \right\}. \quad \ldots\ldots(5)$$

The first two terms of this series form an approximation sufficient for many purposes. This approximation can be arrived at directly by assuming that $1/\sqrt{1 - k^2 \sin^2 \phi} = \sqrt{1 + k^2 \sin^2 \phi}$ and integrating.

From the expression on the right of (5) the multiplier K of $\sqrt{2/g}$ in (9) of § 91 can be calculated. There are more convenient methods of calculating this integral; but it is unnecessary to discuss the subject here. The values of K for different values of k were tabulated by Legendre; for values of $\frac{1}{2}\theta_0$ proceeding by successive steps of 1° from 0° to 90°, a table is given to 4 places of decimals in the *Smithsonian Physical Tables* drawn up by the late Professor Thomas Gray.

When $\frac{1}{2}\theta_0 = 90°$, $\theta_0 = 180°$, so that the particle in the guide tube (not the pendulum) just goes completely round from rest to rest in half a period. The time required for this is infinite; for a range, however, of $\frac{1}{2}\theta_0$, from a deflection of 89° on one side to 89° on the other, the time required is 3·3 times that required for a very small swing from one side of the vertical to the other. Values for other amplitudes can be obtained from the following short table:

$\frac{1}{2}\theta_0$	K	$\frac{1}{2}\theta_0$	K	$\frac{1}{2}\theta_0$	K	$\frac{1}{2}\theta_0$	K
0°	1·5708	5°	1·5738	15°	1·5981	50°	1·9356
1	5709	6	5751	20	6200	60	2·1565
2	5713	8	5785	25	6490	70	2·5046
3	5719	10	5828	30	6858	80	3·1534
4	5727	12	5882	40	7868	90	∞

It is worth noticing that (7) of § 91 shows that the period always lies between the limits $2\pi/n$ and $2\pi \sec \theta_0/n$. For the angular speed of Q about O' in Fig. 36 is $2\dot{\phi}$, and the equation shows that

$$2n > 2\dot{\phi} > 2n \cos \tfrac{1}{2}\theta_0,$$

and the same inequality holds for the mean angular speed of Q. Hence $2\pi/n <$ Period $< 2\pi \sec \theta_0/n$.

93. Revolution of Particle in Vertical Circle. Now let the particle in the circular guiding tube be making complete revolutions under gravity. Here we may have given the time of revolution and be required to find the speed of the particle at any position and the time of describing any part of the circle, or we may have given the speed at top or bottom of the given circle and be required to find the period of revolution, the speed at any point, and the time of describing any part of the circle. If the speed at top of the circle is known, that at the bottom is also known, and *vice versa*. For since the speed v along the circle when the thread makes an angle θ with the vertical is $l\dot{\theta}$, we have

$$v\frac{dv}{dt} = -gl \sin \theta \cdot \frac{d\theta}{dt} \quad \text{..............................(1)}$$

or
$$v^2 = 2gl \cos \theta + C, \quad \text{................................(2)}$$

where C is a constant. Thus if v_1 be the speed at the lowest point ($\theta = 0$), we have $C = v_1^2 - 2gl$.

Hence
$$v^2 = v_1^2 - 2gl(1 - \cos \theta), \quad \text{........................(3)}$$

and thus at the highest point, where $v = v_2$ say,
$$v_2^2 = v_1^2 - 4gl, \quad\dots\dots\dots(4)$$
so that we must have, for the motion to be possible, $v_1^2 > 4gl$.
Now $1 - \cos\theta = 2\sin^2\phi$, if $\phi = \tfrac12\theta$, and therefore
$$v^2 = v_1^2 - 4gl\sin^2\phi. \quad\dots\dots\dots(5)$$
Thus, since $v = ds/dt = l\,d\theta/dt$, we get
$$dt = \frac{2l\,d\phi}{\sqrt{v_1^2 - 4gl\sin^2\phi}} = \frac{2l}{v_1}\frac{d\phi}{\sqrt{1 - \dfrac{4gl}{v_1^2}\sin^2\phi}}. \quad\dots\dots(6)$$

Now it is here known that $4gl/v_1^2 < 1$, and thus if we write $k^2 = 4gl/v_1^2$ we get for the time from the lowest point to the inclination θ,
$$t = \frac{2l}{v_1}\int_0^\phi \frac{d\phi}{\sqrt{1 - k^2\sin^2\phi}} = \frac{2l}{v_1} F(k,\phi). \quad\dots\dots(7)$$
The time for any arc, from $\phi = \phi_1$ to $\phi = \phi_2$, say, is thus
$$t_2 - t_1 = \frac{2l}{v_1}\{F(k,\phi_2) - F(k,\phi_1)\}, \quad\dots\dots(8)$$
and, by (11) of §91, stands in the constant ratio $2\sqrt{gl}/v_1$ to the time of describing the corresponding arc in the oscillatory motion in a vertical circle of the same radius.

Again, from the lowest point to the highest, the time τ is given by
$$\tau = \frac{2l}{v_1}\int_0^{\tfrac{\pi}{2}} \frac{d\phi}{\sqrt{1 - k^2\sin^2\phi}} = \frac{2l}{v_1} F\!\left(k, \frac{\pi}{2}\right). \quad\dots\dots(9)$$

The table in §92 may be used to obtain numerical values in particular cases.

If the speed at the highest point be zero, $v_1 = \sqrt{4gl}$ and $k = 1$; the value of τ is infinite, as we have already seen. Since here
$$\sqrt{1 - k^2\sin^2\phi} = \cos\phi,$$
the integral $\left\{\int d\phi/\cos\phi\right\}$ can be found for any limits 0 and α, if $\alpha < \pi/2$, by ordinary integration.

94. Examples on Motion in a Vertical Circle.

Ex. 1. P is a point on a vertical circle of which AB (reading downward) is the vertical diameter and O is the centre. From a point C taken above A on this diameter produced upward, lines CE, CF, each equal in length to a tangent drawn from C to the circle, are laid off respectively downward and upward along the diameter, and a circle is described on EO as diameter. A line PEQ is drawn from P intersecting the latter circle in Q. Prove that if h, h' be the vertical distances of P and Q below C and F respectively, and P move under gravity g in the first circle with speed due to h, then Q will move in the second circle as would a particle under gravity $g \cdot EO^2/2AO^2$ with speed due to h'.

Ex. 2. Two vertical circles touch one another at their lowest points. B denotes the point of contact and AB, $A'B$ are the coincident diameters, of which $A'B$ has the greater length. A line perpendicular to the vertical diameter cuts the circles in P, P'. Show that if P move under gravity g with speed due to its vertical distance from A', then P' *oscillates* in the larger circle with the speed due to its vertical distance from A and gravity $g \cdot A'B^2/AB^2$.

Ex. 3. Prove that if two particles be projected from the same point with the same speed and in the same direction, but at different times, along a narrow circular tube in which they move without friction, and which has its plane vertical, the line joining them always touches a fixed circle.

Ex. 4. To find the condition that a carriage may "loop the loop," that is pass round a vertical circle or curve, and to find the reaction on the guide.

Regarding the carriage as a particle, we see from § 92, that a particle attached to a cord fixed to the centre of the circle will exert outward pull on the cord at the highest point of the circle, if the value of v^2/r exceed g, where v is the speed at the highest point, and r is the radius of the circle. But if the speed is acquired by the descent of the particle from a starting platform, as is customary in "looping the loop" apparatus, v must be the speed acquired by a particle in falling from the level of the platform to that of the top of the circle, that is if the difference of levels be h, we must have $v^2 = 2gh$, so that the least possible value of the "head" h is $r/2$. The head must be greater than $r/2$ to a sufficient extent to allow for loss of head caused by friction and the resistance of the air.

If the curve traversed by the carriage is not a circle, then r is the radius of the circle of curvature at the highest point. Properly, in the case of a carriage, we ought to take the curve for which the head is reckoned at different points as that in which the centroid of the carriage moves, and in so doing we should still neglect the rotation of the wheels.

The equation of energy of the body moving in the gravitational field is
$$\tfrac{1}{2}mv^2 = mg(y + c),$$
where c is the height of the starting level above the level of the origin from which the vertical distance y is measured downward. Thus, for two distances y, y', the energy equation becomes
$$\tfrac{1}{2}mv^2 - \tfrac{1}{2}mv'^2 = mg(y - y').$$

The reaction against the path, R say, is given by the equation
$$\frac{mv^2}{r} = R + mg \cos \psi,$$

where ψ is the inclination of the normal to the curve at P to the vertical, as in Fig. 37. Thus R is zero if $v^2 = gr \cos \psi$, and the carriage will leave the path in its upward journey at the point where this condition is fulfilled.

We can write the last equation in the form

$$\frac{R}{mg} = \frac{2y - r \cos \psi}{r},$$

where y is the head HP required for the speed v. We then have $PC = r$, $MP = r \cos \psi$, and R vanishes when $PM = 2HP$

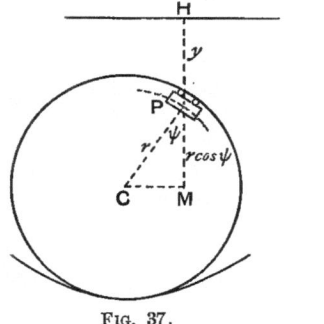
Fig. 37.

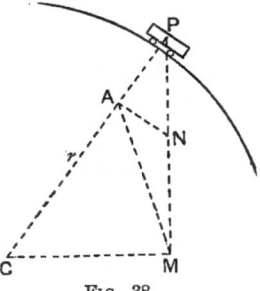
Fig. 38.

When the track is a circle, we see again that for the highest point to be reached $2y$ must be greater than r. At the lowest point of the circle $\cos \psi = -1$, and so $R/mg = (2y + r)/r$. But if at the highest point $2y > r$, at the lowest point $2y + r > r + 4r + r$, that is $(2y + r)/r > 6$. The reaction of the track on the carriage is thus greater than 6 times its weight.

If the carriage be running on the convex side of a curve in a vertical plane, as in Fig. 38, the equation of normal force is

$$\frac{mv^2}{r} = mg \cos \psi - R,$$

or with the same notation as before

$$\frac{R}{mg} = \frac{r \cos \psi - 2y}{r}.$$

Thus R will vanish if $r \cos \psi = 2y$, and will become negative if $r \cos \psi < 2y$, and the carriage can then only be kept on the track by a guard-rail. The figure gives $r = PC$, $MP = r \cos \psi$, and if $MN = 2y$, $R/mg = NP/PC = AP/PM$. Thus R will change sign if MN becomes greater than MP, and the carriage will leave the track unless prevented by a guard-rail.

Ex. 5. At the crown of an arched bridge the curve in which a motor-car passes over it has a radius of 50 feet: at what speed will the wheels of the car just cease to press on the road?

By the last example we have as the condition to be fulfilled $v^2 = gr$, that is $v^2 = 32 \times 50$, or $v = 40$, that is the limiting speed is 40 ft./sec., or 27·27 m./h. The apparent failure of the steering gear may no doubt be sometimes explained in this way. The car running at a high rate of speed passes over a convex part of the road of considerable curvature, and the wheels lose their grip of the surface.

95. Equilibrium of a Plummet under Gravity. Apparent and Real Gravity. A plummet P is hung by a cord of length l from a point fixed relatively to the earth: to find the effect of the earth's rotation. We suppose the earth (Fig. 39) to be a sphere of radius R attracting the plummet at P in the direction towards the centre C with a force G per unit mass. The plummet is in relative equilibrium, and is therefore carried round with the angular speed of the earth in a circle of radius $R \cos L$, where L is the geocentric latitude of P, that is the angle PCE. The plummet is under acceleration $n^2 R \cos L$ towards the centre of the circle in which it moves, and for this a force $mn^2 R \cos L$ is required.

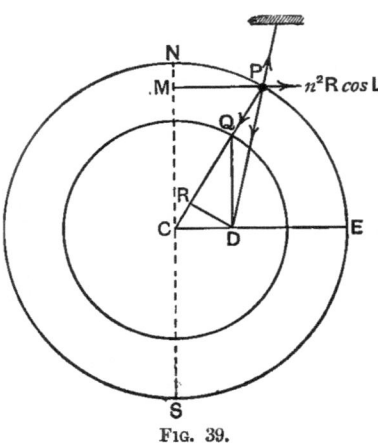

Fig. 39.

This is supplied by the force of gravity mG, which acts towards C; so that we must conceive mG as resolved into two components, one $mn^2 R \cos L$ towards M, and another mg in a direction PD, to be determined, and of such amount that with the first component the resultant is mg. PD is clearly the direction of the cord which supports the plummet.

The sides of the triangle PCD are in the directions of the three forces, and are therefore of lengths proportional to the numerical values of the forces. We thus have

§§ 94, 95]   TRUE AND APPARENT GRAVITY.   169

$\sin \angle CPD / \sin \angle PCD = (n^2 R \cos L)/g$. But $\angle PCD = L$, and therefore
$$\sin \angle CPD = \tfrac{1}{2}\frac{n^2 R}{g} \sin 2L. \quad\quad\quad\quad\quad\quad (1)$$

If, in Fig. 39, $n^2 R$ be represented by CQ, then DQ represents $n^2 R \sin L$, and DR represents $n^2 R \sin L \cos L$ or $\tfrac{1}{2} n^2 R \sin 2L$. If the figure were drawn to scale and CP were taken to represent G, CQ would, as we shall see presently, be only 1/17 of CP.

The direction PD is that of apparent gravity g, and is the line of the plummet-cord. The angle CPD is the deviation of the plumb-line from the true direction of gravity, the direction of G, or, what is the same thing, the excess of the geographical latitude PDE as shown by the inclination of the plumb-line (or the normal to a horizontal mercury surface) to the plane of the equator, over the geocentric latitude L. The acceleration of a particle moving freely under gravity is G; the excess of this over g, and the difference of direction, are however so small that for many purposes, for example an elementary discussion of the flight of projectiles, they may be neglected.

If the earth were not rotating, the plummet at P would be held at rest by a force $mn^2 R \cos L$, applied outwards at P in the direction MP (Fig. 39), without alteration of the direction of the plumb-line, or of the two forces, mG towards C and the pull of the cord mg outwards in the direction DP actually applied to the bob. It is often convenient to put aside the rotation in this way, and consider equilibrium as produced by the introduction of a force acting outward, which is then called the centrifugal force.

The value of $n^2 R \cos L$ is greatest at the equator, and we have in f./s.² units,
$$n^2 R = \left(\frac{2\pi}{86400}\right)^2 21 \times 10^6 = \cdot 111.$$

This is about 1/289 part of the value of G at the equator, and therefore, since $289 = 17^2$, the speed of the earth's rotation would have to be increased to 17 times its present amount in order that the force of gravity might be all employed in giving the necessary centre-ward acceleration to bodies at the equator carried round by the earth. Gravity would then be apparently zero.

In the latitude of Glasgow, $n^2 R \cos L$ is only slightly more than ·062 (f./s.²), and CPD is about $5\tfrac{1}{2}$ minutes of angle.

96. Plummet in Railway Carriage. Apparent Gravity. A plummet is hung in a railway carriage which is subjected to acceleration. The position of equilibrium of the plummet-cord is not along the real vertical, but is inclined to it at an angle depending on the acceleration. If the carriage were running uniformly the equilibrium direction of the plummet would be vertical; but in the case of acceleration there is inclination of the cord, so that the deflection of the plummet is in the opposite direction to that of the acceleration (see Fig. 40). Backward deflection

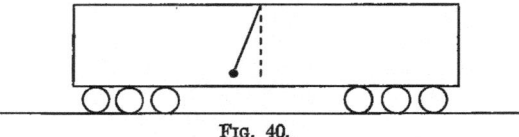

Fig. 40.

accompanies forward acceleration in the line of motion, forward deflection accompanies retardation, outward deflection accompanies motion of the carriage round a curve. The position of equilibrium is that in which the pull exerted by the cord on the bob is just that required to give it the acceleration of the carriage; and if disturbed from that position the plummet will oscillate as a pendulum about it, under a directive force of apparent gravity, differing from the real force of gravity in a manner similar to that in which g was found in the last section to differ from G.

Let α be the equilibrium inclination of the pendulum to the vertical when the acceleration of the carriage is a, and let P be the pull exerted by the cord on the plummet-bob. Then we have

$$ma = P \sin \alpha, \quad mg = P \cos \alpha,$$

so that $\quad \tan \alpha = \dfrac{a}{g}, \quad P = m\sqrt{g^2 + a^2}.$ ....(1)

PLUMB-LINE IN A CARRIAGE.

If the plummet is displaced from this position through an additional angle $\theta - \alpha$ in the plane of α, so that the inclination to the vertical is now θ, its motion relatively to the carriage (that is the motion apparent to an observer in the carriage who takes no cognisance of objects external to it) can be found in the following manner. The horizontal acceleration of the carriage in the direction taken as positive (the line of motion forward say) is a; if the acceleration of the plummet in that direction be $\ddot{x}$, its acceleration relatively to the carriage is $\ddot{x} - a$. If P be the pull applied to the bob by the cord and the deflection be θ, we have $m\ddot{x} = P \sin \theta$, and therefore $m(\ddot{x} - a) = P \sin \theta - ma$. The upward vertical acceleration $\ddot{y}$ is given by

$$m\ddot{y} = P \cos \theta - mg.$$

Thus by Fig. 40, taking the angle the cord there makes with the vertical as θ, we have

$$ml\ddot{\theta} = -(P \sin \theta - ma) \cos \theta + (P \cos \theta - mg) \sin \theta$$

or
$$l\ddot{\theta} = -(g \sin \theta - a \cos \theta). \quad \ldots\ldots\ldots\ldots\ldots(2)$$

But we have seen that if α is the equilibrium inclination of the thread, we have $a = g \tan \alpha$. Hence (1) may be written

$$l \frac{d^2(\theta - \alpha)}{dt^2} = -\frac{g}{\cos \alpha} \sin(\theta - \alpha). \quad \ldots\ldots\ldots\ldots(3)$$

Thus, if $\theta - \alpha$ be small, the motion relative to the carriage is one of simple-harmonic oscillation of the plummet about the inclination α. The period is given by

$$T = 2\pi \sqrt{\frac{l}{g/\cos \alpha}}, \quad \ldots\ldots\ldots\ldots\ldots\ldots(4)$$

that is, the period is that of a pendulum of length l oscillating under the effective gravity $g/\cos \alpha = \sqrt{g^2 + a^2}$, or, as it may be otherwise put, it is the period of a pendulum of length $l \cos \alpha$, under gravity g. If the plummet were deflected slightly sideways from the plane of α, it would oscillate about that plane in the same period $2\pi \sqrt{l \cos \alpha / g}$.

If the carriage be going round a curve so that the bob moves in a circle of radius R at uniform speed v, the plummet is in equilibrium at each instant in the vertical plane through the centre of the curve and the point of suspension, when inclined outward at the angle

$$\alpha = \tan^{-1}(v^2/gR).$$

For the acceleration α is in this case toward the centre of the curve and is v^2/R, so that $a/g = v^2/gR$. The pendulum if disturbed in this plane oscillates about the inclination α in the period

$$T = 2\pi \sqrt{\frac{l}{g/\cos\alpha}}, \quad \ldots\ldots\ldots\ldots\ldots\ldots(5)$$

which, as can easily be seen, is also the period of a small transverse oscillation.

Gravity in the carriage thus seems to have altered in direction by the angle α, and to be increased in intensity in the ratio $\sqrt{1+a^2/g^2}$ to 1.

97. Cycloidal Motion. Cycloidal Pendulum. Consider now motion in a cycloid which has its plane vertical and the tangent at its vertex horizontal. The curve is that traced out by a point P (Fig. 41) of a circle (radius a say) as the circle is rolled without sliding—that is so that the centre of the circle advances a distance $a\theta$ when the circle is turned through an angle θ in its own plane—along a horizontal line AB. If the circle make more than one turn the point traces out successive cycloids which meet in cusps, for example at A and B, for the movement of the point P is there away from or towards the base AB, and the successive cycloids have common vertical tangents. The point I of the circle is at the instant at rest, and therefore the extremity P of IP, regarded as turning about I, is tracing out an element of the curve. It is easy to show that the radius of curvature of the cycloid at P is $2IP = QP = 4a\sin\phi$,

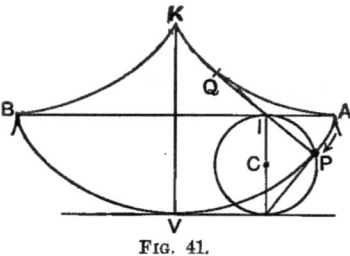

FIG. 41.

if $\phi = \angle AIP$. Hence the arc AP has length $4a(1 - \cos\phi)$, and the distance of P from the vertex V is $4a \cos\phi$, that is $s = 4a \cos\phi$ [see Gibson's *Calculus*, § 146].

Now let a guiding tube in the form and position of the cycloid in Fig. 38 be provided, and let a particle be placed on it at rest in any position P_0. If, as we suppose, there be no friction, the force of gravity along the tube is $mg \cos\phi$, and acts towards the lowest point. We have therefore

$$\frac{d^2 s}{dt^2} = -g \cos\phi = -\frac{g}{4a} s. \quad \ldots\ldots\ldots\ldots\ldots(1)$$

The particle will therefore swing from the position P_0 to another at the same distance from the vertex on the other side, in time $\pi\sqrt{4a/g}$. The whole period will be $2\pi\sqrt{4a/g}$; that is the period is equal to that of a simple pendulum of length $4a$ ($= KV$) vibrating through an infinitesimal arc.

If we differentiate $s = 4a \cos\phi$, we get for the speed, $\dot{s} = -4a \sin\phi \cdot \dot{\phi}$; and for the acceleration,

$$\ddot{s} = -4a \cos\phi \cdot \dot{\phi}^2 - 4a \sin\phi \cdot \ddot{\phi}. \quad \ldots\ldots\ldots(2)$$

Hence we see by (1) that the motion under gravity along the cycloidal guide *from cusp to cusp* is one in which $\dot{\phi}$ has the constant value $\sqrt{g/4a}$, which again gives the period $2\pi\sqrt{4a/g}$. The value of $\ddot{s}$ is here initially $-4a\dot{\phi}^2 = -g$, and remains $-4a \cos\phi \cdot \dot{\phi}^2 = -g \cos\phi$ throughout the motion. Since $\dot{\phi}$ is constant the value of $\dot{s}$ is, in the case stated, everywhere proportional to $\sin\phi$, where ϕ is the angle which the normal to the curve makes with the horizontal. This, as we shall see presently, is an important characteristic of the motion. It shows (since $v^2 = 2gy$, where y is the vertical distance through which the particle has fallen along the guide from rest) that the sine of the angle which the normal to the curve makes with the horizontal (or the tangent to the curve makes with the vertical) is proportional to the square root of the length of the ordinate of the point measured from the line AB joining the cusps. This is a characteristic property of the cycloid.

When the particle starts from P_0, where $\angle AIP = \phi_0$, the value of ϕ at any position P where $\angle AIP = \phi$ is given, as

the reader may verify by the integration of (1), by the equation
$$\dot\phi^2 = \frac{g}{4a}\frac{\cos^2\phi_0 - \cos^2\phi}{\sin^2\phi}, \quad\ldots\ldots\ldots\ldots\ldots(3)$$
which when $\phi_0 = 0$, that is when P_0 is at a cusp, gives $\dot\phi = \sqrt{g/4a}$ as stated above.

A cycloidal pendulum may be realised in the following manner. The evolute of a cycloid consists of the halves of an equal cycloid placed as shown in Fig. 41 [cf. Gibson's *Calculus*, § 146]. Hence if a simple pendulum of length $4a$ be made, and be hung from the cusp of contact of the two halves of the evolute (supposed made as material cycloidal cheeks, with the end of the string clamped between them at K (Fig. 41)), and be made to vibrate, the string will at first be wound upon the cheek on one side, will then unwind itself from that side, next wind itself on the other cheek, then unwind itself, and so on, while the bob moves in an equal cycloid. The motion of the bob, as the student will easily see, is exactly that of the particle in the cycloidal tube discussed above, and the period, whatever the amplitude may be, is $2\pi\sqrt{4a/g}$.

In the construction of such a pendulum the cycloidal cheeks should be made with exactness. Their form is often quite incorrect, especially near the cusp. The length of the pendulum is adjusted by making the string longer than $4a$, and pulling it through between the clamping surfaces, until the bob just reaches to the extremity of one of the cheeks on which the string is wound. It is instructive to hang a circular pendulum of the same length alongside the other, and vibrate them together; when it will be seen that the circular pendulum lags behind the cycloidal for large arcs of vibration.

98. Tautochronous Motion. The discussion, just given, of motion along a cycloid, and the theory of simple-harmonic motion, set forth in §§ 32–34 above, illustrate the fact that the condition $\ddot s = -n^2 s$, is sufficient to ensure that the same time will be taken by a particle to move along any path from rest in any initial position $s = s_0$, to a point of arrival $s = 0$ [s is measured along the path]. The motion is said to be *tautochronous*, and the path for a given field of force is called a tautochrone.

We can prove that the condition is necessary for the case

TAUTOCHRONOUS MOTION.

in which the force depends on the position of the particle. The force must clearly be towards the point of arrival O: let it be $f(s)$. We have $dv = f(s)\,dt$; and therefore
$$v\,dv = -f(s)\,ds.$$
Thus,
$$v_1^2 = -2\int_{s_0}^{s_1} f(s)\,ds = 2\{F(s_0) - F(s_1)\}, \quad \ldots\ldots\ldots\ldots(1)$$
if v_1 be the speed at distance s_1 and $\int_0^s f(s)\,ds = F(s)$.

Hence
$$\frac{dt}{ds} = -\frac{1}{\sqrt{2}}\frac{1}{\sqrt{F(s_0) - F(s)}}, \quad \ldots\ldots\ldots\ldots(2)$$
and if τ be the time of motion of the particle from $s = s_0$ to $s = 0$, we get
$$\tau = \frac{1}{\sqrt{2}}\int_0^{s_0}\frac{ds}{\sqrt{F(s_0) - F(s)}}. \quad \ldots\ldots\ldots\ldots(3)$$

Now let $s = s_0 u$, and the last equation becomes
$$\tau = \frac{1}{\sqrt{2}}\int_0^1 \frac{s_0\,du}{\sqrt{F(s_0) - F(s_0 u)}}, \quad \ldots\ldots\ldots\ldots(4)$$
which for tautochronism must be independent of s_0.

We have
$$\frac{d\tau}{ds_0} = \frac{1}{\sqrt{2}}\int_0^1 \frac{2\{F(s_0) - F(s_0 u)\} - s_0\{F'(s_0) - uF'(s_0 u)\}}{2\{F(s_0) - F(s_0 u)\}^{\frac{3}{2}}}\,du \,; (5)$$
and in order that $d\tau/ds_0$ may vanish, we get the condition
$$2F(s_0) - s_0 F'(s_0) = 2F(s_0 u) - s_0 u F'(s_0 u),$$
that is
$$2F(s) = sF'(s)$$
throughout the motion. Thus we get, by integration,
$$F(s) = Cs^2,$$
that is
$$F'(s) = 2Cs = f(s).$$
The force $f(s)$ is thus proportional to s.

Ex. 1. If the motion of the particle is resisted by a force proportional to the speed, the motion is still tautochronous.

The equation of motion is
$$\ddot{s} + k\dot{s} + n^2 s = 0.$$
If in this we write $s = ue^{-\frac{1}{2}kt}$, we get for the transformed equation
$$\ddot{u} + (n^2 - \tfrac{1}{4}k^2)u = 0.$$

This, when $n^2 > \frac{1}{4}k^2$, is the equation of a tautochronous motion of displacement u. The time required for the passage of the particle to the point $s=0$ from rest at *any* initial distance s_0 is the smallest positive root of the equation

$$\tan(\sqrt{n^2 - \tfrac{1}{4}k^2} \cdot t) = -2\sqrt{n^2 - \tfrac{1}{4}k^2}/k.$$

Ex. 2. If a particle move along a catenary [equation,

$$y = \tfrac{1}{2}c(e^{x/c} + e^{-x/c})]$$

under a force at each point proportional to the ordinate y, and in the direction of y decreasing, the motion is tautochronous for the point of ordinate c, as point of arrival.

Let the force be $n^2 y$. Then the component toward the point of arrival is $n^2 y \, dy/ds = n^2 y s/y = n^2 s$, where s is the distance of the particle at the instant considered from the point of arrival. The proposition is therefore proved. By the last example, it also holds when a resistance proportional to the speed also acts on the particle, and the time of passage is given by an equation similar to that at the end of Ex. 1.

Ex. 3. A particle is constrained to move in an equiangular spiral while acted on by a central force towards the pole of the spiral of amount $n^2 r$, where r is the length of the radius-vector. The component of force along the spiral is $n^2 r \cos\phi$, if ϕ be the constant angle which the radius-vector makes with the tangent. But the distance s, along the curve from the pole, of the point to which the radius-vector is r is $r/\cos\phi$. Hence the component force along the spiral is $n^2 s \cos^2\phi$, which is proportional to s. The motion is therefore tautochronous, and the tautochronism, as before, is unaffected by a resistance proportional to the speed. The time also is found as before.

Ex. 4. Show that a particle moving in an epicycloid or hypocycloid under a central force from or towards the centre of the fixed circle, and proportional to the distance from that point, arrives at the equilibrium position in the same time from any starting point. [The equation of the curve is $r^2 = As^2 + B$, where A and B are constants, and s is the distance along the curve from the equilibrium position of the point at distance r from the centre of force.]

Ex. 5. If the equation of motion of a particle be $\ddot{s} = f(\dot{s}, s)$, where f is a homogeneous function of s and $\dot{s}$ of the first degree, the time from rest at any distance $s = s_0$ to the point of arrival $s = 0$ has the same value.

Consider two initial distances s_0, s_0', and let $s_0' = \kappa s_0$. Since f is homogeneous and of the first degree, the substitution of κs for s' gives $f(\dot{s}', s') = \kappa f(\dot{s}, s)$. Hence the equation $\ddot{s}' = f(\dot{s}', s')$ is converted by this substitution into $\ddot{s} = f(\dot{s}, s)$, the equation for the other motion. One motion therefore differs from the other only in the scale of s, which is in one κ times what it is in the other. If the two motions were started at the same instant, we should have at any subsequent instant $s' = \kappa s$, and s and s' would vanish together. If $s = \phi(t, A, B)$, where

§ 98]   TAUTOCHRONOUS MOTION.   177

A and B are constants, be the finite equation for s, that for s' is $s' = \kappa \phi(t, A, B)$, and the motions are tautochronous.

Ex. 6. The differential equation of tautochronous motion stated in Ex. 5 may be written
$$\ddot{s} = s F\left(\frac{\dot{s}}{s}\right).$$

For $\dot{s}/s$ we write $\dot{u}/f(u)$, and the equation becomes
$$\ddot{u} = \frac{f'(u)}{f(u)} \dot{u}^2 - \frac{\dot{u}^2}{f(u)} + f(u) F\left\{\frac{\dot{u}}{f(u)}\right\}.$$

The last two terms, it is to be noticed, form a homogeneous function of the first degree in $\dot{u}$ and $f(u)$.

The motion begins when $u = 0$, and ends when $f(u) = 0$. For $\dot{u} = 0$ when $\dot{s} = 0$, and since $\dot{s} = \dot{u} s/f(u)$, we see that, as $\ddot{s}$ is not zero when $s = 0$, $s/f(u)$ cannot vanish when $s = 0$. Thus, when $s = 0$, we have $f(u) = 0$, that is at the point of arrival $f(u) = 0$.

It will be observed that the equation just found may be written in the form
$$\ddot{u} = \frac{f'(u)}{f(u)} \dot{u}^2 - \frac{C \dot{u}^2}{f(u)} + f(u) F\left\{\frac{\dot{u}}{f(u)}\right\}.$$

For instead of $f(u)$ we may write $f(u)/C$, where C is any constant; and it is obvious that C cannot appear in the first and last terms.

The theorem stated in this example is due to Lagrange (*Mémoires de Berlin*, 1765, 1770). The proof here given is a version of that due to Bertrand (*Liouville's Journal*, xii. 1847). It is shown by Bertrand that the equation states a sufficient but not necessary condition of tautochronous motion.

Ex. 7. If the equation of motion is
$$\frac{dv^2}{ds} = pv^2 + q,$$
where p and q are given functions of s, prove that the condition of tautochronism is $pq + 2 dq/ds = $ const.

We have here $dv^2/ds = -2\ddot{s} = pv^2 + q$. Thus, by the second form of Lagrange's equation given in Ex. 6, we get, putting $u = s$,
$$\frac{f'(s) - C}{f(s)} = -\tfrac{1}{2} p, \qquad f(s) F\left\{\frac{\dot{s}}{f(s)}\right\} = -\tfrac{1}{2} q.$$

But p and q are functions of s only. We can write $f(s) F\{\dot{s}/f(s)\}$ in the form $A\dot{s} + Bf(s)$, and in the present case $A = 0$. Thus we get for the second of the equations just written and its derivative,
$$B f(s) = -\tfrac{1}{2} q, \qquad B f'(s) = -\tfrac{1}{2} \frac{dq}{ds}.$$

Substitution from these in the first equation gives
$$pq + 2 \frac{dq}{ds} = \text{const.},$$

G. D.   M

178   A TREATISE ON DYNAMICS.   [CH. III.

as stated above. Here, as generally above, s is measured from the point of arrival. If s is measured in the opposite direction, the condition becomes
$$pq - 2\frac{dq}{ds} = \text{const.}$$
It may be proved that this constant is positive.

Ex. 8. If the particle be constrained to move along a given path and be subject to resistance $2\kappa v + \kappa' v^2$: to find the force P along the path at each point which will make the motion tautochronous.

We here suppose v to be the speed along the path towards the point of arrival, so that if s be measured from that point $v = -ds/dt$. The equation of motion is
$$\frac{dv}{dt} + 2\kappa v + \kappa' v^2 = P.$$

Now putting ds/dt for v and multiplying by $e^{-\kappa' s}$, we get
$$-e^{-\kappa' s}\ddot{s} + \kappa' e^{-\kappa' s}\dot{s}^2 - 2\kappa e^{-\kappa' s}\dot{s} = Pe^{-\kappa' s},$$
that is if $u = -e^{-\kappa' s}\dot{s}$, $\ddot{u} + 2\kappa\dot{u} - Pe^{-\kappa' s} = 0$.

The particle will therefore arrive at the point $u = 0$ in the same time, whatever the initial value of u may be, if $-Pe^{-\kappa' s} = n^2 u$, where n^2 is real and positive. But
$$u = \frac{1}{\kappa'}e^{-\kappa' s} + C,$$
and so if u and s begin together, we have $C = -1/\kappa'$. Thus
$$u = \frac{1}{\kappa'}(e^{-\kappa s'} - 1)$$
and
$$P = \frac{n^2}{\kappa'}(e^{\kappa' s} - 1).$$

This theorem is due to Euler. The reader will notice that P has the value $n^2 s$ if κ' be vanishingly small, the result obtained above for zero resistance. We infer from this that the term $2\kappa v$ in the resistance does not affect the tautochronism under the law of force found for zero resistance.

It is supposed here that $n^2 > \kappa^2$, and the time from the initial values of u and s to the point of arrival is the smallest positive root of the equation
$$\tan(\sqrt{n^2 - \kappa^2} \cdot t) = -\frac{\sqrt{n^2 - \kappa^2}}{\kappa},$$
in which it is to be noticed that κ' does not appear. On the other hand the coefficient κ has no influence on the value of the force P. The first of these curious results is noticed by Laplace [*Mécanique Celeste*, t. i. p. 35], who also remarks that the value of the time of passage would not be altered if terms $\kappa'' v^3 + \kappa''' v^4 + \ldots$ were added to the resistance.

The discussion here given is a version of Routh's modification of Laplace's process for the case of the resisted motion of a particle under gravity. [Laplace, *loc. cit.*, Routh, *El. Rigid Dynamics*, § 492.]

Ex. 9. If in the last example the impressed force P be due to gravity we get, measuring z downwards,

$$-g\frac{dz}{ds} = \frac{n^2}{\kappa'}(e^{\kappa's} - 1)$$

or

$$-gz = \frac{n^2}{\kappa'^2}(e^{\kappa's} - \kappa's) + C.$$

If we suppose that $\kappa' = 0$, this equation becomes

$$-gz = \frac{n^2}{2}s^2 + C',$$

the equation of a cycloid. The curve in which the particle is constrained to move must therefore be a cycloid if the impressed force be that of gravity, and there be no resistance depending on the second or higher powers of the speed. This may be compared with the result of § 97 for the cycloidal pendulum.

99. Brachistochrones. The problem of the line of quickest descent, or, to put it more generally, of the path of quickest passage, in a given field of force from one given point in the field to another, is of great interest. It was proposed in 1696 (in the *Acta Erud. Lipsi.*) by John Bernoulli for a particle moving under gravity, and a solution was published by his brother James Bernoulli, in the same journal, in 1697. It seems to have been solved also by John Bernoulli himself and by Leibniz.

The following is a short version of James Bernoulli's solution. In the first place, as the student may easily satisfy himself, the path must lie in the vertical plane containing the two points. Let OGD (Fig. 42) be the curve, and let a small portion of it, CD, be divided into two parts at G; if we assume that the time for each element of the path is a minimum as well as the time for the whole path, then the time along a near element CLD terminated at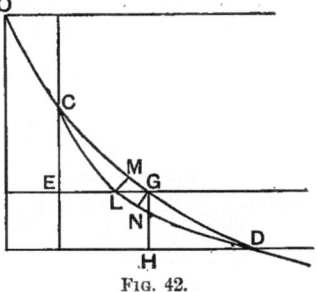

Fig. 42.

C and D must be indefinitely nearly equal to that along CGD. For if we pass gradually to the path of minimum time from paths nearly coinciding with it, there must, from the fact that the time is a minimum, be only a very slight variation from one to the other. The rate of variation of a continuous quantity in the immediate neighbourhood of a maximum or minimum is extremely small—it is absolutely zero at the maximum or minimum itself. Now, in Fig. 42, we may regard CG, GD as straight, the first coinciding with the tangent to the curve at C, the other with the tangent at G; and similarly for CL, LD. Draw LM at right angles to the element CG, and GN at right angles to LD. Then if t, t' be the times of passage along CG and GD, and t_1, t_1' those for CL and LD, we have $t+t'=t_1+t_1'$, and therefore $t-t_1=t_1'-t'$. Also if y and y' be the vertical distances of C and G below O, the starting point, the speeds in the curve at C and G are $\sqrt{2gy}$, $\sqrt{2gy'}$. The latter is also the speed in the adjoining path at L, since LG is horizontal. Thus taking, as we may, the speed along CG and CL as that at C, and the speed along GD and LD as that at G, we have $t-t_1=MG/\sqrt{2gy}$, $t_1'-t'=LN/\sqrt{2gy'}$. But $MG=LG\sin GCE$, $LN=LG\sin DGH$. Calling the first angle ϕ, and the second ϕ', we get finally

$$\sin\phi/v = \sin\phi'/v' \quad \text{or} \quad \sin\phi/\sqrt{2gy} = \sin\phi'/\sqrt{2gy'}.$$

The curve therefore has the property that the speeds along it at successive elements are proportional to the sines of the angles which the tangents to the elements make with the vertical. This, as we have seen (§ 97), is a characteristic property of the cycloid. Since the particle starts from rest at the highest point O, the cycloid has there a cusp. This fact, together with the condition that the final point lies on the curve, determines the cycloid. The cycloidal path is of course not a *free* path. A frictionless guide must be provided.

100. Brachistochrone in Conservative Field of Force. Euler's Theorem. The result just obtained holds for the motion of a particle under any conservative system of coplanar forces. For precisely similar reasoning shows that if θ be the angle which the resultant force F due to the field (that is the resultant of the forces applied to the particle, exclusive of the reaction of the guide) makes with the *normal* to the path at the element ds, then $v=C\cos\theta$, where C is a constant.

We can now find the reaction of the guide on the particle. Since $dv/dt = v\, dv/ds$,

$$mv\frac{dv}{ds} = F\sin\theta, \quad\quad\quad\quad\quad\quad(1)$$

for the reaction gives no component along the path. But $v = C\cos\theta$ gives

$$\frac{1}{v}\frac{dv}{d\theta} = -\frac{\sin\theta}{\cos\theta}. \quad\quad\quad\quad\quad\quad(2)$$

Dividing the former equation by the latter, we obtain

$$\frac{mv^2}{R} = -F\cos\theta, \quad\quad\quad\quad\quad\quad(3)$$

where R is the radius of curvature of the path at ds.

On the left is the force toward the centre of curvature which is supplied by part of the reaction of the guide on the particle. It is important to remark that it is equal and opposite to the normal force with which the particle is pressed against the guide by the field, and which is also balanced by the reaction of the guide. Hence the total reaction is $2F\cos\theta$ toward the centre of curvature, or twice that which would exist if the particle were at rest. This theorem was first given by Euler.

In the cycloid therefore we have

$$\frac{mv^2}{R} = -mg\cos\theta = -mg\sin\phi.$$

In a free path, from one point to the other, we should have

$$\frac{mv^2}{R} = F\cos\theta, \quad\quad\quad\quad\quad\quad(4)$$

that is the field would supply exactly the force on the particle towards the centre of curvature that is required. The concavity of the path would therefore be turned the other way. The brachistochrone would thus be the free path for a system of forces which left the tangential component everywhere unaltered, but reversed the normal component without altering its amount. If the forces of the actual field were replaced by forces represented by the reflection of the former in a mirror containing each element of the path, and perpendicular to the plane of the path at every point, the motion would not be changed, but the guide would be rendered unnecessary.

Conversely, any ordinary free path can be changed into a brachistochrone for a field of force composed of the same tangential component and the normal component *reversed*. For example (see § 126), a particle moves freely in an ellipse under a force directed towards, and varying inversely as the square of the distance of the particle from one of the foci. If this attraction were replaced by a repulsion of *the same amount*, but directed from the *other* focus, the path would become a brachistochrone for the new field. [See a paper by Tait, *Trans. R.S.E.*, 24, 1865.]

101. Variational Method for Brachistochrone under Gravity. It is fairly evident that the motion along the cycloidal guide from one point to the other must be one of least time; but the elementary method adopted above, though instructive in several respects, is defective in that it leads to no general process by which such problems of maxima and minima of integrals as occur in geometry and physics can be solved, and gives no criterion by which to judge whether the result is a maximum or a minimum, or only one of a succession of stationary values. It will be noticed that the problem of the line of quickest descent from one point to another differs from the ordinary questions of maxima and minima dealt with in the differential calculus, for there it is only expressions of known form that are discussed, while in the former we have to find what the expression itself must be, in order that its integral may have a maximum or a minimum value under the circumstances stated.

Thus, in the case of the brachistochrone, it is specified that the integral $\int ds/v$, taken along some path joining the two given points, is to have a minimum value, and we must first discover the form of the path, and so find the manner in which v varies along it, before we can find the least value of the time of passage. As we may have in what follows to employ the method of variations in the discussion of certain problems, we shall give here its solution of the brachistochrone question, in order that the student may understand the notation and form some conception of the general process, which has many applications in higher dynamics.

First, we notice that if we take as rectangular coordinates of an element ds, x horizontal and y vertically downwards from the starting point, we have

$$ds = \{1 + (dy/dx)^2\}^{\frac{1}{2}} dx,$$

and $v = \sqrt{2gy}$. Hence, if t be the time of passage, and $x = a$ be the

BRACHISTOCHRONES.

abscissa of the point of arrival, we have for t the equation

$$t = \int_0^a \sqrt{\frac{1+p^2}{2gy}} \, dx, \quad \ldots\ldots\ldots\ldots(1)$$

where p is written for dy/dx. If we denote $\sqrt{(1+p^2)/2gy}$ by U, we have

$$t = \int_0^a U \, dx. \quad \ldots\ldots\ldots\ldots(2)$$

Here U is a function of y and p, which are both functions of x; we have to find what functions they must be in order that t may be a *minimum*. We therefore impose on y, and consequently also on p, a small variation of value, while x is kept unchanged. It is clear that this will bring about a small change in the course of the curve, which would not be made any more general by also varying x. By equating the effect of this variation (taken to the *first* order of small quantities) on t to zero, we obtain a condition fulfilled by a curve of the shape desired, and a curve of this shape can then be fitted to the given data, and, if it is desired, t calculated. We can then, by carrying the effect of the variation to the second, or, if need be, to a higher order of small quantities, determine whether the condition obtained leads to a maximum or to a minimum, or to neither. The student will observe the similarity of this process to that adopted for ordinary maxima and minima.

Denoting the variation of U by δU, of t by δt, and of y and p by δy and δp, we get

$$\delta t = \int_0^a \delta U \, dx. \quad \ldots\ldots\ldots\ldots(3)$$

But since U contains only y and p,

$$\delta U = \frac{\partial U}{\partial y} \delta y + \frac{\partial U}{\partial p} \delta p, \quad \ldots\ldots\ldots\ldots(4)$$

in which the differential coefficients are partial. Now

$$\delta p = \delta \frac{dy}{dx} = \frac{d}{dx} \delta y, \quad \ldots\ldots\ldots\ldots(5)$$

for by the variation y becomes $y + \delta y$, and therefore dy/dx becomes

$$p + \delta p = d(y + \delta y)/dx = p + d(\delta y)/dx.$$

Thus
$$\delta t = \int_0^a \frac{\partial U}{\partial p} \frac{d}{dx} \delta y \, . \, dx + \int_0^a \frac{\partial U}{\partial y} \delta y \, dx \quad \ldots\ldots\ldots\ldots(6)$$

If we integrate the first term on the right by parts, we obtain

$$\int_0^a \frac{\partial U}{\partial p} \frac{d}{dx} \delta y \, . \, dx = \left[\frac{\partial U}{\partial p} \delta y\right]_0^a - \int \delta y \frac{d}{dx} \frac{\partial U}{\partial p} dx, \quad \ldots\ldots\ldots\ldots(7)$$

where the symbol $[\ ]_0^a$ means that the quantity enclosed is to be evaluated for $x=0$ and $x=a$, and the former value subtracted from the latter. But at each limit y is fixed, and therefore $\delta y = 0$, so that the integrated term vanishes.

184   A TREATISE ON DYNAMICS.   [CH. III.

We get then,
$$\delta t = \int_0^a \left(-\frac{d}{dx}\frac{\partial U}{\partial p} + \frac{\partial U}{\partial y} \right) \delta y \, dx, \quad \ldots\ldots\ldots\ldots\ldots(8)$$

and for the condition sought,
$$-\frac{d}{dx}\frac{\partial U}{\partial p} + \frac{\partial U}{\partial y} = 0. \quad \ldots\ldots\ldots\ldots\ldots(9)$$

Now, differentiating totally, we obtain
$$\frac{dU}{dx} = \frac{\partial U}{\partial p}\frac{dp}{dx} + \frac{\partial U}{\partial y}\frac{dy}{dx} = \frac{d}{dx}\left(p\frac{\partial U}{\partial p}\right) \quad \ldots\ldots\ldots\ldots(10)$$

by the last equation.

Hence
$$U = p\frac{\partial U}{\partial p} + C, \quad \ldots\ldots\ldots\ldots\ldots(11)$$

where C is a constant. Thus U is determined. This equation may be written
$$\sqrt{\frac{1+p^2}{2gy}} = \frac{p^2}{\sqrt{2gy(1+p^2)}} + C$$

or
$$2gy(1+p^2) = 4gc, \quad \ldots\ldots\ldots\ldots\ldots\ldots(12)$$

where c is another constant. This is the differential equation of the curve. Since $v = \sqrt{2gy}$ and $\sqrt{1+p^2} = 1/\sin\phi$, if $\phi = \tan^{-1}(1/p)$, we have
$$v = 2\sqrt{gc}\sin\phi, \quad \ldots\ldots\ldots\ldots\ldots(13)$$

which is the result obtained above by James Bernoulli's elementary process. It is obvious from this result that the curve has a cusp at the starting point.

We can also obtain easily the integral equation of the curve. By (12),
$$p^2 = \frac{2c - y}{y},$$

and therefore
$$dx = \frac{y \, dy}{\sqrt{2cy - y^2}}. \quad \ldots\ldots\ldots\ldots\ldots(14)$$

Integrated, this gives
$$x = -\sqrt{2cy - y^2} + c\cos^{-1}\left(1 - \frac{y}{c}\right) + b, \quad \ldots\ldots\ldots\ldots(15)$$

where b is another constant of integration. This is the equation of a cycloid.

By carrying δU to terms of the second order, we should find the effect of these terms to be positive, and should therefore infer that the condition obtained above renders t a minimum.

102. Variational Method for Brachistochrone in Conservative Field of Coplanar Forces. In the more general case of any system of coplanar forces, we have
$$t = \int_0^a \frac{\sqrt{1+p^2}}{v} dx, \quad \ldots\ldots\ldots\ldots\ldots(1)$$

BRACHISTOCHRONES.

and by precisely the same process as before we get as the condition of least time
$$\frac{d}{dx}\frac{p}{v\sqrt{1+p^2}}+\frac{\sqrt{1+p^2}}{v^2}\frac{\partial v}{\partial y}=0, \quad \ldots\ldots\ldots\ldots\ldots\ldots(2)$$
where it is to be remembered that the first differentiation is total, the second partial. This may be written, if α denote the inclination of the element of path to the horizontal, that is $\alpha = \tan^{-1} p$, in the form
$$\frac{d}{dx}\frac{\sin \alpha}{v} - \frac{1}{\cos \alpha}\frac{\partial}{\partial y}\frac{1}{v} = 0.$$
Hence by reduction, putting $d/dx = \partial/\partial x + p\partial/\partial y$, we get
$$\frac{\cos \alpha}{v}\frac{d\alpha}{dx} = \frac{1}{v^2}\left(\sin \alpha \frac{\partial v}{\partial x} - \cos \alpha \frac{\partial v}{\partial y}\right);$$
or, since $\cos \alpha = dx/ds$, $\sin \alpha = dy/ds$,
$$\frac{mv^2}{R} = mv\left(\frac{\partial v}{\partial x}\frac{dy}{ds} - \frac{\partial v}{\partial y}\frac{dx}{ds}\right). \quad \ldots\ldots\ldots\ldots\ldots\ldots(3)$$
If now the forces, other than those due to the reaction of the guiding curve, be conservative, that is be derivable from a function V of the coordinates as explained in § 50 above, so that the equation of energy
$$T + V = h \quad \ldots\ldots\ldots\ldots\ldots\ldots(4)$$
holds for the motion, we have
$$X = -\frac{\partial V}{\partial x} = mv\frac{\partial v}{\partial x}, \quad Y = -\frac{\partial V}{\partial y} = mv\frac{\partial v}{\partial y}. \quad \ldots\ldots\ldots\ldots(5)$$
Hence (3) becomes $\quad \dfrac{mv^2}{R} = X\dfrac{dy}{ds} - Y\dfrac{dx}{ds} = -F\cos\theta, \quad \ldots\ldots\ldots\ldots\ldots\ldots(6)$

where, as in § 100, θ is the angle between the direction of the resultant force F of the field, at the element ds of the path, and the normal to the element. Hence we have again the theorem stated in § 100, regarding the reaction and the system of forces which would give the same motion unguided.

We can now verify the cosine law of velocity assumed in (2) § 100. From (6) and the relation $mv\, dv/ds = F \sin \theta$, we obtain
$$(R\, dv/ds)/v = -\sin\theta/\cos\theta$$
or
$$\frac{dv}{v} = -\tan\theta\,.\,d\theta,$$
which gives by integration $\quad v = C \cos\theta, \quad \ldots\ldots\ldots\ldots\ldots\ldots(7)$
where C is a constant.

103. Brachistochrone in any Field of Force. If the path is in space of three dimensions and the components of force are X, Y, Z, we have, as before, for the time along the path as prescribed,
$$t = \int \frac{ds}{v}; \quad \ldots\ldots\ldots\ldots\ldots\ldots(1)$$

186 A TREATISE ON DYNAMICS. [CH. III.

and therefore
$$\delta t = \int \frac{v\,\delta ds - ds\,\delta v}{v^2}, \qquad (2)$$

with
$$v\,\delta ds = \dot{x}\,\delta dx + \dot{y}\,\delta dy + \dot{z}\,\delta dz, \qquad (3)$$
$$m\,ds\,\delta v = (X\,\delta x + Y\,\delta y + Z\,\delta z)\,dt. \qquad (4)$$

The latter equation follows from the equation of energy on the supposition that the forces are conservative. Hence, since the operations δd may be taken in the order $d\delta$, as the student may easily convince himself,

$$\int \frac{v\,\delta ds}{v^2} = \int \frac{\dot{x}\,d\delta x + \dot{y}\,d\delta y + \dot{z}\,d\delta z}{v^2}$$
$$= \left[\frac{\dot{x}\,\delta x + \ldots}{v^2}\right] - \int \left\{\delta x\,\frac{d}{dt}\frac{\dot{x}}{v^2} + \delta y\,\frac{d}{dt}\frac{\dot{y}}{v^2} + \ldots\right\} dt. \qquad (5)$$

Again,
$$m\int \frac{ds\,\delta v}{v^2} = \int \frac{X\,\delta x + Y\,\delta y + Z\,\delta z}{v^2}\,dt.$$

Hence, since the integrated terms enclosed in [ ] in (5) vanish when evaluated at the limits—the starting and final points—we obtain by (2), as the condition of a minimum value of t,

$$\delta x\left(m\,\frac{d}{dt}\frac{\dot{x}}{v^2} + \frac{X}{v^2}\right) + \delta y\left(m\,\frac{d}{dt}\frac{\dot{y}}{v^2} + \frac{Y}{v^2}\right) + \ldots = 0, \qquad (6)$$

or, since δx, δy, δz are arbitrary, and this relation must hold whatever values are assigned to them,

$$m\,\frac{d}{dt}\frac{\dot{x}}{v^2} + \frac{X}{v^2} = 0, \quad m\,\frac{d}{dt}\frac{\dot{y}}{v^2} + \frac{Y}{v^2} = 0, \quad m\,\frac{d}{dt}\frac{\dot{z}}{v^2} + \frac{Z}{v^2} = 0. \qquad (7)$$

If we write $v\,d/ds$ for d/dt in these, we obtain

$$\left. \begin{array}{l} mv\dfrac{d}{ds}\left(\dfrac{1}{v}\dfrac{dx}{ds}\right) + \dfrac{X}{v^2} = 0,\ \ldots,\ \ldots, \\[2mm] m\left(v^2\dfrac{d^2x}{ds^2} - v\dfrac{dv}{ds}\dfrac{dx}{ds}\right) + X = 0,\ \ldots,\ \ldots \end{array} \right\} \qquad (8)$$

or

Since the direction-cosines of the tangent to the path at an element ds are dx/ds, dy/ds, dz/ds, and those of the normal in the osculating plane are proportional to d^2x/ds^2, ... (see § 17), we see that if l, m, n are the direction-cosines of a normal to the osculating plane—the binormal—

$$l\frac{dx}{ds} + m\frac{dy}{ds} + n\frac{dz}{ds} = 0,$$
$$l\frac{d^2x}{ds^2} + m\frac{d^2y}{ds^2} + n\frac{d^2z}{ds^2} = 0,$$

and the three equations last obtained give

$$lX + mY + nZ = 0, \qquad (9)$$

so that the resultant of the applied forces lies in the osculating plane.

§ 103]   BRACHISTOCHRONES.   187

If we multiply the first of the equations (8) by d^2x/ds^2, the second by d^2y/ds^2, the third by d^2z/ds^2, and add, we obtain, since

$$1/R = \{(d^2x/ds^2)^2 + \ldots\}^{\frac{1}{2}},$$

$$\frac{mv^2}{R} = -\left(XR\frac{d^2x}{ds^2} + YR\frac{d^2y}{ds^2} + ZR\frac{d^2z}{ds^2}\right)$$

or $\quad\quad \frac{mv^2}{R} = -F\cos\theta,\quad\quad\quad\quad\quad\quad\quad\quad\quad$ ....(10)

where θ is the angle between the direction of the resultant F of the applied forces, and the normal to the element of the path at which the speed is v. This is the theorem already obtained in more restricted cases. As before (§ 102), we might establish the relation

$$v = C\cos\theta. \quad\quad\quad\quad\quad\quad\quad\quad\quad\quad\quad (11)$$

Equation (8) can be modified by writing $mv\,\partial v/\partial x$ for X, $mv\,\partial v/\partial y$ for Y, and $mv\,\partial v/\partial z$ for Z. Thus we obtain

$$\frac{d}{ds}\left(\frac{1}{v}\frac{dx}{ds}\right) = \frac{\partial}{\partial x}\frac{1}{v},\quad \frac{d}{ds}\left(\frac{1}{v}\frac{dy}{ds}\right) = \frac{\partial}{\partial y}\frac{1}{v},\quad \frac{d}{ds}\left(\frac{1}{v}\frac{dz}{ds}\right) = \frac{\partial}{\partial z}\frac{1}{v}. \quad\quad (12)$$

These equations are exactly those of equilibrium of a uniform flexible thread, under tension $1/v$, and in a field of force the components of which are derivable as shown from a function $1/v$ of the coordinates. Any one equation, it is to be noticed, can be derived from the other two.

Now let $vv' = k^2$, where k is a constant, and take a new element of time dt' so that $v' = ds/dt'$. Then, as the student may verify, the equations of motion become

$$\frac{d^2x}{dt'^2} = \frac{1}{2}\frac{\partial v'^2}{\partial x},\quad \frac{d^2y}{dt'^2} = \frac{1}{2}\frac{\partial v'^2}{\partial y},\quad \frac{d^2z}{dt'^2} = \frac{1}{2}\frac{\partial v'^2}{\partial z}. \quad\quad\quad (13)$$

These are obviously the equations of motion of a free particle moving in the brachistochrone, and having speed v' at the point x, y, z at time t'. Take the mass of each particle as unity. The equation of energy of the first is

$$\tfrac{1}{2}v^2 + V = h,$$

that is

$$\tfrac{1}{2}v'^2 = \frac{\tfrac{1}{4}k^4}{-V+h};$$

or, as we may write it, $\quad \tfrac{1}{2}v'^2 + V' = h',\quad\quad\quad\quad\quad\quad$ ....(14)

if $-V' + h' = \tfrac{1}{4}k^4/(-V+h)$.

By this theorem we can pass from brachistochrones to free paths, and *vice versa*. For example, a unit particle moving under a central force F has kinetic energy $\tfrac{1}{2}v^2 = \int F\,dr$. If p be the length of the perpendicular from the centre on the tangent at the point where the speed is v, then $vp = h$. But $v' = k^2/v = k^2p/h$ or $v' = Cp$, where C is a constant. Hence, under a law of force which gives $v' = Cp$, the path will be a brachistochrone. Other applications will be found in the Examples.

104. Conical Pendulum. The conical pendulum consists of an ordinary simple pendulum, the bob of which, however, moves in a horizontal circle (Fig. 43) about the vertical through its point of support, as shown in the diagram.

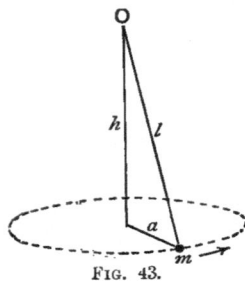

FIG. 43.

If a be the radius of the circle and T the period of revolution, we have $v = 2\pi a/T$. The force on the bob towards the centre of the circle is $m \cdot 4\pi^2 a/T^2$, and must be supplied by the inward pull of the sloping string. Thus, if F be the pull applied by the string to the bob and l be the length of the string, we have

$$F\frac{a}{l} = m\frac{4\pi^2 a}{T^2}. \qquad \ldots\ldots\ldots\ldots(1)$$

But the vertical component of F, that is Fh/l, where h is the height of the point of support above the plane of the circle, must balance mg, so that we have

$$F\frac{h}{l} = mg. \qquad \ldots\ldots\ldots\ldots\ldots\ldots(2)$$

Thus $h/a = gT^2/4\pi^2 a$, and

$$T = 2\pi\sqrt{\frac{h}{g}}, \qquad \ldots\ldots\ldots\ldots\ldots\ldots(3)$$

that is the bob revolves in the period of a simple pendulum of length h.

From this result we can infer the period of a simple pendulum vibrating in the ordinary way through a small arc in a vertical circle. For if a be very small, the circular motion of the bob of the conical pendulum may be regarded as compounded of two simple-harmonic motions at right angles to one another, each being a vibration of the ordinary simple pendulum of length l. Hence, for that pendulum,

$$T = 2\pi\sqrt{l/g}.$$

We shall show later that the motion of the conical pendulum is stable, that is, if the bob be slightly disturbed, say pulled a little out or pushed a little in from the circle by extraneous force, and then left to itself, it will oscillate about its motion of steady revolution in the circle of radius a. The motion of a rigid body, or of a connected system of rigid bodies, which in certain circumstances moves as a conical pendulum, will be discussed in Chapter VII.

105. Double Pendulum. The following pendulum problem is of interest for its physical applications. To the bob B_1 (Fig. 44) of a simple pendulum of length l_1, a second simple pendulum of length l_2 with bob B_2 is attached. The masses of the bobs are m_1, m_2; it is required to find the modes of small vibration in one plane and their periods. We shall see that there are two modes of vibration, and that any actual vibration is compounded of these. Let θ, θ' be the angles, B_1OA_1, B_2CA_2, Fig. 44, which the two threads make with the vertical at time t, and let F_1 be the force applied by the upper string to the bob B_1 of mass m_1, and F_2 that applied by the lower string to the bob B_2 of mass m_2. Then $-F_2$ is the force applied by the lower string to the upper bob. Since the oscillations are

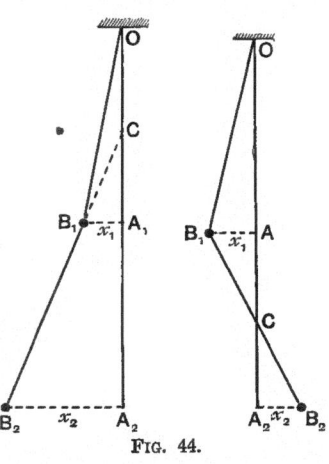

FIG. 44.

small, we may use θ_1 and θ_2 instead of $\sin\theta_1$ and $\sin\theta_2$, and if x_1, x_2 be the horizontal displacements of the bobs from the vertical through the point of support, we can write
$$x_1 = l_1\theta_1, \quad x_2 = l_1\theta_1 + l_2\theta_2.$$
The equations of motion are $m_1\ddot{x}_1 = -F_1\theta_1 + F_2\theta_2$, and $m_2\ddot{x}_2 = -F_2\theta_2$, which, by the values of x_1, x_2 just found, can be written
$$\left.\begin{array}{l} m_1 l_1 \ddot{\theta}_1 = -(m_1+m_2)g\theta_1 + m_2 g\theta_2, \\ m_2(l_1\ddot{\theta}_1 + l_2\ddot{\theta}_2) = -m_2 g\theta_2; \end{array}\right\} \quad\ldots\ldots\ldots\ldots(1)$$
for, since the vertical accelerations are negligible, we have, very approximately,
$$F_1 = (m_1+m_2)g, \quad F_2 = m_2 g. \quad\ldots\ldots\ldots\ldots\ldots\ldots(2)$$

If we now *assume* that the two pendulums vibrate together in the same period, we can settle what the periods of the modes are very easily. For we have then

$$-\frac{\ddot{\theta}_1}{\theta_1} = -\frac{\ddot{\theta}_2}{\theta_2} = \frac{4\pi^2}{T^2}, \quad \ldots\ldots\ldots\ldots\ldots\ldots(3)$$

where T is the mode of vibration adopted by the system. Multiplying both numerator and denominator of the first ratio by l_1, and of the second by l_2, we get, since $l_1\theta_1 = x_1$, $l_2\theta_2 = x_2 - x_1$,

$$\frac{l_2\ddot{\theta}_2}{l_1\ddot{\theta}_1 + l_2\ddot{\theta}_2} = \frac{x_2 - x_1}{x_2}; \quad \ldots\ldots\ldots\ldots\ldots\ldots(4)$$

and therefore, by the second of (1), we have approximately,

$$-\ddot{\theta}_2 = \frac{g(x_2 - x_1)}{x_2 l_2}\theta_2. \quad \ldots\ldots\ldots\ldots\ldots\ldots(5)$$

If the ratio x_1/x_2 is constant, as we here assume it to be, this is the equation of motion of a simple pendulum of length $x_2 l_2/(x_2 - x_1)$ performing small vibrations. Thus

$$T = 2\pi \sqrt{\frac{x_2}{x_2 - x_1} \frac{l_2}{g}}. \quad \ldots\ldots\ldots\ldots\ldots\ldots(6)$$

Hence, if in Fig. 44 we produce the line $B_2 B_1$ back to meet the vertical in C, the length of the equivalent simple pendulum is CB_2 or CA_2. The ratio x_1/x_2 is constant if the displacements x_1, x_2 are in the same phase—and we shall prove immediately that this is the case—and C is a fixed point.

Again, if the deflections θ_1, θ_2 be in opposite directions (as in Fig. 44), we get in the same way $-\ddot{\theta}_2 = g\theta_2(x_1 + x_2)/x_2 l_2$, and

$$T = 2\pi \sqrt{\frac{x_2}{x_1 + x_2} \frac{l_2}{g}}.$$

The point C is now found by the construction in Fig. 44, and the length of the equivalent simple pendulum is, as before, CB_2 or CA_2.

These results, as to the lengths of the equivalent simple pendulums in the two modes of vibration, are due to John Bernoulli, who appears to have been the first to consider this question. [*De Pendulis Multifilibus, Op. Om.* tom. iv. p. 313 *et seq.*]

106. Double Pendulum. We now consider the formal solution of equations (1) of last section, and assume again that the system can vibrate—both parts moving together—in the same period and the same phase, taking account of course of the fact that the deflections are in opposite directions in the second mode; but we shall now justify this assumption by finding an equation for the determination of the periods, the roots of which are proportional to the squares of the reciprocals of the periods, and are real and positive.

Denoting the essentially positive quantities

$(m_1+m_2)g/m_1l_1 + m_2g/m_1l_2$, m_2g/m_1l_2, m_2g/m_2l_2, m_2g/m_2l_2

by a_1, b_1, a_2, b_2 respectively, we can write (1) in the form

$$\left.\begin{array}{l}\ddot{x}_1 = -a_1 x_1 + b_1 x_2, \\ \ddot{x}_2 = a_2 x_1 - b_2 x_2,\end{array}\right\} \quad\ldots\ldots\ldots\ldots\ldots(1)$$

where x_1, x_2 have the same meanings as before. [It will be noticed that here $a_2 = b_2$. These are the equations of motion of the system of two spiral springs shown in Fig. 45.]

Let now $x_1 = A_1 e^{int}$, $x_2 = A_2 e^{int}$ (where $i = \sqrt{-1}$), which will give simple-harmonic motion if n be real. The real part and the imaginary part of e^{int} will satisfy the differential equations separately, as will be found on trial, so that we can easily "realise" the solution. Substituting in (1), we obtain

$$\left.\begin{array}{l}(n^2 - a_1)x_1 + b_1 x_2 = 0, \\ a_2 x_1 + (n^2 - b_2)x_2 = 0.\end{array}\right\} \quad\ldots\ldots\ldots\ldots\ldots(2)$$

These give for the determination of n^2 the equation

$$(n^2 - a_1)(n^2 - b_2) - a_2 b_1 = 0$$

or $\quad n^4 - (a_1 + b_2)n^2 + a_1 b_2 - a_2 b_1 = 0. \ldots\ldots\ldots\ldots(3)$

The roots of this quadratic in n^2 are real if

$(a_1 + b_2)^2 > 4(a_1 b_2 - a_2 b_1)$, that is if $(a_1 - b_2)^2 > -4a_2 b_1$,

which is always the case since a_2 and b_1 are positive. Moreover, the roots are both positive. For the expression on the left of (3) is positive when $n^2 = +\infty$, and also when $n^2 = 0$, since $a_1 b_2 > a_2 b_1$; it is negative when $n^2 = a_1$ and when $n^2 = b_2$. One root, therefore, lies between $+\infty$ and the greater of a_1, b_2 (that is a_1), and the other root lies between the lesser of these (that is b_2) and 0.

Equation (3) also gives, as the student will easily perceive, the two modes of steady vibration of the system as a double conical pendulum.

We can show that when the two connected pendulums are vibrating according to either one of the two modes, the vibrations are in the same phase. For, realising the values of x_1, x_2 assumed above, we write

$$x_1 = K\cos nt + L\sin nt, \quad x_2 = M\cos nt + N\sin nt.$$

Substitution of these values in (2) gives

$$\begin{aligned}\{(n^2-a_1)K+b_1M\}\cos nt+\{(n^2-a_1)L+b_1N\}\sin nt=0,\\ \{(n^2-b_2)M+a_2K\}\cos nt+\{(n^2-b_2)N+a_2L\}\sin nt=0,\end{aligned} \quad (4)$$

and these must hold for all values of t. They will so hold if $(n^2-a_1)(n^2-b_2)-a_2b_1=0$ (which is the equation already found for the determination of n^2), and we obtain

$$\frac{K}{M}=\frac{b_1}{a_1-n^2}=\frac{b_2-n^2}{a_2}, \quad \frac{L}{N}=\frac{b_1}{a_1-n^2}=\frac{b_2-n^2}{a_2}. \quad \ldots\ldots(5)$$

Thus we have $b_1x_2=(a_1-n^2)x_1$, or, which is the same, $a_2x_1=(b_2-n^2)x_2$. Either of these shows that x_1 and x_2 have the same phase in the same mode of vibration. Taking the latter, we get

$$n^2 = \frac{b_2x_2-a_2x_1}{x_2} = \frac{g}{l_2}\frac{x_2-x_1}{x_2}, \quad\ldots\ldots\ldots\ldots\ldots(6)$$

since $b_2 = a_2 = g/l_2$. Thus, for the period, we have

$$T = 2\pi\sqrt{\frac{l_2}{g}\frac{x_2}{x_2-x_1}}, \quad\ldots\ldots\ldots\ldots\ldots(7)$$

which verifies the result otherwise obtained above, as to the length of the equivalent simple pendulum.

107. Double Pendulum. Discussion of Cases. Now it has been proved (§ 106) above that n^2, for one mode of vibration, is greater than a_1 (the greater of a_1 and b_2), and for the other mode is less than b_2. The period is $2\pi/n$, and we see from (7) that in the former case, that of the smaller period, the ratio x_1/x_2 is negative, that is the pendulums are at the same moment deflected in opposite directions, and that in the latter case, when the period has the greater value, the ratio x_1/x_2 is positive, that is the pendulums are at the same moment deflected in the same direction. It is obvious from the action of the forces applied by the cords to the bobs that such a difference of period must exist in the two cases.

If m_1 be very great in comparison with m_2, two cases arise, namely, l_1 small and l_1 large in comparison with l_2. In the former we have, approximately, $a_1 = g/l_1$, and, exactly, $a_2 = b_2 = g/l_2$, while b_1 is very small. Equation (5) of §106 gives approximately $n^2 = a_1 + a_2 b_1/(a_1 - b_2)$, and $n^2 = b_2 - a_2 b_1/(a_1 - b_2)$. Thus the period of the first mode of vibration—which is nearly $2\pi\sqrt{l_1/g}$ and is that for which x_1/x_2 is negative—is diminished in the ratio of $1/\sqrt{1 + a_2 b_1/a_1(a_1 - b_2)}$, and the period of the second mode—which is nearly $2\pi\sqrt{l_2/g}$ and is that for which x_1/x_2 is positive—is increased in the ratio of $1/\sqrt{1 - a_2 b_1/b_2(a_1 - b_2)}$.

In the case of l_1 large in comparison with l_2, we have still, if m_1 be so great as to make b_1 sufficiently small, both these approximations.

In all cases regard must be had to the genesis of the motion, and this will be fully considered later in the discussion of the compound pendulum [Chap. VII.]. But in the case of l_1 large in comparison with l_2, if the large upper pendulum be set into oscillation, and so made to drive the lower pendulum, the period of the former will be little affected, but a steady oscillation of the lower will be set up, and the deflections from the original vertical will be on the same side for both—that is the oscillations of the driven pendulum will be, as we say, *direct*—and the actual period of the driver will be somewhat increased. But if the natural period of the lower pendulum be greater than that of the other, the effect of driving the lower by the upper will be to produce in course of time *inverse* oscillation of the former, that is the deflections will be on opposite sides of the vertical at each instant. The actual period of the driver will be slightly diminished.

108. Physical Analogues of Double Pendulum. We have a physical example in the fact that oceanic tides, produced by the rotation of the earth relatively to the tide-producing bodies, the sun and the moon, are, speaking generally, inverted in low latitudes and direct in high latitudes. The rotating earth is here the driving pendulum. According to what is called the "canal theory" of the tides, the natural period (for an endless canal parallel to the equator) of oscillation of the water in low latitudes (where the canal is longer) is longer and in high latitudes is shorter than that of the tide-producing force, and hence the result stated.

If the free period of the driven pendulum be equal or nearly equal to that of the driver, oscillations of the former of great amplitude will quickly arise. In the tidal case violent oscillations are not found at the latitude of transition from direct to inverted tides: the results of the theory illustrated by the complex pendulum are so modified by friction as to prevent such disturbances (see § 225). A good example, however, is that of two similar pendulums tuned to the same period, and hung opposite one another on the two sides of a plank of wood. When one is set in motion, the other is gradually started by the slight disturbances communicated to the common support. As the motion of the second pendulum increases, that of the first diminishes to almost zero. Then the motion of the second diminishes and that of the first increases, and so on continually until the whole energy has been dissipated in overcoming friction in the air and in the support by which the motion is transferred. The energy is continually exchanged from one pendulum to the other.

A similar case of "sympathy of vibrations" was discussed by Euler in his papers "De Sympathicis Pendulis" (*Nova Comment. Petrop.* xix.). The transference of oscillatory motion from a beam to the scales suspended from its ends and back again was observed by Daniel Bernoulli, and described by him in the *Petersburg Memoirs*. Its theory was given by Euler in the papers referred to: his treatment of the problem and the discussions of later mathematicians have done much to further the theory of the oscillatory motion of connected systems.

DOUBLE PENDULUM.

Lord Kelvin has applied the theory of the complex pendulum to the investigation of the influence of the mode of suspension of a clock or chronometer on the rate of the time-keeper. His paper contains many instructive observations; we can only notice the following. The practice of hanging a watch on a nail (often followed by watch-makers), or in a bag or "watch-holder" hung on a nail, is objectionable, as causing a serious change in the rate of the watch: it is much better to lay it face up on a moderately hard cushion or under a pillow. A marine chronometer should be "firmly attached to the middle of a two feet long plank, with heavy weights near its ends," and this plank should be strapped down on cushions to avoid damage from the tremors of the ship. [See also the worked examples on double pendulums in Chapter VII.]

109. Two Connected Spiral Springs in Same Vertical. The theory of the double pendulum applies also to the arrangement shown in Fig. 45. A mass m_1 is hung by a spring s_1 from a fixed support, and from m_1 is hung a mass m_2 by a spring s_2. If the system be displaced from the equilibrium position along the vertical, vibrations ensue which are given by equations perfectly analogous to those which hold for the double pendulum. For let x_1, x_2 be the downward displacements of m_1, m_2 from the equilibrium position, c_1, c_2 the forces, per unit elongation in each case, which these springs apply to the fastenings at their ends; then if, as we suppose, the masses of the springs be negligible, the spring s_1 pulls upwards on m_1 with a force $c_1 x_1$ and the spring s_2 pulls downwards on m_1 and upwards on m_2 with a force $c_2(x_2 - x_1)$. The equations of motion are therefore

$$\left. \begin{array}{l} m_1 \ddot{x}_1 = -c_1 x_1 + c_2(x_2 - x_1), \\ m_2 \ddot{x}_2 = -c_2(x_2 - x_1), \end{array} \right\} \dots\dots\dots(1)$$

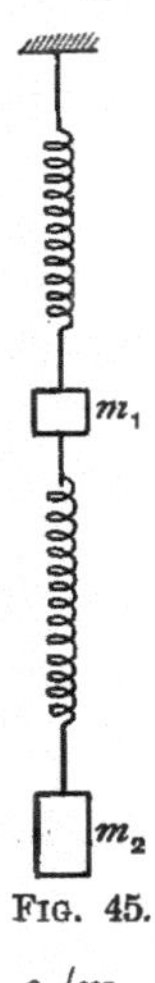

Fig. 45.

or, if we write a_1, b_1, a_2, b_2 for $(c_1+c_2)/m_1$, c_2/m_1, c_2/m_2, c_2/m_2 (so that, as before, $a_2 = b_2$),

$$\ddot{x}_1 = -a_1 x_1 + b_1 x_2, \quad \ddot{x}_2 = a_2 x_1 - b_2 x_2, \dots\dots\dots(2)$$

which are precisely equations (1) of § 106.

The solution is in every respect precisely as before, with a quadratic for n^2 identical with (3) of §106, the roots of which are real and positive. The vibrations are along the vertical, and there are two modes, as above described, one in which the two masses move at each instant in the same direction, the other of shorter period, in which the masses are moving at each instant in opposite directions. The most general motion is compounded of these two motions superimposed.

110. Three or More Connected Springs with Attached Masses. If a third mass be hung from m_2 by a spring s_3, the equations of motion are easily obtained. They are left as an exercise for the student, who may verify that a cubic is now obtained for n^2, the roots of which are real and positive. Thus there are *three* modes of vibration in general, one in which the three masses are all moving at each instant in the same direction, one in which the two lower or the two upper masses move in one direction while the third moves in the opposite direction, and one in which the first and third masses move in the same direction while the second moves in the opposite direction.

Similarly, the case of four or more springs with attached masses might be discussed. If there be p springs with p attached masses, an equation of the pth degree in n^2 gives p distinct modes of vibration.

Lord Kelvin has applied the theory of an arrangement of this kind to the dynamical explanation of the phosphorescence of bodies. To the series of masses thus connected by springs is attached a terminal spring carrying a handle, by means of which a forced vibration of any desired period can be applied. For a description of the apparatus see *Popular Lectures and Addresses*, vol. ii., or *The Baltimore Lectures, passim*.

EXERCISES III.

1. A particle of mass m moves in a spherical bowl without friction. Axes are taken at the centre of the surface, z downwards. Show that the equation of energy can be written

$$\tfrac{1}{2}m(\dot{x}^2+\dot{y}^2+\dot{z}^2)=mgz+h,$$

where h is a constant.

If r be the radius of the bowl, show that the normal force applied by the surface to the particle is given by

$$N = \frac{1}{r}(2h + 3mgz).$$

2. Prove that if C denote the constant double rate of description of area by the projection of the radius drawn from the centre of the bowl to the particle, on a horizontal plane,

$$C^2 = (\dot{x}^2 + \dot{y}^2)(r^2 - z^2) - z^2\dot{z}^2.$$

Hence, show that the equation of energy can be written

$$r^2\dot{z}^2 = 2\left(\frac{h}{m} + gz\right)(r^2 - z^2) - C^2$$

3. The time t for any part of the motion of the particle between the planes $z = z_0$ and $z = z_1$ is given by

$$t = \int_{z_0}^{z_1} \frac{r\,dz}{\pm\sqrt{\phi(z)}},$$

where $\quad\phi(z) = 2\left(\frac{h}{m} + gz\right)(r^2 - z^2) - C^2.$

Prove that $\phi(z) = 0$ has three real roots, one a between $-\infty$ and $-r$, another b between $-r$ and z_0, and a third c between z_0 and $+r$, and that $b + c$ is positive, so that c is always positive. [We have $ab + bc + ca = -r^2$.]

4. Show that if $z = z_0$ initially, where $b < z_0 < c$, the value of z must always lie between b and c.

5. If θ be the angle which the projection of the radius-vector on the horizontal plane through the centre of the surface makes with a fixed horizontal line, find $\dot{\theta}$. If $\dot{z}$ be negative when $z = z_0$ (Ex. 4), show that z will continue to diminish until it reaches the value b, and that then the path of the particle on the surface will have a horizontal tangent. Show further that z will then begin to increase, and will continue to do so until it reaches the value c (when again the particle will be moving horizontally), will again diminish to the value b, and so on continually.

6. Show that the projection of the path on the horizontal plane touches the projection of the circle $z = b$ internally, and the projection of the circle $z = c$ externally, provided both b and c are positive. If, however, b be negative, so that the circle $z = b$ is above and the circle $z = c$ below the centre, show that the path touches both projections externally and the circle $z = 0$ internally.

Prove that if B_1, C_1, B_2 be three successive points of contact with the projections of the circles $z = b, z = c$, the first and third with the

projection of the former circle, and the second with the projection of the latter,
$$\theta_{B_1C_1} = \theta_{C_1B_2},$$
that these angles are described in the same time and correspond to equal areas described by the projection of the radius-vector.

7. Prove that any angle θ_{BC} traversed by the projection of the radius-vector from a point of contact with the projection of the circle $z = b$, to the next point of contact with the projection of the circle $z = c$, is greater than $\pi/2$. [Puiseux, *Journ. de Math.*, 7, 1842.]

We have
$$\theta_{BC} = Cr \int_b^c \frac{dz}{(r^2 - z^2)\sqrt{\phi(z)}},$$
where $\phi(z) = 2(h/m + gz)(r^2 - z^2) - C^2 = 2g(a-z)(b-z)(c-z)$.

But (Ex. 3) $\quad a = -(r^2 + bc)/(b+c),$

so that $\quad \phi(z) = \dfrac{2g}{b+c}(z-b)(c-z)\{z(b+c) + r^2 + bc\},$

and therefore $\quad -C^2 = \dfrac{2g}{b+c}(r-b)(c-r)(r+b)(r+c),$

since $-C^2 = \phi(r)$. These results give
$$\theta_{BC} = r\sqrt{(r^2 - b^2)(r^2 - c^2)} \int_b^c \frac{dz}{(r^2 - z^2)\sqrt{(z-b)(c-z)F}},$$
where $F = z(b+c) + r^2 + bc$, which is positive as z varies from b to c, and has as superior and inferior limits $c^2 + r^2 + 2bc$, $b^2 + r^2 + 2bc$.

Thus, if $\quad I = \int_b^c dz/(r^2 - z^2)\sqrt{(z-b)(c-z)},$

$$\frac{r\sqrt{(r^2 - b^2)(r^2 - c^2)}}{\sqrt{b^2 + r^2 + 2bc}} I > \theta_{BC} > \frac{r\sqrt{(r^2 - b^2)(r^2 - c^2)}}{\sqrt{c^2 + r^2 + 2bc}} I.$$

Now, as the reader may verify,
$$I = \frac{\pi}{2} \frac{\sqrt{(r-b)(r-c)} + \sqrt{(r+b)(r+c)}}{r\sqrt{(r^2 - b^2)(r^2 - c^2)}} = \frac{\pi}{2} \frac{\sqrt{2r^2 + 2bc + 2\sqrt{(r^2 - b^2)(r^2 - c^2)}}}{r\sqrt{(r^2 - b^2)(r^2 - c^2)}},$$
so that θ_{BC} lies between two limits which are both greater than $\pi/2$.

8. Show that as b and c approach equality, θ_{BC} approaches the value $\pi r/\sqrt{r^2 + 3c^2}$.

[The value of θ_{BC} cannot exceed π (Halphen, *Fonct. Ellip.* t. ii., and de Saint-Germain, *Bull. de Sci. Math.*, 1901.]

9. Prove that if the particle is projected horizontally on the surface, in the plane $z = 0$, with speed v_0, the values of θ and t from the starting point are connected by the relation
$$\theta - \frac{1}{2}\frac{v_0}{r} t = \sin^{-1}\frac{v_0\sqrt{z}}{\sqrt{2g(r^2 - z^2)}}.$$

Here $C^2 = v_0^2 r^2$, $2h/m = v_0^2$, and therefore the values of t and θ (Exs. 3 and 7) become

$$t = \int_0^z \frac{r\,dz}{\sqrt{2gz(r^2-z^2)-v_0^2 z^2}}, \qquad \theta = \int_0^z \frac{v_0 r^2 dz}{(r^2-z^2)\sqrt{2gz(r^2-z^2)-v_0^2 z^2}}.$$

From these the result stated can be deduced.

It is to be noticed that the upper limit of $v_0\sqrt{z}/\sqrt{2g(r^2-z^2)}$ is 1, and that therefore z cannot exceed the value given by $2gz^2 + v_0^2 z = 2gr^2$. The value of z is given as an elliptic function of t, and this with the relation stated above enables x, y, and z to be expressed in terms of t. [This theorem is due to Sir George Greenhill.]

10. Reckoning t from the instant at which the particle is at the lowest level it can reach, so that $\dot{z}$ must be negative, prove that, if

$$z = c - (c-b)u^2, \quad k^2 = (c-b)/(c-a), \quad \text{and} \quad \lambda = \sqrt{2g(c-a)}/2r,$$

z is an elliptic function $c - (c-b)\operatorname{sn}^2 \lambda t$, which has the real period

$$\frac{2}{\lambda} \int_0^1 \frac{du}{\sqrt{(1-u^2)(1-k^2 u^2)}}.$$

11. Write down the equations of motion for a position of the particle very close to the bottom of the bowl, and hence show that the x and y equations are

$$\ddot{x} + \frac{g}{r}x = 0, \quad \ddot{y} + \frac{g}{r}y = 0.$$

Hence prove that if when $t=0$, $x=x_0$, $y=0$, $\dot{x}=0$, $\dot{y}=v_0$, the path of the particle is an ellipse of semi-axes x_0, $v_0\sqrt{r/g}$.

12. A particle moves on a concave surface of revolution, the axis of which is vertical. The origin of coordinates z, ρ is taken on the axis; z is measured downward, ρ horizontally, and $z = f(\rho)$ is the equation of the surface. Prove that the energy equation is

$$\tfrac{1}{2}m\{\dot{\rho}^2(1+f'^2) + \rho^2 \dot{\theta}^2\} = mgf(\rho) + h,$$

where f' stands for $f'(\rho)$.

Prove also that the description of areas by the horizontal radius ρ leads to the equations

$$t = \pm \int_{\rho_0}^{\rho} \rho\,d\rho \sqrt{\frac{1+f'^2}{2\rho^2\left\{gf(\rho) + \dfrac{h}{m}\right\} - C^2}},$$

$$\theta - \theta_0 = \pm \int_{\rho_0}^{\rho} C\frac{d\rho}{\rho} \sqrt{\frac{1+f'^2}{2\rho^2\left\{gf(\rho) + \dfrac{h}{m}\right\} - C^2}},$$

where t is the time of passage from the distance ρ_0 from the axis to the distance ρ, and $\theta - \theta_0$ is the angle turned through by the horizontal projection of the radius-vector in the same time.

The square of the resultant speed at time t is

$$\dot{\rho}^2 + \rho^2\dot{\theta}^2 + \dot{z}^2 = \dot{\rho}^2(1+f'^2) + \rho^2\dot{\theta}^2.$$

Eliminating $\dot{\theta}$ from the energy equation by the equation $C = \rho^2\dot{\theta}$, we get the expression for $\dot{t}$, and putting $dt = \rho^2 d\theta/C$, we get the equation for θ.

13. Let α be the angle which the direction of motion at any point makes with a meridian (the intersection with the surface of a vertical plane through the axis of the surface and the point) through the point: prove that

$$C = v\rho \sin \alpha = v_0 \rho_0 \sin \alpha_0,$$

if v_0, ρ_0, α_0 be the initial values of v, ρ, α.
Clearly $\rho\dot{\theta} = v \sin \alpha$, and therefore $v\rho \sin \alpha = C$.

14. Prove that a particle moving under gravity on a surface of revolution with its axis vertical cannot describe a parallel on the surface unless the vertex of the cone of semi-vertical angle $\frac{1}{2}\pi - \beta$, formed by the normals drawn to the surface from points on the parallel, is above the parallel.

It is obvious that the vertex must be as stated, in order that the reaction may balance mg. For equilibrium, we have

$$\frac{v^2}{\rho} \tan \beta = g.$$

But $\cot \beta = -dz/d\rho = -f'(\rho)$. Since z is taken positive downward the vertex of the cone will be above the parallel if $f'(\rho)$ be negative. Thus, we get

$$v = \sqrt{-g\rho f'(\rho)},$$

where ρ is the radius of the parallel and v the speed with which it is traversed.

15. Show that, if $c^2 = C^2 m/2h$, the equations of Ex. 12 become when the particle is under no force, except the reaction of the surface,

$$t = \pm \frac{c}{C}\int_{\rho_0}^{\rho} \rho\, d\rho \sqrt{\frac{1+f'^2}{\rho^2 - c^2}},$$

$$\theta - \theta_0 = \pm c \int_{\rho_0}^{\rho} \frac{d\rho}{\rho} \sqrt{\frac{1+f'^2}{\rho^2 - c^2}}.$$

16. Prove that the particle in this case moves along a geodesic curve on the surface.

The value of v is in this constant and equal to v_0. Also $h = \frac{1}{2}mv_0^2$, and therefore $C^2 m/2h = C^2/v_0^2$. Hence (Ex. 13)

$$\rho \sin \alpha = c.$$

This relation is a characteristic property of a geodesic. [A geodesic is a curve drawn on a surface so that its osculating plane at each point contains the normal to the surface at that point.]

17. Find the path of the particle on a right circular cylinder when no force except the reaction of the surface acts on the particle.

Here ρ is constant, $=a$ say, and therefore $\sin\alpha = c/a$. The path is therefore a helix on the surface. This is otherwise evident.

18. An india-rubber tire of cross-sectional area a is shrunk on the wheel of a motor car, and the tensile force per unit area in the tire is T. If r be the radius of the wheel and P the normal force per unit length of the rim exerted upon the wheel by the tire, show that when the car is at rest $P = aT/r$.

The density of india-rubber is 112 lbs. per cubic foot. If the tensile force in the tire when the car is at rest is 224 pds. per square inch, show that the maximum possible rim-velocity is nearly 65 miles per hour.

19. A particle suspended from a fixed point by a string of length a hangs vertically; it is projected horizontally with speed $\sqrt{7ag/2}$; show that the string will become slack when the particle has risen to a height $3a/2$.

20. A particle is projected from the lowest point of a vertical section of a smooth hollow circular cylinder, of radius r, whose axis is horizontal, so as to move round the inside of the section. Prove that if the velocity of projection is $2\sqrt{gr}$ the particle will leave the circle when the radius through it is inclined to the vertical at $\cos^{-1}(2/3)$.

Prove also that the particle will rise to a total height of $50r/27$ above the point of projection.

21. A particle moves under gravity in a smooth groove in a vertical plane. Write down the equations from which the velocity, and the reaction of the groove on the particle in any position, can be obtained.

If the groove have the form of the parabola $x^2 = 2Ku^2y/g$, with axis vertical and vertex upward, and a particle of unit mass is projected horizontally from the vertex along the groove with speed u, show that at a point where ρ is the radius of curvature, the reaction of the groove on the particle is $u^2(K-1)/\rho$.

22. A particle starts from rest at the highest point of an ellipse of eccentricity e placed with its major axis vertical. Show that if there be no friction the particle will leave the curve at a point for which the cosine, z, of the eccentric angle fulfils the equation

$$e^2z^3 - 3z + 2 = 0.$$

23. A heavy particle moves on the inside of a smooth paraboloid of revolution, axis vertical, vertex downwards, latus rectum $4a$. Prove that when it describes a horizontal circle its angular velocity about the axis is $\sqrt{g/2a}$.

If x_1, x_2 are its greatest and least heights above the vertex, show that the corresponding speeds are $\sqrt{2gx_2}$, $\sqrt{2gx_1}$, respectively. Prove also that when it is at a height x its angular velocity about the axis is

$$(\sqrt{gx_1x_2/2a})/x.$$

24. A train is running smoothly along a curve at the rate of 60 miles an hour, and a pendulum which would ordinarily oscillate seconds is observed to oscillate 121 times in 2 minutes. Show that the radius of the curve in which the train is running is very nearly a quarter of a mile.

25. A heavy particle of mass m moves within a smooth circular tube (radius l) in a vertical plane. It starts with speed V from the lowest point; show that when the line joining the particle to the centre of the tube makes an angle θ with the vertical, the force applied by the particle to the tube is $3mg\cos\theta - 2mg + mV^2/l$.

A carriage of mass 30 pounds moves round the inside of a vertical circular track of radius 8 feet. Its speed when at the lowest point is 40 feet per second. Find the speed at the highest point, and the reaction of the carriage against the track.

26. The bob of a simple conical pendulum of length l, suspended from a point O, is constrained to describe a horizontal circle of radius $\tfrac{1}{2}l$ on the inner surface of a smooth sphere of radius a, of which O is the highest point. If the angular speed of the pendulum be $\sqrt{2g/l}$, determine the stretching force in the pendulum thread, and the thrust on the surface of the sphere.

27. The bob of a simple pendulum is drawn aside through a right angle and let go. Prove that when the thread makes an angle θ with the vertical, the resultant acceleration is $\sqrt{1+3\cos^2\theta}$.

28. Two spiral springs are connected in a vertical series. The two supported masses are 500 grammes each, and each spring is of such strength that 100 grammes produces an extension of 3 cms. Find the period-equation and solve it. Give also the integral equation when the initial displacements are (1) $+1$ cm., $+1$ cm., (2) $+1$ cm., -1 cm., and the initial speeds are zero in each case.

29. A rocket is fired off and rises vertically. If m is the mass burnt, and E the mechanical energy generated per unit time by the burning, prove that the speed of the burnt products relative to the rest of the rocket is $\sqrt{2E/m}$.

30. PQ is a focal chord of a parabola lying in a vertical plane. If PQ is vertical, and TP and TQ are tangents drawn to the parabola at P and Q respectively, show that heavy particles started simultaneously from rest at P and T, and falling along the lines PQ, TQ, will reach Q at the same instant.

31. A number of heavy particles start from rest from a point and slide down straight lines inclined at various angles to the horizontal. Show that the locus of the points reached by them with a given speed is a horizontal plane; show also that the locus of the points reached by them in a given time is a sphere whose highest point is the starting point.

32. A particle falling freely from rest in vacuum acquires a speed L in β seconds. The same particle falls from rest in a medium in which the resistance varies as the speed; its limiting speed is L. Show that the speed after time $\frac{7}{10}\beta$ seconds from the start of the motion is nearly $\frac{1}{2}L$, and that after $\frac{11}{10}\beta$ seconds it is nearly $\frac{2}{3}L$.

33. A particle of mass m moves in a straight line under a constant force F in the direction of motion and a resistance cv^2, where c is a constant and v the speed. Show that if V be the speed acquired in traversing a distance S from rest,
$$S = \frac{m}{2c}\log\frac{F}{F-cV^2}.$$

34. A train moves on a level at V feet per second under a resistance of R pounds per ton given by $R = 6 + \cdot009\,V^2$. Its mass is 100 tons, and a speed of 30 miles per hour is acquired in travelling 1 mile from rest under a constant tractive force F. Show that F is $1\cdot31$ Tons and that the limiting speed is nearly 36 miles per hour.

35. A particle is projected vertically upwards with an initial speed V in a medium whose resistance varies as the square of the speed. If L be the speed for which the resistance offered by the medium is equal to the weight of the particle, show that the time of ascent is $L(\tan^{-1}V/L)/g$, and the distance ascended is $L^2\{\log(1 + V^2/L^2)\}/2g$.

If the speed of projection be small in comparison with k, show that the particle returns to the point of projection with speed $V(1 - V^2/2L^2)$.

36. An engine capable of exerting a maximum pull of P Tons can draw a train weighing M tons with speed V on the level, against resistances which vary as the square of the speed. Prove that the limiting speed of the train when running without steam down a hill inclined at an angle α to the horizontal is $V\sqrt{M\sin\alpha/P}$, and that the maximum speed with which the train can ascend the incline is $V\sqrt{1 - M\sin\alpha/P}$.

37. A ship of 1000 tons displacement is towed at a uniform speed of 15 miles per hour, the pull required being 25 Tons. If the towing rope be slipped, prove that the speed of the ship will fall in five minutes to about $\frac{1}{12}$ of its initial value. [Assume the resistance to vary as the square of the speed.]

38. The engines of a steamer going at full speed are reversed and the steamer is brought to rest in a distance d. Prove that
$$d = (MV^2/2F)\log_e 2,$$
where M is the mass of the steamer, V is full speed, and F is the propelling force (supposed the same for motion ahead and astern). The resistance to the motion is supposed to vary as the square of the speed.

204   A TREATISE ON DYNAMICS.   [CH.

39. On the experimental law that the resistance of similar steamers is proportional to the wetted surface and to the square of the speed, prove that if a 6 ft. model run at a speed of 2 knots in an experimental tank experiences a resistance of 0·2 pound, a similar steamer 600 ft. long and having a displacement of 10000 tons would experience when run at 20 knots a resistance equivalent to an incline of 1/112, and require over 12000 effective horse-power.

40. A ship is steaming at a speed of x knots (relatively to the water) against a tide the speed of which is a knots. If the resistance to motion varies as the nth power of the ship's speed through the water, show that for maximum economy in fuel consumption

$$x = \frac{n+1}{n}a.$$

41. The motion of the bob of a simple pendulum, of length l, is resisted by a force proportional to the speed. The force is equal to the weight of the bob when its speed is $n\sqrt{gl}$, where n is a large number. The pendulum is performing small oscillations. Prove that if $1/n^2$ is negligible, the period is unaffected by the resistance, while the amplitude of the oscillations diminishes in n periods to about $1/20$ of its original value.

42. A thin uniform spherical shell of mass m is filled with a frictionless liquid of the same density. The system descends a rough inclined plane from rest in time t_1, and a solid sphere of the same density and radius makes the same descent in time t_2. If M be the whole mass in each case, show that

$$t_2^2/t_1^2 = 21M/\{15(M-m)+10m\}.$$

43. A system which has one degree of freedom has kinetic energy $T = \frac{1}{2}\mu\dot{\theta}^2$, and potential energy $V = f(\theta)$. Prove that the motion is tautochronous if $V = C\left(\int \mu\, d\theta\right)^2$. [Appell, C.R., 1892.]

Put $\mu\dot{\theta} = s$: then $V = \frac{1}{2}Cs^2$. Hence the theorem by Ex. 8, § 98.

44. Under what condition may the system for which

$$T = \tfrac{1}{2}(A\dot{\theta}^2 + 2B\dot{\theta}\dot{\phi} + C\dot{\phi}^2), \quad V = f(\theta, \phi)$$

where A, B, C are functions of θ and ϕ, be tautochronous? [Appell, *loc. cit.*]

Put $\phi = F(\theta)$, and use the last example.

45. Prove that if a particle move under gravity from rest on one curve in a vertical plane, to another curve in the same plane, in the shortest time, the path is a cycloid which meets the lower curve at right angles and has a cusp on the upper, and that the tangents where the path meets the curve are parallel.

It follows from § 101 that the path is a cycloid, with a cusp as stated. The variation of the time of passage due to displacements of the ends along the curve is to be found. The values of this when first one end, then the other, is fixed must vanish separately, and the results stated are verified.

46. Prove that a given plane curve will be a brachistochrone for a central force $F = \mu/r^n$, and a free path for a central force $\mu'/r^{n'}$, if $n + n' = 2$ and the speed in each case varies as a power of the distance r. [See the last paragraph of § 103.]

47. Show that the lemniscate of Bernoulli is a brachistochrone in a field of potential μr^6, where r is measured from the node. Find the necessary speed.

48. Show that a given plane curve is a brachistochrone for a particle under a central force varying as $p\, dp/dr$ when the speed vanishes with p.

CHAPTER IV.

RESISTED MOTION OF A PARTICLE IN A UNIFORM FIELD OF FORCE.

111. Uniform Field. Resistance kv. We have considered in § 43 the motion of a particle under a force proportional to its distance along its path from a fixed point in the path, and resisted by a force proportional to its speed at each instant, and in §§ 84 ... 86 the rectilineal motion of a particle under a constant force in the line of motion, and resistance varying according to different powers of the speed. We now take the more general case of a projectile in a uniform field of applied force (such as that to which the field of gravity is an approximation), in which a particle is acted on by a force proportional to its mass, and shall suppose that the particle is subject to a resistance according to some power of the speed. For the sake of brevity of reference, we call any direction perpendicular to the field a *horizontal* direction, and refer to any line of applied force as a *vertical*, and speak of the downward or upward vertical according as the direction is with or against the applied force.

We have then, for the horizontal motion of a particle of mass m under a resistance $k\dot{s}$ proportional to the speed $\dot{s}$, the equation

$$m\left(\ddot{x} + k\dot{s}\frac{dx}{ds}\right) = m(\ddot{x} + k\dot{x}) = 0. \quad \ldots\ldots\ldots\ldots\ldots(1)$$

It will be noticed that the component resistance in the direction of x is in this case proportional to $\dot{x}$. The same thing holds of course for $\dot{y}$.

For the motion along the upward vertical, we have

$$m(\ddot{y} + k\dot{y}) = -mg, \quad \ldots\ldots\ldots\ldots\ldots\ldots\ldots(2)$$

where g denotes the uniform force per unit mass on the moving particle. Thus, we have the two differential equations
$$\ddot{x}+k\dot{x}=0, \quad \ddot{y}+k\dot{y}=-g. \quad\ldots\ldots\ldots\ldots\ldots(3)$$

It is clear, in the first place, that $\ddot{y}$ is zero when $\dot{y}$ is such that $k\dot{y}+g=0$, that is when $\dot{y}=-g/k$. Thus, when the particle has a downward speed $=g/k$, the resistance just balances the downward force of gravity, and there is no acceleration. The particle then falls with uniform speed We denote this limit of speed by L.

Integrating (3), and putting $V\cos\alpha$, $V\sin\alpha$ for the initial values of $\dot{x}$, $\dot{y}$, we obtain
$$\dot{x}+kx=V\cos\alpha, \quad \dot{y}+ky=-gt+V\sin\alpha. \quad\ldots\ldots\ldots(4)$$
We multiply by e^{kt}, and again integrate, determining the constants by the conditions that $x=0$, $y=0$ when $t=0$. The results are
$$kx=V\cos\alpha(1-e^{-kt}), \quad ky=-gt+(L+V\sin\alpha)(1-e^{-kt}). \ (5)$$

From the first of these, we get
$$kt=\log\frac{V\cos\alpha}{V\cos\alpha-kx},$$
and therefore the second becomes
$$y=-\frac{L}{k}\log\frac{V\cos\alpha}{V\cos\alpha-kx}+x\left(\frac{L}{V\cos\alpha}+\tan\alpha\right), \ \ldots\ldots(6)$$
which is the equation of the path (the *trajectory*) of a particle projected from the point $x=y=0$, with speed V in a direction inclined at the angle α to a plane drawn through the point of projection perpendicular to the field.

The first of (5) shows that when t is very great, $x=V\cos\alpha/k$, and that then the horizontal velocity is zero. The second of (5) shows that the speed is then L, and that the motion is then vertically downward. Hence a vertical line at distance $V\cos\alpha/k$ from the point of projection is a tangent to the path at a great distance from the origin, measured along the path; that is it is an *asymptote* to the path.

If a tangent to the path be drawn from the point of projection O, to intersect this vertical asymptote in T_0, then, clearly, $V = k \cdot OT_0$. But any point P, at which the speed is v, may be taken as the point of projection. Hence, if the tangent at P (Fig. 46) intersect the vertical asymptote in T, we have $v = k \cdot PT$.

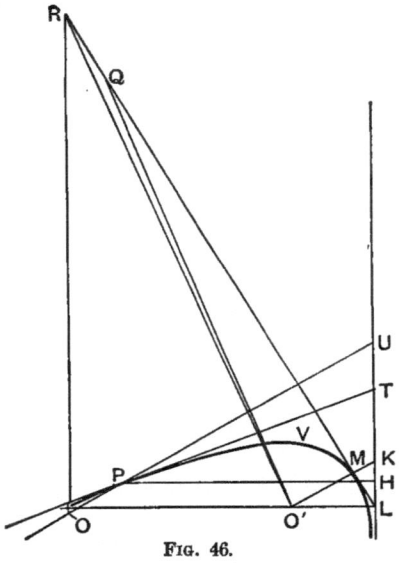

Fig. 46.

[The points O, O' are not on the same level.]

If in (5) we put $t = -\infty$, we find an asymptote at a point far anterior to the point of projection. The inclination of the trajectory there to the axis of x is

$$\tan^{-1}(\dot{y}/\dot{x})_{t=-\infty} = \tan^{-1}\{(L + V\sin\alpha)/V\cos\alpha\};$$

and a line touching the trajectory at the point thus suggested is another asymptote. We shall write β for $\tan^{-1}\{(L + V\sin\alpha)/V\cos\alpha\}$. This asymptote is of much use in the construction of the trajectory.

The equation of the trajectory, with reference to horizontal and vertical axes drawn from any point of the path as origin, can be written

$$y = x\tan\beta - Lt, \quad\ldots\ldots\ldots\ldots\ldots\ldots\ldots(7)$$

which shows that if a line be drawn from any point, P say, at inclination β to the axis of x, a point on the curve whose abscissa with reference to P is x, is, after an interval t, vertically below the corresponding point on the straight line at a distance equal to that which a particle would travel in time t at the speed L. Moreover, the perpendicular distance of the point x, y on the curve from the line $y = x\tan\beta$ is $Lt\cos\beta$.

The component velocity at right angles to this line has thus the constant value $L\cos\beta$. It follows that at the point M (Fig. 46), where the direction of the tangent is perpendicular to the line PU, $y = x\tan\beta$, the speed is $L\cos\beta$, and this is the minimum speed in the path, as we shall see presently.

Differentiating (7) with respect to the time, we obtain

$$\dot{y} = \dot{x}\tan\beta - L, \dots\dots\dots\dots(8)$$

or, if we put ξ, η for $\dot{x}$, $\dot{y}$,

$$\eta = \xi\tan\beta - L, \dots\dots\dots\dots(8')$$

the equation of the hodograph, which is thus a straight line ap (Fig. 47) inclined at the angle β to the axis of x,

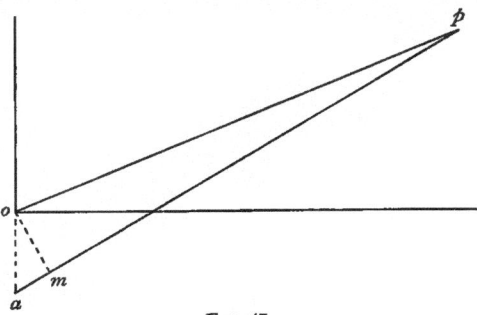

FIG. 47.

and passing through the point $\xi = 0$, $\eta = -L$. The velocity at any point P of the path is represented in magnitude and direction by the line op drawn from the hodographic origin in the direction of the tangent to the path at P to intersect the line (8), that is ap, in p (see Fig. 47). The shortest line

210   A TREATISE ON DYNAMICS.   [CH. IV.

which can be drawn from o to meet the line (8) is the line om which meets the hodograph at right angles. Hence, as stated above, $L \cos \beta$ is the minimum speed.

112. Resistance kv. Trajectory. For the purpose of giving a graphical representation of the path, we calculate the coordinates (1) of the vertex, (2) of the point at which the speed has the least value. By (4) of § 111, $\dot{x} = V \cos \alpha - kx$, hence $\dot{y} = (V \cos \alpha - kx) \tan \beta - L$, and therefore at the vertex, where $\dot{y} = 0$,

$$kx = V \cos \alpha - \frac{L}{\tan \beta} = V \sin \alpha \cot \beta, \quad \ldots\ldots\ldots\ldots(1)$$

since $\tan \beta = (L + V \sin \alpha)/V \cos \alpha$. The horizontal distance of the vertex from the vertical asymptote is thus $L/k \tan \beta$. Again, by (4) of § 111, when $\dot{y} = 0$, $y = -Lt + V \sin \alpha/k$. But by the first of (5) we can eliminate t from the expression for y and obtain with the value of x in (1),

$$ky = -L \log \frac{V \cos \alpha \tan \beta}{L} + V \sin \alpha.$$

If $\dot{x}_0, \dot{y}_0$ denote the initial horizontal and vertical speeds, and v_m the minimum speed, we obtain for the vertex

$$\left.\begin{array}{l} kx = \dot{x}_0 - \dfrac{v_m}{\sin \beta}, \\ ky = \dot{y}_0 - L \log \dfrac{\dot{x}_0 \sin \beta}{v_m}. \end{array}\right\} \ldots\ldots\ldots\ldots\ldots(2)$$

Again, at the point M of minimum speed v_m,

$$\dot{x} = L \cos \beta \sin \beta, \quad \dot{y} = -L \cos^2 \beta.$$

Hence, for this point, since

$$\dot{x} = V \cos \alpha - kx, \quad \dot{y} + ky = -gt + V \sin \alpha,$$

$$\left.\begin{array}{l} kx = \dot{x}_0 - v_m \sin \beta, \\ ky = v_m \cos \beta + \dot{y}_0 - L \log \dfrac{\dot{x}_0}{v_m \sin \beta}. \end{array}\right\} \ldots\ldots\ldots(3)$$

If for any point (for example, the point P) on the trajectory, a line be drawn at inclination β to the horizontal, the intersections of this line, and the tangent at P

with the vertical asymptote, will be at a distance L/k apart, which is the same wherever P may be on the curve. For we find for the distance in question the value

$$\frac{V}{k}(\cos\alpha\tan\beta-\sin\alpha)=\frac{L}{k} \quad\ldots\ldots\ldots\ldots\ldots\ldots(4)$$

by the value of $\tan\beta$. By this means we can draw a tangent to the curve at any point P, the position of which is known. We have only to draw a line from P at the angle β to the horizontal intersecting the vertical asymptote in V, then measure down a distance L/k to a point T on the asymptote. PT is the direction of the tangent at P.

In comparing for a given initial speed the trajectories in different media, each of which resists directly as the speed, we take in each case the vertex V (Fig. 46) as the point of projection, so that the initial speed is horizontal. We have then

$$\tan\beta=\frac{L}{V}=\frac{g}{V}\frac{1}{k} \quad\text{or}\quad k=\frac{g}{V}\cot\beta. \quad\ldots\ldots\ldots\ldots(5)$$

Now the distance of the vertical asymptote from the vertex is V/k. Thus if D denote this distance ($O'L$ in Fig. 46),

$$\tan\beta=\frac{L}{kD} \quad\text{or}\quad k=\frac{L}{D}\cot\beta. \quad\ldots\ldots\ldots\ldots(6)$$

For simplicity we take k as equal to $\cot\beta$, that is we choose the scale of the diagram so that $g/V=1$; (6) shows that this amounts to making in the drawing $D=L$.

113. Construction of Trajectory. We shall now draw the trajectory in this way for $\beta=30°$, and therefore make $k=\sqrt{3}$. We lay down first the vertical asymptote, and choosing a point L upon it lay off the arbitrary length LK. From L we draw the line LQ inclined at 30° to the vertical, and through K draw the line KMO' at right angles to LQ, meeting LQ in M and the horizontal line through L in O'. Then, if we suppose $O'L$ to represent the speed L, the line LQ is the hodograph turned through 90° in the plane of the diagram. Hence, any line $O'Q$ represents the velocity at a point P in the path where the tangent is at right angles to $O'Q$. As the projectile moves in the path, the velocity of Q along the hodograph is the acceleration in the path; and Q moves as a particle in a medium resisting as the first power of the speed.

With the value of k taken, we have for the coordinates of the vertex referred to any origin O on the trajectory,

$$x = \dot{x}_0 \tan\beta - \frac{v_m}{\cos\beta}, \quad y = \dot{y}_0 \tan\beta - L \tan\beta \log\frac{\dot{x}_0 \sin\beta}{v_m} \quad \ldots(1)$$

(where $\dot{x}_0$, $\dot{y}_0$ refer also to the point O), and for the coordinates of the point of minimum speed,

$$\left.\begin{array}{l} x = \dot{x}_0 \tan\beta - v_m \dfrac{\sin^2\beta}{\cos\beta}, \\ y = v_m \sin\beta + \dot{y}_0 \tan\beta - L\tan\beta \log \dfrac{\dot{x}_0}{v_m \sin\beta}. \end{array}\right\} \quad \ldots\ldots(2)$$

Thus, since the distance of the asymptote from the origin O is $\dot{x}_0/k$, the distance of the asymptote from the vertex is $v_m/\cos\beta$. Hence, if we take M as the point of minimum speed, $O'M$ is v_m and $O'L$ is $v_m/\cos\beta$, and the vertex is on the ordinate through O', as already shown above. The coordinates of O' relatively to O are

$$\left.\begin{array}{l} x' = \dot{x}_0 \tan\beta - \dfrac{v_m}{\cos\beta}, \\ y' = \dot{y}_0 \tan\beta - L\tan\beta \log \dfrac{\dot{x}_0}{v_m \sin\beta}. \end{array}\right\} \quad \ldots\ldots\ldots(3)$$

Subtracting y' from the value of y for the vertex, we find that the distance of the vertex from O' is .

$$L \tan\beta \log(1/\sin^2\beta) \quad \text{or} \quad L\tan\beta \times \log_e 4,$$

for $\beta = 30°$. Multiplying the distance LK of the diagram by $\log_e 4$, and laying off a length equal to the result from O' along the vertical, we reach the vertex.

114. Resisted Motion. Tangential and Normal Resolution. We now consider the motion of a projectile under a resistance in its line of motion proportional to a higher power of the speed than the first. It is convenient to use here the tangential and normal resolution of accelerations that has been explained in § 10 above. There it has been shown (1) that the acceleration along the normal to its path at each instant is $v\dot{\phi}$ towards the centre of curvature, where $\dot{\phi}$ is the angular speed (taken positive) with which the tangent is turning at the

§§ 113, 114, 115] RESISTED CURVILINEAR MOTION. 213

point, and (2) that the acceleration in the direction of motion is simply $\dot{v}$. It has also been shown (§§ 10 and 19) that

$$\dot{v} = -v^3 \frac{d^2 t}{ds^2}, \quad v\dot{\phi} = \frac{v^2}{\rho}, \quad \dots\dots\dots\dots\dots(1)$$

where ρ denotes the length of the radius of curvature.

If the resistance per unit mass be some function $f(v)$ of v, we have

$$\dot{v} = -v^3 \frac{d^2 t}{ds^2} = -f(v) - g\sin\psi, \quad \dots\dots\dots\dots\dots(2)$$

where ψ is the angle (Fig. 46) which the forward drawn horizontal line PH at the point makes with the forward drawn tangent PT to the path. But now $\dot{\phi} = -\dot{\psi}$, and therefore, if $u = \dot{x} = v\cos\psi$,

$$-v\dot{\psi} = g\cos\psi, \quad -v^2\dot{\psi} = gv\cos\psi = gu. \quad \dots\dots\dots\dots(3)$$

Also, since the force in the horizontal direction is the resolved part of the resistance in the line of motion,

$$\frac{du}{dt} = -f(v)\cos\psi. \quad \dots\dots\dots\dots\dots(4)$$

The first of equations (3) gives, since $u = v\cos\psi$,

$$-u\dot{\psi} = g\cos^2\psi. \quad \dots\dots\dots\dots\dots(5)$$

Let $\tan\psi$ ($= dy/dx$) be denoted by p; then, if u be known as a function of p, the following relations derived from (5) are useful. Divide (5) by $u^2\cos^2\psi$; then, since

$$\dot{\psi}/u = d\psi/dx \text{ and } (d\psi/dx)/\cos^2\psi = dp/dx,$$

we have
$$-\frac{dx}{dp} = \frac{u^2}{g}. \quad \dots\dots\dots\dots\dots(6)$$

Divided by u, this is
$$-\frac{dt}{dp} = \frac{u}{g}. \quad \dots\dots\dots\dots\dots(7)$$

Again, multiplying (6) by p, we get $-p\,dx/dp = pu^2/g$. But since $p = dy/dx$, $p\,dx/dp = dy/dp$. Hence

$$-\frac{dy}{dp} = p\frac{u^2}{g}. \quad \dots\dots\dots\dots\dots(8)$$

Also $\sqrt{1+p^2} \cdot dx/dp = ds/dp$, where ds is an element of the path.

Hence
$$-\frac{ds}{dp} = \sqrt{1+p^2}\frac{u^2}{g}. \quad \dots\dots\dots\dots\dots(9)$$

Thus the last four equations enable x, t, y and s to be found by direct integration if u is known as a function of p.

115. Resistance = kv^n. We now suppose that $f(v) = kv^n$, where n is some positive integer. If the particle were to fall vertically in the resisting medium, it would finally attain a velocity L, at which the downward acceleration would be zero. Then $kL^n = g$, and therefore $L = (g/k)^{\frac{1}{n}}$. Now, from (4) and (5) of § 114, we obtain, with $f(v) = kv^n$,

$$\frac{du}{d\psi} = \frac{k}{g}v^{n+1} = \frac{k}{g}\left(\frac{u}{\cos\psi}\right)^{n+1}, \quad \ldots\ldots\ldots\ldots\ldots\ldots(1)$$

since $(du/dt)/(d\psi/dt) = du/d\psi$. Thus we have

$$L^n \frac{du}{u^{n+1}} = \frac{d\psi}{(\cos\psi)^{n+1}}. \quad \ldots\ldots\ldots\ldots\ldots\ldots\ldots(2)$$

Integrating from $\psi = \alpha$, to some current value of ψ, we obtain

$$\left(\frac{L}{u}\right)^n - \left(\frac{L}{u_a}\right)^n = -n\int_\alpha^\psi \frac{d\psi}{(\cos\psi)^{n+1}}. \quad \ldots\ldots\ldots\ldots(3)$$

Now $p = \tan\psi$, and therefore $\cos\psi = 1/\sqrt{1+p^2}$, $d\psi = \cos^2\psi \cdot dp$, so that $d\psi/(\cos\psi)^{n+1} = dp/(\cos\psi)^{n-1} = (1+p^2)^{\frac{1}{2}(n-1)}dp$. Hence, starting from the point of projection, we get

$$L^n\left(\frac{1}{u^n} - \frac{1}{u_a^n}\right) = -n\int_{p_a}^p (1+p^2)^{\frac{1}{2}(n-1)}dp. \quad \ldots\ldots\ldots\ldots(4)$$

Here, if n be even, so that $n-1$ is odd, the positive square root of $(1+p^2)^{n-1}$ is to be taken, since the subject of integration is to be positive throughout the possible range of integration, that is from $p = p_a$ to $p = -\infty$.

If the starting point of the integration be the vertex of the path, where $p = 0$, and u_0 now refer to that point, we get, putting

$$F(p) = \int_0^p (1+p^2)^{\frac{1}{2}(n-1)}dp,$$

the equation
$$\frac{L}{u} = \left\{\left(\frac{L}{u_0}\right)^n - nF(p)\right\}^{\frac{1}{n}} \quad \ldots\ldots\ldots\ldots\ldots\ldots(5)$$

or
$$\frac{L}{v} = \frac{1}{\sqrt{1+p^2}}\left\{\left(\frac{L}{u_0}\right)^n - nF(p)\right\}^{\frac{1}{n}}, \quad \ldots\ldots\ldots\ldots(6)$$

which is the polar equation of the hodograph in terms of v and ψ.

116. Particular Cases. Hodograph. Intrinsic Equation of Path. If $n = 1$, $F(p) = p$, and we obtain, still taking the vertex as starting point, $L(1/u_0 - 1/u) = p$, an equation which can also be deduced from (8) of § 111. We have also

$$\frac{L}{v} = \left(\frac{L}{u_0} - p\right)\frac{1}{\sqrt{1+p^2}}, \quad \ldots\ldots\ldots\ldots\ldots\ldots(1)$$

that is
$$\frac{L}{u_0}v\cos\psi - v\sin\psi = \frac{L}{u_0}\xi - \eta = L, \quad \ldots\ldots\ldots\ldots(2)$$

if $\xi, \eta = v(\cos\psi, \sin\psi)$. The hodograph is thus a straight line inclined at the angle $\tan^{-1}(L/u_0)$ to the horizontal, and passing through the points whose horizontal and vertical coordinates are u_0, 0, and 0, $-L$. This result has already been obtained in § 111 above. (See Fig. 46.)

If $n=2$, the law of resistance most nearly fulfilled in a large number of cases in practice,

$$2F'(p) = p\sqrt{1+p^2} + \log(p+\sqrt{1+p^2}).$$

Therefore $\dfrac{L}{v} = \dfrac{1}{\sqrt{1+p^2}} \left\{ \left(\dfrac{L}{u_0}\right)^2 - p\sqrt{1+p^2} - \log(p+\sqrt{1+p^2}) \right\}^{\frac{1}{2}}$, ...(3)

the equation of the hodograph. Expressed in terms of coordinates ξ, η, it is

$$\left(\frac{L}{u_0}\right)^2 \xi^2 - \eta\sqrt{\xi^2+\eta^2} - \xi^2 \log\left\{\frac{1}{\xi}(\eta+\sqrt{\xi^2+\eta^2})\right\} = L^2. \quad\ldots\ldots(4)$$

If $n=3$, $3F'(p) = 3p + p^3$, and so the equation of the hodograph is

$$\frac{L}{v} = \frac{1}{\sqrt{1+p^2}}\left\{\left(\frac{L}{u_0}\right)^3 - (3p+p^3)\right\}^{\frac{1}{3}}$$

or $\left(\dfrac{L}{u_0}\right)^3 \xi^3 - 3\xi^2\eta - \eta^3 = L^3.$ ....(5)

From the nature of the case, ξ cannot have a negative value; its smallest value is zero. It will be seen that each hodograph gives for $\xi=0$, $\eta=-L$. Hence we infer that in each case the path has a vertical asymptote.

If the expression on the right of (5), § 115, be denoted by Q, we have, by equations (6), (8), (9) of § 114 for the equation of the path,

$$x = -\frac{L^2}{g}\int_0^p \frac{dp}{Q^2}, \quad y = -\frac{L^2}{g}\int_0^p \frac{p\,dp}{Q^2}, \quad s = -\frac{L^2}{g}\int_0^p \frac{\sqrt{1+p^2}}{Q^2} dp, \ldots\ldots(6)$$

the last of which is the "intrinsic" equation. For the time of passage, we have, by (7) of § 114,

$$t = \frac{L}{g}\int_0^p \frac{dp}{Q}. \quad\ldots\ldots\ldots\ldots\ldots\ldots\ldots\ldots\ldots\ldots(7)$$

117. Intrinsic Equation of Path for Resistance kv^2. We can find the intrinsic equation of the path for the case of resistance proportional to v^2, as follows. By (4) of § 114, we have

$$\frac{du}{dt} = -kv^2\cos\psi = -ku\frac{ds}{dt}. \quad\ldots\ldots\ldots\ldots\ldots\ldots(1)$$

Hence, dividing both sides by u and integrating, we find

$$u = u_0 e^{-ks}, \quad\ldots\ldots\ldots\ldots\ldots\ldots\ldots\ldots\ldots\ldots(2)$$

if s start from the point at which $u=u_0$. Now, from (3) of § 116, we have

$$\frac{L^2}{u^2} = \frac{L^2}{u_0^2} - p\sqrt{1+p^2} - \log(p+\sqrt{1+p^2}), \quad\ldots\ldots\ldots\ldots(3)$$

and therefore the value of u just found gives

$$\frac{L^2}{u_0^2}(1-e^{2ks})=p\sqrt{1+p^2}+\log(p+\sqrt{1+p^2}), \quad \ldots\ldots\ldots(4)$$

which is the equation sought. The point for which $u=u_0$ is here that for which $p=0$.

The same equation can be obtained at once from the last of (6) (§ 116). For here $Q^2 = L^2/u_0^2 - 2F(p)$, and since

$$F(p)=\int_0^p (1+p^2)^{\frac{1}{2}}dp,$$

$F'(p)=\sqrt{1+p^2}$. Thus, integrating the equation just referred to, we get, since $L^2=g/k$,

$$-s=\frac{1}{2k}\log\frac{L^2}{L^2-2u_0^2F(p)},$$

which agrees with (4).

It is clear from the relation $u=u_0 e^{-ks}$ that as s increases towards $+\infty$, u diminishes towards zero. Equation (4) shows that then p increases numerically towards $-\infty$, that is the motion approaches more and more nearly without limit to the vertical. The path has, like that for the case of resistance simply proportional to speed, a vertical asymptote at a finite distance from the vertex on the right, as shown in Fig. 46. To see that this distance is finite, consider the integral [see (6), § 115]

$$x=-\int_{-q}^{-\infty}\frac{u^2}{g}dp$$

taken from $p=-q$ (where q is a small finite positive quantity) to $p=-\infty$. Then $\dot{x}$ is the horizontal distance between the points for which p has these values. Now, if we take from (5) of § 115 (with the value of $F(p)$ for $n=2$), $L^2/u^2=p^2$ throughout this integration, we shall take L^2/u^2 too small, and therefore u^2 too great. Thus we have

$$x<-\int_{-q}^{-\infty}\frac{L^2}{g}\frac{dp}{p^2},$$

that is $x<1/kq$. Thus x is finite taken between these limits, and must also be finite taken from $p=0$ to $p=-\infty$.

118. Flat Trajectory when Resistance $=kv^2$. If the trajectory be so flat that we may identify s with x, equations (6) of § 114 and (2) of § 117 give for the case of resistance $=kv^2$, the relation

$$-\frac{dp}{dx}=\frac{g}{u_0^2}e^{2kx}=k\left(\frac{L}{u_0}\right)^2 e^{2kx}. \quad \ldots\ldots\ldots\ldots\ldots(1)$$

Hence, integrating and determining the constant by the condition that, when $x=0$, $p=q$, we obtain

$$p=q-\frac{1}{2}\left(\frac{L}{u_0}\right)^2(e^{2kx}-1). \quad \ldots\ldots\ldots\ldots\ldots\ldots(2)$$

Integrating again, and putting $y=0$ when $x=0$, we find

$$y = qx - \frac{1}{4k}\left(\frac{L}{u_0}\right)^2 (e^{2kx} - 2kx - 1) \quad \ldots\ldots\ldots\ldots(3)$$

for the equation of the path.

For the time of flight we get, by (2) of § 117,

$$\frac{dt}{dx} = \frac{1}{u} = \frac{1}{u_0} e^{kx}.$$

Hence, integrating and determining the constant by the condition that when $t=0$, $x=0$, we obtain

$$t = \frac{1}{ku_0}(e^{kx} - 1). \quad \ldots\ldots\ldots\ldots(4)$$

If the resistance to the motion were to cease at the point $x=y=0$, the particle would thereafter move in a parabola of semi-latus rectum $l = u_0^2/g$ (see § 21). Hence we may write (4) in the form

$$t = \frac{1}{k\sqrt{gl}}(e^{kx} - 1). \quad \ldots\ldots\ldots\ldots(5)$$

Equations (3) and (5) are formulae sometimes used by artillerists.

Expanding y from (3) in powers of kx, we get

$$y = qx - \frac{g}{u_0^2}\left(\frac{x^2}{2} + 2k\frac{x^3}{6} + \ldots\right)$$

or

$$y = qx - \frac{x^2}{2l} - 2k\frac{x^3}{6l} - \ldots, \quad \ldots\ldots\ldots\ldots(6)$$

which shows, by the third term on the right, how, in the case of slight resistance, the trajectory deviates from the parabolic form given by

$$y = qx - \frac{x^2}{2l}. \quad \ldots\ldots\ldots\ldots(7)$$

119. Experimental Laws of Resistance to Shot. Ballistic Tables are given in the *Text-Book of Gunnery* used at the Ordnance College, Woolwich, and contain the results of very elaborate experiments made by the Rev. F. Bashforth, B.D., in 1865-1867 and in 1878-1879, by means of a chronograph which enabled the speed at different points in the path of the projectile to be ascertained. We have no space in which to pursue the subject in its more technical aspects, but the reader will find full information in the text-book referred to as to resistances for different speeds and different projectiles, times of flight and distances traversed between different speeds, altitudes attained and so forth, with examples of the solution of practical problems by the tables. One point may however be referred to. No simple law of resistance is found to fit the experimental results. For very low speeds the curves there given show resistance at first nearly proportional to the speed, then resistance increasing more rapidly, a sudden further increase at a little over 1000 feet per second, and then a range from about 1100 ft./sec. to 2200 ft./sec., which the tables show to be one of resistance nearly proportional to the cube of the speed. About 2300 ft./sec. there is a sudden lowering of the upward slope of the curve of resistance, that is at the speed at which air rushes into a vacuous space such as presumably exists at the base of a very quickly moving projectile. When the projectile moves at a higher speed than that of sound—about 1100 ft./sec.— waves produced by its progress cannot outstrip it, and therefore the projectile constantly moves forward into undisturbed air.

Observations were made by Newton in 1687, of the time taken by balls of different diameters and weights (glass shells filled with different materials) to fall a distance of 220 feet from the dome of St. Paul's Cathedral; and it was then found that the resistance at a given speed was proportional to the square of the diameter. This result was confirmed by Bashforth for projectiles of different shapes. Whatever the shape of the shot used—ogival,* hemispheroidal, spherical, or flat headed—the resistance for each shape was proportional to the square of the diameter. The relative resistances may be taken as 2 for flat headed shot, 1·7 for spherical cannon balls, ·95 for modern pointed projectiles, and ·8 for the magazine rifle bullet.

Mr. Bashforth constructed a table of values of a coefficient K, which, used in the equation
$$p = K\left(\frac{v}{1000}\right)^3,$$
gave the resistance p in pounds on an ogival headed shot of 1 inch diameter moving at a speed of v ft./sec. The following short extract gives some of the numbers:

v	K	v	K
100	578·1	1100	106·9
150	385·4	1200	109·6
200	289	1400	104·7
300	192·7	1500	97·9
500	121·9	2000	68·8
1000	75	2800	52

EXERCISES IV.

1. If r denote the retardation produced by the resistance of the air (a given function of the speed) and ψ denote the angle defined in § 114, prove that at a point of minimum speed $r + g \sin \psi = 0$, that where the curvature of the path is greatest (that is, where $\dot{\psi}/\dot{s}$ is

* Shot having a cylindrical body and a pointed head the longitudinal section of which is formed of two arcs of equal circles.

numerically a maximum), $r+\frac{3}{2}g\sin\psi=0$, and that where $\dot\psi$ is numerically a maximum, $r+2g\sin\psi=0$.

2. Let the resistance vary as the speed, and draw through an origin O on the path a line parallel to the oblique asymptote meeting the vertical through a point P on the path in F. Show that if ξ, η denote OF, PF, v_0 be the speed at O, α the elevation at O, and t be the time from O to P, $\xi=(v_0^2+L^2+2Lv_0\sin\alpha)^{\frac{1}{2}}(1-e^{-\kappa t})/k$, $\eta=Lt$.

3. In a medium in which the retardation is kv^2, the length of the arc, measured from the point of projection to any point at which $\tan\psi=p$, is s. If the medium had been non-resisting the length of this arc would have been S. Prove that

$$S=\frac{1}{2k}(e^{2ks}-1).$$

4. Show that if the semi-latus rectum of the unresisted trajectory be l, and α be the angle of elevation,

$$\tan\alpha-p=\frac{1}{2kl}(e^{2ks}-1)$$

for a flat trajectory.

5. A projectile under gravity is resisted by force kv^n. The speeds at the two points where the inclinations of the direction of motion to the horizontal are ψ and $\pi-\psi$ are v_1, v_2, and v is the speed at the vertex. Prove that

$$\frac{1}{v_1^n}+\frac{1}{v_2^n}=\frac{2\cos^n\psi}{v^n}.$$

Prove also that

$$\frac{1}{v_2^n}-\frac{1}{v_1^n}=\frac{2kn}{g}\cos^n\psi\int_0^\psi\sec^{n+1}\psi\,d\psi.$$

6. If the equation of the trajectory be $\cos\psi=f(\rho\cos\psi)$, find the law of resistance.

[Here, by (2) and (4), § 114, $\dot u=-r\cos\psi$, $\dot v=-r-g\sin\psi$, where r is the retardation, so that $rv\,d(\cos\psi)/dv=-g\sin\psi\,d(v\cos\psi)/dv$; and, since $v^2/\rho=g\cos\psi$, $\cos\psi=f(v^2/g)$, so that, since the function f is given, r is found.]

7. If $\rho\cos\psi$ is constant, the path is the catenary of equal strength. Let the concavity be downward. Show that v is constant, and that $r=-g\sin\psi$, so that r is a positive acceleration on the upward slope and a positive retardation on the downward.

8. Apply the result of Ex. 6 to the parabola $\rho\cos^3\psi=2a$.

9. If β have the meaning assigned to it in § 111, prove that if the retardation be kv^3 the speed is a minimum at the point given by the negative root of $p^2-\tan\beta(\tan^2\beta+3)p-1=0$.

CHAPTER V.

FREE MOTION OF A PARTICLE UNDER A FORCE DIRECTED TO A FIXED POINT.

120. Path lies in a Plane. Differential Equation. For a particle moving under the action of a force continually directed towards a fixed point or "centre of force," the equation of motion has been found in §§ 31 and 50. It has been seen that the path lies in a plane, and that the full determination of the motion is theoretically possible when the law of force is given, and the differential equation can be integrated in accordance with the specified initial conditions.

Before proceeding to the discussion of some important particular cases, we give another proof of the fundamental differential equation, including the case in which a force acts on the particle in the line of motion; so that we may have before us all that is necessary to deal with the motion of the particle in a resisting medium, or against such a resisting force as there seems reason to believe may be experienced by a planet absorbing the sun's radiant heat and light, and kept at equilibrium of temperature by its own radiation. [See *Nature*, Aug. 4, 1910.]

Let $1/u$ be the distance of the moving particle P (Fig. 48) at time t from the centre of force O—or, as we call it, the length of the radius-vector—and θ the angle which the line OP makes with a fixed line in the plane of motion. The momentum in the outward direction along the radius-vector is $md(1/u)/dt = -(m\,du/dt)/u^2$. The time-rate of change of this is

$$-\frac{m}{u^2}\frac{d^2u}{dt^2} + 2\frac{m}{u^3}\frac{du}{dt}.$$

ORBITAL MOTION.

The momentum in the forward direction at right angles to the radius-vector is $m\dot{\theta}/u$; and because of this, and the turning round of the radius-vector and lines connected with it at angular speed $\dot{\theta}$, momentum in the outward direction along the radius-vector is growing up at time-rate $-m\dot{\theta}^2/u$ (see §9). Hence the whole rate of growth of momentum along the radius-vector in the position which it occupies at time t is

$$-m\frac{d}{dt}\left(\frac{1}{u^2}\frac{du}{dt}\right) - m\frac{\dot{\theta}^2}{u}.$$

Now let $h = r^2\dot{\theta} = \dot{\theta}/u^2$, so that at the instant the angular momentum about the centre of force is $mh = m\dot{\theta}/u^2$; then $m\dot{\theta}^2/u = mh^2u^3$. Also we have $dt = d\theta/hu^2$, so that the rate of growth of momentum along OP is

$$-m\,hu^2\frac{d}{d\theta}\left(h\frac{du}{d\theta}\right) - mh^2u^3.$$

Hence, if mF is the *inward* force towards the centre, we get

$$\frac{d}{d\theta}\left(h\frac{du}{d\theta}\right) + hu = \frac{F}{hu^2} \quad \ldots\ldots\ldots\ldots\ldots(1)$$

as the radial equation of motion.

121. Effect of Force transverse to Radius-vector. If, as is here supposed, h is not constant, a force transverse to OP in the plane of motion must account for the variation of h. If S be the force, per unit mass of the particle, reckoned positive when in the forward direction, we have $dh/dt = S/u$, or, taking as before the moving particle as timekeeper, that is putting $dt = d\theta/hu^2$, we obtain

$$hu^3\frac{dh}{d\theta} = S. \quad \ldots\ldots\ldots\ldots\ldots\ldots(1)$$

This enables us, when S is known, to write (1) of § 120 in the form

$$\frac{d^2u}{d\theta^2} + u = \frac{F}{h^2u^2} - \frac{S}{h^2u^3}\frac{du}{d\theta}. \quad \ldots\ldots\ldots\ldots(2)$$

Hence, eliminating h, we obtain

$$\frac{d}{d\theta} \frac{\dfrac{F}{u^2} - \dfrac{S}{u^3}\dfrac{du}{d\theta}}{\dfrac{d^2u}{d\theta^2}+u} = \frac{2S}{u^3}. \quad\ldots\ldots\ldots\ldots\ldots(3)$$

In the cases in which the particle is acted on by a force resisting or accelerating in the line of its motion, as well as by a force towards a fixed point O, it is convenient to consider the particle as subject to two component accelerations, one in the forward direction of motion, the other towards O, and to write two corresponding equations of motion. We shall show first that these accelerations can be written in the forms

$$\frac{h}{p^2}\frac{dh}{ds}, \quad \text{and} \quad \frac{h^2}{p^3}\frac{r}{\rho} \quad \text{or} \quad \frac{h^2}{p^3}\frac{dp}{dr},$$

where ρ is the radius of curvature of the path and p the length of the perpendicular let fall from O on the tangent

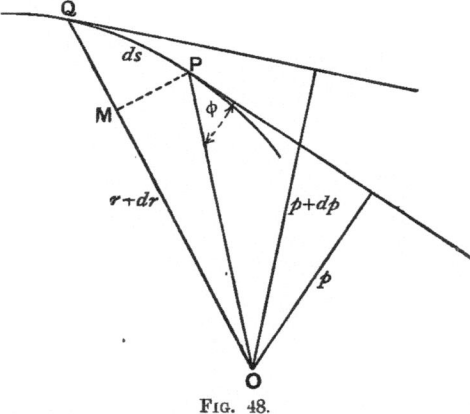

Fig. 48.

to the path at the position P of the particle at time t. For, denoting the tangential and radial accelerations by a_t, a_r, the angle between the radius-vector OP and the

§ 121] ACCELERATION IN ORBITAL MOTION.

tangent at P by ϕ (as shown in Fig. 48), and the radius of curvature at P by ρ, we have by § 10,

$$v\frac{dv}{ds} = a_t - a_r \cos\phi, \quad \frac{v^2}{\rho} = a_r \sin\phi, \quad \dots\dots(4)$$

since $v\,dv/ds$ and v^2/ρ are the rectangular components of acceleration along the tangent in the direction of motion and towards the centre of curvature respectively. The second of these gives, since $\sin\phi = p/r$ and $h = pv$,

$$a_r = \frac{v^2}{\rho}\frac{r}{p} = \frac{h^2}{p^3}\frac{r}{\rho}.$$

But if $p + dp$ be the length of the perpendicular from O on the tangent at a point Q at a distance ds ahead of P on the path, the diagram shows that $dp/r \cos\phi = ds/\rho$, which, since $\cos\phi = dr/ds$, gives $dp/dr = r/\rho$. Hence also

$$a_r = \frac{h^2}{p^3}\frac{dp}{dr} = \frac{h^2}{p^3}\frac{r}{\rho}. \quad \dots\dots\dots\dots\dots\dots(5)$$

We have now, by (4),

$$a_t = v\frac{dv}{ds} + \frac{h^2}{p^3}\frac{dp}{dr}\frac{dr}{ds} = v\frac{dv}{ds} + \frac{h^2}{p^3}\frac{dp}{ds}.$$

But since $v = h/p$, $v\,dv/ds = (h\,dh/ds)/p^2 - (h^2\,dp/ds)/p^3$, and therefore

$$a_t = \frac{h}{p^2}\frac{dh}{ds}. \quad \dots\dots\dots\dots\dots\dots(6)$$

Thus if F be the force toward the point O and S the tangential force in the forward direction, each taken per unit mass of the particle, we have the two equations of motion

$$\frac{h^2}{p^3}\frac{dp}{dr} = F, \quad \frac{h}{p^2}\frac{dh}{ds} = S. \quad \dots\dots\dots(7)$$

If h is constant, S is zero; but the first of these equations still holds, and may be used as an alternative for (1) of § 120.

As an example, let S be a resistance proportional to the speed v, that is, let $S = -kv$. Then $(h\,dh/ds)/p^2 = -kv$.

Multiplying both sides by v ($=ds/dt$) and substituting h^2/v^2 for p^2, we obtain
$$\frac{1}{h}\frac{dh}{dt} = -k,$$
so that $\qquad\qquad h = Ce^{-kt}, \qquad\qquad\qquad\qquad$ (8)

where C is the value of h when $t = 0$.

Again, let $S = -kv^2$; then, after reduction, we get
$$\frac{1}{h}\frac{dh}{ds} = -k,$$
so that $\qquad\qquad h = Ce^{-ks}, \qquad\qquad\qquad\qquad$ (9)

where C is the value of h at the point from which s is measured.

Thus h diminishes exponentially as the time increases in the former case, and as the distance travelled increases, in the latter. The resistance which a planet experiences in its orbit, according to the modern theory of light pressure, is directly proportional to the speed, and therefore h diminishes in that case exponentially as the time increases, according to (8). The coefficient k of the resistance is, however, inversely proportional to the radius of the planet, so that except for a planet of exceedingly small size the effect here calculated is quite insensible.

When S is zero h is constant, and the single differential equation
$$\frac{h^2}{p^3}\frac{dp}{dr} = F, \qquad\qquad\qquad (10)$$
or its equivalent
$$\frac{d^2u}{d\theta^2} + u = \frac{F}{h^2u^2}, \qquad\qquad\qquad (11)$$
determines the motion.

It is useful to remember that, since $v^2 = \dot{s}^2 = r^2\dot{\theta}^2 + \dot{r}^2$, and $h = r^2\dot{\theta} = pv$, we have
$$\left.\begin{array}{l} v^2 = h^2\left\{\left(\dfrac{du}{d\theta}\right)^2 + u^2\right\}, \\[6pt] \dfrac{1}{p^2} = \left(\dfrac{du}{d\theta}\right)^2 + u^2. \end{array}\right\} \qquad (12)$$

122. Speed from Infinity. Exhaustion of Potential Energy. Let us suppose that $F = \mu/r^n$, where μ is a constant (called the *intensity* of the centre) and r is the length of the radius-vector to the position of the particle; and let the particle describe any path in the field of force from a position at distance r_0 from the centre O, to a position at a final distance r_1. If v be the speed of the particle at the instant under consideration, the distance $ds = v\,dt$ is described along the path at P in time dt. If ϕ be the angle which the direction of motion makes with the line drawn from P to the point O, the increase of speed dv is $\mu\cos\phi\,dt/r^n$. But $dt = ds/v$, and therefore $v\,dv = \mu\,ds\cos\phi/r^n$. By Fig. 48 it will be seen that $ds\cos\phi = -dr$, and so $v\,dv = -\mu\,dr/r^n$. Thus we obtain, if $n > 1$ or < 1,

$$\tfrac{1}{2}v_1^2 - \tfrac{1}{2}v_0^2 = -\mu \int_{r_0}^{r_1} \frac{dr}{r^n} = \frac{\mu}{n-1}\left(\frac{1}{r_1^{n-1}} - \frac{1}{r_0^{n-1}}\right). \quad\ldots\ldots(1)$$

This is the equation of energy. On the left is the increase of kinetic energy per unit mass of the particle, and on the right the work done by the force of the field in the displacement. The latter it will be seen is independent of the path of transference.

If the particle start from rest at $r_0 = \infty$, and if $n > 1$,

$$\tfrac{1}{2}v_1^2 = \frac{1}{n-1}\frac{\mu}{r_1^{n-1}}, \quad\ldots\ldots\ldots\ldots\ldots\ldots(2)$$

and v_1 is the speed acquired in the transference of the particle under the action of the field from infinity to the distance r_1. It is called the *speed from infinity* at distance r_1. In the very important case of $n = 2$, we have $v_1^2 = \mu/r_1$. The quantity on the right of (2), multiplied by m, is the amount of potential energy transformed into kinetic energy in the passage of the body of mass m from infinity to the point at distance r_1 from the centre of force. We shall refer to this as the "exhaustion of potential energy from infinity."

The quantity on the right of (1) is the exhaustion of potential energy from distance r_0 to distance r_1, per unit mass.

As an example, we may find the speed from infinity to the surface of the earth, acquired under the influence of the earth's attraction. Here $n = 2$. The speed acquired in time dt at distance r is $\mu\, dt/r^2$, if we suppose the path to be a straight line towards the earth's centre. But at distance r_1, the earth's radius, the speed acquired in time dt is $g\, dt = \mu\, dt/r_1^2$, and therefore $\mu = gr_1^2$. Thus we obtain

$$\tfrac{1}{2}v_1^2 = gr_1 \quad \text{or} \quad v_1^2 = 2gr_1. \quad\quad\quad\quad\quad(3)$$

The speed acquired is therefore that which would be acquired by the particle in falling through a distance equal to the earth's radius under constant acceleration g, equal to that of a falling body at the surface. Taking, as rough values of g and r_1, 32 ft./sec.^{2} and 21×10^6 ft. respectively, we obtain
$$v^2 = 2 \times 32 \times 21 \times 10^6 \text{ ft.}^2/\text{sec.}^2$$
or
$$v = 36700 \text{ ft./sec.} \quad\quad\quad\quad\quad(4)$$
nearly.

When $n > 1$ the contribution made by the term $1/(n-1)r_0^{n-1}$ in (1) is zero for $r_0 = \infty$; but when $n < 1$, this contribution is infinite. We take in that case the speed v_1 acquired by the particle in passing to O, the centre of force, from rest at P_1, distant r_1 from O, and have then

$$\tfrac{1}{2}v_1^2 = \frac{\mu}{1-n}\, r_1^{1-n}. \quad\quad\quad\quad\quad(5)$$

If $n = 1$, both the speed from infinity and the speed from P_1 to O are infinite. We shall see presently how the determination of the orbit in particular cases depends on the speed from infinity.

123. Concavity or Convexity of Orbit towards Centre of Force. It is evident that, if the central force is an attraction, the path, or *orbit* as we shall call it, is concave towards the centre of force. For the attraction is continually causing the direction of motion to deviate from the tangent in the direction *towards* the centre O, that is to bend round O. If the central force is a repulsion the bending is the other way, that is the orbit is convex towards the centre of force. It is easy to arrive at these

§§ 122, 123, 124]   LAW OF DIRECT DISTANCE.   227

results analytically. We have already, § 121, established the equation

$$\frac{h^2}{p^3}\frac{r}{\rho} = \frac{h^2}{p^3}\frac{dp}{dr} = F. \quad\ldots\ldots\ldots\ldots\ldots\ldots(1)$$

It follows that if F is positive, that is, is an attraction, dp/dr is positive (for p is always taken positive), that is p increases with r and diminishes with r, in other words the orbit is concave toward O. If F is negative the force is a repulsion, and p increases or diminishes as r diminishes or increases, and the path is convex toward O.

124. Force varying directly as Distance. Consider a particle moving under the influence of a force which acts along the line joining the position of the particle to a fixed point O, and is proportional to the length r of this line. If μr, where μ is positive, be the magnitude of the force per unit mass of the particle, the equations of motion with reference to axes of x and y with origin at O are

$$\ddot{x} + \mu x = 0, \quad \ddot{y} + \mu y = 0, \quad\ldots\ldots\ldots\ldots\ldots(1)$$

if the force is an attraction, and

$$\ddot{x} - \mu x = 0, \quad \ddot{y} - \mu y = 0, \quad\ldots\ldots\ldots\ldots\ldots(2)$$

if it is a repulsion.

The axes need not be at right angles to one another, and we may choose their directions so that Ox is in the direction of the initial displacement and Oy in that of the initial motion. Thus initially we have $x = a$, $\dot{x} = 0$, $y = 0$, $\dot{y} = v_0$, since the complete solution of either differential equation gives for x or y a value of the form

$$A \cos \sqrt{\mu} t + B \sin \sqrt{\mu} t.$$

For the case of attraction then, we have

$$x = a \cos \sqrt{\mu} t, \quad y = b \sin \sqrt{\mu} t, \quad\ldots\ldots\ldots\ldots(3)$$

where $b = v_0/\sqrt{\mu}$. For these values of x and y satisfy the differential equations and the chosen initial conditions. Eliminating t by the relation $\cos^2\sqrt{\mu} t + \sin^2\sqrt{\mu} t = 1$, we get

$$\frac{x^2}{a^2} + \frac{y^2}{b^2} = 1, \quad\ldots\ldots\ldots\ldots\ldots\ldots(4)$$

the equation of an ellipse of which the axes of coordinates are a pair of conjugate axes and the centre is the centre of force.

In the case of repulsion the complete solution of either differential equation gives for x or y a value of the form $Ae^{\sqrt{\mu}t}+Be^{-\sqrt{\mu}t}$, and, in accordance with this, values of x and y which satisfy the same initial conditions are

$$x=\tfrac{1}{2}a(e^{\sqrt{\mu}t}+e^{-\sqrt{\mu}t}), \quad y=\tfrac{1}{2}b(e^{\sqrt{\mu}t}-e^{-\sqrt{\mu}t}), \quad \ldots\ldots(5)$$

where $b=v_0/\sqrt{\mu}$. From these we get

$$\frac{x^2}{a^2}-\frac{y^2}{b^2}=1, \quad \ldots\ldots\ldots\ldots\ldots\ldots\ldots\ldots(6)$$

the equation of a hyperbola of which the axes of coordinates are conjugate axes, and of which the centre is the centre of force.

The construction of the path in either case is simply the construction of a conic of which a pair of conjugate axes are given in position and magnitude. The reader may verify that the criterion of concavity or convexity stated in last section is satisfied.

It is clear that the period of description of the path is $2\pi/\sqrt{\mu}$ in the case of the ellipse, that is, since twice the area is $2\pi ab \sin\alpha$, where α is the angle between the axes, the double rate of description of area is $\sqrt{\mu}ab\sin\alpha$, or $\sqrt{\mu}ab$ if a, b be the principal semi-axes. In the case of the hyperbola, if we calculate $(x\dot{y}-y\dot{x})\sin\alpha$ from the values of x and y given above, we obtain

$$h=(x\dot{y}-y\dot{x})\sin\phi=\sqrt{\mu}ab\sin\alpha.$$

It will be observed that by (3) the rate of description of area leads in the case of the ellipse to the value $\sqrt{\mu}t$ for the eccentric angle described in any time t, and that the period of revolution depends only on μ, and is therefore the same for all ellipses described about the same centre of force.

125. Examples of Force in Different Cases. The equations

$$F=\frac{h^2}{p^3}\frac{dp}{dr}=\frac{h^2}{p^3}\frac{r}{\rho}$$

are very useful for finding the force when the orbit is given.

§§ 124, 125]   EXAMPLES.   229

Ex. 1. To find F when the orbit is an ellipse with the centre of force at a focus O.

Let r be the distance of a point P on the orbit from O, p, p' the lengths of the perpendiculars from O and the other focus on the tangent at P, and $2a$ the sum of the focal distances of P. Then, for the ellipse $p'/p = (2a-r)/r$, or, since $pp' = b^2$ (where b is the length of the semi-axis minor), $b^2/p^2 = (2a-r)/r$. Thus differentiating, we obtain

$$(dp/dr)/p^3 = a/b^2 r^2,$$

and therefore

$$F = \frac{ah^2}{b^2}\frac{1}{r^2} = \frac{h^2}{l}\frac{1}{r^2},$$

where l is the length of the semi-latus rectum. Thus the force varies as the inverse square of the distance from O.

Ex. 2. Prove that at P (Ex. 1) the curvature, $1/\rho$, of the ellipse has the value $a\sin^3\phi/b^2$, where ϕ is the angle between OP and the tangent at P.

By § 121 we have $1/\rho = (dp/dr)/r = ap^3/b^2 r^3$. But we have similarly from the other focal distance $2a-r$ and perpendicular p',

$$1/\rho = ap'^3/b^2(2a-r)^3.$$

Thus

$$\frac{1}{\rho^2} = \frac{a^2}{b^4}\frac{(pp')^3}{r^3(2a-r)^3} = \frac{a^2}{b^4}\sin^6\phi,$$

since $r\sin\phi = p$, $(2a-r)\sin\phi = p'$. Hence

$$\frac{1}{\rho} = \frac{a}{b^2}\sin^3\phi.$$

Ex. 3. To find F when the orbit is an equiangular spiral with the centre of force at the pole of the spiral.

The equation of the spiral is (see Ex. 3, at end of Chapter I.) $r = ae^{\theta\cot\phi}$, where ϕ is the constant inclination of the tangent to the radius-vector from the origin to the point of contact. We have then

$$p = r\sin\phi \quad \text{and} \quad dp/dr = \sin\phi.$$

Hence

$$F = \frac{h^2}{p^3}\frac{dp}{dr} = \frac{h^2}{\sin^2\phi}\frac{1}{r^3}.$$

Since ϕ is constant, F varies as the inverse cube of the distance r. Since $1/\rho = \sin\phi/r$, F also varies as the cube of the curvature.

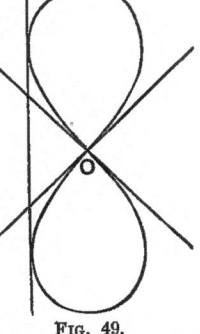

Fig. 49.

Ex. 4. To find F when the orbit is the lemniscate of Bernoulli, and the centre of force is the node of the curve (Fig. 49).

The equation of the curve is $r^2 = a^2\cos 2\theta$. Hence if, as before, ϕ denote the inclination of the tangent to the radius-vector, we have

230   A TREATISE ON DYNAMICS.   [CH. V.

(since $\sin\phi = r\,d\theta/ds$), $1/p^2 = (dr^2 + r^2 d\theta^2)/r^4 d\theta^2 = a^4/r^6$. We get by differentiation for the value of F,

$$\frac{h^2}{p^3}\frac{dp}{dr} = 3\frac{h^2 a^4}{r^7}.$$

The force varies as the inverse seventh power of the distance r. The curvature is $3r/a^2$.

In this case the orbit passes through the centre of force O. At that point the speed is infinite, for it will be seen that the force when the particle is near the origin is along the path and is very great. It will be observed that the acceleration is very great when the particle is approaching the centre, and that the retardation is correspondingly great after the particle has passed the centre, so that at an infinite distance the speed is finite.

Ex. 5. To find the force when the orbit is the curve of which the equation is $r^n = a^n \cos n\theta$.

This curve is the lemniscate when $n = 2$. By the same process as in Ex. 4, we get $1/p^2 = a^{2n}/r^{2n+2}$. Hence

$$F = \frac{h^2}{p^3}\frac{dp}{dr} = (n+1)\frac{h^2 a^{2n}}{r^{2n+3}}.$$

126. Solution of Differential Equation in Various Cases. Energy Relations. We can use the differential equation

$$\frac{d^2 u}{d\theta^2} + u = \frac{F}{h^2 u^2}$$

either to find the force when the orbit is given or to find the orbit when the force is given. In the latter case the differential equation must be solved, and this is not always possible except under special conditions, for example equality of the speed of projection to the so-called speed from infinity.

We now consider first the motion of a particle under gravitational attraction directed towards a fixed point O. In this case $n = 2$, so that $F = \mu u^2$, and the equation of motion is

$$\frac{d^2 u}{d\theta^2} + u = \frac{\mu}{h^2}. \quad\dots\dots\dots\dots\dots\dots(1)$$

The complete solution of this equation is

$$u = \frac{\mu}{h^2} + A\cos(\theta - \alpha), \quad\dots\dots\dots\dots(2)$$

where A and α are constants. (See § 28 above for another method of obtaining this result.)

For $\theta - \alpha = 0$, $u = \mu/h^2 + A$, $r = 1/(\mu/h^2 + A)$, and for $\theta - \alpha = \pi$, $u = \mu/h^2 - A$, $r = 1/(\mu/h^2 - A)$. If the first value of r be denoted by $a(1-e)$ and the second by $a(1+e)$, or the first be denoted by $a(e-1)$ and the second by $-a(1+e)$, according as $\mu/h^2 >$ or $< A$, we obtain in the first case

$$A = \frac{e}{a(1-e^2)}, \quad \frac{\mu}{h^2} = \frac{1}{a(1-e^2)}, \quad \ldots\ldots\ldots(3)$$

and in the second

$$A = \frac{e}{a(e^2-1)}, \quad \frac{\mu}{h^2} = \frac{1}{a(e^2-1)}. \quad \ldots\ldots\ldots(4)$$

In the first case $e < 1$ and in the second $e > 1$. Equation (2) becomes

$$r = \frac{1}{u} = \frac{a(1-e^2)}{1 + e\cos(\theta - \alpha)} \quad \ldots\ldots\ldots(5)$$

in the former case, and

$$r = \frac{1}{u} = \frac{a(e^2-1)}{1 + e\cos(\theta - \alpha)} \quad \ldots\ldots\ldots(6)$$

in the latter. In each case the equation is that of a conic section of which the centre of force is a focus. The curve is an ellipse in the former case and a hyperbola in the latter, the length of the major axis is $2a$ and the eccentricity e in both cases; while $2a(1-e^2)$ is the so-called *parameter* of the ellipse, and $2a(e^2-1)$ that of the hyperbola, that is twice the length of the radius-vector drawn from O at right angles to the major axis.

Now $\quad v^2 = h^2 \left\{ \left(\frac{\partial u}{\partial \theta}\right)^2 + u^2 \right\} = h^2 \frac{1 + e^2 + 2e\cos(\theta - \alpha)}{a^2(1-e^2)^2}. \quad \ldots(7)$

But by what precedes $h^2/a(1-e^2) = \mu$ or $h^2/a(e^2-1) = \mu$, according as $e <$ or > 1, that is according as the curve is an ellipse or a hyperbola. Thus we have

$$v^2 = \mu\left[\frac{2\{1 + e\cos(\theta - \alpha)\}}{\pm a(1-e^2)} \mp \frac{1-e^2}{a(1-e^2)}\right] = \mu\left(\frac{2}{r} \mp \frac{1}{a}\right), \ldots(8)$$

according as the orbit is an ellipse or a hyperbola.

When $e = 1$, the orbit is a parabola, and the equation for v^2 is

$$v^2 = \frac{2\mu}{r}. \quad \ldots\ldots\ldots\ldots\ldots\ldots(9)$$

We shall deal with this case specially when it arises. It is to be noticed that the speed at each point is that from infinity to the point in question. Hence $\sqrt{2\mu/r}$ is called the *parabolic speed*.

It will be shown later [see Ex. 15, § 131] that $m\mu/2a$ is the time-average of the kinetic energy *in either orbit*, so that (8) asserts that the kinetic energy $\frac{1}{2}mv^2$ of the particle at distance r from the centre of force in the hyperbolic orbit exceeds, and in the elliptic orbit falls short of, the exhaustion of potential energy (§ 122) $m\mu/r$, from infinity to the distance r, by the time-average of the kinetic energy in the orbit.

127. Discrimination of Orbit. The speed from infinity to the distance r is, as we have seen (§ 122), $2\mu/r$. Hence we have, by (8) of § 126 (putting now v_∞ for the speed from infinity),
$$v_\infty^2 - v^2 = \frac{\mu}{a} = \frac{h^2}{a^2(1-e^2)}, \quad \ldots\ldots\ldots\ldots(1)$$
in the case of the ellipse, and
$$v_\infty^2 - v^2 = -\frac{\mu}{a} = -\frac{h^2}{a^2(e^2-1)}, \quad \ldots\ldots\ldots\ldots(2)$$
in the case of the hyperbola. Thus the speed from infinity is greater or less than v, according as e is less or greater than 1, that is according as the orbit is an ellipse or a hyperbola, and conversely. Thus a comparison of the speed at any distance with the speed from infinity enables us to discriminate between the two forms of orbit.

The reader may satisfy himself that when the force is a repulsion the only possible orbit is a hyperbola, and that the motion is in the branch which does not contain the focus at which the centre of force is situated. When the force is an attraction the particle moves along the branch within which lies the centre of force.

Now let (1) $r_0 = a(1-e)$, (2) $r_0 = a(e-1)$; then by (5) and (6) of § 126, $du/d\theta = 0$, and $v_0^2 = h^2/a^2(1-e)^2$ in both cases. But $h^2 = \mu a(1-e^2)$ in the first case and $h^2 = \mu a(e^2-1)$ in the second; therefore $v_0^2 = \mu(1+e)/a(1-e)$ in case (1) and $v_0^2 = \mu(e+1)/a(e-1)$ in case (2). This agrees with (8) of §126, which gives in the former case $\frac{1}{2}v^2 = \mu(1/r - 1/2a)$ and in the latter $\frac{1}{2}v^2 = \mu(1/r + 1/2a)$.

Equation (8) of §126 may be taken as that of energy. For we may write it

$$\tfrac{1}{2}mv^2 - m\frac{\mu}{r} = \mp m\frac{\mu}{2a}. \quad\quad\quad\quad(3)$$

On the left we have the kinetic energy $\frac{1}{2}mv^2$ of the particle, and a term, $-m\mu/r$, depending on the position of the particle with reference to the centre of force, which may be taken as the potential energy of the system, while on the right we have a constant, $-m\mu/2a$ or $m\mu/2a$, the constant sum of the kinetic and potential energies.

128. Period of Particle in Orbit. The period of revolution, or time of description, in an elliptic orbit is finite, in a parabolic or hyperbolic orbit it is infinite. If a be the semi-axis major of an elliptic orbit of eccentricity e, the length of the semi-axis minor is $a\sqrt{1-e^2}$, so that the area of the orbit is $\pi a^2\sqrt{1-e^2}$. But twice the rate of description of area is $h = \sqrt{\mu a(1-e^2)}$, so that if T denote the period,

$$T = 2\pi\sqrt{\frac{a^3}{\mu}}, \quad\quad\quad\quad(1)$$

the period of a simple pendulum of length a under acceleration μ/a^2.

It is to be observed that the squares of the periods in different orbits about the same centre of force are by this equation proportional to the cubes of the corresponding values of a. This, as we shall see, is one of the observations made by Kepler regarding the planetary motions.

It is important to remark that by equation (8) of §126 the length a of the semi-axis major depends only on the speed and the distance of the point of projection from the focus. Thus, if a number of particles be projected with the same speed, greater than that from infinity, in different directions from the same point under the attraction of the same centre of force, the major axes of the orbits of the different particles will all be of the same length, and the periods will be the same. The particles will therefore all return after the lapse of a period to the same point.

129. Determination of Orbit from Distance and Velocity, etc.
When the direction and speed of projection, the centre of force and its constant, μ, are given, the orbit can be at once constructed. We join the centre of force O (Fig. 50) with the point P of projection, and calculate the value of $2/R - V^2/\mu$, where R is the distance and V the speed of projection. If the result is positive, the orbit is an ellipse, and the value found is the reciprocal $1/a$ of the length of the semi-axis major. If the result is negative, the orbit is a hyperbola, and the reciprocal $1/a$ of the semi-axis is

$$V^2/\mu - 2/R.$$

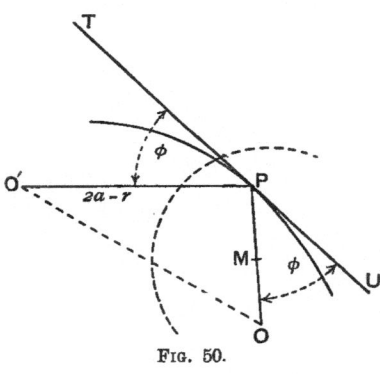

Fig. 50.

Now draw the direction of projection through P and produce it both ways to T and U (Fig. 50). The line so drawn is a tangent to the path. In the case of the ellipse draw from P a line PO', making the angle OPU equal to the angle $O'PT$, and take the length $PO' = 2a - r$. Then O' is the second focus, and the orbit is determined completely. It can be drawn in the usual way. The eccentricity e is the ratio of the length OO' to $2a$.

It is to be observed that any point of an orbit and the velocity there may be taken as the point and velocity of projection. The relation $v^2 = 2\mu/r - \mu/a$ enables the orbit to be drawn if v, r, and μ are given, and the line OP is given in position, provided one other datum is supplied. That may be the direction of the tangent at P, or it may be the condition that the particle shall pass through another given point Q (Fig. 51). In the latter case we find a as described above, and with radius $2a - r$ describe a circle from P as centre in the plane of O, P, Q. Then from Q as centre with radius $2a - r'$ (where $r' = OQ$), we draw another circle which, if it meet the former circle at all, will

§ 129]   CONSTRUCTION OF ORBIT.   235

generally intersect it in two points, O', O''. Either of these points is the second focus of an orbit which passes through O and O'. It will be seen that as Fig. 51 is drawn, if the second focus be O' the two points P, Q are on the same side of the major axis, and that if the second focus O'' be taken, P, Q are on opposite sides of the major axis. If the circles meet in one point O' only, that is if P, O', Q be in line, one orbit only can be drawn; if the two circles neither intersect nor touch, a solution of the problem does not exist.

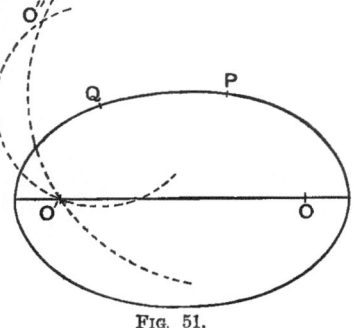

Fig. 51.

To construct a hyperbolic orbit, we draw (Fig. 52) PO' so that $\angle O'PU = \angle UPO$, and take the distance

$$PO' = 2a + OP$$

as the second focus, and again the orbit is determined completely.

It will be seen that both for the ellipse and for the hyperbola, if the plane of motion is fixed, but not the direction of motion, the locus of the second focus is a circle with centre at P. The student may prove that the locus of the centres of the possible orbits is a circle with centre at the middle point M of OP (Fig. 50) and radius $= \tfrac{1}{2}PO'$. If the plane of motion is not fixed, these loci are spheres with centres and radii as stated. [See Ex. 18 below.]

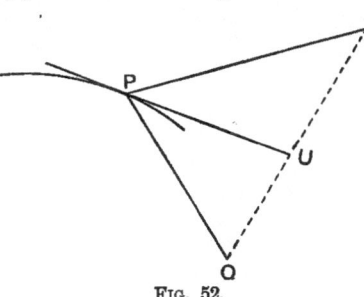

Fig. 52.

If $V^2/\mu = 2/R$ the orbit is a parabola, since a is infinite. The semi-latus rectum, which in the ellipse has length

$a(1-e^2)$, however remains finite. If it be denoted by l, we have for a parabolic orbit, as the student may verify for himself, $h = \sqrt{\mu l}$.

If for a parabolic orbit the focus O and a tangent with point of contact P be given, we join OP (Fig. 53) and draw another line $OT = OP$ to meet the tangent in T. This line is in the direction of the axis of the curve. A perpendicular ON let fall on the tangent and a perpendicular NA on OT, determine the vertex A of the path, and a distance $OD = 2OA$ laid off along OT gives the directrix, to be drawn through D perpendicular to the axis. Further points on the path can be found from the condition that every such point is equidistant from the directrix and focus.

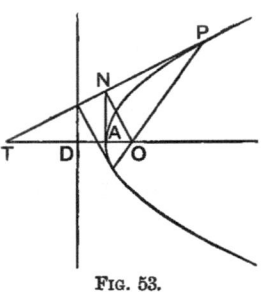

Fig. 53.

130. Newton's Revolving Orbit. If an orbit for a central force $f(u)$ is known, an orbit for the central force $f(u) + \mu_1 u^3$ can be found.

When the force is $f(u)$ the differential equation of the path is

$$\frac{d^2u}{d\theta^2} + u = \frac{f(u)}{h^2 u^2}, \quad \ldots\ldots\ldots\ldots\ldots\ldots\ldots\ldots(1)$$

and if the force is made $f(u) + \mu_1 u^3$, the equation is

$$\frac{d^2u}{d\theta^2} + \left(1 - \frac{\mu_1}{h^2}\right) u = \frac{f(u)}{h^2 u^2}. \quad \ldots\ldots\ldots\ldots\ldots(2)$$

If in this we substitute $d\theta'/\sqrt{1 - \mu_1/h^2}$ (or $d\theta'/k$) for $d\theta$, and put h'^2 for $h^2 - \mu_1$, we obtain

$$\frac{d^2u}{d\theta'^2} + u = \frac{f(u)}{h'^2 u^2}, \quad \ldots\ldots\ldots\ldots\ldots\ldots\ldots(3)$$

a differential equation of the same form as that first written above. Hence if $u = \phi(\theta)$ be the equation of an orbit for the force $f(u)$, $u = \phi(\theta')$ is the equation of an orbit for the force $f(u) + \mu_1 u^3$.

We imagine, thus, the particle to describe the first orbit, and that orbit to revolve at the same time with angular speed $(k-1)\dot{\theta}$ in its own plane about the origin. The path of the particle is then the second orbit required. This is the theorem of Newton's revolving orbit. Or we may suppose the orbit $u = \phi(\theta)$ constructed, and then construct another in which the u for any value θ is the u for an angle $k\theta$ in the former orbit. [*Principia*, Lib. I. Sect. ix.]

131. Examples.

Ex. 1. If $f(u) = \mu u^2$, prove that the orbit for the force $\mu u^2 + \mu_1 u^3$ has the equation
$$r = \frac{+a(1-e^2)}{1+e\cos(k\theta)}.$$

The orbit for the force μ/r^2 has the equation
$$r = \frac{\pm a(1-e^2)}{1+e\cos\theta},$$
where the positive sign is to be taken for an ellipse and the negative for a hyperbola, for which, of course, $e^2 > 1$. The orbit for the force $\mu/r^2 + \mu_1/r^3$ is, by the theorem,
$$r = \frac{\pm a(1-e^2)}{1+e\cos\theta'}.$$

But θ' is the actual vectorial angle θ in the new orbit, corresponding to the radius-vector r, multiplied by h', and so we have
$$r = \frac{\pm a(1-e^2)}{1+e\cos(k\theta)}.$$

Ex. 2. Prove that if the force μr towards or from the centre of a conic be increased by μ_1/r^3, the orbit is changed from
$$\cos^2\theta/a^2 \pm \sin^2\theta/b^2 = 1/r^2$$
to
$$\cos^2(k\theta)/a^2 \pm \sin^2(k\theta)/b^2 = 1/r^2.$$

Ex. 3. To find the law of force towards the same centre, by which the inverse of a given orbit with respect to a circle, with its centre at the centre of force, may be described by a particle.

For the known orbit, we have $F = (h^2 dp/dr)/p^3$, and if F', h', p', r' be corresponding quantities for the inverse, we can, by the relations $r/p = r'/p' = c^2/pr'$, $p = f(r)$ and $h/r^2 = h'/r'^2$, find $F' = (h'^2 dp'/dr')/p'^3$. Or we may derive from the equation $p = f(r)$ of the known orbit the relation $c^2 p'/r'^2 = f(c^2/r')$, and since $F = -\frac{1}{2} dv^2/dr$, write $F' = -\frac{1}{2} h'^2 d(1/p'^2)/dr'$. Between these two last equations p' is eliminated and F' obtained as a function of r' alone.

Ex. 4. Prove that the attractive force F under which a particle describes the inverse of an ellipse, a focus of which is the centre of force, is given by
$$F = +\frac{3ah^2c^2}{b^2}\frac{1}{r^4} - \frac{2h^2c^4}{b^2}\frac{1}{r^5},$$
where the accents used in Ex. 3 are dropped.

Ex. 5. If the centre of the ellipse is the centre of force, prove that
$$F = \frac{c^4h^2}{a^2b^2}\left(\frac{2(a^2+b^2)h^2}{r^5} - \frac{3c^4h^2}{r^7}\right).$$

Ex. 6. When the orbit is the reciprocal of a known orbit, and the centre of force is the same for both: to find the law of force.

In this case $rp' = r'p = c^2$, and if the equation of the known orbit be $r = f(p)$, then $c^2/p' = f(c^2/r')$. As before, also, $F' = -\frac{1}{2}h'^2 d(1/p'^2)/dr'$, and from these relations F' can be determined.

Ex. 7. Show that if the orbit be the reciprocal of a conic, a focus of which is at the centre of force,
$$F = c^4 \frac{8a^2h^2r}{b^4\left(r^2 + \dfrac{c^4}{b^2}\right)^3},$$
and that if the centre be the centre of force,
$$F = \frac{a^2b^2}{c^8}h^2r.$$

Ex. 8. Find F for the pedal of a given orbit, and show that, according as the central pedal or the focal pedal of an ellipse, with centre of force at the focus, is taken,
$$F = h^2\left(\frac{3a^2b^2}{r^7} - \frac{2(a^2+b^2)}{r^5}\right), \quad F = \frac{8a^2h^2r}{(b^2+r^2)^3}.$$

Ex. 9. Find F when the orbit is the pedal of a circle (radius a) with the centre of force at an eccentric point in the plane of the circle distant c from the centre,
$$F = h^2\left(\frac{3a}{r^4} - 2\frac{a^2-c^2}{r^5}\right).$$

Ex. 10. Show that for the cardioid derived from this circle,
$$F = \frac{3ah^2}{r^4}.$$

Ex. 11. Verify the second result of Ex. 8 from the fact that the focal pedal of a conic is the circle described on the major axis as diameter, by finding the force required to give a circular orbit of radius a, when the centre of force is at a distance $\sqrt{a^2-b^2}$ from the centre.

[Most of the foregoing examples are taken from a paper by Curtis, *Mess. Math.* xi. 1881.]

§ 131] EXAMPLES. 239

Ex. 12. Prove that if e be the eccentricity of an orbit described under a force μ/r^2, and v be the speed at a point where ϕ is the angle between the tangent and the radius-vector,

$$\mu a(1-e^2) = v^2 r^2 \sin^2\phi, \quad e^2 = 1 - 2\frac{v^2 r \sin^2\phi}{\mu} + \frac{v^4 r^2 \sin^2\phi}{\mu^2}.$$

(G. W. Hill.)

For brevity, we shall work out for an ellipse. The modifications of the proof for a hyperbola are obvious.

Clearly $h^2 = v^2 r^2 \sin^2\phi$, and it is proved in § 126 that $h^2 = \mu a(1-e^2)$. Hence $\mu a(1-e^2) = v^2 r^2 \sin^2\phi$.

From (5), § 126, we have $e \cos(\theta - \alpha) = a(1-e^2)/r - 1$, so that

$$e \cos(\theta - \alpha) = \frac{v^2 r \sin^2\phi}{\mu} - 1$$

by the former result.

Now produce the tangent and major-axis to meet, and let ψ be the angle of intersection (see Fig. 54). Let fall perpendiculars (lengths pp') from the foci on the tangent. The distance between the foci is $2ae$, and by the figure

$$2ae \cos\psi = (2a - r)\cos\phi + r\cos\phi = 2a\cos\phi.$$

Hence $\qquad e\cos\psi = \cos\phi,$

which is a very useful relation.

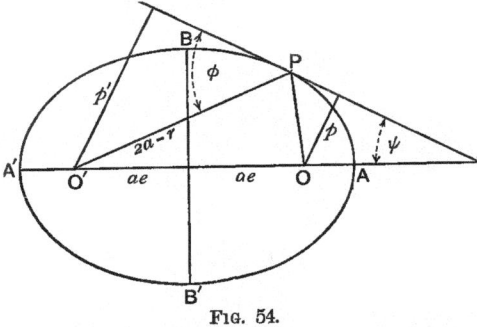

Fig. 54.

Again, $p' - p = (2a - r)\sin\phi - r\sin\phi = 2(a-r)\sin\phi.$ But also

$$p' - p = 2ae \sin\psi.$$

Hence, we have $\qquad ae \sin\psi = (a-r)\sin\phi.$

But in the figure $\angle AOP = \theta - \alpha$, so that $\sin(\theta - \alpha) = \sin(\phi + \psi)$, and therefore

$$e\sin(\theta - \alpha) = e\sin\phi\cos\psi + e\cos\phi\sin\psi = \sin\phi\cos\phi + \frac{a-r}{a}\sin\phi\cos\phi,$$

by the relations just established. Thus

$$e \sin(\theta - \alpha) = r\left(\frac{2}{r} - \frac{1}{a}\right) \sin \phi \cos \phi.$$

But it is proved in §126 that $v^2 = \mu(2/r - 1/a)$, and therefore we get

$$e \sin(\theta - \alpha) = \frac{v^2 r \sin \phi \cos \phi}{\mu}.$$

Squaring this relation and the corresponding one found above for $e \cos(\theta - \alpha)$, and adding, we obtain

$$e^2 = 1 - 2\frac{v^2 r \sin^2 \phi}{\mu} + \frac{v^4 r^2 \sin^2 \phi}{\mu^2}.$$

Ex. 13. A particle describes an elliptic orbit about a centre of force at a focus, in the period $T = 2\pi\sqrt{a^3/\mu}$, where a is the mean distance: to infer the time required by the particle to reach the centre of force if placed at rest at any distance.

It is to be noticed first that the period depends only on the mean distance; hence if we keep a unchanged and make e approach unity, we shall, without altering the period, cause the orbit to approximate to a very narrow ellipse with the centre of force, O, close to one extremity. The motion from the other extremity to very near O is then a path differing little from a straight line towards O. The transverse speed of the particle at the remote extremity of the path is annulled by the small transverse component of the central force, and the generation of motion toward O takes place as if the particle had been given at rest at the remote extremity. Thus we have for the time τ, from a distance $2a$,

$$\tau = \pi \sqrt{\frac{a^3}{\mu}}.$$

If the particle were placed at rest at any other distance $2a'$, we should have for the time τ' required for it to reach the centre of force

$$\tau' = \pi \sqrt{\frac{a'^3}{\mu}}.$$

For instance, if $2a' = a$, the mean distance in the orbit, we get

$$\tau' = \frac{\pi}{2\sqrt{2}} \sqrt{\frac{a^3}{\mu}} = \frac{T}{4\sqrt{2}}.$$

[Thus, if the earth were deprived of its orbital motion at any instant, it would begin to fall into the sun, which it would reach in about 65 days.]

Ex. 14. Verify the results of the preceding example by direct integration from the differential equation

$$\ddot{x} + \frac{\mu}{x^2} = 0.$$

§ 131] EXAMPLES. 241

Ex. 15. To find the value of $\int v^2\,dt$ for a complete period of a particle describing an elliptic orbit under attraction to a focus according to the Newtonian law, and to show that it is independent of the eccentricity of the orbit.

Since $v\,dt = ds$, this integral may be written $\int v\,ds$, and is then called the "action" (per unit mass) for the path along which it is taken. We are to take it once round the orbit. Now we have

$$v^2 = 2\mu\left(\frac{1}{r} - \frac{1}{2a}\right) = \mu\frac{2a-r}{ar} = \frac{\mu}{a}\frac{r'}{r},$$

where r' is the distance of the particle from the "empty" focus. But if p, p' be the lengths of the perpendiculars from the centre of force and the other focus to the position of the particle at the instant considered, we have $r'/r = p'/p$, and therefore, since $pp' = b^2$, $r'/r = p'^2/b^2$.

Hence $$\int v\,ds = \sqrt{\frac{\mu}{a}}\frac{1}{b}\int p'\,ds.$$

But clearly $\int p'\,ds$ taken round the orbit is twice its area, that is $2\pi ab$, and therefore

$$\int v\,ds = 2\pi\sqrt{\mu a}.$$

The action for one revolution is thus $2\pi\sqrt{\mu a}$, and is the same for all orbits, whatever their eccentricities, for which a has the same value. If we denote it by A, then

$$A = 2\pi\sqrt{\mu a} = 2\pi\frac{h}{\sqrt{1-e^2}} = 4\pi^2\frac{a^2}{T}.$$

A is the value of the integral $\int v^2\,dt$ taken over the period T; therefore the time-average of the kinetic energy (per unit mass) of the particle is $A/2T$, and we have

$$\frac{A}{2T} = 2\pi^2\frac{a^2}{T^2} = \frac{\sqrt{\mu a}}{2\sqrt{\frac{a^3}{\mu}}} = \frac{\mu}{2a}.$$

[Thus while the area described about the centre of force by the radius vector is proportional to the time, the area described by the radius vector to the particle from the empty focus is proportional to the action.* It is shown in § 100 that the actual motion of the particle is brachistochronic for a centre of force in the empty focus. Thus the mode of representing the time in the free motion about that focus has become the representation of the action. Now we can write the energy equation (13), of § 127, in the form

$$\tfrac{1}{2}mv^2 \pm \frac{m\mu}{2a} = m\frac{\mu}{r},$$

* Since this Example was written we have found that this fact had been noticed by Tait: *Proc. R.S.E.*, 5, 1865 and *Trans. R.S.E.*, 24, 1865.

G. D. Q

where the upper sign applies to the elliptic and the lower to the hyperbolic orbit. We thus get the curious theorem that the kinetic energy of the particle, at distance r from the same centre of force, in a hyperbolic orbit, of semi-transverse axis a, exceeds, and in an elliptic orbit, of major semi-axis a, falls short of the exhaustion $m\mu/r$ of potential energy from infinity to the distance r (see § 122), by the time-average of the kinetic energy of the elliptic motion. We infer that the ultimate constant velocity in the hyperbolic orbit at a very great distance from the centre of force—that is along the asymptote—is the square root, $\sqrt{\mu/a}$, of twice the time-average of the kinetic energy in the elliptic orbit. Further, since the time along the asymptote at the constant speed $\sqrt{\mu/a}$ is infinite, the mean kinetic energy in the hyperbola is $m\mu/2a$, the same as that in the ellipse. This can be seen to be the case by a consideration of areas in the hyperbola.

It is worth noticing that for one revolution $\int v\,ds = \sqrt{\mu/a}\,b\int ds/p$, so that
$$\int \frac{ds}{p} = 2\pi\frac{a}{b}.$$

Ex. 16. To find the angular speed of a planet about the "empty" focus.

If r, r' be the lengths of the radii from the centre of force and the empty focus to any position of the particle, and $\dot\theta$, $\dot\theta'$ be the corresponding angular speeds, then $r\dot\theta = r'\dot\theta'$. For if ϕ denote, as before, the inclination of the tangent to either radius-vector, we have $\sin\phi = r\,d\theta/ds = r'd\theta'/ds$, and therefore the relation stated. Hence $\dot\theta' = r\dot\theta/r' = h/rr'$, since $\dot\theta = h/r^2$. Now, by the properties of the ellipse, $r = a - ex$, $r' = a + ex$, if x be the distance, parallel to the axis, of P from the centre. Thus we get
$$\dot\theta' = \frac{h}{a^2 - e^2x^2} = \frac{h}{a^2}\left(1 - e^2\frac{x^2}{a^2}\right)^{-1} = \frac{h}{a^2}\left(1 + e^2\frac{x^2}{a^2} + e^4\frac{x^4}{a^4} + \dots\right).$$

Thus if powers of e above the first can be neglected, $\dot\theta'$ may be taken as constant. [See Exercise 4, p. 301, below.]

Ex. 17. To integrate the equation of central orbits for the case of a central force $\mu(a + b\cos 2\theta)/r^2$.

The equation is
$$\frac{d^2u}{d\theta^2} + u = \frac{\mu}{h^2}(a + b\cos 2\theta),$$
which may be written
$$\frac{d^2\left(u - \frac{\mu a}{h^2}\right)}{d\theta^2} + u - \frac{\mu a}{h^2} = \frac{\mu b}{h^2}\cos 2\theta.$$

A particular integral is easily found by substitution to be
$$u - \frac{\mu a}{h^2} = -\frac{\mu b}{3h^2}\cos 2\theta,$$

and this *plus* the complementary function (which satisfies the differential equation when $b=0$) is the complete integral. Thus we get
$$u = A\cos\theta + B\sin\theta + \frac{\mu}{3h^2}(3a - b\cos 2\theta).$$

By putting $x = r\cos\theta$, $y = r\sin\theta$ ($r = 1/u$), we can show that this is an algebraic curve of the fourth degree, unless $b = 0$, when it reduces to a conic.

Let it be given that at the point where $u = c$, $\theta = 0$, the velocity is at right angles to the radius-vector, that is, that the value of $du/d\theta$ is there zero. Then we get
$$c = A + \mu(3a-b)/3h^2 \quad \text{or} \quad A = \{3h^2c - \mu(3a-b)\}/3h^2,$$
and by differentiation and the condition $du/d\theta = 0$, we find $B = 0$. The equation is then
$$u = \frac{1}{3h^2}[\{3h^2c - \mu(3a-b)\}\cos\theta + \mu(3a - b\cos 2\theta)],$$
and the orbit is completely determined.

Ex. 18. To find the locus of the centres of all the orbits that can be drawn for a given centre of force O and given speed V of projection from a fixed point P.

Let R be the distance OP, and suppose for the present that the orbits are ellipses. The value of a is found from the equation $\frac{1}{2}V^2 = \mu(1/R - 1/2a)$, and is $\mu R/(2\mu - V^2 R)$. The second focus lies on the circle described from P (see Fig. 51), with radius $= 2a - R$. If the origin of coordinates be taken at O, and α, β be the coordinates of the point of projection, the equation of the circle is
$$(x - \alpha)^2 + (y - \beta)^2 = (2a - R)^2.$$

The coordinates of the centre of the orbit are $\xi = \frac{1}{2}x$, $\eta = \frac{1}{2}y$, and therefore the equation just written can be put in the form
$$\left(\xi - \frac{\alpha}{2}\right)^2 + \left(\eta - \frac{\beta}{2}\right)^2 = \left(a - \frac{R}{2}\right)^2,$$
which shows that the point ξ, η lies on a circle with centre at the point $\alpha/2$, $\beta/2$, that is the middle point M of OP [Fig. 50]. The radius is $a - R/2$, that is $\frac{1}{2}PO'$, if O' be a second focus.

We have $ae = \frac{1}{2}OO'$, so that
$$a^2e^2 = \xi^2 + \eta^2 = (a - R/2)^2 - \frac{1}{4}(\alpha^2 + \beta^2) + \xi\alpha + \eta\beta = a^2 - aR + \xi\alpha + \eta\beta.$$
Thus
$$e^2 = 1 - \frac{R}{a} + \frac{\xi\alpha + \eta\beta}{a^2},$$
which gives e^2 as depending on ξ, η.

The modification of this process for hyperbolic orbits may be written out by the student.

[The present discussion affords another proof of the expression for e^2 given in Ex. 12. Taking the axis of ξ along OP, we make $\beta = 0$, and the equation of the locus of centres found above may be written
$$\xi^2 + \eta^2 = a^2 - aR + \xi R,$$

since now $\alpha = R$. But Fig. 50 shows that
$$\xi = \tfrac{1}{2}R + (a - \tfrac{1}{2}R)\cos 2\phi = R\sin^2\phi + a\cos 2\phi.$$
Hence
$$\xi^2 + \eta^2 = a^2 - aR(1 - \cos 2\phi) + R^2\sin^2\phi$$
$$= a^2 - 2aR\sin^2\phi + R^2\sin^2\phi.$$
But $\xi^2 + \eta^2 = a^2 e^2$, and $1/a = (2\mu - V^2 R)/\mu R$, and so we get
$$e^2 = 1 - 2\frac{R\sin^2\phi}{a} + \frac{R^2\sin^2\phi}{a^2}$$
$$= 1 - 2\frac{V^2 R\sin^2\phi}{\mu} + \frac{V^4 R^2\sin^2\phi}{\mu^2},$$
as before. It will be noticed that, when $R = a$, this gives $\partial e/\partial\mu = 0$, and also $\partial e/\partial R = 0$ (for then $V^2 a = \mu$).]

132. Acceleration in terms of Tangential and Radial Forces.
Returning now to equations (4) and (7) of § 121, we have
$$v\frac{dv}{ds} = \frac{h}{p^2}\frac{dh}{ds} - \frac{h^2}{p^3}\frac{dp}{ds} = S - F\frac{dr}{ds}. \quad \ldots\ldots\ldots(1)$$
Hence we obtain by integration,
$$\tfrac{1}{2}v^2 = \int_{s_0}^{s} S\, ds - \int_{r_0}^{r} F\, dr, \quad \ldots\ldots\ldots(2)$$
where r_0, s_0, r, s are corresponding values of r and of distance travelled along the path from some chosen point. If F is some function $f(r)$ of r,
$$\tfrac{1}{2}v^2 = \int_{s_0}^{s} S\, ds - \int_{r_0}^{r} f(r)\, dr. \quad \ldots\ldots\ldots(3)$$
Thus, if $S = 0$, v is a function of r, and is the same at the same distance from the centre of force. It follows therefore that when $S = 0$, $du/d\theta$ is the same at the same distance, that is the radius-vector makes the same angle with the tangent. For
$$v^2 = h^2\left\{\left(\frac{du}{d\theta}\right)^2 + u^2\right\},$$
and, since h is constant and v has the same value for the same value of u, $du/d\theta$ must also return to the same value when u does.

Again, by (4), § 121, $v^2/\rho = F\sin\phi$, that is
$$v^2 = 2F \times \tfrac{1}{4} \text{ chord of curvature at position of particle.} \ldots(4)$$

The speed v at any position of the particle in the orbit is thus equal to the speed which the particle would acquire if it traversed from rest, under constant acceleration F, a distance equal to $\frac{1}{4}$ of the length of the chord of curvature. It will be noticed that this theorem holds whether a tangential force S acts or not: the radius of curvature ρ, for a given speed v, however, is affected by such a force.

Since, when $S=0$, the speed is the same at the same distance, and also the angle which the tangent makes with the radius-vector, the chord of curvature and the radius of curvature of the orbit are the same at the same distance from the centre of force.

133. Hodograph of Particle describing Orbit. The relation $v = h/p$ shows that any polar reciprocal of the path, turned through 90°, represents the hodograph of the particle's motion, whatever the orbit may be. When the path is a conic section with the centre of force at a focus, the circle described on the axis of length $2a$ as diameter may be taken as the hodograph, provided the hodographic origin be taken at the "empty" focus, and the direction of motion be taken turned back through 90°. For let O, O' be the foci, of which the former is the centre of force, and a tangent be drawn to the path at any position P. If the tangent meet the circle referred to in M, M', as shown in Fig. 55, the lines OM, $O'M'$ are, by a property of the ellipse, perpendiculars to the tangent, and if p, p' be their lengths, the product pp' is equal to b^2, where b is the length of the minor semi-axis CB, $a\sqrt{1-e^2}$, for the ellipse, and the length of the conjugate semi-axis, $a\sqrt{e^2-1}$, for the hyperbola. Thus we have

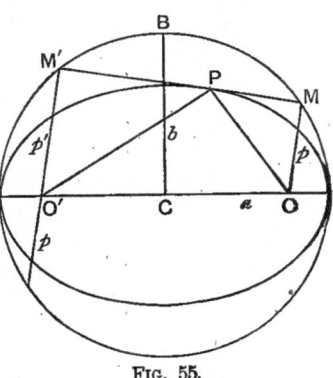

Fig. 55.

$$v = \frac{h}{p} = \frac{h}{a^2(1-e^2)}p' = \frac{1}{a}\sqrt{\frac{\mu}{a(1-e^2)}}p' \quad\ldots\ldots\ldots(1)$$

for the ellipse, and

$$v = \frac{h}{p} = \frac{h}{a^2(e^2-1)} p' = \frac{1}{a}\sqrt{\frac{\mu}{a(e^2-1)}} p' \quad \ldots\ldots\ldots\ldots(2)$$

for the hyperbola. Thus O' is the hodographic origin, and the velocity is represented on the scale indicated in (2) by the line $M'O'$, which is the direction of motion turned forward 90°.

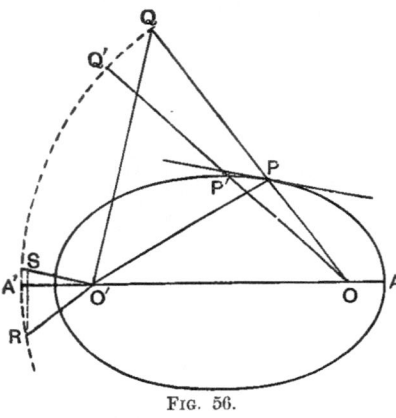

Fig. 56.

A circle of radius $2a$ described from the focus O as centre serves still more conveniently as hodograph. For it will be seen that if the perpendicular $O'M'$ from O' (Fig. 56) be continued to meet the circle in Q, then $O'P = PQ$, and $O'Q = 2p'$. Thus, since $v \propto p'$, we may take $O'Q$ as representing the velocity at P along the tangent to the path turned *back* through 90°. The true direction is $O'S$. Fig. 56, which we shall use in what follows, represents the path and the hodograph thus constructed.

134. Velocity resoluble into Two Components of Constant Amounts. It will be noticed that the velocity represented by $O'Q$ can be resolved into two components $O'O$ and OQ. Of these $O'O$ is fixed both in amount and in direction, the other, OQ, is fixed in amount but changes in direction with OP. The lines $O'R$, RS, perpendicular to OQ and $O'O$ respectively, represent the true directions of these components. We can find their magnitudes very simply from the consideration that their sum must be the speed with which the particle moves at right angles to the line joining it to the centre of force, when the length of that line has its least value. For the ellipse the least length of the line is $a(1-e)$, and the speed is therefore $h/a(1-e)$.

This is made up of two components proportional to the lengths of OO' and OQ, that is to $2ae$ and $2a$. Thus the components are $eh/a(1-e^2) = e\sqrt{\mu/a(1-e^2)} = e\sqrt{\mu a}/b$, and the same divided by e. For the components in the case of the hyperbola we have in the same way,

$$eh/a(e^2-1) = e\sqrt{\mu/a(e^2-1)} = e\sqrt{\mu a}/b,$$

and the same divided by e.

In the latter case, since $e > 1$, the constant speed at right angles to the axis is greater than the component at right angles to the radius-vector, and we see from another point of view why the orbit is closed when $e < 1$ and is infinite when $e > 1$.

As an example of motion with such components as exist for the particle moving round a centre of force, we may take a steamer rounding a buoy moored in a tidal stream which flows past the buoy with constant speed. If the steamer have, besides the motion of the water, always a constant speed at right angles to the direction of the buoy, it will describe a conic section relatively to the land, with the buoy in a focus, just as if it were a satellite moving round a stationary primary which attracts with a force inversely proportional to the square of the distance. If the speed of the stream be greater than that of the steamer, the path will be a hyperbola, and in the contrary case an ellipse. If the two speeds are the same, the orbit is a parabola.

135. Deduction of Law of Force from Form of Orbit and Uniform Description of Area. If we assume that the orbit is an ellipse with the centre of force in a focus O, and that the radius-vector to the particle describes equal areas on the plane of the orbit in equal times, we can prove that the particle is acted on by a force which varies inversely as the square of the distance from the focus. For join the centre O of the circle to Q, then, as the particle moves in time dt along the path from P to an adjacent point P', Q moves along the circle to an adjacent point Q'. The lines $O'Q$, $O'Q'$ (Fig. 56) represent on a certain scale the velocities at the beginning and end of the interval dt. Thus QQ' represents on the same scale the change of velocity which the particle has sustained in the interval. But $QQ' = 2a\dot{\theta}\,dt$ and $h = r^2\dot{\theta}$, so that $QQ' = 2ah\,dt/r^2$. The acceleration is therefore, on the scale of the diagram, $2ah/r^2$, and, since the hodograph, with the lines of construction, is turned back through 90°, is directed towards O. Its absolute value is obtained by multiplying $2ah/r^2$ by the factor $\sqrt{\mu/a(1-e^2)}/2a$ for the ellipse, and is therefore μ/r^2.

In the same way the hyperbolic orbit might be dealt with and the same result obtained.

136. Kepler's Laws. Verification. The manner in which the planets move about the sun was inferred by Kepler from a large number of observations, especially those made of the planet Mars by Tycho Brahe, who preceded him as astronomer at Prague. The results are contained in his *Astronomia Nova*, which appeared in 1629, and though the ideas on dynamics set forth in it are in great part erroneous, this work led to the establishment of the physical theory of gravitation which accounts for the motions of the planets by a consistent dynamical theory. As Newton showed, the planets move in obedience to mutual forces between the different bodies along the lines joining them, and tending to bring them together, a tendency prevented by the relative motions from having the apparently direct and simple effect which the ordinary undynamical intelligence expects.

Kepler in vain endeavoured to fit the observations of positions and times into the hypothesis that each planet moved in a circle with uniform angular speed about an eccentric point, midway between which and the sun the centre of the circle was supposed to lie [see Ex. 16, § 131]. Observing the motion of the earth in the manner indicated in the next paragraph, he noticed that at the points of greatest and least distance from the sun, the earth had speeds inversely as these distances, and (of course with deviation from the hypothesis of uniform angular speed about the eccentric point) concluded that the speed of the earth in the imagined circular orbit was at every point inversely proportional to its distance from the sun. He noticed, moreover, that at the greatest and least distances there was the same rate of description of areas by the radius-vector drawn from the sun to the earth, and was led finally to adopt the law of uniform description of areas for the whole motion. This conclusion, however, he found to be utterly irreconcileable with the hypothesis of a circular orbit when applied to the planet Mars; and so finally he abandoned that hypothesis in favour of the true notion of an elliptic orbit with the sun in a focus. He thus formulated the two laws of the planetary motions:

I. *The radius-vector from the sun to each planet sweeps over equal areas on the plane of the orbit in equal times.*

II. *Planets move round the sun in ellipses which have a common focus at which the sun is situated.*

The observations of Kepler on the motion of the earth can be verified by anyone who cares to examine the tabulated values of the sun's apparent diameter from day to day throughout the year, as they are set forth in the *Nautical Almanac*, and to compare these with the longitudes of the earth's position at different times. The longitude from the perihelion position (the position nearest the sun) is the angle for a planet moving in the plane of the ecliptic denoted by $\theta - \alpha$ in equation (5) of §126. Now the apparent diameter of the sun is the angle which the sun's diameter subtends at the earth, and in radians is d/r, where d is the actual diameter and r the earth's distance from the sun. This apparent diameter is measured in various ways, *e.g.* by observing the time taken by the sun's disk to pass over the cross-wires of a telescope; while the advance of the earth in longitude is obtained for successive equal intervals of time by observing with an equatorial telescope the corresponding changes of the sun's Right Ascension (that is of the angle between a meridian containing the sun's centre and a certain zero meridian— that of the "first point of Aries"). The advance in Right Ascension (say in an hour) is not exactly the same as the advance in longitude, but enables the latter to be calculated, and is roughly proportional to the square of the sun's apparent diameter, as anyone may verify by means of the *Nautical Almanac*.

250   A TREATISE ON DYNAMICS.   [CH. V.

Taking the tabulated values, which, of course, are derived from and checked by observations, we find d/r varying with the longitude from perihelion according to the equation

$$\frac{d}{r} = D\{1 + e\cos(\theta - \alpha)\}, \quad \ldots\ldots\ldots\ldots\ldots(1)$$

where D is a mean value of the apparent diameter for the different positions, that is we have, if l be a constant,

$$r = \frac{l}{1 + e\cos(\theta - \alpha)}, \quad \ldots\ldots\ldots\ldots\ldots(2)$$

which, if $e < 1$, is the equation of an ellipse (see § 126).

The value of e can be calculated with great ease. Take the apparent diameter of the sun when the earth is at perihelion, that is about Dec. 21, and again at Midsummer, June 21, when the earth is at aphelion—these are the greatest and least values. Call them D_1 and D_2. Then we have by (1), $D_1 = D(1 + e)$, $D_2 = D(1 - e)$, and so

$$e = \frac{D_1 - D_2}{D_1 + D_2}, \quad \ldots\ldots\ldots\ldots\ldots(3)$$

which we find to be $8/481 = 1/60$, nearly. Thus the orbit is an ellipse of small eccentricity, that is an ellipse differing perceptibly but not greatly from a circle. Taking the sun's mean distance as 92,600,000 miles, this eccentricity gives as the distance of the focus at which the sun is situated from the centre of the ellipse about 1,540,000 miles, which is rather less than 1·8 times the sun's diameter.

We see then how the law of the elliptic orbit is established for the earth at least; that of the equable description of areas is proved by the fact, referred to above, that the daily or hourly advance in longitude varies directly as the square of the sun's apparent diameter, that is, by what precedes, inversely as the square of the length of the radius-vector. Thus it is verified that $r^2\dot{\theta}$ is constant and $r^2\dot{\theta}$ is twice the rate of description of areas, as has been shown in § 25 above.

By the mean distance of a planet from the sun is meant the length of the major semi-axis. We have already seen that the period of a particle about a centre of force, of constant μ, is $2\pi\sqrt{a^3/\mu}$. Hence, if μ is the same for different particles revolving about centres of force at different distances a_1, a_2, a_3, ..., and T_1, T_2, T_3,... be the periods of revolution,

$$\frac{T_1^2}{a_1^3} = \frac{T_2^2}{a_2^3} = \frac{T_3^2}{a_3^3} = \cdots, \qquad \ldots\ldots\ldots\ldots\ldots(4)$$

and conversely. By comparing the mean distances of the different planets from the sun, measured in terms of the earth's distance, with their periods, Kepler found that this relation of periodic times to mean distances held good, and he enunciated a third law of the planetary motions:

III. *The squares of the periodic times of the different planets are proportional to the cubes of their mean distances from the sun.*

Kepler's third law, dynamically interpreted, thus shows that μ is the same for the forces between the sun and the different planets of the solar system. The law, however, as we shall see presently, requires a correction which could only be foreseen and applied when the dynamical theory had been worked out, and the agreement of which with observation affords a strong confirmation of the truth of the theory.

137. Newton's Dynamical Deductions from Kepler's Laws. From these laws, which, so far as they go, merely state the observational facts of the motions of the planets, Newton made certain dynamical deductions [*Principia*, Lib. I. Props. II. XI. XV.].

(1) From the law of areas: that the force, if any, between the sun and a planet is along the line joining the planet with the sun.

For the product, $mr^2\dot\theta$, of the double rate $r^2\dot\theta$, of description of areas by the mass m of the planet, is the angular momentum of the planet about the centre, and this cannot remain constant under the action of force on the planet in the plane of the orbit unless the force have no moment changing $mr^2\dot\theta$, that is, the force must be in a line through the sun's centre. A component of force perpendicular to the orbit would of course alter the plane of motion, a change which is here supposed not to take place.

(2) From Kepler's law of the elliptic orbit: that the planet is acted on by a force toward the sun which varies, as the planet moves in its orbit, inversely as the square of the distance. The proof of this deduction is contained in § 125, Ex. 1, and again in a simple form in § 135.

(3) From Kepler's third law: that the forces towards the sun on the different planets at any given instant of time are inversely proportional to the squares of the distances of the planets at the instant.

This deduction was proved above, when it was shown that if the squares of the periodic times are proportional to the cubes of the mean distances, μ, the so-called "force of the centre" is the same for all the bodies.

The correction of this law, referred to above, is necessary to take account of the acceleration of the sun towards the planet, which is sensible when the mass of the planet is comparable with the mass of the sun. For if P and S be the masses of the planet and sun, we have, since the force F on the planet towards the sun is equal to the force on the sun towards the planet,

$$\frac{\text{acceleration of sun towards planet}}{\text{acceleration of planet towards sun}} = \frac{F/S}{F/P} = \frac{P}{S},$$

so that if P be very small in comparison with M the sun may be taken as being at rest. In the cases of the large planets, such as Jupiter and Saturn, the masses are so great that they must be taken into account. We shall now show how this may be done.

138. Effect of Mass of Planet. Since the observed motion of a planet is taken with reference to the sun's centre, regarded as at rest, the foregoing theory must be corrected by substituting for the actual acceleration, μ/r^2, of the planet the acceleration with reference to that point. We have seen that, on the supposition that the sun is at rest, the accelerations of the planets along the lines joining them to the sun would be the same at the same distance: let us suppose this to be true in the actual case and compare the result with observation. The *forces* on the different planets are proportional to their masses. Hence we take kS/r^2, where k is a constant and S the mass of the sun, as the force per unit mass on each planet, or its real acceleration, so that $\mu = kS$. The whole force on a planet of mass P is kSP/r^2 at distance r, and this must be equal to the opposite force on the sun. The acceleration of the sun in the opposite direction is therefore kP/r^2. These two oppositely directed accelerations may be taken as relative to the centroid of sun and planet, the position of which cannot be affected by their mutual action.

To enable the theory set forth above to give the motion of a planet relatively to the sun, we must apply to both planet and sun an acceleration kP/r^2 in the direction from planet to sun. This does not alter the relative motion, but cancels the planetward acceleration of the sun and gives $k(S+P)/r^2$ for the sunward acceleration of the planet. Hence, in the application of the foregoing theory, we take μ, for a planet of mass P, equal to $k(S+P)$. Thus we have different values of μ for the different planets in the field of solar attraction. The differences, however, are but slight, since S is great in comparison with every P: for example, $S/P = 332000$ for the earth and $= 1047$ for Jupiter.

If the student does not perceive why the process here described is followed, the following discussion may serve to explain it. The position of the centroid C of the two bodies is not affected by their mutual action, and is convenient, therefore, as a point of reference from which to measure the distances of the sun and planet. We denote these distances by r_1, r_2, and the distance of the planet from the sun is $r_1 + r_2 = r$, say. The two bodies remain in line with their centroid, and so the lines joining their centres to C, remaining as they do parts of one straight line, are turning with the same angular speed $\dot{\theta}$ in the same direction at each instant. Thus, since the forces per unit mass on the sun and planet are respectively kP/r^2, kS/r^2, we have

$$\ddot{r}_1 - r_1\dot{\theta}^2 = k\frac{P}{r^2}, \quad \ddot{r}_2 - r_2\dot{\theta}^2 = k\frac{S}{r^2}. \quad \ldots\ldots\ldots(1)$$

Adding, we get, since $\ddot{r}_1 + \ddot{r}_2 = \ddot{r}$,
$$\ddot{r} - r\dot{\theta}^2 = k\frac{S+P}{r^2}, \quad \ldots\ldots\ldots\ldots\ldots\ldots(2)$$
which is the differential equation of time-rate of variation of momentum along r for either body.

Again, for the angular momentum (per unit mass) of the planet about the centroid, we have
$$r_2^2\dot{\theta} = h_2, \quad \ldots\ldots\ldots\ldots\ldots\ldots\ldots(3)$$
or, since $r_2 = Sr/(S+P)$,
$$r^2\dot{\theta} = h_2\left(\frac{S+P}{S}\right)^2 = h. \quad \ldots\ldots\ldots\ldots\ldots(4)$$
These lead, in the manner already explained, to the differential equation
$$\frac{d^2u}{d\theta^2} + u = k\frac{S+P}{h^2}, \quad \ldots\ldots\ldots\ldots\ldots\ldots(5)$$
where $k(S+P)$ takes the place of μ.

For the period of revolution §128 above gives with this value of μ the equation
$$T = 2\pi\sqrt{\frac{a^3}{k(S+P)}}, \quad \ldots\ldots\ldots\ldots\ldots(6)$$
where a is the mean distance. For another planet of mass P' and mean distance a', the period T' is given by
$$T' = 2\pi\sqrt{\frac{a'^3}{k(S+P')}},$$
if k be the same as in the former case. Thus we obtain
$$\frac{T^2}{T'^2} = \frac{a^3}{a'^3}\frac{S+P'}{S+P}. \quad \ldots\ldots\ldots\ldots\ldots(7)$$

139. Correction of Kepler's Third Law by Theory of Gravitation. Now Kepler's third law asserted, as we have seen, that $T^2/T'^2 = a^3/a'^3$. Equation (6) shows that, according to the theory just explained, this statement is not quite correct. The following table, taken mainly from Maxwell's *Matter and Motion*, shows that observation confirms equation (7). The values of a are the mean distances of the planets expressed in terms of that of the earth, taken as unity; in the same way the periods T are taken. It will be seen that for the planets of smaller mass than that of the earth, $a^3 - T^2$ is very small and negative, while for the much larger planets, Jupiter, Saturn, Uranus and Neptune, it is positive. In proportion to a^3 or to T^2 this difference is greatest for Jupiter, the planet of greatest mass.

We have here referred to the sun and a planet as the two bodies, but of course the same theory is applicable to any primary and a satellite of that primary.

	Mercury.	Venus.	Earth.	Mars.
P,	0·476	0·82	1	0·1073
a,	0·387098	0·72333	1	1·52369
T,	0·24084	0·61518	1	1·88082
a^3,	0·0580046	0·378451	1	3·53746
T^2,	0·0580049	0·378453	1	3·53747
$a^3 - T^2$,	$-0·0000003$	$-0·000002$	0	$-0·00001$

	Jupiter.	Saturn.	Uranus.	Neptune.
P,	317	94·8	14·6	17
a,	5·2028	9·5388	19·1824	30·037
T,	11·8618	29·4560	84·0123	164·616
a^3,	140·832	867·914	7058·44	27100·0
T^2,	140·701	867·658	7058·07	27098·4
$a^3 - T^2$,	$+0·131$	$+0·256$	$+0·37$	$+1·6$

The third law of Kepler is thus corrected by the gravitational theory of the motion of a planet about the sun. This is an important result of the theory of *The Motion of Two Bodies*, as it is called; but it is to be remembered that both the sun and the planet considered are acted on by all the other planets, to say nothing of more distant bodies. While the problem of two bodies is thus comparatively simple, the solution of that of three bodies has so far only been obtained by successive approximations, and the same method has enabled the various perturbations due to the other planets to be evaluated in each case of motion, and tables of the approximate positions of all the planets for future time to be constructed.

140. Weighing the Planets. The determination of the mass of a planet can be effected by this theory if the planet has a satellite the period and distance of which are known. Let the mass of the satellite be m, the period T_1, and the semi-axis major of its orbit a_1. Assuming what observation shows to be the case, that the same constant k applies to the attraction between a planet and its satellite as to the solar attraction, we get

$$T_1 = 2\pi \sqrt{\frac{a_1^3}{k(P+m)}}. \quad\quad\quad\quad\quad\quad\quad\quad (1)$$

On the other hand, for the period of the planet, we have

$$T = 2\pi \sqrt{\frac{a^3}{k(S+P)}}. \quad\quad\quad\quad\quad\quad\quad\quad (2)$$

Therefore
$$\frac{T_1^2}{T^2} = \frac{a_1^3}{a^3} \frac{S+P}{P+m}, \quad\quad\quad\quad\quad\quad\quad\quad (3)$$

and if m be neglected,

$$P = \frac{T^2 a_1^3 S}{T_1^2 a^3 - T^2 a_1^3}. \quad\quad\quad\quad\quad\quad\quad\quad (4)$$

Ex. 1. Take the case of the earth and the moon. We have $T_1/T = 1/13 \cdot 369$, and the mean values of the angles subtended by the earth's radius at the sun's centre and moon's centre are $8 \cdot 8''$ and $57' \, 2''$ respectively, so that $a_1^3/a^3 = (57\tfrac{1}{30})^3 \times 60^3/8 \cdot 8^3$ approximately. Thus we get, neglecting m,

$$\frac{S}{P} = \frac{1}{13 \cdot 369^2} \frac{(57\tfrac{1}{30})^3 \times 60^3}{8 \cdot 8^3} - 1 = 329000.$$

The accepted value of this ratio is slightly greater, 332000.

Ex. 2. A satellite of Saturn makes one revolution about the primary in 16 days (true period 15 d. 22 h. 41 m. 23·2 s.), while the Saturnian year is (see Table, § 139) 10760 days nearly. The radius of the orbit of the satellite subtends at the sun an angle of $176\tfrac{1}{4}$ seconds, so that the ratio a_1/a of the distance of the satellite from the primary to the distance of the latter from the sun is 176·25/206265. Thus we obtain

$$\frac{S}{P} = \left(\frac{16}{10760}\right)^2 \frac{206265^3}{176 \cdot 25^3} - 1 = 3543$$

nearly. The sun's mass thus comes out 3543 times the mass of Saturn. The value accepted is (Young's *Astronomy*) 3502.

In this way the masses of the superior planets have been measured. The miniature solar system which we have in

Jupiter and his family of moons affords in itself examples of Kepler's third law with its Newtonian correction. The observed distances of the moons enable their accelerations to be calculated, and a comparison of these with the acceleration of the planet towards the sun confirms the supposition that it is the same constant k which enters into the value of all the attractions between different planets. This constant, commonly called the *constant of gravitation*, is the force of attraction between two units of mass, say two grammes of matter, concentrated at two points at unit distance, say a centimetre, apart. An experimental comparison of the gravity pull on a body at the earth's surface, with the pull between that body and a sphere of lead,* has enabled the earth's mass to be determined and the value of k to be calculated. For the units just specified it is about 6.7×10^{-8} dynes.

If we alter the units of length, mass, and time to, say L cms., M grammes, T seconds, the value of this constant will be altered in the ratio of 1 to $L^3 M^{-1} T^{-2}$. For the force F, between two masses m, m', at distance r apart, is kmm'/r^2, so that $k = Fr^2/mm'$; and so the multiplier would be as stated. If we take $L=1$, $M=1$, and $T^2 = 10^8/6.7$, k will become 1. Thus the new unit of time would be $10^4/\sqrt{6.7} = 3862$, in seconds, 262 seconds more than an hour. This has been called by M. Lippmann "l'heure naturelle" (*C.R.* 1899), but it would hardly be a convenient interval of time to adopt in practice.

141. Newton's Theory of Universal Gravitation. It occurred to Newton to compare the acceleration of the moon in its orbit relative to the earth with the acceleration of a body falling at the earth's surface. The former can be calculated if the moon's distance from the earth is known, for the orbit is nearly circular, and the average period of revolution has been very exactly determined. In Newton's time, the ratio of the moon's mean distance to the earth's radius was fairly accurately known; the radius of the earth, however, had been very inaccurately estimated, and the moon's distance deduced from it was in error, of course, to the

* See Gray's *Treatise on Physics*, Chap. XIII.

same extent. Thus his calculation of the acceleration of the moon towards the earth was in error, and when multiplied by the proper ratio failed to give as the corresponding acceleration at the surface of the earth a value sufficiently nearly equal to the observed acceleration of a falling body. The comparison was effected on the assumption that the force towards the earth on a particle at or near the surface was the same as it would have been if the matter of the earth had been collected at the earth's centre. Newton laid the calculation aside until, in 1682, he learned at a meeting of the Royal Society that a new measurement of an arc of the meridian had been carried out by M. Picard in France, which increased the former estimate of the earth's radius in the ratio of 7 to 6. Resuming the calculation, he now found very fair agreement between the calculated and observed values of the acceleration of a falling body. He found, in fact, that the acceleration of the moon towards the earth was to the acceleration of a falling body in the inverse ratio of the moon's distance and the earth's radius. It was not, however, until three years later that he published his conclusion that it was the same gravitation that kept the moon in its orbit and caused the fall of a stone at the earth's surface. In the interval he had overcome the difficulty of obtaining a satisfactory proof of the assumption above referred to, on the basis of the theory of universal gravitation to which his investigations had led him. According to this theory there existed a force between every pair of particles of matter, urging each toward the other, which was directly proportional to the product of the masses of the particles and inversely proportional to the square of the distance between them; that, in fact, if m, m' be the masses of two particles (that is portions of matter of dimensions so small in comparison with the distance between any point in one and any point in the other that they might be regarded as concentrated at points) and r the distance just referred to, the mutual force F between them was given by the equation

$$F = k \frac{mm'}{r^2},$$

§ 141]   UNIVERSAL GRAVITATION.   259

where k is a constant—the "constant of gravitation" already referred to—which is the same for every pair of particles. Now, on this principle, Newton at length succeeded in proving that the whole force exerted on a particle of matter in consequence of the presence of a sphere of matter, either uniform in density or made up of concentric shells which were each of uniform density, but differed in density from one another, was the same as if the whole mass were collected at the common centre. The agreement of the two earthward accelerations—that of the moon and a stone at the earth's surface—was strong presumptive proof of the truth of Newton's theory, and later investigations, in which the theory has been applied in an immense number of ways, with in all cases results which agree with observation, have confirmed it in the most complete and triumphant manner.

That the force between two particles is referred to as an attraction is sometimes made a ground of criticism of this theory: for it may be, it is urged, that each body is pushed toward the other. It is true that this might be a perfectly correct way of describing what takes place; but when we say that two bodies A and B mutually attract one another we mean no more than that A is urged toward B and B is urged towards A, with equal forces, in consequence of the presence of the two bodies in the field. The *cause* of gravitational action is in no way prejudged by this mode of referring to the phenomenon.

The comparison made by Newton may be restated as follows, taking the earth as a sphere and neglecting its rotation. If the moon's mean distance from the earth be 383000 kilometres, and its time of revolution be 27·32 mean solar days, its acceleration towards the earth is, in cm./sec.² units,

$$\left(\frac{2\pi}{27\cdot 32 \times 86400}\right)^2 383000 \times 100000 = \cdot 271.$$

The acceleration of a falling body at the surface of the earth, taken as a sphere of radius 6365 kilometres, ought therefore to be, in the same units,

$$\left(\frac{383000}{6365}\right)^2 \times \cdot 271,$$

if it is the same gravitational attraction that keeps the moon in its orbit and causes a stone to fall to the earth. Now we have
$$\left(\frac{383000}{6365}\right)^2 \times \cdot 271 = 982\cdot 4,$$
which is nearly the (uncorrected) value in cm./sec.² units of the acceleration of a body falling freely under gravity at the earth's surface. Laplace (*Mécanique Céleste*, Ire Partie, Lib. II.) calculates from accelerations estimated from the distances the value of the moon's horizontal parallax, and compares the calculated value with the observed value.

142. Does Newtonian Gravitation extend to the Fixed Stars? The question of the extension of the theory of gravitational attraction to the fixed stars is not one that can be settled by means of observation alone. For though it is seen that the components of a binary star revolve round one another, so that it is clear that each component is acted on by a force toward the other, observation cannot decide what the position of the primary of such a pair is with respect to the relative orbit described about it by the secondary. For the apparent orbit is only seen projected on a tangent plane to the celestial sphere at the point, and it is the projected position of the primary that is observed, not the real position. Now the orbits as seen are always ellipses, and the real paths are no doubt also ellipses; they are certainly ellipses if they are plane curves. But the position of the primary is neither at the centre nor at a focus of the ellipse observed. It may, however, be situated at a focus of the real ellipse, for when an ellipse is projected on a plane the foci do not project into foci of the curve obtained by projection, though the centre projects into the centre.

The relative movements of the components of a large number of double stars are known, and these motions are very different in different systems; and we are led to assume that the central force is such that each component describes an elliptic orbit about the other, which depends only upon the position and velocity of the body at the initial instant. If then we take axes Ox, Oy, drawn from the centre of the primary in the plane of the real orbit, we may write for the relative motion of a secondary, the coordinates of which are x, y, the equations

$$m\ddot{x} = -Fx/r, \quad m\ddot{y} = -Fy/r,$$

where $r = \sqrt{x^2 + y^2}$, and inquire what function F is of x, y in order that the orbit may be a conic whatever are the initial values of x, y and of $\dot{x}, \dot{y}$.

This problem was proposed by Bertrand in *Comptes Rendus*, 84, and the same volume of that journal contains solutions by Halphen and Darboux, who have shown by very different methods that two laws, equivalent to those stated in § 158 below, are the only laws of force which give a conic as the orbit for any initial conditions. If the force is assumed to be independent of the vectorial angle,

$$\theta = \tan^{-1} y/x,$$

that is, to be a function of the distance r only, there are only two laws which give always a conic, namely,

$$F = m\mu r \quad \text{and} \quad F = m\mu/r^2.$$

The first of these cannot be the law of force for the components of binary stars, since the primary would then be at the centre of the projected orbit, which is not found to be the case; there remains therefore only the other law, which is that of the Newtonian gravitation.

143. Experimental Illustration of Gravitational Attraction. The motion of a satellite round a primary can be illustrated experimentally for different initial conditions by the following arrangement, in which electrical forces varying inversely as the square of the distance from a fixed point are made to play the part of gravitational forces. Two Leyden jars are arranged on a table with their knobs on the same level, and from two to three feet apart. Between them is hung by a thin fibre of silk a pith ball, or, better, a small silvered bead made of thin glass, so as to be as light as possible. The silk fibre should be at least fifteen or twenty feet long, and the point of support should be adjusted so that the ball may hang about the level of the centres of the knobs, and midway between them. The jars are now removed and charged, one positively, the other negatively, and replaced in the same positions. The small ball will be attracted towards one of the knobs, will touch it, and then be repelled. As it is driven away from that knob it acquires speed under the continual repulsion, and if it moves, as it probably will, towards the other knob, the repulsion is aided by the attraction which the ball also experiences towards the latter centre. Thus the ball arrives in the vicinity of the second knob with a considerable speed in a direction which depends on initial conditions, which are different in different experiments. When it has thus arrived, with what we may call a "speed of projection," at a point near the second knob, it is acted on by the attraction due to the charge on that, and hardly at all by the repulsion due to the charge on the first. The orbit round the second will be clearly seen by the persistence of impressions on the retina, and will take different forms according to the speed and direction of "projection." Sometimes the ball will be seen to pass round the second knob like a comet in its perihelion passage round the sun, passing off in what appears at first to be a long ellipse till it comes again under the influence of the first knob, to be thrown back again, perhaps, to describe a second orbit round the other. Or, on coming into the field of the second knob, the ball may be moving with just the velocity necessary to enable it to describe a circular orbit round the centre of force, which it will do two or three times in quick succession before the adjustment of force and velocity necessary for the circular path has broken down, and the ball falls in on the centre. It will be seen that, except in so far as the charge on the adjacent knob is disturbed by that on the ball, the arrangement, when the ball is near the first knob, is such as to give force varying inversely as the square of the distance from the centres of the knobs. The action of gravity is well-nigh annulled, and this is essential, by making the fibre very long. The spectators should stand some little way off, to prevent disturbances from air-currents, which should be otherwise avoided as far as possible.

144. Elements of an Orbit. The orbit of a planet lies in a plane coinciding more or less nearly with the plane of the ecliptic or path of the earth round the sun. The line of intersection of the plane of the orbit with the ecliptic is called the line of nodes: the nodes are the points on the orbit which lie in the ecliptic. To an eye placed away beyond the north pole of the earth a planet will appear at one node to come from the south to the north side of the ecliptic, and at the other to pass from the north side to the south. The former is called the ascending, the latter the descending node. Let a line be drawn from the sun's centre to the ascending node and another from the same point to the vernal equinox: the angle between these lines is called the heliocentric longitude of the ascending node. Let a line be drawn from the sun's centre to the perihelion position of the planet in its orbit, and another to the vernal equinox, and let these lines be projected on the plane of the ecliptic. The angle between the projections is the

§§ 143, 144, 145]   TIME IN AN ORBIT.   263

heliocentric longitude of the planet's perihelion. The longitude of the planet at a specified instant is defined in the same way by the projections of a line drawn from the sun's centre to the planet and the line to the vernal equinox. These angles are reckoned positive only when measured one way round, so as to avoid confusion.

Thus for the complete determination of an orbit six elements are required:

1. The major semi-axis, a.
2. The eccentricity, e.
3. The inclination of the plane of the orbit to the plane of the ecliptic.
4. The longitude of the perihelion, α.
5. The longitude of the ascending node.
6. The longitude of the planet at a given instant, θ.

145. Time in an Elliptic Orbit. In Fig. 57 let APA' be the orbit, with foci O, O' and centre C, NP the ordinate perpendicular to the major axis AA', to the position P of the particle, meeting when produced the circle described on AA' as diameter in Q. P is joined to O and Q to C and O. As P moves, let the ordinate NPQ accompany it: the point Q is called the *eccentric follower* of P. The angle AOP is called the *true anomaly* of P and the angle ACQ the *eccentric anomaly*. We denote the former by θ and the latter by u. [This is the usual notation, though u is also generally used for $1/r$.]

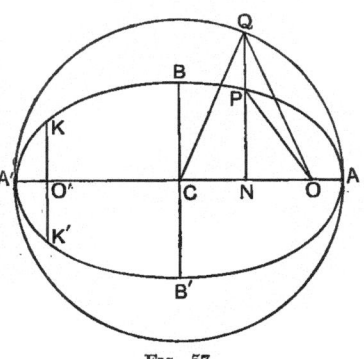

FIG. 57.

The mean angular speed n with which the radius-vector turns as the particle moves is $2\pi/T$. But

$$T = 2\pi\sqrt{a^3/\mu} = 2\pi ab/h, \text{ so that } n = \sqrt{\mu/a^3} = h/ab.$$

The quantity nt, where t is the time in which the particle moves from A to P, is called the *mean anomaly*. We shall now find relations connecting θ, u and nt.

In the first place we may regard the ellipse as derived from the circle in Fig. 57 by shortening every ordinate (as NQ to NP) in the ratio b/a. Hence

$$\text{area } AOP = \frac{b}{a} \text{ area } AOQ = \frac{b}{a}(\text{area } ACQ - \text{area } OCQ)$$

$$= \frac{b}{a}(\tfrac{1}{2}ua^2 - \tfrac{1}{2}a^2 e \sin u).$$

But if t be the time in which the particle moves from A to P, area $AOP = \tfrac{1}{2}ht = \tfrac{1}{2}abnt$. Equating this to the result just found, we get

$$nt = u - e \sin u. \quad \ldots\ldots\ldots\ldots\ldots\ldots\ldots(1)$$

To connect θ with u, we have $NO = a(e - \cos u)$ and also $ON = -OP \cos \theta$, with $OP = a(1 - e \cos u)$, so that

$$ON = a(e \cos u - 1) \cos \theta.$$

Thus we obtain

$$\cos \theta = \frac{e - \cos u}{e \cos u - 1}, \quad \cos u = \frac{e + \cos \theta}{1 + e \cos \theta}.$$

This equation may also be written

$$\left.\begin{array}{c} \dfrac{1 - \cos \theta}{1 + \cos \theta} = \dfrac{1 + e}{1 - e} \dfrac{1 - \cos u}{1 + \cos u} \\[2mm] \tan \tfrac{1}{2}\theta = \sqrt{\dfrac{1+e}{1-e}} \tan \tfrac{1}{2} u. \end{array}\right\} \ldots\ldots\ldots\ldots(2)$$

or

Also we have $\sin u = \sqrt{1 - e^2} \dfrac{\sin \theta}{1 + e \cos \theta}. \quad \ldots\ldots\ldots\ldots(3)$

Finally, by (1), (2) and (3), we obtain

$$nt = 2 \tan^{-1}\left(\sqrt{\frac{1-e}{1+e}} \tan \tfrac{1}{2}\theta\right) - e\sqrt{1-e^2} \frac{\sin \theta}{1 + e \cos \theta}. \quad \ldots(4)$$

From this last equation the time can be reckoned from perihelion when the true anomaly θ is known.

146. Time of Describing any Arc. Lambert's and Euler's Theorems. The time $t_2 - t_1$ of describing any arc from a point P_1, where the radius-vector is r_1, to a point P_2, where the radius-vector is r_2, can be found for any central orbit by the equation

$$t_2 - t_1 = \frac{1}{h}\int_{\theta_1}^{\theta_2} r^2 d\theta, \quad \ldots\ldots\ldots\ldots\ldots\ldots(1)$$

where θ_1 and θ_2 are the angles corresponding to r_1, r_2. The integration can be carried out by the relation connecting r and θ.

For an elliptic orbit the following theorem has been given by Lambert for this case. Let, besides r_1, r_2, the length c of the chord P_1P_2 be known; then, if ϕ, ϕ' be angles defined by the equations $\sin\tfrac{1}{2}\phi = \sqrt{(r_1+r_2+c)/4a}$, $\sin\tfrac{1}{2}\phi' = \sqrt{(r_1+r_2-c)/4a}$,

$$n(t_2 - t_1) = \phi - \sin\phi - (\phi' - \sin\phi'). \quad \ldots\ldots\ldots\ldots(2)$$

To prove it we note first that if u_1, u_2 be the eccentric anomalies for the positions P_1, P_2, we have

$$n(t_2 - t_1) = u_2 - u_1 - e(\sin u_2 - \sin u_1). \quad \ldots\ldots\ldots\ldots(3)$$

Taking ϕ and ϕ' first as undetermined, putting $\phi - \phi' = u_2 - u_1$, and choosing $\phi + \phi'$ so that

$$\cos\tfrac{1}{2}(\phi + \phi') = e\cos\tfrac{1}{2}(u_1 + u_2),$$

we get $\quad n(t_2 - t_1) = \phi - \phi' - (\sin\phi - \sin\phi')$,

the form (2) given to $n(t_2 - t_1)$ by the theorem.

If x_1, y_1, x_2, y_2 be the coordinates of P_1, P_2,

$$c^2 = (x_2 - x_1)^2 + (y_2 - y_1)^2$$
$$= a^2(\cos u_2 - \cos u_1)^2 + b^2(\sin u_2 - \sin u_1)^2$$
$$= 4a^2 \sin^2\tfrac{1}{2}(u_2 - u_1)\{1 - e^2\cos^2\tfrac{1}{2}(u_1 + u_2)\}$$
$$= 4a^2 \sin^2\tfrac{1}{2}(\phi - \phi')\sin^2\tfrac{1}{2}(\phi + \phi').$$

Thus $\quad c = 2a \sin\tfrac{1}{2}(\phi - \phi')\sin\tfrac{1}{2}(\phi + \phi')$,

where the positive value of the square root has of course been taken.

Again,

$$r_1 + r_2 = a(1 - e\cos u_1) + a(1 - e\cos u_2) = 2a\{1 - \cos\tfrac{1}{2}(\phi - \phi')\cos\tfrac{1}{2}(\phi + \phi')\}.$$

Hence $\quad r_1 + r_2 + c = 2a(1 - \cos\phi) = 4a\sin^2\tfrac{1}{2}\phi,$

$$r_1 + r_2 - c = 2a(1 - \cos\phi') = 4a\sin^2\tfrac{1}{2}\phi',$$

that is $\quad \sin\tfrac{1}{2}\phi = \sqrt{\dfrac{r_1 + r_2 + c}{4a}}, \quad \sin\tfrac{1}{2}\phi' = \sqrt{\dfrac{r_1 + r_2 - c}{4a}}. \quad \ldots\ldots(4)$

The theorem is therefore proved. The ambiguity resulting from the radicals in these equations is of no consequence if the positions of P_1, P_2 on the ellipse are known; the student may consider different possible cases for given values of r_1, r_2 and c.

Inserting the value of n, $\sqrt{\mu/a^3}$, in (2), we get

$$t_2 - t_1 = \sqrt{\dfrac{a^3}{\mu}}\{\phi - \phi' - (\sin\phi - \sin\phi')\}. \quad \ldots\ldots\ldots\ldots(5)$$

Now let the eccentricity of the ellipse be increased towards unity, a will increase towards infinity, and the ellipse will approximate to a parabola in the part near the centre of force. When a is very great we may take $\phi - \sin\phi = \frac{1}{6}\phi^3$, $\phi' - \sin\phi' = \frac{1}{6}\phi'^3$, since ϕ and ϕ' are now very small. We have then

$$a^{\frac{3}{2}}(\phi - \sin\phi) = \tfrac{1}{6}(r_1 + r_2 + c)^{\frac{3}{2}}, \quad a^{\frac{3}{2}}(\phi' - \sin\phi') = \tfrac{1}{6}(r_1 + r_2 - c)^{\frac{3}{2}}, \quad \ldots(6)$$

and so find for an ellipse of eccentricity nearly equal to 1 (when P_1, P_2 are taken well on the same side of the minor axis as that on which the centre of force lies), or for a parabola

$$t_2 - t_1 = \frac{1}{6\sqrt{\mu}}\{(r_1 + r_2 + c)^{\frac{3}{2}} - (r_1 + r_2 - c)^{\frac{3}{2}}\}. \quad \ldots(7)$$

This theorem is due to Euler, and was discovered previous to that of Lambert, from which we have here derived it.

It will be observed that we have here proved incidentally that the area of a focal sector of an ellipse, of which the terminal radii are r_1, r_2 and the chord c, has [since $(t_2 - t_1)h =$ twice area described in time $t_2 - t_1$] the value

$$\tfrac{1}{2}a^2\sqrt{1 - e^2}\{\phi - \sin\phi - (\phi' - \sin\phi')\}.$$

Similarly, the area of a focal sector of a parabola for which the same quantities r_1, r_2, c are given is, since h in this case is $\sqrt{\mu l}$, where l is the length of the semi-latus rectum,

$$\tfrac{1}{12}\sqrt{l}\{(r_1 + r_2 + c)^{\frac{3}{2}} - (r_1 + r_2 - c)^{\frac{3}{2}}\}.$$

For a solution of Kepler's Problem—the expansion of the true anomaly θ and the radius-vector r, in terms of the time t—the reader is referred to Routh's *Dynamics of a Particle*, § 476 *et seq.*, or to Tait and Steele's *Dynamics of a Particle*, § 163. The expansion of u in terms of t is given in Gray and Mathews' *Bessel Functions*, Chap. I. p. 4; see also the other books cited.

147. Disturbed Orbits. (1) Tangential Impulse. We now find the effect of a small impulse on the particle in changing the elliptic orbit which it describes about the given centre of force. The impulse may produce an increase of the speed of the particle without changing the direction of motion, or generate a small speed in the direction at right angles to that of motion, or some combination of these.

Let first the impulse be tangential, and change the speed from v to $v + \delta v$ without changing the direction. The distance r of the particle from the centre is thus given, and the problem is to find (1) what change in the eccentricity of the orbit is produced, and (2) the amount of turning of the major axis. The most convenient method

§§ 146, 147]   DISTURBED ORBITS.   267

of dealing with such problems consists in finding first what change is produced in the position of the empty focus. From that the change of eccentricity and the new position of the major axis can be found at once. Let P (Fig. 58) be the position of the particle when the impulse is applied, PT a tangent meeting the axis produced in T, O the centre of force and O' the empty focus. The point A, at which the major axis intersects the orbit, is an apse (§ 152), and the

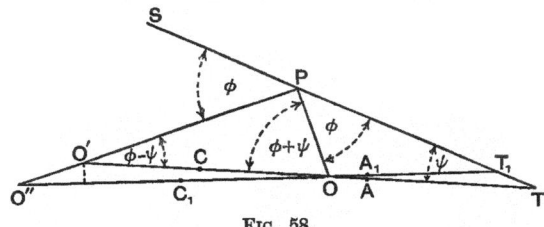

Fig. 58.

alteration of direction of the major axis is often referred to as the change of the position of the apse A. The effect of δv is to change the focus O' to O'', where $O'O''$ is twice the distance δa obtained by differentiating the equation

$$v^2 = \mu\left(\frac{2}{r} - \frac{1}{a}\right),$$

that is
$$\delta a = \frac{2v}{\mu} a^2 \delta v. \quad \ldots\ldots\ldots\ldots\ldots\ldots\ldots(1)$$

Now we have $OP + PO'' = 2(a + \delta a)$, and O'' must lie on PO' produced, since the equal angles OPT, SPO' are unaltered. The distance OO' is $2ae$, and OO'' is $2(a+\delta a)(e+\delta e)$, so that $OO'' - OO' = 2(a\,\delta e + e\,\delta a)$. Now, by Fig. 58,

$$OO'' - OO' = O'O'' \cos \angle OO'P.$$

But if $\phi = \angle OPT = \angle SPO'$ and $\psi = \angle PTO$,
then $\angle OO'P = \phi - \psi$ and $\angle O'OP = \phi + \psi$.

We have, since $O'O'' = 2\delta a$,

$$2(a\,\delta e + e\,\delta a) = 2\delta a \cos(\phi - \psi),$$

that is
$$\delta e = \frac{1}{a}\{\cos(\phi-\psi)-e\}\delta a = \frac{v}{\mu}\{2a\cos(\phi-\psi)-2ae\}\delta v \quad (2)$$

by the value of δa, found in (1) above.

Now, by Fig. 55, $2ae = (2a-r)\cos(\phi-\psi)+r\cos(\phi+\psi)$, and therefore
$$2a\cos(\phi-\psi)-2ae = 2r\sin\phi\sin\psi. \quad\ldots\ldots(3)$$

Also, by the equation for v^2 already used,
$$v/\mu = \sqrt{(2a-r)/\mu ar}.$$

Hence we get
$$\delta e = 2\sqrt{\frac{(2a-r)r\sin^2\phi}{\mu a}}\sin\psi\,\delta v = 2\frac{b}{\sqrt{\mu a}}\sin\psi\,\delta v, \quad\ldots(4)$$

since if p, p' be the lengths of the perpendiculars let fall from O and O' on the tangent at P, $r\sin\phi = p$, $(2a-r)\sin\phi = p'$, and $pp' = b^2$.

Now, to find the change in position of the apse A, we have only to find the alteration of the angle $OTP = \psi$. The figure shows that $2a\cos\phi = 2ae\cos\psi$, so that $e\cos\psi = \cos\phi$, the relation already proved in Ex. 12, §131. In the changes here considered ϕ remains constant, and so
$$\delta e = \frac{\cos\phi}{\cos^2\psi}\sin\psi\,\delta\psi = e\tan\psi\,\delta\psi. \quad\ldots\ldots\ldots(5)$$

Thus we have $\quad e\,\delta\psi = \dfrac{\delta e}{\tan\psi} = 2\dfrac{b}{\sqrt{\mu a}}\cos\psi\,\delta v. \quad\ldots\ldots\ldots(6)$

148. Disturbed Orbit. (2) Normal Impulse. We consider next the effect of a normal impulse, which produces a speed δu in the normal direction inwards. No change, at least to the first order of small quantities, is produced in the speed of the particle, but its direction of motion is turned, as shown in Fig. 59, through the small angle $\delta u/v$. Since the angle OPT is increased by this amount, the line PO' must turn through $2\delta u/v$ to make the angles OPT and $O'PS$ again equal. O' therefore comes to O'', and $PO' = PO''$. Now $O'O'' = PO' \times 2\delta u/v = (2a-r)2\delta u/v$, since $\angle O'PO'' = 2\angle SPS$.

§§ 147, 148]   DISTURBED ORBITS.   269

Then, since $\delta a = 0$,
$$\delta(2ae) = 2a\,\delta e = -O'O''\sin \angle OO'P = -(2a-r)\sin(\phi-\psi)\frac{2\delta u}{v}.$$
But $v = \sqrt{\mu(2a-r)/ar}$, and therefore
$$\delta e = -\sqrt{\frac{(2a-r)r}{\mu a}}\sin(\phi-\psi)\delta u.$$

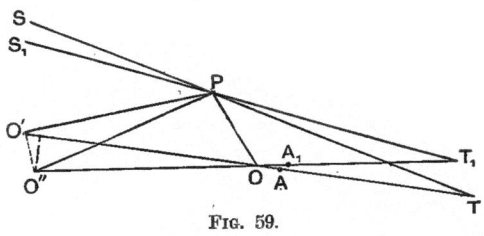

Fig. 59.

Now $(2a-r)/r = \sin(\phi+\psi)/\sin(\phi-\psi)$, and so we get
$$\delta e = -\frac{r}{\sqrt{\mu a}}\sqrt{\sin(\phi+\psi)\sin(\phi-\psi)}\,\delta u = -\frac{r}{\sqrt{\mu a}}\sqrt{\cos^2\psi-\cos^2\phi}\cdot\delta u,$$
that is
$$\delta e = -\frac{br}{\sqrt{\mu a^3}}\cos\psi\,\delta u, \qquad \ldots\ldots\ldots\ldots(1)$$
since $\cos\phi = e\cos\psi$.

For the alteration in the angle ψ, we have
$$\delta\psi = O'O''.\cos(\phi-\psi)/2ae = (2a-r)\cos(\phi-\psi)\delta u/aev.$$
But if x be the abscissa of the point P measured from the centre along the major axis, $\cos(\phi-\psi) = (x+ae)/(2a-r)$. Hence we have
$$e\,\delta\psi = \frac{x+ae}{av}\delta u. \qquad \ldots\ldots\ldots\ldots\ldots(2)$$
If in this we put $1/v = \sqrt{ar/\mu(2a-r)}$, we get
$$e\,\delta\psi = \frac{1}{\sqrt{\mu a}}\sqrt{\frac{r}{2a-r}}(x+ae)\,\delta u,$$
which, since $\sqrt{(2a-r)r\sin^2\phi} = b$, may be written
$$e\,\delta\psi = \frac{r}{b\sqrt{\mu a}}(x+ae)\sin\phi\,\delta u. \qquad \ldots\ldots\ldots\ldots(3)$$

270   A TREATISE ON DYNAMICS.   [CH. V.

Now $2ae \sin \psi = 2(a-r)\sin\phi$, so that $\sin\phi = ae\sin\psi/(a-r)$. Substituting in the last equation, we get, since $a-r=ex$,

$$e\,\delta\psi = \frac{ar}{b\sqrt{\mu a}}\frac{x+ae}{x}\sin\psi\,\delta u. \quad\ldots\ldots\ldots(4)$$

It will be observed that by (4) and (6) of §147 a tangential impulse with the motion (see Fig. 57) increases or diminishes the eccentricity according as the particle, in its motion in the direction $ABA'B'A$, is between B' and B, or between B and B', while the apse advances or recedes according as the particle is between A and A' or between A' and A.

On the other hand, for a normal impulse applied inwards, the eccentricity is diminished or increased according as the particle is between A and A' or between A' and A (see Fig. 57); the apse, on the other hand, advances when the particle is between K' and K, and recedes when the particle is between K and K'.

From the last result we get at once Callandreau's theorem,* that if the orbit of a comet lie within the orbit of Jupiter, so that the comet finds itself near the planet only in the vicinity of aphelion, the disturbing action of Jupiter's attraction is to turn the major axis of the orbit round in the direction of the comet's motion. Here the normal impulse acts outwards, and of course when this is the case, and the tangential impulse retards the motion, the values of de and $e\,d\psi$ found above must be reversed.

If the impulse is in neither the tangential nor the normal direction, it must be resolved into its tangential and normal components, and the effects, found as above, added together.

The effect of continuous action, the law of variation of which is known, can be formed by integration from the results obtained above, in which δv and δu are then to be regarded as the changes of velocity in the tangential and normal directions produced in time dt, over and above those which arise from the displacement in the orbit.

149. Disturbed Orbit.   (3) Change of Intensity of Central Force. So far the constant μ of the centre has been supposed

* Annales de l'Observatoire de Paris, 1892, t. 20.

unaltered. If it be suddenly changed to μ', we must have $v^2 = \mu(2/r - 1/a) = \mu'(2/r - 1/a')$, so that

$$a' = \frac{\mu' a r}{\mu r + 2(\mu' - \mu)a},$$

which gives the length of the new major semi-axis. Since the direction of the motion and the position of the centre of force are not altered, the angle ϕ remains the same, and thus the new position of the empty focus can be found at once from the value of a'. Fig. 58 illustrates this case. If the change $\mu' - \mu$ is a finite one, we get from Fig. 58, since $\angle OPO' = \pi - 2\phi$,

$$4a'^2 e'^2 = (2a' - r)^2 + r^2 + 2r(2a' - r)\cos 2\phi, \dots\dots\dots(1)$$

which gives e'. The change in the position of the apse is shown in the figure.

If the change in μ is small, we see from Fig. 58 that the change in $2ae$ is $2\delta a \cos(\phi - \psi)$, where ϕ and ψ are the angles OPT, OTP, and are related by the equation

$$\delta e = \frac{\delta a}{a}\{\cos(\phi - \psi) - e\}. \dots\dots\dots\dots\dots(2)$$

But we have now, since v^2 is unchanged,

$$\delta a = -a\frac{2a - r}{r}\frac{\delta \mu}{\mu}, \dots\dots\dots\dots\dots(3)$$

so that

$$\delta e = -\frac{2a - r}{r}\{\cos(\phi - \psi) - e\}\frac{\delta \mu}{\mu}. \dots\dots\dots(4)$$

It is interesting to note that if this vanishes, the relation, $2ae = (2a - r)\cos(\phi - \psi) + r\cos(\phi + \psi)$, becomes

$$2a\cos(\phi - \psi) = (2a - r)\cos(\phi - \psi) + r\cos(\phi + \psi),$$

that is $\cos(\phi - \psi) = \cos(\phi + \psi)$ or $\psi = 0$. The change therefore takes place when the particle is at the extremity of the minor axis.

150. Examples of Disturbed Orbits.

Ex. I. A particle describing an elliptic orbit about a focus O is at one end of the latus rectum through O, when the centre of force is suddenly moved a small distance towards the particle: find the alteration of period and the turning of the apse line.

272   A TREATISE ON DYNAMICS.   [CH. V.

Let $\alpha a(1-e^2)$ be the amount of shortening of the length $a(1-e^2)$ of the semi-latus rectum. Now $\frac{1}{2}v^2/\mu = 1/r - 1/2a$, and here $r = a(1-e^2)$. Thus $\delta a = 2a^2 \delta r/r^2$. But $\delta r = -a\alpha(1-e^2)$, and so $\delta a = -2a\alpha/(1-e^2)$, so that a has become $a\{1 - 2\alpha/(1-e^2)\}$. The period has therefore been changed in the ratio of $\{1 - 2\alpha/(1-e^2)\}^{\frac{3}{2}}$ to 1, that is in the ratio of $1 - 3\alpha/(1-e^2)$ to 1.

The shortening of the radius-vector OP is $a\alpha(1-e^2)$ and the shortening of $2a$ is $4a\alpha/(1-e^2)$. Thus the shortening of the radius-vector from the empty focus is

$$4a\alpha/(1-e^2) - a\alpha(1-e^2) = \{4a\alpha - a\alpha(1-e^2)^2\}/(1-e^2).$$

The directions of the radii-vectores are not altered.

Now if θ' be the inclination of the latter radius-vector to the major axis, we have $\sin \theta' = a(1-e^2)/\{2a - a(1-e^2)\} = (1-e^2)/(1+e^2)$. Hence, in consequence of the shortening of the radius-vector just calculated, the second focus is raised above the former major axis a distance

$$[\{4a\alpha - a\alpha(1-e^2)^2\}/(1-e^2)]\sin \theta' = \{4a\alpha - a\alpha(1-e^2)^2\}/(1+e^2).$$

The first focus has been lifted a distance $a\alpha(1-e^2)$; hence relatively the second focus has been lifted a distance

$$\{4a\alpha - a\alpha(1-e^2)^2\}/(1+e^2) - a\alpha(1-e^2) = 2a\alpha(1+e^2)/(1+e^2) = 2a\alpha.$$

Thus the major axis has been turned through the angle $2a\alpha/2ae = \alpha/e$.

Ex. 2. A particle is moving in an ellipse about a centre of attraction in a focus, and the centre of force is transferred to one end of the latus rectum as the particle passes through the other, to find the new orbit.

If we assume that the new orbit is an ellipse and denote the new semi-axis major by a', it comes out negative. The change of the centre of force to the more remote point has therefore made the given speed greater than the speed from infinity for the new centre. The new orbit is therefore a hyperbola, and we must write, if a' be the semi-axis major for the new orbit, and a that for the old,

$$\frac{1}{a(1-e^2)} - \frac{1}{2a} = \frac{1}{2a(1-e^2)} + \frac{1}{2a'},$$

which gives

$$a' = a\frac{1-e^2}{e^2}.$$

Thus the two radii-vectores to the foci are now

$$2a(1-e^2) \quad \text{and} \quad 2a\frac{1-e^2}{e^2} + 2a(1-e^2) = 2a\frac{(1-e^2)(1+e^2)}{e^2}.$$

The distance between the foci is now $2a'e'$, where e' is the new value of the eccentricity: also ϕ, the angle between the tangent and either radius-vector, is such that $\cos 2\phi = -(1-e^2)/(1+e^2)$. Hence, we get

$$4a'^2 e'^2 = 4a^2(1-e^2)^2 \left\{ \frac{(1+e^2)^2}{e^4} + 1 + 2\frac{1-e^2}{e^2} \right\},$$

§ 150]   EXAMPLES.   273

that is $\quad 4a'^2 e'^2 = 4a^2(1-e^2)^2 \dfrac{1+4e^2}{e^4}.$

Hence $\quad e'^2 = 1 + 4e^2.$

If O, O' be the foci in the old orbit, the foci in the new are O_1, O'' (see Fig. 60). The diagram is drawn to scale. Since
$$OL = CL_1 = a(1-e^2), \quad L_1 B_1 = ae^2.$$

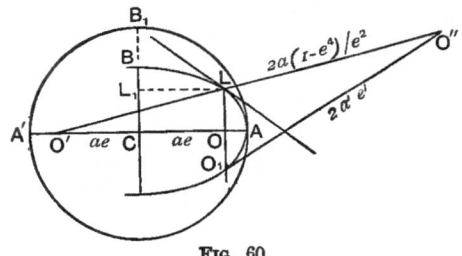

Fig. 60.

Hence, increasing OL in the ratio of CB_1 to $L_1 B_1$, we get $a(1-e^2)/e^2$. Adding to twice this length $2OL$, we obtain LO''.

Ex. 3. A body, the ratio of whose mass to that of the sun is m, falls into the sun. To find the change in the earth's mean distance and in the length of the year.

Differentiating the equation $\frac{1}{2}v^2/\mu = 1/r - 1/2a$ on the supposition that only μ and a vary, we get
$$v^2 \delta\mu/\mu^2 = -\delta a/a^2 \quad \text{or} \quad -\delta a = a^2 v^2 \delta\mu/\mu^2.$$

Inserting the value of v^2/μ, we get
$$\delta a = -a^2 \left(\frac{2}{r} - \frac{1}{a}\right) \frac{\delta\mu}{\mu},$$
which gives the alteration of mean distance consequent on a change $\delta\mu$ in μ. Also here $\delta\mu/\mu = m.$

Again, $T^2 = 4\pi^2 a^3/\mu$, and so by differentiation we get
$$\delta T = \frac{T}{2}\left(3\frac{\delta a}{a} - \frac{\delta\mu}{\mu}\right)$$
or
$$\delta T = -\frac{T}{2}\left(3\frac{v^2}{\mu}a + 1\right)\frac{\delta\mu}{\mu}$$
$$= -\frac{T}{2}\left(\frac{6a}{r} - 2\right)\frac{\delta\mu}{\mu},$$
where as before $\delta\mu/\mu = m.$

For example, if the body falls into the sun at the extremity of the minor axis, we have
$$\delta a = -am, \quad \delta T = -2Tm.$$

G.D.   S

Ex. 4. A body describes an ellipse about a centre of force at a focus when the "intensity of the centre" is suddenly increased in any ratio m; to find the new mean distance and the direction of the line of apsides.

Let a be the mean distance before the increase of intensity, and r the distance of the particle from the centre of force at the instant of change. The energy equation before and after the change has the forms
$$\frac{v^2}{\mu}=\frac{2}{r}-\frac{1}{a}, \quad \frac{v^2}{m\mu}=\frac{2}{r}-\frac{1}{a'},$$
if a' be the new mean distance. Thus we get
$$a=\frac{\mu r}{2\mu-v^2 r}, \quad a'=\frac{m\mu r}{2m\mu-v^2 r}.$$
The new empty focus lies on the line PO', at a distance from
$$P = 2a' - r = v^2 r^2/(2m\mu - v^2 r),$$
and the new line of apsides is the line joining the point thus determined with the focus O.

The new eccentricity e' is given by the equation
$$4a'^2 e'^2 = (2a' - r)^2 + r^2 + 2r(2a' - r)\cos 2\phi,$$
which, by the value of a' found above, becomes
$$e'^2 = \frac{1}{2m^2\mu^2}\{2m^2\mu^2 - 2m\mu v^2 r + v^4 r^2 + v^2 r(2m\mu - v^2 r)\cos 2\phi\}.$$

For instance, take the case of $m=2$ and $r=a$, then
$$2a' - r = v^2 a^2/(4\mu - v^2 a).$$
But now $v^2/\mu = 1/a$, and so
$$2a' - r = \mu a/(4\mu - \mu) = a/3.$$

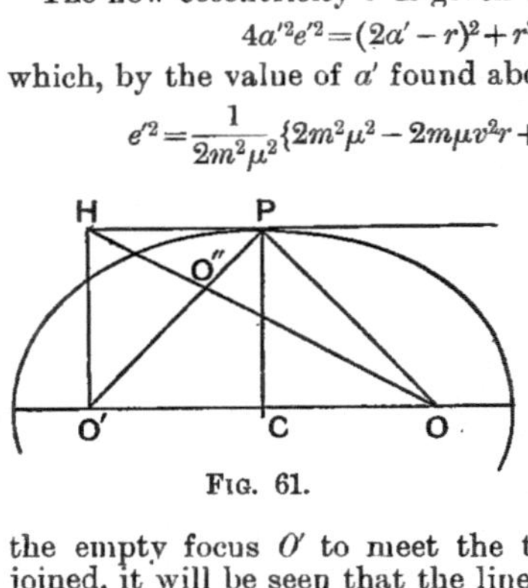

If a diagram (Fig. 61) be drawn of the ellipse with a tangent at an extremity P of the minor axis, and a perpendicular be let fall from the empty focus O' to meet the tangent in H, and $O'P$ and OH be joined, it will be seen that the lines $O'P$, OH meet in a point O'' which is $\frac{1}{3}O'P$ distant from P. But this, as we have seen, is the position of the new empty focus.

Fig. 61.

The equation for e'^2 gives for these values of r and m,
$$e'^2 = \tfrac{1}{4} + \tfrac{3}{4}e^2 = \tfrac{1}{4}(1 + 3e^2).$$

Ex. 5. A body is describing a circle under an attraction towards the centre when the force is suddenly reduced to one half its former value; to find the new path.

We have here $m=\tfrac{1}{2}$, $r=a$, $\cos 2\phi = -1$, $v^2 a = \mu$, and we obtain by the last example, or directly,
$$a' = \infty, \quad e' = 1,$$
and the path is a parabola.

§ 150] EXAMPLES.

Ex. 6. When the ratio is m and the original path is a circle, to find the path.
Again, we have $r=a$, $\cos 2\phi = -1$, $v^2 a = \mu$, and obtain
$$a' = ma/(2m-1), \quad e'^2 = (m-1)^2/m^2,$$
so that $e' = (m-1)/m$.

Ex. 7. A particle describing an ellipse about a centre of force at a focus and is at one end of the minor axis when the centre of force is suddenly shifted a small distance αa towards the particle, to find the change, if any, of the eccentricity, the turning of the line of apsides and the alteration of period.
It has been shown (Ex. 18, § 131) that
$$e^2 = 1 - 2v^2 r \sin^2\phi/\mu + v^4 r^2 \sin^2\phi/\mu^2.$$

It follows that, since $v^2 a = \mu$, $\partial e/\partial r = 0$, when $r = a$. Thus the eccentricity is not altered by the small shift of the centre.
Again, by the equation
$$v^2/\mu = 2/r - 1/a,$$
the change in a is twice the change in r when $r = a$. Thus when r is diminished by αa, $2a$ is diminished by $4\alpha a$. When

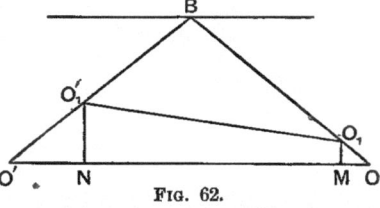
Fig. 62.

the particle is at B, therefore, the centre of force is brought to O_1 and the second focus to O_1', where $O'O_1' = 3OO_1$. Hence (see Fig. 62)
$$NO_1' = 3\alpha a\sqrt{1-e^2}, \quad MO_1 = \alpha a\sqrt{1-e^2}, \quad \text{since} \quad \sin\phi = \sqrt{1-e^2},$$
and therefore the line of apsides $O_1 O_1'$ is inclined to the former at the angle $2\alpha a\sqrt{1-e^2}/2ae = \alpha\sqrt{e^{-2}-1}$.
The alteration of period is from $2\pi\sqrt{a^3/\mu}$ to $2\pi\sqrt{a^3(1-2\alpha)^3/\mu}$, that is to $2\pi(1-3\alpha)\sqrt{a^3/\mu}$. The period is thus diminished in the ratio of $1 - 3\alpha$ to 1.

Ex. 8. A particle describes an elliptic orbit about a centre of force at a focus, and the centre of force is suddenly shifted a small distance αa towards the centre of the orbit: to find the change of eccentricity and the turning of the apsidal line.
The distance r is altered by $-\tfrac{1}{2}\alpha a \cos(\phi+\psi)$, where ψ is the angle between the tangent and the major axis, as shown in Fig. 58. Hence a is shortened by $\alpha a^3 \cos(\phi+\psi)/r^2$, and therefore $2a - r$ is shortened by $\tfrac{1}{2}\alpha a(4a^2 - r^2)\cos(\phi+\psi)/r^2$. Both radii-vectores are turned towards the centre through the angle $\alpha a \sin(\phi+\psi)/r$. Reference to a figure shows that the second focus is carried to the other side of the major axis from the particle through a perpendicular distance

$$(2a-r)\frac{\alpha a}{r}\sin(\phi+\psi)\cos(\phi-\psi) - \tfrac{1}{2}\alpha a(4a^2-r^2)\frac{1}{r^2}\cos(\phi+\psi)\sin(\phi-\psi),$$

and therefore the turning $d\psi$ of the apsidal line is this quantity divided by $2ae$.

Again, the distance between the foci in their new positions is less than the former distance $2ae$ by

$$\alpha a \{1 + \frac{4a^2 - r^2}{2r^2} \cos(\phi + \psi)\cos(\phi - \psi) + \frac{2a - r}{r}\sin(\phi + \psi)\sin(\phi - \psi)\},$$

and this is $-(2a\,\delta e + e\,\delta a) = -2\{a\,\delta e - 2e\frac{\alpha a^3}{r^2}\cos(\phi + \psi)\},$

from which we obtain δe.

Applying these results to the particular case when the particle is at an extremity of the latus rectum through the focus, we notice that to the first order of small quantities $\delta a = 0$, and obtain

$$\delta\psi = \frac{\alpha a}{l}, \quad \delta e = -\alpha,$$

where l is the length of the semi-latus rectum.

To the second order of small quantities we have in the same case $\delta r = \frac{1}{2}r(\delta\phi)^2 = \frac{1}{2}\alpha^2 a^2/l$, and therefore $\delta a = 2\delta r a^2/r^2 = \alpha^2 a^4/l^3$. Thus

$$(a + \delta a)^{\frac{3}{2}} = a^{\frac{3}{2}}(1 + \tfrac{3}{2}\alpha^2 a^3/l^3).$$

The period $2\pi\sqrt{a^3/\mu}$ is thus increased by the fraction $\tfrac{3}{2}\alpha^2 a^3/l^3$ of its former value.

151. Orbit slightly disturbed from Circular Form. In the preceding §§ 147–150, we have considered the effect of a small disturbance of the motion of a particle about a centre of force attracting according to the law μu^2, and have seen that it is to cause the particle to describe a new orbit, the deviation of which from the original orbit is specified by the alterations produced in a, e, and ψ. We now suppose a particle which moves in a circular orbit about a centre of force situated at the centre of the circle, and attracting according to the law μu^n, to be slightly disturbed from its path in such a way that the value of h is not altered.

In the first place, if $1/c$ be the radius of the circular orbit and v the speed of the particle in it, $v^2 c = \mu c^n$, so that $h^2 = v^2/c^2 = \mu c^{n-3}$. Further, the equation of motion is

$$\frac{d^2 u}{d\theta^2} + u = \frac{P}{h^2 u^2} = \frac{u^{n-2}}{c^{n-3}}. \qquad \ldots\ldots\ldots\ldots(1)$$

Now let $u = c(1 + x)$, where x is small. We obtain

$$\frac{d^2 x}{d\theta^2} = -(1 + x) + \{1 + (n-2)x + \ldots\} \qquad \ldots\ldots\ldots(2)$$

or
$$\frac{d^2x}{d\theta^2}+(3-n)x=0, \quad\ldots\ldots\ldots\ldots\ldots(3)$$

if we neglect higher powers of x than the first.
If $3 > n$, this equation has the solution
$$x = A\cos(\sqrt{3-n}\,\theta - \alpha), \quad\ldots\ldots\ldots\ldots(4)$$
where A and α are constants. Thus we have
$$u = c\{1 + A\cos(\sqrt{3-n}\,\theta - \alpha)\}, \quad\ldots\ldots\ldots(5)$$
and as the radius vector turns through the angle $2\pi/\sqrt{3-n}$, the value of u oscillates from the maximum value $c(1+A)$ to the minimum $c(1-A)$ and back again. The value of A is to be found from the conditions of the disturbance to which the orbit is subjected.

To carry the solution to a higher degree of approximation, we write the differential equation as
$$\frac{d^2x}{d\theta^2} = (n-3)\{x + \tfrac{1}{2}(n-2)x^2\}, \quad\ldots\ldots\ldots\ldots\ldots(6)$$
from which all terms above x^2 have been excluded. Substituting the approximate value of x, $A\cos(\sqrt{3-n}\,\theta - \alpha)$, just found in the term in x^2, we get for the differential equation to be solved
$$\frac{d^2x}{d\theta^2} = (n-3)[x + \tfrac{1}{4}(n-2)A^2\{1 + \cos 2(\sqrt{3-n}\,\theta - \alpha)\}]. \quad\ldots\ldots(7)$$
For the solution of this form of equation the student may consult Gibson's *Calculus*, § 170. But he will find by substitution that it is satisfied by
$$x = A\cos(\sqrt{3-n}\,\theta - \alpha) + A^2\{C + D\cos(2\sqrt{3-n}\,\theta - \alpha)\}, \quad\ldots\ldots(8)$$
and will at the same time determine the two additional constants C, D. In the same way the approximation may be pushed still further, but it will be found that the coefficient of θ is no longer a multiple simply of $\sqrt{3-n}$.

If $n > 3$ the solution of (7) is of the form
$$x = Ae^{\sqrt{n-3}\,\theta} + Be^{-\sqrt{n-3}\,\theta},$$
so that unless A is zero x will increase indefinitely with θ. We must therefore regard the circular motion in this case as unstable, and when $n < 3$ as stable, inasmuch as whatever the constants A and α may be the radial deviation can never exceed the values corresponding to the maximum and minimum values of u, $c(1+A)$, $c(1-A)$.

It will be observed that if $n=2$, the differential equation is

$$\frac{d^2u}{d\theta^2}+u=\frac{\mu}{h^2} \quad \text{or} \quad \frac{d^2x}{d\theta^2}+x=0, \quad \ldots\ldots\ldots\ldots\ldots\ldots(9)$$

and x is under no restriction to be small. Thus we have

$$x=A\cos(\theta-\alpha), \quad \ldots\ldots\ldots\ldots\ldots\ldots\ldots\ldots\ldots(10)$$

and
$$u=c\{1+A\cos(\theta-\alpha)\}, \quad \ldots\ldots\ldots\ldots\ldots\ldots(11)$$

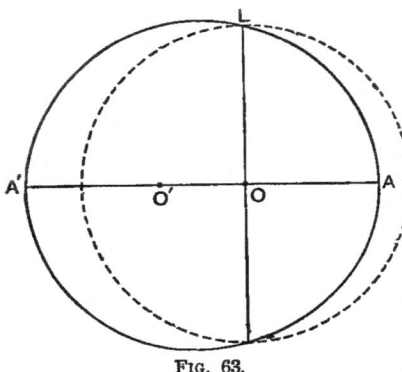

Fig. 63.

the equation of a conic of eccentricity A and semi-latus rectum $1/c$. Thus we get again the solution fully discussed above. But from the present point of view, we regard it (at least when $A<1$) as an oscillatory deviation from the circular orbit, described from the centre of force (a focus of the conic) as centre, with the semi-latus rectum $OL=1/c$ as radius, as shown in Fig. 63. The period of oscillation is that of revolution. For the ellipse which we have when $A\;(=e)<1$, the radial deviation at the point nearest the centre is

$$1/c-1/c(1+A)=e/c(1+e),$$

since $A=e$, and at the point furthest from the centre is

$$1/c-1/c(1-A)=-e/c(1-e).$$

The double rate of description of area retains the value

$$\sqrt{\mu/c}(=\sqrt{\mu a(1-e^2)})$$

in the elliptic orbit which it had in the circular orbit, but the period in the ellipse is

$$2\pi\sqrt{a^3/\mu}=2\pi/\sqrt{\mu c^3(1-e^2)^3},$$

while in the circle it was $2\pi/\sqrt{\mu c^3}$. By this we can reckon easily the alteration of period produced by a slight disturbance of a circular orbit. Thus, if e be very small, the period is changed from

$$2\pi/\sqrt{\mu c^3} \quad \text{to} \quad (2\pi/\sqrt{\mu c^3})(1+\tfrac{3}{2}e^2).$$

If $n=1$, the differential equation of the approximately circular orbit is

$$\frac{d^2x}{d\theta^2}+2x=0, \quad \ldots\ldots\ldots\ldots\ldots\ldots\ldots\ldots\ldots(12)$$

so that for x we have the value

$$x=A\cos(\sqrt{2}\theta-\alpha), \quad \ldots\ldots\ldots\ldots\ldots\ldots\ldots(13)$$

where A is small in comparison with 1, and the equation of the path is
$$u = c(1+x) = c\{1 + A\cos(\sqrt{2}\theta - \alpha)\}. \quad\ldots\ldots\ldots\ldots\ldots(14)$$
The variation of u thus passes through one complete period while the radius-vector revolves through the angle $\sqrt{2}\pi$.

The student may prove that the area swept over by the radius-vector and the period remain unaltered to the second order of small quantities.

152. Theory of Apsides. An apse is a point on the orbit at which it is met at right angles by the radius-vector from the centre of force. The condition fulfilled at an apse is therefore $du/d\theta = 0$, that is u is a maximum or a minimum. A planet is at an apse when in perihelion or aphelion, but not elsewhere in the orbit. At perihelion u is a maximum and r a minimum, at aphelion the reverse is the case.

The radius-vector from the centre of force to an apse is called an *apsidal distance*. We can show that, whatever may be the number of apsides in an orbit or a branch of an orbit, there cannot be more than two apsidal distances, if the central force is a function of the distance alone. For an apse may be taken as the point of projection, and the velocity there as the velocity of projection. If two particles be projected in the plane of the orbit from an apse in the two opposite directions at right angles to the apsidal radius-vector, under a central force which has always the same value at the same distance, the paths of the particles will lie symmetrically on the two sides of that line. Thus every radius-vector on one side will be repeated on the other at an equal angular distance from the apsidal radius. The curve on one side will, in fact, coincide with the image of the curve on the other in a mirror at right angles to the plane of motion and coinciding with the apsidal radius.

Now the radius of curvature at every point of an orbit must be the same for both directions of motion along the tangent at an apse, since $v^2/\rho = F\sin\phi$; and therefore a particle which has reached an apse in its orbital motion will, if its motion were there suddenly reversed, simply return along the path by which it arrived. Thus an apsidal radius-vector divides an orbit into two parts, which lie symmetrically on its two sides. It is clear then, that if we take any three apsidal radii to successive apsides A, B, C, the radius to C is the same as that to A, and the radius to B is repeated again at the next apse in order, D say, and so on. Thus there cannot be more than two apsidal distances in any distinct branch of the orbit, and these are reached alternatively as the particle describes it.

We can prove a somewhat more general proposition analytically as follows. We have

$$v^2 = h^2\left\{\left(\frac{du}{d\theta}\right)^2 + u^2\right\} = -2\int F\,dr.$$

If $F = \mu u^n$, where n is an integer,

$$v^2 = 2\int \mu u^{n-2}\,du = \frac{2\mu}{n-1}u^{n-1} + C. \quad\quad\quad\quad\ldots(1)$$

Hence, for an apse, since there $v^2 = h^2 u^2$, where h is the angular momentum about the centre of force, we get

$$u^{n-1} - \frac{n-1}{2\mu}h^2 u^2 + \frac{n-1}{2\mu}C = 0, \quad\quad\ldots(2)$$

where C is a constant; in fact, it is twice the constant value of the energy of the motion. This is an equation in descending powers of u, if $n > 2$, but whatever n may be the equation can always be so arranged, and as there are only three terms there cannot be more than two mutations of sign of the coefficients. Thus, by Descartes' rule, the equation has no more than two positive roots. Thus there are, *for this law of force*, in all the branches of the curve (if there be more than one branch) not more than two apsidal distances. The case of n a fraction p/q (in its lowest terms), can be dealt with by writing $u = u'^q$, taking care that the sign of F is properly settled when q is even.

Ex. 1. Let the central force be μu^n, where $n > 3$. The value of C is zero when $v^2 = 2\mu u^{n-1}/(n-1)$, that is when the speed is the speed from infinity. To make C positive, therefore, we take

$$v^2 > 2\mu u^{n-1}/(n-1).$$

Then we notice that a superior limit of the positive roots of (2) is a value of u (>0), which makes the expression on the left of (2) positive.

Such a value of u is one which satisfies the equation
$$u^{n-3}=(n-1)\frac{h^2}{2\mu}.$$
Hence $1/u$ cannot be less than a positive root of the equation
$$(1/u)^{n-3}=2\mu/(n-1)h^2.$$
Again, transforming (2) by substituting $1/u$ for u, we get
$$C\frac{n-1}{2\mu}u^{n-1}-\frac{n-1}{2\mu}h^2 u^{n-3}+1=0,$$
and a value of $1/u$ which makes the expression on the left positive is one which satisfies the equation $(1/u)^2=C/h^2$. Thus $1/u$ cannot be greater than the positive root of this equation.

Ex. 2. To find the apsidal angle.

By what has been stated above as to the symmetry of the orbit about each apsidal radius-vector, it is clear that there is only one apsidal angle, that is the angle between two apsidal radii. It can be determined at once when the equation of the curve is known, by differentiating u with respect to θ and putting $du/d\theta=0$. Thus, for the ellipse we have
$$du/d\theta = -e\sin(\theta-\alpha)/a(1-e^2),$$
and this vanishes for $\theta-\alpha=0, \pi, 2\pi, 3\pi, \ldots$. Thus the apsidal angle is π and the apsidal distances are $a(1-e)$, $a(1+e)$.

In the case of the approximately circular orbit, discussed in § 151, it will be seen that the apsidal angle for both the approximations there given is $\pi/\sqrt{3-n}$. For a higher approximation, in which it is found that
$$x=A\cos p(\theta-\alpha)+A^2\{C+D\cos 2p(\theta-\alpha)\}+A^3 E\cos 3p(\theta-\alpha),$$
the values of C, D, E, and p are to be found by substituting in the differential equation, and equating coefficients on the two sides of the result. It is found that
$$p^2=(3-n)\{1-\tfrac{1}{12}(n-2)(n+1)A^2\}.$$
The apsidal angle is then π/p.

[For fuller information regarding the Theory of Apsides and the Classification of Orbits, the student is referred to Routh, *Dynamics of a Particle*.]

153. Centre attracting according to Inverse Cube of Distance. A discussion of the motion of a particle attracted according to the inverse cube of the distance $(F=\mu u^3)$ is very instructive from the point of view of the effect of initial circumstances on the form of the orbit. The differential equation is
$$\frac{d^2u}{d\theta^2}+\left(1-\frac{\mu}{h^2}\right)u=0. \quad\ldots\ldots\ldots\ldots\ldots\ldots\ldots\ldots(1)$$

We may have $1 >, =,$ or $< \mu/h^2$. In the first and last cases we have, if $k = \sqrt{1 - \mu/h^2}$,

$$u = A \cos k(\theta - \alpha), \quad \dots\dots\dots\dots\dots\dots(2)$$
$$u = A_1 e^{k\theta} + A_2 e^{-k\theta} \quad \dots\dots\dots\dots\dots\dots(3)$$

respectively, and in the transition case of $\mu/h^2 = 1$,

$$u = C(\theta - \alpha) \quad \text{or} \quad r(\theta - \alpha)C = 1, \quad \dots\dots\dots(4)$$

where the constants A, A_1, B_1, and C are assigned according to initial conditions.

The speed from infinity to distance R is $\sqrt{\mu}/R = V'$, say. If the particle be projected with speed V at distance R, in a direction inclined at an angle ϕ to the radius-vector, then $h = VR \sin \phi$, and thus $\mu/h^2 = \mu/V^2 R^2 \sin^2 \phi$. The cases enumerated above are therefore those in which $V^2 >, =,$ or $< \mu/R^2 \sin^2 \phi$. If the particle moved in a circle of radius R under the attraction at distance R, we should have for its speed $V_1^2/R = \mu/R^3$ or $V_1^2 = \mu/R^2$, and thus $V_1 = V'$ the speed from infinity. This is called "the speed in the equidistant circle." Thus, according as $V \sin \phi >, =,$ or $<$ the speed in the equidistant circle, we have the three cases enumerated above.

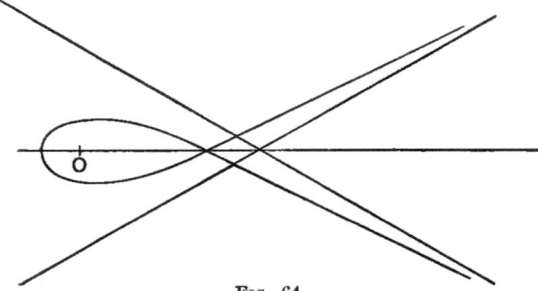

Fig. 64.

(1) $V \sin \phi > V'$, or $1 > \mu/h^2$. Differentiating the expression for u above, we get $du/d\theta = -kA \sin k(\theta - \alpha)$, which vanishes when $\theta - \alpha = n\pi/k$, where n is any integer, 0 included. Measuring θ from the radius-vector for which $n = 0$, we get
$$u = A \cos k\theta \quad \text{or} \quad r \cos k\theta = a \quad \dots\dots\dots\dots(5)$$

for the equation of the path. Each value of α gives a branch of the curve, and these branches occur at successive intervals of π/k. They are all precisely alike in the sense that each in succession is the one before it, turned forward through an angle π/k in its own plane about the centre. The curves are represented in Fig. 64.

(2) $V\sin\phi = V'$, or $\mu/h^2 = 1$. The equation is then
$$r\theta = C, \quad\quad\quad\quad\quad\quad\quad\quad\quad (6)$$
and the curve is known as the reciprocal spiral. It is shown in Fig. 65.

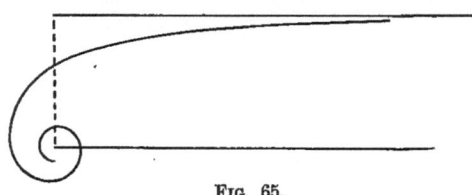

Fig. 65.

(3) $V\sin\phi < V'$ or $1 < \mu/h^2$. Going back to the differential equation, multiplying both sides by $2du/d\theta$ and integrating, we get $(du/d\theta)^2 + u^2 = u^2\mu/h^2 + c$, where c is a constant. Hence
$$\tfrac{1}{2}v^2 = \tfrac{1}{2}\mu u^2 + \tfrac{1}{2}h^2 c = \tfrac{1}{2}V'^2 + \tfrac{1}{2}h^2 c \quad\quad\quad (7)$$
is the energy equation. Initially, $v = V$, and so we have $c = (V^2 - V'^2)/h^2$, and
$$\left(\frac{du}{d\theta}\right)^2 + u^2 = \frac{\mu}{h^2}u^2 + \frac{V^2 - V'^2}{h^2}. \quad\quad (8)$$

If there is an apse, that is if we can suppose that the angle ϕ may take the value $\pi/2$, then $du/d\theta = 0$, and we get
$$k^2 u^2 = \frac{V'^2 - V^2}{h^2}. \quad\quad\quad\quad\quad (9)$$
where k^2 now denotes $\mu/h^2 - 1$.

Thus, with $k = \sqrt{\mu/h^2 - 1}$, the necessary condition for an apse is $V' > V$, and there is no apse if this condition is contradicted. We fall back then on case (1). Assuming the existence of an apse, we take $1/u_0$ for the apsidal distance,

and measure θ from that position of the radius-vector. Thus, for the complete integral written above in (3), we get, since $1/r_0 = u_0$ and $du/d\theta = 0$, for $\theta = 0$, $A_1 = A_2 = 1/2r_0$, and therefore
$$r_0 u = \tfrac{1}{2}(e^{k\theta} + e^{-k\theta}). \qquad (10)$$
Here k is positive, and therefore $du/d\theta$ is positive for all values of θ, that is r diminishes with increase of θ. The curve bends in towards the centre of force, as shown in Fig. 66. There are two branches described in opposite directions from the apse A, and each winds in closer and closer convolutions about the centre of force.

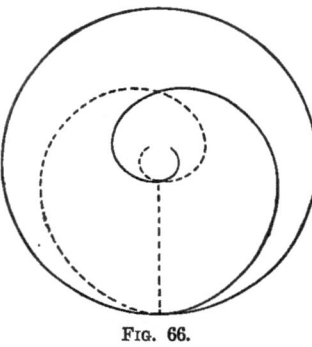

Fig. 66.

Two other sub-cases of Case (3) remain: first, that in which $V = V'$; second, that in which $V > V'$. In the first of these, $du/d\theta = ku$, and therefore
$$r_0 u = e^{k\theta} \qquad (11)$$
is the equation of the curve, which is an equiangular spiral (see Fig. 23, §43). In the remaining case $V^2 > V'^2$, and so we have $(du/d\theta)^2 = (\mu/h^2 - 1)u^2 + (V^2 - V'^2)/h^2$. As we have seen, there is no apse. If we go back to the solution of the differential equation, we get
$$\frac{du}{d\theta} = k(A_1 e^{k\theta} - A_2 e^{-k\theta}), \qquad (12)$$
and, by squaring,
$$\left(\frac{du}{d\theta}\right)^2 = k^2 u^2 - 4k^2 A_1 A_2. \qquad (13)$$
Thus the positive quantity $(V^2 - V'^2)/h^2 = -4k^2 A_1 A_2$, so that in this case A_1, A_2 have opposite signs, and are such that $A_1 A_2 = -(V^2 - V'^2)/4k^2 h^2$. Thus, writing b^2 for $(V^2 - V'^2)/4h^2 k^2$,

we have
$$u = A_1\left(e^{k\theta} - \frac{b^2}{A_1}e^{-k\theta}\right). \qquad (14)$$

Both u and $du/d\theta$ increase without limit as θ increases, and therefore r diminishes. When $\theta = 0$, $u = A_1 - b^2$, and if initially $A_1 = b^2$, then $r = \infty$. Of course $du/d\theta$ may be either positive or negative, and so there are two branches, as in Fig. 67. They have a common asymptote, as shown in the diagram, and the curves are described as shown by the arrows.

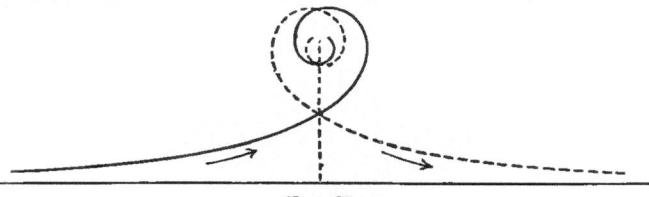

FIG. 67.

By putting $Ae^{k\alpha} = A_1$, $Ae^{-k\alpha} = b^2/A_1$ we get $A = b$ and $k\alpha = \log A_1 - \log b$, so that we can write the equation for u in the form

$$u = A\{e^{k(\theta+\alpha)} - e^{-k(\theta+\alpha)}\} \quad \ldots\ldots\ldots\ldots\ldots\ldots(15)$$

or, changing the initial value of θ, in the form

$$u = A(e^{k\theta} - e^{-k\theta}), \quad \ldots\ldots\ldots\ldots\ldots\ldots(16)$$

which differs from that for the case of $V' > V$ only in the sign of the second term.

The curves for the motions treated in this section are known as Cotes' Spirals (*Harmonia Mensurarum*, 1722).

154. Force varying as Inverse n^{th} Power of Distance. The differential equation for the case of $F = \mu u^n (n > 1)$, namely

$$\frac{d^2u}{d\theta^2} + u = \frac{\mu}{h^2} u^{n-2}, \quad \ldots\ldots\ldots\ldots\ldots\ldots(1)$$

can (except in the case, just treated, of $n = 3$) be integrated by aid of the energy equation when the speed of the particle at every point of its path is the speed from infinity. If this is the case at one point—the point of projection—it will be the case at all. The energy equation can then be written

$$\tfrac{1}{2}v^2 = \tfrac{1}{2}h^2\left\{\left(\frac{du}{d\theta}\right)^2 + u^2\right\} = \frac{\mu}{n-1} u^{n-1}. \quad \ldots\ldots\ldots(2)$$

This gives, after a little reduction,
$$\frac{du}{u\sqrt{au^{n-3}-1}} = d\theta, \quad\ldots\ldots\ldots\ldots\ldots\ldots(3)$$
where $a = 2\mu/(n-1)h^2$.

By the substitution $au^{n-3} = 1/z^2$ (which is only applicable if $n \neq 3$), this transforms into
$$-\frac{dz}{\sqrt{1-z^2}} = \frac{n-3}{2}d\theta, \quad\ldots\ldots\ldots\ldots\ldots(4)$$
which gives
$$\cos^{-1}z = \frac{n-3}{2}(\theta-\alpha), \quad\ldots\ldots\ldots\ldots(5)$$
where α is a constant. Thus the equation of the orbit is
$$r^{\frac{n-3}{2}} = \left(\frac{2\mu}{(n-1)h^2}\right)^{\frac{1}{2}}\cos\frac{n-3}{2}(\theta-\alpha) = c^{\frac{n-3}{2}}\cos\frac{n-3}{2}(\theta-\alpha). \ldots(6)$$

The result of the integration is unaffected by the ambiguity of sign introduced by the radical, which is to be interpreted according to the sign of the initial $du/d\theta$.

This equation shows that when $n > 3$ the path consists of one, two, or more loops, according to the value of n, with a common node at the centre of force, and a maximum radius vector equal to c, which recurs at the angular interval $4\pi/(n-3)$. When $n < 3$ the orbit has infinite branches; for example, when $n = 2$, it is a parabola, and c is the minimum radius-vector.

As another example we take the case of $n = 5$. We have then
$$r = c\cos(\theta-\alpha), \quad\ldots\ldots\ldots\ldots\ldots\ldots(7)$$
the equation of a circle with the centre of force on the circumference. The maximum radius-vector is c, the diameter of the circle.

If $n = 7$ the equation of the curve is
$$r^2 = c^2\cos 2(\theta-\alpha), \quad\ldots\ldots\ldots\ldots\ldots(8)$$
the equation of the lemniscate of Bernoulli (see above, Ex. 4, §125).

In all these cases the condition is imposed that the speed at each point is that from infinity. But the integrations can be effected under other conditions in these and other cases. (Reference may be made to Routh, *Dynamics of a Particle*, and Greenhill, *Elliptic Functions*.)

Ex. 1. Carry out the integration when the force is repulsive, force varying as the inverse n^{th} power of the distance, and the speed at each point is that from the centre of force to the point.

Ex. 2. Integrate the equation of energy when the force is repulsive and varies directly as the nth power of the distance, and the speed at each point is as in Ex. 1.

Ex. 3. If the speed at each point in a central orbit bear a constant ratio to that in an equidistant circle, find the orbit and the law of force (see § 153.)

Ex. 4. The speed and direction of motion at any point and the centre and law of force: find the radius of curvature of the orbit at the point.

Ex. 5. Find the equation of the orbit when $F = \mu u^n + \mu_1 u^3$, where $n > 1$ and $\neq 3$, when the speed in the orbit for $F = \mu u^n$ is equal to the speed from infinity (see § 130.)

155. Different Centres for Same Orbit. Newton's Theorem. Newton proved (*Principia*, Lib. I. Prop. VII. Cor. 3) that if the force towards a centre O, by which an orbit can be described, is known, the force towards a new centre O_1, by which the same orbit is described, can be found. Clearly, the orbit will be described if the force toward the centre of curvature have always the proper value. Let P (Fig. 68) be any point of the orbit, ρ the radius of curvature there, r, r_1 the distances, OP, O_1P, and p, p_1 the lengths of the perpendiculars let fall from O, O_1 on the tangent drawn to the curve at P. Then, if v be the speed at P and F, F_1 the forces which give the same value of v^2/ρ,

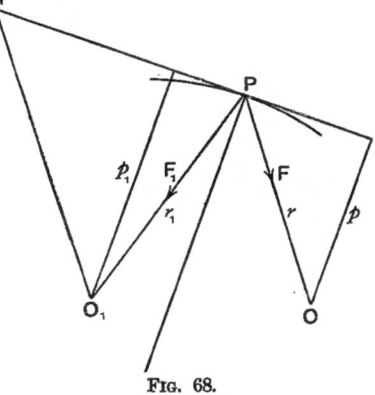

Fig. 68.

$$\frac{v^2}{\rho} = F\frac{p}{r} = F_1\frac{p_1}{r_1}, \text{ so that } \frac{F_1}{F} = \frac{pr_1}{p_1 r}.$$

The double rate of description of area is $h=pv$, under the force F towards O: if the force F_1 towards O_1 is taken for a new speed v', we have $h_1=p_1v'$, so that $v'^2/v^2 = h_1^2 p^2/h^2 p_1^2$, and in this ratio we must increase F_1. Thus, we obtain for the forces towards O and O_1, either of which will enable the orbit to be described,

$$\frac{F_1}{F} = \frac{h_1^2 p^3 r_1}{h^2 p_1^3 r}. \quad\ldots\ldots\ldots\ldots\ldots\ldots\ldots\ldots(1)$$

If we draw from O_1 a line O_1H parallel to OP to meet the tangent in H, then $p_1/p = O_1H/r$, and therefore

$$r^3/p_1^3 = r^3/O_1H^3.$$

Thus
$$\frac{F_1}{F} = \frac{h_1^2}{h^2} \frac{r^2 r_1}{O_1 H^3}. \quad\ldots\ldots\ldots\ldots\ldots\ldots\ldots(2)$$

As an example, take O as the focus of an elliptic orbit at which the centre of force is situated, and let O_1 be the centre of the ellipse. Then $F = \mu/r^2$, and from the geometry of the ellipse we have $O_1H = a$, so that

$$F_1 = \mu \frac{h_1^2}{h^2} \frac{r_1}{a^3}. \quad\ldots\ldots\ldots\ldots\ldots\ldots\ldots(3)$$

Thus the force toward the centre of the ellipse under which the orbit can be described varies directly as the radius-vector r_1, drawn from the centre. Writing $\mu_1 r_1$ for F_1, we get

$$\mu_1 = \mu \frac{h_1^2}{h^2 a^3}. \quad\ldots\ldots\ldots\ldots\ldots\ldots\ldots(4)$$

But when the orbit is described by a particle under a force toward the focus, $h^2 = \mu a(1-e^2)$, so that we obtain

$$h_1^2 = \mu_1 a^4 (1-e^2)$$

or $\qquad h_1 = \sqrt{\mu_1} \cdot ab, \quad\ldots\ldots\ldots\ldots\ldots\ldots\ldots(5)$

where a, b are the principal semi-axes.

156. Hamilton's Theorem. The force toward any centre O_1 (Fig. 69), under which a particle will describe an orbit, is, as we have seen, given by the equation

$$F = \frac{v^2}{\rho} \frac{r}{p} = \frac{1}{\rho} \frac{h^2 r}{p^3}, \quad\ldots\ldots\ldots\ldots\ldots\ldots\ldots(1)$$

§§ 155, 156]   HAMILTON'S THEOREM.   289

where ρ is the radius of curvature at a point P of the orbit to which the radius-vector is r, and p is the length of the perpendicular let fall from O_1 on the tangent at P. Now, if the orbit be a conic of semi-axes ab, and the polar LM of the point O_1 with respect to the conic be drawn, and ϖ, ϖ' denote the lengths of the perpendiculars let fall from P and from the centre of the conic respectively to this polar, it can be proved that

$$\frac{1}{\rho} = \frac{1}{a^2 b^2} \frac{\varpi'^3}{\varpi^3} p^3. \quad \ldots\ldots\ldots\ldots\ldots\ldots\ldots(2)$$

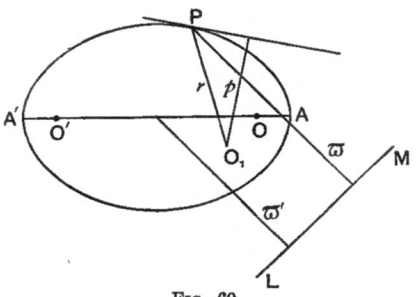

Fig. 69.

In proving this proposition we shall assume that the curve is an ellipse, but the proof may be easily modified to suit any other conic. Let f, g be the coordinates of O_1 with reference to the principal axes; the equation of the polar is

$$\frac{fx}{a^2} + \frac{gy}{b^2} = 1.$$

If x, y be the coordinates of P, the perpendicular from P to the polar has length

$$\varpi = \frac{1 - \dfrac{f}{a^2} x - \dfrac{g}{b^2} y}{\sqrt{\dfrac{f^2}{a^4} + \dfrac{g^2}{b^4}}} = \frac{a^2 b^2 - b^2 fx - a^2 gy}{\sqrt{f^2 b^4 + g^2 a^4}},$$

while that from the centre to the polar has length

$$\varpi' = \frac{a^2 b^2}{\sqrt{f^2 b^4 + g^2 a^4}}.$$

G.D.   T

The length of the perpendicular from O_1 to the tangent at P, of which the equation is

$$\frac{xx'}{a^2}+\frac{yy'}{b^2}=1,$$

is found in the same way to be

$$p=\frac{a^2b^2-b^2fx-a^2gy}{\sqrt{x^2b^4+y^2a^4}}.$$

Hence we get, by (2),

$$\frac{1}{a^2b^2}\frac{\varpi'^3}{\varpi^3}p^3=\frac{a^4b^4}{(x^2b^4+y^2a^4)^{\frac{3}{2}}}. \quad\ldots\ldots\ldots\ldots(3)$$

But if we calculate $1/\rho$ by the usual formula,

$$\frac{1}{\rho}=\frac{\frac{d^2y}{dx^2}}{\left\{1+\left(\frac{dy}{dx}\right)^2\right\}^{\frac{3}{2}}},$$

we find (disregarding sign, since $1/\rho$ is to be taken positive here) precisely this value. Hence by (1) we have

$$F=\frac{h^2}{a^2b^2}\frac{\varpi'^3}{\varpi^3}r. \quad\ldots\ldots\ldots\ldots\ldots\ldots(4)$$

The values of r and ϖ vary from point to point on the curve, the other quantities remain constant. Thus we have the theorem that if O_1 be any centre, a force varying as the distance of O_1 from P, and inversely as the cube of the length of the perpendicular from P on the polar of O_1 and directed towards O_1, will enable the conic to be described. This theorem is due to Sir W. R. Hamilton (*Proc. Royal Irish Academy*, vol. 3).

As an example, let O_1 be the focus of the ellipse. Then the polar of O_1 is the directrix, and

$$\varpi=r/e, \quad \varpi'=a/e.$$

Hence $$F=\frac{h^2}{a^2b^2}\left(\frac{\varpi'}{\varpi}\right)^3 r=\frac{\mu a(1-e^2)}{a^4(1-e^2)}\frac{a^3}{r^3}r=\frac{\mu}{r^2},$$

the known law of force.

157. Second Statement of Hamilton's Theorem. Hamilton's theorem can be put in another form. Still considering a given orbit, let, if possible, two tangents O_1A, O_1B (Fig. 70) be drawn from the proposed centre of force O_1 to the orbit, and from any point P of the orbit let fall perpendiculars to the lines O_1A, O_1B, AB: let the lengths of the first two be denoted by α, β; the length of the third is ϖ since AB is the polar of O_1. Then, by the properties of conics, we have $\alpha\beta = k\varpi^2$, where k is a constant for the conic. Hence, writing κ for $h^2\varpi'^3 k^{\frac{3}{2}}/a^2b^2$, we get

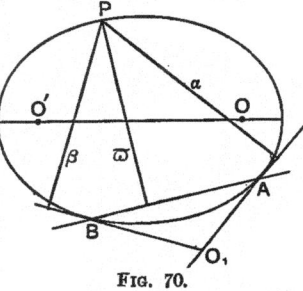

Fig. 70.

$$F = \kappa \frac{r}{(\alpha\beta)^{\frac{3}{2}}}. \quad\quad\quad\quad\quad\quad\quad (1)$$

The equivalence of these two statements of Hamilton's theorem may be seen as follows. The general equation of the second degree referred to O_1 as origin may be written

$$ax^2 + 2hxy + by^2 + 2gx + 2fy + c = 0.$$

The polar of the origin has equation $gx + fy + c = 0$, and therefore if P be any point on the curve of coordinates x, y, the perpendicular from P to this polar has length

$$(gx + fy + c)/\sqrt{f^2 + g^2}.$$

If ξ, η, be the coordinates of the centre of the conic, we obtain by transforming the equation of the conic to the centre as origin,

$$a\xi + h\eta + g = 0, \quad h\xi + b\eta + f = 0 \quad\quad\quad (2)$$

as the conditions that the new f and g should vanish. By these we write the equation of the curve in the form

$$ax^2 + 2hxy + by^2 + g\xi + f\eta + c = ax^2 + 2hxy + by^2 + \frac{\Delta}{ab - h^2} = 0,$$

where $\Delta = abc + 2fgh - af^2 - bg^2 - ch^2$, the result, multiplied by $ab-h^2$, of substituting the values of ξ, η derived from (2) in the expression $g\xi+f\eta+c$. But since ξ, η are the coordinates of the centre, $(g\xi+f\eta+c)/\sqrt{f^2+g^2}$ is the length ϖ' of the perpendicular let fall from the centre on the line $gx+fy+c=0$, the polar of O_1 with respect to the conic. Thus

$$\varpi'\sqrt{f^2+g^2} = \frac{\Delta}{ab-h^2}. \qquad (3)$$

Again, if a_1, b_1 be the lengths of the principal semi-axes of the conic, we get, by turning the axes so as to make the new h vanish,

$$a_1^2 b_1^2 = \frac{(g\xi+f\eta+c)^2}{ab-h^2} = \frac{\Delta^2}{(ab-h^2)^3}.$$

We obtain, therefore,

$$\frac{1}{a_1^2 b_1^2}\left(\frac{\varpi'}{\varpi}\right)^3 = (ab-h^2)\frac{g\xi+f\eta+c}{(gx+fy+c)^3} = \frac{\Delta}{(gx+fy+c)^3}. \quad \ldots(4)$$

But x, y, the coordinates of P, satisfy the equation

$$ax^2 + 2hxy + by^2 + 2gx + 2fy + c = 0,$$

which can evidently be written in the form

$$c(ax^2 + 2hxy + by^2) - (gx+fy)^2 = -(gx+fy+c)^2;$$

that is, if we put $A = g^2-ac$, $B = f^2-bc$, $C = fg-ch$,

$$Ax^2 + 2Cxy + By^2 = (gx+fy+c)^2.$$

We get then, by (1), with the meaning of h in (4), § 156,

$$F = h^2 \frac{r\Delta}{(Ax^2+2Cxy+By^2)^{\frac{3}{2}}}. \qquad (5)$$

Now the equation $Ax^2 + 2Cxy + By^2 = 0$ represents two straight lines O_1A, O_1B meeting the curve at the points A, B in which it is met by the polar of the point O_1. These lines are therefore, if real, tangents to the curve at A, B. If then x, y be, as here, the coordinates of a point P on the curve which does not lie on either line, $Ax^2+2Cxy+By^2$ is, to a factor which is the same for all points on the curve, equal to the products of the lengths of the perpendiculars α, β let fall from P on the lines. The second form of Hamilton's theorem is thus established.

158. Orbit a Conic touching Two Straight Lines drawn from C.F. The very important result follows that if O_1 be any centre of force and O_1A, O_1B be any two lines drawn from O_1, *any* conic touching these two lines is an orbit for the centre of force, and the law of force is given by (5).

Again, if a particle move under the action of a force directed to a fixed point O_1, and varying directly as the distance of the particle from the fixed point and inversely as the cube of its distance from a fixed straight line, the orbit is a conic with respect to which the given straight line is the polar of O_1.

For if a point P in the plane of the two lines O_1A, O_1B, or in the plane of the centre of force O_1 and the fixed straight line, be specified and a velocity at that point be also specified in direction and magnitude, a conic passing through P and touching O_1A, O_1B, or with respect to which the given straight line is the polar of O_1, can be determined, which is an orbit described about the centre of force O_1 under the influence of a force as specified in (4) of §156 or (1) of §157, with velocity at P and direction of curvature as indicated. And every other possible orbit so described will coincide at P with the conic in regard to speed, direction of motion, and curvature, and the variation from P in direction of motion and curvature will be the same in both—that is the two orbits are solutions of the same differential equation which fulfil the same initial conditions. There is only one such solution, and the orbits are identical.

Analytical proofs of propositions equivalent to the statement that the two laws (or rather two versions of the same law) stated above are the only laws which always give conics as orbits have been given by MM. Halphen and Darboux (*Comptes Rendus*, t. 84).

159. Particle acted on by Forces from Several Centres. Bonnet's Theorem. Provided a certain condition is satisfied, a particle can describe a given path under the combined action of any specified system of forces $F_1, F_2, \ldots$ directed to any given fixed points.

Let N and T denote the normal and tangential components of force on the particle, due to these forces. Then

$$N = \Sigma F_k \frac{p_k}{r_k}, \quad T = -\Sigma F_k \frac{dr_k}{ds}, \quad \ldots\ldots\ldots\ldots\ldots\ldots(1)$$

where p_k denotes the length of the perpendicular let fall from the centre for the force F_k to the tangent at P, the position of the particle at the instant considered, and r_k is the distance of P from that centre. Now if ρ be the radius of curvature of the path at P, we have

$$2T = d(v^2)/ds = d(N\rho)/ds.$$

Hence, inserting the values of N and T given above, we get

$$2\Sigma F_k \frac{dr_k}{ds} + \Sigma \frac{d}{ds}\left(F_k \frac{p_k \rho}{r_k}\right) = 0. \quad\quad\quad\quad\quad\quad(2)$$

But we have

$$\frac{1}{p_k^2}\frac{d}{ds}\left(F_k \frac{p_k^3 \rho}{r_k}\right) = \frac{d}{ds}\left(F_k \frac{p_k \rho}{r_k}\right) + 2F_k \frac{\rho}{r_k}\frac{dp_k}{ds} = \frac{d}{ds}\left(F_k \frac{p_k \rho}{r_k}\right) + 2F_k \frac{dr_k}{ds},$$

since $1/\rho = (dp_k/dr_k)/r_k$. Thus the equation just found can be written

$$\Sigma \frac{1}{p_k^2}\frac{d}{ds}\left(F_k \frac{p_k^3 \rho}{r_k}\right) = 0, \quad\quad\quad\quad\quad\quad(3)$$

which is the required condition. Of course, the speed V of projection must be such that $V^2/\rho = N$.

Let $P_1, P_2, \ldots$ be central forces, *each* of which if it acts alone causes a particle to describe a central orbit; then we can prove that any such system of forces acting together will enable the particle to describe the orbit, provided the speed v at any chosen point is given by $v^2 = v_1^2 + v_2^2 + \ldots$, where $v_1, v_2, \ldots$ are the speeds at that point for the separate forces $P_1, P_2, \ldots$. Thus, for the combined forces, the energy is the sum of the energies for the separate forces.

Since each of the forces $P_1, P_2, \ldots$ enables the particle to describe the orbit, we have $v_1^2/\rho = P_1 p_1/r_1$, $v_2^2/\rho = P_2 p_2/r_2$, $\ldots$, $v_1 dv_1/ds = -P_1 dr_1/ds$, $v_2 dv_2/ds = -P_2 dr_2/ds$, $\ldots$. Now, with the value of v stated above, we have

$$\frac{v^2}{\rho} = P_1 \frac{p_1}{r_1} + P_2 \frac{p_2}{r_2} + \ldots, \quad v\frac{dv}{ds} = -\left(P_1 \frac{dr_1}{ds} + P_2 \frac{dr_2}{ds} + \ldots\right), \quad\ldots(4)$$

and the normal and tangential forces required are just furnished by the combined system. This is Bonnet's theorem. [Liouville's *Journal*, t. ix.].

160. Theorem of Curtis. The following is another general theorem with regard to the description of an orbit under combined forces.

If a given path is described by a particle under the separate action of forces $P_1, P_2, \ldots$, which act from fixed centres, it can be described also under the combined action of forces $F_1, F_2, \ldots$ acting from the same centres, provided

$$\Sigma c_k P_k \frac{d}{ds}\left(\frac{F_k}{P_k}\right) = 0, \quad\quad\quad\quad\quad\quad(1)$$

where c_k is the chord of curvature of the path in the direction of P_k. [Curtis, *Mess. Math.* x. 1880].

MULTIPLE CENTRES.

We have, as before,
$$\frac{v_1^2}{\rho}=P_1\frac{p_1}{r_1},\quad \frac{v_2^2}{\rho}=P_2\frac{p_2}{r_2},\ \ldots,\quad v_1\frac{dv_1}{ds}=-P_1\frac{dr_1}{ds},\quad v_2\frac{dv_2}{ds}=-P_2\frac{dr_2}{ds},\ \ldots \quad\ldots(2)$$

If, then, $F_1, F_2, \ldots$, acting from the same centres as $P_1, P_2, \ldots$, enable the particle to describe the path, they must satisfy the simultaneous equations
$$-v\,dv/ds = F_1 dr_1/ds + F_2 dr_2/ds + \ldots,\quad v^2/\rho = F_1\frac{p_1}{r_1}+F_2\frac{p_2}{r_2}+\ldots\ldots(3)$$
and these give the condition
$$2\left(F_1\frac{dr_1}{ds}+F_2\frac{dr_2}{ds}+\ldots\right)+\frac{d}{ds}\left\{\rho\left(F_1\frac{p_1}{r_1}+F_2\frac{p_2}{r_2}+\ldots\right)\right\}=0 \quad\ldots(4)$$
or, with insertion of the values of $p_1/r_1, p_2/r_2, \ldots$ from the first of (2),
$$-2v\frac{dv}{ds}+\frac{d}{ds}\left(\frac{F_k}{P_k}v_k^2\right)=0,$$
that is by the second of (2)
$$-2v\frac{dv}{ds}-2\Sigma F_k\frac{dr_k}{ds}+\Sigma v_k^2\frac{d}{ds}\left(\frac{F}{P_k}\right)=0,\quad\ldots\ldots\ldots(5)$$
from which, noticing that $v_k^2 = P_k c_k$, by § 132, and that the two first terms cancel one another by the first of (3), we get finally equation (1) as the condition to be satisfied [A. H. Curtis, *Mess. Math.* x. 1880].

161. Examples of Multiple Centres of Force.

Ex. 1. Deduce from this theorem the relation
$$\frac{1}{r_1^2}\frac{d}{dr_1}(F_1 r_1^2)=\frac{1}{r_2^2}\frac{d}{dr_2}(F_2 r_2^2),$$
to be fulfilled for two forces F_1, F_2 towards the foci of an ellipse under which acting together a particle can describe the ellipse.

[Note that $\mu/r_1^2, \mu/r_2^2$ directed towards the foci are forces under which the ellipse can be described.]

Show that the general solution of the equation
$$\frac{1}{r_1^2}\frac{d}{dr_1}(F_1 r_1^2)=\frac{1}{r_2^2}\frac{d}{dr_2}\left(F_2 r_2^2\right),$$
which holds for elliptic motion, is
$$r_1^2 F_1 = \int r_1^2\{f_1(r_1)+f_2(2a-r_1)\}dr_1+C_1,$$
$$r^2 F_2 = \int r_2^2\{f(r_2)+f_1(2a-r_2)\}dr_2+C_2,$$
where f_1, f_2 are arbitrary functions and C_1, C_2 are constants, which may be included in the integrals if it is understood that different constants may be used for F_1 and F_2.

Ex. 2. Show that by properly choosing the functions f, we obtain
$$F_1 = \mu\left(\frac{2}{5}r_1^3 - ar_1^2 + \lambda r_1 + \mu_1 r_1^{-2}\right),$$
$$F_2 = \mu\left(\frac{2}{5}r_2^3 - ar_2^2 + \lambda r_2 + \mu_2 r_2^{-2}\right),$$
as forces towards the foci under which a particle can describe the ellipse.

Ex. 3. A particle moves in an ellipse with the speed
$$a\sqrt{\kappa(a-r)/r(2a-r)},$$
where $2a$ is the length of the major axis and κ is a constant: to show that its acceleration consists of two components, one towards the near focus and the other *from* the farther focus, both varying as the inverse square of the distance.

If $r' = 2a - r$, we have $v^2 = \frac{1}{2}a^2(\kappa/r - \kappa/r')$, and $v^2/\rho = \frac{1}{2}a^3 b(\kappa/r - \kappa/r')/(rr')^{\frac{3}{2}}$, since $1/\rho = ab/(rr')^{\frac{3}{2}}$. Now substitute for $2a/(rr')^{\frac{3}{2}}$ the value $(p+p')/\sqrt{pp'}$, and obtain $v^2/\rho = \frac{1}{4}a^2(\kappa p'/r^2 r' - \kappa p/r'^2 r)$, and therefore
$$\frac{v^2}{\rho} = \frac{a^2}{4}\left(\frac{\kappa}{r^2}\frac{p}{r} - \frac{\kappa}{r'^2}\frac{p'}{r'}\right),$$
the first equation, which is consistent with the statement to be proved. This, with
$$v\frac{dv}{ds} = -\frac{1}{4}a^2\left(\frac{\kappa}{r^2}\frac{dr}{ds} - \frac{\kappa}{r'^2}\frac{dr'}{ds}\right),$$
which is at once obtained, establishes the theorem.

It will be noticed that the motion here specified cannot exist except in the half of the ellipse on the same side of the minor axis as the attractive focus. Outside these limits the speed is imaginary.

Ex. 4. Show that a particle will describe an ellipse if its speed along the tangent at any point P is given by
$$v^2 = \frac{1}{ar(2a-r)}\{(\kappa + \kappa')r^2 + 4\kappa a(a-r) - \kappa' ar\},$$
and it is acted on by forces towards the foci.

Ex. 5. Particles of different masses $m_1, m_2, \ldots$, which have speeds $v_1, v_2, \ldots$ at the same point, describe the same path under the action of given forces $F_1, F_2, \ldots$. Show that a particle of any mass M, which has kinetic energy at the same point equal to the sum of the kinetic energies of the particles, will describe the path under the combined action of $F_1, F_2, \ldots$.

Ex. 6. Prove that if a conic section is described under the action of either of two forces directed to the foci, each varying as the inverse square of the distance, or of a force towards the centre and varying directly as the distance, it will describe the curve under the combined action of the same three forces, provided the particle is projected with speed given by

$$v^2 = \frac{1}{a}\left(\mu\frac{r'}{r} + \mu'\frac{r}{r'}\right) + \mu''rr',$$

where r, r' are the focal distances at the point of projection and μ, μ', μ'' the intensities of the centres [Lagrange, *Méc. Anal.* t. ii. sect. vii. § 83].

162. Earth-Moon System disturbed by Action of Sun. We give here an interesting application of the equations of motion, with reference to revolving axes, to the approximate determination of the influence of the sun's attraction in disturbing the motion of the moon relative to the earth. Let S be the position of the sun's centre, supposed to be fixed, and E that of the earth's centre. We take a to denote the distance of the earth from the sun, and x, y, z for the coordinates of the moon's centre M relative to that

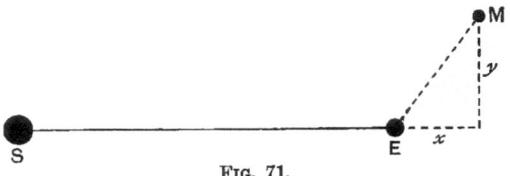

Fig. 71.

of the earth as origin, choosing the direction of x in the prolongation of the line SE, that of y at right angles to SE in the plane of the ecliptic, and taking z as the distance of the moon's centre from that plane. The coordinates of the moon's centre relative to the sun's centre as origin are therefore $a+x, y, z$. The equations of motion of the moon are therefore (see (2), § 14), if X, Y, Z be the component applied forces,

$$\left.\begin{array}{l}\ddot{x} - 2n\dot{y} - y\dot{n} - n^2(a+x) = X,\\ \ddot{y} + 2n\dot{x} + (a+x)\dot{n} - n^2 y = Y,\\ \ddot{z} = Z.\end{array}\right\} \quad \ldots\ldots\ldots\ldots(1)$$

The acceleration of the earth toward the sun is at any given instant $n^2 a$, which is the force per unit mass toward

298   A TREATISE ON DYNAMICS.   [CH. V.

the sun at distance a. Hence the force per unit mass toward the sun on a particle at M is

$$n^2a^3/\{(a+x)^2+y^2+z^2\} = n^2a^3/R^2, \text{ if } R^2=(a+x)^2+y^2+z^2.$$

The components of this in the direction of x, y, z, increasing, are $-n^2a^3(a+x)/R^3$, $-n^2a^3y/R^3$, $-n^2a^3z/R^3$. Since x, y, z are small in comparison with a, these components are approximately $-n^2a+2n^2x$, $-n^2y$, $-n^2z$. Besides these there are the component forces of attraction exerted on the moon by the earth, which, if r denote $\sqrt{x^2+y^2+z^2}$, are $-\mu x/r^3$, $-\mu y/r^3$, $-\mu z/r^3$ per unit mass. Thus, if we suppose $\dot{n}=0$, we have the equations of motion

$$\left.\begin{array}{l}\ddot{x}-2n\dot{y}-\left(3n^2-\dfrac{\mu}{r^3}\right)x=0,\\[4pt] \ddot{y}+2n\dot{x}+\dfrac{\mu}{r^3}y=0,\\[4pt] \ddot{z}+n^2z+\dfrac{\mu}{r^3}z=0.\end{array}\right\} \quad\ldots\ldots\ldots\ldots\ldots(2)$$

Multiplying these equations by $\dot{x}$, $\dot{y}$, $\dot{z}$ respectively, integrating and adding, we get

$$v^2-3n^2x^2+n^2z^2-2\frac{\mu}{r}+C=0,\ldots\ldots\ldots\ldots\ldots(3)$$

which is known as Jacobi's equation of the *relative* energy of the moon's motion.

163. Stability of Earth-Moon System. Hill's Theorem. This result affords an example of a very useful method of assigning limits to the possible relative displacements of the parts of a system. For a given value of v, the body here considered—the moon—must have its centre somewhere on the surface given by (3) of § 162, which intersects the plane of x, y in the curve

$$3n^2x^2+2\frac{\mu}{r}-C=0\ \ \ldots\ldots\ldots\ldots\ldots\ldots(1)$$

or, if $x=r\cos\theta$,

$$3n^2r^3\cos^2\theta-Cr+2\mu=0.\ \ \ldots\ldots\ldots\ldots\ldots(2)$$

If this cubic equation for r has at least one real positive root for every value of θ, the curve possesses a branch closed round the centre, within which the body must always remain. It may be verified by the student that the roots of (2) are all real if $\cos^2\theta < C^3/81n^2\mu^2$. It will be found that when $\theta = \pm\pi/2$, so that $\cos\theta = 0$, the equation has one finite root $r = 2\mu/C$, and two infinite roots, one positive, the other negative. For $\theta = 0$ or π, so that $\cos^2\theta = 1$, one root lies between $2\mu/C$ and $3\mu/C$, and between these values of θ, r alters continuously.

Besides the closed branch, which is oval in shape, the curve has, as shown in Fig. 72, two infinite branches, which have the two lines $3n^2x^2 = C$ as asymptotes. In the space between these infinite branches and the closed branch, v^2 is negative, and v, therefore, a pure imaginary. The body must therefore either be inside the closed branch or outside the two infinite branches, and, if once within the closed branch, can never escape to the space beyond.

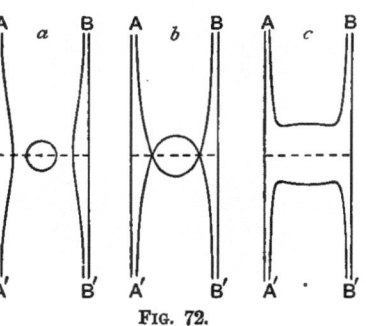

Fig. 72.

The closed branch and the infinite branches are shown in Fig. 72 (a). AA', BB' are the lines $3n^2x^2 = C$. In diagrams a, b, c, the trace of the surface on the plane of xy is shown for the three cases $C^3 >$, $=$, $< 81\mu^2 n^2$. In the second case the oval and the infinite branches meet at the ends of the former, and it appears as if the particle might there escape from the closed branch. But the condition $C^3 = 81\mu^2 n^2$ shows that there both the velocity and the acceleration of the particle are zero. In the remaining case there is no closed curve round the origin, and no upper or lower limit for the distance of the particle from the origin.

Considering the moon's orbit and neglecting its inclination to the ecliptic, we see (§ 126) that $C = \mu/a'$, where a' denotes the length of the semi-axis major, and from this the limits of the branches can be assigned. Mr. G. W. Hill, to whom this discussion is due (*Am. Jour. Math.* vol. i.), has shown that the surface indicated by (3) of § 162 consists of three sheets, one closed around the earth and nearly spherical in shape, another also closed but surrounding the sun, and shaped like an ellipsoid of revolution with semi-axes, in the plane of the ecliptic, rather less in length than the earth's mean distance from the sun, and axis of revolution, about $\frac{2}{3}$ as long, perpendicular to the ecliptic, and a third branch, unclosed in these two directions, surrounding the other two.

Within the space between the two closed sheets and the third, the value of v^2 is negative, so that the moving body must be either outside the latter or inside the former. The radius of the sheet enclosing the earth is about 110 earth-radii; therefore, as the moon is distant from the earth only about 60 earth-radii, it cannot possibly be made by the sun's attraction to part company with the earth.

EXERCISES V.

1. Prove that a body projected from the earth's surface with speed exceeding seven miles per second will not in general return to the earth.

2. Show that the greatest velocity of a planet in its orbit about the sun is to its least velocity as $1+e$ is to $1-e$; and find this ratio for the earth, whose orbit has the eccentricity $e = 0.01677120$.

Find the greatest and least speeds of Halley's comet, taking the eccentricity of the orbit as 0·96173, the mean distance from the sun as 17·96 times the earth's mean distance, and the period as 76·1 years. Verify that this period fulfils Kepler's third law.

3. A particle is placed on the straight line joining two fixed points O, A, and is subject to an attraction towards O and towards A, varying in each case inversely as the square of the distance. Show (i) that there is one position B between O and A at which the particle, if placed there, will be in unstable equilibrium; (ii) that if the particle be projected from any other point C on OB with such a speed as will make it pass through B it will reach A; (iii) that if the speed of projection from C is such that the speed of the particle would vanish at B it will take an infinite time to reach B.

4. Show that if a particle describes an ellipse under the action of a force towards a focus, the angular speed round the other focus varies inversely as the square of the diameter parallel to the direction of motion.

EXERCISES.

5. A particle describes an ellipse under the action of a force toward the centre: prove that the speed is always proportional to the length of the diameter conjugate to that through the particle, and that the sum of the kinetic energies of the particle at the extremities of two conjugate axes is the same for all pairs of conjugate axes.

6. A particle describes a parabola under a force towards the focus: prove that the speed is inversely proportional to the length of the normal intercepted between the point and the axis, and that the sum of the kinetic energies at the extremities of a focal chord is the same for all such chords.

7. Show that in the parabolic orbit specified in the last example the speed of the particle at any point may be resolved into equal components, one perpendicular to the focal distance of the point and the other perpendicular to the axis.

8. A particle describes an ellipse under a force directed to one of the foci: prove that the sum of the speeds at the extremities of a chord parallel to the major axis is inversely proportional to the length of the diameter drawn parallel to the direction of motion at either extremity.

9. A particle moving in an ellipse under the action of a force toward a focus O moves from the greatest distance from O to an extremity of the minor axis in time t, and thence to the least distance from O in time t/k: find the eccentricity of the orbit.

$$[e = \tfrac{1}{2}\pi(k-1)/(k+1).]$$

10. The period of a particle moving in an ellipse is T when the centre of force is at one focus and T' when the centre of force is at the other focus, and the speed at a certain point P is the same in both cases: prove that the focal distances of the point are

$$2aT'/(T+T'), \quad 2aT/(T+T'),$$

where a denotes the mean distance.

11. A particle moves in a circular path in such a manner that the time of describing any arc AP from a fixed point A is proportional to the sum of the length of that arc and the length of the perpendicular let fall from P on the diameter through A: prove that the particle moves under the action of a central force.

12. P is the projection of the centre of a planet on the plane of the ecliptic: prove that P moves as if it were a particle acted upon by a force toward the sun's centre.

13. A particle describes a parabola under the action of a central force directed to the focus. We infer from Ex. 15, § 137, that the time-average of the kinetic energy in the parabolic orbit is zero. Verify this by showing that if A be the area described by the radius-vector in any time t, the ratio A/t tends to zero without limit of closeness as t is made to increase without limit.

14. If the speed of a periodic comet is suddenly increased near its aphelion by a small amount δv, prove that the changes produced in the eccentricity and major axis are given by the equations

$$\delta e = -2\delta v \sqrt{l/\mu}, \quad \delta a = 2\delta v \sqrt{\{a^3(1-e)/\mu(1+e)\}},$$

where the letters have their usual meanings for elliptic motion.

15. A particle is projected from the earth's surface so as to describe a portion of an ellipse whose major axis ($2a$) is $1\cdot5$ times the earth's radius. If the direction of projection makes an angle of $30°$ with the vertical, prove that the time of flight is

$$\tfrac{3}{4}\sqrt{(3a/g)}(\tan^{-1}\sqrt{6}+\sqrt{\tfrac{2}{3}}),$$

where a is the earth's radius, and g is the acceleration due to gravity at the earth's surface. [Find $v^2(=\tfrac{2}{3}gr)$, $e=\sqrt{7}/3$, $\cos\theta = -5/2\sqrt{7}$, by Ex. 12, § 131; then use (4), § 145.]

16. A satellite revolves about a very massive and very distant primary towards which it always turns the same face: prove that in order that a loose particle in contact with the face on the line of centres may remain in contact the condition $M > 3a^3S/r^3$, where M is the mass of the satellite, S that of the primary, a the radius of the satellite and r the distance of the centres of the two bodies apart. Show that the same condition is necessary for the retention of a particle on the line of centres, but on the side turned from the primary.

17. A particle of mass 1 gramme is hung by a very fine quartz fibre 2 metres long, and is at rest with the fibre vertical. A sphere of lead 30 cms. in diameter is suddenly placed with its centre 20 cms. from the particle on the same level. Find the equation of motion of the particle and how far the particle moves towards the sphere in a second. [Density of lead $11\cdot47$ grammes per cub. cm.]

18. Two homogeneous spheres of matter of the same density (22 grammes per cub. cm.), one 30 cms., the other 60 cms. in diameter, have their centres 300 cms. apart and revolve round their common centroid as a double star. Show that the period of revolution is 20 h. 58 m. 22 s.

19. If two homogeneous spheres, of masses E and M, move under their mutual gravitation and that of a fixed homogeneous sphere of mass S, so that the three centres are always in one plane, prove that $(E+M)^2H + EMh$ is constant, where h is the rate at which the radius vector from E to M describes area about E, and H is the double rate of description of area about S by the radius vector from S to the centroid of E and M. What does the relation become if the fixed point is the common centroid of the two bodies?

20. A particle moves under a central force μ/r^2 and is projected with speed v_0 from a point at a distance r_0 from the centre of force in a direction making an angle α with the radius vector. Prove that the apsidal distances are the real roots of the equation for r,

$$Wr^2/(r_0^2\sin^2\alpha - r^2) = \tfrac{1}{2}v_0^2,$$

where W is the work done by the central attractive force as the particle moves from the point of projection to any point r, θ.

21. A thin spherical shell of small radius, moving without rotation, describes a circle of radius R with speed V about a gravitating centre of force O, and when its centre is at a point A, the shell bursts with an explosion which generates speed v in each fragment directly outwards from the centre. Show that the fragments all pass through the line AO within a length

$$8V^3vR/(V^4 - 6V^2v^2 + v^4),$$

and that if v is small the stream of fragments will form a complete ring after a time approximately equal to $\tfrac{1}{3}\pi R/v$.

22. A particle describes an elliptic orbit under a central force towards a focus S. When at distance r from that focus the particle receives a small radial impulse changing the speed by δv. Show that the changes in the mean distance, the eccentricity, and the position of the major axis are

$$\delta a = 2a^2\dot{r}\delta v/\mu, \quad \delta e = h\sin\theta\,.\,\delta v/\mu, \quad \delta\psi = -h\cos\theta\,.\,\delta v/\mu e,$$

where θ is the angle which the radius vector makes with the least radius-vector.

23. A comet moves round the sun in an ellipse of eccentricity e nearly equal to unity. At a point where the radius vector makes an angle θ with the least radius vector the comet has its speed suddenly increased in the ratio $n+1:n$ where n is great, without alteration of direction. Show that if the new orbit is a parabola, e is nearly equal to $1 - (4\cos^2\tfrac{1}{2}\theta)/n$.

24. If the particle of Ex. 22 when at a point P receives the impulse along PM, the perpendicular to the major axis, show that the major axis turns round through the angle $(SM\,.\,PM/SP)\delta v/eh$.

25. A particle acted on by a central attractive force $\mu u^3(c^2u^2+4)$ is projected from an apse at distance c with speed $3\sqrt{2\mu}/2c$: show that the orbit has the equation $r = c\cos\tfrac{1}{3}\theta$, and that the particle arrives at the centre of force after an interval $t = \sqrt{2}\pi c^2/4\sqrt{\mu}$.

26. A particle under a central force $2\mu u^3(1 - a^2u^2)$ is projected from an apse at distance a, with speed $\sqrt{\mu}/a$: prove that the particle is at a distance r after a time

$$\frac{1}{2\sqrt{\mu}}\left\{a^2\log\frac{r+\sqrt{r^2-a^2}}{a} + r\sqrt{r^2-a^2}\right\}.$$

304   A TREATISE ON DYNAMICS.   [CH.

27. If, at any point of an elliptic orbit about a focus, the force ceases to act for a given very short time, find the angle through which the apse line will have turned and the change of the eccentricity, and show that they are respectively proportional to the resolved parts of the force parallel and perpendicular to the apse line.

28. Writing (1), § 153, in the form

$$\frac{d^2u}{d\theta^2} - k^2 u = 0,$$

so that $k^2 = \mu/h^2 - 1$, solve the equation, and hence derive the orbits which exist, according as k is real or imaginary, and according as the coefficients A_1, A_2 in (3), § 153, have the same or opposite signs.

29. Prove that if k be real and the coefficients A_1, A_2 (Ex. 28) have the same sign, the time of passage from the value 0 of the vectorial angle to the value θ is $(a^2/kh)(e^{2k\theta} - 1)/(e^{2k\theta} + 1)$, where a is the distance of the apse from the centre of force.

30. If β be the constant (acute) angle between the tangent to the path and the radius vector, when the orbit is given by (11), § 153 (an equiangular spiral), show that if the vectorial angle be 0 when $u = 2c$, it will have grown to θ in time $(1/4c^2\sqrt{\mu} \cos \beta)(1 - e^{-2k\theta})$.

31. If the motion is given by (6), § 153 (Fig. 65), show that the time taken by the particle to pass to the centre from the extremity of the radius vector inclined at angle θ to the radius vector parallel to the asymptote, on the side of that radius-vector in the direction of motion, is $1/4c^2\sqrt{\mu}\theta$, where $1/2c$ is the distance of the asymptote from the pole.

Show also that if the motion is given by (16), § 153, the time as just specified is given by $(1/2c^2kh)/(e^{2k\theta} - 1)$, where in this case $1/2ck$ is the distance from the pole to the asymptote.

32. Prove that if k be imaginary the time taken by the radius vector to revolve through an angle θ from the apse (at distance $1/2c$) is

$$(1/4c^2h\sqrt{1 - \mu/h^2}) \tan (\sqrt{1 - \mu/h^2}\,\theta).$$

33. A particle describes a central orbit with acceleration μu^4, starting from a point at a distance a from the origin; the direction of motion at the start makes an angle $\pi/4$ with the radius vector, and the speed is the speed from infinity. Find the orbit, and show that the time taken to reach the apse is

$$\sqrt{\frac{3a^5}{\mu}}\left(2 + \frac{3\pi}{4}\right).$$

[The equation of the orbit is $r = a(1 + \sin \theta)$.]

EXERCISES.

34. A particle moving with a central acceleration $\mu(18a^2u^5 - 8u^3)$ starts from a point at distance a from the origin in a direction perpendicular to the radius-vector, and with the velocity from infinity. Show that the equation of the path is

$$r = a \cos 3\theta.$$

35. A particle moves subject to an attraction towards a fixed point O, the attraction per unit mass at the point (r, θ) being

$$\mu(1 + 3\cos 2\theta)/r^2,$$

where r, θ are polar coordinates with O as origin; if at the point $(c, 0)$ the velocity is perpendicular to the radius to the point, and is of magnitude $\sqrt{\mu/c}$, determine the orbit. [Ex. 17, § 131.]

36. A particle under a central attraction $\mu(5u^3 + 6au^4)$ is projected from an apse at a distance a with the speed from infinity; show that the equation of the path is

$$r = \frac{a}{2}\left(1 + \cos\frac{2}{3}\theta\right).$$

If the central attraction be $\mu(5u^3 + 8a^2u^5)$ and the speed of projection from the apse at distance a be $3\sqrt{\mu}/a$, show that the orbit has the equation $r = a\cos\frac{2}{3}\theta$.

37. A particle moves in a smooth tube in the form of a Bernoulli's Lemniscate ($r^2 = a^2\cos 2\theta$), and is attracted to the pole by a force varying as the square of the distance; show that if the speed at the extremity of the axis is that due to a fall from an infinite distance, the force on the tube will be constant.

38. A particle describes an ellipse under the combined action of forces μ/OP^2, $\mu/O'P^2$ towards the foci O, O' and a force $\lambda \cdot CP$ towards the centre C: find the relation connecting μ and λ, and the speed at P. [Ex. 6, § 161.]

39. A particle describes an ellipse under the combined action of two forces towards the foci, each varying according to the law

$$\mu(1/r^2 + r/8a^3),$$

where r is the distance of the position of the particle from either focus. Show that the speed must be $\pi(r^2 + rr' + r'^2)/T\sqrt{rr'}$, where T is the period which the particle would have if the force μ/r^2 towards one focus only acted.

40. A particle describes a parabola under two forces, one constant and parallel to the axis, and the other passing through the focus; prove that the latter force varies inversely as the square of the focal distance. Prove also that if the force through the focus is repulsive, and at the vertex equal to the constant force, the particle will come to rest at the vertex.

41. If the force parallel to the axis in last example is three times the repulsion along the line through the focus, show that the orbit can be a parabola.

Show also that if two particles describe the same parabola under the forces specified, the directions of motion will always intersect in a fixed confocal parabola.

42. Show that if an ellipse be described under an attraction P to the focus O, and an attraction P' to the focus O',

$$\frac{dP'}{dr'} - \frac{dP}{dr} = 2\left(\frac{P}{r} - \frac{P'}{r'}\right),$$

where r, r' are the distances of the particle from the foci S, S' respectively.

43. Prove Newton's theorem by showing that the equations of motion of the particle for the force specified in (2), § 155, give the elliptic path described with areal speed $\frac{1}{2}h_1$ about the centre O_1.

44. A satellite moving round a primary is acted on by a small tangential force in the direction of motion. Show that the satellite will gradually move to a greater distance from the primary, and that while the applied tangential force causes an increase of the total energy, the kinetic energy is diminished by an amount equal to the increase of the total energy.

At any instant the orbital kinetic energy (per unit mass) is $\frac{1}{2}v^2$ and the potential energy $-\mu/a$, if a be the distance from the centre. Take the path as approximately circular; then $v^2/a = \mu/a^2$, and so the equation of energy is

$$\tfrac{1}{2}v^2 - \frac{\mu}{a} = \frac{\mu}{2a}.$$

After an interval of action of the tangential force, the total energy has been changed from $\mu/2a$ to $\mu/2a + W$. The speed has become v' and the distance a'. Hence the energy equation is now

$$\tfrac{1}{2}v'^2 - \frac{\mu}{a'} = \frac{\mu}{2a} + W.$$

But now $v'^2 = \mu/a'$, and so the last equation may be written

$$-\tfrac{1}{2}v'^2 = \frac{\mu}{2a} + W.$$

This, with the first energy-equation, gives $\frac{1}{2}v^2 - \frac{1}{2}v'^2 = W$, that is, the kinetic energy is now less than before by an amount equal to the increase of the total energy.

The reader may consider this slow motion of the satellite outwards by means of the equations of § 121.

The moon is a case in point. A tangential action is exerted in the forward direction on the moon in consequence of the fact that the line of high waters on the earth's surface is not along the radius-vector to the moon, but in advance of that in the direction of the moon's motion. The displaced water, as may easily be seen by means of a figure, gives a forward tangential force on the moon. The additional energy W is derived from the kinetic energy of the earth's rotation.

CHAPTER VI.

MOTION OF A RIGID BODY.

164. Angular Momentum (A.M.) of a Rigid Body. A rigid body is one in which the line joining any two particles of the body (that is two small parts, not two *molecules*), remains unaltered in length, and the angle between every pair of such lines remains unchanged as the body moves.

The motion of a rigid body may be regarded as made up of a motion of the centroid with speeds u, v, w parallel to axes Ox, Oy, Oz, and a rotation of the body with angular speeds $\dot{\theta}_1$, $\dot{\theta}_2$, $\dot{\theta}_3$, about axes parallel to these drawn through the centroid. For an element of the body of mass m, whose coordinates relative to axes through the centroid are x, y, z, has angular momentum $\Sigma\{m(\dot{z}y - \dot{y}z)\}$ about the axis of x through the centroid. Let P_1 (Fig. 73) be the projection of the particle on the plane of yOz, and P_1Q_1, P_1R_1 represent the distances $\dot{y}\,dt$, $\dot{z}\,dt$ which the particle travels parallel to the axes in time dt, being the components, along Oy, Oz of the projection P_1S_1 on the plane yOz of the actual displacement PS of the particle in dt.

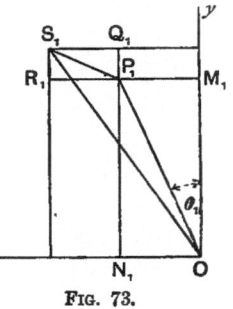

FIG. 73.

The projection OP_1 of the line drawn from the origin to the position P of the particle has turned round through the angle P_1OS_1, which we shall denote for the present by α.

Now, numerically, the angular momentum $m(\dot{z}y - \dot{y}z)dt$ is proportional to

area (rectangle N_1S_1 − rectangle M_1S_1)
= 2 area (triangle OQ_1S_1 − triangle OR_1S_1)
= 2 area (triangle OQ_1S_1 − triangle OP_1Q_1 − triangle $P_1Q_1S_1$)
= 2 area triangle OP_1S_1.

But $OP_1 = r_1$, $OS_1 = r_1 + dr_1$, $\angle P_1OS_1 = \alpha$, and
2 area $OPS_1 = r_1(r_1 + dr_1)\alpha = r_1^2 \alpha$.

Hence $m(\dot{z}y - \dot{y}z)dt = mr_1^2\alpha$, and we get, summing for all the particles, $\Sigma\{m(\dot{z}y - \dot{y}z)\}dt = \Sigma(mr_1^2\alpha)$.

If the body is rigid (in the sense defined above), then, if the line OP_1 drawn for a selected particle turn through an angle α, the lines so drawn for the other particles must all turn through the same angle. If there is no turning at all, the motion of the centroid expresses the whole motion. Hence, putting $\alpha/dt = \dot{\theta}_1$, where $\theta_1 = \angle M_1OP_1$, we get, since $\dot{\theta}_1$ is the same for every particle,

$$\Sigma\{m(\dot{z}y - \dot{y}z)\} = \dot{\theta}_1 \Sigma(mr_1^2).$$

In the same way we get for the other two axes,

$$\Sigma\{m(\dot{x}z - \dot{z}x)\} = \dot{\theta}_2 \Sigma(mr_2^2),$$
$$\Sigma\{m(\dot{y}x - \dot{x}y)\} = \dot{\theta}_3 \Sigma(mr_3^2).$$

Hence the rates of change of angular momentum about the axes are, if the distribution of matter is invariable,

$$\left.\begin{array}{l}\Sigma\{m(\ddot{z}y - \ddot{y}z)\} = \ddot{\theta}_1 \Sigma(mr_1^2),\\ \Sigma\{m(\ddot{x}z - \ddot{z}x)\} = \ddot{\theta}_2 \Sigma(mr_2^2),\\ \Sigma\{m(\ddot{y}x - \ddot{x}y)\} = \ddot{\theta}_3 \Sigma(mr_3^2).\end{array}\right\} \quad\ldots\ldots\ldots\ldots\ldots(1)$$

But there may be alteration of mass of the body, as in the case of a rolling snowball, and from this cause, or from the expansion or contraction of the body with alteration of temperature, r_1, r_2, r_3 may change, though of course this would be a violation of rigidity. We have then

$$\frac{d}{dt}\Sigma\{m(\dot{z}y - \dot{y}z)\} = \ddot{\theta}_1 \Sigma(mr_1^2) + \dot{\theta}\Sigma(\dot{m}r_1^2) + 2\dot{\theta}_1 \Sigma(mr_1\dot{r}_1), \quad (2)$$

with similar equations for the remaining two axes. Any alteration of the motion of the centroid or of its position in the body, due to the addition or withdrawal of mass, must be taken account of by a variation of the angular momentum of the body due to the motion of the centroid.

165. Moments of Inertia about Parallel Axes. The quantities $\Sigma(mr_1^2)$, ... are called the moments of inertia of the body about the axes parallel to Ox, Oy, Oz drawn from the centroid. We may, however, take moments of inertia about any other system of three axes, using the following definition:

The moment of inertia of *any* body or system about a given axis is the sum $\Sigma(mr^2)$ of the products obtained by multiplying each infinitesimal element of mass of the body or system by the square of the distance of the element from the given axis.

We can always find a distance k such that the product Mk^2, where M is the whole mass of the system, is equal to $\Sigma(mr^2)$: k is called the radius of gyration about the given axis.

A simple relation of great practical importance exists between the moment of inertia of any system about a given axis and the moment of inertia about a parallel axis through the centroid. Let m at P (Fig. 74) be an element of mass of

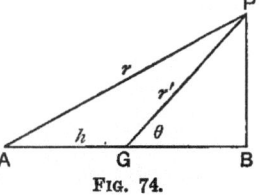

Fig. 74.

the system, and A and G be the points in which a plane drawn through P at right angles to the given axis intersects the given axis and the parallel axis through the centroid. Then $AP = r$, and if h, r', and θ denote the lengths AG, GP, and the angle PGB in the figure, we have

$$r^2 = h^2 + r'^2 + 2hr' \cos \theta.$$

Hence, since h is the same for every particle,

$$\Sigma(mr^2) = Mh^2 + \Sigma(mr'^2) + 2h\Sigma(mr' \cos \theta). \quad \ldots\ldots(1)$$

But $r' \cos \theta = GB$, and GB is the distance, x say, parallel to the fixed line AG, of the mass m from the centroid. Now

$\Sigma(mx) = 0$, by the definition of the centroid; hence

$$\Sigma(mr^2) = Mh^2 + \Sigma(mr'^2) = Mh^2 + Mk^2, \quad\ldots\ldots\ldots(2)$$

where k is the radius of gyration about the parallel axis through the centroid. The theorem thus established may be stated as follows: The moment of inertia of a system about any given axis is equal to the moment of inertia of the system about a parallel axis through the centroid, together with the moment of inertia about the given axis of the whole matter of the system, supposed collected at the centroid.

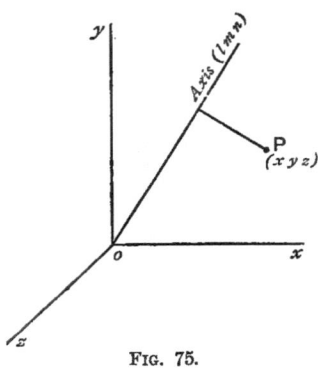

FIG. 75.

166. Calculation of Moments of Inertia. Momental Ellipsoid. We now consider the problem: To find an expression for the moment of inertia of a system about an axis given in position. We shall suppose that the axis passes through the origin and has direction-cosines l, m, n. Then a point P of coordinates x, y, z (Fig. 75) is at a distance from the axis $= \{x^2 + y^2 + z^2 - (lx + my + nz)^2\}^{\frac{1}{2}}$. The square of this distance may be written, among other ways, in the form

$$l^2(y^2 + z^2) + m^2(z^2 + x^2) + n^2(x^2 + y^2) - 2mnyz - 2nlzx - 2lmxy.$$

If we multiply this by the mass, μ say, of an element of the system situated at the point x, y, z, and sum the products for all the elements of the system, we get the moment of inertia of the system about the given axis. Denoting it by I, we have

$$I = \Sigma[\mu\{l^2(y^2 + z^2) + m^2(z^2 + x^2) + n^2(x^2 + y^2)$$
$$- 2mnyz - 2nlzx - 2lmny\}]. \quad\ldots\ldots\ldots(1)$$

This expression is of course, from its formation, essentially positive.

Now let
$$\Sigma\{\mu(y^2+z^2)\} = A, \quad \Sigma\{\mu(z^2+x^2)\} = B, \quad \Sigma\{\mu(x^2+y^2)\} = C,$$
$$\Sigma(\mu yz) = D, \quad \Sigma(\mu zx) = E, \quad \Sigma(\mu xy) = F;$$
then $\quad I = l^2 A + m^2 B + n^2 C - 2Dmn - 2Enl - 2Flm.$ ......(2)

A, B, C are called moments of inertia, D, E, F products of inertia.

If ρ denote a distance measured off along the axis from the origin, and ξ, η, ζ its projections on the axes, we have $l = \xi/\rho$, $m = \eta/\rho$, $n = \zeta/\rho$, and

$$A\xi^2 + B\eta^2 + C\zeta^2 - 2D\eta\zeta - 2E\zeta\xi - 2F\xi\eta = \rho^2 I. \quad ......(3)$$

If we take values of ρ^2 which are inversely proportional to I, $\rho^2 I$ takes a constant value, k^4 say, for different directions l, m, n of the axis. (The meaning of k here is of course distinct from that stated in § 165.) Now the equation

$$A\xi^2 + B\eta^2 + C\zeta^2 - 2D\eta\zeta - 2E\zeta\xi - 2F\xi\eta = k^4, \quad ....(4)$$

is, since the expression on the left is positive, the equation of an ellipsoid. Hence we get the theorem (which seems to have been given first by Cauchy, but is generally ascribed to Poinsot), that the moments of inertia of a material system about different axes drawn through a given point are inversely proportional to the squares of the lengths of the radii-vectores of an ellipsoid, the centre of which is at the point. This is called the *momental ellipsoid*. Since the choice of k is arbitrary, there are any number of similar and similarly situated ellipsoids, any one of which may be taken as a momental ellipsoid.

By the theory of the ellipsoid it is known that when the surface is referred to the principal axes—that is three axes at right angles to one another, which are also normals to the surface—the equation may be written in the form

$$A'\xi^2 + B'\eta^2 + C'\zeta^2 = 1. \quad ....(4)$$

In the most general case the ellipsoid has three unequal axes—the longest (OA, Fig. 76) is in the direction of the axis of least moment of inertia, and the shortest OC in that of the axis of greatest moment of inertia. The intermediate axis has the maximum length of all axes lying in the plane determined by it and the axis of minimum length, but the minimum length for all lying in the plane determined by it and the axis of maximum length.

A momental ellipsoid drawn for the centroid as centre is called a central momental ellipsoid.

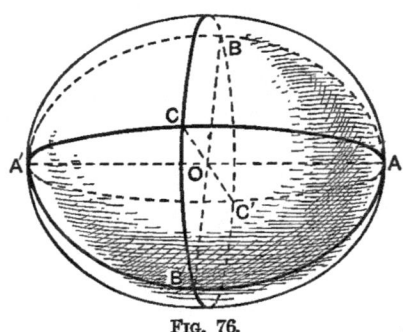

Fig. 76.

167. Principal Axes of Momental Ellipsoid. To find the axes of this ellipsoid, we note that, since a radius-vector has direction-cosines proportional to the coordinates ξ, η, ζ of the point in which the radius-vector meets the surface, these coordinates must, if the radius-vector be a normal, be proportional to the direction-cosines of the normal. But if S denote the expression on the left of (4), § 166, these cosines are proportional to $\partial S/\partial \xi$, $\partial S/\partial \eta$, $\partial S/\partial \zeta$. [For if dx, dy, dz be any displacement along the surface from a point x, y, z, we must have

$$\frac{\partial S}{\partial x}dx + \frac{\partial S}{\partial y}dy + \frac{\partial S}{\partial z}dz = 0, \quad\quad\quad\quad (1)$$

so that $\partial S/\partial x$, ... are proportional to the direction-cosines of a line perpendicular to the displacement dx, dy, dz.] Hence we must have

$$\left. \begin{array}{l} A\xi - F\eta - E\zeta = \kappa\xi, \\ -F\xi + B\eta - D\zeta = \kappa\xi, \\ -E\xi - D\eta + C\zeta = \kappa\eta, \end{array} \right\} \quad\quad\quad\quad (2)$$

where κ is a constant.

By elimination of ξ, η, ζ from equations (2), a cubic equation,

$$\kappa^3 - (A+B+C)\kappa^2 + (AB+BC+CA - D^2 - E^2 - F^2)\kappa$$
$$- (ABC - 2DEF - AD^2 - BE^2 - CF^2) = 0, \ldots\ldots\ldots(3)$$

called the *discriminating cubic*, for the determination of κ is obtained, the three roots of which can easily be proved to be all real; so that there are three axes which can be drawn to the ellipsoid to meet it at right angles, and *each pair of these are at right angles to one another*. They are called the *principal axes* of the ellipsoid. It will be observed that according to (4), § 167, if one of the axes of reference, say that of ζ, be a principal axis, the products D, E of inertia must, from the third of these equations, be zero.

Special cases are (1) that in which two of these axes are of equal length, when also all the axes in the plane of these two are equal, that is, the ellipsoid is one of revolution, and (2) that in which all three axes are equal in length, when the ellipsoid is a sphere.

The roots of (3) substituted successively in (2) enable a set of values of the cosines $\xi/\rho, \eta/\rho, \zeta/\rho$ to be found for each root, which, when used in (4), § 166, enable the length of the axis corresponding to the root to be calculated for an assumed k. The length of this axis is thus found as a function of κ. Hence the roots of the discriminating cubic are independent of the choice of axes, provided the origin is fixed, and therefore the coefficients of the powers of κ in the cubic have the property of *invariance*. These coefficients, the values of which are invariant, that is, independent of the choice of axes, are, as will be seen,

$$A+B+C, \quad AB+BC+CA - D^2 - E^2 - F^2,$$
$$ABC - 2DEF - AD^2 - BE^2 - CF^2.$$

168. Meaning of a Product of Inertia. It is important to gain a clear idea of the meaning and effect of a product of inertia. Consider a body of any form revolving about a shaft, fixed in position and so strong that it is not sensibly disturbed by the action of the body upon it. The body may be of any form whatever; for example, one of the arms of a Watt's steam-engine governor, or the crank-axle of a locomotive, may serve to fix the ideas. The body is attached to the shaft by bearings, the reaction on which we shall also consider. Let any origin O on the central line of the shaft be chosen, and the central line taken as axis of z, while the other axes are taken in a plane at right angles to Oz through O. The coordinates x, y, z of each element of mass are taken for the configuration of the system at a given instant. A particle of mass m at the point $P(x, y, z)$ is moving about Oz in a circle of radius $\sqrt{x^2+y^2}$. Hence, it is under acceleration towards Oz of amount $\omega^2\sqrt{x^2+y^2}$.

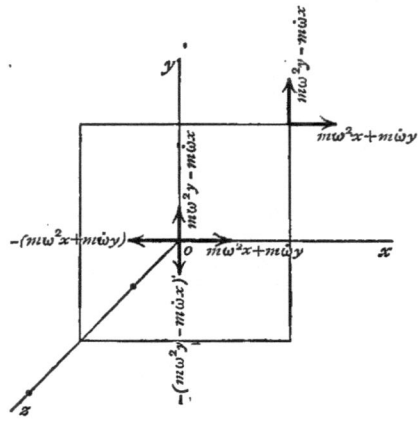

Fig. 77.

This is applied to it through the action of the rest of the body. The particle reacts on the system with an equal and opposite force. This reaction, being outward from Oz, has no moment about Oz, and can be resolved into two components, $m\omega^2 x$ parallel to Ox and $m\omega^2 y$ parallel to Oy. These act as shown in Fig. 77.

Again, if the angular speed is varying there is a force on the particle at P, of amount $m\dot{\omega}\sqrt{x^2+y^2}$, in the direction of motion, and, as before, a reaction of the same amount in the opposite direction on the rest of the system. This reaction has components $m\dot\omega y$, $-m\dot\omega x$ in the direction of Ox and Oy respectively, as shown in Fig. 77.

We shall consider the aggregate of these reactions and their effect, which is to exert certain forces upon the supporting shaft or axle. For this purpose we introduce at the origin O forces $m\omega^2 x + m\dot\omega y$, $m\omega^2 y - m\dot\omega x$ along Ox, Oy with two equal and opposite forces to balance them. The force $m\omega^2 x + m\dot\omega y$ at P and the force $-(m\omega^2 x + m\dot\omega y)$ at O give a couple of moment $m\omega^2 xz + m\dot\omega yz$ about an axis in the direction of Oy, and similarly, the forces $m\omega^2 y - m\dot\omega x$ at P and $-m\omega^2 y + m\dot\omega x$ at O give a couple of moment $-m\omega^2 yz + m\dot\omega xz$ about an axis in the direction of Ox. The forces at P in their action on the body, and ultimately on the axis of support, are equivalent to these two couples, and the two forces at O, $m\omega^2 x + m\dot\omega y$ acting along Ox and $m\omega^2 y - n\dot\omega x$ acting along Oy.

This process, applied to all the particles of the system, reduces the reactions to two resultant couples of moments $\omega^2 \Sigma(mxz) + \dot\omega \Sigma(myz)$, $-\omega^2 \Sigma(myz) + \dot\omega \Sigma(mxz)$ [or as we may write them, $E\omega^2 + D\dot\omega$, $-D\omega^2 + E\dot\omega$, where D, E are the products of inertia $\Sigma(myz)$, $\Sigma(mxz)$], about axes parallel to Oy, Ox and two forces $\omega^2 \Sigma mx + \dot\omega \Sigma my$, $\omega^2 \Sigma my - \dot\omega \Sigma mx$ along Ox, Oy. If $\bar x, \bar y$ be the coordinates of the centroid, these forces become $\omega^2 M\bar x + \dot\omega M\bar y$, $\omega^2 M\bar y - \dot\omega M\bar x$, where M denotes the whole mass of the body. If the products of inertia D, E are zero, the moments of the couples are zero, and there is no couple of reaction given by the resolution with respect to the chosen axes: only the forces $\omega^2 M\bar x + \dot\omega M\bar y$, $\omega^2 M\bar y - \dot\omega M\bar x$ remain applied at O.

169. Reactions of an Unsymmetrical Rotating Body on its Bearings. Free Axis of Rotation. So far only the reactions have been included, and they appear as the reversed mass-accelerations. But the applied forces X, Y on the particle of mass m at P, give couples Xz, $-Yz$ about axes parallel to Oy, Ox respectively, with forces X, Y applied at O. Thus we obtain resultant couples ΣXz, $-\Sigma Yz$ about these axes, and resultant forces ΣX, ΣY at O.

Now let the body be held by two bearings on the axis Oz at distance a_1, a_2 from O, and let X_1, Y_1, X_2, Y_2 denote the components of forces exerted by these bearings respectively on the body. The latter forces and the aggregate of reactions must form a system in equilibrium.

316   A TREATISE ON DYNAMICS.   [CH. VI.

Taking moments about the bearings in succession, we obtain

$$\left.\begin{array}{l} X_1 = -\dfrac{\{M(\omega^2 \bar{x}+\dot{\omega}\bar{y})+\Sigma X\}a_2 - (E\omega^2+D\dot{\omega}+\Sigma Xz)}{a_2-a_1}, \\[6pt] X_2 = \dfrac{\{M(\omega^2 \bar{x}+\dot{\omega}\bar{y})+\Sigma X\}a_1 - (E\omega^2+D\dot{\omega}+\Sigma Xz)}{a_2-a_1}, \\[6pt] Y_1 = -\dfrac{\{M(\omega^2 \bar{y}-\dot{\omega}x)+\Sigma Y\}a_2 - (D\omega^2-E\dot{\omega}+\Sigma Yz)}{a_2-a_1}, \\[6pt] Y_2 = \dfrac{\{M(\omega^2 \bar{y}-\dot{\omega}x)+\Sigma Y\}a_1 - (D\omega^2-E\dot{\omega}+\Sigma Yz)}{a_2-a_1}. \end{array}\right\} \quad\ldots\ldots(1)$$

Along with these, if Z_1, Z_2 be the forces in the direction of Oz applied to the body by the bearings, and Z be the applied force in that direction on the representative particle of mass m at P, we have

$$Z_1 + Z_2 + \Sigma Z = 0. \quad\ldots\ldots\ldots\ldots\ldots\ldots(2)$$

If the bearings be on the axis of z, the force along Oz applied to the body at one bearing can have no moment about the other, and so the conditions $\Sigma(Zx) = \Sigma(Zy) = 0$ must be fulfilled.

Let now the bearings be at equal distances on opposite sides of the plane xOy, then $a_2 = -a_1 = a$, say, and we get

$$\left.\begin{array}{l} X_1 = -\tfrac{1}{2}\{M(\omega^2\bar{x}+\dot{\omega}\bar{y})+\Sigma X\} + \dfrac{E\omega^2+D\dot{\omega}+\Sigma Xz}{2a}, \\[6pt] X_2 = -\tfrac{1}{2}\{M(\omega^2\bar{x}+\dot{\omega}\bar{y})+\Sigma X\} - \dfrac{E\omega^2+D\dot{\omega}+\Sigma Xz}{2a}, \\[6pt] Y_1 = -\tfrac{1}{2}\{M(\omega^2\bar{y}-\dot{\omega}\bar{x})+\Sigma Y\} + \dfrac{D\omega^2-E\dot{\omega}+\Sigma Yz}{2a}, \\[6pt] Y_2 = -\tfrac{1}{2}\{M(\omega^2\bar{y}-\dot{\omega}\bar{x})+\Sigma Y\} - \dfrac{D\omega^2-E\dot{\omega}+\Sigma Yz}{2a}. \end{array}\right\} \quad\ldots\ldots(3)$$

If E denote the resultant of $M(\omega^2\bar{x}+\dot{\omega}\bar{y})+\Sigma X$ in the direction of Ox and $M(\omega^2\bar{y}-\dot{\omega}\bar{x})+\Sigma Y$ in the direction of Oy, and R the resultant of $(E\omega^2+D\dot{\omega}+\Sigma Xz)/a$ in the direction of Ox, and $(D\omega^2-E\dot{\omega}+\Sigma Yz)/a$ in the direction of Oy, these equations show that at one bearing, forces $-\tfrac{1}{2}E$, $\tfrac{1}{2}R$, and at the other bearing, forces $-\tfrac{1}{2}E$, $-\tfrac{1}{2}R$, are applied to the body. The forces applied by the body to the bearings are equal to these forces reversed. The two equal but oppositely directed forces $\tfrac{1}{2}R$, $-\tfrac{1}{2}R$ are entirely due to the products D, E of inertia if there are no applied forces, and in that case vanish when these products are zero. They tend to turn the supporting shaft or axle round in their plane of action.

We have thus an example of the effects of products of inertia on the supporting axis of a rotating body. We may take the driving axle of a bicycle with its pedals, which give products of inertia for an axis through the centroid, or the driving axle of a locomotive with its cranks and attachments as practical examples. It will be observed that the

§§ 169, 170]   EQUATIONS OF ROTATIONAL MOTION.   317

closer together all attachments, such as pedals or cranks, are placed, the smaller are the products of inertia and the resulting couples. Undue spreading out of the parts along the axis of rotation increases the products of inertia, and augments the couple, causing unsteadiness of running.

If we choose the axes Ox, Oy through O so that $\Sigma(mxy)$ is zero, and if at the same time $\Sigma(myz)$, $\Sigma(mzx)$ be each zero, then the three axes of coordinates Ox, Oy, Oz are principal axes of moment of inertia of the body. It will be observed that if O be taken at the centroid $M\bar{x} = M\bar{y} = 0$, and that therefore if the axes Ox, Oy, Oz be principal axes through the centroid, and there be no applied forces, there is no action whatever exerted on the axis of support or exerted by that axis on the body. Hence, in the absence of other forces, the body, if rigid, will, when set rotating about Oz, continue to do so without support. Oz is then what is called a free axis. It will be clear that any principal axis of moment of inertia through the centroid is a free axis.

170. A.M. about any Axis. Equations of Rotational Motion.
Let now the axis OA in the direction l, m, n be one about which the whole system is turning with angular speed ω. The angular momentum H about the axis is given by

$$H = \omega(Al^2 + Bm^2 + Cn^2 - 2Dmn - 2Enl - 2Flm), \quad \ldots(1)$$

or, as we may write it,

$$H = \omega\{l(Al - Fm - En) + m(-Fl + Bm - Dn) + n(-El - Dm + Cn)\}. \quad \ldots(2)$$

But the angular momentum is also $lH_1 + mH_2 + nH_3$, where H_1, H_2, H_3 (the F, G, H of § 71) are the components of angular momentum about the axes of x, y, z. Hence, since ω_1, ω_2, ω_3, the angular speeds about the same axes, are $l\omega$, $m\omega$, $n\omega$ respectively,

$$\left. \begin{array}{l} H_1 = A\omega_1 - F\omega_2 - E\omega_3, \quad H_2 = -F\omega_1 + B\omega_2 - D\omega_3, \\ H_3 = -E\omega_1 - D\omega_2 + C\omega_3. \end{array} \right\} \ldots(3)$$

If L, M, N be the moments of forces about the axes, the time-rates of variation of these components give three equations of the form

$$A\dot{\omega}_1 - F\dot{\omega}_2 - E\dot{\omega}_3 + \dot{A}\omega_1 - \dot{F}\omega_2 - \dot{E}\omega_3 = L ; \quad \ldots\ldots(4)$$

for it will be noticed that as the body is in motion relatively to the axes, the quantities A, B, C, D, E, F cannot be taken as constants.

The equation of the ellipsoid referred to its principal axes may be written

$$A'\xi^2 + B'\eta^2 + C'\zeta^2 = 1, \quad\quad\quad\quad\quad (5)$$

where A', B', C' are the moments of inertia about the principal axes. If l, m, n be the direction-cosines, with reference to the principal axes, of the axis about which the angular speed is ω, the angular momenta about the principal axes are $A'l\omega$, $B'm\omega$, $C'n\omega = A'\omega_1$, $B'\omega_2$, $C'\omega_3$; but it is only when the axes of reference and the principal axes are coincident that these simple values of the components of angular momentum are obtained.

If at the instant under consideration the principal axes coincide with the axes of reference, $A' = A$, $B' = B$, $C' = C$ and $D = E = F = 0$. The equations of motion are now

$$A\dot{\omega}_1 + \dot{A}\omega_1 - \dot{F}\omega_2 - \dot{E}\omega_3 = L, \quad\quad\quad\quad\quad (6)$$

and two others of similar form. It will be noticed that though D, E, F are zero, their time-rates of variation are not in general zero, for the body is changing in position with reference to the axes, and the coincidence of axes existing at time t no longer exists at time $t + dt$.

We now suppose the system to be a rigid body, so that the values of $\dot{A}$, $\dot{F}$, $\dot{E}$ are to be calculated subject to this condition. Since $A = \Sigma\{\mu(y^2+z^2)\}$, $E = \Sigma(\mu zx)$, $F = \Sigma(\mu xy)$,

$$\dot{A} = 2\Sigma\{\mu(y\dot{y}+z\dot{z})\}, \quad \dot{F} = \Sigma\{\mu(\dot{x}y+\dot{y}x)\}, \quad \dot{E} = \Sigma\{\mu(\dot{z}x+\dot{x}z)\}.$$

But since the body is rigid and is turning with angular speeds ω_1, ω_2, ω_3 about the axes,

$$\dot{x} = \omega_2 z - \omega_3 y, \quad \dot{y} = \omega_3 x - \omega_1 z, \quad \dot{z} = \omega_1 y - \omega_2 x, \quad\ldots\ldots(7)$$

so that $y\dot{y} + z\dot{z} = \omega_3 xy - \omega_2 xz$. Hence $\dot{A} = \Sigma\{\mu(y\dot{y}+z\dot{z})\} = 0$, since $D = E = F = 0$ at the instant. Again,

$$\dot{x}y + \dot{y}x = \omega_3(x^2+z^2) - \omega_3(y^2+z^2) + \omega_2 yz - \omega_1 xz,$$

and therefore $\dot{F} = \omega_3(B-A)$.

Similarly $\dot{E} = \omega_2(A-C)$. The equation of motion becomes therefore

$$A\dot{\omega}_1 - (B-C)\omega_2\omega_3 = L. \quad\quad\quad\quad\quad (8)$$

Similar results hold for the other two cases.

§ 170] EQUATIONS OF ROTATIONAL MOTION. 319

Here A, B, C are the moments of inertia about the principal axes, which we have supposed to coincide at the instant with the fixed axes of reference. The angular speeds ω_1, ω_2, ω_3 are those about the fixed axes of x, y, z; but since, obviously, there is no difference between the angular speed about a moving axis and that about a fixed axis with which the moving axis coincides, we may regard ω_1, ω_2, ω_3 as the angular speeds about the principal axes of the momental ellipsoid, which moves with the body. It requires examination, however, to decide whether $\dot{\omega}_1$, the time-rate of variation of the angular speed ω_1 about the fixed axis of x, may be identified with the time-rate of variation of the angular speed about the moving axis; for after the lapse of time dt the moving axis has separated from the fixed axis.

To decide this point, we find, what the angular speed about the moving axis is at time $t + dt$. In time dt the principal axis, which coincided with Ox at time t, has turned round in the plane xOz through the angle $\omega_2 dt$ by the rotation about Oy, and in the plane xOy through the angle $\omega_3 dt$ by the rotation about Oz (Fig. 78). In other words, a line Oa of unit length, which coincided with Ox, has been turned about O so that its outer extremity a has now coordinates 1, $\omega_3 dt$, $-\omega_2 dt$, and these quantities may be taken as its direction-cosines. Hence the cosine of the angle between the new position of this line and the fixed axis, now of direction cosines $l+dl$, $m+dm$, $n+dn$ (about which the angular speed is now $\omega + \dot{\omega}\,dt$), is $l + (m\omega_3 - n\omega_2)dt$, and the angular speed about it is

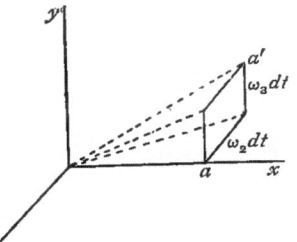

FIG. 78.

$$(\omega + \dot{\omega}\,dt)\{l + (m\omega_3 - n\omega_2)dt\} = (\omega + \dot{\omega}\,dt)l + (\omega_2\omega_3 - \omega_3\omega_2)dt,$$

to the first order of small quantities. Hence $\dot{\omega}l\,dt$ is the change in the angular speed about the moving axis; which is precisely the change which takes place in time dt

in the angular speed about the fixed axis with which the moving axis of Ox coincided at the beginning of that interval of time.

We have thus obtained for a rigid body, moving about the fixed point O, the very important result that the equations of motion with respect to principal axes of moment of inertia passing through the point and *moving with the body* are

$$\left.\begin{array}{l} A\dot{\omega}_1 - (B-C)\,\omega_2\omega_3 = L, \\ B\dot{\omega}_2 - (C-A)\,\omega_3\omega_1 = M, \\ C\dot{\omega}_3 - (A-B)\,\omega_1\omega_2 = N, \end{array}\right\} \quad \ldots\ldots\ldots\ldots\ldots(9)$$

where A, B, C are the principal moments of inertia for the fixed point O. These equations were first given by Euler and are of continual application in the theory of rotational motion. Another proof is given in § 251. [See also Ex. 17, p. 336.]

171. Moments of Inertia in Different Cases. In the previous sections the part which moments of inertia play in the dynamics of a rigid body has been illustrated. We now consider a little in detail the practical subject of the calculation of moments of inertia in different cases.

In the first place we make some deductions from the theorem of the momental ellipsoid. First, we see that, if the principal moments of inertia A, B, C are known, the moment of inertia about an axis, the direction-cosines of which with respect to the principal axes are l, m, n, is $Al^2 + Bm^2 + Cn^2$. Hence, if $A = B = C$, the moment of inertia about the given axis is A. We have such a case in a uniform cube; clearly by symmetry principal moments of inertia for axes passing through the centre are those about the three axes at right angles to the three pairs of opposite sides, and are equal. Thus the moment of inertia about an axis joining two opposite corners of the cube has the same value as that for any one of these axes; in fact the moment of inertia is the same for every axis through the centre of the cube. In this and other such cases consideration of the momental ellipsoid, with the theorem of § 165, enables the moments of inertia about different axes to be found with great ease.

172. M.I. of a Lamina. In the case of a plane lamina, or plate, it is clear that one principal axis is at right angles to the plate, through whatever point as origin axes in different directions are taken. For if ZOZ' be an axis at right angles to the plate, and AOA' an axis inclined at an angle θ to ZOZ', the distance d of any element m from ZOZ' is greater than its distance d' from AOA', since $d' = d \cos \phi$, where ϕ is some angle between 0 and θ. The axis ZOZ' is therefore one of maximum moment of inertia, and the theorem of the momental ellipsoid shows that it meets the ellipsoid at right angles. The other two principal axes therefore lie in the plane of the plate.

If now we take the plane of the plate as that of xy, and any chosen point as the origin through which axes of reference are taken, we get, since $z = 0$ for every particle, $A = \Sigma(\mu y^2)$, $B = \Sigma(\mu x^2)$, $C = \Sigma\{\mu(x^2 + y^2)\}$, whether the axes in the plane of xy are principal axes or not. Thus we have $C = A + B$ for a plate; and however the axes may be taken, provided only that of z be perpendicular to the plate, the products of inertia D and E vanish, and F also vanishes if the axes of x and y are principal axes. The moment of inertia of the plate about an axis through the origin is thus

$$Al^2 + Bm^2 + (A+B)n^2 \quad \text{or} \quad Al^2 + Bm^2 + 2Fmn + (A+B)n^2,$$

and the equation of the momental ellipsoid is

$$A'\xi^2 + B'\eta^2 + (A'+B')\zeta^2 = 1 \quad \ldots\ldots\ldots\ldots(1)$$

or
$$A\xi^2 + B\eta^2 + 2F\xi\eta + (A+B)\zeta^2 = k^4, \quad \ldots\ldots\ldots\ldots(2)$$

according as the axes of x and y are or are not principal axes. As explained above, any constant value can be assigned to k in (2).

173. M.I. of Triangular Plate. As a first example we find the moment of inertia of a uniform triangular plate about any axis in the plane of the plate. The theorem just proved will then enable the momental ellipsoid to be found for any point through which axes are taken in different directions. Let ABC (Fig. 79) be the triangle, OK the axis in its plane, and D, E, F the feet of perpendiculars, of lengths p_1, p_2, p_3, let fall on the axis from the vertices A, B, C. The line AH drawn parallel to OK divides the triangle into two, ABH, AHC, of which we can very easily find the moments of inertia. Taking first ABH, consider a strip LM of breadth du, the length of which is parallel to the axis, and let u be its distance from the axis. The length of the strip is

$$AH(u-p_2)/(p_1-p_2),$$

and its moment of inertia about the axis is the product of this by $\sigma u^2 du$, where σ is the mass of the plate per unit area. Thus the moment of inertia I_1 of the triangle is

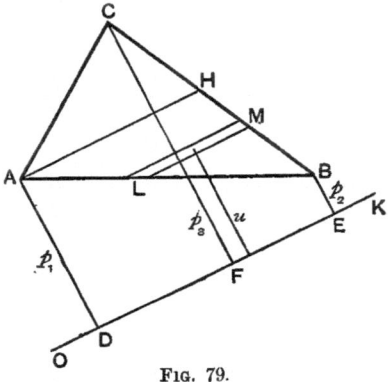

Fig. 79.

$$I_1 = \frac{\sigma \cdot AH}{p_1-p_2} \int_{p_2}^{p_1} (u-p_2) u^2 du$$
$$= \sigma \cdot AH \{ \tfrac{1}{4}(p_1+p_2)(p_1^2+p_2^2) - \tfrac{1}{3} p_2(p_1^2+p_1 p_2+p_2^2) \}. \quad \ldots (3)$$

For the other triangle the length of a strip parallel to the axis and at distance u from it is $AH(p_3-u)/(p_3-p_1)$, and its moment of inertia is

$$\frac{\sigma \cdot AH}{p_3-p_1} \int_{p_1}^{p_3} (p_3-u) u^2 du$$

or $I_2 = \sigma \cdot AH \{ \tfrac{1}{3} p_3 (p_3^2+p_3 p_1+p_1^2) - \tfrac{1}{4}(p_1+p_3)(p_1^2+p_3^2) \}. \quad (4)$

The whole moment of inertia is the sum of these results, or if Δ denote the area of the triangle, that is $\tfrac{1}{2} AH(p_3-p_2)$,

$$I = \tfrac{1}{6} \sigma \Delta (p_1^2+p_2^2+p_3^2+p_2 p_3+p_3 p_1+p_1 p_2) \ldots \ldots (5)$$

or $\quad I = \tfrac{1}{3}\sigma\Delta \left\{ \left(\frac{p_1+p_2}{2}\right)^2 + \left(\frac{p_2+p_3}{2}\right)^2 + \left(\frac{p_3+p_1}{2}\right)^2 \right\}. \quad \ldots(6)$

If OK intersect the triangle, the p or ps on one side have positive numerical values, on the other side negative.

Clearly, (6) gives the moment of inertia, about the axis, of three particles each of mass $\frac{1}{3}\sigma\Delta$, placed at the middle points of the sides. Here we have an example of an *equimomental system*. In every way, as regards moment of inertia, this system of particles is equivalent to the triangular plate.

If we consider two perpendicular axes through O and in the plane of the triangle, and call one of these the axis of x and the other the axis of y, the ordinates of the vertices will be y_1, y_2, y_3, and their abscissae x_1, x_2, x_3, and we shall have for the moment of inertia about Ox,

$$I_x = \tfrac{1}{3}\sigma\Delta \left\{ \left(\frac{y_1+y_2}{2}\right)^2 + \left(\frac{y_2+y_3}{2}\right)^2 + \left(\frac{y_3+y_1}{2}\right)^2 \right\}, \ldots\ldots(7)$$

and for the moment of inertia about Oy,

$$I_y = \tfrac{1}{3}\sigma\Delta \left\{ \left(\frac{x_1+x_2}{2}\right)^2 + \left(\frac{x_2+x_3}{2}\right)^2 + \left(\frac{x_2+x_1}{2}\right)^2 \right\}. \ldots\ldots(8)$$

If now we take an axis through O in the plane of the triangle and inclined at an angle θ to the axis Ox, the distances of the vertices from that axis are

$$y_1 \cos\theta - x_1 \sin\theta, \ldots,$$

and the moment of inertia can be written down by substituting these values for p_1, p_2, p_3 in the expression found above. It will be found to have the form

$$A\cos^2\theta + B\sin^2\theta - 2F\sin\theta\cos\theta, \ldots\ldots\ldots(9)$$

where

$$A = \tfrac{1}{12}\sigma\Delta[\{(y_1+y_2)\}^2 + \ldots], \quad B = \tfrac{1}{12}\sigma\Delta[\{(x_1+x_2)\}^2 + \ldots],$$
$$F = \tfrac{1}{12}\sigma\Delta\{(x_1+x_2)(y_1+y_2) + \ldots\}.$$

Hence the equation of the momental ellipsoid is

$$A\xi^2 + B\eta^2 - 2F\xi\eta + (A+B)\zeta^2 = k^4, \ldots\ldots\ldots(10)$$

where A, B, F have the values here stated. Of course the common factor $\tfrac{1}{3}\sigma\Delta$ may be neglected; and, according to the value assigned to the parameter k, different, but similar and similarly situated, ellipsoids are obtained.

174. M.I. about Axes at any Point parallel to Principal Axes at Centroid. The moment of inertia of a system with reference to principal axes through the centroid G being $Al^2 + Bm^2 + Cn^2$, we can find the relation of this to the moment of inertia with reference to parallel axes through any other point. Consider an axis in the direction l, m, n and passing through an origin O whose coordinates with reference to the axes through the centroid are a, b, c. The square of the distance h of the centroid from this axis is $a^2 + b^2 + c^2 - (la + mb + nc)^2$, and the square of the distance of an element of mass μ at the point x, y, z (referred to the axes drawn from G) is

$$(x-a)^2 + (y-b)^2 + (z-c)^2 - \{l(x-a) + m(y-b) + n(z-c)\}^2.$$

Thus the value of I is

$$\Sigma[\mu\{(x-a)^2 + (y-b)^2 + (z-c)^2 - (l(x-a) + m(y-b) + n(z-c))^2\}],$$

which, since $\Sigma\mu = M$, the total mass of the system, and $\Sigma(\mu x)$, $\Sigma(\mu y)$, $\Sigma(\mu z)$ are zero, may be written in the form

$$I = M\left\{l^2\left(\frac{A}{M} + b^2 + c^2\right) + m^2\left(\frac{B}{M} + c^2 + a^2\right) + n^2\left(\frac{C}{M} + a^2 + b^2\right) - 2mnbc - 2nlca - 2lmbc\right\}. \quad \ldots\ldots\ldots\ldots(1)$$

It will be noticed that this differs from $Al^2 + Bm^2 + Cn^2$ by Mh^2, so that we have here another proof of the theorem of § 165.

Taking then distances from $O(a, b, c)$ along the axes drawn from O for different values of l, m, n, each of such a length ρ that the product of the expression just obtained by ρ^2 has the same value, k^4, for all axes drawn through O, and putting $\xi = l\rho$, $\eta = m\rho$, $\zeta = n\rho$, we obtain for the equation of a momental ellipsoid referred to axes drawn from O parallel to the principal axes at G,

$$\left(\frac{A}{M} + b^2 + c^2\right)\xi^2 + \left(\frac{B}{M} + c^2 + a^2\right)\eta^2 + \left(\frac{C}{M} + a^2 + b^2\right)\zeta^2 - 2bc\eta\zeta - 2ca\zeta\xi - 2ab\xi\eta = \frac{k^4}{M}. \quad \ldots\ldots\ldots\ldots(2)$$

It appears therefore that the ellipsoid, with centre at the point O, has its principal axes otherwise directed than are those of the central ellipsoid. But the terms in $\eta\zeta, \ldots$ vanish if the point $O(a, b, c)$ is on one of the principal axes at G, and then the principal axes at O are parallel to those at G.

Equation (2) can be written in the form

$$A\xi^2 + B\eta^2 + C\zeta^2 - k^4 + M(a^2+b^2+c^2)(\xi^2+\eta^2+\zeta^2) \\ - M(a\xi+b\eta+c\zeta)^2 = 0. \quad\ldots\ldots\ldots\ldots\ldots(3)$$

Here ξ, η, ζ refer to the origin O; but if we go back to the origin G, we see that the equation of a momental ellipsoid referred to principal axes at G may be written

$$A\xi^2 + B\eta^2 + C\zeta^2 - k^4 = 0.$$

Hence denoting the expression on the left, taken for the parallel axes at O, by S, the equation of the ellipsoid is

$$S + M(a^2+b^2+c^2)(\xi^2+\eta^2+\zeta^2) - M(a\xi+b\eta+c\zeta)^2 = 0. \quad(4)$$

175. Examples of M.I. We take now some examples of the calculation of moments of inertia for particular cases, considering only axes drawn through the centroid of the distribution of matter, inasmuch as the moments of inertia for other axes can then be found with great ease by the theorem of § 165.

1. *A straight rod of length $2a$ and uniform mass μ per unit length.* Here the axis of the rod and any two axes at right angles to the length and to one another are principal axes. The ellipsoid is in fact one of revolution. Let the moment of inertia about the axis of the rod be A: that about a perpendicular axis is

$$2\int_0^a \mu x^2 dx = \tfrac{2}{3}\mu a^3 = \tfrac{1}{3}Ma^2, \quad\ldots\ldots\ldots\ldots\ldots\ldots(1)$$

if $M = 2a\mu$, the whole mass of the rod.

The moment of inertia about an axis through the centroid G in the direction l, m, n is therefore $Al^2 + \tfrac{1}{3}Ma^2(m^2+n^2)$, and the equation of a momental ellipsoid is

$$A\xi^2 + \tfrac{1}{3}Ma^2(\eta^2+\zeta^2) = 1. \quad\ldots\ldots\ldots\ldots\ldots\ldots(2)$$

The thinner the rod the smaller is A, and therefore the longer the axis of revolution of this ellipsoid in comparison with the other axes. The equation

$$\eta^2 + \zeta^2 = 1 \quad\ldots\ldots\ldots\ldots\ldots\ldots\ldots\ldots\ldots(3)$$

may be used as that of a momental ellipsoid for all axes which are not coincident with that of the rod, if the rod be very thin.

2. *A thin rectangular plate of length $2a$ and breadth $2b$ and of uniform mass μ per unit area.* We suppose the plate first divided into thin rods each parallel to the sides of the plate, and calculating I for one of these rods, about the longitudinal axis of the plate, find then by integration I for the whole plate about that axis. Let y be the distance of a strip of breadth dy from the axis: then its mass is $2\sigma a\, dy$, and I for the strip is $2\sigma a y^2 dy$. Hence for the whole plate

$$I = 4\sigma a \int_0^b y^2 dy = \tfrac{4}{3}\sigma a b^3 = M\frac{b^2}{3} \quad\quad\quad\quad (4)$$

if $M = 4\sigma a b$, the mass of the plate.

Similarly the moment of inertia about a transverse axis in the plane of the plate is $Ma^2/3$. It follows from the theorem of plane plates (§ 172) that for an axis perpendicular to the plate through G,

$$I = \tfrac{1}{3}M(a^2 + b^2), \quad\quad\quad\quad (5)$$

and for an axis through G in the direction l, m, n,

$$I = \tfrac{1}{3}M\{(b^2 l^2 + a^2 m^2 + (a^2 + b^2)n^2\}. \quad\quad\quad\quad (6)$$

The equation of a momental ellipsoid is therefore

$$b^2 \xi^2 + a^2 \eta^2 + (a^2 + b^2)\zeta^2 = 1. \quad\quad\quad\quad (7)$$

3. *A uniform block bounded by rectangular sides.* Let its length, breadth and thickness be $2a, 2b, 2c$, and its mass per unit volume ρ. Suppose it divided into thin plates parallel to the breadth and length, and let the distance of one such plate from the parallel middle plane be z, and its thickness dz. Then, for the plate about an axis through its centroid parallel to its length, $I = 4\rho ab^3 dz/3$; to this, by § 165, we have to add $4\rho abz^2 dz$ to get the value of I for the plate about the longitudinal axis of the block. Taking twice the integral of their sum from $z = 0$ to $z = c$, we obtain for the whole block

$$I = 8\rho abc\,\frac{b^2 + c^2}{3} = M\frac{b^2 + c^2}{3}. \quad\quad\quad\quad (8)$$

Similarly the values of I for axes parallel to the breadth and thickness are $\tfrac{1}{3}M(a^2 + c^2)$, $\tfrac{1}{3}M(a^2 + b^2)$.

Thus for an axis in the direction l, m, n,

$$I = \tfrac{1}{3}M\{(b^2 + c^2)l^2 + (c^2 + a^2)m^2 + (a^2 + b^2)n^2\}, \quad\quad\quad\quad (9)$$

and the equation of a momental ellipsoid is

$$(b^2 + c^2)\varsigma^2 + (c^2 + a^2)\eta^2 + (a^2 + b^2)\zeta^2 = 1. \quad\quad\quad\quad (10)$$

4. *A thin uniform plate bounded by an ellipse of semi-axes a, b.* The principal axes in this case are clearly the major and minor axes of the elliptic boundary, and an axis at right angles to the plane. Taking first the major axis, a strip parallel to it at distance y, and of breadth dy, has $2\sigma a(1 - y^2/b^2)^{\frac{1}{2}} y^2 dy$ for its moment of inertia. For by the equation $x^2/a^2 + y^2/b^2 = 1$ of the ellipse, the length of the strip is $2a(1-y^2/b^2)^{\frac{1}{2}}$. Hence for the whole disk,

$$I_x = 2\sigma a \int_{-b}^{b} \left(1 - \frac{y^2}{b^2}\right)^{\frac{1}{2}} y^2 \, dy = 2\sigma ab^3 \int_{-\frac{\pi}{2}}^{\frac{\pi}{2}} \sin^2\theta \cos^2\theta \, d\theta, \quad \ldots\ldots(11)$$

if $y^2/b^2 = \sin^2\theta$. The integral can be found at once by integration by parts, and we obtain

$$I_x = \pi\sigma ab \frac{b^2}{4} = M \frac{b^2}{4}, \quad \ldots\ldots\ldots\ldots\ldots\ldots\ldots\ldots(12)$$

where $M = \pi\sigma ab$, the mass of the disk.

Similarly, for the minor axis,

$$I_y = M \frac{a^2}{4} \quad \ldots\ldots\ldots\ldots\ldots\ldots\ldots\ldots\ldots(13)$$

The moment of inertia about the third axis, I_z, is given by the relation $I_z = I_x + I_y$, and we have

$$I_z = M \frac{a^2 + b^2}{4} \quad \ldots\ldots\ldots\ldots\ldots\ldots\ldots\ldots(14)$$

Thus, for an axis in the direction l, m, n,

$$I = \tfrac{1}{4} M(b^2 l^2 + a^2 m^2 + (a^2 + b^2) n^2), \quad \ldots\ldots\ldots\ldots\ldots(15)$$

and the equation of a momental ellipsoid is

$$b^2 \xi^2 + a^2 \eta^2 + (a^2 + b^2)\zeta^2 = 1, \quad \ldots\ldots\ldots\ldots\ldots\ldots(16)$$

the equation already found for a rectangular plate.

These results are of course, with $a^2 = b^2$, applicable to a circular disk.

5. *A uniform ellipsoid of semi-axes a, b, c.* The equation of the surface is
$$\frac{x^2}{a^2} + \frac{y^2}{b^2} + \frac{z^2}{c^2} = 1,$$

and evidently the axes of x, y, z are the principal axes. We find first I for the axis of x, and for that purpose divide the ellipsoid up into elliptic disks parallel to the plane of x, y through the centre. Let z be the distance of such a disk from the plane of x, y. The area of the disk is $\pi ab(1 - z^2/c^2)$, and its moment of inertia about an axis in its own plane through its centroid parallel to that of x is $\tfrac{1}{4}\pi\sigma ab^3(1 - z^2/c^2)^2$. Hence the moment of inertia about the x-axis of the ellipsoid is

$$\sigma ab(1 - z^2/c^2)\{z^2 + \tfrac{1}{4}b^2(1 - z^2/c^2)\}.$$

We get, taking twice the integral of this from $z = 0$ to $z = c$,

$$I_x = \tfrac{4}{3}\pi\rho abc \frac{b^2 + c^2}{5} = M \frac{b^2 + c^2}{5}. \quad \ldots\ldots\ldots\ldots\ldots(17)$$

Similarly we obtain

$$I_y = M \frac{c^2 + a^2}{5}, \quad I_z = M \frac{a^2 + b^2}{5}. \quad \ldots\ldots\ldots\ldots\ldots(18)$$

The moment of inertia of a uniform sphere about a diameter is thus $\frac{2}{5}Mr^2$, where r is the radius.

The moment of inertia of the ellipsoid about an axis in the direction l, m, n is thus given by

$$I = \tfrac{1}{5}M\{(b^2+c^2)l^2 + (c^2+a^2)m^2 + (a^2+b^2)n^2\}, \quad\ldots\ldots\ldots\ldots(19)$$

and the equation of a momental ellipsoid is

$$(b^2+c^2)\xi^2 + (c^2+a^2)\eta^2 + (a^2+b^2)\zeta^2 = 1. \quad\ldots\ldots\ldots\ldots\ldots(20)$$

6. *An ellipsoidal shell.* It is sometimes necessary to use the moment of inertia of a thin spherical or ellipsoidal shell. This we can obtain by differentiation from the moments of inertia found above. For take

$$I_x = \tfrac{4}{15}\pi\rho abc(b^2+c^2) = \tfrac{1}{5}M(b^2+c^2), \quad\ldots\ldots\ldots\ldots\ldots\ldots(21)$$

which has been found above for a solid ellipsoid of uniform density ρ. Let the axes be increased in length by small amounts da, db, dc; then, neglecting small quantities of the second order, we get

$$dI_x = \tfrac{4}{15}\pi\rho abc\left\{(b^2+c^2)\left(\frac{da}{a}+\frac{db}{b}+\frac{dc}{c}\right) + 2(b\,db + c\,dc)\right\}. \quad\ldots\ldots(22)$$

The former mass is $M = \tfrac{4}{3}\pi\rho abc$, the increase of mass, dM, is

$$\tfrac{4}{3}\pi\rho abc\,(da/a + db/b + dc/c);$$

hence we can write the equation just found in the form

$$dI_x = \tfrac{1}{5}dM \cdot (b^2+c^2) + \tfrac{1}{5}Md(b^2+c^2), \quad\ldots\ldots\ldots\ldots\ldots(23)$$

which we might have obtained at once from the second form of I_x in (17). Similar results hold of course for I_y, I_z.

If the axes be increased in the proportion of their lengths so that $da/a = db/b = dc/c = d\lambda$, say, we get

$$dI_x = \tfrac{4}{3}\pi\rho abc(b^2+c^2)d\lambda = 5I_x d\lambda. \quad\ldots\ldots\ldots\ldots\ldots\ldots(24)$$

The moment of inertia of a thin spherical shell about a diameter is thus $\tfrac{2}{3}Mr^2$, if M is the mass of the shell and r its radius.

If the moments of inertia of thick shells bounded by concentric surfaces are required, the moments of inertia of the solid ellipsoids which coincide with the outer and inner surfaces of the shells must be calculated and the required moments of inertia found by subtraction.

176. Condition that an Ellipsoid may be a Momental Ellipsoid. While a momental ellipsoid, or, rather a series of momental ellipsoids, can be found for any point taken in relation to a given material system, it is not the case that to every ellipsoid that can be described there corresponds a material system of which it is a momental ellipsoid. For (except in the limiting case in which one principal moment of inertia is zero and the other two principal moments are equal) the sum of any two principal moments of inertia is greater than the third. Take say $A+B-C$. We have

$$A = \Sigma\{\mu(y^2+z^2)\}, \ldots\ldots,$$

and so $A+B-C = \Sigma\{\mu(y^2+z^2+z^2+x^2-x^2-y^2)\} = \Sigma(2\mu z^2)$, which is positive, and the same thing can be proved for $A+C-B$ and $B+C-A$. Thus, unless the sum of the squares of the reciprocals of the lengths of any two of the principal axes of the given ellipsoid is greater than the square of the reciprocal of the length of the third, the given ellipsoid cannot be a momental ellipsoid of any material system.

177. Foci of Inertia. Let the principal moments of inertia at the centroid, G, of a given material system be A, B, C, and let A, the moment about the axis of x, be greater than B, the moment about the axis of y. On the axis of x take two points O_1, O_2 (Fig. 80), one on each side of the centroid, at a distance $O_1G = GO_2 = \sqrt{(A-B)/M}$. Since O_1 and O_2 lie on a principal axis through G, the principal axes at either point are parallel to the principal axes at G. The moment about the axis of x is A for each point, while that about the axis of y at O_1 or O_2 is

$$B + M(A-B)/M = A.$$

Thus the moment of inertia is the same for every axis at O_1 or O_2 in the plane of xy, that is the momental ellipsoids with centres at

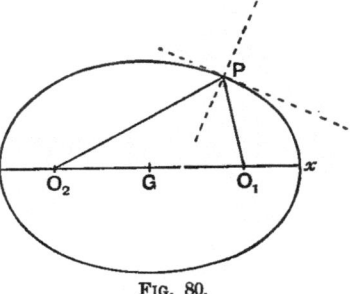

Fig. 80.

O_1 or O_2 are ellipsoids of revolution. The points O_1, O_2 are called *foci of inertia*.

If we take any point P in the plane of two of the principal axes at G, it can be proved that one of the principal axes at that point is perpendicular to the plane. For let the plane be that of x, y, and let h, k be the co-ordinates of P, and x, y, z the coordinates, with reference to the principal axes through the centroid, of an element of mass μ. We have then for an axis through P parallel to Gz, the products of inertia

$$\Sigma\{\mu(x-h)z\}, \quad \Sigma\{\mu(y-h)z\},$$

which are both zero since $\Sigma(\mu xz) = \Sigma(\mu yz) = 0$, and $\Sigma(\mu z) = 0$, for the axes at G are principal axes and G is the centroid. Hence the proposition stated.

Again, taking the plane of x, y at G, let Gx (Fig. 80) be the axis about which the moment of inertia is $A (> B)$, and O_1, O_2 be the foci of inertia. Then, if we take any point P in the plane and join it with O_1, O_2, the moments of inertia about O_1P and O_2P are the same in amount, and one principal axis at P has been shown to be at right angles to the plane O_1PO_2. The other two must be the internal and external bisectors of the angle O_1PO_2. For if a momental ellipsoid be described from P as centre it will meet the plane O_1PO_2 (the plane xGy) in an ellipse, and the radii-vectores from P through O_1, O_2 will be equal in length. The principal axes of the ellipse are the bisectors referred to. Thus if an ellipse or hyberbola be described through P with O_1 and O_2 as foci, the two principal axes at P required are the tangent and normal to the curve at P as shown in the figure.

178. Ellipsoid of Gyration. Finally may be noted here some theorems regarding other ellipsoids which also represent conveniently the moments of inertia of a material system about different axes through a specified point. For example, if, M being the total mass, we write Mk_1^2, Mk_2^2, Mk_3^2 for the moments of inertia A, B, C about principal axes through the specified point, we may use the equation of the momental ellipsoid in the form

$$k_1^2\xi^2 + k_2^2\eta^2 + k_3^2\zeta^2 = 1. \quad \ldots\ldots\ldots\ldots\ldots\ldots(1)$$

The quantities k_1, k_2, k_3 are called *radii of gyration* of the system about the principal axes.

It is convenient sometimes to use the ellipsoid

$$\frac{\xi^2}{A} + \frac{\eta^2}{B} + \frac{\zeta^2}{C} = \frac{1}{M}, \quad \ldots\ldots\ldots\ldots\ldots\ldots(2)$$

§§ 177, 178] ELLIPSOID OF GYRATION. 331

which is said to be *reciprocal* to the momental ellipsoid
$$A\xi^2 + B\eta^2 + C\zeta^2 = 1, \quad\quad\quad\quad\quad (3)$$
and is called the *ellipsoid of gyration*. With the constant term on the right chosen as $1/M$, where M is the whole mass, the ellipsoid represents moments of inertia about different axes through its centre in the following manner. For every such axis two parallel planes can be drawn to touch the ellipsoid and be perpendicular to the axis. These planes are at the same perpendicular distance p from the centre, and the moment of inertia about the axis is Mp^2.

For the direction-cosines of the normal l, m, n, say, are given by the equations
$$l, m, n = \frac{\frac{\xi}{A}, \frac{\eta}{B}, \frac{\zeta}{C}}{\left(\frac{\xi^2}{A^2} + \frac{\eta^2}{B^2} + \frac{\zeta^2}{C^2}\right)^{\frac{1}{2}}}. \quad\quad\quad (4)$$

Hence, if ξ, η, ζ be the coordinates of a point in which a tangent plane touches the surface, the length of the perpendicular is
$$l\xi + m\eta + n\zeta = p = \frac{1}{M(\xi^2/A^2 + \eta^2/B^2 + \zeta^2/C^2)^{\frac{1}{2}}}. \quad (5)$$

But since $l/(\xi/A) = m/(\eta/B) = n/(\zeta/C)$, we get by squaring the fractions, multiplying the numerator and denominator of the first squared fraction by A, of the second by B, and of the third by C, and then adding numerators and denominators,
$$\frac{l^2A + m^2B + n^2C}{1/M} = \frac{1}{\xi^2/A^2 + \eta^2/B^2 + \zeta^2/C^2} = M^2 p^2 \quad\ldots\ldots(6)$$
by (5). Hence we have
$$l^2A + m^2B + n^2C = Mp^2, \quad\quad\quad\quad\quad (7)$$
which is the proposition stated above. Thus the perpendicular p on the tangent plane is exactly the radius of gyration of the body about the axis with which the perpendicular coincides. In this lies the convenience of this mode of representation.

It will be seen that if k_1, k_2, k_3 be the principal radii of gyration, we can write the ellipsoid of gyration in the more compact form,

$$\frac{\xi^2}{k_1^2} + \frac{\eta^2}{k_2^2} + \frac{\zeta^2}{k_3^2} = 1. \quad\quad\quad\quad\quad\quad\quad\quad (8)$$

This ellipsoid is said to be *reciprocal* to the momental ellipsoid, (1) above, for the following geometrical reason. Let the momental ellipsoid be constructed, and concentric with it a sphere of such radius that it lies wholly within the ellipsoid. Then taking any point P on the momental ellipsoid, draw the polar plane of P with reference to the sphere, that is the plane which contains the points of contact of all tangent planes to the sphere which pass through P. Then if we cause the point P to travel over the momental ellipsoid, we get a succession of polar planes which all touch a second ellipsoid—envelope it, as it is said. This second ellipsoid is coaxial with the first and reciprocal to it. The ellipsoid of gyration, (2) or (8), may be regarded as thus produced with a suitable choice of the radius of the sphere of reference.

179. Equimomental Cone. Theorem of Binet. At any point P, the principal moments of inertia at which are A, B, C, the axes for which the moment of inertia has the same value I form a cone of which the principal diameters are the principal axes at P. For if l, m, n be the direction-cosines of an axis about which the moment is I, we have $l^2 A + m^2 B + n^2 C = I$ or $l^2(A-I) + m^2(B-I) + n^2(C-I) = 0$. Multiplying by $\rho = \xi/l = \eta/m = \zeta/n$, we get

$$(A-I)\xi^2 + (B-I)\eta^2 + (C-I)\zeta^2 = 0, \quad\quad\quad\quad\quad\quad (1)$$

which is the equation of a cone, called an equimomental cone, on which lie the axes in question through P. The principal axes of this surface are coincident with the principal axes of the momental ellipsoid at P, since there are no terms involving the products of coordinates $\xi\eta, \eta\zeta, \zeta\xi$. Different equimomental cones are obtained for different values of I, but it is to be carefully remarked that all have this property.

To further determine the principal axes of moment of inertia at any point P, we consider the surfaces which pass through P and are confocal with the ellipsoid of gyration which has its centre at G (the central ellipsoid of gyration), which for brevity we shall refer to as the ellipsoid E. The equation of a surface through P confocal with E is

$$\frac{x^2}{k_1^2 + \lambda} + \frac{y^2}{k_2^2 + \lambda} + \frac{z^2}{k_3^2 + \lambda} = 1. \quad\quad\quad\quad\quad\quad (2)$$

Its principal sections have the same foci as those of the ellipsoid E. Equation (2) may be regarded as a cubic equation for the determination of λ, for any given fixed real values of x, y, z. There is no difficulty in proving that all three roots are real, and that one is less than the least of k_1^2, k_2^2, k_3^2 and negative or positive according as P is within or without E, while the other two roots are both negative, and have numerical values which, taken positive, lie one between the greatest and next greatest and the other between the least and next least of k_1^2, k_2^2, k_3^2. Thus, if k_1^2, k_2^2, k_3^2 be in order of magnitude, the greatest first, $k_1^2+\lambda$, $k_2^2+\lambda$, $k_3^2+\lambda$ are all positive for the first root, $k_1^2+\lambda$ is positive and $k_2^2+\lambda$, $k_3^2+\lambda$ are negative for the second, and $k_1^2+\lambda$, $k_2^2+\lambda$ are positive and $k_3^2+\lambda$ is negative for the third. The surface represented by the equation is an ellipsoid when the first root is used as the value of λ, a hyperboloid of two sheets when the second root is taken, and a hyperboloid of one sheet in the third case. Thus through any point whatever can be drawn these three surfaces confocal and therefore coaxial with the ellipsoid E. It can easily be proved that at the point of intersection the normals to the three surfaces are mutually perpendicular. Moreover, the normals to the hyperboloids at P are tangents to the lines of curvature of the confocal ellipsoid at the same point, that is, the intersections of the surface by the two planes at right angles to one another which contain the radii of greatest and least curvature of the ellipsoid at the point.

Now, from the specified point P, at which it is required to find the principal axes, draw a tangent cone to *any* surface confocal with E. To fix his ideas the student may take the confocal ellipsoid. This cone is the locus of the intersections of planes which all pass through P and touch the surface. Take

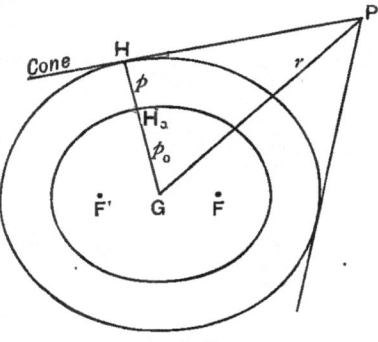

FIG. 81.

any one of these planes and calculate its distance from G. If l, m, n be the direction-cosines of a normal to the plane from G, the square of this distance is, by (2),

$$l^2(k_1^2+\lambda) + m^2(k_2^2+\lambda) + n^2(k_3^2+\lambda) = l^2 k_1^2 + m^2 k_2^2 + n^2 k_3^2 + \lambda. \quad \ldots\ldots(3)$$

Thus if (Fig. 81) a perpendicular from G meet the tangent plane at H and a parallel tangent plane to E in H_0, and we write p, p_0 for GH and GH_0, we get $\lambda = p^2 - p_0^2$. This interprets λ, and we see that it is the same for all tangent planes drawn from P to the same surface confocal with E.

But if we write $GP^2 = r^2$, we have $PH^2 = r^2 - p^2$. Hence, by § 165, if we take the moment of inertia of the body about GH, namely Mp_0^2, the moment of inertia about a parallel axis through P is

$$Mp_0^2 + M(r^2 - p^2) = M(r^2 - \lambda). \quad \ldots\ldots\ldots\ldots\ldots\ldots\ldots\ldots(4)$$

Thus $r^2 - \lambda$ is the square of the radius of gyration about the axis parallel to GH through P, and hence the axes drawn through P parallel to all the axes GH, corresponding to planes through P enveloping the surface characterised by λ, form an equimomental cone with P as vertex, and the principal axes at P are those of this cone.

Such an equimomental cone can be drawn by enveloping any one of the confocal surfaces by planes through P, and we have seen that the principal axes of all such cones coincide. We may therefore use any one of the three confocal surfaces which intersect in P. In this case the equimomental cone has one axis at P perpendicular to the surface which it envelopes; and thus, by drawing an equimomental cone to envelope each surface, we see that the three principal axes at P are normals to the three confocal surfaces which these intersect. This is Binet's theorem.

EXERCISES VI.

1. Prove that if the mass of a system is symmetrically distributed on the two sides of a plane, a pair of principal axes lie in that plane for every point of it.

2. A uniform plate is in the form of a regular polygon. Prove that its M.I. about an axis through its centre at right angles to its plane is $\frac{1}{6}M(r'^2 + 2r^2)$, where r, r' are the radii of the inscribed and circumscribed circles.

3. Find the M.I. of a uniform elliptic plate, of semi-axes a, b, and mass m, round an axis at right angles to its plane and passing through an end of a diameter inclined at an angle θ to the major axis. Find also the M.I. about a tangent to the elliptic boundary at the extremity of the diameter specified [Ex. 4, § 175].

4. Prove that the M.I. of a homogeneous right circular cone about an axis through the centroid perpendicular to the axis of figure is $\frac{3}{80}M(h^2 + 4a^2)$, where a is the radius of the base and h the height of the cone from base to vertex.

Prove also that the M.I. about the axis of figure is $\frac{3}{10}Ma^2$. Hence find the M.I. about an axis l, m, n through the centroid, and the equation of the central M.E. Find also the M.E. for the vertex.

5. Prove that in a momental ellipsoid the length of the shortest of the three axes is not less than that of the perpendicular let fall from the centre on the line joining the extremities of the other two axes.

6. A uniform elliptic lamina of mass M is loaded with two particles each of mass m placed at the extremities of the minor axis. Find what condition must be fulfilled in order that the principal axes for any point on the boundary of the lamina may be the tangent and normal at the point.

7. Prove that a body of given density and of mass M will have minimum M.I. about an axis through a given point if it is a sphere with its centre at the point.

8. Prove that the M.I. of a uniform hemispherical shell is the same for every axis through the centre. Hence show that the same thing is true for axes drawn through the vertex of the surface.

9. A uniform plate is bounded by a parabola ($y^2 = 4ax$) and a straight line perpendicular to the axis at distance c from the vertex: prove that the M.I. of the plate about the axis of symmetry is $\frac{24}{15}Mca$, and about the tangent at the vertex is $\frac{3}{7}Mc^2$. Hence find the M.E. for the vertex.

10. A solid ellipsoid may be regarded as made up of infinitely thin similar and similarly situated ellipsoidal shells, each of uniform density. This density varies as the distance from the centre along the axis a. Show that the M.I. about that axis is $\frac{2}{3}M(b^2+c^2)$, where M is the mass of the ellipsoid. [Equation (24), § 175. Put $b=pa$, $c=qa$, $\rho=ka$, where p, q, k are constants.]

11. Show that the foci of inertia for a uniform elliptic lamina lie on the minor axis at distances from the centre each equal to $\frac{1}{2}ae$.

12. A rigid body has its mass M symmetrically distributed on the two sides of a vertical plane and revolves under gravity about an axis at right angles to the plane of symmetry. At the instant considered the angular speed is ω: show that the resultant forces on the axis are $M(\omega^2 h + g\cos\theta)$ outwards along the perpendicular let fall from the centroid on the axis and $Mg\sin\theta . k^2/(h^2+k^2)$ at right angles to this perpendicular, where h is the distance of the centroid from the axis, k the radius of gyration about a parallel axis through the centroid, and θ the inclination of the perpendicular to the vertical.

13. If the perpendicular from the centroid to the axis of rotation have an initial inclination α to the vertical, show that the forces are respectively

$$\frac{Mg}{h^2+k^2}\{(3h^2+k^2)\cos\theta - 2h^2\cos\alpha\}, \quad Mg\frac{k^2}{h^2+k^2}\sin\theta.$$

Hence show that the resultant stress is a minimum when $\theta=\alpha$.

14. A planet of mass M has a satellite of mass m which revolves about it at a constant distance r. The planet has moment of inertia I about a diameter and rotates with angular speed n about an axis perpendicular to the orbit. Show that the A.M. of the system about its centroid is $In + 2\sqrt{\kappa}Mm(M+m)^{-\frac{1}{2}}r^{\frac{1}{2}}$, where κ is the force of attraction between two particles of unit mass at unit distance apart.

15. Show that the total energy E kinetic and potential of the planet and satellite in Ex. 14 is given by
$$E = \tfrac{1}{2} In^2 - \tfrac{1}{2}\kappa Mmr^{-1} + C,$$
where C is a constant.

16. A body turns about a fixed point with angular speeds ω_1, ω_2, ω_3 about axes fixed in space. Show that the kinetic energy T is given by
$$T = \tfrac{1}{2}(A\omega_1^2 + B\omega_2^2 + C\omega_3^2 - 2D\omega_2\omega_3 - 2E\omega_3\omega_1 - 2F\omega_1\omega_2),$$
and verify that the equations of motion are
$$\frac{d}{dt}\frac{\partial T}{\partial \omega_1} = L, \quad \frac{d}{dt}\frac{\partial T}{\partial \omega_2} = M, \quad \frac{d}{dt}\frac{\partial T}{\partial \omega_3} = N.$$
[See § 170.]

17. By means of equation (1), § 9, and the values of H_1, H_2, H_3 (F, G, H of § 9) given in § 170, find the general equations of motion with respect to moving axes for a rotating body.

Also by (1), § 9, taking for F, G, H the angular speeds ω_1, ω_2, ω_3 about the moving axes, and for L, M, N the angular speeds about fixed axes with which the moving axes at the instant coincide, prove that $\dot{\omega}_x = \dot{\omega}_1$, $\dot{\omega}_y = \dot{\omega}_2$, $\dot{\omega}_z = \dot{\omega}_3$. [See also § 170.]

18. If the axes of x and z are the axes of greatest and least M.I. for the origin, in the case of any material system, prove that the equimomental cones intersect the M.E. in curves which, projected on the planes of yz and xy, give ellipses, and projected on the plane of xz give hyperbolas.

19. Find the locus of P (§ 179) so that the moment of inertia with respect to the principal axis (Pz, say) at the point may have a constant value Mk^2.

By (4), § 179, the M.I. about a principal axis of the surface is $M(r^2 - \lambda)$, where λ is a root of equation (2) of that section, and $r^2 = x^2 + y^2 + z^2$. Now here $Mk^2 = M(r^2 - \lambda)$, so that $\lambda = r^2 - k^2$. Substituting in (2), we get for the required locus
$$\frac{x^2}{r^2 - k^2 + k_1^2} + \frac{y^2}{r^2 - k^2 + k_2^2} + \frac{z^2}{r^2 - k^2 + k_3^2} = 1$$
a surface of the fourth degree. If for (1) on the right we substitute $(x^2 + y^2 + z^2)/r^2$, and put $a^2 = k^2 - k_1^2$, $b^2 = k^2 - k_2^2$, $c^2 = k^2 - k_3^2$, the equation takes the form
$$\frac{a^2 x^2}{a^2 - r^2} + \frac{b^2 y^2}{b^2 - r^2} + \frac{c^2 z^2}{c^2 - r^2} = 0,$$
the well-known equation of the wave-surface.

20. Find the condition that a given straight line
$$(x-\alpha)/l = (y-\beta)/m = (z-\gamma)/n$$
may be a principal axis at some point, and find the coordinates x, y, z of the point.

The line must be a normal to the quadric surface, (2) § 179, which passes through the point and is confocal with the central ellipsoid, and therefore, if we put $\mu = x/l(k_1^2 + \lambda) = y/m(k_2^2 + \lambda) = z/n(k_3^2 + \lambda)$, and substitute the values of x, y, z which these give in the equation of the line, we get $\mu = (\alpha/l - \beta/m)/(k_1^2 - k_2^2) = (\beta/m - \gamma/n)/(k_2^2 - k_3^2)$, which is the condition required.

The value of μ is thus known, and so x, y, z can be found. The value of λ is assigned by substituting the values of x, y, z in the equation of the quadric. This gives $\lambda + l^2 k_1^2 + m^2 k_2^2 + n^2 k_3^2 = 1/\mu^2$.

21. Prove that in the plane $\alpha x + \beta y + \gamma z - 1 = 0$ there is a point for which it is a principal plane of the M.E. (with centre at the point) of a given material system. Prove that if A, B, C be the principal moments for the centroid, the coordinates of the point are those of the intersection of the plane with the straight line
$$x/\alpha - A = y/\beta - B = z/\gamma - C.$$

22. Prove that a straight line drawn on a uniform thin plate is a principal axis of M.I. for some point on the line. Find the point if the straight line pass through the centroid.

23. A principal axis at a point P meets a principal axis for a point Q in a point R. Two planes are drawn through P and Q respectively perpendicular to these principal axes. Show that their line of intersection is a principal axis for the point in which it meets the plane PQR.

24. Ox, Oy and Ox', Oy' are two pairs of rectangular axes in the same plane, and θ is the angle xOx'. The moments about the first pair are A, B, and the product of inertia $\sum(mxy)$ is zero. Prove that $\sum(mx'y') = \tfrac{1}{2}(A - B)\sin 2\theta$, where $\theta = \angle xOx'$.

CHAPTER VII.

APPLICATIONS OF DYNAMICAL PRINCIPLES.

180. Practical Applications. In the present chapter we shall deal with a considerable number of illustrations of dynamical principles, drawn as far as possible from practical affairs, such as mechanical traction, workshop appliances, and various contrivances made use of in the industries or in daily life. By practical examples drawn from ordinary experience and from engineering and the arts generally, the relations of the different fundamental ideas, and indeed their precise significance, are made clear, and by a careful study of these the student can obtain a hold of the subject which no mere study of abstract formulae can provide.

We shall in this chapter use gravitational or practical units in many examples, and shall distinguish between a force equal to that of gravity on a pound or a ton—or briefly a force of one pound, or one ton—and the mass or weight of a pound or a ton by the use of an initial capital for Pound or Ton in the former case.

There can be no question that the use of the word *weight* in the Act of Parliament defining the standard pound, and the process of comparing masses by weighing, renders difficult and inconvenient the restriction of the word *weight* to forces. The combination foot-ton and the like are in no danger of being misapprehended.

181. Acceleration in the Direction of Motion. We take first the simple case in which the acceleration of a body along the path in which it moves is alone considered. And here we consider a body moving without rotation as that is explained in § 45 above, or only the motion of the

centroid of a body which does not fulfil that condition. Acceleration is rate of growth of velocity of a body. When the component in the line of motion is of uniform amount a, the speed which grows up in t units of time is at. If this is in addition to the speed u which the body had at the beginning of the interval of time, the speed at the end is v, where
$$v = u + at. \quad \ldots\ldots\ldots\ldots\ldots\ldots\ldots\ldots\ldots(1)$$

As has been already explained, speeds are measured in centimetres per second (cm/s), in feet per second (f/s), in miles per hour (m/h), or in knots (k). An acceleration of amount a may be a rate of growth of $a\,f/s$ per second (written $a\,f/s^2$, or of $a\,m/h$ per second (written $a\,m/hs$) or of a knots per hour ($a\,k/h$), or of a knots per minute ($a\,k/m$). It is to be clearly understood that acceleration is not velocity, but rate of growth of velocity, and has in every case its own direction which does not depend on the direction of motion, but on the action of other bodies which produces it. The speed in a given direction which grows up in time t depends on the average value for that time of the acceleration in that direction, and on the magnitude of the interval of time t. If that average value be a, or if the acceleration in the specified direction is uniform and of amount a, the speed in that direction, produced in the interval t, is at; and if we desire to specify the units, it will be written $at\,.\,f/s$, $at\,.\,m/h$, or $at\,.\,k$ as the case may be. This will be done when necessary: it is undesirable to encumber our equations by *always* inserting the units specification.

When the acceleration of a body in the direction of motion is uniform in amount, the average speed during time t is $\frac{1}{2}(u+v) = u + \frac{1}{2}at$, and the distance travelled in the time is given by
$$s = \tfrac{1}{2}(u+v)t = ut + \tfrac{1}{2}at^2. \quad \ldots\ldots\ldots\ldots\ldots(2)$$
If in this we substitute $(v-u)/a$ for t, we get
$$as = \tfrac{1}{2}v^2 - \tfrac{1}{2}u^2. \quad \ldots\ldots\ldots\ldots\ldots\ldots(3)$$

Of course u may denote an initial speed which is negative and a may at the same time denote a positive acceleration—as when an engine exerts a forward pull on a train moving backward; or the initial speed may be positive while a denotes a negative acceleration (a retardation)—as when a train approaching a station is being slowed down by the action of the brakes. The direction taken positive is a mere matter of convenience; the formulae hold in all cases, with proper interpretation of course when numerical values of the quantities symbolised are inserted.

182. Motion of a Railway Train. Time lost in Stoppages. If now F denote the force applied to the body and R the resistance to motion due to gravity, friction, etc., and these be constant, the whole work done by F in time t is Fs, and the part of this spent in increasing the kinetic energy is $(F-R)s$. But if W be the weight of the body in pounds or tons, $F-R = Wa$, and so

$$(F-R)s = Was = \tfrac{1}{2}Wv^2 - \tfrac{1}{2}Wu^2. \quad\ldots\ldots\ldots\ldots(1)$$

In the specification of units here employed, the unit of force is that which gives unit of acceleration to the unit of weight, a pound, or a gramme, or a ton, and so the unit of work or energy, may be expressed as lb. $(f/s)^2$ or ton $(f/s)^2$, as the case may be.

Let, however, the force of gravity on a weight of 1 lb. be taken, as it often is, as the unit of force, then, since this force gives to the 1 lb. weight let fall under gravity a downward acceleration of which the numerical reckoning is g, the values of F and R are the former values divided by g. Roughly, $g = 32 f/s^2$. The unit of work when F and g are reckoned in the units now specified is 1 ft. lb., the work done in overcoming a force equal to the gravity of 1 lb. through a space of 1 foot. We have then in *ft. lbs.*

$$(F-R)s = \frac{1}{2}\frac{W}{g}v^2 - \frac{1}{2}\frac{W}{g}u^2, \quad\ldots\ldots\ldots\ldots(2)$$

where it is to be clearly understood that W is the number of lbs. which the body weighs.

As an example of what precedes, we take the case of an express train fitted with continuous brakes, which is brought to rest before entering on a block, and started again after the block has been declared clear. If the speed of the train was 60 miles an hour, and the brakes, and other resistances, produced a retardation of 3 *m/hs*, if

§§ 181, 182, 183]   DYNAMICS OF RAILWAY TRAIN.   341

the train remained at rest 2 minutes, and was then started and regained its full speed under uniform acceleration in travelling 1 mile, it is required to find the running time lost. The student may construct the speed diagram for such a case. The ordinates of the curve are speeds, and the abscissae are times measured from a convenient zero. The distance travelled in any time is numerically equal to the area contained between the curve, the line of abscissae, and the terminal ordinates for the interval of time. The graph for a journey, including stoppages between which the maximum speed is attained, is a succession of curves rising from and falling again to the line of abscissae, with gaps between. The length of a gap along the line of abscissae is the duration of the stop. The distance lost in the running of the train is the area of the gap between the straight line of maximum speed, the line of abscissae, and the curve. If this latter area is measured in any way, the running time lost is got by division by the full uniform speed of the train.

The time required to bring the train to rest is 20 seconds, and the distance traversed in stopping is, since the average speed is 30 m/h, or 44 f/s, $880f$ or $1/6$ of a mile. The time taken to start is 120 seconds, and so the whole time from the instant of application of the brakes to that of regaining full speed is $(20+120+120)$sec. or 260 sec. In this time, at full speed, the train would have travelled $260 \times 88f = 4\frac{1}{3}m$. But $1\frac{1}{8}$ mile is actually traversed, so that the loss of distance is $3\frac{1}{6}$ miles. For this $3\frac{1}{6}$ minutes would be required, and this is the exact loss of running time.

The formulae established above have not been referred to in this simple computation, and the student is strongly recommended to avoid using formulae, and as far as possible to use his own common sense, which amounts indeed to constructing his formulae as he wants them.

183. Work done on Trains. Tractive Force. Positive work is not done *by* the resistances in stopping the train, work is done *against* these resistances by the train itself, and its kinetic energy is correspondingly diminished: this may be regarded as *negative* work done by the resistances.

Work is again done by the engine in starting the train up to its full speed, and the kinetic energy is regained, while, moreover, work is done in overcoming resistances with a resulting equivalent in potential energy if the train has been raised against gravity, in heat generated in overcoming friction, and a small amount in aerial and other vibrations in the noise of the train and the shaking of the ground—but this is also finally transformed intò heat.

The available tractive force which can be exerted by an engine is the forward force exerted by the rails against backward slipping of the wheels, and is proportional to the weight of the engine and the coefficient of friction or "adhesion" (§ 201) between the wheels and the rails. Let the engine in the example of § 182 weigh 80 tons, and the whole weight be available for adhesion (as in a tank engine with 5 pairs of wheels coupled), then in ordinary English weather the adhesion will enable a tractive force of 16 Tons to be developed. The resistance R on the level is only about $\frac{1}{2}$ per cent. of the weight of the train. If, however, as we here suppose, the train in this example weighs 200 tons, and is on a somewhat steep gradient up which it must be taken, the total resistance may be very considerable. We take it here as 9·8 Tons in all. Thus $F - R = 6\cdot2$, in Tons.

The work done by the engine, in bringing the train (including of course the engine itself) from rest to its full speed, amounts, at this value of F, to 16×5280, or 84480, foot-tons, and the kinetic energy of the train at full speed is this diminished in the ratio of 6·2 to 16, that is 32736 f.-t.

Let the time of regaining speed be t and that of coming to rest t'. The total resisting force during t' was $B + R$, if B denote the brake resistance, and the momentum destroyed was Wv. The same momentum was regained in the time t by the action of the force $F - R$. Hence, with gravitational units of force,

$$Wv = (B+R)gt' = (F-R)gt,$$

and therefore
$$t + t' = \left(\frac{W}{B+R} + \frac{W}{F-R}\right)\frac{v}{g} \quad \ldots\ldots\ldots\ldots\ldots\ldots(1)$$

Also
$$t + t' = \frac{B+F}{B+R}t = \frac{B+F}{F-R}t'. \quad \ldots\ldots\ldots\ldots\ldots(2)$$

§§ 183, 184]   EFFECT OF ROAD SURFACE.   343

The two forms of the last equation show that the total resistance, $B+R$, which is applied during the time t' of stopping, would if it acted during the time t of regaining speed, as well as the time of losing it, t', destroy as much momentum as a force $F+B$ would generate in the interval t, and, alternatively, that this latter force acting during the interval t' would generate just as much momentum as would the force $F-R$ (the actual momentum-generating force during t') in the whole time $t+t'$.

If s, s' be the distances travelled by the train in the times t, t', then, since the kinetic energy, $Wv^2/2g$, is annulled by the resistance $B+R$ in the distance s', and regained by the action of the force $F-R$, over the distance s, we have

$$\tfrac{1}{2}W\frac{v^2}{g}=(B+R)s'=(F-R)s, \qquad (3)$$

and so
$$s+s'=\left(\frac{W}{B+R}+\frac{W}{F-R}\right)\frac{v^2}{2g}. \qquad (4)$$

Also
$$s+s'=\frac{B+F}{B+R}s=\frac{B+F}{F-R}s'. \qquad (5)$$

The energy spent in overcoming brake resistance in the stop is Bs', and from the last result we get

$$Bs'=Fs-R(s+s'), \qquad (6)$$

which of course is self-evident.

184. Effect of Nature of Road Surface on Vehicular Traffic. These equations, and especially the last, show that diminution of R must be accompanied by increase of brake power if the time and distance of stopping are not to be increased. The resistance R, here taken as constant, depends to a certain extent on the air resistance to the motion of the train, as well as on the state of the road, and this part is smaller the lower the speed. The adhesion to which F is due is not altered in the case of a railway by improvements of the road; but the provision of a hard smooth surface on an ordinary road makes motor-cars skid, and prevents horses from obtaining that grip of their feet on the ground which is necessary for the development of any given forward force F. In this last case both F and

R are diminished, and s, the space traversed in bringing the speed up to any required value, becomes great, so that the general speed of traffic is diminished.

185. Efficiency of Brakes. Brakes *as such* are only effective if the wheels continue to revolve, as the energy of motion is consumed in overcoming the frictional resistance between the brake-shoe or band and the surface against which it is pressed. If the brake be applied too firmly the wheels will be locked and skid along the rails, and the braking action is then that of the friction between the rails and the sliding wheels. The occurrence of this state of things is rendered all the more likely by the diminution of the bite of the wheels, in consequence of a greasy state of the track; and a stream of sand should be poured on that surface, before the brakes are more than moderately applied.

If the coefficient of friction between the brake-shoe, supposed applied to the revolving surface of the wheel, be the same as that between the wheel and the rail, the thrust of the shoe against the surface must not be so great as the thrust of the wheel against the rail; otherwise the revolution of the wheel will be opposed by a moment of forces as great as or greater than that causing it to revolve, and skidding will begin. If the coefficient of friction between the wheel and the road be smaller than that between the wheel and the brake-shoe, the stoppage of revolution will occur for a smaller thrust of the brake-shoe than that of the wheel against the rail. Thus the limit of action of brakes applied to the wheels is that at which the wheel skids, and some form of emergency brake which will then check the motion of the carriage along the rail is necessary. Magnetic brakes actuated by an electric current have been proposed and used; but no emergency brake used on steep hills should depend on the rotation of the wheels for its action.

186. Time of Train from Station to Station. It is of importance to determine the time in which under given conditions of load, brake power, road resistance, weight of engine, etc., a given journey from one station to another can be performed. If the distance is not too great the speed will not rise above that which it is desirable on account of curves, or for other reasons, should not be exceeded. The solution of the problem is given by the equations written above (§ 183), in which the two intervals of time t, t' are now to be supposed to occur in the order here stated. The distance $s+s'$ ($=c$, say) is fixed, and so are all the other quantities, W, F, B, R, so that the highest speed attainable is given by the equation

$$v = \sqrt{\frac{2gc}{W}\frac{(B+R)(F-R)}{B+F}} \quad \ldots\ldots\ldots\ldots\ldots(1)$$

derived from (3) (§ 183). The time is therefore $2c/v$ or

$$t+t' = \sqrt{\frac{2cW}{g}\frac{B+F}{(B+R)(F-R)}}. \quad \ldots\ldots\ldots\ldots(2)$$

Ex. 1. A train weighing 200 tons has brake power which, as ordinarily used, stops it in $\frac{1}{3}$ of a mile from a speed of 60 miles an hour under additional resistance R. If $R = 9\cdot8$ Tons, show that $B = 4$ Tons nearly. If $F = 12$ Tons, show also that for $c = 2$ miles $t+t' = 264$ secs.

The highest speed attained according to this example is in feet per second $4 \times 5280/264$, or about 55 m/h. In actual working of a local heavy train between stations two or three miles apart, the slowing down would be effected more gradually, and so the brakes would be applied sooner, and the speed attained would be less, and the time of running somewhat lengthened.

Of course for runs of any length the speed must not rise above the limit required for safety, and must be reduced before passing curves of any sharpness. (See § 190 for some results based on the Salisbury accident of 1906.)

Ex. 2. Find the distance travelled (according to the data in last example) up to the instant of shutting off steam and applying the brakes, and the highest speed attained.

Ex. 3. Find the horse-power developed by the engine in accelerating the train, and the energy and horse-power absorbed by the brake in stopping it.

If the time $t+t'$ between two stations at a distance c is fixed, F must be determined so as to take a train of given weight W under resistance R and with brake power B, from one to the other in the allotted time. The student may verify from the equations given above that

$$F = \frac{R(B+R)g(t+t')^2 + 2cBW}{(B+R)g(t+t')^2 - 2cW}.$$

Ex. 4. With the former values of W, B, R, find the least value of F so that the train may be taken a distance of 4 miles in 6 minutes. [$F=12\cdot2$ Tons.]

Ex. 5. Find the least value of F for a train of 100 tons, resistance 0·5 p.c. of load on level, and brake power used that necessary to stop the train from 60 miles an hour in $\frac{1}{3}$ mile on the level, if the train is to be carried on the level 4 miles in 6 minutes. [$B=6\cdot375$ Tons.]

Ex. 6. An engine can pull a train weighing M tons at a speed V on the level, against resistances which vary as the square of the speed, the engine exerting a pull of P tons weight. Prove that the limiting speed of the train when running without steam down a plane inclined at an angle α to the horizon is $V\sqrt{M\sin\alpha/P}$. What is the maximum speed with which the engine can draw the train up the incline?

Ex. 7. An engine of M tons when working at H horse-power draws n carriages, each of weight M' tons, at the uniform speed of v miles per hour. Supposing the resistance on the engine and in each carriage to be proportional to the weight, show that the pull on the coupling connecting the engine to the first carriage is

$$\frac{75}{448}\frac{HnM'}{(M+nM')v}\text{ Tons.}$$

Ex. 8. On a certain branch railway there are between the termini of the branch five stations at nearly equal distances of 2 miles; find for engine and train, etc., as in Ex. 1 (except that the resistance is that on the level and only 0·5 p.c. of the load, and the engine gives a total force F of 3 Tons), and 3 minute stops at the intermediate stations, how long the journey on the branch would take.

The curve of speed plotted against time is, on the merely approximately true supposition of constant resistances, a succession of straight lines, so that the distance travelled between any two stops is $\frac{1}{2}v(t+t')$. If, however, the speed be plotted against distance, the curve consists of a periodic succession of parts in contact at their extremities: each part consists of two parabolic arcs which meet the line of abscissae at right angles, at the vertices in fact of the parabolas.

The distance run from the instant of starting to that of shutting off steam and applying the brakes is the fraction $(B+R)/(B+F)$ of the distance 2 miles, between stations, and the time occupied is the same fraction of the time, $t+t'$ seconds, from start to stop. [$t+t'=268\cdot3$; time of journey, 41·8 minutes.]

187. Dynamics of Self-Propelled Vehicle on Straight Road. If the wheel-base of a self-driven four-wheeled vehicle—for example a motor-car or motor-bus—have length b feet, and height of C.G. h feet, the bite of the driving wheels on the ground and the consequent forward force (of F Tons, say) exerted on the wheels and through them on the vehicle, alters the distribution of the weight between the front and hind wheels to the extent given by the equation

$$Fh = wb, \qquad (1)$$

where w is the weight in tons taken off the front wheels and added to the load on the hind wheels. If then the weights on the hind and front wheels be W_1, W_2 respectively, when the driving power is off and the vehicle is unbraked, and μ be the coefficient of adhesion (or friction), we have $F = \mu(W_1 + w)$, that is by the former equation

$$F = \frac{\mu b W_1}{b - \mu h}. \qquad (2)$$

For a constant force F given by this equation, the acceleration is $\mu b W_1 g / (b - \mu h)(W_1 + W_2)$ and the speed attained and distance travelled in time t from rest are given by

$$v = \frac{\mu b W_1}{(b - \mu h)(W_1 + W_2)} gt, \quad s = \frac{1}{2} \frac{\mu b W_1}{(b - \mu h)(W_1 + W_2)} gt^2. \quad (3)$$

Thus the time required to get up a given speed v and the distance travelled in that time are

$$t = \left(1 + \frac{W_2}{W_1}\right)\left(\frac{1}{\mu} - \frac{h}{b}\right)\frac{v}{g}, \quad s = \left(1 + \frac{W_2}{W_1}\right)\left(\frac{1}{\mu} - \frac{h}{b}\right)\frac{v^2}{2g}. \quad \ldots(4)$$

When the power is taken off and brakes are applied to the hind wheels to stop the car, the retarding force F, say, takes weight w off the hind wheels and throws it on the front wheels according to the same relation $Fh = wb$. But F is now given by the equation $F = \mu(W_1 - w)$, and so we have

$$F = \frac{\mu b W_1}{b + \mu h}. \qquad (5)$$

Thus, for the time and distance of stopping from speed v, we have

$$(t, s) = \left(1 + \frac{W_2}{W_1}\right)\left(\frac{1}{\mu} + \frac{h}{b}\right)\left(\frac{v}{g}, \frac{v^2}{2g}\right). \quad \ldots(6)$$

If the vehicle is only slowed down from speed v to speed u, the values of t and s are to be found for the slowing down and the speeding up again from the equations

$$(t, s) = \left(1 + \frac{W_2}{W_1}\right)\left(\frac{1}{\mu} + \frac{h}{b}\right)\left(\frac{v-u}{g}, \frac{v^2-u^2}{2g}\right),$$
$$(t, s) = \left(1 + \frac{W_2}{W_1}\right)\left(\frac{1}{\mu} - \frac{h}{b}\right)\left(\frac{v-u}{g}, \frac{v^2-u^2}{2g}\right) \quad \ldots\ldots\ldots(7)$$

respectively.

In a motor-car the height h is not very great, though it varies with the number of people in it; thus the change of load on the wheels is small. On a motor-bus, however, the height h is considerable, and varies a good deal according to the distribution of the passengers between the inside and on the top.

In the case of a horse-drawn vehicle of any kind, the value of W_1 for forward pull is the weight of the horses. For stopping the case is different according as the hind wheels, or the front wheels, or both, are braked, and as the horses exert or not a backward push. In the last case, of course, only the shaft-horses can be taken account of.

Ex. A motor-bus weighs 9 tons with passengers; 6 tons are on the hind wheels and 3 tons on the front wheels, without driving or retarding force applied. It is driven and braked from the hind wheels and is limited to a speed of 10 miles per hour. Taking the adhesion coefficient as $\frac{1}{5}$, and the height of the c.g. and the length of the wheelbase as 5 feet and 15 feet, find the time and distance for starting and stopping, and the time occupied in a journey of 300 yards between two stopping stations.

Here we have $v = 44/3$ (ft./sec.), and

$$\left(1 + \frac{W_2}{W_1}\right)\left(\frac{1}{\mu} - \frac{h}{b}\right) = 7, \quad \left(1 + \frac{W_2}{W_1}\right)\left(\frac{1}{\mu} + \frac{h}{b}\right) = 8.$$

Hence, for starting, $t = 3\frac{5}{24}$ (sec.), $s = 23\cdot5$ (ft.), and for stopping $t = 3\frac{19}{24}$ (sec.), $s = 26\cdot9$ (ft.).

Thus $6\frac{7}{8}$ seconds are occupied with starting and stopping and 50·4 feet are traversed in the time. There remain 849·6 feet to be travelled at 10 miles per hour, that is 44/3 feet per second, and for this 57·9 seconds are required, making in all 64·8 seconds as the time spent in travelling the 300 yards.

In this way, with an allowance for the duration of each stop, the time required for any specified journey can be found.

188. Dynamics of Vehicle on a Curve. A vehicle, such as a bicycle or a motor-car, moving round a curve on the level, or on a track inclined inward towards the centre of

VEHICLE ON CURVE.

the curve, affords an example of the relative equilibrium referred to in § 95. We take first a level track on which the vehicle, a motor-car say, of weight W, moves so that its centre of gravity describes a circle of radius r with speed v. The force toward the centre of the curve required to give the acceleration v^2/R towards that point is Wv^2/R. That is supplied by the action of the ground transverse to the vehicle brought into play by the continual change of direction of the motion. The force thus applied is equivalent to a force Wv^2/R towards the centre of the curve, applied at the C.G., and a couple of moment Wv^2d/R, where d is the height of the C.G., tending to capsize the car *outwards*. This capsizing couple is balanced by the action of the weight of the car and the vertical forces applied by the ground to the wheels on the two sides; for these vertical forces are, as we shall see presently, unequal.

If b be the breadth of the wheel-base, and P, Q the upward forces on the inner and outer pairs of wheels, we have, taking moments about the line of contacts of (1) the inner wheels, (2) the outer wheels,

$$Wv^2\frac{d}{R}+\frac{1}{2}Wbg=Qb, \quad -Wv^2\frac{d}{R}+\frac{1}{2}Wbg=Pb. \quad\ldots\ldots(1)$$

Hence the forces applied to the wheels are

$$P=W\frac{gbR-2v^2d}{2bR}, \quad Q=W\frac{gbR+2v^2d}{2bR}. \quad\ldots\ldots\ldots(2)$$

We see then that the inner wheels will just cease to bear on the ground, that is, the car will be in imminent danger of upsetting, when $2v^2d=gbR$; that is, when

$$v^2=\frac{1}{2}\frac{b}{d}gR. \quad\ldots\ldots\ldots\ldots\ldots\ldots\ldots\ldots\ldots\ldots(3)$$

Ex. Take the case of a motor-car for which d is 30 inches and b 5 feet, turning a corner of a street 30 feet wide on the level (that is in a curve of 15 feet radius). We get in feet per second

$$v=\sqrt{\frac{1}{2}\frac{60}{30}32\times 15}=21\cdot 9,$$

or slightly less than 15 miles per hour, as the limiting speed at which the wheels on the inner side just cease to press, and the car is on the point of upsetting.

The force Wv^2/R is, if the weight of the car W be taken as 2 tons, 143360 in lb. ft./sec² units, or the gravity of 4480 lbs., that is, as it happens in this case, just the force of gravity on the weight of the car. It is the force towards the centre of the curve applied by the ground to the tires, and therefore also the force applied by the tires to the ground—the force tending to produce skidding. If the ground is too slippery to allow this force to be produced, the car will skid.

189. Bicycle on Curve on Banked Track. We now consider the more general case of a vehicle on a track canted over towards the centre of the curve to obviate risk of upsetting. For a bicycle on such a track, the condition of greatest safety is adjustment of the speed so that the plane of the bicycle shall be normal to the slope of the track, and therefore no transverse force along the slope be applied to the tires. The reaction of the track on the machine is then upwards in the plane of the frame, and balances the resultant of the outward centrifugal force Wv^2/R, and the downward force of gravity Wg, which acts in the same plane. Then $\tan\alpha = v^2/gR$. If α be given, we can find v from $v^2 = gR/\tan\alpha$.

Ex. 1. If the radius of the curve be 120 feet, find the cant of the track for a racing speed of 40 miles per hour. [$\alpha = 48\frac{3}{5}°$.]

A bicycle is said to have run from a steeply canted track to a vertical bounding wall on the outside of the slope, described a curve on the wall and returned to the track without losing contact with the wall or the rider losing his balance. The path described on the wall was no doubt convex upward as well as outward.

Ex. 2. If R be the radius of the circle which the bicycle describes, and ϕ the limiting angle of friction [§ 201], show that equilibrium is possible with the bicycle frame inclined to the normal to the track if $gR\tan(\alpha+\phi) > v^2 > gR\tan(\alpha-\phi)$.

Ex. 3. Prove that it is possible for a cyclist to travel round the inside of a vertical cylinder, if the frame of the bicycle is inclined to the horizontal at the angle $\tan^{-1}(gR/v^2)$, provided v be so great that this angle does not exceed ϕ.

190. Locomotive on Curve with Super-elevated Rail. We shall now consider a locomotive on a curve the outer rail of which has an elevation h about the inner. This is called the *super-elevation*, and is arranged of course to suit the average speed of trains which pass the curve; and if the curve is at all sharp a maximum speed is prescribed which is not to be exceeded by drivers. In 1906 a terrible accident took place at Salisbury station on a curve of 528 feet radius, to a boat express which was rounding the curve at an excessive speed. The locomotive simply capsized outwards on its side; and twenty passengers of the train were killed and many injured. The theory which we give for a locomotive on rails is at once applicable to a motor-car or other vehicle, by substitution of $\tan \alpha$ (where α is the "cant" of the track) for the ratio h/b.

Taking P and Q (Fig. 82) as the upward forces exerted at right angles to the wheel-base on the two sets of side wheels by the inner and outer rails respectively, b as the breadth of the wheel-base (the "gauge" of the rails), d as the distance of the C.G. from the wheel-base, and using α for a moment in

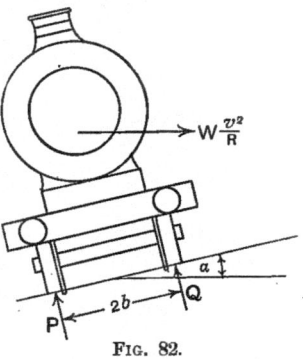

Fig. 82.

the sense of $\tan^{-1}(h/b)$, we get, by taking moments of the forces acting as shown in the figure, (1) about the outer rail, (2) about the inner rail, the equations

$$2bP = W\left\{g(b\cos\alpha + 2d\sin\alpha) - (2d\cos\alpha - h)\frac{V^2}{R}\right\}, \\ 2bQ = W\left\{g(b\cos\alpha - 2d\sin\alpha) + (2d\cos\alpha + h)\frac{V^2}{R}\right\}.$$ (1)

But $\cos\alpha = \sqrt{b^2 - h^2}/b$, $\sin\alpha = h/b$, and therefore these equations become

$$2bP = \frac{W}{bR}\{gR(b\sqrt{b^2-h^2} + 2hd) - (2d\sqrt{b^2-h^2} - hb)v^2\}, \\ 2bQ = \frac{W}{bR}\{gR(b\sqrt{b^2-h^2} - 2hd) + (2d\sqrt{b^2-h^2} + hb)v^2\}.$$ (2)

From these expressions the force on the rail (or on the ground) exerted by the wheels on either side can be found, and, by putting $P=0$, we can find the value of v for which the inner wheels just cease to press on the rail (or the ground). Of course when there is zero force on the inner rail, the state is one of extreme danger, and the speed should fall far short of that which throws all the weight on the outer rail. The speed of 30 miles an hour at the Salisbury curve gives, according to the example below, five parts of the weight on the outer rail and four parts on the inner, and is probably high enough. For transverse oscillations of the engine are inevitably set up, which produce alternate increase and diminution of the weight on either rail, and it is evident that, if the speed is so high as to approach the critical value, the equilibrium will be endangered by every oscillation. And if it happen that a considerable oscillation, set up by any cause, is so timed as to be assisted by some other disturbance, the equilibrium may be destroyed, and capsizing or derailment take place.

In the theory here given no account is taken of the effect of the parallelism of the axles of the driving and trailing wheels, which renders pure rolling of the wheels on both sides impossible when a curve is being traversed. The engine has no differential gearing like that provided in a motor-car; and, besides, in the case of a six-coupled locomotive the different wheels overlap the rails to different extents. All these things tend to the production of oscillations which might be a source of danger at speeds considerably below the critical speeds.

Ex. For the locomotive of the Salisbury accident b was 59 inches, and d had approximately the same value: the weight of the engine was 53·2 tons with water in the boiler-tubes and men on the foot-plate. The radius of the curve was 528 feet, and the super-elevation h was 3·5 inches. Verify the following table of weights on the rails at different speeds.

Speed.	Inner rail.	Outer rail.
30 m/h	23·9 tons	29·3 tons
40	19·3	33·9
50	13·4	39·8
60	6·3	47
67·3	0	53·2

§§ 190, 191]   RIFLE BULLET.   353

Ex. Verify the following table of super-elevation h which would just give zero weight on the inner rail for different speeds on the Salisbury curve:

Speed.	Super-elevation.	Speed.	Super-elevation.
15 m/h	-27 inches	60 m/h	-2 inches
30	-21	67·3	$+3\cdot5$ (Salisbury)
40	-17	70	5·2
50	$-9\cdot3$	80	14

191. Variation of Speed of Rifle Bullet in Air. The speed of a shot from a rifled gun is affected by the air. To determine the air resistance for different kinds of shot, and different speeds, an elaborate series of experiments was made by Mr. Bashforth in 1865-70, and again in 1878-79. Screens placed at equal intervals were pierced in succession, and the instants electrically recorded on an accurate chronograph which had the advantage of acting continuously.

Let s be the horizontal distance of any point in the trajectory from a chosen zero, then we assume, and the assumption is found by experience to be sufficiently accurate in many cases, that the time of flight from the zero point to the point at distance s is given by

$$t = t_0 + as + bs^2, \quad \ldots\ldots\ldots\ldots\ldots\ldots\ldots\ldots\ldots (1)$$

where t_0 is the time-interval from the time-zero to the instant of reaching the zero of s. Here t is taken as a function of s, and accordingly we adopt s as the independent variable in reckoning speed and acceleration as in § 19. We have

$$v = \frac{1}{\frac{dt}{ds}} = \frac{1}{a + 2bs}$$

and

$$\frac{dv}{dt} = -\frac{d^2 t}{ds^2} v^3 = -\frac{2b}{(a+2bs)^3}. \quad \ldots\ldots\ldots\ldots\ldots\ldots (2)$$

Thus we obtain the value $-dv/dt$ of the retardation as the product of two factors, one of which is v^3 and the other a constant, so that dv/dt varies as v^3. Once a and b have been determined with the needful accuracy, the speed and retardation at any point of the path can be found.

If we take three consecutive screens of a series, the $(m-1)$th, mth and $(m+1)$th of the series, at a distance l from the first to the second and from the second to the third, and note the times t_{m-1}, t_m, t_{m+1} of arrival of the projectile at these in succession, we have, taking the zero of s at the middle screen,

$$t_{m-1} = t_0 - al + bl^2, \quad t_m = t_0, \quad t_{m+1} = t_0 + al + bl^2,$$

so that $t_{m+1} - t_{m-1} = 2al, \quad t_{m+1} + t_{m-1} - 2t_m = 2bl^2, \quad \ldots\ldots\ldots\ldots (3)$

and therefore $a = \dfrac{t_{m+1} - t_{m-1}}{2l}, \quad b = \dfrac{t_{m+1} + t_{m-1} - 2t_m}{2l^2}.$

G.D.   Z

It will be seen that $1/a$, the speed at the middle screen, is exactly the mean speed for the passage from the first screen to the third of the set. The retarding force on the projectile if W is its weight is

$$R = 2W \frac{t_{m+1} + t_{m-1} - 2t_m}{l^2} \frac{v^3}{g}$$

in Pounds, if W is weighed in pounds, and the same unit of length is used for l, v and g, and the same unit of time is used for $t_{m+1}, \ldots, v$ and g.

That the speed at the middle point of any distance $2s$ traversed is the mean speed for that distance, (that is, has the value $2s/t_{2s}$ where t_{2s} is the time taken to traverse $2s$), if $dv/dt = -kv^3$, can easily be proved. We have $v\,dv/ds = -kv^3$, and therefore $(dv/ds)/v^2 = -k$; and if v_0 be the speed at the initial end of $2s$ and v_{2s} the speed at the other extremity, we get, by integration,

$$\frac{1}{v_{2s}} - \frac{1}{v_0} = 2ks. \qquad\qquad\qquad\qquad (4)$$

Similarly the speed at the middle point is given by

$$\frac{1}{v_s} - \frac{1}{v_0} = ks. \qquad\qquad\qquad\qquad (5)$$

Again we have $dv/dt = -kv^3$, and therefore $(dv/dt)/v^3 = -k$, and this gives, by integration,

$$\frac{1}{v_{2s}^2} - \frac{1}{v_0^2} = 2kt, \qquad\qquad\qquad\qquad (6)$$

if t be the interval of time occupied in traversing $2s$. Thus we obtain by (4), (6) and (5)

$$\frac{2s}{t} = \frac{\dfrac{1}{v_{2s}} - \dfrac{1}{v_0}}{\dfrac{1}{2}\left(\dfrac{1}{v_{2s}^2} - \dfrac{1}{v_0^2}\right)} = \frac{2v_0 v_{2s}}{v_0 + v_{2s}} = \frac{v_0}{1 + v_0 ks} = v_s.$$

As remarked in § 119, the results of Mr. Bashforth's experiments show that for speeds from $1100\,f/s$ to $2200\,f/s$, the resistance is very nearly proportional to v^3.

192. Effect of Small Periodic Variation of Uniform Speed: (1) Time-Periodic, (2) Space-Periodic. The effect of a simple harmonic variation of an otherwise uniform speed is of considerable practical importance. The motion of a boat is periodically disturbed by the action of the oars, the motion of a steamship by the variation of the action of the screw which occurs with every revolution of the engines. These variations are too complicatedly periodic

PERIODIC VARIATION OF SPEED.

to be completely represented by a single harmonic term, but such a term gives a first approximation to the effect. It is to be observed that they are *time-periodic*, that is the speed v is capable of being represented by the equation
$$v = v_0 + v_1 \sin nt, \quad\quad\quad\quad\quad\quad\quad (1)$$
where in general v_1 is small in comparison with v_0. The interval of time—the period—in which the variation goes through a cycle of changes is $2\pi/n$.

In this case the distance s travelled in the interval $2\pi/n$ is simply $v_0 2\pi/n$, that is the distance which the body would have travelled if there had been no periodic disturbance. For we have
$$s = \int_0^{2\pi/n} (v_0 + v_1 \sin nt) dt = \frac{2\pi}{n} v_0, \quad\quad\quad (2)$$
since the integral of the harmonic term vanishes. Thus v_0 is the mean speed of advance for any time containing a whole number of time-intervals each equal to $2\pi/n$. Just as much time is gained when $\sin nt$ is positive as is lost when $\sin nt$ is negative, and this is obvious without calculation.

This, however, is not the case when the variation of speed is *space-periodic*, as when a ship passes over a succession of waves of equal length, or better (since the wave motion varies with time as well as with distance), when a bicycle or motor-car traverses a series of regular up and down undulations of the road, so that the speed is given by the equation
$$v = v_0 + v_1 \sin mx, \quad\quad\quad\quad\quad (3)$$
where x is distance travelled forward from some chosen point in the path. The length of an undulation is $2\pi/m$. The distance travelled in a period is now given by
$$\int (v_0 + v_1 \sin mx) dt$$
taken over the interval of time occupied in traversing an undulation.

It is easy to see without calculation that the time gained when $\sin mx$ is positive is less than that lost when $\sin mx$ is negative. A boat is driven at speed v through water which is flowing at speed v'. The speed of the boat relative to the land is $v-v'$ against the stream and $v+v'$ with the stream. To travel a distance s with the stream takes time $s/(v+v')$, and if the boat then travels the same *distance* against the stream, the time taken is $s/(v-v')$. The time required for the distance $2s$, half travelled with the stream and half against the stream, is thus $s/(v+v')+s/(v-v')=2s/v(1-v'^2/v^2)$, which is greater than $2s/v$, the time required when v' is zero. When $v'=v$ the time is infinite, for in the second half of the journey the boat then makes no headway against the stream. If v' be small in comparison with v, this expression is approximately $(2s/v)(1+v'^2/v^2)$. We shall show that in the case of the periodic variation the factor $1+v'^2/v^2$ is replaced by

$$1+\tfrac{1}{2}v'^2/v^2.$$

The time required to traverse an undulation is t, given by the equation

$$t=\int_0^{2\pi/m}\frac{dx}{v}=\int_0^{2\pi/m}\frac{dx}{v_0+v_1\sin mx},\quad\ldots\ldots\ldots\ldots(3)$$

where $v_1 < v_0$. For the calculation of this integral, the transformation $u=\tan\tfrac{1}{2}mx$ may be employed (see Gibson's *Calculus*, § 117), but care must be taken in evaluating for the limits. It will be found that the integral has the value $2\pi/m\sqrt{v_0^2-v_1^2}$, or provided v_1/v_0 is small,

$$t=\frac{2\pi}{mv_0}\left(1+\frac{1}{2}\frac{v_1^2}{v_0^2}\right).\quad\ldots\ldots\ldots\ldots\ldots\ldots\ldots(4)$$

The time in the undisturbed motion is $2\pi/mv_0$, and the increase caused by the term $v_1\sin mx$ is thus $50v_1^2/v_0^2$ per cent.

193. Small Periodic Variations of Speed of Ship. Effect of Relative Motion of Parts of Ship. It will be seen that it conduces to uniformity of speed in the first case, that of *time-periodic* variation of speed, to have everything in the boat or ship made quite fast, so that the periodic variation of the driving force which gives rise to the term $v_1\sin nt$ may have as little effect as possible. For if any part of the boat or cargo be loose and move relatively to the boat, its inertia is in whole or in part withdrawn from the reaction against acceleration or retardation, and the change is greater in consequence, that is, the amplitude v_1 of the harmonic term is increased.*

Moreover, though the time-periodic change does not affect the average speed it makes the boat, as we shall see, more difficult to drive, so that for the same mean speed the rowers or the engines must work at a greater rate. The swing of the oars forward and backward which produces a corresponding backward and forward swing of the boat is more or less nearly counteracted by the swinging of the bodies of the rowers.

On the other hand, in the case of space-periodic variations of speed, due to waves or undulations in the path pursued, *the value of v_1 is fixed*, and consequently the smaller the mass which takes up the periodic change completely, the more nearly does the momentum as a whole remain uniform. Thus everything should in such a case be as loose as possible, even to the masts.†

194. Activity with periodically Varying Speed. The rate of working, or activity, of the propulsive force is easily calculated in each of these cases. We shall suppose, what is approximately true for a ship, that the resistance R to motion is proportional to the square of the speed, that is, that $R = \mu W v^2$, where W is the weight of the vessel and μ a coefficient. If, then, F be the propulsive force applied at any instant, we have

$$W\dot{v} = F - R$$
or
$$F = W(\dot{v} + \mu v^2). \quad \ldots\ldots\ldots\ldots\ldots\ldots\ldots(1)$$

---

*Sir George Greenhill (*Notes on Dynamics*) quotes Joseph Pitts' *Account of Mohammetans* (1704) regarding the pirates of Algiers whose galleys then infested that part of the Mediterranean, ". . . so careful are they that nothing may hinder their speed, that they will scarce suffer any Person in the Ship to stir, but all must sit stock-still, unless Necessity otherwise require. And all things that are capable of any motion must be fasten'd or unhang'd (even the smallest weight), lest the Pursuit should be something retarded thereby."

† "Pipe the hammocks down and each man place shot in them, slack the stays, knock up the wedges and give the masts play."—Sir Edward Berry's orders on board the "Foudroyant" when in chase of the "Le Généreux," Feb. 18, 1800 (Mahon's *Life of Nelson*, ii. p. 25).

The rate of working is thus Fv or $\mu W v^3 + W v \dot{v}$.

To find the average activity, we integrate this over one complete period of a variation and divide by the time occupied. For the time-periodic variation, we have

$$Fv = \mu W(v_0 + v_1 \sin nt)^3 + W(v_0 + v_1 \sin nt) n v_1 \cos nt. \quad \ldots(2)$$

When this is expanded, we get

$$Fv = \mu W v_0^3 + 3\mu W v_0 v_1^2 \sin^2 nt + \ldots \quad \ldots\ldots\ldots\ldots(3)$$

The terms which are not written down on the right are all such as, when integrated over the time $2\pi/n$, give a zero result. Thus

$$\int_0^{2\pi/n} Fv \, dt = \mu W v_0^3 \frac{2\pi}{n} + \frac{3}{2} \mu W v_0 v_1^2 \frac{2\pi}{n}. \quad \ldots\ldots\ldots(4)$$

Dividing this by $2\pi/n$, we get for the mean value A_m of the activity the equation

$$A_m = \mu W v_0^3 \left(1 + \frac{3}{2} \frac{v_1^2}{v_0^2}\right). \quad \ldots\ldots\ldots\ldots\ldots\ldots(5)$$

The first factor is the activity for uniform speed v_0; and it appears, therefore, that the periodic variation brings about an increase of activity amounting to $150 v_1^2/v_0^2$ per cent. of the uniform activity.

The propulsive force F is given by

$$F = \mu W v^2 + W \dot{v} = \mu W(v_0^2 + 2v_0 v_1 \sin nt + v_1^2 \sin^2 nt)$$
$$+ W v_1 n \cos nt. \quad \ldots\ldots(6)$$

Neglecting the term in v_1^2 and writing

$$F = F_0\{1 + k\sin(nt + \epsilon)\},$$

we obtain

$$F_0 = \mu W v_0^2, \quad F_0 k \cos \epsilon = 2\mu W v_0 v_1, \quad F_0 k \sin \epsilon = W v_1 n, \ldots(7)$$

so that $k \cos \epsilon = 2\dfrac{v_1}{v_0}$, $\quad k \sin \epsilon = \dfrac{W v_1 n}{F_0}$, $\quad \tan \epsilon = \dfrac{W v_0 n}{2 F_0}$. $\ldots\ldots(8)$

In the other case considered, that of space-periodic variation of speed, we shall calculate the work done in traversing the distance $2\pi/m$—the length of an undulation

§§ 194, 195] PASSAGE OF CARRIAGE OVER OBSTACLE. 359

—and then, dividing by the time $2\pi(1+v_1^2/v_0^2)/mv_0$, which we have seen is occupied in traversing that distance, we shall obtain the mean activity. Thus

$$\int_0^{2\pi/m} F\,dx = \int_0^{2\pi/m} (\mu W v^2 + W\dot{v})\,dx. \quad\ldots\ldots\ldots\ldots(9)$$

But $\qquad v^2 = v_0^2 + 2v_0 v_1 \sin mx + v_1^2 \sin^2 mx,$

and $\qquad \dot{v} = v_1 m \cos mx \cdot \dot{x} = m v_1 \cos mx (v_0 + v_1 \sin mx).$

Inserting these values in the integral to be found, we note that no term makes any contribution to the integral except the group of two $\mu W(v_0^2 + v_1^2 \sin^2 mx)$. Thus we get

$$\int_0^{2\pi/m} F\,dx = \mu W v_0^2 \frac{2\pi}{m}\left(1 + \frac{1}{2}\frac{v_1^2}{v_0^2}\right). \quad\ldots\ldots\ldots\ldots(10)$$

Dividing this by the time $2\pi(1+\frac{1}{2}v_1^2/v_0^2)/mv_0$, we get simply $\mu W v_0^3$ for the mean activity, that is, the mean activity is not affected by the space-rate of variation of v. Nevertheless, as the time of traversing any given distance across such undulations is, if the distance is great in comparison with $2\pi/m$, increased by $50v_1^2/v_0^2$ per cent., the energy expended is increased in the same proportion; so that besides the delay there results an increased cost of propulsion.

Denoting in this case the force F by $F_0\{1 + k\sin(nt + \epsilon)\}$, we have, neglecting as before terms in v_1^2,

$$F_0 = \mu W v_0^2, \quad F_0 k \cos \epsilon = 2\mu W v_0 v_1, \quad F_0 k \sin \epsilon = m W v_0 v_1, \ldots(11)$$

so that

$$k \cos \epsilon = 2\frac{v_1}{v_0}, \quad k \sin \epsilon = \frac{m W v_0 v_1}{F_0}, \quad \tan \epsilon = \frac{m W v_0^2}{2 F_0}. \ldots(12)$$

195. Work done in the Passage of a Carriage over an Obstacle. Extra Work on a Causeway. Effect of Springs. We now consider the passage of the wheel of a carriage over an obstacle in its track. We suppose that the radius of the wheel is r, and the height of the obstacle h, and that the centre of the wheel, before impact occurs, is moving with speed v horizontally. If W be the weight of the wheel and the part of the carriage and its load which rests upon it, the kinetic energy of the wheel and its load is $\frac{1}{2}Wv^2$ in absolute units. When impact with the obstacle occurs the direction of motion is changed, for the wheel at that instant begins to turn about the point of contact B with the obstacle (see Fig. 83); but the radius to this point is inclined, at an angle $\alpha = \cos^{-1}(1 - h/r)$, to the radius which at the same instant has its outer extremity in contact with the horizontal plane along which the wheel was rolling. Just before impact the momentum associated with the wheel was Wv in the horizontal direction; just after the impact with the obstacle the momentum is in the direction CD and is of amount $Wv\cos\alpha$. For the impulse applied to the wheel cannot alter the angular momentum about the point of contact B, and this just before impact was proportional to $Wv\cos\alpha$. The centre of the wheel now gradually ascends through a height h, and the speed changes from $v\cos\alpha$ to u, say. Let now the average forward force in the direction of motion, on the wheel and its associated load, be F, and the resistance be R. During the ascent the centre of the wheel travels a distance $r\alpha$, and the forward displacement of each part of the load will also be $r\alpha$, if, as the wheel mounts the obstacle, the load is displaced so that its centroid remains vertically above the axle. We suppose this to be the case, and that the forward speed u when the obstacle has just been surmounted is v. This involves the supposition that the energy of rotation of the wheel is not altered. Then the principle of energy gives

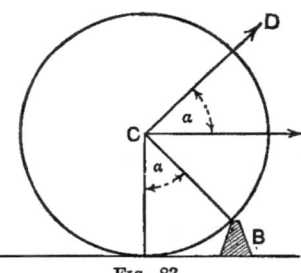

Fig. 83.

$$(F - R)r\alpha = Wgh + \tfrac{1}{2}Wv^2\sin^2\alpha \quad \ldots\ldots\ldots\ldots\ldots(1)$$

On the left we have the work done by external forces in making the wheel surmount the obstacle, and on the right that work is seen to be made up of two parts, Wgh the gain of potential energy and the part $\frac{1}{2}Wv^2\sin^2\alpha$ due to the sudden change of direction of motion—the *jerk*. But

$$\sin^2 \alpha = 2h/r - h^2/r^2,$$

and so $\qquad (F-R)r\alpha = Wgh + Wv^2\left(\dfrac{h}{r} - \dfrac{h^2}{2r^2}\right). \quad\ldots\ldots\ldots\ldots(2)$

In general the second term on the right is the more important. For example, if a wheel 4 feet in diameter carrying a load of 10 cwt. pass over a pebble an inch high, at a speed of 10 miles an hour ($44/3\,f/s$), we get, taking 1 cwt. as the unit of mass, $Wgh = 10 \times 32 \times \tfrac{1}{12} = 26\tfrac{2}{3}$ (or in foot-pounds, $93\tfrac{1}{3}$) and $Wv^2h/r = 10 \times 44^2/12 \times 2 \times 9 = 90$, nearly (or in foot-pounds, 313).

Let now the wheel descend again to its former level. The force F in the direction of motion has not the same value as before: we suppose it to be such that the speed of the centre of the wheel, when contact with the horizontal plane has been resumed, is still the same. By the same process as before, we get

$$(F-r)r\alpha = -Wgh + Wv^2\left(\dfrac{h}{r} - \dfrac{h^2}{2r^2}\right). \quad\ldots\ldots\ldots\ldots(3)$$

Hence, since h is small in comparison with r, the work done in passing over the obstacle is $2Wv^2h/r$. It is directly as the height of the obstacle and inversely as the radius of the wheel. A high wheel is therefore better adapted for the easy running of a springless vehicle on a rough road. Thus two-wheeled vehicles in which the whole weight is borne by one axle are made, whether springs are used or not, with higher wheels than four-wheeled vehicles, where of course the load raised by the passing of a wheel over an obstacle is only one fourth of the whole.

The work spent in overcoming obstacles is diminished by the use of springs, which prevent to a great extent sudden change of direction of motion of any part of the load on the wheels, and so diminish the expenditure of work from that cause. It will now be seen how it is that the work spent in propelling a vehicle over a causeway exceeds that necessary for the same speed on a smooth road, and how this is diminished by the use of springs for the support of the body of the vehicle on the axle, or by the use of pneumatic tires on the wheels.

196. Condition that a Vehicle on Wheels may surmount an Obstacle. If the carriage is not acted on by any external forces, it will be stopped by the obstacle of height h unless a certain condition is fulfilled. Let us suppose that the two wheels of a cart or gig encounter an obstacle of height h at the same instant, a plank, for example, laid across the road, and that no tractive force is at the moment being exerted. Let r be the radius of each wheel and k its radius of gyration about its axis. The angular momentum of the two wheels about the summit of the obstacle is at the instant of impact

$$2Wv(r-h) + 2Wk^2v/r.$$

Hence, if ω be the angular speed of turning of the wheels about their points of contact with the obstacle, we have

$$2W(r^2 + k^2)\omega = 2Wv(r-h) + 2Wk^2v/r,$$

and therefore $\omega = v\{r(r-h) + k^2\}/r(r^2 + k^2)$, so that the kinetic energy of the wheels just after the impact is

$$Wv^2\{r(r-h) + k^2\}^2/r^2(r^2 + k^2).$$

Further, if there is load W' on the axle which has the same displacement, its kinetic energy just after impact is $\frac{1}{2}W'v^2(r-h)^2/r^2$. The obstacle will be surmounted if the sum of these kinetic energies is at least equal to the potential energy $(W + W')gh$ given to the whole mass by the elevation h. We must have therefore

$$v^2\left\{ W\frac{\{r(r-h)+k^2\}^2}{r^2(r^2+k^2)} + W'\frac{(r-h)^2}{r^2} \right\} > 2(W+W')gh. \quad\ldots(1)$$

This is in agreement with (2), §195. The wheel, without load, will surmount the obstacle if

$$\frac{v^2}{2g} > \frac{r^2(r^2+k^2)h}{(r(r-h)+k^2)^2} \quad\ldots\ldots\ldots\ldots\ldots\ldots(2)$$

197. Proper Height of Buffers, or of a Line of Draught. Rotary Inertia. Another problem regarding vehicles is that of the proper height of the buffers of a railway carriage or

§§ 195, 196, 197] PROPER HEIGHT OF BUFFERS. 363

of the line of forward pull exerted on such a carriage, or of the draught on a cart or waggon. For this it is necessary to take account of the rotary inertia of the wheels.

Consider a carriage the body of which with load weighs W tons, and the wheels of which, n in number, each weigh w tons, and have radius of gyration k and radius r. We shall prove that the effective inertia of the carriage is $W + nw(1 + k^2/r^2)$. Let P be the forward resultant force applied to the carriage, and f the backward force exerted at the rails on a wheel in consequence of friction. We introduce at the axle of each wheel a forward and a backward force each equal to f, so that there acts on the wheel a couple of moment fr, and a backward force f on the axle. Thus if $\dot{\omega}$ be the angular acceleration of the wheel, we have $wk^2\dot{\omega} = fr$. But if the wheel rolls forward on the rail without slipping, $\dot{\omega} = \dot{v}/r$, and so we get
$$wk^2\dot{v} = fr^2.$$

Now for the linear acceleration $\dot{v}$, we have, applying the resultant force $P - nf$ at the centroid of the whole system of body of carriage and wheels, $P - nf = (W + nw)\dot{v}$, that is,
$$P = \left(W + nw\frac{k^2 + r^2}{r^2}\right)\dot{v}. \quad\quad\ldots\ldots\ldots\ldots\ldots(1)$$

The quantity in brackets is the effective inertia of the whole carriage, including the wheels, and thus has the value stated above. The resultant force required to give the *body of the carriage and load only* the acceleration $\dot{v}$ is therefore
$$W\dot{v} \text{ or } PW/\{W + nw(k^2 + r^2)/r^2\}.$$

Let us now suppose that P is applied to the carriage, so that this resultant has its line of action through the centroid of the *body and load* of the carriage at height h, say, above the level of the axles. Let h' be the height of the line of action of P above that level; then taking moments about a transverse horizontal axis at that level, we get $Ph' = PhW/\{W + nw(k^2 + r^2)/r^2\}$ or
$$h' = \frac{Wh}{W + nw\dfrac{k^2 + r^2}{r^2}}. \quad\quad\ldots\ldots\ldots\ldots\ldots(2)$$

This is the proper height of the buffers or the coupling above the level of the axles. The carriage will, if this adjustment is made, be free from oscillations about a transverse horizontal axis when started or stopped suddenly, and be more unlikely to leave the rails. Caution should be observed with waggons loaded so that the centroid of the carriage itself and the load is abnormally high, to avoid the setting up of such oscillations by collisions between buffers or sudden tugs on the couplings. When a locomotive is started the pull on its couplings, and the tangential pull of the rails on the wheels applied at their points of contact, give a couple which throws the weight of the engine and boiler to a greater extent on the hindwheels than before, until the moment of the couple is counteracted (see § 187).

Another way of regarding this matter is to consider the carriage as consisting of mass W, the centroid of which is at the height h above the axles, together with mass $nw(k^2+r^2)/r^2$ with centroid on the level of the axles. The centroid of this system is at height h' above the axles, and the force P is applied at this level.

The force $PW/\{W+nw(r^2+k^2)/r^2\}$ applied at height h above the axles gives acceleration $\dot{v}$ to W, the force

$$P\{nw(k^2+r^2)/r^2\}/\{W+nw(r^2+k^2)/r^2\},$$

applied at the height of the axles, supplies

$$P(nwk^2/r^2)/\{W+nw(r^2+k^2)/r^2\}$$

to give the same acceleration to the mass nw of the wheels, and
$$Pnw/\{W+nw(r^2+k^2)/r^2\}$$
to annul the backward force of amount $nf=nwk^2\dot{v}/r^2$ applied at the axles, according to the specification of the couples which produce the rotational acceleration of the wheels.

198. Effective Inertia of Wheeled Vehicle or of Train of Wheelwork. The effective inertia of any connected system, for example a locomotive, including its wheels and the parts moving with them, a bicycle, or a train of wheelwork which has a motion of translation, may be found in the

§§ 197, 198]   EFFECTIVE INERTIA OF WHEELS.   365

following manner. Let the system consist of different parts of weights $w_1, w_2, \ldots$, let W be the total weight, and v be the speed of the centroid of the whole system. The total kinetic energy is that of the whole system moving with the speed of the centroid together with the sum of the kinetic energies of the motions of the parts relative to the centroid. Thus, if the relative speeds of the parts referred to be $v_1, v_2, \ldots$ in any direction, we have

$$\text{K.E.} = \tfrac{1}{2}(Wv^2 + w_1 v_1^2 + w_2 v_2^2 + \ldots).$$

We may write this

$$\text{K.E.} = \tfrac{1}{2}v^2\left(W + w_1\frac{v_1^2}{v^2} + w_2\frac{v_2^2}{v^2} + \ldots\right), \quad \ldots\ldots\ldots\ldots(1)$$

and

$$W + w_1\frac{v_1^2}{v^2} + w_2\frac{v_2^2}{v^2} + \ldots$$

is the effective inertia of a body moving with only translational speed v, which would have the same kinetic energy.

If some of the parts, or a group of parts forming a wheel, or a set of equal wheels, say, have rotation, $\tfrac{1}{2}\Sigma(w_k v_k^2)$ becomes $\tfrac{1}{2}(\Sigma w_k)k^2\omega^2$, where Σw_k is the weight of the group, k is the radius of gyration and ω the angular speed of rotation, about the axle of a wheel. Then if the speed of the rim of the wheel about the centre be v, and the diameter of the wheel be d, we have $\omega^2 = 4v^2/d^2$, and therefore

$$\tfrac{1}{2}(\Sigma w_k)k^2\omega^2 = \tfrac{1}{2}(\Sigma w_k)4k^2v^2/d^2.$$

If the speed of the rim be not v, but nv, we get

$$\tfrac{1}{2}(\Sigma w_k)k^2\omega^2 = \tfrac{1}{2}(\Sigma w_k)4k^2n^2v^2/d^2,$$

and n is the speed-ratio.

Take for example a bicycle with two equal wheels, a crank axle with attached sprocket wheel, and a chain running at a speed depending on the gear of the machine. We have here $\tfrac{1}{2}Wv^2$ for the forward motion of the machine and rider as a whole; $\tfrac{1}{2}W_1 k_1^2 \omega_1^2$, where ω_1 is the angular speed and k_1 the radius of gyration of either wheel, and W_1 is the weight of the pair, for the kinetic energy of the two wheels; $\tfrac{1}{2}W_2 k_2^2 \omega_2^2$ for the kinetic energy of the crank-axle, cranks and sprocket; $\tfrac{1}{2}W_3 v_3^2$, where W_3 is the weight and v_3 the speed of the chain, and, in strictness, a fourth term, for the motion of the legs of the rider.

If d_1 be the diameter of the wheels, measured by the same unit as k_1, say in inches, and the crank-axle be geared up to a diameter d_2, that is so that $\omega_2 = v/d_2$, and if d_3 be the diameter of the toothed wheel by which the chain drives the hind wheel of the bicycle, we have

$$\text{K.E.} = \frac{1}{2}\left(W + W_1\frac{4k_1^2}{d_1^2} + W_2\frac{4k_2^2}{d_2^2} + W_3\frac{d_3^2}{d_1^2}\right)v^2, \quad \ldots\ldots\ldots(2)$$

and so the expression within the brackets is the effective inertia. It is this that the net force of traction, the force applied to the driving wheel by the ground *minus* resistance, has to overcome in giving acceleration to the system.

Similarly if a train of wheelwork receive angular acceleration $\dot{\omega}$ by the action of a couple of moment L applied at a main axle, and $\dot{\omega}_1, \dot{\omega}_2, \ldots$ be the resulting angular accelerations of the wheels in the train geared in succession, we have

$$L = wk^2\dot{\omega} + w_1 k_1^2 \dot{\omega}_1 + \omega_2 k_2^2 \dot{\omega}_2 + \ldots$$
$$= (wk^2 + w_1 k_1^2 n_1^2 + \omega_2 k_2^2 n_2^2 + \ldots)\dot{\omega}, \quad \ldots\ldots\ldots\ldots(3)$$

where $w, w_1, w_2, \ldots$ are the weights on the main and successive axles, $k, k_1, k_2, \ldots$ the radii of gyration, and $n_1, n_2, \ldots$ the speed-ratios of the successive wheels to the first. The effective moment of inertia I of the train is thus given by

$$I = wk^2 + w_1 k_1^2 n_1^2 + \omega_2 k_2^2 n_2^2 + \ldots, \quad \ldots\ldots\ldots\ldots\ldots(4)$$

that is the moment of inertia of a single wheel and axle in which L would generate the angular acceleration $\dot{\omega}$ has this value.

199. Motion of a Wheeled Vehicle on an Inclined Plane. The motion of a vehicle on an inclined plane—for example of a railway carriage on a gradient—may be determined from (1), § 197, which enables account to be taken of the inertia of the wheels. The gradient is measured by the rise h of the track in a distance l travelled along it. When h and l are measured in the same units, the inclination α

VEHICLE ON INCLINED PLANE.

of the track to the horizontal is given by $\sin\alpha = h/l$. Thus, for a gradient of 1 in 20, we have $\sin\alpha = 1/20$.

The value of P in (1), §197, is then $(W+nw)g\sin\alpha - R$, where $Wg+nwg$ is the force of gravity in absolute units on the whole weight, and R is the resistance to motion, apart from the backward pull applied to the carriage at the contacts of the wheels with the rails, which has been taken account of in forming the equation referred to. Thus, if the only applied force be that due to gravity,

$$\left(W+nw\frac{k^2+r^2}{r^2}\right)\dot{v} = (W+nw)g\sin\alpha - R \quad \ldots\ldots(1)$$

or $$\left(W+nw\frac{k^2+r^2}{r^2}\right)\ddot{\theta} = \frac{1}{r}\{(W+nw)g\sin\alpha - R\}, \ldots(2)$$

where $\ddot{\theta}$ is the rate of increase of $\dot{\theta}$, the angular speed of turning of the wheels, supposed to be rolling without slipping. If these equations be multiplied by v ($=ds/dt$, where s is distance measured along the slope in the direction of motion) and $\dot{\theta}$ respectively, and R be supposed constant, they become directly integrable, and we obtain

$$\left.\begin{array}{l}\dfrac{1}{2}\left(W+nw\dfrac{k^2+r^2}{r^2}\right)v^2 = \{(W+nw)g\sin\alpha - R\}s + C, \\ \dfrac{1}{2}\left(W+nw\dfrac{k^2+r^2}{r^2}\right)\dot{\theta}^2 = \dfrac{1}{r}\{(W+nw)g\sin\alpha - R\}\theta + \dfrac{C}{r^2},\end{array}\right\} \quad (3)$$

where C is a constant. If v, s, $\dot{\theta}$, θ be v_0, s_0, $\dot{\theta}_0$, θ_0 initially, we have

$$\left.\begin{array}{l}\dfrac{1}{2}\left(W+nw\dfrac{k^2+r^2}{r^2}\right)(v^2 - v_0^2) \\ \qquad = \{(W+nw)g\sin\alpha - R\}(s-s_0), \\ \dfrac{1}{2}\{Wr^2 + nw(k^2+r^2)(\dot{\theta}^2 - \dot{\theta}_0^2)\} \\ \qquad = \{(W+nw)g\sin\alpha - R\}r(\theta - \theta_0).\end{array}\right\} \quad (4)$$

The first of these equations may be written also in the form

$$\left.\begin{array}{l}\tfrac{1}{2}(W+nw)(v^2 - v_0^2) + \tfrac{1}{2}nwk^2(\dot{\theta}^2 - \dot{\theta}_0^2) \\ \qquad = \{(W+nw)g\sin\alpha - R\}(s-s_0).\end{array}\right\} \quad (5)$$

These are equations of energy; on the left-hand side is the kinetic energy gained in descending the distance $s - s_0$ along the incline from initial speed v_0; on the right is the loss of potential energy and the work done against the resistance R. In the last form of the equation the kinetic energy is separated into two parts—the translational kinetic energy of the whole moving system and the energy of rotation of the wheels about their axes.

200. Rolling of a Solid of Revolution on an Inclined Plane under Gravity. For the motion of a solid of revolution or "wheel" rolling down the incline under gravity, without resistance, we have

$$\tfrac{1}{2}wv^2 + \tfrac{1}{2}wk^2\dot\theta^2 = wgs \sin\alpha, \ldots\ldots\ldots\ldots\ldots(1)$$

if the motion has started from rest. Since there is supposed to be no slipping we have here $\dot\theta = v/r$. Thus the speed v acquired from rest is less than that which would be acquired by the body in sliding frictionlessly down a distance s along a slope of the same inclination, in the ratio of r to $\sqrt{r^2 + k^2}$. From (1), we obtain also

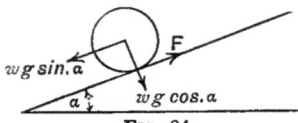

Fig. 84.

$$\tfrac{1}{2}w\left(1 + \frac{k^2}{r^2}\right)(v^2 - v_0^2) = wg(s - s_0)\sin\alpha, \ldots\ldots\ldots(2)$$

where $s - s_0$ is the distance traversed by the centroid while the speed increases from v_0 to v.

These results may of course be obtained directly. At the centroid a force $wg \sin\alpha$ acts down the plane, and at the point of contact a force F acts up the plane. Hence for the motion of the centroid, we have

$$w\dot v = wg \sin\alpha - F. \ldots\ldots\ldots\ldots\ldots\ldots\ldots\ldots(3)$$

Again for turning about the centroid, we get

$$wk^2\ddot\theta = Fr; \ldots\ldots\ldots\ldots\ldots\ldots\ldots\ldots(4)$$

or if there be pure rolling, since then $\ddot\theta = \dot v/r$

$$wk^2\dot v = Fr^2. \ldots\ldots\ldots\ldots\ldots\ldots\ldots\ldots\ldots(5)$$

With the value of F given by (4) inserted (3) becomes
$$w\left(1+\frac{k^2}{r^2}\right)\dot{v}=wg\sin\alpha \quad\ldots\ldots\ldots\ldots\ldots\ldots(6)$$
from which multiplying by v and integrating we derive
$$\tfrac{1}{2}w\left(1+\frac{k^2}{r^2}\right)(v^2-v_0^2)=wg(s-s_0)\sin\alpha$$
which is (2). Also (3) and (6) give F.

By (6) the value of $\dot{v}$ is uniform, and so the time of motion can be obtained as in uniformly accelerated motion.

The "wheel" may be any solid of revolution with matter symmetrically distributed about its centre. For example, it may be a uniform sphere of radius r, in which case $k^2=\tfrac{2}{5}r^2$, and we have
$$\tfrac{1}{2}w\tfrac{7}{5}v^2=\tfrac{7}{10}wv^2=wgs\sin\alpha. \quad\ldots\ldots\ldots\ldots\ldots(7)$$
The effective inertia of the sphere is thus increased by rolling in the ratio of 7/5. For a thin hoop the equation is, since $k^2=r^2$,
$$\tfrac{1}{2}w\,2v^2=wv^2=wgs\sin\alpha, \quad\ldots\ldots\ldots\ldots\ldots(8)$$
so that the effective inertia is $2w$.

If the wheel is a uniform disk, $\tfrac{2}{3}(k^2+r^2)/r^2=1$, so that the effective inertia is increased in the ratio of 3/2. This is an approximate estimate for the wheels of railway carriages.

Ex. 1. Two spheres have the same external diameter and the same weight. One is a gilded sphere of brass and the other a hollow shell of gold. Compare the speeds acquired in the same time from rest by the two spheres in rolling down an inclined plane through the same distance. Thus one sphere may be distinguished from the other.

Ex. 2. A rough homogeneous sphere of radius r is placed within a hollow cylindrical garden roller of radius R and comes to rest at the lowest point. The roller is suddenly set rolling on a level track so that its centroid moves with speed V. Show that the sphere will roll completely round the interior of the roller if $V^2>\tfrac{27}{7}g(R-r)$.

[If the line from the centre of the sphere to the point of contact with the roller make an angle θ with the vertical at time t, the angular speed of the sphere is $(R-r)\dot\theta/r - V/r$. Hence find the equations of motion].

201. Sliding Motion of a Body along an Inclined Plane with Friction. The approximate laws of friction between dry solids are no doubt known to the student, but they may be here recapitulated.

(1) Friction acts always tangentially to the surface of contact of two bodies in the direction to annul or prevent relative motion. Thus a body resting on an inclined plane is prevented from sliding down if the inclination is less than a certain limiting value. Just sufficient resisting force is developed to prevent motion, and this force, which must equal $wg \sin \alpha$, if w be the weight of the body and α the inclination of the plane to the horizontal, increases until $wg \sin \alpha = \mu wg \cos \alpha$, where μ is a coefficient depending on the nature of the surfaces in contact. Thus $\mu = \tan \alpha$, and α is called the limiting angle of friction.

When pure rolling is possible just enough friction is developed to make $r\dot{\theta} = v$. (See § 204).

(2) Friction is independent of the extent of the surfaces in contact.

(3) Friction is independent of the relative speed of the surfaces in contact.

(4) Friction at each part of the surface of contact is proportional to the normal force with which the two surfaces there press against one another, that is, if F be the friction and N the normal force, $F = \mu N$, where μ is the "coefficient of friction." [Thus in the case of the inclined plane and body resting on it referred to in (1), the normal force N is $wg \cos \alpha$ and $\mu = \tan \alpha$. The angle α, at which the body begins to slide, thus enables the coefficient of friction to be determined for any two substances if the inclined plane is made of one, and the body placed upon it is made of the other.]

The value of μ thus obtained is, however, rather greater than that which an experiment with an inclined plane gives, if there is sensible relative motion. For it is found that if the plane is held at the limiting angle, and the body is started down the plane with a small speed, it will have a slight acceleration, showing that now the value of F is somewhat under $wg \sin \alpha$. Experiment has shown that the value of the coefficient of friction—nearly constant for finite speeds—increases for a small range of values of v as v is diminished towards zero.

Let now an inclined plane make an angle $\beta > \alpha$ with the horizontal, and let a body of weight w be placed upon it. For simplicity we shall suppose for the present that the body is a particle. The particle will slide down along the line of greatest slope of the plane through the initial position, that is along a line at right angles to the intersection of the inclined plane with a horizontal plane at the place. The equation of motion is

$$w\dot{v} = wg \sin\beta - \mu wg \cos\beta \qquad \qquad (1)$$

or $\qquad \dot{v} = g(\sin\beta - \mu \cos\beta) = g \sec\alpha \sin(\beta - \alpha), \quad \ldots (2)$

since $\mu = \tan\alpha$. Thus the acceleration is the same as if there were no friction, the inclination were $\beta - \alpha$, and gravity were increased to $g \sec\alpha$.

If the motion start from rest,

$$v = gt \sec\alpha \sin(\beta - \alpha), \qquad \qquad (3)$$

and the distance s traversed in time t is given by

$$s = \tfrac{1}{2}gt^2 \sec\alpha \sin(\beta - \alpha). \qquad \qquad (4)$$

But the equation for v gives $t = v/g \sec\alpha \sin(\beta - \alpha)$, and so

$$\tfrac{1}{2}v^2 = sg \sec\alpha \sin(\beta - \alpha), \qquad \qquad (5)$$

or, as we may write it, the equation of energy

$$\tfrac{1}{2}wv^2 = wgs \sec\alpha \sin(\beta - \alpha). \qquad \qquad (6)$$

This might have been obtained at once by the principle of energy. The loss of potential energy is $wgs \sin\beta$, the work done against friction is $wgs \tan\alpha \cos\beta$: the excess of the former over the latter is the gain $\tfrac{1}{2}wv^2$ of kinetic energy.

If the body is drawn up the inclined plane through the distance s, the work spent is

$$wgs(\sin\beta + \mu \cos\beta) = wgs \sec\alpha \sin(\beta + \alpha).$$

We may regard the downward motion through s, and the upward displacement of the body restoring it to its starting position as a "stroke" of the arrangement regarded as a machine. The work spent in the stroke is

$$wgs \sec\alpha \sin(\beta + \alpha),$$

that gained is $\qquad wgs \sec\alpha \sin(\beta - \alpha),$

372   A TREATISE ON DYNAMICS.   [CH. VII.

and therefore the efficiency of the arrangement is
$$\sin(\beta-\alpha)/\sin(\beta+\alpha).$$
In Fig. 85, $AB = s$,
$\angle BAD = \beta$, $\angle CAD = \angle DAE = \alpha$,
and $BCDE$ is a vertical line. Then
efficiency $= BC/BE$.

Some of these results have already been obtained for a particle in § 89.

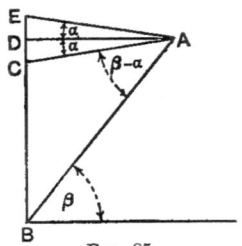

Fig. 85.

A wheel rolling on a rail is always opposed by a small couple called the *couple of rolling friction* (proportional to the normal force) which is here neglected.

202. Railway Carriage at Rest on Incline: Front or Back Wheels Braked. It is important to notice that the equations of motion of a particle along an inclined plane without friction are exactly those of an extended body mounted on very small wheels or castors which roll along the plane. This is obvious from the equations for $\dot{v}$ and v^2, (2) and (5), § 199, in which, if k^2 be made very small, the quantity $W + nw(k^2 + r^2)/r^2$ becomes $W + nw$, the whole weight of the body. In the case of an extended body like a long railway carriage, supported on two sets of wheels, one at each end of the carriage, the action against the plane exerted by each set of wheels depends on the distribution of the matter composing the carriage and its load. If that be uniform on the whole along the carriage, or equally distributed on the wheels, and there be unresisted acceleration down the plane, each set of wheels (rotary inertia neglected) will exert a total force of $\frac{1}{2}(W+nw)g\cos\beta$ in absolute units on the plane at right angles to its direction, and an equal and opposite reaction will be exerted on the wheels.

It is otherwise when one set of wheels is braked and the carriage is at rest on the incline. Then the reactions are as shown in Figs. 86 and 87, according as the lower or upper wheels are braked. If, as we suppose to be the case, the carriage is just prevented from sliding down, the full frictional force is developed at the braked wheels, and

§§ 201, 202] VEHICLE ON INCLINE. 373

if the total reaction there be N (Fig. 86) or N' (Fig. 87) the force F is $N \tan \alpha$ or $N' \tan \alpha$ as the case may be. To find N' and N we have, taking moments about the contacts of the wheels (supposed coinciding in a point at each end at distance $2l$ apart), and putting h for the distance of the C.G. from the wheel-base,

$$\left. \begin{array}{l} 2lN = (W+nw)g(l\cos\beta + h\sin\beta), \\ 2lN' = (W+nw)g(l\cos\beta - h\sin\beta). \end{array} \right\} \quad \ldots\ldots\ldots(1)$$

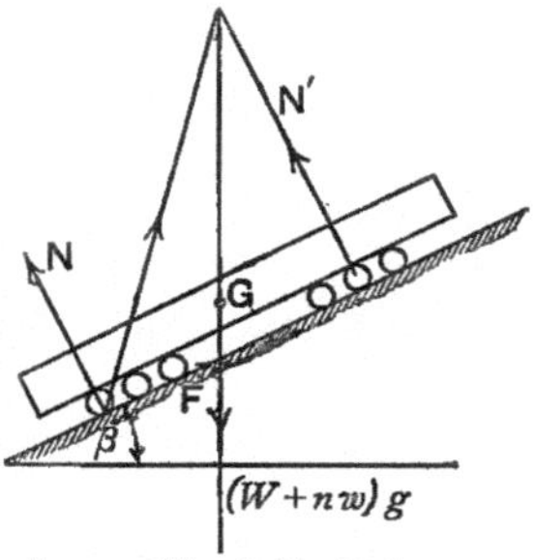

Lower Wheels Braked
FIG. 86.

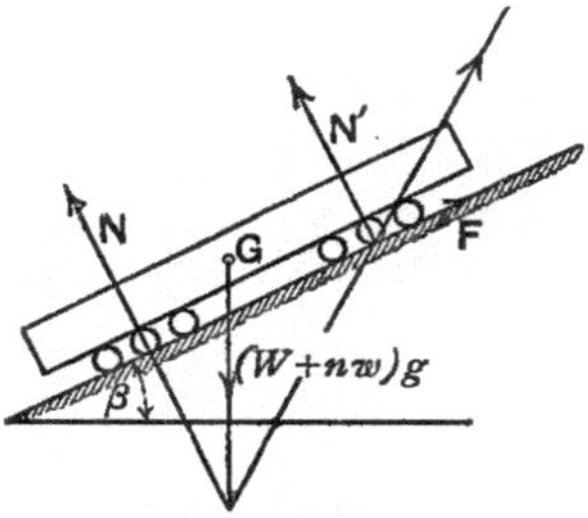

Upper Wheels Braked
FIG. 87.

Thus the friction in the first case, that of the front-wheels braked, is

$$F = \tfrac{1}{2}(W+nw)g(\cos\beta + \tfrac{h}{l}\sin\beta)\tan\alpha, \quad \ldots\ldots\ldots(2)$$

and in the other case, when the hind wheels are braked,

$$F = \tfrac{1}{2}(W+nw)g(\cos\beta - \tfrac{h}{l}\sin\beta)\tan\alpha. \quad \ldots\ldots\ldots(3)$$

In each case, of course, $F = (W+nw)g\sin\beta$, since the component of gravity along the plane is balanced. It appears, therefore, that when the carriage is at rest it is more easily held when the front wheels are braked than when the hind wheels are. The reaction at the braked wheels in each case makes an angle α with the normal to the plane as shown in the diagrams. The value of β, the inclination of the plane to the horizontal, for which the carriage can just be held by the brakes on one set of wheels is therefore greater in the first case than in the second.

374   A TREATISE ON DYNAMICS.   [CH. VII.

If h/l be small, we may neglect terms multiplied by that factor, and then each value of F is the same, namely, $\frac{1}{2}(W+nw)g\cos\beta\tan\alpha$, and the limiting inclination may be taken as the same whether the fore or the hind wheels are braked.

As will be seen from the diagrams, the carriage is held in equilibrium in each case by three forces in one plane (N', $(W+nw)g$, $N/\cos\alpha$ in one case, and N, $(W+nw)g$, $N'/\cos\alpha$ in the other), and it is a well-known proposition that when a rigid body is thus held in equilibrium the forces either meet in a point or are parallel. The forces are not parallel; they therefore meet in a point as shown in the figures.

203. Railway Carriage in Motion on Incline. One Set of Wheels Braked. We now consider the more general case in which the carriage has acceleration $\dot{v}$ along the incline. The equations of motion according as the front or the hind wheels are braked are

$$\left.\begin{array}{l}(W+nw)\dot{v}=(W+nw)g\sin\beta-N\tan\alpha,\\(W+nw)\dot{v}=(W+nw)g\sin\beta-N'\tan\alpha.\end{array}\right\}\quad\ldots\ldots(1)$$

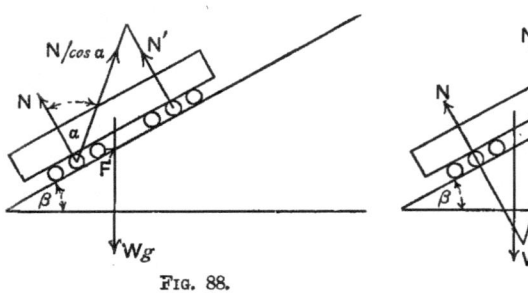
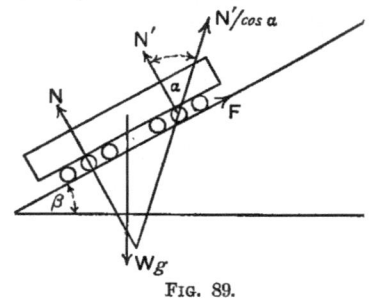

FIG. 88.   FIG. 89.

Thus, for a given inclination β of the plane, we get different values of $\dot{v}$ according to the wheels braked. To find these values we note that we have now the equations of moments

$$\left.\begin{array}{l}2lN=(W+nw)\{g(l\cos\beta+h\sin\beta)-\dot{v}h\},\\2lN'=(W+nw)\{g(l\cos\beta-h\sin\beta)+\dot{v}h\}.\end{array}\right\}\quad\ldots\ldots(2)$$

When the hind wheels are braked these equations become by the value of $\dot{v}$ given by (1) and reduction,

$$N = (W+nw)g \cos\beta \, \frac{l+h\tan\alpha}{2l+h\tan\alpha},$$
$$N' = (W+nw)g \cos\beta \, \frac{l}{2l+h\tan\alpha}.$$ ....(3)

When the front wheels are braked the equations become in the same way, by the value of $\dot{v}$ in (1),

$$N = (W+nw)g \cos\beta \, \frac{l}{2l-h\tan\alpha},$$
$$N' = (W+nw)g \cos\beta \, \frac{l-h\tan\alpha}{2l-h\tan\alpha}.$$ ....(4)

It is to be observed (see § 96) that a plummet hung in a railway carriage has its cord in the direction of the resultant of $\dot{v}$ reversed and g downward. No matter how $\dot{v}$ occurs, whether with one or the other set of wheels braked, or with the carriage resisted in some other way, a value of α can be found which will enable the equation (2), § 201 above,

$$\dot{v} = g \sec\alpha \sin(\beta-\alpha), \quad \ldots\ldots\ldots(5)$$

to be satisfied. With this meaning of α, we have

$$\frac{\dot{v}}{g} = \frac{\sin(\beta-\alpha)}{\cos\alpha}; \quad \ldots\ldots\ldots\ldots(6)$$

and therefore the angle DAE (Fig. 90), which the resultant AD of $\dot{v}$ reversed and g makes with the normal AE to the incline, is α. Thus AD is the direction of the apparent vertical to observers in the carriage, and relatively to that the true vertical, as shown by buildings, etc., in the neighbourhood, will seem to be inclined. In this direction a man can stand upright in the carriage without support, and to it the free surface of water in equilibrium in the carriage is perpendicular.

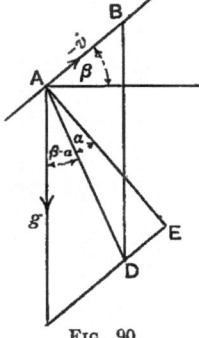

FIG. 90.

204. Solid of Revolution Rolling and Sliding on Horizontal Plane. A uniform solid of revolution held with its axis horizontal, while spinning about its axis with angular speed $\dot{\theta}_0$, is projected along a horizontal plane with speed v_0 perpendicular to the axis. The speeds $\dot{\theta}_0$, v_0 are in the directions shown in Fig. 91: to find the motion.

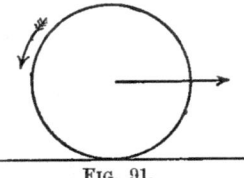

FIG. 91.

Let w be the weight of the solid and wg therefore the upward force applied by the plane to the solid. The force μwg acts in the direction opposed to the motion at the line, or point, of contact. The motion of the centroid is given by the equation

$$w\dot{v} = -\mu wg. \qquad (1)$$

Again, the angular motion about the axis has the equation

$$wk^2\ddot{\theta} = -\mu wgr, \qquad (2)$$

where $\ddot{\theta}$ is the angular acceleration.

Integrating, we get for the speeds at time t,

$$v - v_0 = -\mu gt, \qquad (3)$$

$$k^2(\dot{\theta} - \dot{\theta}_0) = -\mu grt, \qquad (4)$$

so that $k^2\dot{\theta} - rv$ is constant. We denote this by A. That A is constant might have been inferred at once from the fact that the angular momentum of the body about the contact with the plane must remain unaltered, since the forces applied by the plane to the solid all pass through the contact.

Initially the speed of the part of the solid in contact with the plane is $v_0 + r\dot{\theta}_0$, and at time t the contact is moving with speed

$$v + r\dot{\theta} = v_0 + r\dot{\theta}_0 - \mu gt\left(1 + \frac{r^2}{k^2}\right), \qquad (5)$$

which vanishes when

$$t = \frac{v_0 + r\dot{\theta}_0}{\mu g} \frac{k^2}{k^2 + r^2}. \qquad (6)$$

§ 204] COMBINED ROLLING AND SLIDING. 377

From this instant onward pure rolling exists, and provided a certain condition is fulfilled, the solid returns towards the place of projection at a uniform speed. The speed v of the centroid is zero by (3) when $t = v_0/\mu g$; but, as we shall see, v will not vanish unless this instant occurs before that of the production of pure rolling. The angular speed when $v = 0$ is $(k^2\dot\theta_0 - v_0 r)/k^2$, and if this has the same sign as at first the body will turn back.

The angular speed at the instant of the beginning of pure rolling is found by inserting the value of t from (6) in (4). Thus we get for that instant,

$$\dot\theta = \frac{k^2\dot\theta_0 - v_0 r}{k^2 + r^2} = \frac{A}{k^2 + r^2}. \qquad (7)$$

From this it appears that if $v_0 r > k^2\dot\theta_0$, the angular speed will have changed sign before rolling has been set up. The distance s of the centroid from the point of projection at the same instant is given by

$$\begin{aligned}s &= \frac{v_0 + r\dot\theta_0}{2\mu g} \frac{k^2}{(k^2+r^2)^2} \{v_0(k^2+2r^2) - k^2 r\dot\theta_0\} \\ &= \frac{v_0 + r\dot\theta_0}{2\mu g} \frac{k^2}{(k^2+r^2)^2} \{v_0(k^2+r^2) - Ar\}.\end{aligned} \qquad (8)$$

Thus s is positive or negative according as

$$v_0(k^2 + 2r^2) > \text{ or } < k^2 r\dot\theta_0.$$

If it is positive and likewise $k^2\dot\theta_0 > v_0 r$, the body will, when pure rolling begins, be rotating in the same direction as at first, and will roll back to the starting point with uniform speed. But if $k^2\dot\theta_0 < v_0 r$, the body will roll still further away and will not return. This is the condition referred to above, for then [see (6)]

$$v_0/\mu g > (v_0 + r\dot\theta_0)k^2/\mu(k^2+r^2)g.$$

On the other hand, if $k^2 r\dot\theta_0 > v_0(k^2 + 2r^2)$, s is negative, that is the body has had the speed of its centroid reversed, and been brought back *beyond* the starting point before the setting up of pure rolling. If then $k^2\dot\theta_0 > v_0 r$, the body will be rotating in the same direction as at first, and will roll still further away from the starting point. The

378   A TREATISE ON DYNAMICS.   [CH. VII.

condition $k^2 r \dot\theta_0 > v_0(k^2 + 2r^2)$ precludes the possibility of the case $k^2 \dot\theta_0 < v_0 r$, which therefore cannot be associated with a negative value of s.

If the solid returns the time t' occupied in retraversing s is given by $s/\dot\theta r$, by (8), that is $t' = s(k^2 + r^2)/Ar$. Thus

$$t' = \frac{v_0 + r\dot\theta_0}{2\mu g} \frac{k^2}{k^2 + r^2} \frac{v_0(k^2 + r^2) - Ar}{Ar}. \quad \ldots\ldots\ldots(9)$$

To find the whole time from projection to return, we have to add to this the value of t. Thus if $A = k^2\dot\theta_0 - v_0 r$,

$$t + t' = \frac{v_0 + r\dot\theta_0}{2\mu g} \frac{k^2}{k^2 + r^2} \frac{v_0(k^2 + r^2) + Ar}{Ar} = \frac{(v_0 + r\dot\theta_0)^2}{2\mu g} \frac{k^4}{k^2 + r^2} \frac{1}{Ar}, \quad (10)$$

If the body, before projection in the same direction as before, is spinning the other way, the motion of mixed sliding and rolling will go on until pure rolling is set up, and the rolling motion will then continue to carry the body farther and farther from the point of projection.

Ex. 1. Prove that in the latter case $v_0 r + k^2 \dot\theta_0$ is constant, that pure rolling is set up after a time $\pm(v_0 - r\dot\theta_0)k^2/\mu g(k^2 + r^2)$, according as $v_0 >$ or $< r\dot\theta_0$, that the angular speed is then $(v_0 r + k^2\dot\theta_0)/(k^2 + r^2)$, and

$$\pm(v_0 - r\dot\theta_0)k^2\{Ar + (k^2 + r^2)v_0\}/2\mu g(k^2 + r^2)^2,$$

where $A = v_0 r + k^2 \dot\theta_0$ is the distance described in the time here stated.

Ex. 2. If the solid be given underhand spin, as in Fig. 91, and be projected up a plane inclined at the angle β to the horizontal, show that, so long as pure rolling does not exist, the equations of motion are

$$\dot v = -g(\mu \cos\beta + \sin\beta), \quad k^2 \ddot\theta = -\mu g r \cos\beta,$$

that (unless pure rolling has first set in) the solid will ascend for a time $t = v_0/g(\mu\cos\beta + \sin\beta)$, and a distance $\tfrac12 v_0^2/g(\mu\cos\beta + \sin\beta)$, that pure rolling will begin after a time

$$t' = (v_0 + r\dot\theta_0)k^2/g\{\mu(k^2 + r^2)\cos\beta + k^2 \sin\beta\},$$

from the instant of projection, with angular speed

$$\{k^2\dot\theta_0(\mu\cos\beta + \sin\beta) - v_0 r\mu\cos\beta\}/\{(k^2 + r^2)\mu\cos\beta + k^2\sin\beta\}.$$

Find the condition that $t' > t$. Find also the whole time from the instant of projection to that of return to the starting point.

Ex. 3. The solid, still with initial underhand spin, is projected down the inclined plane of last example: find the equations of motion and show that, if $\mu\cos\beta > \sin\beta$, and pure rolling has not begun, $v = 0$

when $t = v_0/g(\mu \cos\beta - \sin\beta)$. Prove that at that instant the solid is rotating in the same direction as at first, and will therefore turn back, provided $\mu > \tan\beta/(1 - v_0 r/k^2\theta_0)$. Prove also that pure rolling will never begin unless $\mu > k^2 \tan\beta/(k^2+r^2)$.

Ex. 4. A uniform cylinder of radius r, revolving with angular velocity ω about its axis, is gently laid with its axis horizontal on a horizontal table. If the coefficient of friction between the cylinder and table be μ, show that the cylinder will slip for a time $r\omega/3\mu g$, and then roll with angular velocity $\omega/3$.

Ex. 5. A shaft on loosely fitting bearings, radius a feet, carries a weight of W lbs. If $\mu = \tan\phi$, show that the resisting couple is $Wa \sin\phi$, in pound foot units.

205. Compound Pendulum. Any rigid body movable about a horizontal axis may be used as a compound pendulum, provided the centroid does not coincide with the axis about which the body is pivoted. A wheel mounted with its axis horizontal and put out of balance by a weight attached to the rim may serve as an example. The position of stable equilibrium of the body is that in which the centroid is in

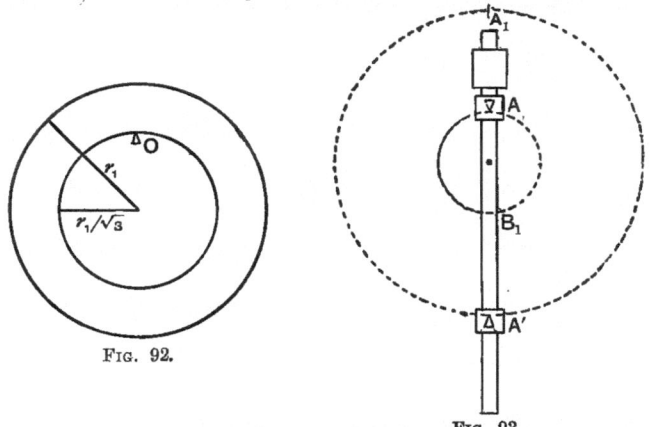

FIG. 92.

FIG. 93.

the lowest possible position. For when the body is deflected a little way from that position and left to itself at rest, the forces upon it have a moment causing it to return to that position, that is the forces tend to bring it into the position of minimum potential energy consistent with rotation about the fixed axis when the moment vanishes.

Generally a compound pendulum constructed as such is a body supported on a horizontal line of knife-edges, and so shaped that its parts are symmetrically distributed about a plane through the centroid at right angles to the knife-edges which are also symmetrically placed with regard to that plane. Fig. 92 shows one form—a massive ring of rectangular section supported on an upturned knife-edge which touches it along one of the generating lines of its inner cylindrical surface. Fig. 93 shows a more usual form with attached knife-edges and sliding weight.

206. Theory of Compound Pendulum (C.P.). Equivalent Simple Pendulum. We shall suppose first that the body is provided with a cylindrical bearing of radius c (Fig. 94) supported on a horizontal surface, so that at any instant of its motion the body is rolling on that surface and turning therefore at the instant about a generating line of the cylinder. We denote by h the distance of the centroid of the body from the axis of the cylinder and by Wk^2 the moment of inertia of the body about an axis through the centroid parallel to that of the cylinder. Then, if the deflection of the line through the centroid perpendicular to the axis from the vertical be θ, the moment of inertia about the instantaneous axis is

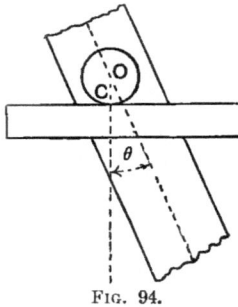

Fig. 94.

$$W(k^2 + h^2 + c^2 - 2hc \cos \theta).$$

The forces on the body are (1) the resultant force of gravity acting vertically downward through the centroid, and (2) the reaction R of the axis. The latter has no moment about the axis, and thus Wg is the only force concerned in altering a deflection from the vertical position, for we assume that there is no friction at the axis which exerts a moment on the pendulum, for example no couple due to what is called "rolling friction" (see § 201). $Wgh \sin \theta$ is then the moment of Wg about the instantaneous axis of ..... turning, and tends to produce angular momentum in the direction of diminishing θ, and the angular momentum at the moment is $W(k^2+h^2+c^2-2hc\cos\theta)\dot\theta$. We have therefore

$$W(k^2+h^2+c^2-2hc\cos\theta)\ddot\theta+2Whc\sin\theta\,.\,\dot\theta^2=-Wgh\sin\theta,$$

and therefore

$$(h^2+k^2+c^2-2hc\cos\theta)\ddot\theta+2hc\sin\theta\,.\,\dot\theta^2+gh\sin\theta=0\ ...(1)$$

for the equation of motion.

In the case of small oscillations we replace in this $\cos\theta$ by 1, $\sin\theta$ by θ, and ignore the term in $\dot\theta^2$. Thus we obtain

$$\{(h-c)^2+k^2\}\ddot\theta+gh\theta=0 \quad ....(2)$$

as the equation of motion, which is precisely that of a simple pendulum, of length l, given by

$$l^2=\frac{(h-c)^2+k^2}{h}. \quad ....(3)$$

If the pendulum is suspended on knife-edges supported on hard plates, we may take c as zero, and then

$$l=\frac{h^2+k^2}{h} \quad ....(4)$$

is the length of a simple pendulum, which would, in the absence of air-resistance, oscillate through any angular range whatever in the same period as that of the compound pendulum in oscillations of the same angular range.

Should the pendulum consist of several parts of weights $w_1, w_2, \ldots$, of which it is convenient to consider the moments of inertia, and moments of forces about the given axis, separately, then if $h_1, h_2, \ldots$ be the distances of the centroids $G_1, G_2, \ldots$ of these parts from the axis of suspension and $k_1, k_2 \ldots$ the radii of gyration about the axis A, we have

$$W(h^2+k^2)=w_1(h_1^2+k_1^2)+w_2(h_2^2+k_2^2)+\ldots.$$

Also, if the perpendiculars from $G_1, G_2, \ldots$ to the axis A make at the instant under consideration angles $\theta_1, \theta_2, \ldots$

with the vertical, we have

$$Wgh \sin \theta = w_1 gh_1 \sin \theta_1 + w_2 gh_2 \sin \theta_2 + \ldots, \quad \ldots\ldots(5)$$

so that
$$\frac{l}{\sin \theta} = \frac{w_1(h_1^2 + k_1^2) + w_2(h_2^2 + k_2^2) + \ldots}{w_1 h_1 \sin \theta_1 + w_2 h_2 \sin \theta_2 + \ldots}. \quad \ldots\ldots\ldots(6)$$

The compound pendulum of Fig. 92 consists of a ring of iron of rectangular section, made of quarter-inch boiler or ship plate, well hardened after construction. The inner and outer surfaces are truly coaxial cylinders, and the ring, as already stated, oscillates on an upturned knife-edge touching it in a generating line of the inner surface. If r_1, r_2 be the inner and outer radii, the moment of inertia about the axis of figure is

$$\left(\frac{m}{2}\pi r_2^4 - \frac{m}{2}\pi r_1^4\right), \text{ or } \frac{1}{2}m\pi(r_2^2 - r_1^2)(r_2^2 + r_1^2),$$

where m is the weight of the plate per unit of area, that is, the M.I. is $\frac{1}{2}W(r_2^2 + r_1^2)$, where W is the whole weight, and the moment of inertia about a generating line of the inner cylinder is $\frac{1}{2}W(r^2 + 3r_1^2)$. The period is therefore given by

$$T = 2\pi \sqrt{\frac{r_2^2 + 3r_1^2}{r_1 g}}.$$

207. Suspension Axes and Oscillation Axes. Interchangeability. Suppose the pendulum to be hanging in stable equilibrium, while capable of turning about an axis A (Fig. 93) at distance h from the centroid G, and let a circle be imagined to be described from the centroid as centre with h as radius, in the plane in which the centroid moves. Now let the pendulum as it hangs be imagined connected, if necessary, by a framework of negligible mass, rigidly attached to the pendulum with an axis through B parallel to A, and then to be loosed from the axis at A so as to be free to turn about that at B. The period of unresisted oscillation about B for any range of deflection will be the same as the period for the same range about A.

If another circle be described from G as centre in the same plane as before with $l-h$ (or $l-h+c$) as radius, a

§§ 206, 207]   COMPOUND PENDULUM.   383

perpendicular let fall from G to any of the equivalent axes $A, B, \ldots$, and produced backward, will meet the second circle in a point $A', B', \ldots$. Then $l = AA' = BB' = \ldots$. The points $A, B, \ldots$ have been called centres of suspension for the pendulum, and $A', B', \ldots$ centres of oscillation.

The pendulum has, as will be shown presently, the same period of oscillation about a parallel axis through $A', B', \ldots$ that it has about the axis through A, or any of the equivalent axes through $B, C, \ldots$. This is the principle of "convertibility of the centre of oscillation and suspension"; but the principle is often so expressed as to suggest that for a certain period there is only one centre (or axis) of suspension and a corresponding centre (or axis) of oscillation.

As generally made with fixed knife-edges compound pendulums admit of only one axis of suspension being used, and the problem is then that of finding the centre of oscillation which corresponds, and some range of variation of that is provided for by a sliding weight which can be fixed in different positions on the pendulum. But as a matter of dynamics there are an infinite number of equivalent *axes* and corresponding oscillation *axes*, or, as they would be more properly called, *conjugate axes*.

It is convenient to have an arrangement to illustrate this, and one has been made as follows. A sheet of steel-plate, thick enough to remain rigidly plane, is loaded with a diametral bar across the centroid formed by two strips of steel riveted to its two sides. Holes of equal size, large enough to admit an upturned knife-edge projecting from a fixed support, are bored with their centres in a circle round the centroid, and another concentric row of similar holes is made nearer the centroid, so that the radii of the circles touched by the outer edges of the holes in the two series have the radii h and $l-h$ for the arrangement when used as a compound pendulum. The outer series of holes is cut first, and then the position of the second series is fixed with allowance for the material to be cut away. The cross-bar is made a little too long at first, and the arrangement is finally "tuned" to agreement of period by filing a little away from each end. The same period of oscillation is given whatever hole is used for the suspension of the body on the knife-edge.

The theorem of convertibility of axes referred to above is proved as follows. The period T is given by

$$T = 2\pi\sqrt{\frac{h^2+k^2}{gh}} = 2\pi\sqrt{\frac{l}{g}}, \quad\ldots\ldots\ldots\ldots\ldots(1)$$

where $l = (h^2+k^2)/h$. This last equation can be written in either of the forms

$$h^2 - hl + k^2 = 0, \quad (l-h)^2 - (l-h)l + k^2 = 0, \ldots\ldots(2)$$

so that, if h is one root of the equation, $l-h$ is the other. The sum of the roots is l and their product is k^2, as affirmed by the quadratic equation. We infer that if l be the length of the equivalent simple pendulum for the distance h from the centroid to the axis, it is also the length of the equivalent simple pendulum for the distance $l-h$. Thus for the infinite series of parallel axes, for which l has a given value, there is a conjugate series at distance $l-h$ from the centroid, for which l has the same value.

If h be chosen very great $l-h$ will be correspondingly small, and the periods will be the same; and when h is infinite $l-h$ will be zero, and the periods in both cases will be infinitely long. Hence, if we diminish h from infinity $l-h$ will be increased from zero, and the periods will be diminished; and clearly the two distances coincide when the period is a minimum. We have then $l = l-h$, or $l = 2h$ and $h = k$, so that $l = 2k$ is the smallest length of the equivalent simple pendulum.

If the matter of the pendulum be concentrated in two particles, one of weight $Wk^2/(h^2+k^2)$ at the centre of suspension O and the other of weight $Wh^2/(h^2+k^2)$ at a point L at distance $l = (h^2+k^2)/h$ from the suspension, the period will be the same. This arrangement, as was pointed out by Maxwell (*Matter and Motion*), is kinetically equivalent to the compound pendulum. For if the compound pendulum have its suspension at O and its centre of oscillation at L, the two centroids coincide, the moments of gravity forces, and the moments of inertia about O, are the same. The moments of inertia about an axis through the common centroid are the same, and therefore the moments of inertia about any axis whatever are the same.

208. Experimental C.P. A compound pendulum used for experiment is generally furnished with two pairs of knife-edges, one pair fixed relatively to the pendulum and a movable pair, and also with a sliding weight to enable the distribution of matter in the pendulum to be altered, and the experimenter is required to arrange the apparatus so that the pendulum swings about the two pairs of knife-edges in the same period. In the Repsold pendulum the sliding weight is within a containing tube, which keeps the external form the same for all distributions of the mass, in order to avoid inequalities of air-resistance. This resistance may be regarded as made up of two parts, a true frictional resistance and a dragging of air with the pendulum, by which its inertia is virtually increased. Further, the pendulum being immersed in the air has its gravity virtually diminished by the buoyancy of the air displaced. We shall show presently how the virtual increase of mass and the effect of buoyancy may be estimated.

The adjustment of the period of swing about the two axes to equality is made easier by hanging a simple pendulum alongside the compound one (when the latter is made to oscillate about the fixed knife-edges) and altering its length until the two just keep pace. The position of the second pair of knife-edges should then be shifted to a distance from the first equal to the length of the simple pendulum thus found; and this, with a slight correction for the change produced by the sliding piece carrying the knife-edges, will give the required arrangement. The distance of one line of knife-edges from the other is then l, and, if the period T of small oscillations be determined, g can be calculated from the equation

$$g = \frac{4\pi^2}{T^2} l. \quad \dots \dots \dots \dots \dots \dots \dots \dots (1)$$

This method of determining g was carried out by Captain Kater (*Phil. Trans. R.S.* 1818). In preference to a simple pendulum he carried a compound pendulum from place to place, and so made a gravity survey over a considerable part of the country.

It will be clear from Fig. 93 that besides A and A' there are in the same line AA' two other points, A_1, B_1, at which the second knife edge can be placed to give the same period. The student is not likely to place the second knife-edge at A_1, but occasionally he hits on B_1 as the position. This, it will be seen, gives $2h$, not l, as the distance between the two lines of knife-edges. Thus, twice one root of (2), § 207, generally the greater root, is obtained and taken as l; the student ought to be advised of his error by the absurdly large value of g then given by (1).

209. Buoyancy and Air-Drag of C.P. The buoyancy and air-drag modify the equations as follows. Let w be the weight of air displaced by the pendulum, that is the weight of the air at the density of the surrounding atmosphere, which fills a volume equal to that of the pendulum: the assumption is made that the air dragged with the pendulum is proportional to w. This assumption is derived from the fact that, for example, an infinitely long cylinder moving with uniform speed u in a direction at right angles to its length in an infinite incompressible frictionless fluid, has an apparent kinetic energy greater than that corresponding to the mass of the cylinder by $\frac{1}{2}wu^2$: in the case of a sphere moving in any direction on such a fluid, the excess of energy is $\frac{1}{4}wu^2$, for an ellipsoid it is κwu^2, where κ is a coefficient depending on the direction of motion relatively to the principal axes.

We take then k' such a length that wk'^2 is the increase of moment of inertia of the pendulum, supposed of symmetrical outward shape, and situated about positions of the knife-edges, symmetrical about the centre of figure, and giving nearly equal periods T_1, T_2. The buoyancy of the air is a force wg acting upwards through a point which is called the *centre of buoyancy* of the immersed body, and this for a pendulum in which the knife-edges are symmetrically placed, as here supposed, is at a distance $(h_1 + h_2)/2$ from either axis, if h_1, h_2 now denote the distances of the centroid of the pendulum from the two knife-edges. Thus the moment of inertia is increased to $W(h_1^2+k^2)+wk'^2$, and the moment of forces is diminished to $Wgh_1 - \tfrac{1}{2}wg(h_1+h_2)$, about the first knife-edge. Similar expressions hold for the other knife-edge. The lengths l_1, l_2 of the equivalent simple pendulum for the two knife-edges are given by

$$l_1 = \frac{W(h_1^2+k^2)+wk'^2}{Wh_1 - \tfrac{1}{2}w(h_1+h_2)} = \frac{g}{4\pi^2} T_1^2,$$
$$l_2 = \frac{W(h_2^2+k^2)+wk'^2}{Wh_2 - \tfrac{1}{2}w(h_1+h_2)} = \frac{g}{4\pi^2} T_2^2. \qquad \ldots\ldots\ldots\ldots(1)$$

By means of these equations, we can eliminate $Wk^2+wk'^2$, and so find an equation for g containing a small correction term, depending on the value of w, which can be approximated to more or less nearly in various particular cases; and this, with or without the term depending on w/W may be used to find g, when the distances h_1, h_2 giving periods T_1, T_2 are measured. We find

$$g = \frac{8\pi^2(h_1+h_2)}{T_1^2+T_2^2+\left(1-\frac{w}{W}\right)\frac{h_1+h_2}{h_1-h_2}(T_1^2-T_2^2)}. \qquad \ldots\ldots\ldots(2)$$

This divided by $4\pi^2$ is the length of the equivalent simple pendulum which would have a period equal to unity, and divided by π^2 it gives the length of the equivalent simple pendulum which would beat seconds. The length is thus expressed in terms of h_1, h_2, T_1, T_2 and the ratio w/W. The latter furnishes a small correction term, which can be estimated more or less nearly in different cases, according to the shape of the pendulum.

For a clock-pendulum the air carried with the bob is the only thing regarded, and then it is sufficient to take it as a particle added at the centroid of the bob. The weight added is some fraction μ of the weight w of air displaced, and so the equation for the corrected value l' of the length of the equivalent simple pendulum is

$$l' = \frac{W(h^2+k^2)+\mu wh^2}{(W-w)h} = l\left\{1+\frac{w}{W}\left(1+\mu\frac{h}{l}\right)\right\}, \qquad \ldots\ldots(3)$$

where $l=(h^2+k^2)/h$, the uncorrected length. If the bob is a cylinder moving at right angles to its length, μ may be taken as 1, though this supposition is rendered inaccurate by the fact that the cylinder is of finite length, and the atmosphere in which it moves is limited by the clock-case. For a spherical bob μ may be taken as $\frac{1}{2}$. The factor of w/W is the ratio of the specific gravity of air to that of the material of the bob, and if the bob be of lead the ratio is about 8000. Thus, taking $h/l=1$ and $\mu=\frac{1}{2}$ for a spherical bob $(w/W)(1+\mu h/l)=3/16000$, so that a clock regulated by such a pendulum, of the length l to beat seconds, would, in consequence of buoyancy and air-drag combined, lose about 8 seconds in 24 hours.

Very accurate sidereal clocks at observatories are now enclosed in partly exhausted air-tight cases, so that this correction may not fluctuate as it would otherwise do with the barometric pressure, owing to alterations produced in the ratio w/W.

210. Examples on the Compound Pendulum.

Ex. 1. A compound pendulum is formed of a uniform rod of length $2l$ and mass m loaded with a mass m' at each extremity. Find the length of the equivalent simple pendulum for vibrations about a horizontal axis at right angles to its length. Find also the position of this axis when the period has its least value.

Let the distance of the axis from the centroid be h. The length L of the equivalent simple pendulum is then given by

$$L=\frac{(\tfrac{1}{3}m+2m')l^2+(m+2m')h^2}{(m+2m')h}.$$

This equation may be written

$$h^2-Lh+\frac{\tfrac{1}{3}m+2m'}{m+2m'}l^2=0.$$

The roots of this quadratic in h cannot be imaginary, and therefore the least possible value of L is to be found from the relation

$$(m+2m')L^2=4(\tfrac{1}{3}m+2m')l^2.$$

If $m=m'$, this gives $9L^2=28l^2$, or $3L=2\sqrt{7}l$. We have then $h=\tfrac{1}{3}\sqrt{7}l$. If the axis of suspension intersects the rod, it divides the rod into segments in the ratio of $3-\sqrt{7}$ to $3+\sqrt{7}$.

Ex. 2. A homogeneous sphere rolls within a hollow right circular cylinder which is fixed. Find the time of a small oscillation of the sphere about the lowest position.

COMPOUND PENDULUM.

The centre of the sphere moves in a circle of radius $R-r$, where R is the radius of the cylinder and r that of the sphere. Let ψ be the inclination to the vertical of the perpendicular from the centre of the sphere to the axis of the cylinder, and $\dot{\theta}$ the angular speed of the sphere at any instant. Then we have (Fig. 95), noticing that $\dot{\theta}$ and $\dot{\psi}$ are in opposite directions

$$r\dot{\theta} = (R-r)\dot{\psi}.$$

The kinetic energy of the sphere (weight w) is

$$\tfrac{1}{2}w(R-r)^2\dot{\psi}^2 + \tfrac{1}{5}wr^2\dot{\theta}^2 = \tfrac{7}{10}w(R-r)^2\dot{\psi}^2$$

by the relation between $\dot{\theta}$ and $\dot{\psi}$. The potential energy in the position indicated is $wg(R-r)(1-\cos\psi)$. Hence if α is the extreme value of ψ,

$$\tfrac{7}{10}w(R-r)^2\dot{\psi}^2 = wg(R-r)(\cos\psi - \cos\alpha);$$

and we get, by differentiation,

$$\tfrac{7}{5}(R-r)\ddot{\psi} + g\sin\psi = 0.$$

The period of a small oscillation is therefore $2\pi\sqrt{\tfrac{7}{5}(R-r)/g}.$

The problem may also be solved as follows. The sphere is turning at the instant about the point of contact A with the cylinder. Hence, if $\ddot{\theta}$ be the angular acceleration,

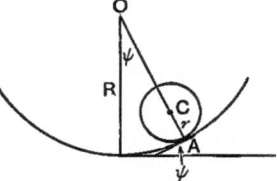

Fig. 95.

$$\ddot{\theta} = \frac{-wgr\sin\psi}{\tfrac{2}{5}wr^2 + wr^2} = -\frac{5}{7}\frac{g\sin\psi}{r}.$$

But, by the relation between $\dot{\theta}$ and $\dot{\psi}$, we have $\ddot{\theta} = (R-r)\ddot{\psi}/r$. Substituting in the equation just found for $\ddot{\theta}$, we get

$$\ddot{\psi} + \frac{5}{7}\frac{g}{R-r}\sin\psi = 0,$$

the same equation as before.

Ex. 3. A uniform plank, of length l, balances on a fixed horizontal cylinder of radius R: the length of the plank is at right angles to the axis of the cylinder. If the plank is set rocking without slipping, show (neglecting the thickness of the plank) that the period is that of a simple pendulum of length $\tfrac{1}{12}l^2/R$. Derive also the energy equation.

The plank rolls without slipping: at time t let it be inclined at an angle θ to the equilibrium position: the radius to the point of contact now makes an angle θ with the vertical, and if G be the centroid, and D the point of contact (Fig. 96), $DG = R\theta$. Hence, if W be the weight of the plank,

$$W(\tfrac{1}{12}l^2 + R^2\theta^2)\ddot{\theta} = -WgR\theta\cos\theta,$$

or, when θ is small,
$$\ddot{\theta} + \frac{gR}{\tfrac{1}{12}l^2}\theta = 0,$$

that is, the length of the equivalent simple pendulum is $\tfrac{1}{12}l^2/R$.

390 A TREATISE ON DYNAMICS. [CH. VII.

The kinetic energy of the rod is $\frac{1}{2}W(\frac{1}{12}l^2 + R^2\theta^2)\dot\theta^2$; and at time t the point of contact of the rod is at a distance $R(1-\cos\theta)$ above the centre of the cylinder. Hence, the centroid is at a distance

$$R\theta\sin\theta + R(1-\cos\theta)$$

above C. The potential energy may therefore be taken as

$$Wg\{R\theta\sin\theta + R(1-\cos\theta)\}.$$

Let α be the extreme value of θ, for which, of course, $\dot\theta=0$. The equation of energy is

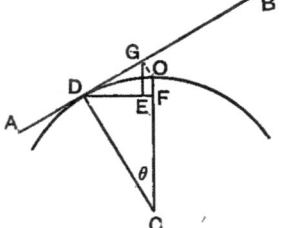

FIG. 96.

$$\tfrac{1}{2}W(\tfrac{1}{12}l^2 + R^2\theta^2)\dot\theta^2 + WgR\{(\theta\sin\theta - \alpha\sin\alpha) - (\cos\theta - \cos\alpha)\} = 0.$$

Ex. 4. A uniform plank 13 feet long is balanced on a horizontal log of circular section, 4 feet in diameter, and two boys of equal mass seated at its ends use it as a "see-saw." Taking the mass of the plank as 40 lbs. and that of each boy as 84 lbs., and regarding the plank as a thin rod and the boys as particles each at a distance of 6 feet from the middle of the plank, show that the period of a small oscillation is 4·43 seconds.

Ex. 5. Show that if the internal and external radii of the ring pendulum described in § 205 be r_1 and r_2, the length of the equivalent simple pendulum l is given by

$$l = \frac{1}{2}\frac{r_2^2}{r_1} + \frac{3}{2}r_1.$$

If the mechanic in cutting the ring has made r_1/r_2 have nearly an assigned ratio (so that only the outside diameter is measured), show that a small error in this ratio has zero effect on the calculated length of the equivalent simple pendulum when the ratio has the value $\sqrt{3}/1$.

Ex. 6. At a point P in the line joining the centre of suspension O and the centre of oscillation of a compound pendulum a mass w is attached. It is required to find the change in the length l of the equivalent simple pendulum, and to show that if the mass w be small it produces the greatest change in l when attached at a point halfway between the two centres.

Without the additional mass $l=(h^2+k^2)/h$. When w is attached the moment of forces for a deflection θ becomes $(Wgh+wgx)\sin\theta$, where x is the distance of P from O. The moment of inertia becomes

$$W(h^2+k^2)+wx^2.$$

Hence if $l+y$ denote the new value of l, and ρ the ratio w/W, we have

$$y = \frac{h^2+k^2+\rho x^2}{h+\rho x} - l = \frac{hl+\rho x^2}{h+\rho x} - l.$$

Thus y vanishes when $x=0$, and when $x=l$, and is a maximum when $x=l/2$, if ρ be small.

Clocks are sometimes regulated by varying a small mass placed on a shelf carried by the pendulum. It is here shown that the shelf should be midway between the two centres.

Ex. 7. If y denote the excess of the length of the equivalent seconds pendulum when the mass w is at distance x from the centre of suspension over the length when the mass w is at distance a, show that the graph formed with values of y as ordinates and values of x as abscissae, is a hyperbola, of which the asymptotes are the lines
$$x=0, \quad x=y.$$
We have here
$$y = \frac{hl+\rho x^2}{h+\rho x} - \frac{hl+\rho a^2}{h+\rho a} = \frac{hl+\rho x^2}{h+\rho x} - L,$$
which leads to the equation
$$\rho x^2 - \rho xy - \rho Lx - hy - h(L-l) = 0,$$
the graph of which is clearly a hyperbola. The terms of the second degree $\rho x^2 - \rho xy$ equated to zero give the asymptotes, which are therefore the lines
$$x=0, \quad x-y=0.$$

This relation can be used to graduate a metronome, an instrument for beating time in music. The period is altered by changing the position of a sliding weight, which is comparable with the whole vibrating mass.

Ex. 8. A compound pendulum is formed of a sphere as bob, consisting of a uniform shell of iron filled with water, and suspended on knife-edges attached to a rod rigidly connected with the spherical shell.

If we neglect the friction of the shell on the water we must take the water as a mass every particle of which has at each instant the same *velocity* as the centroid. Hence if W be the weight of the water, W_1 that of the shell and rod, h the distance of the centroid of the whole and h' the distance of the centre of the sphere from the knife-edges, k the radius of gyration of the solid part *about the knife-edges*, we get
$$l = \frac{Wh'^2 + W_1 k^2}{(W+W_1)h}.$$

211. Reactions due to Accelerations. Case of C.P. It is important to find the reactions due to the accelerations impressed on the different parts of a body or system moving in any manner, as these give the forces which are exerted by each different part on the rest of the system, and when properly summed lead to expressions for the forces exerted on the supports of the system. As an example we take here the compound pendulum; but the same process may easily be applied to any swinging body, such for example as a ship in a seaway. Any small part of weight w_1, say, at a point P_1 at distance r_1 from the axis of suspension has, in the motion of the pendulum at any instant, an acceleration $r_1\dot\theta_1^2$ in the direction towards the axis, and an acceleration $r\ddot\theta_1$ in the direction of θ increasing, if θ_1 be the inclination to the vertical of the perpendicular let fall from the point P_1 to the axis about which the pendulum turns. For a positive value of θ_1 that of $\ddot\theta_1$ is negative, and *vice versa*, so that the acceleration $r\ddot\theta_1$ is really always in the direction of diminishing θ_1.

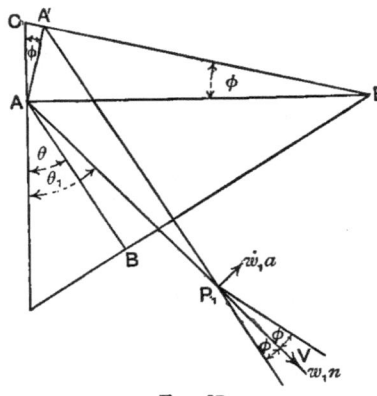

FIG. 97.

The corresponding forces are $w_1 r_1 \dot\theta_1^2$ and $w_1 r_1 \ddot\theta_1$. These are forces applied to the part by the rest of the system. Now we have $w_1 r_1 \ddot\theta_1 = -wg \sin\theta + P_1$, $w_1 r_1 \dot\theta_1^2 = -wg \cos\theta + R_1$, where P_1 is the force tangential to the circular motion in the direction of increasing θ_1, and R_1 is the inward radial force, both applied to w_1 by the body itself. Hence

$$w_1 r_1 \ddot\theta_1 + w_1 g \sin\theta_1 = P_1, \quad w_1 r_1 \dot\theta_1^2 + w_1 g \cos\theta_1 = R_1. \quad \ldots(1)$$

The addition can be carried out graphically, by drawing vectors from the point P_1 to represent the mass-accelerations of w_1 *reversed*, and then combining with these the vertically downward vector $w_1 g$. The vector obtained is equilibrated by that given by the P, R forces in their actual directions. The latter vector represents the resultant of the forces applied to the body by the axis, since the resultant of the internal forces is zero.

Thus, in Fig. 97, the symbols $w_1 a$, $w_1 n$ indicate the two reversed vectors so drawn for w_1 at the point P_1. The resultant is the vector V inclined at an angle $\tan^{-1} a/n$ to the line AP_1 produced. Now, since the angular acceleration $\ddot{\theta}$, and the angular speed $\dot{\theta}$, are the same for every part of the oscillating body at any instant, this angle is the same for every radius-vector AP drawn from the axis to the position of an element. Thus the resultant of the reversed mass-accelerations is, at every point, along the forward tangent to the equiangular spiral of equation $re^{\tan^{-1} a/n}$, $(r = AP)$, drawn through the point from a pole at A. This result is due to Sir George Greenhill (*Notes on Dynamics*).

With this is to be combined the uniformly directed vector wg. This can be done by constructing another spiral of the same angle $\phi = \tan^{-1}(a/n)$ from a new pole A' found by the following process. We draw AB inclined to the vertical at the angle θ, which represents the deflection of the pendulum at the instant (so that AB is a line which would be vertical in the equilibrium position of the body), and make $AB = l$, the length of the equivalent simple pendulum, and on the upward vertical through A take a point C, such that $AC = g/\dot{\theta}^2$. Then through B we draw a line at right angles to AB, to meet a horizontal line through A in E, shown in Fig. 97. C is then joined to E and a perpendicular AA' let fall to CE. Then, as can easily be shown, $\angle AEC = \angle A'AC = \phi$, and A' is a new pole from which, by means of an equiangular spiral of the same equation as before, we can represent for every part of the body in the plane of the diagram, the vector compounded of the reversed mass-accelerations wa, wn, and the downward vector wg.

For we have, at P_1, by the equations of motion,

$$w_1 a = w_1 g A P_1 \sin \theta / l = w_1 g A P_1 / AE, \quad w_1 n = w_1 g A P_1 / AC$$

by construction, and therefore $a/n = AC/AE$. But
$$a/n = \tan \phi,$$
and thus the construction gives $\angle AEC = \phi$. The resultant of a, n and g at P_1 is
$$a/\sin \phi = g(AP_1/AE)/(AA'/AE) = gAP_1/AA'. \quad \ldots\ldots(2)$$
Again, for w_2 at A' the resultant vector is evidently vertically upwards, by the spiral, and its amount is
$$w_2 a_2/\sin \phi = w_2 g(AA'/AE)/(AA'/AE) = w_2 g. \quad \ldots\ldots(3)$$
Hence, if with this be compounded the vector $w_2 g$ downwards, the resultant is zero. Since the resultants of a and n for the two points P_1 and A' are by (2) proportional to the lengths of the lines AP_1 and AA' (at A' the resultant is g upwards), and are inclined to one another at the same angle as are these two lines, the result of compounding the downward acceleration g with a and n at P_1 is the same as that of compounding a vector represented by AP_1, with a vector equal and opposite to one represented by AA', and is a vector represented in the same way by $A'P_1$. Thus the resultant at P_1 is inclined to $A'P_1$ at the angle ϕ, and is proportional to $A'P_1$, and so for other points. A' is thus the pole of a new spiral by which the resultants at other points may be found graphically.

It is to be observed that, since a and n vary as the pendulum swings, the positions of E, C, and A' also change. For example, in the middle of a swing $\dot{\theta}^2$ has its maximum value, and AC its least, while, since $a = 0$, ϕ is then zero. Thus E is infinitely far off from A, for the deflection θ is zero, and B is on the vertical through A, and the pole A' is at C. At the end of a swing $\dot{\theta}$ is zero and $\phi = \pi/2$, so that A' is at E, the position of which is that given by the construction when θ is the whole amplitude of deflection.

By resolving the forces P_1, R_1 horizontally and vertically, and summing for the whole body, we find the components in these directions of the whole force exerted on the body in consequence of its internal connections and the action of its support. These are partly purely internal forces, and partly forces transmitted through the body from the axis of support. Since the purely internal forces equilibrate one another, we shall obtain by a summation of the forces described above the equilibrant of the whole system of forces *applied to the body* by the axis of support, and therefore also the reaction of the body on the axis.

Thus, for the total force in the direction of x, taken positive when taken along AE in Fig. 97, applied to the body by the axis, we have

$$\left. \begin{array}{l} X = \Sigma P_1 \cos \theta_1 - \Sigma R_1 \sin \theta_1 = \Sigma w_1 r_1 \ddot{\theta}_1 \cos \theta_1 - \Sigma w_1 r_1 \dot{\theta}^2 \sin \theta \\ = Wh \cos \theta \cdot \ddot{\theta} - Wh \sin \theta \cdot \dot{\theta}^2, \end{array} \right\} (4)$$

and for the total force in the vertically downward direction

$$\left. \begin{array}{l} Y = - \Sigma P_1 \sin \theta_1 - \Sigma R_1 \cos \theta_1 = - Wh \sin \theta \cdot \ddot{\theta} \\ - Wh \cos \theta \cdot \dot{\theta}^2 - Wg, \end{array} \right\} \dots (5)$$

which give

$$\left. \begin{array}{l} X = Wg \dfrac{h^2}{h^2 + k^2} \sin \theta \cos \theta - h \dot{\theta}^2 \sin \theta, \\[2pt] Y = - Wg - Wh \dot{\theta}^2 \cos \theta + Wg \dfrac{h^2}{h^2 + k^2} \sin^2 \theta. \end{array} \right\} \dots (6)$$

Besides the forces here calculated the axis may apply to the pendulum, a couple depending on the manner in which it is attached to the axis. An overhanging pendulum, for example, turning about an axle carried in a bearing before or behind the plane in which the centroid moves, applies a couple to the bearing, and a reaction couple must be applied by the bearing to the axis to keep it horizontal.

212. Theory of Impulsive Forces. Impulse. An impulsive force is a force of very great amount F applied to a body during a very short interval of time τ: a blow from a hammer, the impact of a common-shot on an armour plate, are examples. The smallness of τ makes the change of momentum produced in that time by ordinary forces applied to the body, such as the force of gravity, vanishingly small in comparison with the time integral

$$\int_0^\tau F \, dt$$

of the impulsive force F. The change of momentum

produced by the impulsive force is equal to this integral, which is called the *impulse*; and though, as a rule, the manner of variation of F within the interval τ is unknown, the value of the integral can be calculated, or observed experimentally, in many practical cases. We shall take some examples, and then consider how the equations of motion of a system are to be modified in the case of impulsive forces.

213. Collision of Inelastic Bodies. Theory of Pile-Driver. We consider here collision between *inelastic* bodies. These are bodies which after impact remain in contact, so that two rigid bodies which impinge on one another move afterwards as one rigid body, or, if there be any relative motion, there is no elastic deformation of either to be extinguished by frictional resistance to vibrations. As an example, consider the impact of a wooden mallet on a chisel used to cut wood or soft stone. There is little or no elastic deformation, or "rebound," of the mallet, the momentum which it possessed before impact is distributed between the mallet and the chisel just after impact, and the kinetic energy of the system is then used up in the cut made. If the mallet rebounded from the chisel there would be a greater forward momentum of the chisel just after the blow, and that would be useful in making a slight cut in hard and resistent material like steel and granite, and for this reason it is found advantageous to substitute a steel hammer for the mallet. We shall return to the discussion of this example. Anything like a complete discussion of the impact of elastic bodies involves the theory of vibrations of an elastic solid, and therefore we do not enter on the subject in the present treatise.

Consider now an inelastic "pile"—a beam of wood pointed at the lower end—which is being driven into the ground by successive blows of a hammer, or pile-driver, of weight W let fall from a height h above the head of the pile. The speed of the hammer at the beginning of the impact is $\sqrt{2gh}$, if the friction of the guide and of the air be disregarded. Hence the momentum is then $W\sqrt{2gh}$.

Just after the impact the hammer and pile have the common speed v given by the equation

$$v = \frac{W}{W+w}\sqrt{2gh}. \qquad (1)$$

For the momentum of the pile has been increased from zero to wv, and that of the hammer has been diminished from $W\sqrt{2gh}$ to Wv. Hence we have

$$W(\sqrt{2gh} - v) = wv,$$

which gives the equation just written down. We have in this case

$$\int_0^\tau F dt = wv = \frac{Ww}{W+w}\sqrt{2gh}. \qquad (2)$$

Now let the pile descend a short distance d in consequence of the blow. The energy expended is

$$\tfrac{1}{2}(W+w)v^2 + (W+w)gd.$$

But if R be the space-average of the resistance of the material to the downward progress of the pile, the work done is Rd. Hence, inserting the value of v just found, we get

$$Rd = \frac{1}{2}\frac{W^2}{W+w}2gh + (W+w)gd$$

or
$$\{R - (W+w)g\}d = \frac{W^2}{W+w}gh. \qquad (3)$$

The average upward thrust R' on the hammer during the penetration d is different from R. For that we have in the same way

$$(R' - Wg)d = W\left(\frac{W}{W+w}\right)^2 gh. \qquad (4)$$

The quantity $(W+w)gd$ is small in comparison with the right-hand side of (3), and therefore this quantity in (3), and Wgd in (4), may be omitted without seriously impairing the accuracy of the values of R and R'.

From (3) it follows that the weight which must be applied to the top of the pile, so that it may descend by dead weight alone, is

$$W\left(\frac{W}{W+w}\frac{h}{d} + 1\right).$$

The method of dead weight is adopted for the sinking of caissons, which for several reasons cannot be driven down by blows from a hammer. It is to be observed that if, after a little penetration, a smaller resistance than R were offered to the pile, the dead weight would be too great and the pile would go down "with a run."

The discussion here given for a pile is applicable to the driving of nails by a hammer, though here the action between the nail and the hammer is elastic. A wooden hammer does not drive nails well, even if it is made of very hard wood, for the head of the nail deforms the hammer face, and energy is lost thereby, which in the case of the steel hammer is utilised in causing the nail to penetrate the wood.

214. Energy-Change in Inelastic Impact. Advantage of Heavy or Light Hammer. The error, which is not uncommon, of equating the kinetic energy of the hammer just before impact to the work done in causing the pile or nail to penetrate the ground or wood is to be avoided. The first action is one of redistribution of momentum, and this has been effected before penetration to any sensible distance has taken place, so that the resistance of the material has not been sensibly brought into play.

In the impact itself a loss of kinetic energy of amount

$$E = Wgh - \frac{W^2}{W+w}gh = \frac{Ww}{W+w}gh \quad \ldots\ldots\ldots\ldots(1)$$

takes place, and it is noteworthy that for a hammer and pile or nail, of given weights, it is always the same fraction of the whole kinetic energy just before impact. This is expended in deforming the head of the pile and, to a much less extent, the face of the hammer. It is important to observe that the energy lost bears to the whole kinetic energy available the ratio $w/(W+w)$, which is nearly equal to unity, or to zero, according as W is small or great in comparison with w. Thus the hammer should have a weight W, great in comparison with that of the pile, or nail, for then very nearly the whole available kinetic energy will be utilised in causing the penetration desired. On the other hand, if w be great in comparison with W, or of the same order of magnitude, nearly the whole or a large part of the kinetic energy available will be expended in deforming the head of the body struck.

Hence if the object is to indent, or fashion the surface of a body according to any pattern, by hammer blows, the hammer should have mass W *small* in comparison with the mass w of the body struck, as then the available kinetic energy is expended in producing the result required. Thus a blacksmith uses a small hammer to give detail of form to the surface of a piece of iron, and employs a sledge hammer to drive a steel chisel through the material, softened by heat, when he cuts a thick bar in two, and also a sledge hammer when a bar is to have its cross-section much reduced or altered.

215. Duration of Impact. How far a Pile should be Driven. From (1), § 214, and (4), § 213, we can obtain the distance, a say, by which the pile is shortened in consequence of the blow. For the energy $Wwgh/(W+w)$ lost from the hammer in the impact must be equal to the work $R'a$ done by the force R' exerted by the hammer on the pile. Hence

$$a = \frac{Wwgh}{(W+w)R'} = \frac{w(W+w)}{W^2} d, \quad \ldots\ldots\ldots\ldots\ldots(1)$$

by the approximate value of R' from (4), § 213. From this result we see that, according as W is great or small in comparison with w, the distance a is small or great in comparison with d.

The times t_1, t_2, τ of traversing the spaces h, d, a can be compared. First we have $t_1 = \sqrt{2h/g}$. Again, the time-average of the speed during the interval t_2 is

$\tfrac{1}{2}v = \tfrac{1}{2}\sqrt{2gh}\, W/(W+w)$, so that $t_2 = 2d(W+w)/W\sqrt{2gh}$.

But $t_1 = 2h/\sqrt{2gh}$, and therefore

$$\frac{t_2}{t_1} = \frac{W+w}{W} \frac{d}{h}. \quad \ldots\ldots\ldots\ldots\ldots\ldots\ldots(2)$$

The momentum lost in time τ by the hammer is

$$\sqrt{2gh}\, Ww/(W+w),$$

and the action R' of the pile on the hammer is
$$W\{W/(W+w)\}^2 gh/d.$$
But $\qquad R'\tau = \sqrt{2gh}\,Ww/(W+w),$
and therefore
$$\tau = \sqrt{\frac{2}{gh}}\,\frac{w(W+w)}{W^2}\,d = \sqrt{\frac{2}{gh}}\,a = \frac{a}{h}t_1. \quad\ldots\ldots\ldots(3)$$

Thus, if a is very small in comparison with h, that is, if only a slight deformation of the pile is produced, the time of redistribution of the momentum is very short, and the impulsive force R' (which is approximately equal to the resistance R to penetration, if W/w be great) is very large—enough to overcome through a short distance the resistance of the substance. This explains the advantage of a hammer in cutting metal or marble or granite, though it is to be remembered that the impact of a steel hammer on a steel chisel is not a case of the impact of inelastic bodies. In the case of marble or granite, which are brittle, the impulsive wedge-action may start a crack in the material, which extends so that a large piece is splintered off.

The resistance of ground to penetration by a pile frequently increases as the pile is driven deeper; there is, of course, additional resistance due to friction, if the ground presses against the sides of the pile. If L be the load, in tons or pounds, according to the unit adopted for W and w to be carried, the driving may be stopped when the value of R has risen above Lg, that is, when
$$L\frac{d}{h} < \frac{W^2}{W+w}.$$

The chain used to raise the hammer of the pile-driver applies a lifting force equal to $W(g+\alpha)+F$, where α is the upward acceleration and F is the friction of the slide. At starting on its upward journey the weight W has a considerable acceleration, but this falls off and the weight is finally brought to rest, or nearly so, at the top of the slide by the action of F.

216. Equations of Motion of System under Impulses. We now consider a system of particles acted on by impulsive forces. Let the components of one of a set of impulses applied to the system be P, Q, R, in the directions of the axes, and let the components of velocity of a particle of mass m at the point x, y, z be changed from $\dot{x}_0, \dot{y}_0, \dot{z}_0$ to $\dot{x}, \dot{y}, \dot{z}$ in the very short time-interval τ. If we insert the impulsive forces in the equations of §§ 60, 75, or regard the forces there specified as impulsive, and integrate over the duration τ of the impulse, we get

$$\Sigma\{m(\dot{x}-\dot{x}_0)\} = \Sigma P, \quad \Sigma\{m(\dot{y}-\dot{y}_0)\} = \Sigma Q, \\ \Sigma\{m(\dot{z}-\dot{z}_0)\} = \Sigma R. \quad \ldots\ldots(1)$$

Any ordinary forces, coexisting with the impulsive forces, have zero integrals over the vanishingly small time τ.

Similarly, we get for the equations of moments,

$$\Sigma[m\{(\dot{z}-\dot{z}_0)y-(\dot{y}-\dot{y}_0)z\}] = \Sigma(Ry-Qz), \\ \Sigma[m\{(\dot{x}-\dot{x}_0)z-(\dot{z}-\dot{z}_0)x\}] = \Sigma(Pz-Rx), \\ \Sigma[m\{(\dot{y}-\dot{y}_0)x-(\dot{x}-\dot{x}_0)y\}] = \Sigma(Qx-Py), \quad \ldots(2)$$

where the summations on the left are to be taken over all the particles of the system, and on the right over all the impulses. The impulses P, Q, R are supposed to be applied from without at certain points to the system. But, in general, the particles are connected by internal links, or fulfil certain conditions of configuration, and, therefore, changes of velocity in general occur throughout the system.

The last three equations break up into two sets, one with reference to parallel axes through the centroid, for which the equations are precisely (2), on the understanding that the origin is now at the centroid, and the set

$$M(\dot{\zeta}\eta - \dot{\eta}\zeta) = \eta\Sigma R - \zeta\Sigma Q, \quad M(\dot{\xi}\zeta - \dot{\zeta}\xi) = \zeta\Sigma P - \xi\Sigma R, \\ M(\dot{\eta}\xi - \dot{\xi}\eta) = \xi\Sigma Q - \eta\Sigma P, \quad (3)$$

where ξ, η, ζ are the coordinates of the centroid with reference to the given axes, and M is the whole mass Σm of the system.

By the properties of the centroid we can write (1) in the form,

$$M(\dot{\xi}-\dot{\xi}_0) = \Sigma P, \quad M(\dot{\eta}-\dot{\eta}_0) = \Sigma Q, \quad M(\dot{\zeta}-\dot{\zeta}_0) = \Sigma R. \quad \ldots(4).$$

For a rigid body the equations of moments become
$$Mk_x^2(\dot\phi - \dot\phi_0) = \Sigma S_x r_x, \quad Mk_y^2(\dot\chi - \dot\chi_0) = \Sigma S_y r_y,$$
$$Mk_z^2(\dot\psi - \dot\psi_0) = \Sigma S_z r_z, \quad\quad\quad\quad\quad\quad\quad\quad\quad \ldots\ldots(5)$$

where ϕ, χ, ψ are the angles which perpendiculars let fall from any point, xyz, to the axes of x, y, z, make with the axes of y, z, x respectively. The lengths of these perpendiculars are r_x, y_y, r_z, and

$$(S_x, S_y, S_z) = \{(R\cos\phi - Q\sin\phi)r_x,$$
$$(P\cos\chi - R\sin\chi)r_y, \quad \ldots\ldots(6)$$
$$(Q\cos\psi - P\sin\psi)r_z\}.$$

The values of ϕ, χ, ψ are different for perpendiculars drawn from different points, but if the body be rigid, $\dot\phi$, $\dot\chi$, $\dot\psi$ must be the same for all. The perpendiculars may therefore be supposed drawn from the centroid to the given axes.

217. Impulse applied to Compound Pendulum. Consider now a compound pendulum hanging vertically on its axle, or on knife-edges, and let it receive a horizontal impulse in the vertical plane through the centroid at right angles to the axis of turning. We can prove that, if the line of application of the impulse pass through the centre of oscillation, no shock will be applied to the axle or bearing by which the body is supported. We suppose that the duration τ of the impulse is so short that whatever change of motion of a body is produced by an impulse applied to it is brought about before the body has moved through any perceptible distance, or turned through any sensible angle.

Now the change of motion of the centroid of a body, whether rigid or not, effected in any time, is the same (§ 60) as it would have been if all the forces on the body had been applied to a free particle of mass equal to the mass of the body; and so if the horizontal component of the reacting impulse at the axis be I' (measured as before by the time integral of an impulsive force), and v be the change of speed of the centroid in the direction of the impulse, we have
$$Wv = I - I'. \quad\quad\quad\quad\ldots\ldots(1)$$

§§ 216, 217, 218] THEORY OF IMPULSIVE MOTION.

Again, the moment of the impulse about the axis must be equal to the angular momentum generated about the axis, so that if a be the distance of the line of application of I from the axis,
$$Ia = Wvh + Wk^2 \frac{v}{h},$$
since v/h is the angular speed generated. Thus we have
$$Ia = Wv\frac{h^2+k^2}{h} = Wvl = (I - I')l, \quad \ldots\ldots\ldots\ldots (2)$$
by (1). Thus we get
$$I' = I\left(1 - \frac{a}{l}\right), \quad \ldots\ldots\ldots\ldots\ldots\ldots (3)$$
and I' is positive or negative according as a is $<$ or $>l$. Thus if $a = l$, $I' = 0$, and there is no shock to the axis.

There is no vertical component of *impulse* called into play. The production of angular speed v/h about the axis calls into play a *force* towards the axis, of amount $Whv^2/h^2 = Wv^2/h$, on the body, and a reaction of the same amount on the support; but this being a force of finite amount, depending as it does on v/h, cannot in any very short time produce a sensible change of momentum.

218. Impulse applied to Rod on Smooth Table. Impulse on Pivot. Consider a rod of length $2h$ resting on a horizontal table. If the rod be of uniform weight per unit length and friction be absent, it will, if struck at one end A by an impulse along the table at right angles to the length of the rod, begin to turn about a point B, at a distance of $\frac{4}{3}h$ from A. B is the centre of oscillation of the rod as a compound pendulum hung from the point A, and if the rod is struck by an impulse at C, directed as before, it will begin to turn about A. In neither case will there be any impulse or shock applied to an axle at the point of turning. The proof is similar to that given above for the compound pendulum.

Let I be the impulse and v the speed of the centroid produced. Then if W be the weight of the rod, we have
$$Wv = I. \quad \ldots\ldots\ldots\ldots\ldots\ldots\ldots\ldots (1)$$
If the rod turn about a point A at distance x from the end

struck, the angular speed is $v/(x-h)$. Hence, taking moments about the point A, we get

$$Ix = Wv(x-h) + W\frac{h^2}{3}\frac{v}{x-h}, \quad \ldots\ldots\ldots\ldots(2)$$

or, substituting the value Wv of I on the left, and rejecting the common factor Wv,

$$xh = \tfrac{4}{3}h^2. \quad \ldots\ldots\ldots\ldots\ldots\ldots\ldots\ldots\ldots(3)$$

Thus we obtain $x = \tfrac{4}{3}h$, and the statement made above as to the point of turning is verified. Moreover, this result has been obtained on the supposition that no impulse, except that at the end, has been applied to the rod, and we infer that if there had been a pivot at the point B, it would have experienced no shock.

But let a pivot be provided at a distance x_1 from the end, so that the rod is constrained to turn about it, and let the impulse I be applied at the end as before. If I' be the impulse now applied to the rod by the pivot, in the direction parallel to that of I, we have

$$Wv = I + I' \quad \ldots\ldots\ldots\ldots\ldots\ldots(4)$$

and $$Ix_1 = Wv(x_1 - h) + W\frac{h^2}{3}\frac{v}{x_1 - h}. \quad \ldots\ldots\ldots\ldots(5)$$

These equations, since x_1 is now fixed, enable us to determine I' and v. We see first that if $x_1 = h$, v must be zero; this is obvious without calculation, for then the centroid is fixed and its speed v is zero. It will be seen that the equation reduces to

$$I' = Wv\frac{3hx_1 - 4h^2}{3x_1(x_1 - h)}, \quad \ldots\ldots\ldots\ldots\ldots(6)$$

which vanishes when $x_1 = \tfrac{4}{3}h$. For v we get the equation

$$Wv = \frac{3x_1(x_1 - h)}{3x_1^2 - 6hx_1 + 4h^2}I. \quad \ldots\ldots\ldots\ldots(7)$$

Ex. 1. Verify that when $x_1 = \tfrac{4}{3}h$ the kinetic energy is a minimum for given speed u of the end struck.

The angular speed is u/x_1, and the moment of inertia about the pivot is $W\{\tfrac{1}{3}h^2 + (x_1 - h)^2\}$. Hence the kinetic energy is

$$\tfrac{1}{2}W\{\tfrac{1}{3}h^2 + (x_1 - h)^2\}u^2/x_1^2,$$

and this, by the ordinary criterion, is a minimum when $x_1 = \tfrac{4}{3}h$.

Ex. 2. Show that if the impulse I applied to the end of the rod be given, the kinetic energy is a maximum when $x_1 = \frac{4}{3}h$.

It will be observed that in this case u is not given but depends on the value of I. But the kinetic energy is still $\frac{1}{2}Wu^2\{\frac{1}{3}h^2+(x_1-h)^2\}/x_1^2$, and since $u = x_1 v/(x_1-h)$, we have $Wu^2 = Wv^2 x_1^2/(x_1-h)^2$. Thus, by (7), we get for the value of the kinetic energy,

$$\frac{1}{2}\left\{\frac{x_1^2}{\frac{1}{3}h^2+(x_1-h)^2}\right\}^2\frac{I^2}{W}.$$

We have seen that the reciprocal of the fraction in the brackets is a minimum when $x_1 = \frac{4}{3}h$, hence the fraction is a maximum for that value of x_1. But I^2/W is given, and so the kinetic energy is a maximum.

These examples illustrate by particular cases a general theorem of maximum and minimum energy of a system set in motion by impulses, which we shall explain later.

Ex. 3. An impulse I is applied at the distance $x = \frac{4}{3}h$ from one end of the rod; prove that turning will begin about that end. We have again for the motion of the centroid $I = Wv$, and if the rod begins to turn about a point in itself, or in line with it on the table, at distance x from the point struck, we have, taking moments about that point, $Ix = Wv(x-\frac{1}{3}h) + W\frac{1}{3}h^2v/(x-\frac{1}{3}h)$. Substituting Wv for I, we obtain $x(x-\frac{1}{3}h) = (x-\frac{1}{3}h)^2 + \frac{1}{3}h^2$, or $\frac{1}{3}h(x-\frac{1}{3}h) = \frac{1}{3}h^2$, that is $x = \frac{4}{3}h$. The rod therefore begins to turn about the farther extremity from the point struck.

The student may easily experiment on this subject in any smith's shop or engineering laboratory. Let him take a uniform bar of iron, measure off two-thirds of its length from one end, and mark the point. Then, gripping it by the farther extremity from the mark, let him strike the bar forcibly against the edge of an anvil, at a point a little beyond the mark to allow for his grip of the bar. He will feel little or no jar from the blow. But if the point of the bar which strikes the anvil be much farther off, or much nearer the hand, the jar will be very unpleasant.

Again, if the bar is held at a distance of two-thirds of its length from one end, and is then made to strike the anvil, there will be a very perceptible jar, unless the point of collision is the farther extremity of the bar.

Ex. 4. Show that a uniform sphere, oscillating about a point on its surface under gravity, has a period equal to that of a simple pendulum of length equal to ·7 of the diameter of the sphere.

Hence explain why the cushion of a billiard table is at a height above the table equal to ·7 of the diameter of a billiard ball.

219. Double Compound Pendulum. We take next the problem of two compound pendulums, one hinged to the other, like a bell and its clapper. To deal with this we take axes as in the last problem, and denote by x, y the coordinates of the point of attachment of the second pendulum to the first (so that $x^2 + y^2 = l^2$, where l is the distance of the hinge from the fixed point O), by hx/l, hy/l the coordinates of the centroid of the first pendulum (distant h from O) and by ξ, η the coordinates of the centroid of the second pendulum. We suppose that the hinge is on the line from O through the first centroid. We have $x = l \sin \theta$, $y = l \cos \theta$, $hx/l = h \sin \theta$, $hy/l = h \cos \theta$, $\xi = l \sin \theta + a \sin \phi$, $\eta = l \cos \theta + a \cos \phi$, where θ, ϕ are the angles which the line in each pendulum through the centroid and the hinge makes with the vertical, and a is the distance of the centroid of the second pendulum from the hinge. These lines are supposed to remain in one plane—the plane of vibration.

We have then

$$\begin{aligned} \frac{h}{l}\dot{x} &= h\cos\theta\,.\,\dot{\theta}, \quad \frac{h}{l}\dot{y} = -h\sin\theta\,.\,\dot{\theta}, \\ \dot{\xi} &= l\cos\theta\,.\,\dot{\theta} + a\cos\phi\,.\,\dot{\phi}, \quad \dot{\eta} = -l\sin\theta\,.\,\dot{\theta} - a\sin\phi\,.\,\dot{\phi}, \\ \frac{h}{l}\ddot{x} &= -h\sin\theta\,.\,\dot{\theta}^2 + h\cos\theta\,.\,\ddot{\theta}, \quad \frac{h}{l}\ddot{y} = -h\cos\theta\,.\,\dot{\theta}^2 - h\sin\theta\,.\,\ddot{\theta}, \\ \ddot{\xi} &= -l\sin\theta\,.\,\dot{\theta}^2 - a\sin\phi\,.\,\dot{\phi}^2 + l\cos\theta\,.\,\ddot{\theta} + a\cos\phi\,.\,\ddot{\phi}, \\ \ddot{\eta} &= -l\cos\theta\,.\,\dot{\theta}^2 - a\cos\phi\,.\,\dot{\phi}^2 - l\sin\theta\,.\,\ddot{\theta} - a\sin\phi\,.\,\ddot{\phi}. \end{aligned} \quad \ldots(1)$$

The angular momentum of the first pendulum about O is clearly $W_1(h^2 + k_1^2)\dot{\theta}$, if W_1 be the mass and k_1 the radius of gyration of the pendulum about the centroid in the plane of motion. The angular momentum of the second pendulum about O is, if k_2 be the radius of gyration about the centroid as before,

$$W_2(\dot{\xi}\eta - \dot{\eta}\xi) + W_2 k_2^2 \dot{\phi} = W_2\{l\cos\theta\,.\,\dot{\theta} + a\cos\phi\,.\,\dot{\phi}\}(l\cos\theta + a\cos\phi) \\ + (l\sin\theta\,.\,\dot{\theta} + a\sin\phi\,.\,\dot{\phi})(l\sin\theta + a\sin\phi) + k_2^2\dot{\phi}\},$$

that is

$$W_2(\dot{\xi}\eta - \dot{\eta}\xi) + W_2 k_2^2 \dot{\phi} = W_2\{l^2\dot{\theta} + (a^2 + k_2^2)\dot{\phi} + al\cos(\phi - \theta)(\dot{\theta} + \dot{\phi})\}. \quad (2)$$

The total angular momentum of the system about O is thus

$$W_1(h^2 + k_1^2)\dot{\theta} + W_2\{l^2\dot{\theta} + (a^2 + k_2^2)\dot{\phi} + al\cos(\phi - \theta)(\dot{\theta} + \dot{\phi})\}.$$

The time-rate of change of this equated to the total moment of the forces of gravity gives an equation of motion

$$\left.\begin{aligned} W_1(h^2 + k_1^2)\ddot{\theta} + W_2\{l^2\ddot{\theta} + (a^2 + k_2^2)\ddot{\phi} + al\cos(\phi - \theta)(\ddot{\theta} + \ddot{\phi}) \\ - al\sin(\phi - \theta)(\dot{\phi}^2 - \dot{\theta}^2) = -\{W_1 gh\sin\theta + W_2 g(l\sin\theta + a\sin\phi)\}. \end{aligned}\right\} \quad (3)$$

We obtain another equation of motion by calculating the angular momentum of the second pendulum about the *fixed point of space* coinciding with the point of attachment to the first at any instant, and equating the time-rate of change of that to the moment $W_2 ga \sin \phi$

§ 219] COMPOUND PENDULUM: EXAMPLES.   407

about that position. The angular momentum is $W_2\{\dot{\xi}(\eta-y)-\dot{\eta}(\xi-x)\}$, and in taking the time-rate of change of this, we must regard x, y as constant. We thus obtain, as the reader may verify,

$$W_2\{(a^2+k_2^2)\ddot{\phi}+al\cos(\phi-\theta)\ddot{\theta}+al\sin(\phi-\theta)\dot{\theta}^2\} = -W_2 ga\sin\phi. \quad (4)$$

Subtracting this from (3), we get

$$\left.\begin{array}{r}W_1(h^2+k_1^2)\ddot{\theta}+W_2\{l^2\ddot{\theta}+al\cos(\phi-\theta)\ddot{\phi}-al\sin(\phi-\theta)\dot{\phi}^2\}\\ =-(W_1h+W_2l)g\sin\theta.\end{array}\right\} \quad\ldots\ldots(5)$$

We may take (4) and (5) as the equations of motion.

A chain of n pendulums vibrating about parallel axes, the first pendulum attached to a fixed point, the second pivoted on the first, the third on the second, and so on, can be dealt with in the same way. The rate of change of angular momentum of the nth, about the instantaneous position of its pivot, is first found and equated to the moment of the forces of gravity on the nth pendulum about that pivot, which gives one equation: then the nth and $(n-1)^{th}$ are taken together as one system turning about the pivot on the $(n-2)^{th}$, and an equation of motion found as before; and so on until the n pendulums are taken together, and n equations in all are obtained.

Ex. 1. A plane lamina rests on a horizontal table between which and the lamina there is no friction. The lamina is pivoted to one end of a horizontal rod which turns about a vertical axis at its other end. If the rotation of the rod be uniform, show that the motion of the lamina relatively to the rod is that of a simple pendulum of length equal to $(a^2+k_2^2)g/al\dot{\theta}^2$, where a is the distance of the centroid of the lamina from its pivot, k_2 the radius of gyration of the lamina about an axis at right angles to its plane through the centroid, l the length of the rod, and $\dot{\theta}$ its uniform angular speed.

Ex. 2. An inextensible thread of negligible mass and length a has one end attached to a point on the rim of a vertical wheel of mass M, radius l, and radius of gyration k about its axis, and carries at the other end a particle of mass m. Find the equations which determine the small oscillations of the system about the position of stable equilibrium. Prove that the two principal periods are $2\pi/n_1$, $2\pi/n_2$, where n_1, n_2 are the real positive roots of the equation

$$Mk^2an^4-(Mk^2+mal+ml^2)gn^2+mlg^2=0.$$

Ex. 3. Two equal uniform rods AB, CD have each mass m and length $2a$. The ends A, C and B, D are connected by threads of negligible mass and length l, and the system is hung in a vertical plane on a horizontal axis passing through the centroid of the rod AB. If the latter rod be set in rotation about the axis, it is required to find the subsequent motion.

The rod AB revolves with uniform speed, while the centroid of CD moves as would a simple pendulum of length l.

220. Small Vibrations of Double Pendulum. If now in the double pendulum we suppose θ and ϕ to be so small that we may write θ, ϕ for $\sin\theta$, $\sin\phi$, 1 for $\cos(\phi-\psi)$, and neglect terms in $\dot\theta^2$, $\dot\phi^2$, we obtain (§ 219)

$$\left.\begin{array}{l}al\ddot\theta+(a^2+k_2^2)\ddot\phi+ag\phi=0,\\ \left(h^2+k_1^2+\dfrac{W_2}{W_1}l^2\right)\ddot\theta+\dfrac{W_2}{W_1}al\ddot\phi+\left(h+\dfrac{W_2}{W_1}l\right)g\theta=0.\end{array}\right\}\ \ldots\ldots(1)$$

Writing b, d, e for the coefficients in the first of (1), and c, ρb, f for those in the second, as they stand in each case, we get

$$\left.\begin{array}{l}b\ddot\theta+d\ddot\phi+e\phi=0,\\ c\ddot\theta+\rho b\ddot\phi+f\theta=0,\end{array}\right\}\ \ldots\ldots\ldots\ldots\ldots\ldots\ldots\ldots(2)$$

where $\rho=W_2/W_1$. If now we put $\theta=A\sin(nt+\alpha)$, $\phi=B\sin(nt+\alpha)$, and substitute in these last equations, we obtain

$$\left.\begin{array}{l}bAn^2+dBn^2-eB=0,\\ cAn^2+\rho bBn^2-fA=0,\end{array}\right\}\ \ldots\ldots\ldots\ldots\ldots\ldots\ldots(3)$$

which by elimination of A and B give

$$(cd-\rho b^2)n^4-(ce+fd)n^2+ef=0,\ \ldots\ldots\ldots\ldots\ldots(4)$$

a quadratic equation for n^2 which, since $cd>\rho b^2$, has two positive roots. Thus, as before, we get two modes of vibration of different frequencies, one, the mode of greater period $2\pi/n_1$, in which both pendulums are deflected at the same instant in the same direction from the vertical, the other, of smaller period $2\pi/n_2$, in which they are deflected in opposite directions.

Solving (4), we get

$$\left.\begin{array}{l}n_1^2=\dfrac{1}{2(cd-\rho b^2)}\{ce+fd-\sqrt{(ce-fd)^2+4\rho ef b^2}\},\\ n_2^2=\dfrac{1}{2(cd-\rho b^2)}\{ce+fd+\sqrt{(ce-fd)^2+4\rho ef b^2}\},\end{array}\right\}\ \ldots\ldots(5)$$

which, since $cd>\rho b^2$, proves that n_1^2 and n_2^2 are real and positive. The complete solutions of the differential equations (2) are thus

$$\left.\begin{array}{l}\theta=A_1\sin(n_1t+\alpha_1)+A_2\sin(n_2t+\alpha_2),\\ \phi=B_1\sin(n_1t+\alpha_1)+B_2\sin(n_2t+\alpha_2).\end{array}\right\}\ \ldots\ldots\ldots\ldots(6)$$

The constants A, B for each frequency are connected by a fixed relation, namely, $B_1=\kappa_1 A_1$, $B_2=\kappa_2 A_2$. Multiplying the first of (3) by ρb and the second by d, and subtracting, we obtain the ratio $B/A=\{fd-(cd-\rho b^2)n^2\}/b\rho e$, so that

$$\left.\begin{array}{l}B_1=\dfrac{fd-(cd-\rho b^2)n_1^2}{b\rho e}A_1=\kappa_1 A_1,\\ B_2=\dfrac{fd-(cd-\rho b^2)n_2^2}{b\rho e}A_2=\kappa_2 A_2.\end{array}\right\}\ \ldots\ldots\ldots\ldots\ldots(7)$$

Thus
$$\left[\begin{array}{c}\kappa_1\\\kappa_2\end{array}\right] = \frac{1}{2b\rho e}\{-(ce-fd) \pm \sqrt{(ce-fd)^2+4b^2\rho ef}\}.\quad\ldots\ldots\ldots\ldots(8)$$

Thus κ_1 is essentially positive and κ_2 essentially negative. Multiplying these values together, we obtain

$$\kappa_1\kappa_2 = -\frac{f}{e\rho}.\quad\ldots\ldots\ldots\ldots\ldots\ldots\ldots\ldots(9)$$

It is important to notice that if $ce=fd$, the values of κ_1 and κ_2 are equal in numerical value but have opposite signs, and further that, when the relation $ce=fd$ is not fulfilled, the imposition of the value 1 on either of the coefficients κ_1, κ_2 makes the other have the value $-f/e\rho$. [See also Föppl, *Technische Mechanik*, Bd. VI.]

221. Double Compound Pendulum under Special Conditions. Bell and Clapper. We shall now work out some examples of what precedes.

Ex. 1. Find the values of the constants of integration and the complete solution for small motions, when the initial values are $\theta_0, \phi_0, \dot\theta_0, \dot\phi_0$.

We obtain easily from equations (6) of § 220,

$$\theta_0 = A_1\sin\alpha_1 + A_2\sin\alpha_2, \quad \phi_0 = \kappa_1 A_1\sin\alpha_1 + \kappa_2 A_2\sin\alpha_2,$$
$$\dot\theta_0 = n_1 A_1\cos\alpha_1 + n_2 A_2\cos\alpha_2, \quad \dot\phi_0 = n_1\kappa_1 A_1\cos\alpha_1 + n_2\kappa_2 A_2\cos\alpha_2,$$

from which to find $A_1\sin\alpha_1, A_2\sin\alpha_2, A_1\cos\alpha_1, \ldots$. Thus we have

$$\theta = \frac{1}{\kappa_2-\kappa_1}\left\{-\frac{\dot\phi_0-\kappa_2\dot\theta_0}{n_1}\sin n_1 t + \frac{\dot\phi_0-\kappa_1\dot\theta_0}{n_2}\sin n_2 t \right. \\ \left. -(\phi_0-\kappa_2\theta_0)\cos n_1 t + (\phi_0-\kappa_1\theta_0)\cos n_2 t\right\},\quad(1)$$

with for ϕ the same expression, modified by multiplying the first and third terms by κ_1, and the second and fourth by κ_2. Hence

$$\phi-\theta = \frac{1}{\kappa_2-\kappa_1}\left[-(\kappa_1-1)\left\{\frac{\dot\phi_0-\kappa_2\dot\theta_0}{n_1}\sin n_1 t + (\phi_0-\kappa_2\theta_0)\cos n_1 t\right\}\right. \\ \left. +(\kappa_2-1)\left\{\frac{\dot\phi_0-\kappa_1\dot\theta_0}{n_2}\sin n_2 t + (\phi_0-\kappa_1\theta_0)\cos n_2 t\right\}\right].\quad(2)$$

If we impose the condition that $\theta_0=\phi_0=0$, we get

$$\theta = \frac{1}{\kappa_2-\kappa_1}\left\{-\frac{\dot\phi_0-\kappa_2\dot\theta_0}{n_1}\sin n_1 t + \frac{\dot\phi_0-\kappa_1\dot\theta_0}{n_2}\sin n_2 t\right\},$$

with the same expression for ϕ, modified by multiplying the first term by κ_1 and the second by κ_2. Also in this case,

$$\phi-\theta = \frac{1}{\kappa_2-\kappa_1}\left\{-(\kappa_1-1)\frac{\dot\phi_0-\kappa_2\dot\theta_0}{n_1}\sin n_1 t + (\kappa_2-1)\frac{\dot\phi_0-\kappa_1\dot\theta_0}{n_2}\sin n_2 t\right\}.\quad(3)$$

From these last results we draw at once the conclusion that if both pendulums be started with the same angular speed $\dot{\theta}_0 = \dot{\phi}_0$, $\phi - \theta$ will remain zero, if $\kappa_1 = 1$. The coefficient κ_2 will then have the value $-f/e\rho$ (see (9) § 220). These are therefore the conditions that the two pendulums should continue to vibrate as one, if started together as one pendulum.

Such an arrangement of a bell and its clapper would, if started as here supposed, fail to give any relative motion of the parts, and the bell would not ring. We shall, however, consider the failure of a bell more fully presently.

If in (2) we assume that $\kappa_1 = 1$, $\theta_0 = 0$, but do not suppose that ϕ_0 is zero, we get

$$\phi - \theta = \frac{\dot{\phi}_0 - \dot{\theta}_0}{n_2} \sin n_2 t + \phi_0 \cos n_2 t, \quad\quad\quad\quad\quad (4)$$

of which the maximum value is $\sqrt{(\dot{\phi}_0 - \dot{\theta}_0)^2 + n_2^2 \phi_0^2}/n_2$. Thus, if the arrangement is such that $\kappa_1 = 1$, then, although the second pendulum may have an initial deflection ϕ_0, the relative deflection cannot exceed the maximum value here stated, which it will be seen approximates to ϕ_0 if n_2 be great, that is, if the period of the second pendulum vibrating alone is short. Thus the relative deflection remains very nearly ϕ_0, and the two pendulums still practically vibrate as one. This result still holds when $\dot{\phi}_0 = 0$.

Ex. 2. Prove that if the condition $ce = fd$ is fulfilled, the values of κ_1, κ_2 are $\sqrt{f/\rho e}$, $-\sqrt{f/\rho e}$, and of n_1, n_2 are $\sqrt{fd - \sqrt{\rho e f b^2}}/\sqrt{cd - \rho b^2}$, $\sqrt{fd + \sqrt{\rho e f b^2}}/\sqrt{cd - \rho b^2}$, respectively. Find the finite equations of motion for this case.

Ex. 3. If $\rho \ (= W_2/W_1)$ be small, prove that to a first approximation $n_1 = \sqrt{f/c}$, $n_2 = \sqrt{e/d}$, and to a second approximation

$$n_1 = \sqrt{\{fd(ce - fd) - \rho e f b^2\}/(ce - fd)(cd - \rho b^2)},$$
$$n_2 = \sqrt{\{ce(ce - fd) + \rho e f b^2\}/(ce - fd)(cd - \rho b^2)}.$$

Ex. 4. A rod of length $2a$ is suspended by a string of length l attached at one end of the rod, from a fixed point O.

Show that if the inclinations of the string and the rod to the vertical at time t be θ and ϕ, the equations of motion are

$$l\ddot{\theta} + a\cos(\phi - \theta)\ddot{\phi} - a\sin(\phi - \theta)\dot{\phi}^2 + g\sin\theta = 0,$$
$$\tfrac{4}{3}a\ddot{\phi} + l\cos(\phi - \theta)\ddot{\theta} + l\sin(\phi - \theta)\dot{\theta}^2 + g\sin\phi = 0.$$

Hence find the equations for small motions, and show that the equation of frequencies is

$$(an^2 - 3g)(ln^2 - 4g) - 9g^2 = 0.$$

Show that this equation has four real roots, and write down the complete integral equations.

222. Driving and Driven Pendulums. Forced Vibrations.

The corresponding values of κ_1, κ_2 in the Ex. 3 are approximately $\kappa_1 = bf/(ce-fd)$, $\kappa_2 = -(ce-fd)/b\rho e$. The value $\sqrt{f/c}$ of n_1 is very nearly $\sqrt{hg/(h^2+k_1^2)}$, that is, $\sqrt{g/L}$, where L is the length of the equivalent simple pendulum for the first pendulum oscillating alone, and $\sqrt{e/d}$ is the same thing for the second pendulum. Thus the two fundamental periods of the system are simply those of the two pendulums, each hung up alone.

If, then, $\rho = W_2/W_1$ be small, and the double pendulum be started from rest with $\theta_0 = \phi_0 = 0$, and $\dot{\phi}_0 = 0$, by imparting an initial angular speed $\dot{\theta}_0$ to the first pendulum, we have, by (1) above and the approximate values of κ_1, κ_2,

$$\theta = \sqrt{\frac{c}{f}}\,\dot{\theta}_0 \sin\sqrt{\frac{f}{c}}\,t + \frac{b^2\rho ef\dot{\theta}_0}{(ce-fd)^2}\,\sqrt{\frac{d}{e}} \sin\sqrt{\frac{e}{d}}\,t. \quad \ldots\ldots\ldots\ldots(1)$$

Since ρ is here supposed small, and it is assumed that there is no approach to fulfilment of the condition $ce-fd=0$, the second term makes only a small addition to the first term, which is the main value of θ; but so far as the second term goes it varies in the period $2\pi\sqrt{d/e}$.

The value of ϕ is obtained from that of θ by multiplying the first term by κ_1 and the second by κ_2, that is,

$$\phi = \frac{bf\dot{\theta}_0}{ce-fd}\sqrt{\frac{c}{f}}\sin\sqrt{\frac{f}{c}}\,t - \frac{bf\dot{\theta}_0}{ce-fd}\sqrt{\frac{d}{e}}\sin\sqrt{\frac{e}{d}}\,t. \quad \ldots\ldots\ldots\ldots(2)$$

Of course, if the effect on the period of oscillation is required with exactness, the more closely approximate values of n_1, n_2 must be used.

If the second pendulum has a very short equivalent simple pendulum, $\sqrt{c/f}$ may be so great in comparison with $\sqrt{d/e}$, that the main part of ϕ is represented by the first term, and this varies in the period of the first pendulum. This, of course, is what we should anticipate without calculation; the massive upper pendulum acts as driver, and the small attached pendulum is driven in the period of the other, and acquires a steady amplitude of vibration of considerable amount, while the vibration of the driving pendulum is but little affected. The term, however, in the value of ϕ, which has the period of the second pendulum, is great in comparison with the corresponding term in the value of θ.

It is to be observed that here ϕ has for its main term the same sign as θ, or the opposite sign, according as $ce > fd$ or $ce < fd$, that is according as the period of the natural vibration of the driving pendulum is greater or less than that of the driven.

223. Theory of Seismographs.

The principle of the Gray-Milne seismograph, and of other seismographic apparatus for registering earth vibrations may be regarded as that of the double pendulum in the case here discussed; but the motion of such apparatus falls more naturally under the category of *forced* vibrations. The moving earth or building, however, may be considered to be the driver and the pendulum of the instrument, which has naturally a long period, as driven. The period, $2\pi\sqrt{c/f}$, of the driving vibrations is very short, so that $\sqrt{c/f}$ is small, and $2\pi\sqrt{d/e}$ is relatively great. The condition that W_2/W_1 is negligible holds here, of course, so that we need only include vibrations due to the earth itself in θ, for there can be no sensible reaction exerted by the apparatus on the earth. We have thus

$$\theta = A \sin\left(\sqrt{\frac{f}{c}}\, t + \alpha_1\right). \quad\ldots\ldots\ldots\ldots\ldots\ldots(3)$$

The effect of this on the seismograph is to produce a vibration $\phi = \kappa_1 \theta$, along with which will be free vibrations of the seismograph itself, in its much longer period $2\pi\sqrt{d/e}$. All these will be registered by the apparatus, but there is no difficulty in distinguishing those due to the earth or building from those of the instrument. We have thus

$$\phi = \kappa_1 \theta + B \sin\left(\sqrt{\frac{e}{d}}\, t + \alpha_2\right). \quad\ldots\ldots\ldots\ldots\ldots(4)$$

The value of κ_1 is $bf/(ce - fd) = (b/e)/(c/f - d/e) = 4\pi^2(b/e)/(T_1^2 - T_2^2)$ if $T_1 = 2\pi\sqrt{c/f}$, $T_2 = 2\pi\sqrt{d/e}$. Thus

$$\phi = -4\pi^2 \frac{b}{e} \frac{\theta}{T_2^2 - T_1^2} + B \sin\left(\sqrt{\frac{e}{\alpha}}\, t + \alpha_2\right). \quad\ldots\ldots\ldots\ldots(5)$$

We may write this, putting $b/e = l/g$, in the form

$$\phi = -\frac{4\pi^2 l \theta}{g(T_2^2 - T_1^2)} + B \sin\left(\frac{2\pi}{T_2} t + \alpha_2\right), \quad\ldots\ldots\ldots\ldots\ldots(6)$$

since T_2 is very much greater than T_1 in almost all cases. The quantity $l\theta$ is the linear displacement of the point of suspension of the seismograph pendulum, whether placed horizontal or vertical (see § 226). The relation of the amplitude of the vibrations, as registered, to the actual amplitude, can thus be calculated.

224. Bell and Clapper. Returning now to the bell and its clapper, it will be observed that if W_2/W_1 be very small, as it is in this case, and if l be not very great, we may neglect in (2), § 220, the term multiplied by this ratio. We have then

$$al\ddot{\theta} + (a^2 + k_2^2)\ddot{\phi} + ag\phi = 0,$$
$$(h^2 + k_1^2)\ddot{\theta} + hg\theta = 0.$$

These are identical equations if

$$\theta = \phi,\ \ddot{\theta} = \ddot{\phi},\ \text{and}\ a = hl,\ al + k_2^2 = k_1^2.$$

The length of the equivalent simple pendulum is then for the first (the bell) vibrating alone,

$$(h^2 + k_1^2)/h = a + k_1^2/a = a + (al + k_2^2)/a = l + a + k^2/a = l + L,$$

§§ 223, 224, 225]   FORCED VIBRATIONS.   413

where L is the length of the equivalent simple pendulum for the second (the clapper) vibrating alone.

The two pendulums if started together with $\theta = \phi$, and $\dot\theta = \dot\phi$, will thus vibrate so that θ remains equal to ϕ, if the distance of the centre of oscillation of the second from the point of suspension O of the system, when the centroids are in line, is equal to the distance of the centre of oscillation of the first pendulum from the same point. Thus, if the first pendulum is a bell and the second its clapper, and the conditions of starting are as stated, the bell will not ring. One way of curing a bell from behaving in this way would be to lengthen its clapper considerably. This is said to have been done for a bell in the Cathedral of Cologne.

225. Forced Vibrations. The subject of forced vibrations referred to above is of great importance. Examples of it are found in the phenomena of the tides, which are oscillations of the water on the earth's surface and of the earth's substance, produced by the periodic action of forces which are not to any appreciable extent controlled by the earth itself, in such a way as to enable tidal vibrations to have any of the free periods of such disturbances. A ship is made to vibrate by the revolution of the more or less unbalanced parts of the engines, and it is made to pitch in the period of the waves it passes over, and to roll in the period of the waves that pass under it transversely. In a great number of such cases it will be seen that the control of the driven body by the driving oscillator is absolute: the energy of the latter is practically unlimited, or, at least, the part abstracted by the driven body is so small a fraction of the whole that no modification of the driving oscillations is noticeable. It is otherwise, however, in such cases as a pendulum driven by another pendulum of energy of motion comparable with that which the former possesses when in full swing. Take, for example, a beam and scales, in which the beam oscillates about its knife-edges (when the scales hardly swing about their suspensions), in nearly the same period as that in which the scales swing alone. When the beam is set oscillating the scales gradually increase their pendulum swing about the extremities of the beam, which in its turn comes to rest, to begin oscillating again as the scales in their turn become the driver, and so on. Thus, if the system is left to itself, a continual backward and forward transfer of energy takes place, from the beam to the scales, from the scales to the beam, and so on, until all the energy has been transformed into heat by the friction which retards the motion throughout.

This is the problem referred to in § 108 as having been discussed by Euler. It is obviously an example of the double pendulum of which the theory is given above. The reader may now work it out for himself and trace the energy changes, leaving friction out of account.

226. Simple Pendulum with Vibrating Support. As an example of forced vibrations, we take first the case of a simple pendulum hung from a point P, which is constrained to vibrate in a horizontal direction about a mean position O (Fig. 98), so that its distance x from that point is given by the equation $x = a \sin pt$. Let l be the length of the cord, m the mass of the bob, ϕ the angle which the thread makes with the vertical at any instant, and P the pull which the cord exerts on the bob. The horizontal distance of the bob from O at time t is $x + l \sin \phi$, and the vertical distance $l \cos \phi$. Hence the equations of horizontal and vertical motion are

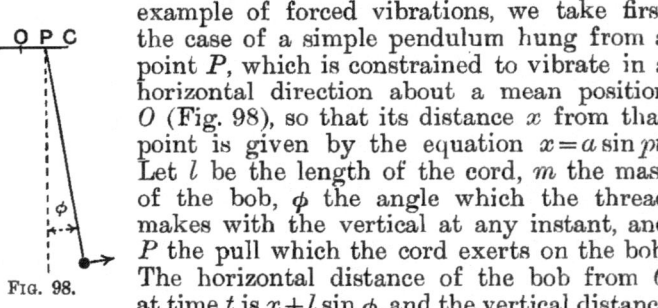

Fig. 98.

$$m\frac{d^2}{dt^2}(x + l \sin \phi) = -P \sin \phi,$$

$$m\frac{d^2}{dt^2}(l \cos \phi) = -P \cos \phi + mg$$

or
$$\left.\begin{array}{l} m(\ddot{x} + l \cos \phi \cdot \ddot{\phi} - l \sin \phi \cdot \dot{\phi}^2) = -P \sin \phi, \\ m(-l \sin \phi \cdot \ddot{\phi} - l \cos \phi \cdot \dot{\phi}^2) = -P \cos \phi + mg. \end{array}\right\} \quad \ldots(1)$$

Multiplying the first of these by $\cos \phi$, the second by $\sin \phi$, and subtracting the second product from the first, we eliminate P and obtain

$$l\ddot{\phi} + g \sin \phi = -\ddot{x} \cos \phi, \quad \ldots\ldots\ldots\ldots\ldots\ldots(2)$$

which, if ϕ is always small, may be written

$$\ddot{\phi} + \frac{g}{l}\phi = -\frac{\ddot{x}}{l}. \quad \ldots\ldots\ldots\ldots\ldots\ldots(3)$$

FORCED VIBRATIONS.

But $\ddot{x} = -p^2 x$, and hence this equation of motion is really

$$\ddot{\phi} + \frac{g}{l}\phi = p^2\frac{a}{l}\sin pt. \quad\ldots\ldots\ldots\ldots\ldots\ldots(4)$$

We now assume that $\phi = A \sin pt$ is a particular solution of this differential equation. Substituting, we obtain

$$A(g/l - p^2) = p^2 a/l, \text{ so that } A = (p^2 a/l)/(g/l - p^2).$$

But if T_1 be the period of the forced oscillation of the point of suspension, and T_2 the natural period of the pendulum, $p^2 = 4\pi^2/T_1^2$, $g/l = 4\pi^2/T_2^2$, and we get

$$A = -\frac{4\pi^2 a}{g(T_2^2 - T_1^2)} = -\frac{T_2^2}{T_2^2 - T_1^2}\frac{a}{l}. \quad\ldots\ldots\ldots\ldots(5)$$

Thus, adding the complementary function to the particular solution, with the value of A just found, we obtain

$$\phi = -\frac{4\pi^2}{g(T_2^2 - T_1^2)}a\sin pt + B_1 \sin\sqrt{\frac{g}{l}}t + B_2 \cos\sqrt{\frac{g}{l}}t \quad\ldots(6)$$

or $$\phi = -\frac{4\pi^2}{g(T_2^2 - T_1^2)}a\sin\frac{2\pi}{T_1}t + C\sin\left(\frac{2\pi}{T_2}t - \alpha\right), \quad\ldots\ldots(7)$$

where C and α are constants. This, as the reader should notice, agrees with (5) of § 223, for the quantity $l\theta$ (l has there a different signification) which occurs in the first term of ϕ in that equation is clearly the present $a \sin pt$.

It is important to observe that, if $T_2 > T_1$, the forced vibration term in the solution is opposite in phase to the exciting vibration, and that the amplitude of the latter is altered in the ratio of $4\pi^2$ to $g(T_2^2 - T_1^2)$, a ratio which is greater the more nearly the two periods coincide. Examples are a plank of wood, which when floating in water has a very short free period, and follows at once the motions of the waves in a seaway, and a vessel, the period of rolling of which is greater than the half period of the waves in a seaway, and which therefore oscillates in the opposite phase to what must be regarded as the exciting oscillation in this case. Other examples are the driven pendulums discussed in § 107.

227. Agreement of Natural Period with Forced Period: Resonance. When, however, the two periods—the natural period T_2 of the pendulum and the impressed period T_1 given by the motion of the point of support—coincide, the particular integral which we have assumed is not applicable. We now assume that $\phi = At \cos pt$ is a solution. Substituting in the differential equation,

$$\ddot{\phi} + g\phi/l = M \sin pt \quad (M = p^2 a/l),$$

we find that $A = -M/2p$, and therefore we have

$$\phi = -a\frac{p}{2l} t \cos pt + B_1 \sin \sqrt{\frac{g}{l}}\, t + B_2 \cos \sqrt{\frac{g}{l}}\, t,$$

with $p = \sqrt{g/l}$, or, by the values of T_1, T_2 given above, which are now equal ($= T$, say),

$$\phi = \frac{4\pi^3}{T^3}\frac{a}{g} t \sin\left(\frac{2\pi}{T} t - \frac{\pi}{2}\right) + C \sin\left(\frac{2\pi}{T} t - \alpha\right). \quad \ldots\ldots(1)$$

Thus the "forced" part of the oscillation is a vibration of frequency $p/2\pi$, a quarter of a period behind the exciting vibration in phase, and of amplitude increasing uniformly with the time. The exciting vibration is given by $x = a \sin pt$, and therefore at $t = 0$ we have $x = 0$. The forced part of ϕ represents the oscillation of the pendulum, which has grown up in time t from rest through the action of the point of support; and it is not difficult to see how the difference of phase arises. For at $t = 0$ the pendulum hangs vertical with the bob at rest, and the point of support is then moving with maximum speed, towards the right, let us say. As soon as the cord becomes inclined the bob is made to follow, and angular speed $\dot{\phi}$ of the cord begins to grow up, and continues to do so as the speed of the point of support falls off, until when the latter point has its furthest displacement towards the right the value of $\dot{\phi}$ has become a maximum, and the cord is now again vertical, *because the natural period of vibration of the pendulum is equal to that of the variation of x, and a quarter period of both has elapsed since $t = 0$*. From this instant the slope of the thread is towards the right, and the speed of the bob towards the right begins to diminish, and is zero when the point of support has come back to its middle position, and again the pendulum motion is a quarter period behind that of the point of support. Then motion of the bob towards the left begins, and continues until the point of support has returned to its middle position, and so on. At each swing the exciting action is repeated, and the appearance of the factor t in the amplitude is explained.

We have here an example of *resonance*, by which a body is set into violent oscillation by an exciting vibrator, the period of which nearly agrees with the free period of the body. But it is to be observed that in the particular case of the pendulum, as in others, the results of the theory given above, and of the parallel theory that holds for these other cases, are modified by the frictional and other resistances to motion that exist. The theory of forced oscillations with friction proportional to speed is given in § 235 below.

228. Examples of Resonance. Examples of resonance occur in all parts of physics. The column of air in a sea-shell, or in an organ pipe, picks out from a confused mixture of vibrations in the air that vibration which suits its period, and if there is energy enough available, sounds quite loudly its own proper note. The student may experiment by sounding different notes in a room in which there is a piano, the keys of which, in order to lift the dampers from the strings, are held down by a bar of wood laid along the keyboard. The notes, if they are in unison with notes of the piano, will be echoed by the strings, which will continue to be heard after the exciting sounds have ceased.

Again, a ship which lies broadside on to waves in a sea-way is set into forced vibration, in being made to roll from side to side in the half-period of the waves, and, if the natural period of rolling (the time of what is commonly called two rolls) of the ship in still water agree with the period of the wave, the angle of the inclination of the ship may be carried dangerously near the limit of the ship's stability. It is also to be remembered that while there may be no such coincidence of periods when the ship is disabled and rolling "in the trough of the sea," or steaming in a direction parallel to the wave-crests, it may arise when the ship steams obliquely across the direction of the waves, because then the period of the wave at the ship is altered by the relative motion. Thus H.M.S. *Devastation* lying broadside on to waves having a period of about 11 seconds, rolled through a maximum angle of $6\frac{1}{2}°$ to windward and $7\frac{1}{2}°$ to leeward, or through a total angle of 14°. She was then made to steam obliquely away from the waves at a speed of 7½ knots, when she was found to roll 13° to windward, and 14½° to leeward, or through a total angle of 27½° [Sir William White's *Naval Architecture*, p. 242]. Thus the period of the wave and the ship's "natural period" of rolling much more nearly synchronised in the latter case than in the former. The rolling of a ship is greatly modified by resistance, and the irregularities of the waves tend besides to prevent the full effects of synchronism from being experienced. Often an almost imperceptible but regular swell in calm weather will, if synchronism exist, produce a much greater effect than waves in a heavy sea. "Admiral Sir Cooper Key observed that the vessels of the *Prince Consort* class were made to roll very heavily by an almost imperceptible swell, the period of which was just double that of the ship" [Sir William White, *loc. cit.*]. The ship's period in this quotation is half the complete period.

It has also been observed that in the rolling of ships produced by a regular succession of waves the amplitude of deflection alternately increases to a maximum and diminishes to a minimum. This is due to alternate coincidence and opposition of the forced and free oscillations. If the ratio T_1/T_2 of the periods be expressed by p/q, where p and q are two whole numbers which have no common factor, then $pT_2 = qT_1$ (and no smaller multiples of T_1 and T_2 can satisfy this equation), and so in every interval of time pT_2 or qT_1 agreement or disagreement of phase between the forced and free oscillations will recur.

If the student attempts to deal with the problem of § 226 by the method of energy, he will see that the pendulum is not what has been called in § 65 a "self-contained system," for it receives energy from the exciting vibrations. The rate of receipt of energy can be estimated, but that involves the introduction of the pull of the thread on the bob, and then the method of solution coincides with that adopted above.

229. Examples of Forced Vibration.

Ex. 1. Show that P, the pull exerted by the cord on the bob (§ 226), has the value mg, if small quantities of the second order are excluded, and only the forced vibration is considered.

Find also the value of P when small quantities of the second order are taken into account.

Ex. 2. The point of suspension of a simple pendulum has forced simple harmonic motion in a horizontal line, of period ½ sec. and amplitude 1 inch. If the natural period of the pendulum be 1 sec., find the amplitude of the forced vibration. [R.N.C. 1909.]

By (6) § 223, the angular amplitude in radians is $4\pi^2 a/g(T_2^2 - T_1^2)$, where a is the amplitude of the forced vibration, T_1 the forced period,

§§ 228, 229] FORCED VIBRATIONS. 419

T_2 the natural period, and g the acceleration produced by gravity in a falling body at the place [say $32\frac{1}{6}$(ft/sec.^{2})]. The angular amplitude in radians is therefore

$$\frac{9 \cdot 87 \times 4}{12 \times 32\frac{1}{6} \times \frac{3}{4}} = \cdot 136, \text{ nearly.}$$

But $g/4\pi^2$ is the length of the simple pendulum, and therefore the linear amplitude of the forced vibration is $a/(T_2^2 - T_1^2) = 1/(1 - 1/4) = 1\frac{1}{3}$, in inches.

Ex. 3. An instrument for the detection of vertical oscillations has been made as follows (Fig. 99). A strong post with attached bracket stands on a massive base which supports the whole apparatus. From the bracket hangs a spiral or other spring with its lower end attached to a horizontal lever, at a point distant l from a pivot, or knife-edge, about which the lever turns. The lever is loaded with a mass which can be clamped at different distances from the pivot, and which gives the lever and attachments a large moment of inertia about the pivot. The spring is so stretched that the lever is horizontal when the apparatus is in equilibrium. It is required to find the natural period of free vibration of this spring-lever arrangement, and explain how it can be used for detecting vertical vibrations. [R.N.C. 1909.]

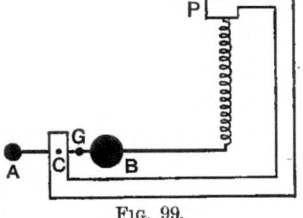

Fig. 99.

Let the arrangement rest in equilibrium with the lever horizontal, and let the moment of inertia about the pivot be Mk^2, and the moment of the whole weight about the same axis be Mgh. Further, let the equilibrium elongation of the spring, beyond that produced by its own weight, be s, and the pull in consequence exerted on the lever be F. We have then $Fl = Mgh$ for equilibrium. Let the elongation of the spring be increased from s to $s + x$; then the upward pull applied by the spring is increased to $F(s+x)/s$, and the moment of this about the pivot is $F(s+x)l/s$. If x be, as we here suppose, a small elongation, the opposing moment of forces is Mgh, and so the net moment giving angular acceleration $\ddot{\theta} = \ddot{x}/l$ to the lever is $Fxl/s = Mghx/s$. The equation of motion is therefore

$$-\frac{\ddot{x}}{l} = \frac{Mghx}{Mk^2 s} = \frac{ghx}{k^2 s},$$

that is, $\qquad \ddot{x} + \dfrac{ghl}{k^2 s} x = 0.$

Thus the free period of small oscillations is $2\pi \sqrt{k^2 s/ghl}$, and the length of the equivalent simple pendulum is $k^2 s/hl$. By making l very small, that is, by attaching the spring at a point very close to the pivot, the period of free vibration can be made very great.

420   A TREATISE ON DYNAMICS.   [CH. VII.

This apparatus was proposed as a vertical motion seismograph by the late Professor Thomas Gray (see *Trans. Seis. Soc.*, Japan, 1879). The arrangement enables a long period to be obtained without the use of an inconveniently long spring.

Writing, now, n^2 for ghl/k^2s, so that $n/2\pi$ is the frequency of vibration, let the support from which the spring is suspended, and the base carrying the lever, etc., be subjected to a vertical vibration, the displacement in which is $\xi = a\sin pt$ at time t. If x be the distance at the same instant of the point of attachment of the lever below the level of the pivot, and the acceleration $\ddot{\xi}$ be in the opposite direction to $\ddot{x}$, we have, at the instant, elongation of the spring $= x$, and so the moment of forces producing angular acceleration is $Mghx/s$. The angular acceleration is then $(\ddot{x}+\ddot{\xi})/l$, and the equation of motion is $-(\ddot{x}+\ddot{\xi})/l = ghx/k^2s$. This may be written in the form

$$\ddot{x} + n^2 x = -\ddot{\xi} = p^2 a \sin pt.$$

The forced vibrations are therefore given by the integral equation

$$x = \frac{p^2 a}{n^2 - p^2} \sin pt,$$

and this, if the natural vibrations are negligible, is the equation of the vibrational motion of the arrangement. The period is that of the forced oscillation, and the amplitude is $p^2 a/(n^2 - p^2)$.

The lever writes, by means of a pen fixed upon it at a convenient point, the vertical oscillations of that point on a vertical ribbon of paper carried on a suitable holder placed on the base of the apparatus. The paper is carried past the pen by clockwork, and the relative motion of the lever and the supporting frame-work is thus registered. The period of natural vibration is generally much longer than $2\pi/p$, and the forced oscillations are thus easily separable in the record from the natural vibrations, and their period can be determined from the rate of motion of the paper. The equation for x gives the reducing factor by which a can be found from the registered amplitudes.

230. Examples of Mutually Influencing Vibrations. Ex. 1. Oscillations of Balance and Case of a Watch. The bending of the spiral hair-spring caused by the deflection of the balance from the equilibrium position gives rise to a return couple, the moment of which is proportional to the angular deflection θ multiplied by a constant, E say, depending on the elasticity of the spring. Thus $E\theta$ is the moment of the couple, and if wk^2 be the moment of inertia of the balance-wheel and the hair-spring which swings with it, the equation of motion is

$$\ddot{\theta} + \frac{E}{wk^2}\theta = 0, \quad \dotfill (1)$$

and this, for properly shaped springs, is very nearly true, even for somewhat large values of θ. The period of oscillation is therefore $2\pi/\sqrt{E/wk^2}$, and the frequency, f say, is $\sqrt{E/wk^2}/2\pi$.

§§ 229, 230, 231] FORCED VIBRATIONS. 421

We shall suppose, for simplicity, that the balance wheel has its axis through the centroid of the rest of the watch. If then the watch be hung with its face horizontal by a sling attached to a long fine cord, the torsion in which may be neglected, or be laid on its back on a smooth table, it will, when the balance swings round in one direction through an angle θ, swing in the opposite direction through an angle ϕ given by the equation $wk^2\theta = WK^2\phi$, where WK^2 is the moment of inertia of the watch (without the balance-wheel), for turning about a vertical axis through the centroid. For the hair-spring exerts on the balance and the rest of the watch forces which have equal and opposite moments, and so *throughout the motion* we have $wk^2\ddot\theta = WK^2\ddot\phi$, so that $wk^2\theta = WK^2\phi$.

The deflection of the balance-wheel is now $\theta + \phi$, and so the equation of motion is

$$\ddot\theta + \frac{E}{wk^2}(\theta+\phi) = \ddot\theta + E\left(\frac{1}{wk^2} + \frac{1}{WK^2}\right)\theta = 0. \quad \ldots\ldots\ldots\ldots(2)$$

Thus the period is changed from

$$2\pi\sqrt{wk^2/E} \text{ to } 2\pi\sqrt{wk^2}/\sqrt{E(1+wk^2/WK^2)},$$

and the frequency from f to $f(1+wk^2/WK^2)^{\frac{1}{2}}$. Thus the watch goes more quickly.

A pocket chronometer belonging to Archibald Smith of Jordanhill (presented by the Admiralty for his work on the Deviations of the Compass in Iron Ships) when thus suspended was found to gain 1 second in 1299. In this case the ratio of frequencies was 1300/1299, and therefore $\frac{1}{2}wk^2/WK^2$ was approximately 1/1299, that is, the moment of inertia of the watch was about 649 times that of the balance-wheel. [Lord Kelvin, "On the Rate of a Clock or Chronometer as Influenced by the Mode of Suspension," *Popular Lectures and Addresses*, vol. ii.]

231. Ex. 2. Watch hung by Bifilar Suspension. Theory of Bifilar. A watch is hung with its face horizontal by two threads each of length l attached at their upper ends to two points on the same level at a distance $2a$ apart. The lower ends are symmetrically attached to the watch at a distance $2r$ apart. It is required to find the effect of the vibrations of the support on the rate of the watch.

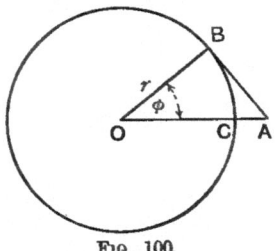

Fig. 100.

It will be clear that when the watch is hanging in equilibrium each thread is inclined to the vertical at the angle $\sin^{-1}\{(a-r)/l\}$. When the watch is turned through an angle ϕ about the vertical through its centre, the inclination of each thread to the vertical is $\sin^{-1}AB/l$. Hence if P be the pull applied by each thread the two threads together apply a couple to diminish

θ, of which the moment is $P \cdot AB/l \cdot a \sin \angle OAB$ (Fig. 100). But $\sin \angle OAB / \sin \phi = r/AB$, and the moment of the couple is $2Par \sin \phi/l$.

Now, if, as we shall suppose to be the case, l be great in comparison with r and a, we have $2P = (W+w)g$, since the vertical acceleration will then be small. Here W is the weight of the watch (without the balance) and the sling, and w is the weight of the balance. Hence if K be the radius of gyration of the watch and sling, and k that of the balance, the equation of motion, if the watch is not going, is

$$(WK^2 + wk^2)\ddot{\phi} + (W+w)\frac{ar}{l}g \sin \phi = 0. \quad \ldots\ldots\ldots\ldots (3)$$

Thus, for small motions, the frequency is

$$\sqrt{(W+w)(arg/l)/(WK^2+wk^2)}/2\pi.$$

We shall denote this by F, so that

$$4\pi^2 F^2(WK^2+wk^2) = (W+w)arg/l. \quad \ldots\ldots\ldots\ldots (4)$$

If now the balance be vibrating, and its deflection from the position which it occupies when everything is at rest be θ, the equation of motion of the watch, etc., without the balance, is

$$WK^2\ddot{\phi} + (W+w)\frac{ar}{l}g\phi + E(\phi - \theta) = 0, \quad \ldots\ldots\ldots\ldots (5)$$

and that of the balance alone is

$$wk^2\ddot{\theta} - E(\phi - \theta) = 0. \quad \ldots\ldots\ldots\ldots (6)$$

If the balance were vibrating alone the equation of motion would be $wk^2\ddot{\theta} + E\theta = 0$, and the frequency of vibration would be

$$\sqrt{E/wk^2}/2\pi = f,$$

say. Thus $E = 4\pi^2 f^2 wk^2$.

The two equations of motion (5) and (6) are satisfied by

$$\theta = A \sin 2\pi nt, \quad \phi = B \sin 2\pi nt \quad \ldots\ldots\ldots\ldots (7)$$

(so that n is the frequency), provided the equations

$$\left. \begin{array}{r} -4\pi^2 n^2 WK^2\phi + (W+w)\frac{ar}{l}g\phi + E(\phi - \theta) = 0, \\ -4\pi^2 n^2 wk^2\theta - E(\phi - \theta) = 0, \end{array} \right\} \quad \ldots\ldots\ldots (8)$$

hold simultaneously. The necessary condition for this is

$$\frac{B}{A} = \frac{E}{-4\pi^2 WK^2 n^2 + (W+w)\frac{ar}{l}g + E} = \frac{E - 4\pi^2 wk^2 n^2}{E}. \quad \ldots\ldots (9)$$

Substituting for E and $(W+w)arg/l$, the values

$$4\pi^2 f^2 wk^2 \quad \text{and} \quad 4\pi^2 F^2 (WK^2+wk^2),$$

found above, we have

$$\frac{B}{A} = \frac{f^2 - n^2}{f^2} = -\frac{wk^2 f^2}{-WK^2 n^2 + F^2(WK^2+wk^2) + wk^2 f^2}. \quad \ldots\ldots (10)$$

§ 231] FORCED VIBRATIONS. 423

If $1+e$ be put for $1+wk^2/WK^2$, equation (10) may be written in the form
$$\{n^2-(1+e)F^2\}\{n^2-(1+e)f^2\}-eF^2f^2(1+e)=0. \quad\ldots\ldots\ldots(11)$$

This equation in n^2 has two positive roots, one between $+\infty$ and the greater of $(1+e)F^2$ and $(1+e)f^2$, and another between the smaller of these and 0. For when $n^2=+\infty$, the left-hand side is positive, when $n^2=(1+e)F^2$, or $n^2=(1+e)f^2$, it is negative, and when $n^2=0$, it is again positive.

We see therefore that if n be greater than $F\sqrt{1+e}$, or greater than $f\sqrt{1+e}$, it must be also greater than the other, and the watch gains. But (10) shows that then B/A is negative, that is, the watch and balance are then deflected in opposite directions at each instant. On the other hand, if n be less than $F\sqrt{1+e}$, or less than $f\sqrt{1+e}$, it must also be less than the other, and the watch loses. Then A/B is positive, and the watch and balance swing in the same direction at each instant.

It is important to consider what will happen if the bifilar suspension is held at rest while the watch goes, and is then left to itself. The discussion of the analogous case in § 107 above answers this question. The watch becomes the driving pendulum, and we see that if the natural period of the bifilar be greater than that of the watch balance, the two vibrations, that set up in the bifilar arrangement and the vibration of the balance, will be in opposite phases and the watch will gain. This case can be arranged for by placing the upper points of attachment of the threads sufficiently close together, so as to make the value of F^2, which varies as a, small enough. The mode of vibration is shown in Fig. 44, where the upper pendulum represents by analogy the watch balance, and the lower pendulum the bifilar pendulum.

On the other hand, if the natural period of the bifilar arrangement be smaller than that of the watch balance—and this can be arranged for by placing the upper ends of the threads sufficiently far apart—the vibration set up by the going of the watch, and that of the balance will be in the same phase, and the watch will lose. The mode of vibration is represented by the diagram of two pendulums in Fig. 44, where, as before, the upper pendulum corresponds to the watch balance, and the lower to the bifilar pendulum.

This last result is of great importance in its bearing on the proper mode of supporting a clock which is intended to keep accurate time. Very frequently the supporting framework from which the pendulum is suspended is not sufficiently massive, while it is rigid enough to have a short period of free vibration. The result is that the going of the clock is influenced by the mode of suspension just as that of the watch is in the second case just considered.

Ex. 3. Prove that if the watch be hung by the ring from a nail (as a watch under adjustment sometimes is in a watchmaker's shop) so that it oscillates like a compound pendulum under the influence of the vibrations of the balance, the equations of motion are

$$wk\ddot{\theta}^2 - E(\phi - \theta) = 0,$$
$$W(K^2 + h^2)\ddot{\phi} + (W + w)gh\phi + E(\phi - \theta) = 0,$$

where h is the distance of the common centroid of watch and balance from the point of suspension.

Hence show that the frequencies (values of n) of vibration are given by the equations

$$\frac{wk^2 f^2}{-W(K^2+h^2)n^2 + F^2\{W(K^2+h^2)+w(k^2+h^2)+f^2wk^2\}} = \frac{f^2 - n^2}{f^2} = \frac{\phi}{\theta},$$

where $F^2 = (W+w)gh/\{WK^2 + wk^2 + (W+w)h^2\}4\pi^2$, and $f^2 = E/4\pi^2 wk^2$ are the squares of the natural frequencies of free vibrations of the watch hanging on the nail with the works stopped, and of the balance vibrating with the watch at rest.

Approximate values of n^2 are $f^2 + (wk^2/WK^2)f^2/(f^2 - F^2)$, and $F^2 - (wk^2/WK^2)f^2/(f^2 - F^2)$. The frequency of oscillation and beat of the watch is n in the two cases.

It will be noticed that in all these problems no account has been taken of the effect of the motions of other parts of the watch than the balance, e.g. of the escapement, etc. These motions must, of course, affect the results to some extent.

Ex. 4. A carriage of weight W, mounted on side springs at a distance b apart, oscillates about a longitudinal axis mid-way between the springs and on a level with their top: if the c.o. of the oscillating body be at a height h above the springs, and its radius of gyration about a parallel axis through the centroid be k, and the springs be compressed a distance c when the load upon them is in equilibrium, find the period of small oscillations.

If the compression be x at any instant during an oscillation, the return force of the springs on one side will be $\frac{1}{2}Wx/c$. One spring will be under compression, the other under stretch, and therefore the carriage will be acted on by a "righting couple," due to the springs, of moment $\frac{1}{2}Wbx/c$. The angle of inclination is then $2x/b$, and if we call this θ, the moment of the couple is $\frac{1}{4}Wb^2\theta/c$. Besides this a couple is applied in consequence of displacement of the c.o. This has moment $Wgh\sin\theta$, and tends to increase θ. Thus the equation of motion for small oscillations is

$$(h^2 + k^2)\ddot{\theta} + g\frac{b^2 - 4ch}{4c}\theta = 0.$$

The period of oscillation is $2\pi\sqrt{4c(h^2+k^2)/(b^2-4ch)g}$, and the length of the equivalent simple pendulum is $(h^2+k^2)/(b^2/4c-h)$. The period is thus greater the greater h and the greater c; but b^2 must be greater than $4ch$ to ensure return to the equilibrium position.

232. Dependence of Steadiness of a Vehicle on Period of Vibration. For steadiness, a long period of free vibration is essential: a carriage mounted on stiff springs (that is, for which c is small) with its C.G. low, will vibrate in a short period, and its motion will be unpleasant. Thus, if the carriage is hung low on the springs, these must not be stiff or the motion will be very uneasy. Care, however, must be taken not to turn corners quickly if the C.G. is high, otherwise the carriage may capsize. [See § 190.]

The C.G. of a locomotive, or of a railway carriage, is made fairly high to ensure easy running; the righting moment of a ship, for small angles of heel to one side or the other, is usually made so small, that in a moderate sea the period of rolling is long. But the ship is so constructed that, as the angle of heel increases, the righting moment increases more rapidly, so that there may be no risk of capsizing in a heavy sea, or, when a succession of waves passes transversely under the ship, the period of which may nearly coincide with the free period of rolling of the ship.

Lord Kelvin's compass card is made exceedingly light, and most of the weight is distributed round the rim, which is kept in shape by radial silk threads under tension. The card has thus a large moment of inertia, and therefore a long period of free vibration, thus ensuring great steadiness.

233. Pendulum with Point of Support in Vertical Vibration. If the point of support is subjected to a vertical vibration instead of a horizontal one, we can write down the equations of motion in a similar way to that used in § 226. We have in this case
$$y = a \sin pt,$$
and the equations of motion become then
$$\left. \begin{aligned} m(l \cos \phi \cdot \ddot{\phi} - l \sin \phi \cdot \dot{\phi}^2) &= -P \sin \phi, \\ m(\ddot{y} - l \sin \phi \cdot \ddot{\phi} - l \cos \phi \cdot \dot{\phi}^2) &= -P \cos \phi + mg, \end{aligned} \right\} \quad \ldots(1)$$

which give
$$\ddot{\phi} + \frac{g}{l} \sin \phi = -\frac{\ddot{y}}{l} \sin \phi$$

or
$$\ddot{\phi} + \left(\frac{g}{l} - \frac{p^2}{l} a \sin pt \right) \sin \phi = 0. \quad \ldots\ldots\ldots\ldots\ldots(2)$$

For small motions this is
$$\ddot{\phi} + \left(\frac{g}{l} - p^2 \frac{a}{l} \sin pt \right) \phi = 0, \quad \ldots\ldots\ldots\ldots\ldots(3)$$

an equation which, if a is of sensible amount, does not represent simple harmonic motion of the pendulum.*

A uniform circular motion of the point of support will, if it take place in a horizontal plane, give rise to a forced conical motion of the pendulum; if it is performed in a vertical plane, no true vibrational motion will result. The student may try attaching a small pendulum to the centre pin of the pedal of a bicycle turned upside down, and then causing the crank axle to revolve steadily. The student may write down the theory of a C.P. hung from the crank.

234. Pendulum Motion retarded by Friction. If friction retards the pendulum motion, the results are modified in an interesting manner. The typical equation of the forced oscillating displacement of a single body, whatever the nature of the displacement may be, when the motion is resisted in proportion to the speed, can be written

$$\ddot{\xi} + \kappa \dot{\xi} + n^2 \xi = p^2 a \sin(pt + \alpha), \dots\dots\dots\dots(1)$$

where $a \sin(pt+\alpha)$ is the displacement of the type considered, whatever it may be, at time t in the exciting vibration, $2\pi/n$ is the period of the vibrator acted on, and x, ξ are the similar displacements in the exciting and excited vibrations respectively.

We assume that $\xi = A \sin(pt + \beta)$ is a particular solution of the differential equation, and find by substitution that this value of ξ satisfies the equation if

$$A = \frac{p^2 a}{\sqrt{(n^2 - p^2)^2 + \kappa^2 p^2}}, \quad \tan \beta = \frac{(n^2 - p^2) \tan \alpha - \kappa p}{n^2 - p^2 + \kappa p \tan \alpha}. \dots(2)$$

For the equation found by substitution gives on the left terms in $\sin(pt+\beta)$, $\cos(pt+\beta)$, the aggregate of which are equal to $p^2 a \sin(pt+\alpha)$; and since the equation must hold for all values of t, we are entitled to equate the coefficients of $\sin pt$, $\cos pt$ on the two sides. This process gives the values of $\tan \beta$ and A written above, as the

* Equation (3) belongs to the class of linear differential equations in which the coefficients of the terms are harmonic functions of the independent variable. This class of equations is discussed in various treatises.

student should verify. We have then only to add the complementary function to complete the solution, which is therefore, if $n^2 > \tfrac{1}{4}\kappa^2$,

$$\xi = \frac{p^2 a}{\sqrt{(n^2-p^2)^2 + \kappa^2 p^2}} \sin(pt+\beta)$$
$$+ e^{-\tfrac{1}{2}\kappa t}(\beta_1 \sin n't + \beta_2 \cos n't), \quad \ldots\ldots(3)$$

where $n' = \sqrt{n^2 - \tfrac{1}{4}\kappa^2}$. The condition $n^2 > \tfrac{1}{4}\kappa^2$ must hold if the body is to be capable of vibrating about the position of equilibrium when left entirely to itself after displacement. If $\tfrac{1}{4}\kappa^2 > n^2$, the body will, when left in the displaced state,

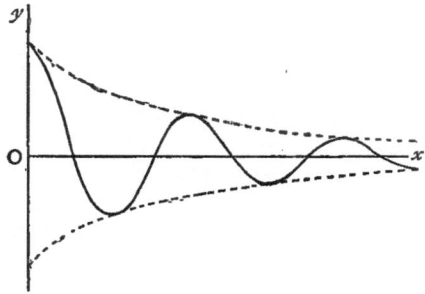

Fig. 101.

gradually lose its displacement according to the exponential law $e^{-\tfrac{1}{2}(\kappa + \sqrt{\kappa^2 - 4n^2})t}$, thus losing it all in an infinite time, but the greater part of it in a moderate interval of time. As it is, the free oscillations once started are gradually wiped out by the exponential multiplier $e^{-\tfrac{1}{2}\kappa n t}$ in the manner shown by Fig. 101.

235. Resonance modified by Friction. Tidal Example. It will now be seen more clearly what happens when the periods $2\pi/p$ and $2\pi/n$, of the exciting vibrations and the free vibrations, coincide. The forced vibrations do not, as might at first sight appear from (6), §226 above, become infinite in amplitude; the amplitude approximates to pa/κ, as p and n tend to coincidence. Thus, according to the canal theory of the tides, with friction left out of account, the excess of the natural period in a canal parallel to the equator, above that of the forced tidal wave at the place, causes the tides to be inverted in low latitudes, while in sufficiently high latitudes where this excess has become negative, the tides are direct, and at the latitude of transition the tides are infinite. The effect of friction is to modify these results profoundly, and to bring them into something like agreement with actual fact.

What takes place is this. It will be seen from the equations found above, that

$$\tan(\alpha-\beta)=\frac{\kappa p}{n^2-p^2}.$$

By comparing the values of t for which $\sin(pt+\alpha)$ and $\sin(pt+\beta)$ are equal to unity, it will be found that at the equator, where $n<p$, the phase of the tide is behind that of the tide-producing action by an angle $\alpha-\beta$, lying between $\pi/2$ and π; in other words, high water occurs later at any place than the maximum of the tide-producing action, by the time-interval corresponding to this angle. But without friction the angle would have been π, and therefore, relatively to the state of affairs, with no friction, the existence of friction has set the phase forward by an angle in value between 0 and $\pi/2$.

As we go to higher latitudes, where still $n<p$ but by a less amount, $\alpha-\beta$ alters until at the latitude of transition it becomes $\pi/2$. At still higher latitudes $\alpha-\beta$ lies between $\pi/2$ and 0, and high water occurs later than the maximum of the tide-producing action by the corresponding time-interval. But without friction the time of high water, and that of maximum tide-producing action, would have coincided—the tides would have been *direct*; relatively to this state of things, the existence of friction has retarded high water by the interval of time corresponding to a phase-angle between 0 and $\pi/2$.

236. Ballistic Pendulum. The theory and use of the ballistic pendulum, invented by Benjamin Robins in 1740 for measuring the speed of musket bullets, afford excellent illustrations of the principles of momentum and energy. Fig. 102 shows an old form of the pendulum which has been used for many years in the Natural Philosophy Department of the University of Glasgow. Improved forms have been made by Mr. A. Mallock, but the old arrangement will serve as a good example of this application of the principle of constancy of angular momentum.

In the first form a heavy cylindrical bob is hung horizontally by a rigid framework from a fixed horizontal support. The upper cross-bar of the framework has a knife-edge at each end turned downward to rest on hardened steel plates, and give a horizontal axis, at right angles to the axis of figure of the bob, about which the whole framework and bob can turn as a rigid body.

The bob consists of an outer shell of boiler plate, with the top front part removable to allow the interior to be got at. About two-thirds of the cylinder is filled with lead; the remainder, which is in front, is filled by a block of wood.

The bullet is fired as nearly as possible along the axis of the bob, and, after piercing the wood in front, is received by the lead, from which the splinters of the bullet are prevented by the wood in front from rebounding into the room. The pendulum is deflected by the blow through an angle which is measured by the length of a tape drawn out by the deflection. The tape is attached to the bob at a point just below it and is held just firmly enough to prevent slipping of more than the right amount by a spring which grips it on the same level, just at the point of attachment to the pendulum, when in the position of stable equilibrium. The tape drawn out measures the chord of the arc of deflection, for a radius equal to the

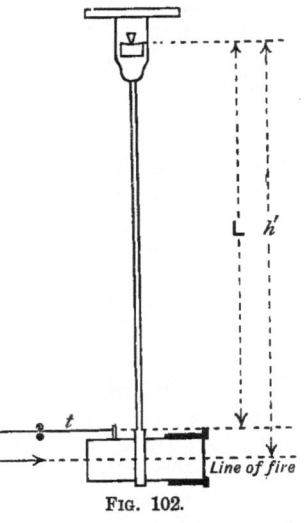

FIG. 102.

distance of the point of attachment of the tape from the line of knife-edges.

For the theory of the ballistic pendulum we require the principles of angular momentum and energy. Let the distances of the centroid, the line of fire, and the point of attachment of the tape from the knife-edges be h, h', L respectively, the weights of the pendulum and bullet W, w, and l the length of tape drawn out. Then before the collision the angular momentum of the bullet, flying with speed v, is wvh' about the line of knife-edges. When collision occurs the pendulum takes over this angular momentum to the amount $Wk^2\omega$, if Wk^2 be the moment of inertia and ω the initial angular speed of the pendulum about the line of knife-edges. The bullet, moving with the pendulum, and supposed to remain at the same distance as before from the knife-edges, retains the amount $wh'^2\omega$ of angular momentum, for $h'\omega$ is now the speed of the bullet. Hence, since the action and reaction between the bullet and pendulum cannot change the angular momentum of the whole system about the axis of turning, we have

$$wvh' = (Wk^2 + wh'^2)\omega \quad \text{or} \quad \omega = wvh'/(Wk^2 + wh'^2). \quad \ldots(1)$$

We have here assumed, what is to all intents and purposes correct, that the transfer of angular momentum has been completed before the pendulum has been sensibly deflected from its initial position. The angular speed ω has been generated, but the pendulum has not had time to turn through any appreciable angle from its initial position.

The turning system has kinetic energy of amount

$$\tfrac{1}{2}(Wk^2 + wh'^2)\omega^2 = \tfrac{1}{2}w^2v^2h'^2/(Wk^2 + wh'^2),$$

in absolute units, by the value of ω found above. This enables the pendulum to go on turning, until, at a deflection θ, the whole kinetic energy has been turned into potential energy, by the raising of the pendulum to a higher level on the whole. The centroid has been raised through the vertical distance $h(1 - \cos\theta)$, and the bullet through a height $h'(1 - \cos\theta)$. The potential energy is thus

$$(Wh + wh')g(1 - \cos\theta)$$

§ 236] BALLISTIC PENDULUM. 431

in the same units. Hence we have the energy equation
$$\frac{1}{2}\frac{w^2v^2h'^2}{Wk^2+wh'^2}=(Wh+wh')g(1-\cos\theta) \\ =2(Wh+wh')g\sin^2\tfrac{1}{2}\theta, \quad (2)$$
and so we get
$$v^2=4\frac{(Wh+wh')(Wk^2+wh'^2)g\sin^2\tfrac{1}{2}\theta}{w^2h'^2}\quad\ldots\ldots(3)$$

The value of k^2 has been, it is understood, previously found by allowing the pendulum to oscillate through a small angle about its knife-edges, and determining its period of oscillation, with and without a massive cylinder of weight W_1, which can be attached below the bob with its axis of figure parallel to the knife-edges in the plane through these and the centroid. This cylinder can be made fairly long and thin, so that its diameter may be neglected. If T, T_1 be the periods of the pendulum alone and with the cylinder attached, and h_1, the distance of the axis of the cylinder from the line of knife-edges, we have, by the theory of the compound pendulum,

$$k^2/h=gT^2/4\pi^2,\quad (k^2+W_1h_1^2/W)/(h+W_1h_1/W)=gT'^2/4\pi^2.$$

Thus we have two equations from which to find k^2 and h. When h is found we can use the value $k^2=ghT^2/4\pi^2$, in the equations for v^2. If l be the length of tape drawn out, we have $2L\sin\tfrac{1}{2}\theta=l$ or $\sin\tfrac{1}{2}\theta=l/2L$. Making these substitutions in (3), we obtain

$$v^2=\frac{(Wh+wh')(Wg^2hT^2+4\pi^2wh'^2g)l^2}{4\pi^2w^2h'^2L^2}\quad\ldots\ldots(4)$$

for the calculation of v.

For the sake of the example we have worked out the exact value of v^2, with neglect, of course, of the resistance of the air, which it is difficult to estimate. In view of this neglect, and of the smallness of the ratio of w to W, we may leave out of account the effect of the retention of the bullet in the pendulum, and obtain,

$$v^2=W^2h^2g^2T^2l^2/4\pi^2w^2h'^2L^2$$
or
$$v=\frac{1}{2\pi}\frac{WhgT}{wh'L}l.\quad\ldots\ldots(5)$$

It is of no consequence what units of weight and length are used except for l. If l be measured in feet, and the second be the unit of time used for g and T, we get v in f/s.

In the Glasgow pendulum $W = 25855$ grammes, $h = 37\cdot 6$ inches, $h' = 42$ inches, $L = 47$ inches, $T = 2\cdot 0690$ secs. A Jacob rifle was used of which the bullet weighed 45·5 grammes. Thus, for a bullet of weight w grammes, $v = 5189 l/w$. (f/s) when l is reckoned in feet, and for the Jacob bullet $v = 45.17. l f/s$. The charge of powder was usually 65 grains or 4·18 grammes, and the speed was about 900 f/s.

The ballistic pendulum is sometimes used with the rifle screwed into position under the bob, and the pendulum then measures the angular momentum of recoil, from which the speed of the bullet can be deduced, but only with some uncertainty due to the fact that the powder gases which leave the rifle after the bullet also produce recoil. This may be allowed for by estimating the extra recoil in various cases, by comparison with the results obtained with the apparatus used as described above; but there does not seem to be any very good reason for deviating from the latter method.

EXERCISES VII.

1. An iceboat is mounted on runners so that it can make no leeway, that is can only move in the fore-and-aft direction. If the direction of the lower edge of the sail, drawn forward from the foot O of the mast, make an angle α with the direction of motion, OV drawn in the latter direction represent the speed of the boat, inclined to the *windward* direction at an angle β, and OW drawn in the proper direction represent the actual speed of the wind, show that VW represents the apparent wind at the boat, and must be parallel to the sail if the boat is at full speed.

If a circle be described about the triangle OVW, show that, for a given wind and fixed angle α, this is a fixed circle, and that the maximum speed of the boat is $OW \operatorname{cosec} \alpha$, and the course is then so directed that the wind blows at an angle α abaft the beam. Show also that if the speed of the boat be resolved into two components, one to true windward and one at right angles to that direction, the windward component is greatest when $\beta = \frac{1}{4}\pi + \frac{1}{2}\alpha$. Hence prove that, if the sail can be set so that $\alpha = \sin^{-1}\frac{1}{3}$, the maximum speed of the boat is three times the speed of the wind, and the boat travels to windward as fast as the wind blows in the opposite direction. (Greenhill.)

2. A train weighing W tons starts from rest under a net forward pull of P Tons, and in t seconds acquires a speed of v f/s and travels a distance of s feet. It is brought to rest at the next station in t' seconds and s' feet by a retarding force of P' Tons. Show that

$$Ps = Wv^2/2g = P's', \quad Pt = Wv/g = P't', \quad \tfrac{1}{2}v = (s+s')/(t+t').$$

It is required to run trains of 100 tons weight on a level electric railway, with stations half a mile apart, at an average speed of 12 miles an hour, including a half-minute stop at each station. Prove that the electric locomotives must weigh *at least* an additional 8 tons, if the coefficients of adhesion be $\frac{1}{5}$, and the trains be fitted with continuous brakes (so that if necessary the whole adhesion of the train with locked wheels may be utilised to stop). (Greenhill.)

3. A locomotive of weight M has two pairs of wheels (radius a) such that the moment of inertia of either pair (including axle) about the axis of rotation is A. The engine exerts a couple (moment G) on the forward axle. Prove that if both pairs of wheels bite at once when the engine starts, the friction capable of being called into play between one of the forward wheels and the rail must not be less than $\tfrac{1}{2}G(A+Ma^2)/a(2A+Ma^2)$: also prove that if the only action between an axle and its bearings is a couple of moment proportional to the angular speed of the axle, the final friction called into play between a forward wheel and the rail is $G/4a$. [Forces exerted by the rails are, F forward on the pair of driving wheels, and F' backward on the other pair. Hence $(Ma^2+2A)\dot{\omega} = G$, $Ma\dot{\omega} = F - F'$, $F'a = A\dot{\omega}$.]

4. Prove that the horse-power consumed in maintaining a flywheel, weighing W tons, revolving N times a minute in bearings a feet in diameter, is $2240\pi a N W \sin \phi / 33000$, if $\tan \phi$ be the coefficient of friction.

Prove that if the flywheel is left to itself it will come to rest after making $\pi k^2 N^2/1800 a g \sin \phi$ turns in $\pi k^2 N / 900 a g \sin \phi$ minutes, where k is the radius of gyration of the wheel about the axle. [Ex. 5, § 204.]

5. A truck consists of a framework with the wheels and springs, which carries a box above it hinged along the front of the truck. The box is filled with material so that it may be regarded as a uniform rectangular block of length $2a$, height $2b$, and mass M, with its centroid G at a distance h from the line of hinges. If the truck be suddenly stopped, find the speed so that the box may just turn over.

Prove that if the box thus turns over, the horizontal and vertical components of force on the hinges vanish when the plane through the line of hinges and G is inclined at the angles $\sin^{-1}(2/3)$ and $\sin^{-1}(1/3)$ respectively, and that the total force on the hinges has a minimum value $\tfrac{1}{4}\sqrt{7/11} \cdot Mg$ when the angle is $\sin^{-1}(20/33)$.

6. A pulley (weight M) has a fine cord wrapped round a groove (radius a) in its edge and its middle plane is coincident with that of a fixed vertical pulley over which the cord is passed in a groove (radius b). The free end of the cord carries a weight, M', and the parts of the cord depending from the fixed pulley are vertical. Find the motion.

Let MK^2 be the M.I. of the first pulley about its axis mk^2 that of the fixed pulley, T, T' the forces applied to the latter, by the cord, α, α' the downward linear accelerations of the movable pulley and the weight respectively. Let also $\dot{\omega}$ be the angular acceleration of the first pulley. The equations of motion are

$$MK^2\dot{\omega} = T\alpha, \quad M\alpha = Mg - T, \quad M'\alpha' = M'g - T', \quad mk^2\alpha' = (T' - T)b^2.$$

The reader may verify that since $\dot{\omega}a - \alpha' = \alpha$, these equations give

$$\alpha = \frac{\left(M'a^2 + (M-M')K^2 + m\dfrac{k^2}{b^2}\right)g}{(M+M')K^2 + M'a^2 + m\dfrac{k^2}{b^2}(K^2 + a^2)},$$

$$\alpha' = \frac{(M'a^2 - (M-M')K^2)g}{(M+M')K^2 + M'a^2 + m\dfrac{k^2}{b^2}(K^2 + a^2)}.$$

T and T' are determined by $T = M(g - \alpha)$, $T' = M(g - \alpha')$.

Any mass may be rigidly attached to the movable pulley, provided its centroid coincide with that of the pulley, and a principal axis with that of rotation. M is then the total mass at that end of the cord.

Find the motion of M in this example when the cord to which the unrolling pulley is attached is held at the upper end by a fixed point.

7. A body of moment of inertia Mk^2 about an axis round which it rotates with angular speed ω impinges on a particle of mass M'. The line of action of the shock is perpendicular to the axis of rotation and at a distance r from it.

Find the momentum communicated to M' and the value of r that this may be a maximum, on the supposition that just after the impact the bodies are moving in contact.

The speed of M' is $Mk^2r\omega/(M'r^2 + Mk^2)$, which is a maximum when $r = k\sqrt{M/M'}$. [Equate angular momenta before and after impact.]

8. A cord is wound round a vertical wheel (weight M, radius of groove a, and M.I. MK^2) which is free to turn about its axis which is fixed. A weight M' is attached to the free end of the cord. To find the acceleration of the system and determine at what distance from the axis M' must act so that the angular acceleration may be a maximum.

[The linear acceleration of M' is $M'a^2g/(MK^2 + M'a^2)$, and the angular acceleration of the wheel is $M'ag/(MK^2 + M'a^2)$. The latter is a maximum when $a = K\sqrt{M/M'}$.]

9. A heavy rod, free to move only in a vertical line, presses with its lower end on a smooth wedge which can slide along a smooth horizontal plane. If m be the mass of the rod, m' that of the wedge, and α the inclination of the face of the wedge to the horizon, show that the acceleration of the wedge is $mg \tan\alpha/(m' + m\tan^2\alpha)$.

10. An inclined plane of mass M and angle α can move without friction on a horizontal plane. A uniform sphere of mass m and radius a is placed on the incline and *rolls* down under the action of gravity. Prove that if x be the distance rolled over on the inclined plane by the sphere in time t, the horizontal displacement of the inclined plane in the same time is $mx\cos\alpha/(M+m)$, and

$$x = \frac{5(M+m)gt^2\sin\alpha}{14(M+m) - 10m\cos^2\alpha}.$$

11. A horizontal platform is kept moving with S.H.M. of amplitude c. A uniform cylinder of radius a is placed gently on the platform, with its axis horizontal and perpendicular to the motion of the platform.

Determine the motion of the cylinder, supposing the friction developed to be sufficient to ensure pure rolling of the cylinder on the plane. Prove that if the platform is at rest when the cylinder is placed upon it, the cylinder rocks over a strip of breadth $4c/3$.

12. The door of a railway carriage which has its hinges (supposed smooth) on the side of the door towards the engine stands open at right angles to the train, when the train starts off with uniform acceleration f. Show (neglecting any action of the air) that the door closes in time

$$\sqrt{\frac{a^2+k^2}{2af}} \int_0^{\frac{1}{2}\pi} \frac{d\theta}{\sqrt{\sin\theta}},$$

with a final angular speed $\sqrt{2af/(a^2+k^2)}$, where $2a$ is the breadth of the door, and k the radius of gyration about a vertical axis through the centroid.

13. A uniform rod is turning (without friction) about one extremity on a horizontal table and drives before it a particle of mass equal to its own, which starts from rest indefinitely near to the fixed extremity of the rod: show that when the particle has described a distance r along the rod, its direction of motion makes with the rod the angle

$$\tan^{-1}\theta = k/\sqrt{r^2+k^2}.$$

Why does the particle move outward along the rod?

14. A uniform solid spherical ball of mass m and radius a is at rest in a cylindrical garden roller of radius b, when the roller is seized and made to roll along the level with uniform speed V. Find the motion of the ball, supposing that it does not slip on the roller.

Prove that the inclination θ of the line of centres to the vertical varies as does the inclination to the vertical of the thread of a simple pendulum of length $\frac{7}{5}(b-a)$, and the ball will lose contact with the roller when $\theta = \frac{1}{17}\{10 - 7V^2/(b-a)g\}$. Hence find V so that the ball may just go completely round.

15. The wheel of an Atwood's machine is supported by placing the two ends of its axle in the well-known manner on two pairs of overlapping friction wheels or rollers: to work out the theory of the machine and explain the action of the rollers.

Let L be the moment of frictional forces applied to the axle (radius a, moment of inertia MK^2) of the wheel, T, T' ($T > T'$) the pulls applied to the rim of the wheel by the cord on the two sides. Hence if $\Omega =$ angular speed of wheel at time t,

$$MK^2\dot{\Omega} = (T - T')R - L.$$

Let the sum of the frictional couples on the axles of the rollers be L', and the sum of the moments of the rollers about their axes $4\mu k^2$. The angular speed of each roller is $\Omega R/r$, and therefore

$$4\mu k^2 \dot{\Omega} = L\frac{r^2}{aR} - L'\frac{r}{R}.$$

Elimination of L between these two equations gives

$$\left(MK^2 + 4\mu k^2 \frac{aR}{r^2}\right)\dot{\Omega} = (T - T')R - L'\frac{a}{r}.$$

But if $\alpha (= R\dot{\Omega})$ be the linear acceleration of m downwards and m' upwards,

$$(m + m')\alpha = (m - m')g - (T - T').$$

Hence
$$\alpha = \frac{(m - m')g - L'\dfrac{a}{rR}}{m + m' + M\dfrac{K^2}{R^2} + 4\mu k^2 \dfrac{a}{Rr^2}}.$$

If the radius a of the axle be small in comparison with both r and R, the effect of the frictional couple L' becomes negligible. The rollers therefore prevent friction from causing any sensible dissipation of energy. In many pieces of mechanism ball-bearings are used for this purpose. The theory of friction rollers here given requires modification for such bearings, since the balls are displaced bodily as they roll in the ball-races; but the action is similar. The couple L' is avoided by having no bearings for the balls, but on the other hand the motion of the balls is retarded by friction in the "races."

In Atwood's machines, as usually made, the ends of the axle are enormously too thick. A short length at each end should be turned down to the thickness of a darning needle.

16. Find the length of the shortest equivalent simple pendulum for a uniform solid hemisphere oscillating about an axis parallel to the base in a plane through the centroid perpendicular to the base.

17. A uniform rod of mass m and length $2a$ is hung from a fixed point by a fine cord of length l attached to one end, and the system moves in a vertical plane through the fixed point. Find the exact equations of motion, and prove that the equation of frequencies ($n/2\pi$) for small oscillations is

$$aln^4 - g(4a + 3l)n^2 + 3g^2 = 0.$$

18. Solve Ex. 17 when the string is replaced by a uniform rod, of mass μ and length $2l$, to which is freely jointed at the outer extremity the rod of mass m and length $2a$.

VII.]   EXERCISES.   437

19. Two uniform and equal rods AB, BC, freely jointed at B, are moving forward in line with speed v, the direction of motion being perpendicular to the lengths of the rods. If A is suddenly fixed, show that the speed of the middle point of AB is immediately reduced to $\frac{9}{14}v$, the angular speeds of AB, BC are made $9v/14a$, $-3v/14a$, respectively, and the kinetic energy is reduced by $\frac{1}{7}$ of its original value.

20. Determine the speed acquired by a block of wood, weighing W lb., free to move in a straight line, when struck directly by a bullet weighing w lb. moving with a speed of v feet per second; and prove that if the bullet is imbedded a feet, the resistance of the wood to the bullet, supposed uniform, is in Pounds $Wwv^2/(W+w)2ga$.

Prove also that the time of penetration is $2a/v$ seconds, during which time the block travels through a distance of $wa/(W+w)$ feet.

21. A railway carriage of weight W and moving with speed v impinges on a carriage of weight W' at rest. The force necessary to compress a buffer to the full extent l is equal to the force of gravity on a weight w. Assuming that the compression is proportional to the force, prove that the buffers will not be fully compressed if

$$v^2 < 2wgl(1/W + 1/W').$$

If the yielding of the backing against which the buffers are driven be neglected, prove that when v exceeds the limit stated the ratio of the final speeds is

$$\{Wv - \sqrt{2w\,W'gl/(1+W'/W)}\}/\{Wv + \sqrt{2w\,Wgl/(1+W/W')}\}.$$

Let the speed v be just sufficient for driving the buffers home, and let the common speed of the carriages when this is done be v'. Then by the principle of energy $(W+W')v'^2 = Wv^2 - 2mgl$. But $(W+W')v' = Wv$, and so $v^2 = 2wgl(1/W + 1/W')$. A smaller value of v would not give complete compression of the buffers.

If this value of v be exceeded, let the final speeds be v_1, v_2. Then finally the kinetic energy is what it was at first, and so

$$Wv_1^2 + W'v_2^2 = Wv^2.$$

Also $Wv_1 + W'v_2 = Wv$. Hence if $\rho = v_1/v_1$ we get

$$W(W\rho^2 + W')/(W\rho + W')^2 = 1,$$

or $\rho = (W - W')/2W$, which is zero when $W = W'$. But at the instant of complete compression of the buffers we have $(W+W')v'^2 = Wv^2 - mgl$, $(W+W')v^1 = Wv$, and therefore

$$Wv^2 = 2wgl(1 + W/W'),\ W'v^2 = 2wgl(1 + W'/W),$$

and the ratio can be written as stated.

22. A thin lamina moves, without rotation and unimpeded by friction, in contact with a horizontal plane, when a point A at distance x from the centroid is suddenly fixed. Prove that the speed of the centroid is changed to $vx^2 \sin\theta/(k^2 + x^2)$, where v denotes the original speed of the lamina, k its radius of gyration about a vertical axis through the centroid, and θ the angle between the original direction of motion and the line from the centroid to the point A.

[The angular momentum about the point of space with which A coincides at the instant cannot be changed by the fixing.]

CHAPTER VIII.

ROTATIONAL MOTION.

237. Motion of a Rigid Body about a Fixed Point. When a rigid body turns round an axis every point of the body receives a displacement in a circle, the centre of which is on, and the plane of which is at right angles to the axis: these displacements are all in the same direction round the axis, and are proportional to the distances of the points from it. An example is the turning of a wheel about a stationary axis.

The particles of the body retain the same configuration relative to one another, since clearly the particles in any plane whatever containing the axis retain the same configuration relative to one another, and the particles in any plane perpendicular to the axis remain also in the same relative positions as the plane turns.

At any instant while such a displacement is taking place, all the particles have speeds, in the coaxial circles which are their paths, proportional to the radii of these circles; that is, the perpendiculars to the axis from the different points are all turning with the same angular speed in the same direction.

We can prove that any displacement of a rigid body, one point of which is fixed, can be effected by a rotation of the body about a definite axis passing through the point and fixed in the body. Describe a spherical surface in the body with the fixed point O as centre, and let the displacement be one (however effected) in which points A, B of a spherical sheet of the body (centre O), are carried to $A'B'$. [The student should construct a suitable Figure.] The different points of the sheet do not alter their relative positions. Join A and A', B and B', by arcs of great circles, and through the middle points C, D of these arcs draw great circles on the spherical sheet meeting AA', BB' at right angles. These will meet in two diametrically opposite points I, I' on the spherical surface. Join AI, BI, $A'I$, $B'I$. The body might have been carried from the initial to the final position by a rotational displacement about the line II'. For by this turning A is carried to A' and B to B', and it is clear that the particles which lay on the part of the spherical surface bounded by the spherical triangle ABI are in the same relative positions on the part bounded by $A'B'I$; and all the particles in the spherical surface are in the same relative positions.

238. Every Rigid Body Displacement parallel to Fixed Plane is equivalent to a Rotation. A rigid body is displaced in such a way that a plane A fixed in the body, initially and finally coincides with a plane B fixed in space, and three points (not in line) in A come from P, Q, R to P', Q', R': it is clear that the displacement, whatever it may be, could be effected by first displacing the body so that every point of the plane A receives a displacement equal and parallel to PP', and then turning the body round an axis through P' at right angles to the plane B, until Q, R coincide with Q', R'. [Here again the reader should draw the necessary Figure.]

This displacement may also be effected by a turning, of the same amount and in the same direction, about an axis at right angles to the plane B. For, except in an extreme case, the lines joining P, P' and Q, Q' will not be parts of the same straight line. Excluding that case (in which no change of direction of lines in the body is involved), let these lines be drawn, and their middle points C, D be found, and lines perpendicular to PP', QQ' drawn through C and D. These meet in a point I. A turning about an axis through I at right angles to the plane B would evidently bring the three points P, Q, R to P', Q', R', and likewise all other points of the body from their initial to their final positions.

If s denote the displacement PP', and θ the angle of turning, which is clearly the same in both the modes of effecting the displacement described above, the co-ordinates of I in the plane B are evidently $PC = s$ and $CI = \frac{1}{2}s/\tan\frac{1}{2}\theta$, to be measured from C so that the angle $PIC (= \frac{1}{2}\theta)$ is in the direction of turning.

If the displacement s be the small displacement effected in time dt with speed $\dot{s}$, we have $PP' = \dot{s}\,dt$, and if $d\theta$ be the angle of turning, we have $CI = \dot{s}\,dt/d\theta$. The displacement might be effected in time dt by a turning about the axis at I, with angular speed $\dot{\theta}$, such that $\dot{\theta}\,dt = d\theta$. We have then $CI = \dot{s}/\dot{\theta}$. The axis through I is then the *instantaneous axis* about which the body may be regarded as turning.

239. Any Rigid Body Displacement is equivalent to that of a Nut on a Certain Screw. We can prove that any displacement whatever of a rigid body can be effected by a displacement of the body without rotation (a translation) parallel to a certain direction; and a rotation about an axis parallel to that direction. For the displacement can be effected by displacing the body without rotation, so that a point in it initially at P is transferred to its final position P', and then rotating the body about some axis through P'. The different points of the body in the latter displacement move in planes at right angles to the axis, and the direction of the axis and the angle of turning are independent of the choice of the point P. The former displacement, the translation PP', can be resolved into two components, PM and MP', at right angles to one another, of which MP' is at right angles to the axis of the rotational displacement. But, as we saw in § 238, the displacement MP', and the rotation about an axis through P' at right angles to MP', may be replaced by a turning about a parallel axis. Hence the displacement can be effected as specified in the proposition.

The two displacements may be supposed effected together, in such a manner that the amount of turning effected is always proportional to the translation; that is, the body may be regarded as having the motion of a nut along a screw, so that each point of the body moves in a helix. If s be the distance which measures the translation, and θ the angle which measures the turning, the ratio s/θ is the advance of the body per radian turned through, the "pitch" of the screw, while $2\pi s/\theta$ is the advance per complete turn, called the "step" (often also the *pitch*) of the screw. Thus all the helices in which the points of the body move have the same pitch. If the motion is a pure rotation $s=0$, and the pitch and step are zero; if the motion is a pure translation $\theta=0$, and the pitch and step are infinite.

The motion of a rigid body has been discussed very fully from this point of view by Sir Robert Ball in his *Theory of Screws*, which the reader may consult for further particulars. We shall find this mode of regarding the subject illustrated later by the theorem of the central axis [see § 247 below. In Chap. XI. below the central axis of a system of forces is considered. The system is reduced to a "wrench," a single force along the central axis, and a couple about a line parallel to the central axis]. That the central axis is a single determinate line will be proved in § 247.

240. Motion of a Rigid Body parallel to a Given Plane. Space and Body Centrodes. We have seen (§ 238) that any small displacement of a rigid body, which is moving parallel to a fixed plane, may be produced by turning the body through an angle $d\theta$ about an instantaneous axis which meets the fixed plane in the point I. To find I, we take two points P and Q in a plane in the body coinciding with the fixed plane, and apply the construction described in § 238. Since PP', QQ' are very short lines, the construction can be carried out by drawing two lines from P and Q, perpendicular respectively to the direction of motion at P and the direction of motion at Q. These meet at I. The points P and Q are obviously turning about I: the reader may prove that any other point in the body is turning about the axis drawn through I at right angles to the fixed plane.

As the body moves continuously the positions of the

instantaneous axis change in space and in the body. Thus, taking their intersections with the fixed plane, and with the plane in the body which moves in coincidence with it, we get two curves which are called respectively the *space-centrode* and the *body-centrode* (C_s, C_b). We can find their equations in the following manner.

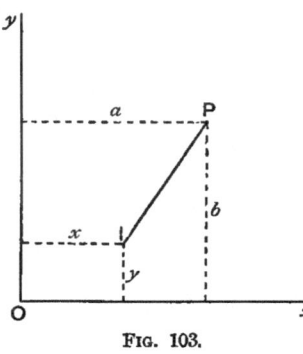

Fig. 103.

Take two axes Oxy in the fixed plane, as shown in Fig. 103. Let I be the intersection (coordinates x, y) of the plane by the instantaneous axis, and P any point (coordinates a, b). Then if l be the distance IP, and u, v the components of velocity of P, θ the inclination of IP to Ox, we have

$$-u = l\dot\theta \sin\theta = \dot\theta(b-y), \quad v = l\dot\theta \cos\theta = \dot\theta(a-x).$$

Hence $\qquad x = a - \dfrac{v}{\dot\theta}, \quad y = b + \dfrac{u}{\dot\theta}$. ....(1)

If a, b, u, v are known functions of the time, we can eliminate the time between these two equations, and thereby obtain the equation of C_s.

To find the equation of C_b, take two axes of ξ, η fixed in the plane of the body which moves in coincidence with the fixed plane, and let ξ, η be the coordinates of I with reference to these axes. Let θ have the same meaning as before, and θ' denote the angle at the instant between the fixed axis Ox and the axis of ξ. The coordinates of P are now $\qquad \xi + l\cos(\theta - \theta'), \quad \eta + l\sin(\theta - \theta')$,

and therefore, since

$$l\cos\theta = a - x = v/\dot\theta, \quad l\sin\theta = b - y = -u/\dot\theta,$$

they are

$$\xi + (v\cos\theta' - u\sin\theta')/\dot\theta, \quad \eta - (u\cos\theta' + v\sin\theta')/\dot\theta.$$

§§ 240, 241]   MOTION OF A RIGID BODY.   443

If now P be the origin of the ξ, η coordinates, we get
$$\xi = \frac{1}{\dot{\theta}}(u \sin \theta' - v \cos \theta'), \quad \eta = \frac{1}{\dot{\theta}}(u \cos \theta' + v \sin \theta'), \ldots (2)$$
which give the equation of C_b by elimination of the time.

The two curves C_s, C_b (Fig. 104) are two series of points such that, as the body moves, the points of the second series come in succession into coincidence with corresponding points of the first series, and each in doing so comes to rest *at the instant*, though, as the body moves continuously, it does not remain at rest for any *interval* of time, however short. At the instant of rest it coincides with the point I of the instantaneous axis. After an interval of time dt has elapsed, the instantaneous axis has passed to another position I', and another point P' of the body coincides with it.

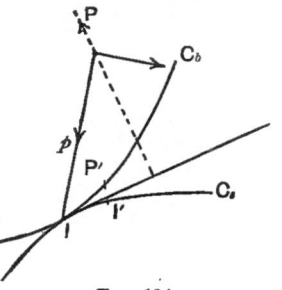

Fig. 104.

241. Velocity and Acceleration of Body-Point. The velocity of the point of C_b at the instant of coincidence with I is zero; its acceleration has in general a definite finite value. If $\dot{s}$ be the speed with which the point I moves along the curve C_s, it is plain that this is also the speed with which the position of the instantaneous axis moves along C_b. For clearly the distance IP' is equal to II', if P', I' be the points in the two curves which coincide after the interval dt. The curve C_b may be regarded as rolling without slipping along C_s, as a wheel rolls without slipping along a rail, and the distance which the instantaneous axis travels along the circle of contact of the wheel in any time is equal to the distance which it travels along the rail.

Now, since the curve C_b may be regarded as turning about I, the point P', at distance from $I = \dot{s}\,dt$, has speed $\omega \dot{s}\,dt$ (where $\omega = \dot{\theta}$) at right angles to IP', and this speed is annulled in the interval of time dt, in which P' travels to I'. Thus the acceleration of the point P' infinitely near

P is $\omega \dot{s}$, in the direction perpendicular to the curve C_s, opposed to that along which P' approaches the curve just before arrival. For a point P' on C_b, but on the other side of P, the acceleration is also $\omega \dot{s}$, in the same direction as before. It may be affirmed of course that P' has an acceleration $\omega^2 \dot{s}\, dt$ towards I, but this is infinitely small in comparison with $\omega \dot{s}$.

If P (Fig. 104) be *any* point in the body, in the plane for which the centrodes are drawn, and at distance r from P, the velocity of P is $r\omega$ at right angles to IP. Hence, relatively to I, the acceleration of P consists of two components $r\dot{\omega}$ at right angles to IP, and $r\omega^2$ in the direction from P towards I. But after dt, P is turning about I', and we must take account therefore of the acceleration of the point of the body coinciding with I. Thus we must add to the acceleration of P a component $\dot{s}\theta$, in the direction of the normal IN drawn to C_B (Fig. 105). That direction is also indicated by the dotted line through P in Fig. 104.

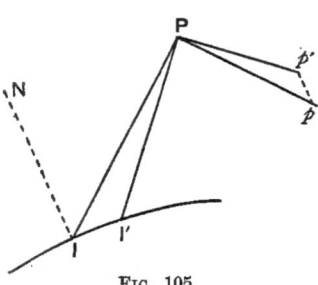

FIG. 105.

Or the acceleration may be found as follows (Fig. 105). From I, I' draw lines to the position of P for I, and lay off Pp, Pp' to represent $r\omega$, $r'\omega$; the geometrical difference $p'p$ between these lines represents the change in $r\dot{\theta}$ due to the displacement in dt from I to I'. The other changes produced are $r\dot{\omega}\, dt$ and $r\omega^2 dt$, the directions of which have been specified. But Pp, Pp' are proportional to IP, $I'P$, and the angle pPp' is equal to the angle IPI'. Hence the triangles IPI', pPp' are similar, and, since IPp is a right angle, pp' is at right angles to II'. Thus we have $pp' = II'. Pp/IP = \dot{s}\, dt . r\omega/r = \dot{s}\omega\, dt$. Thus the acceleration due to the motion of I along the space-centrode is $\dot{s}\omega$, and is parallel to the direction IN.

242. Curvature of Path of Body-Point. We can apply these results to find the curvature of the path described

MOTION OF A RIGID BODY.

by any point of the body. For, (Fig. 106), let the curve C_b roll on the curve C_s in the plane of the paper, and C, D be the centres of curvature of the two curves at the point of contact I. Then, if I' and P' are corresponding points, we have arc $IP'=$ arc II', and if the arcs be those traversed in time dt, $\dot{s}\,dt = IC \cdot \angle ICP' = ID \cdot \angle IDI'$. Let $IC = \rho$, $ID = \rho'$, and we have

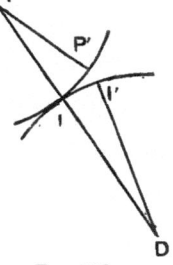

$$\angle ICP' + \angle IDI = \dot{s}\,dt\left(\frac{1}{\rho} + \frac{1}{\rho'}\right).$$

But this is the angle turned through by the body in time dt, and therefore

$$\omega = \dot{s}\left(\frac{1}{\rho} + \frac{1}{\rho'}\right). \quad \ldots\ldots\ldots(1)$$

FIG. 106.

This is on the supposition that, as shown in Fig. 106, the curvatures are oppositely directed. If the curvature of C_s be in the same direction as that of C_b,

$$\omega = \dot{s}\left(\frac{1}{\rho} - \frac{1}{\rho'}\right), \quad \ldots\ldots\ldots\ldots\ldots(2)$$

and, of course, $\rho' > \rho$. We get then for the acceleration of the body-point at I, the value

$$\omega\dot{s} = \omega^2\frac{\rho\rho'}{\rho+\rho'}, \quad \text{or} \quad \omega\dot{s} = \omega^2\frac{\rho\rho'}{\rho'-\rho}, \quad \ldots\ldots\ldots(3)$$

according as the curvatures are opposed or in the same direction. Also $\dot{s}/\omega = \rho\rho'/(\rho'\pm\rho)$.

For the point P (Fig. 105) in the body the total acceleration in the direction PI is, by the results obtained above, $\omega^2 r - \dot{s}\omega\cos\phi$, if ϕ denote $\angle PIN$. Thus

$$\omega^2 r - \dot{s}\omega\cos\phi = \omega^2 r^2/R,$$

where R is the radius of curvature of the path of P at the instant. Thus

$$\frac{1}{R} = \frac{\omega^2 r - \dot{s}\omega\cos\phi}{r^2\omega^2} = \frac{1}{r} - \frac{1}{r^2}\frac{\rho\rho'}{\rho'\pm\rho}\cos\phi. \quad \ldots\ldots(4)$$

This expression for the curvature vanishes if

$$r = \rho\rho' \cos \phi/(\rho' \pm \rho), \quad \ldots\ldots\ldots\ldots\ldots\ldots(5)$$

that is for all points on a circle in the body-plane touching both curves at I, and of diameter $\rho\rho'/(\rho' \pm \rho)$. All such body-points therefore pass points of inflexion in their paths at the same instant.

243. Signs of Angular Displacements. The direction of turning of a body about an axis is positive or negative according to the manner in which it is regarded. Thus the direction of turning of a flywheel may be taken as positive or negative according to the side from which it is viewed. Seen from one side the motion of the top (supposing the wheel vertical) is from right to left, seen from the other side it is from left to right. We usually take the former direction, or, to make the distinction applicable to all cases, the counter-clock direction, as positive, the clock direction as negative.

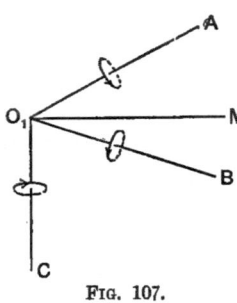

FIG. 107.

If we have to take account of turnings about a number of parallel axes, for example the turning of each of the wheels of a train of wheelwork, we may, viewing the arrangement from either side, reckon all those moving in the counter-clock direction as having a positive turning motion, and all those moving the other way as having a negative turning motion.

Again, when we have a number of axes in different directions which all pass through one point or origin, it is convenient to settle in each case, according to convenience, a direction from the origin outward along the axis, which is to be regarded as positive. Let O_1A, O_1B, O_1C, ... be these directions chosen as positive. Then, regarding the turning about each axis from the point $A, B, C, \ldots$, it is classed as positive or negative according as it is in the counter-clock direction or in the clock direction. Thus, in the figure the rotations about O_1A and O_1B appear

§§ 242, 243, 244]   MOTION OF A RIGID BODY.   447

to an eye situated at A and B respectively, counter-clock rotations, and are to be reckoned positive, while that about O_1C is in the clock direction, and is to be reckoned negative.

As already noticed in § 76, the turning of a rigid body about an axis is one in which each point of the body moves at right angles to the perpendicular drawn from the point to the axis, in the same way round for each point, and through a distance $\omega\, dt\, .\, p$, where $\omega\, dt$ is the (infinitely small) angle of turning, the same for all points, effected in time dt in consequence of the angular speed ω, and p is the length of the perpendicular. The arrangement of the particles and their relative distances are evidently undisturbed by this motion.

244. Composition of Angular Displacements. The displacement of a point P of a rigid body, due to a turning of the body through any small angle $\omega\, dt$ above any axis, say O_1A, being equal to the product $\omega\, dt\, .\, p$ of the angle turned through into the perpendicular distance of P from the axis O_1A, is numerically equal to the moment of a force $F = \omega\, dt$, acting along the axis, about the point P, or about an axis at P at right angles to the plane of O_1A and P. This leads to the conclusion that angular speeds about different axes (that is angular velocities) are to be compounded like forces of the same numerical amounts along the same axes. The theorems regarding the composition of angular velocities might be inferred from those of composition of forces, but for clearness we shall give a separate investigation.

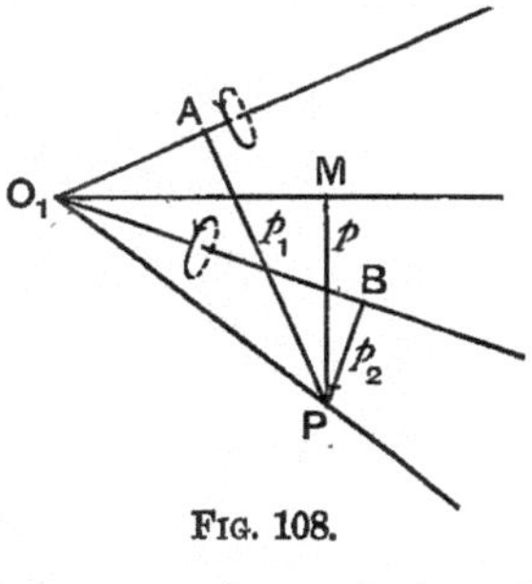

Let first P be a point on O_1M, and consider the motion of P, due to the turnings in an element of time dt, in consequence of angular speeds ω_1, ω_2, about O_1A and O_1B, in the directions shown by circular arrows in Fig. 108. Let PA, PB be perpendiculars from P on OA, OB, and denote the lengths of these perpendiculars by p_1, p_2. By

FIG. 108.

the turning $\omega_1 dt$ about $O_1 A$ the point P is depressed below the plane of the paper a distance $\omega_1 dt \cdot p_1$, and by the turning $\omega_2 dt$ about $O_1 B$ it is raised above the paper a distance $\omega_2 dt \cdot p_2$. The point P will be undisturbed if $\omega_1 p_1 = \omega_2 p_2$, that is if $\omega_1/\omega_2 = \sin \beta/\sin \alpha$, where α, β denote the angles AOP, BOP, and r the distance $O_1 P$. The same thing can be proved for any point lying in the line $O_1 M$, and for no other set of points. The line $O_1 M$ is thus an axis about which the body may be regarded as turning: this will be seen more clearly from what follows.

Let now P be *any* point in the plane AOB, which also contains $O_1 M$, and let PA, PB, PM, of lengths p_1, p_2, p, be perpendiculars let fall from P on $O_1 A$, $O_1 B$, $O_1 M$ (Fig. 108). Denoting the angle $PO_1 M$ by θ, and, as before, $O_1 P$ by r, and the angles $AO_1 M$, $MO_1 B$ by α, β, we have for the displacement of P, due to the turnings about OA and OB, the expression

$$dt(\omega_1 p_1 + \omega_2 p_2) = r\, dt \{\omega_1 \sin(\theta + \alpha) + \omega_2 \sin(\theta - \beta)\},$$

which may be written

$$r \sin \theta \cdot dt(\omega_1 \cos \alpha + \omega_2 \cos \beta),$$

since $\omega_1 \sin \alpha - \omega_2 \sin \beta = 0$, as we have already seen. If then we write

$$\omega = \omega_1 \cos \alpha + \omega_2 \cos \beta, \quad \dots\dots\dots\dots\dots(1)$$

we have for the displacement the expression $\omega\, dt \cdot p$.

Now $\omega_1 \cos \alpha + \omega_2 \cos \beta$ would, in the case of forces ω_1, ω_2 along the lines $O_1 A$, $O_1 B$, be recognised as the resultant of the forces, acting along OM, since the relation

$$\omega_1 \sin \alpha = \omega_2 \sin \beta$$

would show that there was no component of force at right angles to $O_1 M$. Hence we take $\omega_1 \cos \alpha + \omega_2 \cos \beta$, the result as we say of resolving ω_1, ω_2 about $O_1 M$, as the *resultant angular speed*, and the turning at this angular speed is about $O_1 M$, the line which we have seen remains at rest when the two turnings specified about $O_1 A$, $O_1 B$ are superimposed.

Now let P be taken at a distance h from the plane AOB. Fig. 108 will serve for this case also. We have to show that the displacement of P, compounded of those due to

§§ 244, 245]   MOTION OF A RIGID BODY.   449

the two turnings $\omega_1 dt$, $\omega_2 dt$ about the axes $O_1 A$, $O_1 B$, is equal to that produced by the single turning

$$(\omega_1 \cos \alpha + \omega_2 \cos \beta) dt$$

about OM, which is so situated in the plane $AO_1 B$ that

$$\omega_1 \sin \alpha = \omega_2 \sin \beta.$$

First consider the displacement $\omega_1 dt \cdot p_1$: this is at right angles to the perpendicular from P on OA, and lies in a plane at right angles to the plane AOB and containing that perpendicular. Evidently it can be resolved into two components, one at right angles to the plane AOB, and one parallel to the latter plane. Let P_0 be the projection of P on the plane AOB and r_0 the distance OP_0. Then, if θ is the angle $P_0 O_1 M$, the two components just specified are

$$r_0 dt \cdot \omega_1 \sin(\theta + \alpha) \quad \text{and} \quad \omega_1 h \, dt.$$

Similarly we have for the components due to the turning $\omega_2 dt$ about $O_1 B$ the expressions $r_0 dt \cdot \omega_2 \sin(\theta - \beta)$ and $\omega_2 h \, dt$. It has already been proved that the displacement $\omega \, dt \cdot p_1 = r_0 dt \{\omega_1 \sin(\theta + \alpha) + \omega_2 \sin(\theta - \beta)\}$. There remain the components $\omega_1 h \, dt$, $\omega_2 h \, dt$. These are parallel to the perpendiculars from P_0 on $O_1 A$ and $O_1 B$ respectively, and since they are proportional to ω_1, ω_2 have a resultant in the direction of the perpendicular from P_0 on OM. The magnitude of that resultant is $h \, dt (\omega_1 \cos \alpha + \omega_2 \cos \beta)$, that is $\omega h \, dt$. Hence it has been proved that the displacement at P, compounded of the independent displacements due to the two rotations specified, is identical with the displacement at the same point due to the resultant rotation, that compounded of the rotations ω_1, ω_2 about $O_1 A$, $O_1 B$.

The rotations about $O_1 A$, $O_1 B$ may be each the result of compounding the rotations about a pair of axes, and so on, so that the rotation about $O_1 M$ may be the resultant obtained by compounding the rotations about any number of axes given in position.

245. Turning about any Axis expressed by Component Turnings about Three Rectangular Axes. We shall now show that if a rigid body turns with angular speed ω about an axis $O_1 M$, passing through any point O_1, the same motion is produced by the displacement due to independent turnings at angular speeds $l\omega$, $m\omega$, $n\omega = p$, q, r, about three fixed axes $O_1 x_1 y_1 z_1$ at right angles to one another, and making angles with $O_1 M$, the cosines of which are l, m, n.

The distance ϖ of any point P (coordinates x, y, z with reference to axes $O_1 xyz$) of the body from $O_1 M$ is

$$\{x^2 + y^2 + z^2 - (lx + my + nz)^2\}^{\frac{1}{2}}.$$

Hence the displacement effected in dt is this multiplied by $\omega\, dt$, that is

$$\omega\varpi\, dt = dt\{(mz - ny)^2 + (nx - lz)^2 + (ly - mx)^2\}^{\frac{1}{2}} \atop = dt\{(qz - ry)^2 + (rx - pz)^2 + (py - qx)^2\}^{\frac{1}{2}}. \quad (1)$$

The expression on the right can easily be seen to be equivalent to the three displacements of the point P, $p\sqrt{y^2 + z^2}.dt$, $q\sqrt{z^2 + x^2}.dt$, $r\sqrt{x^2 + y^2}.dt$, due to the turning through the angles $p\, dt$, $q\, dt$, $r\, dt$ about the axes of the set $O_1 x_1 y_1 z_1$ respectively, where each turning is supposed to be effected independently of the others, from the same initial position of the body. The three displacements resulting from these turnings are not generally at right angles to one another, but they give the displacements parallel to the axes as follows:—$pz\, dt$ and $py\, dt$ parallel to $O_1 y_1$ and $O_1 z_1$, the components of $p\sqrt{y^2 + z^2}.dt$, $-qx\, dt$ and $qz\, dt$ parallel to $O_1 z_1$ and $O_1 x_1$, the components of $q\sqrt{z^2 + x^2}.dt$, and $-ry$ and rx parallel to $O_1 x_1$ and $O_1 y_1$, the components of $r\sqrt{x^2 + y^2}.dt$.

246. Component Linear Velocities of Point in Turning Body. The rates of displacement of the point P parallel to the axes are therefore $qz - ry$, $rx - pz$, $py - qx$; and so we have the equations

$$u = qz - ry, \quad v = rx - pz, \quad w = py - qx, \quad \ldots\ldots(1)$$

which are useful in many applications.

These are component velocities of the point P due to the rotations of the body about the axes. From them we can obtain at once the expressions for the components of velocity for a set of mutually rectangular axes $Oxyz$ which are turning with angular speeds p, q, r about Ox, Oy, Oz

respectively. For we may suppose these axes fixed in the rigid body, and, in the course of their turning with it, to be at time t in coincidence with the fixed axes $O_1x_1y_1z_1$. The motion of the particle P, if that particle is fixed in the body, has in consequence of the rotation of the body the components just written down.

But if the particle at P be moving in the body, and we now regard x, y, z as the coordinates of P relative to the moving axes at the instant, which of course we may do, since at the instant the axes are coincident with the fixed axes, the components $\dot{x}$, $\dot{y}$, $\dot{z}$, relative to the moving axes, give the rates of displacement of the particle in the body with respect to axes fixed in it and therefore moving with it. The components u, v, w of the velocity with respect to the fixed axes $O_1x_1y_1z_1$ are therefore given by

$$u = \dot{x} + qz - ry, \quad v = \dot{y} + rx - pz, \quad w = \dot{z} + py - qx. \quad \ldots(2)$$

Thus if we draw the vector OP, the components of the motion of the outer extremity, P, are given by these equations. The terms $qz - ry, \ldots$, are those which depend on the motion of the system of axes $Oxyz$, those, in fact, due to the motion of the rigid body here supposed to carry the axes, and with them also the point P. Thus $qz - ry, \ldots$ are called by French writers the components of the velocity of *entraînement*; perhaps they may be termed the components of *co-velocity*.

If the origin of the moving axes does not coincide with that of the fixed axes, the values of u, v, w require no modification, provided the two systems are parallel and the origin O is not in motion. If, however, O is in motion with components u_0, v_0, w_0, the equations become, as the reader may easily convince himself,

$$\left. \begin{array}{l} u = \dot{x} + u_0 + qz - ry, \quad v = \dot{y} + v_0 + rx - pz, \\ w = \dot{z} + w_0 + py - qx. \end{array} \right\} \quad \ldots\ldots(3)$$

Then the components of the velocity of *entraînement* are

$$u_0 + qz - ry, \quad v_0 + rx - pz, \quad w_0 + py - qx.$$

The same results may be obtained in the following manner. Let the fixed axis O_1X_1 at time t make angles,

the direction-cosines of which are α, β, γ, with the axes OX, OY, OZ, and let the projection of O_1O on the axis O_1X_1 be x_0. Then if x_1 be the projection of O_1P on O_1X_1, we obtain
$$x_1 = x_0 + \alpha x + \beta y + \gamma z, \quad \ldots\ldots\ldots\ldots\ldots(4)$$
and therefore
$$\dot{x}_1 = \dot{x}_0 + \alpha \dot{x} + \beta \dot{y} + \gamma \dot{z} + \dot{\alpha} x + \dot{\beta} y + \dot{\gamma} z. \quad \ldots\ldots\ldots(5)$$
But if the directions of $Oxyz$ coincide with those of $O_1x_1y_1z_1$, then $\alpha = 0$, $\beta = \gamma = \pi/2$, and, since $d(\cos\theta)/dt = -\sin\theta \cdot \dot{\theta}$, $\dot{\alpha} = 0$, $\dot{\beta} = 0$, $\dot{\beta} = -r$, $\dot{\gamma} = 0$, $\dot{\gamma} = q$, and therefore, writing u for $\dot{x}_1$, and u_0 for $\dot{x}_0$, we get
$$u = \dot{x} + u_0 + qz - ry. \quad \ldots\ldots\ldots\ldots\ldots(6)$$
Similar expressions are obtained in the same way for v and w.

247. Central Axis. Let, now, the point P be fixed in the body so that $\dot{x} = \dot{y} = \dot{z} = 0$. Then u_0, v_0, w_0 are the same for all points of the body, and are the components of a motion of translation of the body as a whole parallel to the fixed axes with which the moving axes at the instant coincide. We can find for each instant a line in the body which fulfils the condition that the motion at every point of it is in the direction of the axis of resultant angular velocity. The equations of the line are

$$\frac{qz - ry + u_0}{p} = \frac{rx - pz + v_0}{q} = \frac{py - qx + w_0}{r}. \quad \ldots\ldots(1)$$

It is called the *central axis of the motion*. Its equation depends on the components u_0, v_0, w_0 of the translational motion, and the components p, q, r of angular velocity, just as the central axis defined in §343 below for forces depends on the resultant of a set of forces and their moments about the axes.

It may be observed that the central axis is the locus of points for which the resultant speed

$$v = \{(qz - ry + u_0)^2 + (rx - pz + v_0)^2 + (py - qx + w_0)^2\}^{\frac{1}{2}} \quad (2)$$

is a minimum. For if this expression be differentiated partially with respect to x, y, z, and the derivatives be equated to zero, we get exactly the equation of the line.

§§ 246, 247, 248] CENTRAL AXIS: EXAMPLES.   453

With respect to the fixed axes, to which $Oxyz$ are parallel, the equations of the central axis are

$$\left.\begin{array}{l}\dfrac{q(z_1-z_0)-r(y_1-y_0)+u_0}{p}=\dfrac{r(x_1-x_0)-p(z_1-z_0)+v_0}{p}\\=\dfrac{p(y_1-y_0)-q(x_1-x_0)+w_0}{r}.\end{array}\right\} \quad (3)$$

If we denote the common value of these ratios by V/ω, V/ω is the ratio of the rate of displacement of a point of the body parallel to the central axis to the rate of rotation around it, the pitch of the screw at the point (see § 239). If $V=0$, the body has motion of rotation only, if $\omega=0$ the motion is of translation only.

248. Examples on Central Axis and Rotation.

Ex. 1. Planes are drawn through any two points P, Q of a rigid body at right angles to the trajectories of these points, and meet the central axis A in M, N. Show that M, N are the feet of the perpendiculars let fall from P, Q to the central axis, and that

$$MN = PQ \cos(PQ, A). \text{[Chasles.]}$$

No generality is lost by taking the central axis A as the axis of x, the coordinates of P as x_1, 0, z_1, and the coordinates of Q as x_2, y_2, z_2. The point P has speeds u_0 parallel to the axis of x, $-\omega z_1$ parallel to the axis of y, and zero parallel to the axis of z. The corresponding speeds of Q are u_0, $-\omega z_2$, ωy_2. Hence the equation of a plane through P at right angles to the trajectory of P is

$$u_0(x-x_1)-\omega z_1 y = 0,$$

which meets the central axis in the point $x=x_1$.

Again, the equation of a plane through Q normal to the trajectory of that point is
$$u_0(x-x_2)-\omega z_2(y-y_2)+\omega y_2(z-z_2)=0,$$
that is, $$u_0(x-x_2)-\omega z_2 y+\omega y_2 z=0,$$

which meets the central axis in the point $x=x_2$.

Hence the first part of the proposition is proved. The second is self-evident, since MN is the projection of PQ on the axis A.

Ex. 2. From an arbitrary origin, say the origin O of coordinates, are drawn three vectors OA, OB, OC, representing in magnitude and direction the velocities at three points P, Q, R of the body: to show that the central axis is at right angles to the plane of the three points A, B, C, and to find the intersection of the central axis with that plane.

If the coordinates of the three points be x_1, y_1, z_1, x_2, y_2, z_2, x_3, y_3, z_3, the coordinates of A, B, C are

$$u_0 + qz_1 - ry_1, \quad v_0 + rx_1 - pz_1, \quad w_0 + py_1 - qx_1$$

for A, with similar expressions for B and C, to be obtained by changing the suffixes to 2 for B and to 3 for C. If we denote these three sets of coordinates by ξ_1, η_1, ζ_1, ξ_2, η_2, ζ_2, ξ_3, η_3, ζ_3, we get for the equation of the plane ABC,

$$\begin{vmatrix} x, & y, & z, & 1 \\ \xi_1, & \eta_1, & \zeta_1, & 1 \\ \xi_2, & \eta_2, & \zeta_2, & 1 \\ \xi_3, & \eta_3, & \zeta_3, & 1 \end{vmatrix} = 0.$$

The coefficient of x in this is $\eta_1(\zeta_2 - \zeta_3) + \eta_2(\zeta_3 - \zeta_1) + \eta_3(\zeta_1 - \zeta_2)$, and the coefficients of y and z can be written down by symmetry. Substituting the values of the coordinates, we find that these three coefficients are respectively p, q, r multiplied by a common factor. Hence the direction-cosines of the normal to the plane are proportional to p, q, r, and the proposition is proved.

The completion of the example is left to the student.

Ex. 3. A rigid body is turning about a fixed point O; show that if the instantaneous axis of rotation, OI, is fixed in the body it is also fixed in space, and conversely.

Let the direction-cosines of a fixed axis Ox_1, referred to the moving axes, be l, m, n. Then the angle between OI and Ox_1 has cosines $\alpha = (lp + mq + nr)/\omega, \ldots$ Hence

$$\dot{\alpha} = \frac{1}{\omega}(l\dot{p} + m\dot{q} + n\dot{r} + \dot{l}p + \dot{m}q + \dot{n}r) - \frac{\dot{\omega}}{\omega^2}(lp + mq + nr).$$

If the axis OI is fixed in the body, we must have, however p, q, r may change, $p/\omega = k_1$, $q/\omega = k_2$, $r/\omega = k_3$, where k_1, k_2, k_3 are constants. Hence $\dot{p}/\dot{\omega} = p/\omega$, $\dot{q}/\dot{\omega} = q/\omega$, $\dot{r}/\dot{\omega} = r/\omega$. Thus

$$\omega(l\dot{p} + m\dot{q} + n\dot{r}) = (lp + mq + nr)\dot{\omega},$$

and therefore
$$\dot{\alpha} = \frac{1}{\omega}(\dot{l}p + \dot{m}q + \dot{n}r).$$

Now for the motion of a point of coordinates x, y, z, we have $u = qz - ry$, $v = rx - pz$, $w = py - qx$. Take a point on the axis Ox_1, at unit distance from the origin; its coordinates with respect to the moving axes are l, m, n. The values of u, v, w therefore give

$$\dot{l} = nq - mr, \quad \dot{m} = lr - np, \quad \dot{n} = mp - lq,$$

and so $\dot{l}p + \dot{m}q + \dot{n}r = 0$. Thus $\dot{\alpha} = 0$, that is the angle which OI makes with the axis Ox_1, is constant, if $(p, q, r)/\omega$ remain constant; and Ox_1 may be any fixed axis. The direct proposition is therefore proved.

§ 248]   ROTATIONAL MOTION: EXAMPLES.   455

To prove the converse, we begin with $\dot{\alpha}=0$ and note that we have also $\dot{l}p+\dot{m}q+\dot{n}r=0$. Hence we obtain

$$\omega(l\dot{p}+m\dot{q}+n\dot{r})=\dot{\omega}(lp+mq+nr)$$

or
$$l(\omega\dot{p}-\dot{\omega}p)+m(\omega\dot{q}-\dot{\omega}q)+n(\omega\dot{r}-\dot{\omega}r)=0,$$

which must hold for all values of l, m, n. Thus we have $p/\omega=\dot{p}/\dot{\omega}, \ldots$, the conditions that the axis should be fixed in space.

Ex. 4. Prove that if a body be turning about a fixed point, the angular acceleration about an axis, the cosines of which with respect to the moving axes are l, m, n, is $l\dot{p}+m\dot{q}+n\dot{r}$. If ω_1 be the angular speed about the axis in question, we have $\omega_1=lp+mq+nr$. Hence $\dot{\omega}_1=l\dot{p}+m\dot{q}+n\dot{r}+\dot{l}p+\dot{m}q+\dot{n}r$. But in last example it is proved that $\dot{l}p+\dot{m}q+\dot{n}r=0$, and therefore we have

$$\dot{\omega}_1=l\dot{p}+m\dot{q}+n\dot{r}.$$

Ex. 5. A body moves along a curve in space in the following manner. A point fixed in the body describes the curve, and three lines fixed in the body and intersecting in that point are always directed so that the first is along the tangent to the curve in the direction of motion, the second along the principal normal, and the third at right angles to the osculating plane. These lines are at right angles to one another and in the order named form a system of moving axes $Oxyz$, in which the turning is from y to z, z to x and x to y. It is required to find the angular speeds about the axes.

Let the radius of curvature at any position of the body be ρ, and the radius of torsion—that is the reciprocal of the rate at which the osculating plane is turning round the tangent per unit distance travelled along the curve—be τ, and let s, the distance travelled along the curve from $t=0$ to the instant considered, be $f(t)$. According to the sign usually given to the analytical expression denoted by τ, the rate of turning of the body about Ox is $-\dot{s}/\tau=-f'(t)/\tau$. The rate of turning about the radius of curvature is zero, since the changes in the direction of the tangent lie wholly in the osculating plane for the instant. Finally, the rate of turning in the osculating plane is that about the binormal as an axis, and is $\dot{s}/\rho=f'(t)/\rho$. Hence we have

$$p=-f'(t)/\tau, \quad q=0, \quad r=f'(t)/\rho.$$

To find the equations of the central axis, we note that the axis of x here taken has, with reference to axes $O_1x_1y_1z_1$, direction-cosines $d\xi/ds$, $d\eta/ds$, $d\zeta/ds$, where ξ, η, ζ are the coordinates of the position at time t of the point which moves along the curve. The cosines of the y-axis are

$$\rho(d^2\xi/ds^2, \, d^2\eta/ds^2, \, d^2\zeta/ds^2),$$

and of the z-axis,

$$\rho(d\eta/ds \cdot d^2\zeta/ds^2 - d\zeta/ds \cdot d^2\eta/ds^2), \ldots\ldots$$

Calling these three sets of cosines a, b, c, a', b', c', a'', b'', c'', and putting x_1, y_1, z_1 for the coordinates of a point P of the body, we get

$$x=a(x_1-\xi)+\ldots, \quad y=a'(x_1-\xi)+\ldots, \quad z=a''(x_1-\xi)+\ldots,$$

456   A TREATISE ON DYNAMICS.   [CH. VIII.

and therefore the equations of the central axis are

$$q\{a''(x_1-\xi)+\ldots\}-r\{a'(x_1-\xi)+\ldots\}=p\frac{V}{\omega}-\dot{s},$$

$$r\{a\ (x_1-\xi)+\ldots\}-p\{a''(x_1-\xi)+\ldots\}=q\frac{V}{\omega},$$

$$p\{a'(x_1-\xi)+\ldots\}-q\{a\ (x_1-\xi)+\ldots\}=r\frac{V}{\omega},$$

where p, q, r have the values found for them above, and V is $\dot{s}\cos(\omega, s)$.

Ex. 6. Prove that if the ratio $\rho/\tau = \text{const.}$, the curve in the last example is a helix traced on a cylinder.

If we draw axes from a fixed point parallel to the moving axes $Oxyz$, then, since ρ/τ is constant, the line through O parallel to the central axis is fixed relatively to the system of axes. It is therefore fixed in space (see Example 3), and therefore the axis Ox makes a constant angle with the instantaneous axis, which remains fixed in direction as the body moves.

249. Accelerations of Point in Rotating Body. Equations of Motion. In precisely the same way if we set up a vector from O, the components of which along the axes $Oxyz$, that is, parallel to Ox, Oy, Oz, are u, v, w, we obtain the components of acceleration in terms of x, y, z, p, q, r, $\dot{x}, \dot{y}, \dot{z}, u_0, v_0, w_0$, and their rates of variation. If the components of acceleration along the fixed axes be a_x, a_y, a_z, we have

$$\left.\begin{aligned}a_x &= \dot{u}+qw-rv = \ddot{x}+\dot{u}_0+2q\dot{z}-2r\dot{y}+\dot{q}z-\dot{r}y\\&\qquad\qquad\qquad\qquad+p(qy+rz)-(q^2+r^2)x,\\a_y &= \dot{v}+ru-pw = \ddot{y}+\dot{v}_0+2r\dot{x}-2p\dot{z}+\dot{r}x-\dot{p}z\\&\qquad\qquad\qquad\qquad+q(rz+px)-(r^2+p^2)y,\\a_z &= \dot{w}+pv-qu = \ddot{z}+\dot{w}_0+2p\dot{y}-2q\dot{x}+\dot{p}y-\dot{q}x\\&\qquad\qquad\qquad\qquad+r(px+qy)-(p^2+q^2)z.\end{aligned}\right\} \ldots(1)$$

The first two terms on the right in these expressions are the components of relative acceleration, the next two terms, $2(q\dot{z}-r\dot{y})$, $2(r\dot{x}-p\dot{z})$, $2(p\dot{y}-q\dot{x})$, form the components of what is called the complementary acceleration, and the three groups of four terms remaining form the components of the acceleration of *entraînment* or *co-acceleration*. Thus, denoting

$$\dot{q}z-\dot{r}y+p(qy+rz)-(q^2+r^2)x$$

by a_{xc}, $2q\dot{z}-2r\dot{y}$ by a'_{xc}, and so on, we have
$$a_x = \ddot{x}+a_{xc}+a'_{xc}, \quad a_y = \ddot{y}+a_{yc}+a'_{yc}, \quad a_z = \ddot{z}+a_{zc}+a'_{zc},$$
where $\dot{u}_0$, $\dot{v}_0$, $\dot{w}_0$ are supposed included in $\ddot{x}$, $\ddot{y}$, $\ddot{z}$.

Thus, if X, Y, Z be forces on a particle at P, the equations of motion are
$$\left.\begin{array}{c}m\ddot{x}+ma_{xc}+ma'_{xc}=X, \quad m\ddot{y}+ma_{yc}+ma'_{yc}=Y,\\ m\ddot{z}+ma_{zc}+ma'_{zc}=Z.\end{array}\right\} \ldots(2)$$

These equations may be written
$$m\ddot{x}=X+X_c, \quad m\ddot{y}=Y+Y_c, \quad m\ddot{z}=Z+Z_c, \quad \ldots\ldots(3)$$
where $X_c = -m(a_{xc}+a'_{xc})$, ... Thus the equations of motion are now of the form for axes at rest, but the force in each case is the applied force, with a force added sufficient to produce an acceleration equal and opposite to $a_{xc}+a'_{xc}$, ...

It will be noticed that the components a'_{xc}, a'_{yc}, a'_{zc} represent a vector at right angles to the plane of the vector (p, q, r) (the instantaneous axis about which the body is turning with angular speed $\omega = \sqrt{p^2+q^2+r^2}$) and the vector $v_r = \sqrt{\dot{x}^2+\dot{y}^2+\dot{z}^2}$ (where $\dot{x}$, $\dot{y}$, $\dot{z}$ include $\dot{x}_0$, $\dot{y}_0$, $\dot{z}_0$ if these exist), that is, the vector representing the relative velocity. Its magnitude is $2\omega v_r \sin(\omega, v_r)$, where (ω, v_r) is the angle between the positive direction of the instantaneous axis and that of v_r, and its sense is that in which the turning ω tends to carry the outer end of the vector v_r.

250. Angular Momenta. By (2), §71, the components of angular momentum about the fixed axes $O_1x_1y_1z_1$ are given by the equations
$$\left.\begin{array}{c}H_1 = \Sigma\{m(\dot{z}y-\dot{y}z)\}, \quad H_2 = \Sigma\{m(\dot{x}z-\dot{z}x)\},\\ H_3 = \Sigma\{m(\dot{y}x-\dot{x}y)\},\end{array}\right\} \ldots\ldots(1)$$
and therefore by (1), §246, we have
$$H_1 = p\Sigma\{m(y^2+z^2)\} - q\Sigma(mxy) - r\Sigma(mxz), \quad \ldots\ldots(2)$$
with similar expressions for H_2, H_3. But $\Sigma\{m(y^2+z^2)\}, \ldots$ are the moments of inertia about the axes and are denoted by A, B, C, while $\Sigma(myz), \ldots$ are products of inertia and are denoted by D, E, F. Hence
$$\left.\begin{array}{c}H_1 = Ap - Fq - Er, \quad H_2 = Bq - Dr - Fp,\\ H_3 = Cq - Ep - Dq.\end{array}\right\} \ldots\ldots(3)$$

When the axes are principal axes of moment of inertia $D=E=F=0$ and

$$H_1=Ap, \quad H_2=Bq, \quad H_3=Cr. \quad \ldots\ldots\ldots\ldots(4)$$

The kinetic energy T is given by

$$\begin{aligned}T &= \tfrac{1}{2}\Sigma[m\{(qz-ry)^2+(rx-pz)^2+(py-qx)^2\}] \\ &= \tfrac{1}{2}[p^2\Sigma\{m(y^2+z^2)\}+q^2\Sigma\{m(z^2+x^2)\} \\ &\qquad\qquad +r^2\Sigma\{m(x^2+y^2)\} \\ &\qquad -2qr\Sigma(myz)-2rp\Sigma(mzx)-2pq\Sigma(mxy)],\end{aligned} \quad \ldots(5)$$

and so by (2) $\quad \dfrac{\partial T}{\partial p}=H_1, \quad \dfrac{\partial T}{\partial q}=H_2, \quad \dfrac{\partial T}{\partial r}=H_3. \quad \ldots\ldots\ldots\ldots(6)$

Also clearly $\quad T=\tfrac{1}{2}(pH_1+qH_2+rH_3). \quad \ldots\ldots\ldots\ldots\ldots(7)$

A proof in all respects similar to that given in § 244 above for the composition of angular velocities might be framed to show that the angular momentum about the axis, the direction-cosines of which are proportional to H_1, H_2, H_3, is $(H_1^2+H_2^2+H_3^2)^{\frac{1}{2}}$, and that, if this be called H, the angular momentum about any axis inclined at an angle θ to that of H is $H\cos\theta$; but the subject has already been discussed in § 71.

It has been proved in § 75 that the time-rate of change of angular momentum, about any axis, is equal to the sum of the moments of the impressed forces about the axis, or, as it is sometimes put, to the moment of the impressed couple about that axis. This holds whether or not the system is a rigid body.

251. Representation of A.M. as a Vector. Rates of Change of A.M. about Moving Axes. It is convenient to measure a distance from O along any axis OA, OB, ..., in the positive direction, in length numerically equal to the angular momentum, or angular speed, or moment of forces, as the case may be, about the axis. The points $A, B, \ldots$ may be the outer terminal points of these distances or vectors, and will show by their displacements as time passes, how the direction or the numerical value of the directed quantity represented by the vector is varying.

Now, the time-rates of change of angular momentum for the fixed axes $O_1x_1y_1z_1$ have been found in § 72 above, and if these be denoted by $\dot{H}_1, \dot{H}_2, \dot{H}_3$, the time-rate of change of angular momentum about any axis O_1N, the direction cosines of which with reference to $O_1x_1y_1z_1$ are l, m, n, is $l\dot{H}_1+m\dot{H}_2+n\dot{H}_3$. Also, in § 170 have been derived the rates of growth of angular momentum for a rigid body, about the principal axes of moment of inertia supposed fixed in the body, and therefore turning with angular speed p about O_1x_1, q about O_1y_1, and r about O_1z_1 ($\omega_1, \omega_2, \omega_3$, in § 170).

For the case of angular momentum referred to a system of axes $Oxyz$ turning with angular speed $\theta_1, \theta_2, \theta_3$ about fixed axes, with which the moving axes at the instant coincide, we can find the equations of motion by an application of the method explained in § 9 above. We shall denote the components of angular momentum referred to the system of rotating axes by h_1, h_2, h_3, and identify these with the directed quantities L, M, N referred to in § 9. The symbols L, M, N, thus set free, we shall use to represent the moments of impressed forces—the impressed couples—about the axes. Thus we get, if the origin O be at rest,

$$\left.\begin{aligned}\dot{h}_1-\theta_3h_2+\theta_2h_3&=L,\\ \dot{h}_2-\theta_1h_3+\theta_3h_1&=M,\\ \dot{h}_3-\theta_2h_1+\theta_1h_2&=N.\end{aligned}\right\} \quad\ldots\ldots\ldots\ldots\ldots\ldots(1)$$

If the axes are fixed in space $\theta_1, \theta_2, \theta_3$ are zero, and the expressions on the left reduce to their first terms. If the axes are fixed in the body, then $\theta_1, \theta_2, \theta_3$ are the angular speeds, p, q, r say, of the body at the instant about these axes fixed in itself. If moreover the axes fixed in the body coincide with the principal axes of moment of inertia of the body, we have $h_1=Ap, h_2=Bq, h_3=Cr$, so that the equations of motion become

$$\left.\begin{aligned}A\dot{p}-(B-C)qr&=L,\\ B\dot{q}-(C-A)rp&=M,\\ C\dot{r}-(A-B)pq&=N,\end{aligned}\right\} \quad\ldots\ldots\ldots\ldots (2)$$

which are the Euler's equations, found in § 170 by another method. These give only the rates of change of the angular momenta, so that the body is either turning about a fixed point, for which the principal axes are taken, or the translational motion is ignored.

252. Body with One Point fixed. Deductions from Euler's Equations. From these equations we can obtain some important results. Multiply the first equation by p, the second by q, and the third by r, and add. The sum on the left is $Ap\dot{p}+Bq\dot{q}+Cr\dot{r}$, so that

$$Ap\dot{p}+Bq\dot{q}+Cr\dot{r} = Lp+Mq+Nr. \quad \ldots\ldots\ldots\ldots(1)$$

The kinetic energy T is given by the equation

$$T = \tfrac{1}{2}(Ap^2+Bq^2+Cr^2), \quad \ldots\ldots\ldots\ldots\ldots\ldots(2)$$

so that the equation just obtained can be written

$$\frac{dT}{dt} = Lp+Mq+Nr. \quad \ldots\ldots\ldots\ldots\ldots\ldots\ldots(3)$$

The quantity on the right is the time-rate at which work is being done by the impressed couples as the body moves, and this is the time-rate of growth of the kinetic energy. Hence, if $L=M=N=0$, the system moves subject to the condition that the kinetic energy is constant.

If we multiply the first Euler's equation by Ap, the second by Bq, and the third by Cr, we get

$$A^2p\dot{p}+B^2q\dot{q}+C^2r\dot{r} = LAp+MBq+NCr. \quad \ldots\ldots(4)$$

The square, h^2, of the resultant angular momentum is given by
$$h^2 = A^2p^2+B^2q^2+C^2r^2, \quad \ldots\ldots\ldots\ldots\ldots\ldots(5)$$

and therefore the equation just found can be written

$$\frac{dh}{dt} = \frac{1}{h}(LAp+MBq+NCr), \quad \ldots\ldots\ldots\ldots\ldots(6)$$

that is, the time-rate of growth of resultant angular momentum is equal to the resultant moment of the impressed couples about the axis of resultant angular momentum. If
$$L=M=N=0,$$

the resultant angular momentum (H below) remains constant

in amount, and its axis (OH say) unchanged in direction as the body moves. The axis of resultant angular velocity OI, the instantaneous axis, is not, however, stationary, and the value of ω ($=\sqrt{p^2+q^2+r^2}$) also varies.

253. Body with One Point fixed. Relation of Axis of Resultant A.M. and Instantaneous Axis. The cosine of the angle between the axes OH and OI (angle POH in Fig. 109, below) is $(Ap^2+Bq^2+Cr^2)/H\omega$, that is, if T be the kinetic energy, $2T/H\omega$. Now, if $L=M=N=0$, both T and H are constant, and we have then $\omega \cos IOH = 2T/H$, a constant.

The direction-cosines of a normal to the plane of IOH are $\{(B-C)qr,\ (C-A)rp,\ (A-B)pq\}/\omega H \sin IOH$, and so the resultant couple, or rate of growth of angular momentum, represented by

$$\{(B-C)^2q^2r^2+(C-A)^2r^2p^2+(A-B)^2p^2q^2\}^{\frac{1}{2}},$$

lies in the plane IOH, and its magnitude is $\omega H \sin IOH$. This is sometimes called the centrifugal couple, or couple due to centrifugal forces. For we can write Euler's equations in the form
$$A\dot{p} = L + (B-C)qr, \ \ldots, \quad \ldots\ldots\ldots\ldots\ldots\ldots(1)$$
and then $(B-C)qr, \ldots$, appear as moments of centrifugal couples. On the other hand, we have interpreted $-(B-C)qr, \ldots$, above as the rates of growth of angular momentum about the instantaneous positions of the principal axes, due to the motion of the body. In fact, the angular momentum H about the axis OH resolves into two components $\omega H \cos \theta$ along OI and $\omega H \sin \theta$ at right angles to OI, and the turning with angular speed ω about OI gives a rate of growth of angular momentum

$$\omega H \sin IOH = \{(B-C)^2q^2r^2+(C-A)^2r^2p^2+(A-B)^2p^2q^2\}^{\frac{1}{2}} \ (2)$$

about an axis at right angles to the plane IOH.

The reader may consider for the sake of the analogy the equation of radial acceleration in the motion of a particle in a plane,
$$m(\ddot{r} - r\dot{\theta}^2) = F, \quad \ldots\ldots\ldots\ldots\ldots\ldots\ldots(3)$$
where F is the outward impressed force along the radius-vector from the origin. We may consider the term $mr\dot{\theta}^2$ either as appearing in the rate of growth of momentum

$-mr\dot{\theta}^2$ along the radius-vector, due to the turning with angular speed $\dot{\theta}$, and consequent momentum $mr\dot{\theta}$ transverse to the radius-vector, or as a centrifugal force $mr\dot{\theta}^2$ added to F, which gives the rate of growth of momentum due to the rate at which $m\dot{r}$ is changing, according to the equation

$$m\ddot{r} = F + mr\dot{\theta}^2.$$

254. Motion of a Rigid Body under No Forces. We now go on to consider very shortly the motion of a rigid body under no forces, by means of the momental ellipsoid, according to the method of Poinsot. We may suppose one point of the body to be fixed in space; but the conclusions will be applicable in other cases, for example to the oscillations and rotations, with respect to the centroid, of a quoit, or of a stick thrown into the air, since these relative motions are not affected by the action of gravity when the body is free in the air.

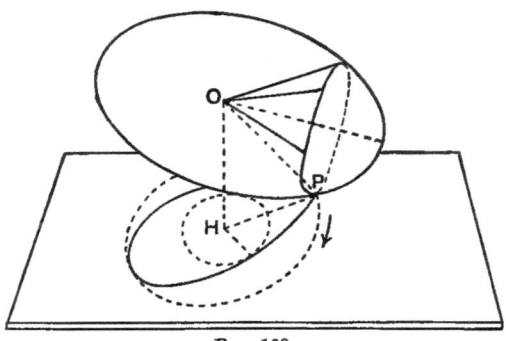

Fig. 109.

First, we prove that the angular speed about OI is proportional to the length of the radius-vector of the momental ellipsoid (M.E.) (described for the body about O as centre), with which OI coincides. For let OI intersect the M.E. in P, and x, y, z be the coordinates of P with respect to the principal axes of the ellipsoid. Then, since p, q, r are the angular speeds about the principal axes, we have

$$p/x = q/y = r/z = \omega/OP.$$

The square of each of these ratios can be written
$$(Ap^2+Bq^2+Cr^2)/(Ax^2+By^2+Cz^2).$$
But the numerator of this is $2T$, where T is the kinetic energy, and by the equation of the ellipsoid we can put
$$Ax^2+By^2+Cz^2=1.$$
Thus we get
$$\frac{\omega^2}{OP^2}=2T, \quad\ldots\ldots\ldots\ldots\ldots\ldots\ldots\ldots\ldots(1)$$
a constant.

Again, the value of $\omega\cdot\cos IOH$ is constant. For
$$\cos IOH = 2T/\omega H,$$
since the direction-cosines of OI are proportional to p, q, r and those of OH to Ap, Bq, Cr, and therefore
$$\omega\cos IOH = \frac{2T}{H}, \quad\ldots\ldots\ldots\ldots\ldots\ldots\ldots(2)$$
and T and H are both constant from the condition $L=M=N=0$.

255. Invariable Plane and Invariable Line. Rolling of M.E. on Invariable Plane. The perpendicular from the centre O on the tangent plane at P has direction-cosines proportional to Ax, By, Cz, that is to Ap, Bq, Cr. The perpendicular therefore coincides with OH. Its length is $1/(A^2x^2+B^2y^2+C^2z^2)^{\frac{1}{2}}$, that is $\omega/(OP.H)$, which, by (1), § 254, has the constant value $\sqrt{2T}/H$. The M.E. thus always touches a plane perpendicular to the axis of resultant angular momentum H at the distance $\omega/(OP.H)$, or $\sqrt{2T}/H\,(=\varpi)$, from the centre of the ellipsoid. The plane through O at right angles to OH is frequently called the *invariable plane*. In this plane an impulsive couple, of moment H, which instituted the motion from rest would have to be laid. The fixed line OH is called the *invariable line*.

The M.E. is turning about the instantaneous axis OI, which is coincident with OP. At P the M.E. is in contact with a fixed plane parallel to the invariable plane, and so rolls on that plane. The angular velocity about OP may be resolved into two, an angular velocity of amount
$$\omega\cos IOH = 2T/H$$

about OH and an angular velocity of amount $\omega \sin IOH$ about an axis OG, the intersection of the plane HOI with the invariable plane. If then we suppose the invariable plane to turn with the M.E. about OH with speed $2T/H$, the motion of the ellipsoid relative to that plane will then be simply that of rolling about OG with angular speed

$$\omega \sin IOH.$$

In the course of the motion, OG describes in the body a cone, and in space a portion of the invariable plane about O. The angle turned through by the invariable plane will give the time.

Ex. 1. Prove that the ellipsoid

$$\frac{A}{1+Ah}x^2 + \frac{B}{1+Bh}y^2 + \frac{C}{1+Ch}z^2 = 1,$$

which is confocal with the M.E., touches a plane parallel to the invariable plane in a point Q, the coordinates of which are

$$x = R(1+Ah)p, \quad y = R(1+Bh)q, \quad z = R(1+Ch)r,$$

where $R = 1/(2T + hH^2).$

Also prove that the line OH intersects this plane of contact in a point L, at a distance $\sqrt{2T + hH^2}/H$, a constant.

Ex. 2. Calculate the speed of the point Q, that is $\omega \cdot OQ \sin QOI$ for any instant, and hence the angular speed $\omega \sin QOI/\sin QOL$, of Q round OL at the same instant, and show that this angular speed reduces to hH.

[This gives Sylvester's measure of the time required by the body to perform any part of the motion; namely the angle turned through by Q about the line OL, divided by hH.]

Ex. 3. Prove that the line OG describes a cone in the body.

Let G be the projection of P on the invariable plane. Then $GP = \varpi$. Also if the coordinates of G with reference to the principal axes be ξ, η, ζ, we have, since GP is parallel to OH,

$$(\xi - x)/Ax = (\eta - y)/By = (\zeta - z)/Cz = \mu, \text{ say}.$$

Also, since OG is perpendicular to OH, $Ax\xi + By\eta + Cz\zeta = 0$. The first set of relations give $\xi = x + \mu Ax$, $\eta = y + \mu By$, $\zeta = z + \mu Cz$. Multiplication of these by Ax, By, Cz gives $Ax^2 + By^2 + Cz^2 + \mu(A^2x^2 + B^2y^2 + C^2z^2) = 0$, or $\mu = -\varpi^2$ (since $Ax^2 + By^2 + Cz^2 = 1$, $A^2x^2 + B^2y^2 + C^2z^2 = 1/\varpi^2$). Thus $x = \xi/(1-\varpi^2 A)$, $y = \eta/(1-\varpi^2 B)$, $z = \zeta/(1-\varpi^2 C)$, which, substituted in $Ax\xi + By\eta + Cz\zeta = 0$, gives

$$\frac{A\xi^2}{\varpi^2 A - 1} + \frac{B\eta^2}{\varpi^2 B - 1} + \frac{C\zeta^2}{\varpi^2 C - 1} = 0,$$

the equation of a cone.

256. Polhode and Herpolhode. As the M.E. rolls on the fixed plane referred to above, the successive points of contact trace out two loci, one on the ellipsoid, the other on the plane. The former is called the *polhode*, the latter the *herpolhode*. The former is the locus of points on the ellipsoid, the tangent planes at which are at a constant distance from O. If ϖ as before be the constant length $\sqrt{2T}/H$ of this perpendicular, we have the equations

$$Ax^2 + By^2 + Cz^2 = 1, \quad A^2x^2 + B^2y^2 + C^2z^2 = \frac{1}{\varpi^2}, \quad \ldots(1)$$

which give the equation

$$A(2AT - H^2)x^2 + B(2BT - H^2)y^2 + C(2CT - H^2)z^2 = 0, \quad (2)$$

the equation of a cone fixed in the body. This is called the *body-cone*. It rolls on a cone fixed in space, the *space-cone*, the intersection of which with the fixed plane of contact is the herpolhode. The cone is imaginary unless $H^2/2T$, that is $1/\varpi^2$, lies between the greatest and the least of A, B, C.

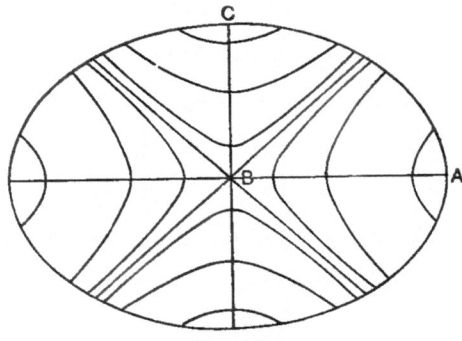

Fig. 110.

If C be the greatest moment of inertia and A the least, then $1/\varpi^2 = A$ or $1/\varpi^2 = C$ converts the equation of the cone into

$$B(A - B)y^2 + C(A - C)z^2 = 0 \quad \ldots(3)$$

or

$$A(A - C)x^2 + B(B - C)y^2 = 0, \quad \ldots(4)$$

each of which represents a pair of imaginary planes, in the

former case meeting in the axis of x, in the latter case in the axis of z.

The cone degenerates into two real planes if $1/\varpi^2 = B$, where B is the intermediate moment. We have then

$$A(A-B)x^2 - C(B-C)z^2 = 0. \quad \ldots\ldots\ldots\ldots(5)$$

These two planes intersect on the axis of intermediate moment, and they separate the polhodes which are closed curves surrounding the axes of greatest and least moment, as shown roughly in Fig. 110. Their intersections with the M.E. are therefore called the *separating polhodes*.

257. Stability of Motion of Rigid Body under No Forces. It has been shown in § 169 that an axis of principal moment of inertia is an axis of free rotation for a body under no impressed forces. The figure shows that if the body be set rotating about the axis of greatest or least moment, any slight deviation of the axis of rotation from the principal axis will not result in any further large divergence of the axes; the instantaneous axis moves in the body so that its intersection with the M.E. describes the small closed curve of points at the same distance ϖ from the centre. But if the body be set rotating about an axis nearly coinciding with the axis of intermediate moment, the axis of rotation will wander off in the body along the polhode, which it will be seen passes nearly to the opposite side of the ellipsoid before returning to the original position. The motion is therefore stable in either of the former cases and unstable in the latter. If the body rotates exactly about either the axis of greatest or the axis of least moment, the polhode is a mere point.

258. Projections of the Polhodes. If we eliminate z between the two equations (1) and (5) of § 256, we obtain

$$A(A-C)x^2 + B(B-C)y^2 = \frac{1}{\varpi^2}\left(1 - \frac{C}{B}\right).\ldots\ldots\ldots(1)$$

Whether C be the greatest or the least moment the locus, which is the projection of the polhode on a plane at right angles to the axis of z, is an ellipse. The ratio of the x-axis of the ellipse to the y-axis is $\sqrt{B(B-C)/A(A-C)}$, and is therefore more nearly a circle the nearer A and B are to equality. But if $B-C$ and $A-C$ be very unequal, the axes of the ellipse differ widely, and in one direction there will be a comparatively large displacement of the instantaneous axis in the body. For the highest degree of stability, therefore, we should have in this case $A=B$.

Eliminating y between the equations (1) and (2) of § 256 to project the polhode on the plane of xz, we get

$$A(A-B)x^2 - C(B-C)z^2 = \frac{1}{\varpi^2}(1-B\varpi^2), \quad \ldots\ldots\ldots(2)$$

the equation of a hyperbola. For $1 > B\varpi^2$, we get one hyperbola, and for $1 < B\varpi^2$ the conjugate. The asymptotes are the two lines

$$A(A-B)x^2 - C(B-C)z^2 = 0, \quad \ldots\ldots\ldots\ldots(3)$$

that is the lines

$$\left. \begin{array}{l} \sqrt{A(A-B)}\,x + \sqrt{C(B-C)}\,z = 0, \\ \sqrt{A(A-B)}\,x - \sqrt{C(B-C)}\,z = 0, \end{array} \right\} \ldots\ldots\ldots(4)$$

which are the projections of the separating polhodes.

259. Form of the Herpolhode. With regard to the herpolhode we have not space to go into detail. It is a curve consisting of different parts, which correspond to the successive repetitions of the polhode, and from the manner of its description, by the rolling of the ellipsoid, it must always have its concavity turned towards the foot of the perpendicular from the centre of the ellipsoid to the plane of contact, and therefore cannot have a point of inflexion. The distance of the point of contact at any instant from the foot H of the perpendicular from the centre is $\sqrt{OP^2 - \varpi^2}$, and it is evident from the form of the polhode as displayed by its projections just indicated, that OP varies between a maximum and a minimum value, in each fourth part of its description. Thus, the distance $HP = \sqrt{OP^2 - \varpi^2}$ similarly varies, and so the herpolhode is a curve lying between two circles which have the projection of the centre of the M.E. as their common centre, and touching the outer circle internally and the inner externally, as shown in Fig. 109. The herpolhode is not in general, however, a closed or re-entering curve; unless the angle turned through by HP, from contact of the herpolhode with one circle to contact with the other, be commensurable with 2π, the curve will not be repeated.

When $\varpi^2 = 1/B$, the intermediate moment, the herpolhode has an interesting form shown in Fig. 110. The polhode then passes through the extremity of the principal axis OB of the M.E., and is therefore one of the ellipses which form the separating polhodes. When the extremity of the axis OB is in contact with the fixed plane, $HP = 0$, and so the radius of the inner limiting circle is zero.

Let the motion of the M.E. begin at any point of the polhode distant from the extremity of the axis OB, say at the maximum value of OP, then the motion consists, as we have seen (§ 255), of a spin about an axis through the point of contact, of angular speed $2T/H$, and a rolling motion about the line HP with angular speed $\omega \sin IOH$. As the ellipsoid moves and the point of contact approaches B, the motion becomes more and more one of spin merely, and so the herpolhode consists of a succession of constantly diminishing arcs of a spiral closing down on a pole P. The spiral is a double one, but only one half of it is described by the point of contact. (See Ex. 4, § 260 below.)

260. Examples on Motion of Rigid Body.

Ex. 1. If ρ be the distance HP, then from the equations

$$x^2 + y^2 + z^2 = \rho^2 + \varpi^2, \quad Ax^2 + By^2 + Cz^2 = 1, \quad \varpi^2(A^2x^2 + B^2y^2 + C^2z^2) = 1,$$

fulfilled by the coordinates of the point of contact of the M.E. with the plane on which it rolls, prove that

$$x^2 = \frac{BC(C-B)(\rho^2 - \alpha)}{(A-B)(B-C)(C-A)}, \quad y^2 = \frac{CA(A-C)(\rho^2 - \beta)}{(A-B)(B-C)(C-A)}, \quad z^2 = \dots,$$

where $\alpha = -\dfrac{(\varpi^2 B - 1)(\varpi^2 C - 1)}{\varpi^2 BC}, \quad \beta = \dots, \quad \gamma = \dots$.

Ex. 2. By means of the relations $p/x = q/y = r/z = \omega/OP = \sqrt{2T}$ (§ 254), prove that Euler's equations may be written for the case of no forces in the form

$$A\dot{x} - \sqrt{2T}(B-C)yz = 0, \quad B\dot{y} - \sqrt{2T}(C-A)zx = 0, \dots.$$

Hence show that
$$\rho\dot\rho = -\sqrt{2T}.xyz\frac{(A-B)(B-C)(C-A)}{ABC},$$
and by the last example that
$$\rho\dot\rho = \sqrt{2T}\sqrt{-(\rho^2-\alpha)(\rho^2-\beta)(\rho^2-\gamma)},$$
from which ρ^2 can be found in terms of t.

Ex. 3. By calculating the rates of description of area by the projections of the radius-vector OP on the coordinate planes (that is, $y\dot z - z\dot y$, $z\dot x - x\dot z$, $x\dot y - y\dot x$), and taking the sum of the projections of these on the plane of contact, show that if $\dot\phi$ be the rate of increase of the vectorial angle ϕ corresponding to the radius-vector $\rho = HP$ of a point of the herpolhode,
$$\rho^2\dot\phi = \frac{\sqrt{2T}}{\varpi}\left(\frac{\varpi^2 A-1}{BC}Ax^2 + \frac{\varpi^2 B-1}{CA}By^2 + \frac{\varpi^2 C-1}{AB}Cz^2\right),$$
and that this, by Example 1 above, reduces to
$$\rho^2\dot\phi = \varpi\sqrt{2T}(\rho^2 + E),$$
where $E = (\varpi^2 A-1)(\varpi^2 B-1)(\varpi^2 C-1)/\varpi^4 ABC = -\sqrt{-\alpha\beta\gamma}/\varpi$.

Hence show that the differential equation of the herpolhode is
$$\frac{d\phi}{d\rho} = \frac{\varpi(\rho^2+E)}{\rho\sqrt{-(\rho^2-\alpha)(\rho^2-\beta)(\rho^2-\gamma)}}.$$

Ex. 4. In the case (§ 259 above) in which $\varpi^2 = 1/B$, show that this differential equation reduces to
$$\frac{d\phi}{d\rho} = \frac{1}{\sqrt{B}\rho\sqrt{\beta^2-\rho^2}},$$
and that therefore
$$\frac{1}{\rho} = \frac{e^{\phi\sqrt{\beta/B}} + e^{-\phi\sqrt{\beta/B}}}{2\sqrt{\beta}},$$
so that the curve has the form shown in Fig. 66. (See equation (10), § 153.)

[These examples are mainly due to a Note by M. Darboux in Despeyrous' *Traité de la Mécanique*.]

Ex. 5. From Euler's equations of motion of a rigid body turning about a fixed point under the action of no forces, deduce the stability of the motion, when the axis of greatest or the axis of least moment of inertia is the instantaneous axis.

Let the axis of rotation coincide with OA, then the equations of motion are $A\dot p = 0$, $B\dot q = 0$, $C\dot r = 0$. If, however, the axis deviate slightly from OA, and the angular speeds be $p_0 + p'$, q, r, where p', q, r are small, then we can show that in certain circumstances q, r can never become large. The equations of motion are now, if products of small quantities be neglected, $A\dot p' = 0$, $B\dot q - (C-A)rp_0 = 0$, $C\dot r - (A-B)p_0 q = 0$. Differentiating the second equation and eliminating $\dot r$ between the result

470 . A TREATISE ON DYNAMICS. [CH. VIII.

and the third equation, we obtain

$$\ddot{q} + \frac{(A-C)(A-B)}{BC} p_0^2 q = 0. \quad \ldots\ldots\ldots\ldots\ldots\ldots(1)$$

Now, if $(A-C)(A-B)$ be positive, that is, if either $A>B>C$ or $C>B>A$, this equation can be written

$$\ddot{q} + n^2 q = 0, \quad \ldots\ldots\ldots\ldots\ldots\ldots\ldots\ldots\ldots(2)$$

where $n^2 = (A-C)(A-B)p_0^2/BC$ is real and positive. If initially $q = q_0$ and $\dot{q} = \dot{q}_0$, we get

$$q = q_0 \cos nt + \frac{\dot{q}_0}{n} \sin nt. \quad \ldots\ldots\ldots\ldots\ldots\ldots(3)$$

But initially $\dot{q}_0 = (C-A)r_0 p_0/B$, and therefore

$$q = q_0 \cos nt + \frac{C-A}{Bn} r_0 p_0 \sin nt. \quad \ldots\ldots\ldots\ldots(4)$$

Thus if, as we suppose, q_0 and $\dot{q}_0$ be small initially, q can never acquire more than the small value given by the last equation, and a similar result can be found for r. The instantaneous axis therefore remains in proximity to OA. This will be seen more clearly if we find the position of the instantaneous axis. By the relation $B\dot{q} = (C-A)rp_0$, we get for r the equation $r = B\dot{q}/(C-A)p_0$, or

$$r = r_0 \cos nt + \frac{Bn}{A-C} \frac{q_0}{p_0} \sin nt. \quad \ldots\ldots\ldots\ldots\ldots(5)$$

Hence, for the angle AOI which the instantaneous axis makes with OA, we have

$$\tan AOI = \frac{\sqrt{q^2 + r^2}}{p_0}. \quad \ldots\ldots\ldots\ldots\ldots\ldots\ldots(6)$$

For the angle AOH which the axis of resultant angular momentum OH makes with OA, we have

$$\tan AOH = \frac{\sqrt{B^2 q^2 + C^2 r^2}}{A p_0}. \quad \ldots\ldots\ldots\ldots\ldots\ldots(7)$$

Thus, if A be the greatest moment, the fixed cone lies within the moving cone.

Ex. 6. Show that if A be the greatest or least moment, and $B = C$, that the instantaneous axis describes in the body a right cone round OA, the axis of figure, and that this cone rolls on a right cone fixed in space.

We have here $n^2 = (A-B)^2 p_0^2/B^2$ or $n = (A-B)p_0/B$. The equations for q and r become

$$q = q_0 \cos nt - r_0 \sin nt, \quad r = r_0 \cos nt + q_0 \sin nt,$$

or

$$q = R \cos(nt+e), \quad r = R \sin(nt+e),$$

where $R = \sqrt{q_0^2 + r_0^2}$ and $\tan e = r_0/q_0$. The resultant of q and r is therefore an angular speed about an axis which lies in the plane of B and C, and makes an angle $nt+e$ with the axis OB. That angle increases at rate n, and the resultant axis moves round from OB

§ 260] ROTATIONAL MOTION : EXAMPLES.   471

towards OC, that is, in the direction of the rotation about OA, if $A>B$, and in the contrary direction if $A<B$.

It is clear from the Poinsot representation of the motion that as the M.E. (here of revolution) moves, the instantaneous axis must make always the same angle with the invariable line OH. Hence OI describes a right cone in space, that is, the cone fixed in the body rolls on a right cone fixed in space. If $A>B$, n is positive, and the axis OI moves round OA in the body in the direction of rotation. The angle which OI makes with OA is

$$\tan^{-1}(\sqrt{q_0^2+r_0^2}/p_0),$$

that is, $\tan^{-1}(R/p_0)$, that which OH makes with OA is $\tan^{-1}(BR/Ap_0)$, which is less or greater than the former according as $A>B$ or $<B$. Thus the fixed cone lies within the moving cone in the former case, and the concave side of the latter cone rolls on the convex side of the former. In the other case, the convex surface of the moving cone rolls on the convex surface of the fixed cone. The two cases are shown in Fig. 111, (a) and (b).

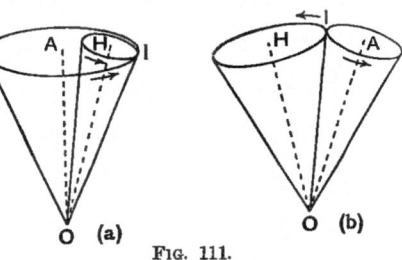

Fig. 111.

Ex. 7. Discuss the motion of a symmetrical quoit, and of a long thin cylinder.

When the quoit is thrown into the air its centroid moves in a parabola, if the resistance of the air be supposed insensible ; but the motion of the body relative to the centroid is unaffected by gravity, and is the same as if that point were fixed. The moment A about the axis of figure is very much greater than the moment B, and so if the quoit when it is thrown is given a rapid rotation about the axis of figure it preserves that rotation unchanged, except by the air resistance, and the direction of the axis only changes comparatively slowly, if at all. The action of the air is thus rendered nearly the same throughout the flight, and the mark aimed at is more certainly reached. The fixed and moving curves are as shown in Fig. 111 (a).

The motion of the cylinder illustrates the other case in which $A < B$. Here again there is stability in the case of rapid rotation about the axis of figure. A juggler throwing knives or other elongated bodies from one hand to the other, or to another performer, gives in the act of throwing the necessary rotation about the axis of figure, which therefore remains nearly fixed in direction, and the body can be caught with ease and certainty.

An elongated rifle bullet rotating rapidly about its axis of figure, and preserving the direction of that axis constant during the flight, is another example of this case. (See Chapter IX.)

EXERCISES.

1. Compound two screw motions about rectangular axes, Ox, Oy, if ω_1, ω_2 be the angular speeds, and p_1, p_2 the pitches of the screws. Prove that resultant angular speed is about a line OP in the plane xOy inclined at the angle $\theta = \tan^{-1}(\omega_2/\omega_1)$ to Ox, and that there are two linear speeds,

$$\omega_1 p_1 \cos\theta + \omega_2 p_2 \sin\theta \text{ along } OP_1 \quad \text{and} \quad \omega_1 p_1 \sin\theta - \omega_2 p_2 \cos\theta$$

at right angles to OP.

Show that the former of these and the resultant angular speed give a screw motion about OP of pitch $p = p_1 \cos^2\theta + p_2 \sin^2\theta$.

2. Prove that the motions of Ex. 1 give a single screw motion of angular speed $\sqrt{\omega_1^2 + \omega_2^2}$ about a line $O'P'$ through the axis of z parallel to OP at a distance $z = \frac{1}{2}(p_1 - p_1)\sin 2\theta$ from the plane xOy.

Show that this line may be constructed as follows: Take two points A, B on the axes Ox, Oy equidistant from O, such that the distance between them is $p_1 - p_2$. Through AOB describe a circle; the centre is C, the mid-point of AB. Let OP intersect the circle in P, and join CP. Then $\angle AOP = \theta$, $\angle ACP = 2\theta$. Let fall a perpendicular PD on AB, then $DP = \frac{1}{2}(p_1 - p_2)\sin 2\theta$. Now draw perpendicular to the plane of the circle a line PP' of length equal to DP, and a line from P' parallel to PO to meet Oz in O'. The line $O'P'$ is the axis of the single screw which represents the motion.

3. Show that if the angle θ of Ex. 2 be varied uniformly by variation of ω_1, ω_2 while p_1, p_2 are kept unchanged, the successive positions of $O'P'$ trace out a surface of which the equation is

$$2z(x^2 + y^2) = (p_1 - p_2)xy.$$

The successive positions of $O'P'$ are the generators of the surface.

4. Show that the pitch p (Ex. 1) of the screw for any generator of the cylindroid is inversely proportional to the square of the radius-vector in the given direction of the conic

$$p_1 x^2 + p_2 y^2 = C,$$

where C is a constant. When is it possible to have generators for which the pitches of the screws are zero, so that the motion is of pure rotation?

5. From Exs. 3 and I, § 260, prove that

$$\phi = \frac{2T}{H} + \frac{(2AT - H^2)(2BT - H^2)(2CT - H^2)}{2HTABC}\cos^2\zeta,$$

where ζ is the inclination of the instantaneous axis to the invariable line.

Hence show that if the M.E. be written in the form

$$Ax^2 + By^2 + Cz^2 = M\epsilon^4,$$

and OK be the radius-vector of the ellipsoid parallel to the projection on the invariable plane of the radius-vector to the point of contact of the ellipsoid with the plane on which it rolls,

$$\dot{\phi} = \frac{H^3 M \epsilon^4}{2ABCT} \frac{1}{OK^2}.$$

It has been seen (§ 254) that the first part of $\dot{\phi}$, that is $2T/H$, is the angular speed with which the plane through the invariable line and the radius-vector to the point of contact is turning about the invariable line. The remainder of $\dot{\phi}$ arises from the other component of the turning about the instantaneous axis.

6. To find the motion of the principal axes OA, OB, OC in space.

Let θ be the angle which OA makes with OI: the motion of a point P on OA at unit distance from O is at right angles to the plane AOI with speed $\omega \sin \theta$. Let ϕ be the inclination of the plane AOI to AOL: the speed of P at right angles to AOL is $\omega \sin \theta \cos \phi$. Now let a denote the angle AOL, and ξ_1 be the angle at which the plane AOL is inclined to a plane through OL and fixed in space. The speed of P at right angles to AOL is therefore also $\dot{\xi}_1 \sin a$. Hence

$$\dot{\xi}_1 \sin a = \omega \sin \theta \cos \phi.$$

But a, θ are the sides of a spherical triangle the vertices of which are the intersections of OL, OA, OI with a sphere of unit radius described about O as centre, and ϕ is the angle between these sides at P. If ζ (see Ex. 5) be the third side, $\sin a \sin \theta \cos \phi = \cos \zeta - \cos a \cos \theta$. Hence $\dot{\xi}_1 \sin^2 a = \omega \cos \zeta - \omega \cos a \cos \theta$. But $\omega \cos \zeta$ is the turning about OL, that is $2T/H$, and $\omega \cos \theta = \omega_1$. Hence

$$\dot{\xi}_1 \sin^2 a = \frac{2T}{H} - \omega_1 \cos a = \frac{2T}{H} - \frac{H}{A} \cos^2 a,$$

since $\omega_1 = H \cos a / A$. This gives the rate at which the plane AOL is turning away from a plane intersecting it in OL and fixed in space. Similar results hold for the planes BOL, COL, inclined at the angles b, c to the fixed plane.

7. Show that if the invariable line OL make angles with the principal axes the cosines of which are a, β, γ, Euler's equations, for a body with one point fixed and under no forces, may be written in the form $BC\dot{a} - H(B-C)\beta\gamma = 0$, with two similar equations.

Taking along with the equations of last Example, written in the form

$$\dot{a} - H(1/C - 1/B)\beta\gamma = 0, \ldots,$$

the equations of Ex. 6,

$$(1 - a^2)\dot{\xi}_1 = \frac{2T}{H} - \frac{Ha^2}{A}, \ldots,$$

show that if two bodies of principal moments A, B, C, A', B', C', be initially placed with their principal axes parallel and be set in motion by parallel impulsive couples H, H' which fulfil the relation $H(1/C - 1/B) = H'(1/C' - 1/B')$, ..., prove that after any time t the principal axes will still be equally inclined to the axes of the couples.

8. Prove that if the kinetic energies of the two bodies in Ex. 7 be T, T',

$$\frac{H}{A} - \frac{H'}{A'} = \frac{H}{B} - \frac{H'}{B'} = \frac{H}{C} - \frac{H'}{C'} = 2\left(\frac{T}{H} - \frac{T'}{H'}\right),$$

and hence that the angles between the corresponding planes AOL, $A'OL'$, ... will increase at constant rate $2(T/H - T'/H')$.

9. A body free to turn about a fixed point is impulsively set into motion: to find the equations of motion about principal axes fixed in the body.

[Let L, M, N denote the time-integrals of the impulsive couples L, M, N, and use Euler's equations.]

10. To find when an impulse applied in a given straight line to a body movable about a fixed point produces no rotation of the body about a perpendicular from the fixed point to the line.

Take the direction of the impulse as Ox and the perpendicular as axis Oz. Then, impulse about $Oz = 0$, and $\omega_3 = 0$, if $D = E = 0$. Oz is then a principal axis for the sections xOz, yOz.

11. Find the direction of the axis of the impulse of moment H in order that the initial kinetic energy of the body may be a maximum.

Here $T = \frac{1}{2}(L^2/A + M^2/B + N^2/C)$. Let $A > B > C$, then clearly T will have its greatest value if N be made equal to H, and $L = M = 0$. The impulse should be applied about the axis of least M.I.

12. To find the values of L, M, N for fixed axes. These are given by (3), § 170. They are

$A\omega_1 - F\omega_2 - E\omega_3 = $ L, $\quad -F\omega_1 + B\omega_2 - D\omega_3 = $ M, $\quad -E\omega_1 - D\omega_2 + C\omega_3 = $ N,

where ω_1, ω_2, ω_3 are the angular speeds of the body about the axes, and A, B, C, D, E, F are the moments and products of inertia. If the motion does not take place from rest, then for ω_1, ω_2, ω_3 we must write $\omega_1 - (\omega_1)_0$, $\omega_2 - (\omega_2)_0$, $\omega_3 - (\omega_3)_0$.

13. An impulse H applied at a point P of a rigid body movable about a fixed point O gives that point a speed V; to find the instantaneous axis.

The direction of V must be at right angles to OP since O is fixed. Hence the direction of V may be taken as Ox, and OP as Oz. Then (§ 246) $V = \omega_2 z - \omega_3 y$, $0 = \omega_3 x - \omega_1 z$, $0 = \omega_1 y - \omega_2 x$. But $z = OP$, $x = y = 0$, and therefore $V = \omega_2 z$, $\omega_1 = 0$. Also $N = 0$, that is, $C\omega_3 = D\omega_2$, or $\omega_3 = DV/Cz$. Hence show that the instantaneous axis lies in the plane yOz, and makes an angle $\tan^{-1}(C/D)$ with Oz.

CHAPTER IX.

TOPS AND GYROSTATS. GYROSTATIC ACTION IN MACHINERY.

261. Symmetrical Top moving about Fixed Point. Equations of Motion. As a preliminary to the discussion of the theory and some of the applications of gyrostatic action, we consider the motion of a body which turns about a fixed point, and is under the action of gravity. We suppose the body to be symmetrical as regards distribution of mass about an axis which passes through the point of support, and which we shall call the *axis of figure*. The body is in fact a top, and its position may be taken as that represented in Fig. 112. O is the fixed point and OC is the axis of figure, which is inclined at an angle θ to the vertical OZ. Two other axes OD, OE, at right angles to one another and to OC, are taken as axes of reference. These are not fixed in the body, but one of them, OD, is at right angles to the plane ZOC, the other, OE, lies in that plane. They move with the plane ZOC.

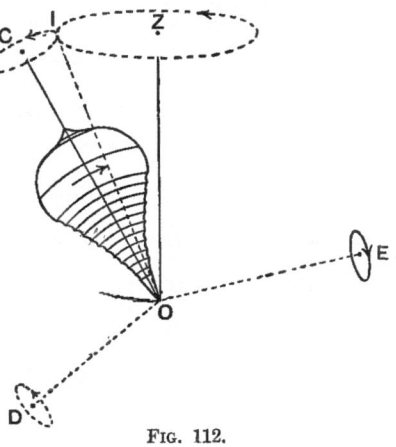

Fig. 112.

We suppose the motion to consist of a spin of angular speed ω about the axis OC, relative to the plane ZOC, a turning of the top about OD at angular speed $\dot\theta$, and a turning of the plane ZOC with angular speed $\dot\psi$ about OZ, all in the directions (clockwise as seen from O, Fig. 112) of the arrows in the circles surrounding the axes. The angle ψ may be taken as that which a horizontal line in the plane ZOC makes with a fixed horizontal line.

Now $\dot\psi$ may be resolved into two, $\dot\psi\cos\theta$, $\dot\psi\sin\theta$, about OC, OE respectively. Hence the total angular speed, n, about OC is $\omega+\dot\psi\cos\theta$. The A.M. about OD is $A\dot\theta$, about OE is $A\dot\psi\sin\theta$, and about OC is $Cn=C(\omega+\dot\psi\cos\theta)$, if C be the moment of inertia about OC and A that about OD or OE.

The turning of the plane ZOC about the vertical is frequently called the *precession* of the top, for a reason which will be explained in § 275 below. Sometimes the turning about OE is referred to as precession. In the discussion of gyrostats we shall regard motions about different axes, perpendicular to the axis of figure, as precessions, according to convenience. The context will make clear the sense in which the term is used.

Now let a vector OH be drawn from O in the proper direction and of the proper length to represent the resultant A.M. of the top: the *velocity* of H is the resultant rate of change of A.M. in direction and magnitude. The speed with which the extremity H of that vector is moving in any direction in space is the rate at which A.M. is growing up in that direction. This of course is partly due to the time-rate of increase of length of OH, partly due to its change of direction in consequence of the motion of the axes about which the components of OH are reckoned. We now proceed to calculate this speed for the moving axes OD, OE, OC themselves.

Taking first OD, we notice that gravity exerts about that axis, in any of its positions, a moment $Wgh\sin\theta$, if the distance of the centroid of the top from O be h, and the weight of the top be W. This is one expression for the rate of growth of A.M. about OD. Another expression is obtained by estimating the several parts of this rate of growth. These are: (1) $A\ddot{\theta}$ due to increasing angular speed about OD, (2) the rate of production of A.M. about the instantaneous position of OD in consequence of the motion. [In what follows the instantaneous position of OD, or of OE, which are both definite directions in space, will be referred to as simply OD or OE, when an axis is referred to as moving toward or from either, and the reader will kindly supply the proper interpretation.] The turning about OE with angular speed $\dot{\psi}\sin\theta$ moves the axis OC round towards OD, and therefore produces a rate, $Cn\dot{\psi}\sin\theta$, of growth of A.M. about OD. Similarly the turning about OC moves OE away from OD, and therefore A.M. is growing about OD, at rate $-A\dot{\psi}^2\sin\theta\cos\theta$. Thus the total rate of growth of A.M. about OD is $A\ddot{\theta}+(Cn-A\dot{\psi}\cos\theta)\dot{\psi}\sin\theta$, and equating this to $Wgh\sin\theta$, we get the equation of motion

$$A\ddot{\theta}+(Cn-A\dot{\psi}\cos\theta)\dot{\psi}\sin\theta = Wgh\sin\theta, \quad\ldots\ldots(1)$$

which will have many applications in what follows.

We notice next that there is no moment of forces about the axis of figure. The rate of growth of angular momentum consists (1) of $A\dot{\psi}\cos\theta\,.\,\dot{\theta}$ due to the turning of OE towards the instantaneous position of OD, and (2)

$$-A\dot{\theta}\dot{\psi}\cos\theta$$

due to the turning of OD away from the position of OC by the rotation about OE. The total rate due to the motion is thus $A\dot{\theta}\dot{\psi}\cos\theta - A\dot{\theta}\dot{\psi}\cos\theta$ or zero, and since there is no moment of forces, we have

$$C\dot{n}=0. \quad\ldots\ldots\ldots\ldots\ldots\ldots\ldots\ldots(2)$$

Therefore n and Cn are constants throughout the motion.

Further, about OE there is also no moment of forces. There is, however, rate of change of angular momentum $A\,d(\dot{\psi}\sin\theta)/dt$ because of rate of change of angular speed about OE, and of change of inclination θ of the axis to the vertical. In consequence of the motion there is, as the method already employed shows, rate of growth of angular

momentum $A\dot\theta\dot\psi\cos\theta - Cn\dot\theta$. Thus we get the equation
$$A\sin\theta . \ddot\psi + (2A\dot\psi\cos\theta - Cn)\dot\theta = 0. \quad\ldots\ldots\ldots\ldots(3)$$
This equation, it will be seen, expresses the fact that the angular momentum about the vertical OZ undergoes no change, that is
$$Cn\cos\theta + A\dot\psi\sin^2\theta = G, \quad\ldots\ldots\ldots\ldots\ldots(4)$$
where G is a constant. We thus see that (4) is a first integral of (3).

By writing a for $2Wgh/A$ and b for C/A, we put equations (1) and (3) in a somewhat simpler form, which is convenient
$$\left.\begin{array}{l}\ddot\theta + (bn - \dot\psi\cos\theta)\dot\psi\sin\theta = \tfrac{1}{2}a\sin\theta,\\ \ddot\psi\sin\theta + (2\dot\psi\cos\theta - bn)\dot\theta = 0.\end{array}\right\}\ldots\ldots\ldots\ldots(5)$$

We have also as two first integrals of these, (4) derived from the second of (5), and the equation of energy. The latter is evidently
$$\tfrac{1}{2}\{A(\dot\theta^2 + \dot\psi^2\sin^2\theta) + Cn^2\} + Wgh\cos\theta = E, \ldots\ldots\ldots(6)$$
if the position of zero potential energy be that for which $\theta = \pi/2$, and E be the constant sum of energies.

262. "Spherical" Top. If $C = A$ all the moments of inertia are equal, and we have what is called a *spherical top*, though that does not mean that the top is of spherical shape. Now, if we write An' for Cn, we can put the equations of § 261 in the form
$$\ddot\theta + (n' - \dot\psi\cos\theta)\dot\psi\sin\theta = \frac{Wgh}{A}\sin\theta,$$
$$\ddot\psi\sin\theta + (2\dot\psi\cos\theta - n')\dot\theta = 0,$$
with the integral equation corresponding to the second of these, namely,
$$n'\cos\theta + \dot\psi\sin^2\theta = \frac{G}{A}.$$

Thus, so far as these equations are concerned, we may suppose the actual top replaced by a spherical one, provided A remains the same, and the actual rotational speed n is changed to n', where $n' = nC/A = bn$; in other words, that

n has been increased by $n(C-A)/A$. As these equations give the whole motion, there is no loss of generality in supposing the top spherical.

It is to be noticed, however, that the kinetic energy is not given by this substitution, for $Cn'^2 = C^3n^2/A^2$.

263. Rise and Fall of Top. Putting now for brevity,
$$\alpha = (2E - Cn^2)/A, \quad \beta = G/A, \quad z = \cos\theta,$$
we obtain the equations of energy and angular momentum in the form
$$\left.\begin{array}{r}\dot{\theta}^2 + \dot{\psi}^2(1-z^2) = \alpha - az, \\ \dot{\psi}(1-z^2) = \beta - bnz.\end{array}\right\} \quad \ldots\ldots\ldots\ldots\ldots(1)$$

Eliminating $\dot{\psi}$ between these equations, we get
$$\dot{z}^2 = (\alpha - az)(1-z^2) - (\beta - bnz)^2 = f(z). \ldots\ldots\ldots(2)$$

The cubic expression $f(z)$ is negative when $z = -\infty$, $z = \pm 1$, and positive when $z = +\infty$. It is also positive when z has its initial value z_0, say, which must be between -1 and $+1$. Two roots of the equation $f(z) = 0$ lie therefore one, z_1, between -1 and z_0, another, z_2, between z_0 and $+1$, and the third, z_3, between $+1$ and ∞. The last is not relevant to the question, since $-1 < z < +1$. We have therefore
$$\dot{z}^2 = a(z - z_1)(z_2 - z)(z_3 - z). \ldots\ldots\ldots\ldots\ldots(3)$$

The product of the three factors is positive since $\dot{z}^2$ is positive: the third factor is obviously positive, and therefore z must lie between z_1 and z_2. We have taken z_2 as the greater of the two roots z_1, z_2. Hence, as $\dot{z}$ alters the angle θ varies also, but is always such that $\cos\theta$ lies between the limits z_1, z_2.

From (3) z can be found as an elliptic function of the time t, and thus the top rises and falls periodically.

264. Path of Point on Axis of Top. By elimination between $\dot{z} = \sqrt{f(z)}$ and $\dot{\psi} = (\beta - bnz)/(1-z^2)$, we get
$$\frac{d\psi}{dz} = \frac{\beta - bnz}{(1-z^2)\sqrt{f(z)}}, \quad \ldots\ldots\ldots\ldots\ldots(1)$$
from which ψ can be obtained in terms of z by quadrature.

Let a sphere of radius 1 be drawn round O as centre, and call Z_1, the point in which the vertical through O intersects the sphere, the *pole* of the sphere (Fig. 113). Then, if P be a point in which the axis of the top meets the surface, the projection OP on the radius OZ_1 is the value of z, and the distance of P from that radius is $\sqrt{1-z^2}$.

The tangent of the inclination i of the line traced by P on the unit sphere to the meridian Z_1P at any position is $-(\beta-bnz)/\sqrt{f(z)}$, in which the value of $\sqrt{f(z)}$ is taken $+$ or $-$ according to the sign of $\dot{z}$. This expression shows that the path of P is at right angles to the meridian

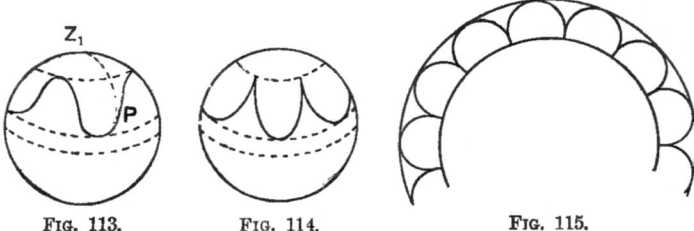

FIG. 113. FIG. 114. FIG. 115.

whenever z has one or other of the values z_1, z_2, unless it should happen that at either limit $z=\beta/bn$. Thus the path lies between the two parallel circles on the unit sphere corresponding to z_1, z_2. When $z=\beta/bn$ at one of these circles, the path of P has cusps as shown in Fig. 114. As we shall show, this can only be the case at the upper circle.

FIG. 116.

The form of the projection on a horizontal plane is shown in Fig. 115 for the second case.

If the value of β/bn lie outside the limits z_1, z_2, $\beta-bnz$ must always preserve the same sign as P moves. But if β/bn lie between z_1 and z_2 the path will have the form shown in Fig. 116, from which the changes of sign and value in $\tan i$ can be traced. To settle whether when $z(=\beta/bn)$ lies between -1 and $+1$, it also lies between z_1 and z_2, we have only to consider the value which this gives to $f(z)$, that is $\dot{z}^2$, which of course must be positive. By (2) § 263 we have, if $z = \beta/bn$,

$$f(z) = \left(\alpha - a\frac{\beta}{bn}\right)\left(1 - \frac{\beta^2}{b^2n^2}\right), \quad \ldots\ldots\ldots\ldots(2)$$

in which the second factor is positive. Hence if the first factor is positive β/bn lies between z_1 and z_2. The condition is therefore $\beta/bn < \alpha/a$.

There is, however, the case in which this factor vanishes; β/bn is then equal to one of the limits z_1, z_2. To find which we substitute in $f(z)$, $\alpha = a\beta/bn$, and get

$$f(z) = \frac{1}{bn}(\beta - bnz)\{a(1-z^2) - bn(\beta - bnz)\}. \quad \ldots\ldots(3)$$

If we equate the right-hand side to zero, we see that one root of the equation is given by the first factor. The second factor is zero if $\beta - bnz = a(1-z^2)/bn$. But $a(1-z^2)/bn$ is positive, and therefore $\beta - bnz$ must also be positive if this equality holds, that is, $z < \beta/bn$, with n positive. We see then that if one of the roots z_1, z_2 of $f(z) = 0$ be β/bn, it must be the greater root. Thus the cusps are at the upper circle as stated above.

The conclusion thus analytically obtained for the position of the cusps is obvious from considerations of energy. For at either limiting circle the term in the kinetic energy depending on $\dot{\theta}$ is zero. The potential energy, however, has its maximum value at the upper limiting circle, and its minimum value at the lower. At the lower circle therefore it is impossible for $\dot{\psi}$ to be zero, otherwise the kinetic energy would, for the *minimum* of potential energy, be *reduced* to the constant part $\frac{1}{2}Cn^2$, depending on the spin about the axis of figure. But, since the total energy does not vary, the kinetic energy must have its greatest value at the lower limiting circle. Hence the cusps, if they occur, are connected with the reduction of the kinetic energy to the constant part in consequence of the adjustment of the maximum of potential energy to the value $E - \frac{1}{2}Cn^2$.

The dynamical reason for the form of the path in Fig. 116 is clear from (1) above, the second of (1) of § 263. If the two roots of $f(z) = 0$ be such that before reaching the *upper* limit of value, $\cos\theta$ becomes so great that $Cn\cos\theta$ exceeds G or $bnz > \beta$, then $\dot\psi(1-z^2)$ must become negative. In other words, the turning about the vertical must be reversed from the direction which it had at the lower limit of $\cos\theta$, where $Cn\cos\theta < G$.

It is here assumed that the diagram of the third case, that in which β/bn lies between z_1 and z_2, is shown in Fig. 116 (c). The positive advance in the value of ψ in each period is there shown as greater than the negative. This can be proved, but we leave the discussion for the present.

265. Top started with Rapid Rotation and Zero Precession. Let it be supposed that initially $\dot\theta = 0$, $\theta = \theta_0$ (and therefore $\cos\theta_0 = z_0$), $\dot\psi = 0$, and n very great. Then

$$E = \tfrac{1}{2}Cn^2 + Wgh\cos\theta_0.$$

Thus, initially, $\alpha = az_0$, $\beta = bnz_0$. Afterwards, when the inclination of the axis of the top to the vertical is θ, we have
$$\tfrac{1}{2}A(\dot\theta^2 + \dot\psi^2\sin^2\theta) = Wgh(\cos\theta_0 - \cos\theta) \quad\ldots\ldots\ldots(1)$$
or, as we now write it,

$$\dot\theta^2 + \dot\psi^2(1-z^2) = a(z_0 - z). \quad\ldots\ldots\ldots\ldots\ldots\ldots\ldots(2)$$

Also $\quad\dot\psi(1-z^2) = \beta - bnz = bn(z_0 - z). \quad\ldots\ldots\ldots\ldots(3)$

We have seen that $\dot z^2 = (\alpha - az)(1-z^2) - (\beta - bnz)^2$, and therefore, by the values of α, β given by the initial conditions in this case, we have

$$\dot z^2 = a(z_0 - z)\left\{1 - z^2 - \frac{b^2n^2}{a}(z_0 - z)\right\}. \quad\ldots\ldots\ldots(4)$$

The second relevant root, z_1 say, will cause the factor $1 - z^2 - b^2n^2(z_0-z)/a$ to vanish. Hence

$$z_0 - z_1 = a\,\frac{1-z_1^2}{b^2n^2}. \quad\ldots\ldots\ldots\ldots\ldots\ldots(5)$$

It follows that if n be great $z_0 - z_1$ must be small. Hence the axis of the top moves between two close right cones which have OZ_1 for their common axis.

Now consider the value of ψ. We have

$$\dot\psi = bn\frac{z_0 - z}{1 - z^2}. \quad\quad\quad\quad (6)$$

By the value of $z_0 - z_1$ just obtained we can write this in the form

$$\dot\psi = \frac{a}{bn}\frac{z_0 - z}{z_0 - z_1}\frac{1 - z_1^2}{1 - z^2}. \quad\quad\quad (7)$$

The quantities $z_0 - z$, $z_0 - z_1$ are both small: their ratio depends on the value of z. The value, however, of the ratio $(1 - z_1^2)/(1 - z^2)$ is (since z can differ but little from z_1) very nearly 1. We see from (2) that $z_0 > z_1$, that is, z_0 is the value of z for the *upper* limiting circle, and z_1 is that for the lower.

We notice that when $z = z_0$, that is at the upper circle, $\dot\psi = 0$, or the curve of intersection of the axis with the spherical surface is that shown in Fig. 115, for it is clear from (2), (3) and (7) that $\dot\psi^2(1 - z^2)$ is small in comparison with $\dot\theta$ when z approximates to z_0, though both $\dot\theta$ and $\dot\psi$ approach zero, and the path meets the upper circle in a series of cusps.

Again, when $z = z_1$, we have $\dot\psi = a/bn = 2Wgh/Cn$. We shall see that the average value of $\dot\psi$ is Wgh/Cn in this case.

266. Approximate Solution for Rapidly Rotating Top. In the present case, $\theta_1 - \theta_0$ is small, and θ lies between θ_0 and θ_1. Let $\theta = \theta_0 + \eta$, where η is a small quantity. We get $\cos\theta = \cos\theta_0 - \eta\sin\theta_0$, that is, $z = z_0 - \eta\sin\theta_0$. Now, substituting in (4), § 265, we get, neglecting terms affected by the factor η/n^2, and remembering that $1 - z_0^2 = \sin^2\theta_0$,

$$\dot\eta^2 = a\eta\sin\theta_0 - b^2 n^2 \eta^2. \quad\quad\quad\quad (1)$$

From this we obtain

$$bn\, dt = \frac{d\eta}{\left\{\dfrac{a^2\sin^2\theta_0}{4b^4 n^4} - \left(\eta - \dfrac{1}{2}\dfrac{a\sin\theta_0}{b^2 n^2}\right)^2\right\}^{\frac{1}{2}}},$$

and so $\eta = a \sin\theta_0 (1-\cos bnt)/2b^2n^2$. Hence we have

$$\theta = \theta_0 + \frac{a \sin\theta_0}{2b^2n^2}(1-\cos bnt), \quad \ldots\ldots\ldots\ldots(2)$$

and therefore

$$\theta_1 = \theta_0 + \frac{a}{b^2n^2}\sin\theta_0. \quad \ldots\ldots\ldots\ldots\ldots\ldots(3)$$

It only remains to determine $\dot\psi$. We have
$\dot\psi = bn(z_0-z)/(1-z^2)$
$\quad = bn\{\cos\theta_0 - \cos(\theta_0+\eta)\}/\sin^2(\theta_0+\eta) = bn\eta/\sin\theta_0.$

Hence $\quad\quad\quad \dot\psi = \dfrac{a}{2bn}(1-\cos bnt). \quad\ldots\ldots\ldots\ldots\ldots(4)$

This gives $\dot\psi = 0$ when $t=0$, for then $\theta=\theta_0$, and $\dot\psi = a/bn$ when $t=\pi/bn$. This agrees with the statement in § 265.

The motion expressed by (2) and (4) is one of oscillation about a steady motion with constant values θ_0 and $a/2bn$ ($= Wgh/Cn$) of θ and $\dot\psi$. We shall prove later that the steady motion is stable. Meanwhile we note that the period of oscillation about the state of steady motion is

$$2\pi/bn = 2\pi A/Cn.$$

267. Reaction of Top on Support.

Ex. It is required to find the horizontal and vertical forces exerted on the support by a rapidly rotating top, supposing the point of support O to be fixed.

If the azimuthal motion is insensible, the outward horizontal force exerted by the support on the top is $Wh(\ddot\theta\cos\theta - \dot\theta^2\sin\theta)$. The vertical force is $-Wg + Wh(\ddot\theta\sin\theta + \dot\theta^2\cos\theta)$. Hence the forces exerted on the ground are

$$X = -Wh(\ddot\theta\cos\theta - \dot\theta^2\sin\theta), \quad Y = Wg - Wh(\ddot\theta\sin\theta + \dot\theta^2\cos\theta). \ldots(1)$$

But by (2) of § 266,

$$\ddot\theta = \tfrac{1}{2}a\sin\theta_0\cos bnt, \quad \dot\theta^2 = \frac{a^2}{4b^2n^2}\sin^2\theta_0\sin^2 bnt.$$

Putting $\cos\theta_0$, $\sin\theta_0$ for $\cos\theta$, $\sin\theta$, we get

$$\left.\begin{aligned}X &= -\tfrac{1}{2}Wha\sin\theta_0\left(\cos\theta_0\cos bnt - \frac{a}{2b^2n^2}\sin^2\theta_0\sin^2 bnt\right),\\ Y &= Wg - \tfrac{1}{2}Wha\sin^2\theta_0\left(\cos bnt + \frac{a}{2b^2n^2}\cos\theta_0\sin^2 bnt\right).\end{aligned}\right\}\ldots\ldots(2)$$

As noticed above, this takes no account of the azimuthal motion with angular speed $\dot{\psi}$. For this motion there must be applied through the centroid the inward force

$$Wh\sin\theta\,\dot{\psi}^2 = Wha^2\sin\theta_0(1-\cos bnt)^2/4b^2n^2.$$

Hence an outward force of this amount is applied by the top to the support, and this must be added to the value of X given above.

268. Top on Perfectly Smooth Plane. So far we have supposed the point O fixed. If, however, the top be supported on a plane which offers no resistance to the motion of the point O, we notice that no horizontal force is applied to the top, and that therefore if the centroid G is initially at rest horizontally, it will remain at rest. We may apply the preceding discussion to this case, if we take the centroid G as the fixed point and modify the equations to take account of the vertical motion of G. The axes are taken as before, but through G.

Let F be the vertical reaction of the plane on the point O of the top. Then we have, by the reasoning in § 261,

$$A\ddot{\theta} + (Cn - A\dot{\psi}\cos\theta)\dot{\psi}\sin\theta = Fh\sin\theta. \quad\ldots\ldots\ldots\ldots(1)$$

But $h\sin\theta\,.\,\dot{\theta}$ is the speed of G vertically downwards. Hence

$$W\frac{d}{dt}(h\dot{\theta}\sin\theta) = Wg - F$$

or $$F = Wg - Wh(\sin\theta\,.\,\ddot{\theta} + \cos\theta\,.\,\dot{\theta}^2). \quad\ldots\ldots\ldots\ldots\ldots\ldots(2)$$

Substituting this value of F in (1), we get

$$(A + Wh^2\sin^2\theta)\ddot{\theta} + Wh^2\sin\theta\cos\theta\,.\,\dot{\theta}^2 + (Cn - A\dot{\psi}\cos\theta)\dot{\psi}\sin\theta \brace = Wgh\sin\theta, \quad\ldots(3)$$

which takes the place of (1) of § 261.

The equation of constancy of angular momentum about the vertical, through G in this case, is the same as (4), § 261,

$$Cn\cos\theta + A\dot{\psi}\sin^2\theta = G. \quad\ldots\ldots\ldots\ldots\ldots\ldots\ldots(4)$$

The kinetic energy in the present case is

$$\tfrac{1}{2}\{Wh^2\sin^2\theta\,.\,\dot{\theta}^2 + A(\dot{\theta}^2 + \dot{\psi}^2\sin^2\theta) + Cn^2\},$$

and the potential energy is $Wgh\cos\theta$, as before. The equation of energy therefore is

$$\tfrac{1}{2}\{(A + Wh^2\sin^2\theta)\dot{\theta}^2 + A\sin^2\theta\,.\,\dot{\psi}^2 + Cn^2\} + Wgh\cos\theta = E. \quad\ldots(5)$$

We remember that Cn is constant, and write by (4),

$$\dot{\psi} = (G - Cn\cos\theta)/A\sin^2\theta.$$

Thus the equation of energy can be written in the form

$$\frac{1}{2}\left\{(A + Wh^2\sin^2\theta)\dot{\theta}^2 + \frac{(G - Cn\cos\theta)^2}{A\sin^2\theta} + Cn^2\right\} + Wgh\cos\theta = E, \ldots(6)$$

in which $\dot{\psi}$ does not appear. If now we write z for $\cos\theta$ in this, we get, after reduction,

$$A\{A + Wh^2(1-z^2)\}\dot{z}^2 = -(G - Cnz)^2 + 2A(c - Wghz)(1-z^2), \quad \ldots\ldots(7)$$

where $2c = 2E - Cn^2$, a constant. It will be noticed that c is the whole energy *minus* the energy of the rotation of the top about its axis of figure.

From this t can be expressed in terms of z by integration; but the discussion is beyond our limits of space.

269. Examples on the Motion of a Top.

Ex. 1. Prove that, if we write $z = z_1 \cos^2\phi + z_2 \sin^2\phi$, (3) of § 263 reduces to
$$\dot{\phi}^2 = m^2(1 - k^2 \sin^2\phi),$$
where
$$k^2 = \frac{z_2 - z_1}{z_3 - z_1}, \quad m^2 = \frac{1}{2}\frac{g}{l}(z_3 - z_1),$$

if $l = A/Wh$. [Thus t can be found as an elliptic integral of the first kind.]

Also prove that if $\phi = \operatorname{am} nt$,
$$z = \cos\theta = z_1 \operatorname{cn}^2 mt + \cos\beta \operatorname{sn}^2 mt.$$

[Greenhill, *Elliptic Functions*, § 210.]

Ex. 2. Prove that
$$A\dot{\psi} = \frac{G - Cn\cos\theta}{\sin^2\theta} = \frac{1}{2}\frac{G+Cn}{1+\cos\theta} + \frac{1}{2}\frac{G-Cn}{1-\cos\theta},$$
so that
$$A\dot{\psi} = \frac{1}{2}\frac{G+Cn}{1+z_1+(z_2-z_1)\operatorname{sn}^2 mt} + \frac{G-Cn}{1-z_1-(z_2-z_1)\operatorname{sn}^2 mt}$$

Also by (4), § 268, show that
$$\left(\frac{G+Cn}{A}\right)^2 = 2\frac{g}{l}(1+z_1)(1+z_2)(1+z_3), \quad \left(\frac{G-Cn}{A}\right)^2 = 2\frac{g}{l}(1-z_1)(1-z_2)(1-z_3),$$
so that if
$$k^2 \operatorname{sn}^2 v_1 = -\frac{z_2-z_1}{1+z_1}, \quad k^2 \operatorname{sn}^2 v_2 = \frac{z_2-z_1}{1-z_1},$$
$$\frac{d \cdot i\dot{\psi}}{d(mt)} = \frac{\frac{\operatorname{cn} v_1 \cdot \operatorname{dn} v_1}{\operatorname{sn} v_1}}{1 - k^2 \operatorname{sn}^2 v_1 \cdot \operatorname{sn}^2 mt} + \frac{\frac{\operatorname{cn} v_2 \cdot \operatorname{dn} v_2}{\operatorname{sn} v_2}}{1 - k^2 \operatorname{sn}^2 v_2 \cdot \operatorname{sn}^2 mt}.$$

[Greenhill, *loc. cit.*]

Ex. 3. Prove that the axis of the top keeps time with the beat of a simple pendulum of length $L = l/\frac{1}{2}(z_2 - z_1)$, suspended from a point at height $\frac{1}{2}l(z_1+z_2)$ above O, so that a point on the pendulum at distance l^2/L from the point of suspension moves so as to be always at the same level as the centre of oscillation of the top. [Greenhill.]

MOTION OF TOP: EXAMPLES.

Ex. 4. A top is rotating rapidly about the axis of figure and performing small oscillations about a state of steady motion at inclination θ_0 of its axis to the vertical. Find the distance described by the point P (Fig. 113) on the unit sphere in the period of vibration.

By (2) and (4) of § 266, we have

$$(\dot{\theta}^2 + \sin^2\theta_0 \dot{\psi}^2)^{\frac{1}{2}} = (a \sin \theta_0/bn)\sin \tfrac{1}{2}bnt,$$

and this is approximately the speed of P. Hence integrating over a period $2\pi/bn$, we get for the distance s travelled by P,

$$s = 4\frac{a}{b^2n^2}\sin \theta_0 = 8\frac{\mu}{bn}\sin \theta_0,$$

if we denote the mean value of $\dot{\psi}$, that is $a/2bn$, by μ.

The distance travelled in a period by the centroid of the top is therefore $8\mu h \sin \theta_0/bn$.

Ex. 5. A symmetrical top is held at rest on a rough horizontal plane, with its axis inclined at an angle θ_0 to the vertical, and an angular speed n about the axis of figure is given to it by unwinding a string. The top is then left to itself. Show that the inclination θ oscillates between θ_0 and $\cos^{-1}\{1-\sqrt{1-2p\cos\theta_0+p^2}\}$, where

$$p = 4\,WghA/C^2n^2.$$

Ex. 6. Prove that the distance β described by the point P (Fig. 113) on the unit sphere fulfils the equation

$$(C^2n^2 - 4\,WghA\cos\theta_0)\tan\beta = 4\,WghA\sin\theta_0.$$

By (1), § 263, we have $\dot{\theta}^2 + \dot{\psi}^2\sin^2\theta = \alpha - a\cos\theta$, and this is $\dot{\phi}^2$ if $\dot{\phi}$ be the rate at which the axis of the top is changing direction. Hence

$$\dot{\phi} = \sqrt{\alpha - a\cos\theta}.$$

But we have also, by elimination of $\dot{\psi}$ between the two equations (1) of § 263, $\dot{\theta} = \sqrt{\alpha - a\cos\theta - \{(\beta - bn\cos\theta)/\sin\theta\}^2}$, and therefore

$$\frac{d\phi}{d\theta} = \frac{\sqrt{\alpha - a\cos\theta}\cdot\sin\theta}{\sqrt{(\alpha - a\cos\theta)\sin^2\theta - (\beta - bn\cos\theta)^2}}.$$

But, initially, $\theta = \theta_0$, and $\dot{\theta} = \dot{\psi} = 0$; and therefore

$$\alpha = a\cos\theta_0, \quad \beta = bn\cos\theta_0.$$

Substituting in the last equation, reducing, and writing p for $\tfrac{1}{2}b^2n^2/a$, we get
$$\frac{d\phi}{d\theta} = \frac{\sin\theta}{\sqrt{1 - 2p\cos\theta_0 + p^2 - (p - \cos\theta)^2}}.$$

Now, at the other limit θ_1 of θ we have $\cos\theta = p - \sqrt{1 - 2p\cos\theta_0 + p^2}$, and therefore we get, by integration,

$$\phi = \sin^{-1}\frac{p - \cos\theta}{\sqrt{1 - 2p\cos\theta_0 + p^2}} + C,$$

488   A TREATISE ON DYNAMICS.   [CH. IX.

and for β the value of this integral between the limits $\theta = \theta_0$ and $\theta = \cos^{-1}\{p - \sqrt{p^2 - 2p\cos\theta_0 + 1}\}$. Hence

$$\beta = \sin^{-1}\frac{\sqrt{p^2 - 2p\cos\theta_0 + 1}}{\sqrt{p^2 - 2p\cos\theta_0 + 1}} - \sin^{-1}\frac{p - \cos\theta_0}{\sqrt{p^2 - 2p\cos\theta_0 + 1}}$$

or
$$\beta = \tfrac{1}{2}\pi - \sin^{-1}\frac{p - \cos\theta_0}{\sqrt{p^2 - 2p\cos\theta_0 + 1}}.$$

This is, of course, also the measure of the angle turned through by the axis of the top on the surface traced out by the axis.

The expression found for β gives

$$\cos\beta = \frac{p - \cos\theta_0}{\sqrt{p^2 - 2p\cos\theta_0 + 1}},$$

and it follows that
$$\sin\beta = \frac{\sin\theta_0}{\sqrt{p^2 - 2p\cos\theta_0 + 1}}.$$

Hence, we have $(p - \cos\theta_0)\tan\beta = \sin\theta_0$, the relation to be proved.

270. Steady Motion of Top Rapidly Rotating about a Fixed Point. Stability of Steady Motion. It is proved in § 266 above, that if a top be set spinning about its axis of figure at a high speed and then be left to itself, with one point fixed, it will perform small oscillations about a state of steady motion between narrow limits of θ, the smaller of which is the initial inclination of the axis of figure to the vertical. But as an example of a method which is of frequent application, another discussion is here given.

We have, § 261, the equations

$$\left.\begin{array}{l} A\ddot{\theta} + (Cn - A\dot{\psi}\cos\theta)\dot{\psi}\sin\theta = Wgh\sin\theta, \\ Cn\cos\theta + A\dot{\psi}\sin^2\theta = G. \end{array}\right\} \quad \ldots\ldots(1)$$

We notice first that if θ be changed slightly by action which has no moment about the vertical,

$$d(Cn\cos\theta + A\dot{\psi}\sin^2\theta) = 0. \quad \ldots\ldots\ldots\ldots\ldots(2)$$

The peculiarity of steady motion is that θ is permanently constant, so that $\ddot{\theta} = 0$. Hence $\dot{\psi}$ must be constant also: let its value be μ. We get therefore by the first of (1) for steady motion, the equation

$$(Cn - A\mu\cos\theta)\mu = Wgh. \quad \ldots\ldots\ldots\ldots\ldots(3)$$

The factor $\sin\theta$ is dropped as we do not suppose that $\theta = 0$.

§§ 269, 270, 271] STABILITY OF TOP. 489

This is a quadratic equation in μ. The condition that its roots should be real is that $C^2n^2 > 4A\,Wgh\cos\theta$. Unless this condition is fulfilled, steady motion is not possible. For example, a top cannot spin upright in steady motion unless $C^2n^2 > 4A\,Wgh$. We shall return to this question presently.

Now let the steady motion be deviated from, so that the inclination becomes $\theta + \alpha$, where θ is the steady value, and the azimuthal motion, or *precession* as we shall call it (see § 275), becomes $\mu + \eta$. Substituting in the first of (1) and in (2) multiplied by $\sin\theta$, combining the results and using (3), we obtain, as the reader may verify,

$$A^2\mu^2\ddot{\alpha} + (A^2\mu^4 - 2Wgh A\mu^2 \cos\theta + W^2g^2h^2)\alpha = 0. \quad \ldots\ldots\ldots\ldots(4)$$

The quantity in brackets can be written as the sum of two squares, and is therefore positive. Hence the deviation from steady motion is simple harmonic. The period is

$$T = \frac{2\pi A\mu}{(A^2\mu^4 - 2Wgh A\mu^2 \cos\theta + W^2g^2h^2)^{\frac{1}{2}}}.$$

If the motion had been unstable, the period would have been imaginary. The result shows that if a top is in steady motion, and is slightly disturbed without violation of (2), the motion is then one of oscillation about the state of steady motion, in a period which is shorter the greater the spin. The period here obtained is a more exact value than that, $2\pi A/Cn$, found in § 266, to which, however, it reduces if the terms in μ^4, μ^2 be neglected.

The two values of μ given by (3) are

$$\mu = \frac{Cn}{2A\cos\theta}\left(1 \pm \sqrt{1 - \frac{4A\,Wgh}{C^2n^2}\cos\theta}\right).$$

Either of these values of μ is possible and may be realised by starting the top properly. The smaller root, which approximates to Wgh/Cn, or, more exactly, to $Wgh\{1 + (A\,Wgh\cos\theta)/C^2n^2\}/Cn$, when n is great, is that which applies when the top is held with its axis inclined at some angle θ to the vertical, set into rapid rotation by the unwinding of a string, and then left to itself. The motion is not then strictly steady, but is one of oscillation through a small range of θ, and a range of μ from twice the initial value of $\dot{\psi}$ to zero. For truly steady motion, the top must, besides being set into rapid rotation, have given to it at starting the proper amount of azimuthal motion μ.

271. Graphical Representation of Condition of Stability of Steady Motion. The dynamical stability can be illustrated by a very elegant geometrical construction due to Sir George Greenhill. In Fig. 117 OC is the vertical, OC' the axis of the top. OC and OC' are made of lengths to represent respectively the angular momentum

G about the vertical, and the angular momentum Cn about the axis of figure. These are components of an angular momentum OK in the plane COZ, obtained by drawing lines in that plane at right angles to OC and OC', and the line OK to their point of meeting K. KM is also drawn vertically, and KN is drawn parallel to OC' to meet OC in N.

[From K the line KH at right angles to CK is drawn to represent $A\dot\theta$; and so OH represents the resultant angular momentum.]

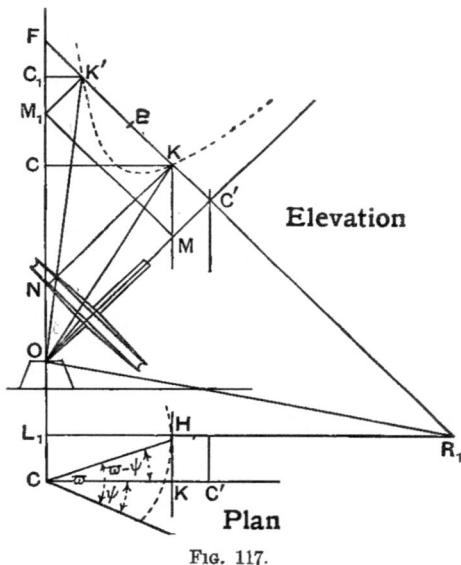

Fig. 117.

OK is equivalent either to the two components OC', $C'K$ or to the two OC, CK. Now $C'K$ is $A\dot\psi\sin\theta$, so that

$$CK = OC'\sin\theta - C'K\cos\theta = (Cn - A\dot\psi\cos\theta)\sin\theta.$$

Also $$MK = ON = C'K/\sin\theta = A\dot\psi,$$

and $$NC = Cn\cos\theta - A\dot\psi\cos^2\theta = (Cn - A\dot\psi\cos\theta)\cos\theta.$$

Thus $$NK = Cn - A\dot\psi\cos\theta.$$

Now, if the motion is steady, $\dot\theta = 0$, and H coincides with K. Let the steady value of $\dot\psi$ be μ. The point K then moves round OC, keeping θ constant, at such a speed that angular momentum in the

direction of the motion of K, measured by the speed of K in that direction, grows at rate $CK \cdot \mu = Wgh \sin \theta$. But
$$CK = (Cn - A\mu \cos \theta) \sin \theta,$$
and therefore we have
$$(Cn - A\mu \cos \theta)\mu = Wgh,$$
the quadratic equation for μ found in § 270 above.

By the diagram,
$$\mu = \frac{Wgh}{CK} \sin \theta = \frac{Wgh}{NK} \quad \text{and} \quad \mu = \frac{ON}{A} = \frac{MK}{A}.$$

Thus we get $MK \cdot NK = A\,Wgh$, and thus, for OC with the given length and inclination θ to the vertical, K lies on a hyperbola of which OC and OC' are the asymptotes.

If E be the middle point of $C'F$, we get
$$C'E^2 - KE^2 = C'K \cdot KF = KM \cdot NK \cdot \sin \theta \tan \theta = Wgh \sin \theta \tan \theta.$$

If the line $C'K$ intersect the hyperbola again in K', another value μ' of the azimuthal angular speed exists for K', and is the larger root of the equation.

When the roots are equal the line $C'K$ touches the hyperbola. Then $KM = \tfrac{1}{2}OF$, $KN = \tfrac{1}{2}OC'$, and therefore
$$A\,Wgh = KM \cdot NK = \tfrac{1}{4}OF \cdot OC' = \tfrac{1}{4}C^2n^2 \sec \theta.$$

Hence $Cn = 2\sqrt{A\,Wgh \cos \theta}$, $\mu = 2\,Wgh/Cn$. It will be seen that the hyperbola depends only on the angle θ, so that if OC' be too short $C'K$ will fall below the vertex of the branch of the curve shown dotted in the diagram, and steady motion will be impossible. The roots of the quadratic are then imaginary.

What happens, when the top is started with the given A.M. Cn, at a given inclination θ with $\dot{\theta}$ and $\dot{\psi}$ zero, is, first (since the term $\tfrac{1}{2}Cn^2$ of the kinetic energy remains unaltered, while terms $\tfrac{1}{2}A\dot{\theta}^2$ and $\tfrac{1}{2}A\dot{\psi}^2 \sin^2 \theta$ are called into existence at the expense of the potential energy) a sinking of the axis below the inclination θ. This sinking continues while $\dot{\theta}$ increases, and $\ddot{\theta}$, at first a maximum, diminishes until when $\ddot{\theta}$ is zero $\dot{\theta}$ is a maximum. At that instant $\dot{\psi}$ has the steady motion value μ, as appears from (1) of § 270. Fig. 117 shows that at the starting of the top K lies within the hyperbola, and that when $\ddot{\theta}=0$ the value of $\dot{\psi}$ is the smaller root of the steady motion equation just referred to. It cannot possibly be the greater root unless a sufficiently large initial value of $\dot{\psi}$ is given to make
$$(Cn - A\dot{\psi} \cos \theta)\dot{\psi} > Wgh,$$
when, by (1), § 270, $A\ddot{\theta}$ must be negative, and the axis will rise toward the point K.

After $\dot{\theta}$ has thus become a maximum, and K has reached the hyperbola, the axis continues to sink, and $\ddot{\theta}$ becomes negative. We have then $(Cn - A\dot{\psi}\cos\theta)\dot{\psi} > Wgh$, and $\dot{\psi}$ increases, until it attains a maximum value just when the absolute value of $\ddot{\theta}$ is greatest, as we see from (3) of § 261, for then $\dot{\theta}=0$, and therefore $\ddot{\psi}=0$. Then the absolute value of $\ddot{\theta}$ diminishes, a negative value of $\dot{\theta}$ grows up and the axis rises.

Unless the initial position is such that the line $C'K$ intersects the hyperbola, there does not exist a value of $\dot{\psi}$, with which if the top were started it would continue in steady motion.

272. Additional Couple about OD. Effect of forcing Precession above Free Value. Now let an additional couple N about OD be applied to the top, say by the action of a ring similar to that which constrains the model in Fig. 121, so that the whole moment about OD is $Wgh\sin\theta + N$, and let the top be in steady motion in these circumstances. We have then the equation

$$(Cn - A\mu\cos\theta)\mu\sin\theta = Wgh\sin\theta + N$$

or
$$\frac{N}{\sin\theta} = -A\mu^2\cos\theta + Cn\mu - Wgh. \quad\ldots\ldots\ldots\ldots(1)$$

If μ_1, μ_2 ($\mu_1 > \mu_2$) be the roots of the equation

$$A\mu^2\cos\theta - Cn\mu + Wgh = 0,$$

we can write (1) in the form

$$\frac{N}{\sin\theta} = A\cos\theta(\mu_1 - \mu)(\mu - \mu_2) = \frac{KM \cdot NK}{A} - Wgh \quad\ldots(2)$$

by § 271 above. According as N is positive or negative μ does or does not lie between μ_1 and μ_2, that is, the point K in Fig. 117 does or does not lie within the hyperbola which gives the values of μ for *free* steady motion. But if N be positive, it must arise from the exertion of a force by the ring on the axis tending to increase θ, so that the axis presses upwards against the ring, that is, the outer end of the axis tends to rise. On the other hand, if N be negative, the point K in Fig. 117 lies outside the hyperbola, and the axis tends to fall from the ring.

In free steady motion no ring is required, but it is now clear that any increase of the precessional speed μ from the value μ_2 will, in the absence of constraint such as that

EFFECT OF PRECESSION.

given by the ring, cause the outer end of the axis to rise, and that any decrease of μ will cause the axis to fall.

It is shown in § 261 that A.M. is produced by the motion about the axes OC, OE at rate $(Cn - A\dot\psi \cos\theta)\dot\psi \sin\theta$, and so we have the equation of free steady motion

$$(Cn - A\mu\cos\theta)\mu\sin\theta = Wgh\sin\theta,$$

which can be written, without change of signs,

$$A\cos\theta(\mu_1 - \mu)(\mu - \mu_2) = 0. \dots\dots\dots\dots\dots(1)$$

If this equation is fulfilled because $\mu = \mu_2$, the smaller root of the quadratic in μ, any sudden increase in μ, without change in θ, must give the quantity on the left a positive value, that is make $(Cn - A\dot\psi\cos\theta)\dot\psi\sin\theta$ *exceed* $Wgh\sin\theta$, and so by (1), § 261, $A\ddot\theta$ must be negative, that is $\dot\theta$ begins to acquire a negative value, and the top rises. On the other hand, if the equation is fulfilled because $\mu = \mu_1$, the greater root, any increase of μ beyond that value will make

$$(Cn - A\dot\psi\cos\theta)\dot\psi\sin\theta - Wgh\sin\theta$$

acquire a negative value, that is $A\ddot\theta$ must be positive; in other words, $\dot\theta$ begins to acquire a positive value, and the top falls. Similarly diminution of μ from the values μ_2, μ_1 causes the top to fall and rise respectively.

It is important to notice that the common rule "hurrying the precession causes the top to rise, delaying the precession causes the top to fall" is not, as it is usually given, correct. The effect of either depends on whether the smaller or the larger of the two possible values of μ is that of the steady motion. In the majority of cases which occur in experiments with tops, it is the smaller value of μ which characterises the motion,

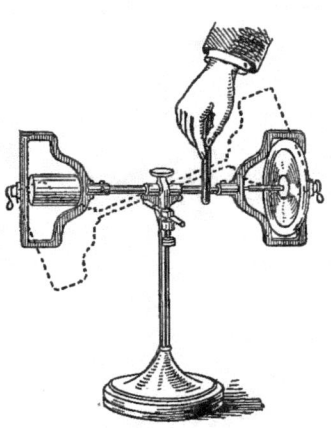

FIG. 118.

and so the rule in its ordinary form gives results in accordance with experiment.

Fig. 118 shows the effect of imposing precession about a vertical axis in a balanced gyrostat. Precession about a horizontal axis is produced.

273. Reaction of Ring-Guide or Space-Cone on Top. If, as in the model of Fig. 121 and in the toy shown in Fig. 119, the top be furnished with a material cone or axle, fixed round the axis of figure, which rolls on a cone fixed in space represented by the ring in Fig. 121 or the curved wire of Fig. 119, and the point of support be at the centroid, the couple on the top must be applied by the pressure of the fixed against the moving cone. The circle of the points of contact on the moving cone is the polhode on the top, and the fixed ring or curved wire is the herpolhode. (See Chap. VIII.)

The pressure of the axle on the ring-guide, that is of one polhode on the other, is to be found from the calculation of the rate of growth of A.M. given in § 261. This is the rate of displacement of the extremity H of the vector OH representing the A.M., and is clearly about an axis at right angles at once to the axis of figure and to the vertical, an axis, therefore, which may be represented by the axis OD of Fig. 112. For OH is always in the plane ZOC of Fig. 112, which is perpendicular to the path of the point I of the instantaneous axis along the guide.

But the A.M. grows in the direction OD at rate

$$A\ddot{\theta} + (Cn - A\dot{\psi}\cos\theta)\dot{\psi}\sin\theta,$$

and therefore, if N be the couple,

$$A\ddot{\theta} + (Cn - A\dot{\psi}\cos\theta)\dot{\psi}\sin\theta = N, \quad \ldots\ldots\ldots\ldots(1)$$

or if the motion is steady,

$$(Cn - A\mu\cos\theta)\mu\sin\theta = N. \quad \ldots\ldots\ldots\ldots\ldots(2)$$

This equation is sometimes written in this connection[*] in the form
$$\{C\omega - (A - C)\mu\cos\theta\}\mu\sin\theta = N, \quad \ldots\ldots\ldots\ldots(3)$$

---

[*] See Klein and Sommerfeld, *Theorie des Kreisels*, p. 173, where, however, a different mode of derivation is used.

where ω is the rate of turning of the top relatively to the plane ZOC (§ 261).

If $A = C$, we have the steady precessional motion, under couple N, of a spherical top, that is, the equation is

$$C(n - \mu \cos \theta)\mu \sin \theta = N, \dots\dots\dots\dots\dots(4)$$

as in § 272 above. We shall see below that the term introduced by the inertia of the *case* of a gyrostat enables a similar equation of steady motion to be obtained for that form of top (§ 281).

The pressure on the ring is N/l if l denote the distance of the point of contact of the axle with the ring from the point of support.

If a slight push or blow be given to the axis of the top, an impulsive couple is applied which produces an increase of the component $A\dot\psi \sin \theta$ of A.M. about the axis OE, that is, changes $\dot\psi$ to $\dot\psi + \delta\dot\psi$, if θ is kept unchanged by the guide. This increase in $\dot\psi$ makes the rate of growth of A.M. about OD more rapid than is accounted for by the couple N, and so the top endeavours to turn about OD in the direction to keep the rate of change of A.M. the same as before, that is so as to press with so much greater force against the guide, that the enhanced value of N is that required for the greater precession. [The reader should as an exercise verify this by the consideration of an actual case, drawing the momentum axes, and determining the sense of the couple N.]

274. Explanation of Clinging of Axle of Top to Curved Guide. The action of the top shown in Fig. 119 is very curious, but its explanation may be made out easily from the above discussion. The axle rolls round the curved guide following all the convolutions, however sharply curved, and on coming to the end of the guide in one direction turns rapidly round the end of the wire and rolls back on the other side. The axle has been described as clinging to the wire like a piece of iron to a magnet.

For simplicity we have supposed that there is no gravitational couple on the top. The action of the guide may be analysed as follows. Consider a right circular cone with the vertical through O as axis and the line OI as a generator; a short element of the guide at the point of contact is at the intersection of the guide and a circular section of the cone. Such a cone may be made to pass through any element of the guide, and θ is now the semi-vertical angle of that cone. The element will in general give a component of action on the axis of the top in the plane through the axis of the cone.

We have for the couple applied to the axle in the plane through OI, the equation

$$A\ddot{\theta} + (Cn - A\dot{\psi}\cos\theta)\dot{\psi}\sin\theta = N. \quad\ldots\ldots\ldots\ldots(5)$$

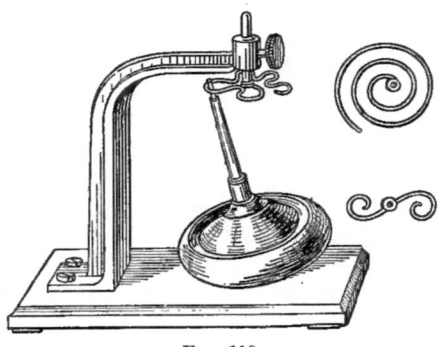

Fig. 119.

Besides this couple N, a reactional couple in the tangent plane to the cone through OI is applied to the top. For clearly a component F of reaction of the guide acts on it at I with or against the direction of motion along the circular section, according to the angle between the section and the guide, and F and $-F$ inserted at the point of support give a couple of moment N', the axis of which is at right angles to OI, in the plane COI. This can be resolved into two components $N'\sin\alpha$, $N'\cos\alpha$ ($\alpha = IOC$) about OC and OE (at right angles to OC) in the plane COI. The former couple of comparatively small moment alters the speed of rotation, the latter gives change of $\dot{\psi}$ at numerical rate

$$\ddot{\psi}\sin\theta = N'\cos\alpha,$$

where $\dot\theta$ is negligible. The axle therefore presses more or less on the guide from this cause.

There is also a frictional couple which in general splits into two components, one with or against N, and the other helping or retarding $\dot\psi$, according to the direction of the guide.

Now let the axle come to a discontinuity in the guide, for example one of the ends. The couple N may be regarded as there suddenly annulled, and therefore (since any thing like steady motion ceases) $A\ddot\theta$ as taking at the same time a value
$$-(Cn - A\dot\psi \cos\theta)\dot\psi \sin\theta,$$
the value of $A\ddot\theta - N$ just before the discontinuity is arrived at. In other words, the motion may be regarded as disturbed by an outward force N/l applied at I to the axle. Thus $\dot\theta$ grows up rapidly, and the axle moves outward.

But as the axle moves outward owing to $\dot\theta$, a rate R of growth of A.M. about OE would be produced, were it not for another motion of the top. There is now no couple about OE, and therefore, in order to keep R zero, the top must turn about OE, and in the direction, as will be seen from the figure, to bring the axle against the end of the wire, across which the axle will roll, until the next sharp corner is reached. In this way the axle rolls round the end of the guide, while the space-cone of angle θ changes position rapidly.

When the end has been rounded the precession becomes again nearly steady, but the axle now presses against the other side of the wire. The precession is now in the opposite direction, and the axle therefore again presses against the wire, but in the opposite direction to that in which it formerly pressed at the same place.

A similar explanation accounts for the hard pressing of the axle against the guide where θ increases or diminishes rapidly, as it does in a guide like that of Fig. 119.

275. Astronomical Precession. The term precession as applied to the motion of a top or gyrostat is derived from the "precession of the equinoxes" caused by what becomes a conical motion of the earth's axis, if the translational motion of the earth in its orbit is reduced to zero. For the earth is a top, rotating about an axis inclined at an angle of 66° 33' to the plane of the ecliptic, that is the plane of the motion of the earth's centre. While the earth thus rotates, the differential attraction of the sun on the two halves of the earth's equatorial protuberance, that turned towards the sun and that turned away from the sun—to take the earth at perihelion or at aphelion—exerts a couple which tends to bring the earth's equator into coincidence with the ecliptic, by turning it about a diameter at right angles to the radius-vector from the earth's centre to the sun. This couple plays the part of the couple about the axis OD (Fig. 112) applied by gravity to the top. The result is the same; just as the top does not fall down, but has an azimuthal motion in virtue of the couple, so that the axis of rotation, if the motion is steady, moves in a right cone, so the earth's axis does not approach perpendicularity to the ecliptic, but, relative to the earth's centre regarded as a fixed point, has a conical motion in space about a line drawn from the earth's centre to the pole of the ecliptic, which answers to the vertical OZ in the case of the top (Fig. 120). The angular speed of a point on the earth's axis about the axis of the cone is $M/Cn \sin \theta$, where M is a certain mean value of the moment of the couple referred to above as applied by the sun's attraction. This is exactly analogous to the value $Wgh \sin \theta / Cn \sin \theta$, which the theory of the top gives for the precessional motion of angular speed ψ_0 about the vertical. The conical motion of the earth's axis has a period of 26,000 years, and causes the astronomical phenomenon of *precession of the equinoxes*, that is the continual revolution of the line of equinoxes in the plane of the ecliptic.

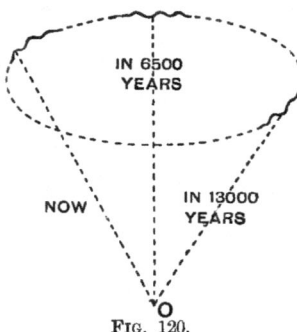

FIG. 120.

This is illustrated by Fig. 121, which shows a terrestrial globe with the lower half cut away, and the upper part

§ 275] ASTRONOMICAL PRECESSION. 499

loaded so that it can turn about a point of support at the centre, with the pin P in contact with the inside of the horizontal ring RP at the top. The pin P is the upper end of a cone fixed on the body, having its vertex at the centre O of the globe; this cone rolls on a cone fixed in space. The latter cone is represented by the ring RP, which is enough to guide the moving cone: all the rest is cut away, but it is understood that the vertex in this case is also at the centre.

As then the globe turns about the axis of figure the cone P rolls on the fixed cone, and travelling round the axis of figure describes a cone in space, in the model a cone of 23° 27′ semi-vertical angle. The equator of the globe is shown by the dark line intersecting a meridian through P in N. The upper surface of the rim, to which the supports

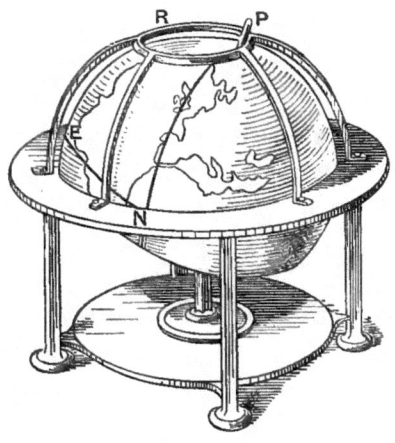

FIG. 121.

of the ring R are attached, represents the plane of the ecliptic, and the point N represents the intersection of the equator with that plane. N therefore represents an equinox. As the globe revolves in the counter-clock direction (as seen from outside P) the pin P rolls round the ring in the clock direction, and so the point N moves from right to left along the ecliptic, in the direction to meet the rotation, that is to make the equinox occur earlier in time. This is the precession of the equinoxes, which is thus completely illustrated by the model.

Ex. Supposing the model enlarged to the size of the earth and to spin with the same speed as the earth, find the diameter at the north pole of the cone fixed in the earth with vertex at the centre, which, rolling on the internal surface of a cone of semi-vertical angle 23° 27′

with its vertex also at the centre of the earth, gives precessional motion of 26,000 years' period.

The rolling of a cone fixed in the body on a cone fixed in space represents exactly the steady motion of a top. The body as it rotates about the axis of figure with speed n has each point of that axis carried round the vertical OZ with angular speed $\dot\psi_0$. The point I in Fig. 112 is therefore, in consequence of the rotation about OC, being carried in the direction from the reader, while, in consequence of the turning about OZ, it is being carried towards the reader. Let the position of I be so chosen that the one motion just counteracts the other. Then, as we shall show, the body is turning about the line OI, which is the instantaneous axis.

276. Rolling of Body-Cone on Space-Cone. As shown in the figure, I lies on two circles described about OZ and OC as axes. Denote the angle IOC by α, then $ZOI = \theta - \alpha$. The radii of the two circles are $OI \sin(\theta - \alpha)$ and $OI \sin\alpha$. But I has speed at right angles to the paper, of amount $n \cdot OI \sin\alpha$, due to the rotation about OC and speed

$$\dot\psi \sin\theta \cdot OI \cos\alpha,$$

due to the rotation $\dot\psi \sin\theta$ about OE. Thus we have

$$\tan\alpha = \frac{\dot\psi \sin\theta}{n}. \quad\quad\quad\quad\quad\quad (1)$$

The resultant angular speed is thus about OI, and is

$$\sqrt{n^2 + \dot\psi^2 \sin^2\theta}.$$

OI always lies in the vertical plane ZOC, which turns round OZ with angular speed $\dot\psi_0$. Hence, if θ does not vary neither does α, and OI moves round OZ in the cone of semi-vertical angle $IOZ = \theta - \alpha$, the cone fixed in space.

It will be noticed that the moving cone rolls in this case on the convex surface of the cone fixed in space, and that therefore precessional, or azimuthal, motion is in the same direction as the rotation. In the case of the earth, the moving cone rolls on the concave surface of the fixed cone, that is inside the latter. If this be called positive precession, that of the top is negative.

BODY-CONE AND SPACE-CONE.

We can now analyse the motion in the following manner, which gives a geometrical picture of what takes place. Consider two axes OA and OB fixed in the body, at right angles to one another and to OC, and therefore principal axes about which the moment of inertia is A, to coincide with OD and OE, and let a short interval of time τ elapse. The moving cone has rolled forward on the fixed cone, and the instantaneous axis is now OI'. The change of direction IOI' on the surface of the cone is towards the position which OA occupied at the beginning of τ, that is towards the position then of OD. The angle IOI' is clearly

$$\dot\psi\tau \sin(\theta - \alpha).$$

By the turning of OI towards OD in this way the angular speed about the position of OA at the initial instant of τ has (as we see by the principle already frequently applied) been increased by

$$\sqrt{n^2 + \dot\psi^2 \sin^2\theta} \cdot \cos\{\pi/2 - \dot\psi\tau \sin(\theta - \alpha)\},$$

that is by $\quad \sqrt{n^2 + \dot\psi^2 \sin^2\theta} \cdot \dot\psi\tau \sin(\theta - \alpha).$

[The semi-vertical angle of the cone has in the time τ been increased by $\dot\theta\tau$, but this has only moved the instantaneous axis parallel to the plane ZOC, and therefore can have produced no effect on the angular speed about OA.]

Now the figure shows that

$$\sin(\theta - \alpha)/\sin\theta = (n - \dot\psi \cos\theta)/\sqrt{n^2 + \dot\psi^2 \sin^2\theta},$$

so that the change of angular speed just calculated is

$$\dot\psi\tau(n - \dot\psi \cos\theta)\sin\theta.$$

[For $n - \dot\psi \cos\theta$ is the angular speed about OC relative to the plane ZOC, and therefore $(n - \dot\psi \cos\theta)\sin\alpha$ is balanced by $\dot\psi \sin(\theta - \alpha)$, so that

$$\sin(\theta - \alpha)/\sin\alpha = (n - \dot\psi \cos\theta)/\dot\psi.$$

But $\sin\theta/\tan\alpha = n/\dot\psi$, and therefore

$$\sin(\theta - \alpha)/\sin\theta = (n - \dot\psi \cos\theta)/(n/\cos\alpha)$$
$$= (n - \dot\psi \cos\theta)/\sqrt{n^2 + \dot\psi^2 \sin^2\theta}.]$$

To this change of angular speed falls to be added any change $\ddot{\theta}_T$ which has grown up in the angular speed $\dot{\theta}$. The total rate of growth of angular speed about the instantaneous position of OA is therefore

$$\ddot{\theta} + \dot{\psi}(n - \dot{\psi}\cos\theta)\sin\theta;$$

and this is the rate of change of the angular speed about OA in its position at the instant. We have proved (§ 170) that this is also the rate of change of the angular speed about OA as it moves with the body.

The angular acceleration about the axis OD, the instantaneous position of which was taken as coinciding with that of OA, is uninfluenced by the rotation of the body with angular speed $n - \dot{\psi}\cos\theta$ relative to the plane ZOC, and is therefore simply $\ddot{\theta}$.

The reader may in like manner find the position of the axis OH of resultant A.M., and find the equations of motion from a consideration of its motion.

277. Motion of a Top deduced from Euler's Equations. The equations of motion of a top, with reference to the special axes OC, OD, OE which have been used above, are often obtained by means of Euler's equations, and to complete the discussion we indicate how that is done. We have to use axes fixed in the body: one of these is OC, the others are OA, OB, which are in the plane of OD and OE (see Fig. 122). Since OE moves with the plane ZOC, we may take EOB as the angle through which the body in its turning about OC has outstripped the plane ZOC. Denoting this angle by ϕ, we have $\dot{\phi} = \omega$, the angular speed relative to ZOC. Putting p, q for the angular speeds about OA and OB, and $r(=n)$ for that about OC, we have

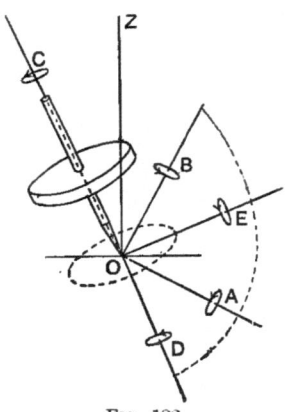

Fig. 122.

$$p = \dot{\theta}\cos\phi + \dot{\psi}\sin\theta\sin\phi, \quad q = -\dot{\theta}\sin\phi + \dot{\psi}\sin\theta\cos\phi. \quad (1)$$

The Eulerian equations are therefore

$$A\dot{p}-(A-C)qr = Wgh\cos\phi\sin\theta,$$
$$A\dot{q}-(C-A)rp = -Wgh\sin\phi\sin\theta, \quad\Big\}\ \ldots\ldots\ldots(2)$$
$$A\dot{r}=0.$$

Hence $r = \dot{\phi}+\dot{\psi}\cos\theta = \omega+\dot{\psi}\cos\theta$ is constant.

Substituting the values of p, q, r in the first two equations, multiplying the first equation by $\cos\phi$, and the second by $\sin\phi$, and subtracting the second product from the first, we get, after reduction,

$$A\ddot{\theta}+(Cn-A\dot{\psi}\cos\theta)\dot{\psi}\sin\theta = Wgh\sin\theta, \ \ldots\ldots(3)$$

which is (1) of § 261.

Multiplying the first equation obtained by the substitutions by $\sin\phi$ and the second by $\cos\phi$, and adding the results, we obtain

$$A\ddot{\psi}\sin\theta+(2A\dot{\psi}\cos\theta-Cn)\dot{\theta}=0, \ \ldots\ldots\ldots\ldots(4)$$

or (3) of § 261.

The last found equation, if multiplied by $\sin\theta$, is directly integrable, and the result is the equation of constancy of momentum about the vertical OZ.

The reader may also verify that if the first equation of (1) be multiplied by p, the second by q, the third by r, and the results be added, the equation obtained is directly integrable and yields the equation of energy.

It will be noticed that by the values of p and q in (1) we have when ϕ is zero, and OA and OB therefore coincide with OD and OE,

$$\dot{p}=\ddot{\theta}+\dot{\psi}(n-\dot{\psi}\cos\theta)\sin\theta,\ \dot{q}=\ddot{\psi}\sin\theta-\dot{\theta}(n-2\dot{\psi}\cos\theta).(5)$$

The first of these agrees with the value obtained otherwise in § 276, and the second can be obtained in a similar manner.

The reader should also obtain them by the method of § 9, proceeding as shown in § 261.

The reader should also carefully note the fact here illustrated, that $\dot{p},\ \dot{q},\ \dot{r}$, the angular accelerations with respect to fixed axes with which the moving axes OA, OB, OC coincide at the instant, are also (see § 170 above) the angular accelerations with respect to the moving axes

504   A TREATISE ON DYNAMICS.   [CH. IX.

OA, OB, OC. In other words, the change in dt of angular speed about OA, OB or OC in their new positions is the same as for the fixed axes, with which at the initial instant of dt they coincided. On the other hand, while the angular accelerations about the fixed axes, with which OD and OE coincide at the instant, are the values stated above in the equations for $\dot{p}$, $\dot{q}$, the accelerations about the *moving* axes OD, OE are simply $\ddot{\theta}$, and $d(\dot{\psi} \sin \theta)/dt$. The former is less than $\dot{p}$ by $\dot{\psi}(n - \dot{\psi} \cos \theta) \sin \theta$, and the latter greater than $\dot{q}$ by $(n - \dot{\psi} \cos \theta)\dot{\theta}$.

278. Gyrostats. Motion of a Gyrostat. The theory of a top given above applies with some slight modifications to the motion of a *gyrostat*, that is, a fly-wheel mounted in a case or on a framework, and set into rapid rotation about its axis. Figs. 123, 124, and 125 show different gyrostats made for different purposes. The first shows a fly-wheel with heavy rim, mounted on an axis the ends of which are carefully rounded points held in cup bearings, adjustable

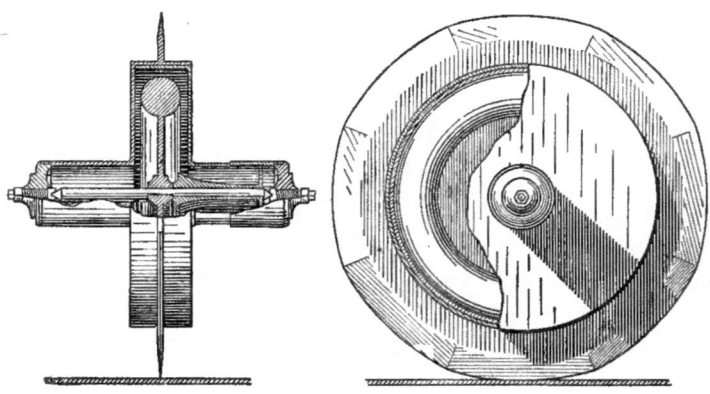

Fig. 123.

by screws, and secured by locking nuts which prevent any possibility of loosening of the bearings as the wheel revolves. The bearings are attached to a case shaped to enclose the wheel and its axis; so that the central part

§§ 277, 278]   GYROSTATS.   505

is a wide and shallow cylinder with at each side a longer, narrower cylinder surrounding the axle. Round the wide cylindrical box is a projecting edge, on which in the diagram the gyrostat is shown resting.

A part of the case surrounding the axis is cut away to allow the thread by which the spin is generated to be passed round the axle. A strong fine cord about 6 or

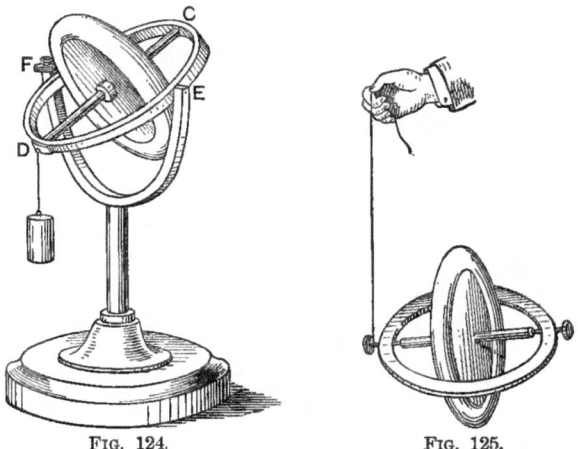

Fig. 124.   Fig. 125.

7 yards long has one end passed round the axle, and the two ends are then knotted together. The cord is then passed over the over-hanging pulley of a small electric motor, so that the plane of the now endless string is at right angles to the axis, and the string is crossed to give it a better grip of the axle. The motor is now started while the gyrostat is held by the operator, who pulls only slightly at first, so as not to stop the motor. After a time the fly-wheel will have been got into motion, and the string is cut by a blow from a sharp knife near where it is running to the axle, and runs off.

A simpler form is that familiar to nearly everybody as a scientific toy, in which the case is reduced to a ring carrying the fly-wheel bearings, and provided with a stand on which the gyrostat can be placed in different positions.

The gyrostatic action of a bicycle wheel is familiar to every one. The angular momentum of such a wheel is great though its speed of rotation be small. A simple form of gyrostat (or rather top) may be constructed, as suggested by Sir George Greenhill, by mounting a bicycle wheel at one end of a straight rod as axle, and hanging it from a fixed point by a universal joint at the other end. The wheel can then be spun by a stick placed between the spokes, and the phenomena of precession, reactions, etc., studied. The gyrostatic action of the wheels of a vehicle (a rapidly moving motor-car or railway carriage, for example), moving round the curve, gives a couple aiding centrifugal force to upset the vehicle, which must be balanced by the reaction of the ground or rails. The reader may calculate this couple by the methods explained below.

279. Gyrostatic Stability. Two positions of a gyrostat which experiment and theory show are stable are indicated

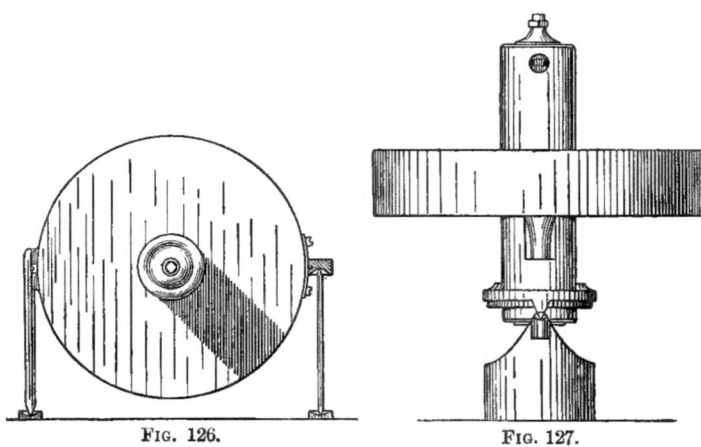

Fig. 126.   Fig. 127.

in Figs. 126, and 127. In the first, the gyrostat is supported on two stilts, one rigidly attached to the case and parallel to the plane of the wheel, the other merely a stiff wire with rounded points, the upper of which rests loosely in

§§ 278, 279]   GYROSTATIC STABILITY.   507

a hollow in the projecting arm seen in the diagram. The lower ends of the stilts rest on a metal plate. If the gyrostat is free to oscillate in azimuth, it will be stable when thus supported.

In the second case, the gyrostat is supported on gimbals, with its axis nearly vertical. It can thus turn its axis away from or towards the vertical in any direction. It has in fact two freedoms to turn from the vertical, one about the axis of each gimbal ring. The upright position is thoroughly stable when the fly-wheel is spinning. The remarkable fact will be proved below that the gyrostat must be unstable for *both* freedoms when the fly-wheel is not rotating, otherwise it cannot be made completely stable by rotation. In point of fact only an even number of freedoms can be rendered stable by the angular momentum.

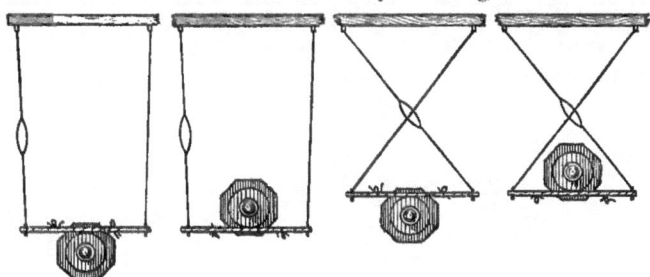

Fig. 128.

In Fig. 128 a gyrostat is shown supported on a bifilar sling, arranged in different ways. In the third and fourth diagrams of this figure the two threads are crossed by putting one through a ring placed in the other. Here azimuthal oscillations are possible. It is clear that the inclinational equilibrium in 1 and 3 is stable without rotation; in 2 and 4 it is rendered stable by rotation of the fly-wheel. The azimuthal equilibrium in 3 and 4 is only rendered stable by rotation. These arrangements are due to Lord Kelvin. [See Thomson and Tait's *Natural Philosophy*, § 345x.]

One of the most striking experiments which can be made with a gyrostat is that shown, carried out in slightly different ways, in Figs. 125, and 129. In Fig. 129 the cased gyrostat is shown hung by its rim, while a weight is hung from one end of the part of the case surrounding the axis. The gyrostat thus supported is pulled by the weight, so that it is acted on by two equal and vertical forces at a considerable distance apart, and would, if the wheel were not rotating, turn round so as to bring the centre of gravity of the whole under the supporting thread.

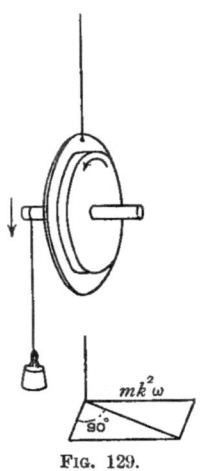

FIG. 129.

But if the wheel is in rapid rotation, the axis of rotation remains approximately horizontal while the whole revolves about a vertical axis. The axis of rotation of the fly-wheel turns round in a horizontal plane, that is to say, turning is produced about an axis perpendicular at once to the axis of rotation, and to the axis about which the vertical forces tend to turn the gyrostat. One almost naturally expects (though any other behaviour of the gyrostat than that which actually takes place would be really unnatural), the axis to be tilted down. This does not happen; the axis moves round sideways. The result is not, however, more wonderful than the azimuthal motion of an ordinary top under the action of gravity.

The same thing is shown in Fig. 125, and perhaps in the latter case more strikingly. The whole gyrostat is hung by a cord attached outside the containing ring, and by its weight pulls the centre of gravity down. As before, the axis, if free to do so, turns round in azimuth.

It is to be noticed that the direction of this azimuthal turning of the whole gyrostat is (like that of the top under gravity) always towards making the fly-wheel face in the direction in which it would face if the rotational motion of the wheel were produced by the turning moment, or torque, due to the weight of the gyrostat and the pull in the supporting cord. As the vertical line of action of the weight moves round with the gyrostat, the turning in

§ 279]   EXPLANATION OF PRECESSION.   509

azimuth goes on continuously, and is always towards giving to the system angular momentum about the axis round which gravity tends to generate such momentum.

We shall refer to this azimuthal motion as the *precession* of the gyrostat, according to the analogy between it and the precession of the equinoxes, explained in § 275 above.

The precession may be explained in an elementary way as follows. Consider a ring of balls contained in a circular tube as shown in Fig. 130. Let the balls move round in the tube in the direction shown by the arrows, while a couple acts tending to turn the whole system round the axis AB, so that C comes forward towards the reader. A ball when at B has no A.M. about AB, but as it rises above AB it will, if the ring have any turning about that line, be made to take up such A.M. The ball will therefore press against the tube in the direction from the reader.

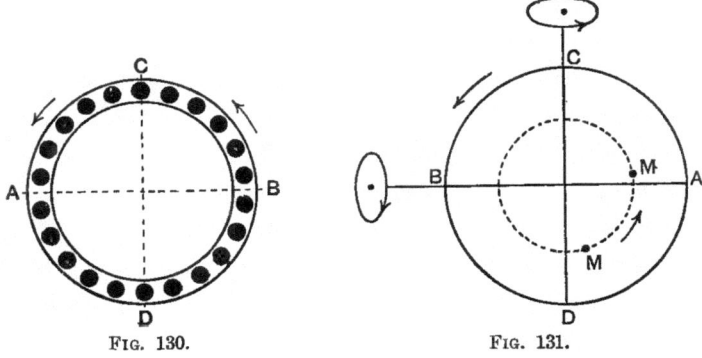

FIG. 130.   FIG. 131.

Similarly, a ball below the level of B losing its A.M. as it rises presses against the tube in the same direction. The right-hand half of the tube is thus pressed away from the reader.

It will be seen in the same way that the balls in the left-hand half press on the tube towards the reader. Thus the tube is made to take a precessional motion about CD.

The directions of the motions are shown by the circles in Fig. 131.

280. Experiments with Gyrostats. Rising and Falling of Ordinary Top. If the gyrostat is held in the hand with the axle in the line of the outstretched arm, and an attempt is made to strike a sudden downward blow with it, as with a mallet, the gyrostat gives a violent sideways wrench. The explanation of this is obvious. The downward turning of the gyrostat gives a rapid rate of production of angular momentum about a vertical axis, while the action of the operator has a moment, not about a vertical, but about a horizontal axis. The gyrostat as a whole, therefore, moves round sideways about a vertical axis in the proper direction to annul the production of angular momentum about that axis.

When the gyrostat is supported by a cord, or on a glass plate or stone slab, so that a couple is applied to it by gravity tending to change the direction of the axis of rotation, it will be noticed that when the precessional motion is impeded by applying a couple round the vertical axis, the gyrostat at once begins to fall down, and that if a couple is applied in the opposite direction, that is so as to hurry up the precession, the axis actually rises. It is thus, as was long ago pointed out by Jellett in his *Theory of Friction*, that a top is made to rise in the first part of its spin and fall in the latter part. In the first part of the spin the rotation is so rapid that the point of contact of the peg with the surface of the stone slab is moving relatively to that surface in the direction opposite to that indicated for the precession in Fig. 132, so that the friction applied to the top gives a couple about its axis hurrying up the precession; in the latter part the spin is so slow that the point of contact is moving the other way, so that the couple due to friction delays the precession, and the

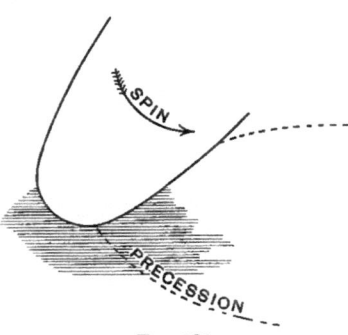

FIG. 132.

§ 280]   EXPERIMENTS WITH GYROSTATS.   511

top falls. [It is very instructive to experiment with two identical tops, one with a peg ground sharp, the other with a well-rounded peg. The former, if supported on a glass or marble slab, does not rise up from its initial inclined position—the latter does.] A dynamical explanation of all this will be found later; and the phenomena here described, though apparently not directly connected with the subject, will help to make clear the dynamical discussion.

Another experiment, which it is convenient to describe here, is made with the gyrostat (Fig. 133, § 283) spun as before. It is provided with a pair of trunnions, attached at extremities of a diameter to the edge surrounding the case in the plane of the fly-wheel. These rest in bearings on the two sides of this rectangular frame of wood; and the gyrostat when thus supported, and the frame held level, has its axis nearly vertical. Moreover, the centre of gravity of the gyrostat (wheel and case) is almost exactly in the plane through the trunnions at right angles to the axis of rotation, so that there is little or no stability due to gravity with either end of the axis uppermost.

The direction of rotation of the fly-wheel is shown by the arrow-head marked on the case. If then, holding the tray in his hands, the operator carries it with the gyrostat round in azimuth in the direction in which the wheel is rotating, the gyrostat remains at rest so long as the azimuthal motion imposed on the whole system coincides with the rotation; but if the azimuthal motion is reversed, the gyrostat at once capsizes so as to bring its rotational motion into coincidence with the azimuthal motion. This will also afford an illustration of the theory of the instrument.

Finally, consider the arrangement in Fig. 137, (like that of Fig. 129 without the attached weight). A gyrostat has the centre of gravity of the fly-wheel and the case (which is supposed to be symmetrical on the two sides of the fly-wheel) at the centre of the fly-wheel. The fly-wheel is spun rapidly, and the gyrostat is hung at the lower end of a long vertical steel wire, so that the axis of rotation is very nearly, if not quite, horizontal. If the gyrostat is turned round in azimuth, so that the wire is twisted, and is then left to itself, it swings in azimuth about the vertical in consequence of the torsional elasticity of the wire, performing also inclinational oscillations in the same period, and the period of this torsional vibration is much greater than that of the vibrations which the same system would execute if the fly-wheel had no rotation. The moment of inertia of the gyrostat round the vertical axis is virtually enormously increased.

This arrangement is analogous to that of a large and very rapidly rotating fly-wheel supported in a certain way on board ship, with its axis across the horizontal line about which the ship rolls. If this wheel were of great enough moment of inertia and rotated sufficiently rapidly, it would virtually increase the moment of inertia of the rolling vessel and lengthen the period of rolling. The virtual increase of moment of inertia is proportional to the square of the angular momentum of the fly-wheel. This arrangement will be referred to again later.

281. Equations of Motion of Gyrostat. The equations given in § 261 above for the motion of a top require modification for a gyrostat to take account of the fact that only part of the instrument—the fly-wheel—has the angular speed n about the axis of figure. We suppose, however, that the distribution of matter is symmetrical about the axis of the fly-wheel, that the wheel has moment of inertia C about its axis, and that the rest of the arrangement, which we shall call the *case*, has moment of inertia C' about the same axis. Frequently a point on the axis of the gyrostat may be taken as fixed; we shall denote then by A the moment of inertia of the whole about an axis through that point at right angles to the axis of figure. We refer to Fig. 112.

First, then, we suppose that the angular speed n is only taken by the fly-wheel, while the case turns with the angular speed ψ about the vertical. The angular speed of the case is thus $\psi \cos \theta$ about the axis of figure and $\psi \sin \theta$ about OE, and the whole system turns about OD

with angular speed $\dot{\theta}$. The A.M. about OD is $A\dot{\theta}$, about OE it is $A\dot{\psi}\sin\theta$, and about OC it is $Cn + C'\dot{\psi}\cos\theta$. Thus the rate of growth of A.M. about OD is $(Cn + C'\dot{\psi}\cos\theta)\dot{\psi}\sin\theta$ due to the turning about OE, and $-A\dot{\psi}^2\sin\theta\cos\theta$ due to the turning with angular speed $\dot{\psi}\cos\theta$ about OC. A.M. therefore grows about the instantaneous position of OD at total rate

$$A\ddot{\theta} + \{Cn - (A - C')\dot{\psi}\cos\theta\}\dot{\psi}\sin\theta = Wgh\sin\theta. \quad\ldots(1)$$

In a similar way the reader may calculate the total rate of growth of A.M. about the instantaneous position of OE, and, since there is no moment of forces about OE, verify the equation

$$A\ddot{\psi}\sin\theta + \{2(A - C')\dot{\psi}\cos\theta - Cn\}\dot{\theta} = 0. \quad\ldots\ldots(2)$$

As before, we notice that this equation of motion is derivable from that of constancy of A.M. about the vertical through the fixed point, which is now

$$(Cn + C'\dot{\psi}\cos\theta)\cos\theta + A\dot{\psi}\sin^2\theta = G. \quad\ldots\ldots(3)$$

Equations (1) and (2) are exactly the same as those obtained in §261, with $A - C'$ substituted for A in the terms within brackets on the left, but not in the first term in each case.

282. Steady Motion of Gyrostat. Period of Oscillation about Steady Motion. We may find, in precisely the same manner as for the ordinary top, the condition of steady motion at a constant inclination θ of the axis to the vertical, and the period of a small oscillation of the gryostat about steady motion. The equation of steady motion is

$$\{Cn - (A - C')\mu\cos\theta\}\mu = Wgh. \quad\ldots\ldots\ldots(1)$$

The period of oscillation is

$$T = \frac{2\pi\mu\{(A\sin^2\theta + C'\cos^2\theta)A\}^{\frac{1}{2}}}{\{W^2g^2h^2 - 2Wgh\mu^2(A - C')\cos\theta + A(A - C')\mu^4\}^{\frac{1}{2}}\sin\theta} \quad\ldots(2)$$

If $C' = 0$, this reduces to the period obtained for the ordinary top.

It is interesting to notice that the top may be so constructed that $C' = A$. In that case, the equation of steady motion is
$$Cn\mu = Wgh, \quad \quad \quad \quad \quad \quad \quad \quad (3)$$
and there is only one possible value of μ. The period becomes
$$T = \frac{2\pi\mu A}{Wgh \sin \theta} = \frac{2\pi A}{Cn \sin \theta}. \quad \quad \quad \quad (4)$$

283. Gyrostat with Axis Vertical, Stable or Unstable according to Direction of Azimuthal Motion. We now take some cases of gyrostatic motion. First, let the gyrostat be supported (as shown in Fig. 133) by two trunnions screwed to the projecting edge in the plane of the fly-wheel on a wooden tray as shown. The axis of the fly-wheel is very nearly vertical, and the wheel is spinning rapidly in the direction of the arrow shown on the upper side of the case. The centre of gravity of the whole instrument is nearly on the level of the trunnions, so that there is no stability due to gravity.

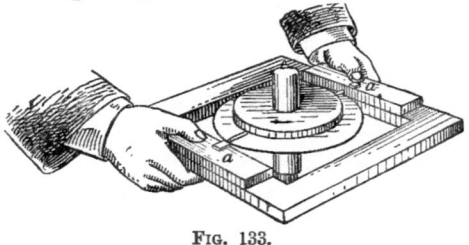

FIG. 133.

If now the tray be carried round horizontally with constant angular speed μ in the direction of spin, the gyrostat remains quite stable. If, however, it be carried round in the opposite direction, the gyrostat immediately turns on its trunnions and capsizes so that the other end of the axis is uppermost, and if the azimuthal motion is continued in the same direction, the gyrostat is now stable. It will be observed that the fly-wheel is now spinning in the direction of the azimuthal motion. Hence the gyrostat is in stable equilibrium when the azimuthal motion is in the same direction as the rotational motion.

This result follows from equation (1) adapted to fit this particular case. It will be seen that the terms $mgh\sin\theta$ and $A\mu^2\sin\theta\cos\theta$ are small in comparison with $Cn\mu\sin\theta$, the former because h is practically zero and the latter because μ is small in comparison with n.

Hence the equation is

$$A\ddot{\theta} + Cn\mu\theta = 0. \qquad\qquad\qquad (1)$$

The solution of this differential equation, if n and μ be in the same direction so that $n\mu$ is positive, is oscillatory motion of period $2\pi\sqrt{A/Cn\mu}$ about the vertical position, so that this position is stable.

On the other hand, if n and μ have opposite signs the solution of the differential equation is of another form, curiously connected with the former, but representing a different state of things. It shows that if the gyrostat is disturbed from the vertical position of its axis it tends to pass further away from it; the instrument capsizes.

These results are indeed indicated by the differential equation. The moment $Cn\mu\theta$, producing rate of change $A\ddot{\theta}$ of A.M., is in the first case in the direction to check motion away from the vertical position and to bring the gyrostat back to that position, while in the other case $Cn\mu\theta$, having the opposite sign, produces A.M. in the direction away from the vertical.

It will be seen that in this arrangement of the gyrostat it has only one freedom of motion as regards inclination of the axis to the vertical; it can turn about the trunnions but not about a horizontal axis at right angles to the line of the trunnions. Hence, as we shall now show, it cannot have complete dynamical stability. [See § 284.]

284. Gyrostat on Gimbals. Gyrostatic Pendulum: Analogy of Motion of Electron in Magnetic Field. Consider the arrangement shown in Fig. 127 of a gyrostat on gimbals. One end of the part of the case which surrounds the axis carries knife-edges in a line at right angles to the axis and intersecting it. These knife-edges are pivoted on a ring, which itself carries knife-edges at right angles to the bearings on which the former rest, and these in their turn rest on bearings carried by a second but fixed ring, or on a fixed support as shown in the figure. The gyrostat is shown with its axis vertical, and the two sets of knife-edges enable it to turn about one horizontal axis or about the other, or about both at the same time, so as to be inclined to the vertical in any desired azimuth. The two pairs of knife-edges are not exactly, but nearly, on the same level. The part of the case surrounding the axis may be supposed prolonged so as to give any required "preponderance" Wgh to the gyrostat above either axis.

Let the total mass which turns about the axes formed by the knife-edges be W and W', the heights of the centroids above (or distances from) the axes be h, h', the moments of inertia about the axes be A, A', the respective angular deflections (supposed small) be ψ, ϕ, and the moment of inertia and angular speed of the fly-wheel be C, n. We get then, by the process so often employed for the rates of growth of A.M. about the axes, fixed in the present case,
$$\left.\begin{array}{l} A\ddot{\psi} + Cn\dot{\phi} = Wgh\psi, \\ A'\ddot{\phi} - Cn\dot{\psi} = W'gh'\phi, \end{array}\right\} \quad \ldots\ldots\ldots\ldots\ldots(1)$$

or, if we write $B = Wgh$, $B' = W'gh'$,
$$\left.\begin{array}{l} A\ddot{\psi} + Cn\dot{\phi} - B\psi = 0, \\ A'\ddot{\phi} - Cn\dot{\psi} - B'\phi = 0. \end{array}\right\} \quad \ldots\ldots\ldots\ldots\ldots(2)$$

Now let $\psi = ae^{i\nu t}$, $\phi = be^{i\nu t}$. Then, by substitution, we get
$$\left.\begin{array}{l} i^2\nu^2 Aa + i\nu Cnb - Ba = 0, \\ i^2\nu^2 A'b - i\nu Cna - B'b = 0, \end{array}\right\} \quad \ldots\ldots\ldots\ldots(3)$$

and therefore, since $i^2 = -1$,
$$(\nu^2 A + B)(\nu^2 A' + B') - \nu^2 C^2 n^2 = 0. \quad \ldots\ldots\ldots\ldots(4)$$

The quantities A, B, A', B' are all positive according to the supposition made above, and the roots of the quadratic in ν^2 are real and positive if the inequality
$$(C^2 n^2 - AB' - A'B) > 4AA'BB'$$
is satisfied. This is the condition of complete dynamical stability, for, if it be fulfilled, ψ and ϕ represent simple

§ 284]   GYROSTATIC PENDULUM.   517

harmonic deflections from the position in which the axis of the gyrostat is at right angles to both lines of knife-edges—in the diagram the upright position. Each deflection may have either of the two periods given by the two real roots ν_1^2, ν_2^2 of (4). The motion is therefore stable, and there are two modes of vibration which the gyrostat may take either separately or in combination.

It is important to notice that if (contrary to the figure of course) B, B' have opposite signs and the product B, B' therefore be negative, one of the roots of the quadratic in ν^2 is positive, the other negative; and consequently there is only one possible mode of stable motion, for the negative root of the quadratic in ν^2 gives an imaginary period.

Let now $h = h'$, $W = W'$, $A = A'$, and let $n_1, -n_1, n_2, -n_2$ be the four roots of the determinantal equation in v; then, since the real and imaginary parts of $x = ae^{ivt}$, $y = be^{ivt}$ must separately satisfy the differential equations, and since the expressions for the ratio a/b exhibited above give $a = ib$, we get

$$\left.\begin{array}{l}\psi = L_1 \cos n_1 t + L_1' \sin n_1 t + L_2 \cos n_2 t + L_2' \sin n_2 t,\\ \phi = L_1 \sin n_1 t - L_1' \cos n_1 t + L_2 \sin n_2 t - L_2' \cos n_2 t,\end{array}\right\}\ldots(5)$$

where L_1, L_1', L_2, L_2' are arbitrary constants.

We see that the first terms on the right give a circular motion of a point on the axis in the period $2\pi/n_1$, that the second terms give a circular motion of the same period in the opposite direction, and that the third and fourth terms give circular motions in opposite directions in the period $2\pi/n_2$. The radii of the circular paths are the values of L_1, L_1', etc.

If we combine two of these circular motions, say those given by the first two terms, or the last two terms, on the right of equations (5), we get Fig. 134 as the path of a point of the axis of the gyrostat. [The rays are not drawn in to the centre.] For here the radii are equal, the periods unequal, and the motions of the circular components oppositely directed. If we take the motions given by the first and third, or by the second and fourth terms in each equation, the path is as shown in Fig. 135. Here everything is as before, but the circular components are in the same direction. The resultant radius bisects the angle between

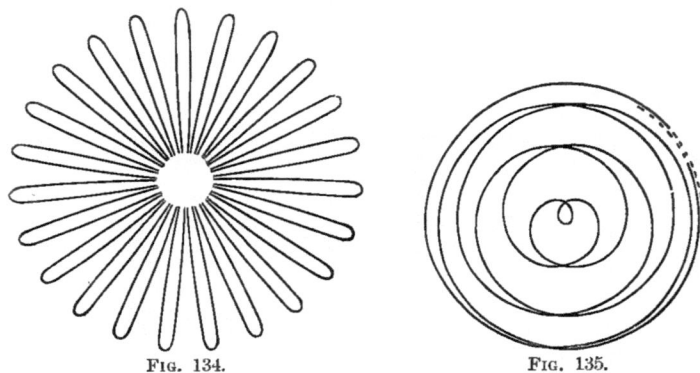

Fig. 134. Fig. 135.

the component radii, and the resultant angular speed is the mean of the components.

When the two motions exist together, we have the path shown in Fig. 136. There the present arrangement inverted is represented by a pendulum with a fly-wheel rotating about the axis of figure contained in the bob, so that there is gravitational stability for both displacements apart from rotation. The theory is essentially the same in both cases. In the pendulum, however, the universal gimbal joint is replaced by a short piece of steel wire which bends easily but resists torsion very greatly.

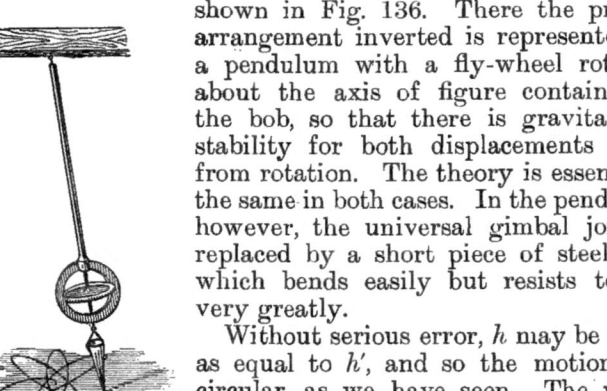

Fig. 136.

Without serious error, h may be taken as equal to h', and so the motions are circular, as we have seen. The period of describing the circle in one motion is $2\pi/n_1$ and in the other $2\pi/n_2$. The student may verify that in the case of the gyrostatic pendulum shown in Fig. 136, where the

whole mass may be regarded as concentrated at the centroid, provided the fly-wheel have moment of inertia C, the periods are $4\pi/(2p+k)$ and $4\pi/(2p-k)$, where $p=\sqrt{g/h}$, $k=Cn/Wh^2$ (supposed small). For equations (2) may be written
$$\ddot{x}+k\dot{y}+p^2x=0, \quad \ddot{y}-k\dot{x}+p^2y=0. \quad\quad\quad\quad(6)$$
With proper analogues for k and p^2 these are precisely the approximate equations of motion of an electron in a magnetic field. In the electromagnetic case, the value of k is, if the magnetic inductive capacity of the medium be taken as unity, $\epsilon H/m$, where ϵ is the charge and m the effective inertia of the electron and H is the magnetic field intensity.

In the case referred to above, in which one of the inclinational modes is stable and the other unstable without rotation of the fly-wheel, one of the elliptic or circular motions just discussed is possible, the other is not; for in the latter case the period, as we have seen, is imaginary. This, in point of fact, is the general theorem, of which the action of the gyrostat supported on trunnions with its axis vertical, as described and explained in § 283, is a particular case.

It will be noticed that while *complete* stability is conferred on a gyrostat if it is unstable as regards both its freedoms without rotation, this is not the case when only one freedom is unstable. This is a case of a general theorem, which asserts that for a holonomous system (§ 302) only an even number of degrees of freedom can be rendered stable by rotation.

It was proposed in 1870, by Sir Henry Bessemer, to obtain a steady cabin for a cross-channel steamer by placing it on a gyrostat with its axis vertical and supported on fore-and-aft trunnions. This plan was bound to fail; for it will be seen from what has been set forth above, that while the arrangement was stable when the ship's head was turning in one direction, it could not be stable when the ship was turning in the opposite direction. A gyrostat has, however, been successfully applied recently by Herr Schlick to mitigate the rolling of a ship (see § 288 below).

285. Gyrostatic Action of Rotating Bodies on their Bearings.

It will now be evident that if the gyrostat is so fixed on bearings that the motion, which the change of direction to which its axis is subjected tends to bring about, is made impossible, a couple preventing the motion will be brought into play and applied to the bearings by the framework to which they are attached. The magnitude of this couple is $Cn\mu$, where n is the angular velocity of the fly-wheel and μ is the angular velocity with which its axis is changing direction. For, take a distance OC along the axis of rotation from the centre of the fly-wheel, say to represent the A.M. Cn. Then OC is turning with angular speed μ towards a line at right angles to OC, OD, say. The rate of production of A.M. about OD is therefore $Cn\mu$. The gyrostat will tend to turn about OD *in the direction to annul this rate of growth of* A.M., and can only be held in equilibrium when the couple applied to it in the opposite direction is $Cn\mu$. Then this couple it is that produces the rate of growth of A.M.

In this way the equation of motion can be written down at once in each of a number of practical cases which we shall now consider.

A good example is a dynamo armature of large moment of inertia, rotating with velocity n about its axis placed athwartships, while the ship rolls with angular velocity μ. The armature tends to turn about a vertical axis, but is prevented by fore-and-aft forces applied to the ends of the axle by the front and back of the bearings. This couple is always of just the amount to produce the rate of growth of A.M. which, in consequence of the changing direction of the axis of rotation, is being generated about an axis at right angles to the deck. It tends to shear the bearings off the deck, and is reversed when the ship rolls back, and varies in amount as the angular velocity of rolling varies. If the bearings are in the fore-and-aft direction the rolling of the ship has no effect, but the pitching causes equal and opposite forces to be applied to the two bearings. These forces are again in the plane of the deck, but are in this case across the ship. If the bearings are at all loose, this alternating action upon them may have serious effects.

Ex. A dynamo, the armature of which weighs half a ton, has a radius of gyration of 2 feet and is revolving at 240 revolutions a minute. If the axis is athwartships, and the ship rolls through a total range of 30° in a period of 10 seconds (what is commonly reckoned two periods of rolling or "two rolls"), find the moment of the couple on the bearings.

In ton-foot units the moment of inertia is 2. The maximum angular speed of rolling, that at the middle of the roll, is in radians $2\pi \times 15/(10 \times 57\cdot 3) = 3\pi/57\cdot 3 = \cdot 165$. The angular speed of the fly-wheel is in radians 8π. Hence the couple in a plane parallel to the deck which is called into play is in ton-foot units

$$2 \times 8\pi \times \cdot 165/32 \text{ or } \cdot 26.$$

If the length of the axis between the centre of the bearings is 2 feet, each bearing will be acted on by a force of $\tfrac{1}{8}$ of a Ton.

286. Virtual Increase of Moment of Inertia of Vibrating Body produced by Gyrostat. To illustrate the gyrostatic couple brought into play by constrained precession of the axis of rotation and the method here used for its calculation, we take the following problem, which was dealt with by Lord Kelvin at the meeting of the British Association at Montreal in 1884. A long vertical torsion wire had a gyrostat, with axis horizontal, attached to its lower end in such a way that the gyrostat turned with the wire, when that turned about its axis. The wire was attached at a point of the rim, in the plane of the fly-wheel (Fig. 137). A twist was given to the wire, and the system of gyrostat and wire then performed torsional oscillations about the vertical. When the fly-wheel was made to rotate rapidly the period was found to be increased in the ratio of $\sqrt{A' + C^2n^2/Mga}$ to $\sqrt{A'}$, where A' denotes

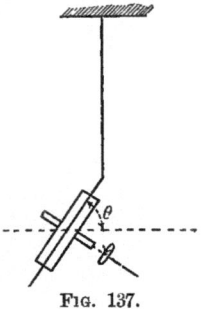

Fig. 137.

the moment of inertia of the gyrostat about a diameter of the fly-wheel, Cn the A.M. of the wheel, M the weight of the gyrostat, and a the distance of the point of attachment of the wire from the centre O of the wheel.

Let the lower end of the wire be turning with angular speed $\dot{\phi}$, the rate at which the wire is untwisting. Let, as before, a distance OC from the centre along the axis of the wheel represent the A.M. Cn; the rate of growth of A.M. about a horizontal axis OA, in the plane of the wheel and at right angles to OC, towards the instantaneous position of which OC is turning, is the horizontal speed $\dot{\phi} \cdot OC$ of the extremity C of the line, that is $Cn\dot{\phi}$.

The gyrostat turns about the point of attachment of the wire so as to place the centroid at each instant sufficiently far out of the line of the wire to give a gyrostatic couple about OA. The wire will not remain quite vertical, but if it is long the deviation from verticality may be neglected. Let the tilt of the gyrostat from the horizontal be θ, supposed also small. [It is exaggerated in the Fig. 137.] Then the couple about OA is $Wga\theta$. We have therefore

$$A\ddot{\theta} - Cn\dot{\phi} = -Wga\theta, \quad\ldots\ldots\ldots\ldots\ldots\ldots(1)$$

where A is the moment of inertia of the gyrostat about a horizontal axis through the point of attachment at right angles to the plane of the vertical and the axis.

But the angular speed $\dot{\theta}$ produces A.M., about the downward vertical along the wire, at rate $Cn\theta$, and the untwisting of the thread produces A.M. about the same line at rate $A'\ddot{\phi}$. Hence we have

$$A'\ddot{\phi} + Cn\dot{\theta} = -\tau\phi, \quad\ldots\ldots\ldots\ldots\ldots\ldots(2)$$

where τ is the torsional rigidity of the wire.

Now at starting $\dot{\theta}$ is zero when $\dot{\phi} = 0$; and we have thereafter θ a maximum, and $\ddot{\theta}$ also at its greatest numerical value, when ϕ is greatest numerically. Thus, as θ is always small, we may neglect $A\ddot{\theta}$ in comparison with $-Cn\dot{\phi}$. Substituting then the value $\dot{\phi}Cn/Wga$ derived from (1) in (2), we get the differential equation

$$\left(A' + \frac{C^2n^2}{Wga}\right)\ddot{\phi} + \tau\phi = 0.$$

The motion is therefore simple harmonic in period

$$T = 2\pi\sqrt{\frac{C^2n^2/Wga + A'}{\tau}}. \quad\ldots\ldots\ldots\ldots\ldots(3)$$

If n be great, the period is greatly increased by the rotation. The moment of inertia of the gyrostat regarded as a torsional vibrator hung on the wire is virtually $C^2 n^2 / Mga + A'$; when there is no rotation of the fly-wheel, the moment of inertia is simply A'.

287. General Theory of Vibrator containing Gyrostat. In view of various practical problems, we give here a rather more detailed discussion of equations (1) and (2) of § 286. Let

$$\theta = k e^{iat}, \quad \phi = K e^{iat},$$

then, by substitution, we obtain

$$\left. \begin{array}{l} i^2 a^2 k A - i a K C n + W g a k = 0, \\ i^2 a^2 K A' + i a k C n + K \tau = 0, \end{array} \right\} \quad \dots\dots\dots\dots\dots (1)$$

so that
$$\frac{k}{K} = \frac{i a C n}{i^2 a^2 A + W g a} = -\frac{i^2 a^2 A' + \tau}{i a C n}. \quad \dots\dots\dots\dots\dots (2)$$

Thus, we have the equation [see (4), § 284]

$$(A' a^2 - \tau)(A a^2 - Wga) - C^2 n^2 a^2 = 0, \quad \dots\dots\dots\dots\dots (3)$$

a quadratic equation in a^2. Thus there are four values of a, namely, $a_1, a_2, -a_1, -a_2$, and the complete solution of the equations (1) and (2) of § 286 for the initial conditions $\phi = \phi_0$, $\theta = 0$, $\dot\phi = \dot\theta = 0$ is given by
$$\theta = k_1 \sin a_1 t + k_2 \sin a_2 t, \quad \phi = K_1 \cos a_1 t + K_2 \cos a_2 t, \dots\dots\dots (5)$$

where, since when $t = 0$, $\phi = \phi_0$, and $\theta = 0$, we must have

$$a_1 k_1 + a_2 k_2 = 0, \quad K_1 + K_2 = \phi_0. \quad \dots\dots\dots\dots\dots (6)$$

Now, by (2), we have *in any case*,

$$\left. \begin{array}{l} \dfrac{k_1}{K_1} = \dfrac{i a_1 C n}{i^2 a_1^2 A + W g a} = -\dfrac{i^2 a_1^2 A' + \tau}{i a_1 C n}, \\[6pt] \dfrac{k_2}{K_2} = \dfrac{i a_2 C n}{i^2 a_2^2 A + W g a} = -\dfrac{i^2 a_2^2 A' + \tau}{i a_2 C n}, \end{array} \right\} \quad \dots\dots\dots\dots\dots (7)$$

so that, again, in any case whatever,

$$\frac{K_1}{K_2} = -\frac{(i^2 a_2^2 A' + \tau)(i^2 a_1^2 A + Wga)}{i^2 a_1 a_2 C^2 n^2} \frac{k_1}{k_2}.$$

In the present case $k_1 a_1 = - k_2 a_2$, and so putting -1 for i^2, we get

$$\frac{K_1}{K_2} = -\frac{(A' a_2^2 - \tau)(A a_1^2 - Wga)}{C^2 n^2 a_1^2} = -1. \quad \dots\dots\dots\dots\dots (8)$$

We might have supposed the wire at rest without torsion and the

gyrostat at rest initially, but tilted through an angle θ_0. Then we should have had
$$\left.\begin{array}{l}\phi = K_1 \sin \alpha_1 t + K_2 \sin \alpha_2 t, \\ \theta = k_1 \cos \alpha_1 t + k_2 \cos \alpha_2 t,\end{array}\right\} \quad \ldots\ldots\ldots\ldots\ldots\ldots(9)$$
with the condition
$$K_1 \alpha_1 + K_2 \alpha_2 = 0, \quad k_1 + k_2 = \theta_0. \quad \ldots\ldots\ldots\ldots\ldots(10)$$
Then we should have found also
$$\frac{k_2}{k_1} = -\frac{(A'\alpha_2^2 - \tau)(A\alpha_1^2 - Wga)}{C^2 n^2 \alpha_2^2}. \quad \ldots\ldots\ldots\ldots\ldots(11)$$

It will be noticed that if $A\alpha_1^2$ be small in comparison with Wga (which in § 286 was supposed to be the case), the two frequencies of vibration have approximately the common value
$$\frac{1}{2\pi}\sqrt{\frac{Wga\tau}{C^2 n^2 + A' Wga\tau}},$$
so that the period is
$$T = 2\pi\sqrt{\frac{C^2 n^2 + A' Wga\tau}{Wga\tau}}, \quad \ldots\ldots\ldots\ldots\ldots(12)$$
the result obtained above [3, § 286].

If the angular momentum Cn of the fly-wheel is zero, (3) becomes
$$(A'\alpha^2 - \tau)(A\alpha^2 - Wga) = 0. \quad \ldots\ldots\ldots\ldots\ldots(13)$$
The first factor gives the period $2\pi\sqrt{A'/\tau}$ of the free oscillations of the wire and the attached gyrostat, when the fly-wheel is at rest and the gyrostat is moving only in azimuth with the lower end of the wire: the second factor gives the period $2\pi\sqrt{A/Wga}$ of the free pendulum oscillations which the gyrostat can perform about the point of attachment to the wire, when the wire is held at rest. By means of these periods, or the corresponding frequencies, the quantities τ, Wga can be eliminated from the equations set forth above.

288. Gyrostatic Controller of Rolling of Ship: Schlick's Apparatus. The solution here given is applicable to the oscillations of a ship in which is fixed a gyrostat G, as shown in Fig. 138. When the ship is upright and the gyrostat in equilibrium, the axis of the fly-wheel is vertical. The wheel is pivoted in a frame F, as shown. The frame turns on the bearings $b_1 b$, and a weight W gives the arrangement gravitational stability. In an arrangement of this kind, devised by Herr Otto Schlick to diminish the rolling of a ship, a brake pulley B surrounds the axis bb, about which the frame turns, and friction of a graded amount is applied by a special device. The brake damps out the free oscillations of the system and also serves to reduce the forced oscillations. But the action of the brake must not be so violent as to prevent the swinging of the gyrostat, as that would annul the inertia effect, which is of the greatest importance for the forced oscillations, according to the principle illustrated in § 287.

If the ship is set rolling in still water, the theory of the motion

§§ 287, 288] GYROSTATIC CONTROLLER. 525

is precisely that set forth above. For τ/A', Wga/A we write $4\pi^2 F'^2$, $4\pi^2 f^2$, where F, f are the frequencies of the free oscillations of the ship and gyrostat, the first oscillating with the gyrostat rigidly fixed within it, the second when the ship is at rest, in both cases without rotation of the fly-wheel. A', A are the moments of inertia of the ship and fly-wheel for the axes about which the ship rolls and the gyrostat frame turns. The equation of periods, (3) of § 287, is thus

$$(\alpha^2 - 4\pi^2 F'^2)(\alpha^2 - 4\pi^2 f^2) - \frac{C^2 n^2}{AA'} \alpha^2 = 0. \quad \ldots\ldots\ldots\ldots\ldots(1)$$

Similarly the other equations may be modified.

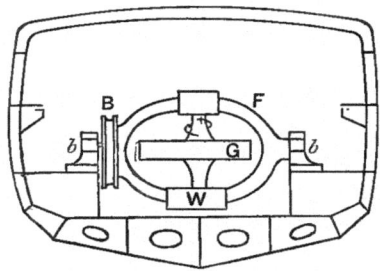

FIG. 138.

When the ship rolls in a sea-way, the main oscillations of the ship are forced oscillations of the period of the waves, and the natural period of the ship is so increased by the gyrostat that any resonance effect, due to near agreement between the period of the waves and that of the ship, which might exist without rotation of the fly-wheel, is rendered impossible. The differential equations of small oscillations are, as we see at once from what has been stated above,

$$\left. \begin{array}{l} A'\ddot{\phi} + N'\dot{\phi} - Cn\dot{\theta} + M\phi = C' \cos pt, \\ A\ddot{\theta} + N\dot{\theta} + Cn\dot{\phi} + Wga\theta = 0, \end{array} \right\} \quad \ldots\ldots\ldots\ldots\ldots(2)$$

where A, A' are the moments of inertia of the gyrostat for the axis b, b and the ship for the longitudinal axis about which she rolls, $N\dot{\theta}$ is the frictional couple applied to the gyrostat frame by the brake B and otherwise, $N\dot{\phi}$ is the frictional couple applied by the water to the ship as she rolls, M is the righting moment per unit of the angle θ of heel, Wga is the "preponderance" of the weight W, C' is the amplitude, and $p/2\pi$ is the frequency of the forced rolling produced by the waves.

The forced oscillations are given by supposing $\phi = Ke^{ipt}$, $\theta = ke^{ipt}$. Substituting in the differential equations, we get

$$K(-A'p^2 + iN'p + M) - ikpCn = C', \quad k(-Ap^2 + iNp + Wga) + iKpCn = 0.$$

Here it is to be remembered p is fixed in value: the coefficients K, k are complex quantities. The reader may solve for K and k, and realise then the solution of the differential equations. The reader will find in *Nature* for March 12, 1908, some numerical solutions by Professor Perry for such an apparatus.

To complete the solution, the expressions already obtained for the oscillation in still water are of course to be added. In practice the frictional resistance, due to the action of the water on the ship, may be neglected, and the results may therefore be simplified by putting $N' = 0$. Of course N is not made so great as to render the gyrostatic action ineffective: it is possible to have it small enough for this and yet large enough to give through the relative motion of the ship and gyrostat a sufficient damping out of the free oscillations, and to reduce the forced oscillations.

Just as the turning of the wire produced tilting of the gyrostat, so the rolling of the vessel causes turning of the gyrostat about the axis bb, and this may set up or augment pitching of the vessel. For a full account of the action of this important appliance the student may consult Klein and Sommerfeld's *Theorie des Kreisels*, Bd. V. (Leipzig, 1910). See also a theoretical paper by Herr Föppl in the *Transactions of the Institution of Naval Architects* for 1904.

289. Foucault's Apparatus to show Earth's Rotation. Gilbert's Barygyroscope. The theory of a method originally proposed by Foucault and by Sire, of using a properly mounted gyrostat to show the rotation of the earth, will now be easily understood. Let the gyrostat be supported on an axis, as on the tray in the experiment in § 283 above, in the plane of the wheel, and passing through the centre of gravity. Suppose this axis to be fixed horizontally east and west so that the axis of rotation can move in the plane of the meridian. Then the slow turning motion of the earth supplies the angular speed μ. If the gyrostat be so placed that the direction of spin of the fly-wheel is in the direction of the rotation of the earth, we have precisely the same equation as before,

$$A\ddot{\theta} + Cn\mu\theta = 0, \quad\quad\quad\quad\quad\quad\quad (1)$$

when θ is small. The gyrostat then turns on its bearings, so that its axis moves in the meridian, and oscillates about the direction of the earth's axis in the period $2\pi\sqrt{A/Cn\mu}$, where n is the angular speed of spin of the gyrostat and μ the angular speed of the earth's rotation.

The same simple considerations give the complete solutions in nearly every other case, for example for Foucault's gyrostat with axis of rotation in a horizontal plane [now converted, with axis elastically constrained to horizontality, into a non-magnetic but powerfully directive marine compass (*Nature*, July 20, 1911)], and for Gilbert's barygyroscope, also for demonstrating by a gyrostat the earth's rotation. [See Ex. 8, p. 547.]

In this a gyrostat is supported on bearings, as in Foucault's experiment, fixed horizontally east and west; but it is given a certain adjustable amount of gravitational stability through the centre of gravity being beneath the line of bearings.

Let λ (Fig. 139) be the (north) latitude of the place, and the axis of rotation of the fly-wheel be inclined at an angle θ (lower end, say, towards the south) to the vertical at the place P. The angular speed, ω say, of the earth's rotation can be resolved into two components, one, $\omega \sin(\lambda + \theta)$, about the axis of the fly-wheel, the other, $\omega \cos(\lambda + \theta)$, about a line at right angles to this axis, and drawn towards the north. If n and ω be similarly directed, the component $\omega \cos(\lambda + \theta)$ gives a precessional motion which, for a proper value of θ, will equal $Wgh \sin \theta$. At this inclination there will be equilibrium, and then, as in the cases considered above, $Cn \cos(\lambda + \theta) = Wgh \sin \theta$. Hence

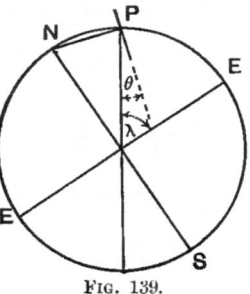

Fig. 139.

$$\tan \theta = \frac{Cn\omega \cos \lambda}{Cn\omega \sin \lambda + Wgh}. \quad \ldots\ldots\ldots\ldots\ldots\ldots(2)$$

If the spin be reversed the inclination is to the other side of the vertical, and of amount θ' given by

$$\tan \theta' = \frac{Cn\omega \cos \lambda}{Cn\omega \sin \lambda - Wgh}. \quad \ldots\ldots\ldots\ldots\ldots\ldots(3)$$

This deviation θ or θ' must be taken into account when a gyrostat is used as a clinometer, or to give an artificial horizon.

Ex. Let the line of bearings of the barygyroscope be placed in a horizontal direction inclined at an angle ϕ to the east to west horizontal direction, and the inclination of the axis of rotation of the gyrostat to the vertical be θ. Prove that

$$\tan\theta = \frac{Cn\omega\cos\lambda\cos\phi}{Cn\omega\sin\lambda + Wgh}. \qquad (4)$$

The components of ω about the vertical and about the horizontal in the meridian are $\omega\sin\lambda$ and $\omega\cos\lambda$. The latter has a component $\omega\cos\lambda\cos\phi$ about a horizontal axis towards the east of north at right angles to the line of bearings. This, in its turn, gives an angular speed about an axis perpendicular at once to the horizontal axis just specified and to the axis of rotation, of amount $\omega\cos\lambda\cos\phi\cos\theta$. The component $\omega\sin\lambda$, about the vertical, gives a component, $\omega\sin\lambda\sin\theta$, about the axis last mentioned. The precessional angular speed about that axis is therefore $\omega(\cos\lambda\cos\phi\cos\theta - \sin\lambda\sin\theta)$. Hence, since the couple about that axis has moment $Wgh\sin\theta$, we have

$$Cn\omega(\cos\lambda\cos\phi\cos\theta - \sin\lambda\sin\theta) = Wgh\sin\theta,$$

and therefore

$$\tan\theta = \frac{Cn\omega\cos\lambda\cos\phi}{Cn\omega\sin\lambda + Wgh}. \qquad (4)$$

Here it is supposed that n and ω are the same way round. If they are not, the denominator has the value $Cn\omega\sin\lambda - Wgh$, and the upper end of the axis is turned towards the south, instead of to the north as in the former case.

290. The Brennan Monorail Car. In this invention gyrostatic action is used to keep a carriage in stable equilibrium on a single rail, and the apparatus is entirely self-acting. It forms at once the nerve-system which detects the need for the application of a righting couple to the carriage, and mechanism by which the couple is applied. Two gyrostats are placed in the carriage with their axes in line, and transverse to the rail, as shown in Fig. 140. The wheels W, W' are driven by motors and revolve about the axes AA, $A'A'$, at the same speed in opposite directions, as indicated by the arrows. The wheels are enclosed in cases C, C', from which the air has been exhausted, and which turn about the axes BB, $B'B'$. The system can turn as a whole about the axis O which is parallel to the rail. By means of two segments, B, B', above the apparatus, the gyrostats are made to take equal and opposite precessions, when any precession occurs; then, of course, the axes cease to be in line.

When the car is upright and in equilibrium, the gyrostats are upright, with their axes in line transverse to the rail.

§§ 289, 290]   MONORAIL CAR.   529

Suppose, now, a couple to be applied to the car, say by a gust of wind, or the displacement of part of the load, so as to tilt the car over on the rail, to the right, say. In consequence of the rotation the axes of the wheels retain their directions, and the carriage turns relatively to the gyrostats. This brings the shelf D, which is fixed to the car, into contact with the spinning axis R of the left-hand gyrostat,

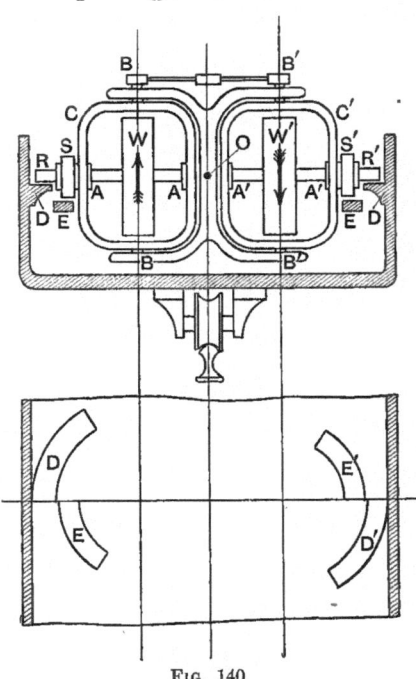

Fig. 140.

and the axes begin to be tilted. Each gyrostat therefore begins to produce by its motion A.M. about a vertical axis, and the gyrostats therefore precess in opposite directions. This precession is assisted by the couple exerted by the force of friction on R, enhanced by slipping of the rapidly revolving spindle R on the shelf D, which is in the direction of forward motion of R, that is, in the direction

G.D.   2 L

away from the reader, with the result that a restoring couple is applied to the shelf D, and therefore to the car. This couple, which is due to the acceleration of the precession, is sufficient to arrest the tilting and turn the car in the opposite direction.

The shelf D extends away from the reader, and on the right there is a corresponding shelf D' extending towards the reader, as shown by the plan, on which the end R' of the spindle acts in the case of a deflection to the left, as explained above for R. There are two other shelves E, E' which are arranged to come into contact with rollers S, S', mounted on sleeves turning loosely on the spindles. The shelf E extends inwards towards the reader, the shelf E' outwards.

It will be clear that in consequence of the precession of the gyrostats brought about by the pressing of the shelf D on the end R of the rotating spindle, the roller S' has been brought over the shelf E'. Consequently, as the car swings over to the left in consequence of the couple applied by the gyrostats, the roller S' comes into contact with E'. Precession in the opposite direction to the former precession is caused, but there is not now any *accelerating* couple, but really a retarding one, since the roller sleeve turning round on and supporting the spindle applies a friction couple to the gyrostats *resisting* the precession, which, it is to be remembered, is now back towards the mid-position. The gyrostatic axes do not, however, greatly alter their inclination to the horizontal while precession occurs in obedience to the couple applied by the pressure of the shelf on S'.

As precession goes on, the axes of the gyrostats are brought once more into the line RR', with R lowered. They go beyond the mid-position and R' begins to roll on the shelf D', and so applies a frictional couple to the gyrostat, just as R did before, with the result that the gyrostats now begin to turn over and apply a couple to the car from left to right. The car tilts over, and the roller S comes into contact with the shelf E, the axles are brought once more into line, R presses on D and rolls along it as before, and a couple to the left is applied to

§§ 290, 291] GYROSTATIC ACTION OF TURBINES. 531

the car, and so on. Thus the car vibrates about an equilibrium position under the deflecting couple, that is a position in which it is heeled over to meet the couple (supposed still existing) through angles which rapidly diminish in amount. Finally, the vibration has been wiped out, and the car stands in the new position of equilibrium. Thus the car is held over against the deflecting couple, if that is maintained constant.

When the car runs on a curve the two gyrostats exert equal and opposite gyrostatic actions, and the car takes the curve without the gyrostatic resistance which a single gyrostat would have applied, and which would have been very inconvenient.

The mode of action of the gyrostats on the car has been modified in various ways by Mr. Brennan in later models; but the principle is perhaps sufficiently explained in the description here given of the arrangement which he exhibited to the Royal Society in May 1907. [See the article by Professor Perry, in *Nature* for March 12, 1908.]

291. Gyrostatic Action of Turbines in Steamers. Interest in the gyrostatic action in steamers in which the main propelling engines are of the steam turbine type was excited at the time of the *Cobra* disaster, and a series of letters from engineers and others appeared in the technical journals. These letters were informing in very varying degree, but the general conclusion come to was no doubt correct, that the gyrostatic action could not produce any breaking moment so great as to affect a ship's safety. For example, to break the ship, as the *Cobra* apparently was broken, by a breaking moment applied to it in a vertical plane, the ship's head would have had to turn round at an impossible rate. Rolling could bring no gyrostatic action into play, the axes of the turbines being fore and aft; pitching would produce a moment no doubt, as will be seen, much greater than the former, but tending to bend the vessel in a *horizontal* plane, that is, about vertical lines.

The following discussions are based on authoritative estimates of the data necessary for the calculation of the gyrostatic moments applied in possible circumstances to the hull (1) of a large Atlantic liner (the *Carmania*), (2) of a torpedo-boat destroyer, and (3) of a cross-channel steamer.

The mode of calculation will be clear from the preceding discussion. When, for example, the ship's head turns round, the direction of the axis of the rapidly revolving turbines is changed at a rate μ, the μ of the equations above; that is a precession of speed μ about a vertical axis is imposed. But to correct the generation of A.M. about an athwartship axis, which this produces, the turbines make an effort to turn about that axis, and so a couple is applied to the ship, and an equal and opposite couple to the turbines. Hence the turbines may be regarded as having a precession of angular speed μ in azimuth produced by the couple just referred to, which, therefore, has the moment $Cn\mu$, if Cn be the A.M. of the turbines.

If the turbine rotors be equal in all respects, and run at the same speed, but in opposite directions, the total couple exerted on the ship, as a whole, will be zero. But each turbine will exert a couple on the ship at the bearings, and an opposite couple will give the precession μ to the turbine. Internal stresses will be exerted on the ship in consequence of the opposite couples, and the stresses will be a self-balancing system within the ship.

A corresponding action of course takes place when the ship is pitching with angular speed μ.

For the *Carmania*,* the total weight of the rotors, three in number, may be taken as 200 tons, and the radius of gyration as 4 feet, so that in ton-foot units, the moment of inertia of the rotor on each wing-shaft is 1280, on the supposition that the weight of each rotor is $\frac{2}{5}$ of the whole, and the moment of inertia of the rotor on the centre shaft is therefore 640. The number of revolutions is 200 per minute, and therefore the value of μ is $20\pi/3$, in radians per second. The ship's head can be turned through $\frac{3}{4}$ of a degree, or about $\frac{1}{75}$ of a radian in a second. Hence the gyrostatic couple of moment $Cn\mu$ which must be

* For these data we are indebted to Mr. W. J. Luke, of Messrs. John Brown & Co., Limited, Shipbuilders, Clydebank, who built the *Carmania*.

§ 291]   GYROSTATIC ACTION OF TURBINES.   533

applied by the ship to each wing-rotor to give it the precession which the turning of the ship involves, and therefore also the moment of the equal and opposite couple exerted on the ship, is $1280 \times 20\pi \times \frac{1}{3} \times \frac{1}{75} \times \frac{1}{32} = 11\cdot2$, in ton-foot units; that is, the moment is that which would be produced by a force of 11·2 Tons acting at an arm of 1 foot, or a couple of ·28 ton acting at an arm of 40 feet. Such a couple cannot have any perceptible effect in straining the ship.

If we take 12° as the range of pitching, and the period as 6 seconds, the maximum angular speed is

$$2\pi \times 6/(6 \times 57\cdot3) = 1/9,$$

in radians per second, and this is to be substituted for the 1/75 in the above calculation. The couple is thus 8·3 times the former couple, or 2·3 Tons at an arm of 40 feet: still quite a small couple when regarded from the point of view of breaking the ship, even if relatively as lightly built as was the *Cobra*. The engines of the *Cobra* were, of course, very small as compared with those here considered. The gyrostatic couple due to pitching is, however, reversed twice in each (double) period of pitching. For a range of pitching half as much again, and a period of 9 seconds, the gyrostatic action would just be the same.

If there were only two shafts, one right-handed, the other left-handed, the moments applied to the ship would be equal and in opposite directions. Of course, internal stresses of a kind easily analysed would be set up in the structure. These would tend to produce alternately compression and extension at the bow, and extension and compression at the stern, athwartships in each case; but they would be quite negligible.

For three shafts, if two turn one way, and the third the other way, and the weight of the turbines be supposed distributed among them in the ratio of two parts to each wing-shaft and one part to the centre shaft, the resultant gyrostatic couple is much less than $\frac{1}{2}$ of that calculated above, inasmuch as the radius of gyration of the centre rotor is only 3 feet. The couple may be taken as 9/32 of that due to each wing-shaft. The couples due to the wing-rotors being oppositely directed at each instant, will produce internal stresses, which can only be of importance in the event of their coinciding in period with a free oscillation of the ship as an elastic structure, an event which seems very unlikely.

If, however, one wing-shaft be driven ahead, the other astern at full speed, so that the direction of rotation is the same in both, and the centre shaft be stopped, the gyrostatic couple (due to pitching) applied to the ship will be twice that due to each wing-shaft, or 186 Tons at an arm of 1 foot. If the centre shaft be at the same time driven full speed ahead, the couple will be that just stated, with 9/32 of its amount added or subtracted, according as the centre shaft runs in the same direction as the wing-shafts, or in the contrary direction. If the centre shaft is run at diminished speed, the latter couple must be diminished in proportion.

For a destroyer the weight of each rotor may be taken as 6 tons, the radius of gyration as 2 feet, and the revolutions 900. This gives moment of inertia, in ton-foot units, 24 for each rotor on wing-shafts. The angular velocity is 30π in radians per second, and the angular velocity with which the ship can be turned round is $3°$ per second or $\frac{1}{19}$ of a radian per second. The gyrostatic couple for the two rotors running in the same direction would be $48 \times 30\pi \times \frac{1}{19} \times \frac{1}{32} = 7\cdot 4$, that is, 7·4 Tons at an arm of 1 foot.

With the same period and range of pitching the gyrostatic couple for the destroyer would be about twice the couple just calculated.

Here, again, to get the true values of the resultant couple, we must take one-half, or, if the vessel has triple screws, some other fraction of the values just found.

For a cross-channel steamer, the following data have been furnished by the Hon. C. A. Parsons: weight of each L.P. rotor 7 tons, radius of gyration 21 inches, speed 700 revolutions. The moment of inertia of each rotor is thus $7 \times 1\cdot 75^2$, or 21·4 in ton-foot units, and the speed is $70\pi/3$, in radians per second. The maximum gyrostatic couple of each rotor, for the same amplitudes and periods

§§ 291, 292] GYROSTATIC ACTION OF MACHINERY. 535

of pitching as those supposed above, is thus above 1·8 Tons acting at an arm of 1 foot.

If the turbine on the centre shaft has, as Mr. Parsons states it has in this class of vessel, less than half the mass of the others, the resultant couple on the ship will be less than one-half of that just calculated.

The stresses seem quite insignificant. Their only importance, if they have any, must be in their rapid reversal and the consequent forced vibration of the structure. Danger is not likely to arise from near agreement of the period of this forced vibration with that of some natural free period of the structure, but this is a question for naval architects. Nor are natural vibrations in the rotor itself likely to correspond in period with that of the gyrostatic couple. [See a paper by Dr. Henderson, *Transactions of the Inst. of Engineers and Shipbuilders in Scotland*, 1905.]

292. Gyrostatic Couple on a Locomotive or Carriage. Gyrostatic couples of practically insignificant amount have been found for a new locomotive recently built in Glasgow, part of which consists of a rapidly rotating steam-turbine and dynamo mounted with their common axes in the "fore-and-aft" direction. Numerical particulars cannot be given here, but the couples due to passing round curves, or over parts of the track where the gradient is changing, can have but little effect on the running of the engine.

Ex. 1. A carriage, which has wheels of total moment of inertia C and radius a, runs on a curve of radius R with speed v: find the gyrostatic couple on the train.

The angular speed of a wheel is v/a, and the A.M. of the wheels is Cv/a. Hence A.M. is being generated by each wheel of amount $Cv/na \cdot v/R = Cv^2/naR$ per second, if n be the number of wheels, about an axis drawn from the wheel in the direction *backwards* along the track. In order to counteract this, the carriage will tend to turn about this axis in the direction *outwards* from the centre, until the couple required to produce A.M. at the rate due to the turning is applied to the carriage by the excess of pressure on the outer rail. Thus the gyrostatic action provides a couple of moment Cv^2/aR, which tends to upset the carriage in the same direction as the couple due to centrifugal force, and is balanced with the latter by the action of the rails.

If the track is on the level, and b be the gauge, the excess of thrust exerted on the wheels by the outer rail over that exerted by the inner rail, is Cv^2/baR. The ratio of this to the centrifugal force Mv^2/R, where M is the weight of the carriage, is C/Mab, and is obviously very small.

Ex. 2. Work out the action of the steam-turbine referred to above as mounted on a carriage with its axis in the fore-and-aft direction.

The A.M. of the turbine may be denoted by Cn, where n is the angular speed of rotation. As the carriage moves forward on a curve, there is a rate of production Cnv/R of A.M. about an axis in the direction of the radius of the curve at the position of the turbine at the instant. This throws more weight on the front wheels and less on the back, or *vice versa*, according to the direction of rotation and of turning in the curve, until the reaction couple applied to the carriage by the rails has moment Cnv/R. If d be the distance between the front and back sets of wheels, the difference of weights borne is Cnv/Rd, which is the fraction $Cnv/MgRd$ of the weight M of the carriage.

If the locomotive, with the "fore-and-aft" turbine, referred to above, is not on a curve but on a convex part of the track, of radius of curvature R, there will be a rate of production of A.M. of amount Cnv/R about a normal to the track at each instant. If the rotation is in the counter-clock direction, as seen by an observer standing behind the carriage, the rate of growth of A.M. is about the outward normal, and so the rear of the carriage tends to slew round towards the observer's left, and the front towards his right. The reverse is the case with reversed rotation, or with concavity of the track.

293. Drift of a Projectile. The turbine thus moving forward while rotating, may be compared to a projectile fired from a rifled gun. The rotation of the projectile is right handed in that case as looked at by an observer at the firing point, and the shot drifts in its trajectory, which is convex upwards, towards the right. But with this direction of rotation of the turbine, the front of the carriage would turn towards the left; so that the idea of the projectile as a gyrostat moving forward on a convex track with its axis in the direction of motion throws no light on the drift of the projectile.

The cause of this drift is not yet fully understood, but it is connected with the rotation, as its direction is reversed with that of the rotation. It amounts to ·25, 1·1, 4·4, 11·5 metres on ranges of 500, 1000, 2000, 3000 metres respectively. Since the rapidly spinning projectile tends to keep the direction of its axis unchanged, it is presently moving forward on the convex trajectory with its axis in the plane of the trajectory, but pointing a little upward relatively to the path. Thus it has a motion in the direction of the axis together with a lateral component. Hence, by § 80, a couple is applied by the air tending to increase this obliquity of the axis of spin to the direction of motion; but, as the projectile spins rapidly about its axis, it precesses about the instantaneous position of the axis of resultant momentum, as explained in § 294, with of course modification of the resistance in consequence. As a result the projectile moves forward in air, and relatively to the path its point is directed slightly upward and to the right, and the shot is continually deflected towards the right by a side thrust applied by the air.

294. Stability of Rotating Projectile in Air. We now consider the stability of a rotating projectile in an unlimited frictionless liquid.* Let the projectile rotate about its axis of figure with angular speed n, so that its A.M. about that axis is Cn. By § 80 the projectile will experience a couple depending on its motion with speed v in the axial direction, and in a direction perpendicular to the axis with speed u. The moment of the couple is

$$(c_2 - c_1)uv,$$

where c_1, c_2 are the effective inertias in the directions of v and u respectively, what are denoted by M_1, M_2 in § 80 above.

Now let the shot have precessional angular speed μ about an axis parallel to the direction of the resultant momentum, that is, the resultant of $c_1 v$ and $c_2 u$. This is the direction of the impulse which would be required to produce these components of momentum. If θ be the angle which this direction makes with the axis of figure,

$$\tan \theta = c_2 u / c_1 v.$$

We suppose the motion to be steady. The shot now "precesses" as if it were an ordinary top (Fig. 112) spinning about a fixed point O with the line of resultant momentum vertical, and endowed with A.M. Cn about the axis of figure, and an *effective* A.M. $A\mu \sin \theta$, about an axis OE, at right angles to the axis of figure OC, and in the vertical plane containing OC. The couple N acts about an axis represented in the case of the top by OD.

For steady motion, § 272 above gives the equation

$$(Cn - A\mu \cos \theta)\mu \sin \theta = N. \quad \ldots\ldots\ldots\ldots\ldots\ldots\ldots(1)$$

Now, since $N = (c_2 - c_1)uv$ and $\tan \theta = c_2 u / c_1 v$, we have

$$N = \frac{c_1}{c_2}(c_2 - c_1)v^2 \tan \theta,$$

and therefore (1) becomes

$$(Cn - A\mu \cos \theta)\mu = \frac{c_1}{c_2}(c_2 - c_1)v^2 \sec \theta, \quad \ldots\ldots\ldots\ldots\ldots(2)$$

for we do not suppose that $\theta = 0$, which would mean that the shot did not swerve from the axial direction of motion given to it by the gun.

---

* The discussion here given is a version of that by Sir George Greenhill (see "Gyroscope and Gyrostat," *Encyc. Brit.*, 10th edition, vol. xxix.), to whom most of recent investigation in this subject is due.

The roots of the last equation are real if

$$\frac{n^2}{v^2} > 4\frac{A}{C^2}\frac{c_1}{c_2}(c_2 - c_1), \quad\quad\quad\quad\quad\quad\quad\quad (3)$$

which gives the least value of n compatible with stability. In what follows, we assume that n has the value given by converting this inequality into an equation.

Now we can put $\quad c_1 = M + M'\alpha, \quad c_2 = M + M'\beta, \quad\quad\quad\quad\quad (5)$

where M' is the weight of the displaced fluid and α, β are coefficients depending on the shape of the body. Thus

$$c_2 - c_1 = M'(\beta - \alpha).$$

If β be the angle of rifling and d the diameter of the bore at the muzzle of the gun,

$$\left.\begin{array}{l} \tan^2\beta = \dfrac{1}{4}\dfrac{n^2}{v^2}d^2 = \dfrac{A}{C^2}\dfrac{c_1}{c_2}(c_2 - c_1)d^2 \\[6pt] = \dfrac{A}{C^2}\dfrac{c_1}{c_2}M'd^2(\beta - \alpha). \end{array}\right\} \quad\quad\quad\quad (5)$$

If k_1, k_2 be the radii of gyration of the body about the axis of figure, and the other axis about which the body revolves with angular speed $\mu\sin\theta$, we have, writing κ for M'/M,

$$C = Mk_1^2, \quad A = Mk_2^2 + M'k'^2_2$$

and $\quad\quad \tan^2\beta = (k_2^2 + \kappa k'^2_2)\dfrac{d^2}{k_1^4}\dfrac{1 + \kappa\alpha}{1 + \kappa\beta}\kappa(\beta - \alpha). \quad\quad\quad\quad (6)$

Now we may apply this theory to a shot in air, and in that case we may neglect $M'k'^2_2/M$ in comparison with k_2^2, and write

$$\tan^2\beta = d^2\frac{k_2^2}{k_1^4}\kappa(\beta - \alpha), \quad\quad\quad\quad\quad\quad\quad\quad (7)$$

which, if α and β are known, gives a lower limit to the angle of rifling required for stability. Into the calculation of α and β for an ellipsoid, for which alone the discussion has been completed, we cannot here enter. [See Greenhill, article on "Hydromechanics," *Encyc. Brit.*, 10th edition.]

For an automobile torpedo completely submerged and without buoyancy $M' = M$ and $c_1 = M(1 + \alpha)$, $c_2 = M(1 + \beta)$, so that

$$\frac{C^2 n^2}{v^2} = 4M^2(k_2^2 + k'^2_2)\frac{1 + \alpha}{1 + \beta}(\beta - \alpha).$$

The A.M., Cn, is supplied by a rapidly rotating fly-wheel in the torpedo with its axis along the axis of figure and running at a very high speed, about 150 revs. per sec. In the Obry self-steering torpedo, when the axis of the torpedo turns relatively to that of the gyrostat, mechanism actuated by compressed air and started by the gyrostat brings a rudder into action to restore the projectile to its course. In the Whitehead-Howell torpedo, the gyrostatic apparatus (axis perpendicular to direction of motion) both detects the deflection from the course and applies the restoring couples.

295. Rolling of a Solid of Revolution on Horizontal Plane. Let O (Fig. 141) be the point of contact of the solid with the horizontal plane, G the centroid, GC the axis of figure, and draw a vertical through G meeting the horizontal plane in M, and a perpendicular from O to the axis of

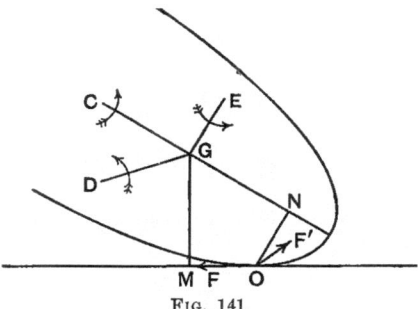

Fig. 141.

figure meeting it in N. Denote GN by x and ON by y. Let F, F' be the components of friction at O, the former acting along the intersection of the horizontal plane and the vertical plane, and the latter at right angles to the vertical plane as shown, and let R be the reaction of the plane on the solid at O. What is called pivot-friction (by the Germans "boring friction"), the resistance to *spinning* of the solid on the plane, is here neglected. For a body resting on what may be regarded as a point its moment is very small. Let θ be the inclination of GC to the upward vertical.

Now take axes at G, one along GC, the second, GD, at right angles to the plane GOC, and the third, GE, at right angles to GC in the plane GOC, all as shown in the figure. If the solid turn about GC and CD with angular speeds n and $\dot{\theta}$, and about the vertical with angular speed $\dot{\psi}$ counter-clockwise to one looking downward, the angular momenta about the axes just specified are Cn, $A\dot{\theta}$, $A\dot{\psi}\sin\theta$. Hence, for the rate of growth of A.M. about GD, we get, by the process used in § 261, the expression $A\ddot{\theta}+(Cn-A\dot{\psi}\cos\theta)\dot{\psi}\sin\theta$. Now the total moment of forces about GD is clearly

$$R(x\sin\theta-y\cos\theta)-F(x\cos\theta+y\sin\theta),$$

so that we get the equation

$$A\ddot{\theta}+(Cn-A\dot{\psi}\cos\theta)\dot{\psi}\sin\theta=R(x\sin\theta-y\cos\theta)\\-F(x\cos\theta+y\sin\theta)....(1)$$

Again, as in § 261, we see that the rate of growth of A.M. about GE is $A\ddot{\psi}\sin\theta+(2A\dot{\psi}\cos\theta-Cn)\dot{\theta}$, and the only force with moment about GE is F'. Hence we get

$$A\ddot{\psi}\sin\theta+(2A\dot{\psi}\cos\theta-Cn)\dot{\theta}=F'x. \quad\ldots\ldots\ldots(2)$$

The motion of the axes produces no change of A.M. about GC, and therefore

$$C\dot{n}=-F'y. \quad\ldots\ldots\ldots\ldots\ldots\ldots\ldots(3)$$

Now let u, v be the speeds of the centroid parallel to OM and perpendicular to the plane GOC respectively. Then, since O is supposed to be at rest,

$$u=MG.\dot{\theta}=(x\cos\theta+y\sin\theta)\dot{\theta}, \quad v=yn-\dot{\psi}x\sin\theta....(4)$$

Here v is taken in the direction DG. The rates of change of momentum in these directions and along MG are given by

$$M(\dot{u}+v\dot{\psi})=F, \quad M(\dot{v}-u\dot{\psi})=F', \quad M\ddot{\xi}=R-Mg. \ldots(5)$$

These equations give the whole motion. A relation between x and y is given of course by the form of the surface.

For steady motion $\ddot{\theta}=0$, $\dot{\theta}=0$, $\dot{u}=0$, $\ddot{z}=0$, $\ddot{\psi}=0$, so that $\dot{\psi}=\mu$, a constant, $F'=0$, $-F=M\mu(\mu x\sin\theta-ny)$, $R=Mg$. Hence (1) becomes

$$\{(C+My^2)n-(A+Mx^2)\mu\cos\theta\}\mu\sin\theta\\+Mxy(n\mu\cos\theta-\mu^2\sin^2\theta)=Mg(x\sin\theta-y\cos\theta). \ldots(6)$$

Since in steady motion $\dot{u}=\dot{v}=0$, we have by the first of (5), and the value of F for steady motion,

$$v=ny-\mu x\sin\theta,$$

that is v is constant. The direction of v turns round with uniform angular speed μ, and therefore G moves in a circle, and M in a parallel circle in the horizontal plane. But μv is the acceleration of M towards the centre of the circle, that is if r be the radius $\mu v = v^2/r$ and $r = v/\mu$. Thus

$$r = \frac{ny}{\mu} - x \sin \theta. \quad \ldots\ldots\ldots\ldots\ldots\ldots\ldots(7)$$

The azimuthal motion μ is in the counter-clock direction to an observer looking from above on the solid, and therefore the circle has the position shown in Fig. 132.

296. Rising and Falling of Top Spinning on Rounded Peg. We see that a top supported on a rounded peg rises under certain circumstances. Initially the top is spun in various ways, generally by throwing it from the hand so that it alights on the ground on its peg. The speeds u, v, $\dot{\psi}$ are small as a rule, the speed of rotation n is large. The result is that the friction F' is for the turning indicated in Fig. 141 in the direction there shown, and is as great as the force R can make it: for the point of contact of the solid, owing to the rapid rotation, slips back on the plane, and the friction is not limited to that required for pure rolling.

The total couple given by friction resolves into the two components on the right of equations (1) and (2); one accelerates the precession, the other reduces the spin about the axis of figure. The axes GC, GD, GE show, by the directions in which they are drawn from G, the sense of the angular momentum about each. Now the acceleration of the precession produces A.M. about the axis GD towards which the precession is carrying the axis GC, with its A.M. of amount Cn, so fast that the rate of growth

$$(Cn - A\dot{\psi} \cos \theta)\dot{\psi} \sin \theta$$

of A.M. is greater than the applied couple producing A.M. about GD; and therefore $A\ddot{\theta}$ is negative, that is the centroid of the solid, if $\dot{\theta}$ before was zero, is now rising. If $\dot{\theta}$ is still positive, it is now diminishing, and the action is towards raising the centroid of the solid.

We can study this quantitatively by means of the equations. Multiplying both sides of (2), § 295, by $\sin \theta$

and substituting the value of F' given by (3), we obtain

$$\frac{d}{dt}(A\dot{\psi}\sin^2\theta + Cn\cos\theta) + Cn\frac{x - y\cot\theta}{y}\sin\theta = 0. \quad \ldots\ldots(1)$$

Now let the solid roll on a part of its surface, including the extremity of the axis of figure, which may be taken as spherical of radius a, and let c be the distance of G from the centre of curvature. We have then

$$(x - y\cot\theta)/(y/\sin\theta) = c/a,$$

so that we get from (1), by integration, the result

$$A\dot{\psi}\sin^2\theta + Cn\left(\cos\theta + \frac{c}{a}\right) = Cn_0\left(\cos\theta_0 + \frac{c}{a}\right), \quad \ldots\ldots(2)$$

where the constant expression on the right is the initial value of the quantity on the left, for initially

$$\theta = \theta_0, \quad n = n_0, \quad \dot{\psi} = 0.$$

Now n is being continually diminished by friction, and if we suppose n large and therefore $\dot{\psi}$ small, there will be a value of $n = n_0(\cos\theta_0 + c/a)/(1 + c/a)$. But, as the reader may verify from (2), for this value of n, $\theta = 0$, that is the body is spinning with its axis vertical. If this value of n satisfy the condition (§ 270 above) $C^2n^2 > 4AWgh$, steady motion in the upright position is possible; the top will rise up and "sleep" in the vertical position.

297. Disk or Hoop on Horizontal Plane, Oscillations about Steady Motion. For a circular disk or hoop rolling without slipping on a horizontal plane, equations (1) and (2), § 295, become, since $x = 0$ and $y = a$, the radius of the circular edge

$$\left.\begin{array}{c} A\ddot{\theta} + (Cn - A\dot{\psi}\cos\theta)\dot{\psi}\sin\theta = -a(R\cos\theta + F\sin\theta), \\ \dfrac{d}{dt}(A\dot{\psi}\sin^2\theta) - Cn\dot{\theta}\sin\theta = 0, \\ C\dot{n} = -F'a, \end{array}\right\} \quad \ldots\ldots(1)$$

with $\quad M(\dot{u} + v\dot{\psi}) = F, \quad M(\dot{v} - u\dot{\psi}) = F', \quad M\ddot{\zeta} = R - Mg,$

where (§ 295) $u = a\dot{\theta}\sin\theta$, $v = an$, $\zeta = a\sin\theta$. Thus

$$Ma(\ddot{\theta}\sin\theta + \dot{\theta}^2\cos\theta + n\dot{\psi}) = F, \quad Ma(\dot{n} - \dot{\theta}\dot{\psi}\sin\theta) = F' \quad \ldots\ldots(2)$$

OSCILLATIONS OF ROLLING DISK.

Hence we obtain for the first of (1),

$$\left.\begin{aligned}(A+Ma^2)\ddot{\theta}+\{(C+Ma^2)n-A\dot{\psi}\cos\theta\}\dot{\psi}\sin\theta+Mga\cos\theta&=0,\\ \frac{d}{dt}(A\dot{\psi}\sin^2\theta)-Cn\dot{\theta}\sin\theta&=0,\\ (C+Ma^2)\dot{n}-Ma^2\dot{\theta}\dot{\psi}\sin\theta&=0.\end{aligned}\right\}\ ...(3)$$

Now, let the motion be steady. Then $\ddot{\psi}=0$, $\dot{\theta}=0$, $\ddot{\theta}=0$, $u=0$, $\dot{u}=0$, $\dot{v}=0$, $\dot{n}=0$, and we get

$$\{(C+Ma^2)n-A\mu\cos\theta\}\mu\sin\theta+Mga\cos\theta=0\ \ ....(4)$$

with $v=na$.

For a uniform circular disk, $C=\tfrac{1}{2}Ma^2$, $A=\tfrac{1}{4}Ma^2$, and for a hoop, $C=Ma^2$, $A=\tfrac{1}{2}Ma^2$.

Now, let n', θ', μ be steady values of n, θ, $\dot{\psi}$ and $n'+\nu$, $\theta'+\alpha$, $\mu+\dot{\beta}$ be the values at any instant for a slight deviation from steady motion. Then equations (1) become

$$\left.\begin{aligned}(A+Ma^2)\ddot{\alpha}+\{(C+Ma^2)\nu-A\dot{\beta}\cos\theta'+A\alpha\mu\sin\theta'\}\mu\sin\theta'\\ +\{(C+Ma^2)n-A\mu\cos\theta'\}(\dot{\beta}\sin\theta'+\mu\alpha\cos\theta')\\ -Mga\alpha\sin\theta=0,\\ A\ddot{\beta}\sin\theta'+(2A\mu\cos\theta-Cn)\dot{\alpha}=0,\\ (C+Ma^2)\dot{\nu}-Ma^2\dot{\alpha}\mu\sin\theta'=0.\end{aligned}\right\}\ ...(5)$$

From the last equation, we get

$$(C+Ma^2)\nu=Ma^2\alpha\mu\sin\theta',\ \ ....(6)$$

since there can be no constant of integration. Substituting in the first equation, we obtain

$$\left.\begin{aligned}(A+Ma^2)\ddot{\alpha}+(Ma^2\alpha\mu\sin\theta'-A\dot{\beta}\cos\theta'+A\alpha\mu\sin\theta')\mu\sin\theta'\\ +\{(C+Ma^2)n-A\mu\cos\theta'\}(\dot{\beta}\sin\theta'+\mu\alpha\cos\theta')\\ -Mga\alpha\sin\theta=0.\end{aligned}\right\}\ ...(7)$$

Putting now $\alpha=r\sin(pt-f)$, $\beta=s\cos(pt-f)$, and substituting in the last equation, we obtain

$$\frac{s}{r}=\frac{\{(C+Ma^2)n-A\mu\cos\theta'\}\mu\cos\theta'+(A+Ma^2)(\mu^2\sin^2\theta'-p^2)-Mga\sin\theta'}{\{(C+Ma^2)n-2A\mu\cos\theta'\}p\sin\theta'}.\ \ ....(8)$$

Again, substituting in the second of (5), we get

$$\frac{s}{r}=\frac{2A\mu\cos\theta'-Cn}{Ap\sin\theta'}.$$

The value of p^2 can now be obtained by equating the two values of s/r. It is given by the equation

$$p^2=\frac{A\{(K+Ma^2n)\mu\cos\theta'+L\mu^2\sin^2\theta'-Mga\sin\theta'\}+(K-A\mu\cos\theta')(K+Ma^2n-A\mu\cos\theta')}{AL},\ \ ....(9)$$

where $K = Cn - A\mu \cos \theta'$, $L = A + Ma^2$. Here $\theta < \pi/2$, and therefore p^2 is positive if n be great enough. Thus, there is a real period of vibration, and the motion is dynamically stable, if the rotation be sufficiently rapid.

If $n = 0$ and $\theta = \pi/2$, that is, if the body only turn in azimuth with its axis horizontal, as a coin spins with its plane vertical on a table, we have
$$p^2 = \frac{(A + Ma^2)\mu^2 - Mga}{A + Ma^2}, \quad \ldots\ldots\ldots\ldots\ldots\ldots\ldots(10)$$

which is evidently positive if μ be sufficiently great. This shows, moreover, that for a coin spinning very rapidly, the period of an oscillation about the vertical position is approximately the period of the azimuthal rotation, for then $p^2 = \mu^2$ nearly.

For a hoop the equation for p^2 reduces to
$$p^2 = \frac{8na(n - \mu \cos \theta') + 3a\mu^2 - 2g \sin \theta'}{3a}. \quad \ldots\ldots\ldots\ldots\ldots(11)$$

If the hoop is spinning about the vertical so that $n = 0$, we get
$$p^2 = \mu^2 - \frac{2}{3}\frac{g}{a}. \quad \ldots\ldots\ldots\ldots\ldots\ldots\ldots\ldots\ldots\ldots\ldots(12)$$

298. Condition that a Disk or Hoop may Roll Upright in Straight Line. In the steady motion of the hoop, the radius of the circle in which the centroid moves is na/μ, which agrees with (7), § 295, for here $x = 0$. The radius of the circle in which the point of contact with the horizontal plane moves is therefore

$$na/\mu + a \cos \theta = a(n + \mu \cos \theta)/\mu.$$

This also holds for a circular disk in steady motion in the same way.

In order that the disk may roll upright stably along a straight line, we see from (11), § 297, that
$$p^2 = \frac{C(C + Ma^2)n^2 - AMga}{A(A + Ma^2)}. \quad \ldots\ldots\ldots\ldots\ldots\ldots(1)$$

The condition therefore is $n^2 > \dfrac{AMga}{C(C + Ma^2)}. \quad \ldots\ldots\ldots\ldots\ldots\ldots\ldots\ldots(2)$

For a hoop this is $\quad n > \sqrt{\dfrac{g}{4a}}, \quad \ldots\ldots\ldots\ldots\ldots\ldots\ldots\ldots\ldots\ldots(3)$

and for a uniform disk it is $\quad n > \sqrt{\dfrac{g}{3a}}. \quad \ldots\ldots\ldots\ldots\ldots\ldots\ldots\ldots\ldots\ldots(4)$

The hoop is therefore more stable than the disk, requiring for the same radius less speed of rotation, in the ratio of $\sqrt{3}$ to 2, in order to remain upright.

EXERCISES IX.

1. A heavy flywheel is pivoted at the extremities of a horizontal diameter AOB, and this diameter is carried round a vertical axis through its centre O with uniform angular speed μ. At a point P at distance a from the centre on a diameter at right angles to AB an additional weight w is attached. Find the equation of motion.

Take as axes OA, OP and the axis OC of the wheel drawn from O on the other side of the vertical from OP. If θ be the inclination of OP to the downward vertical, the angular speeds about OP and OC are $\mu\cos\theta$ and $\mu\sin\theta$, while the angular momenta are $A\mu\cos\theta$ and $(C+wa^2)\mu\sin\theta$. The total rate of growth of A.M. about OA is therefore, by § 9, $-(A+wa^2)\ddot{\theta}+(C+wa^2)\mu^2\sin\theta\cos\theta - A\mu^2\cos\theta\sin\theta$, and the moment of applied forces is $wga\sin\theta$. The equation of motion is
$$(A+wa^2)\ddot{\theta} - (C+wa^2-A)\mu^2\cos\theta\sin\theta = -wga\sin\theta.$$

2. A top is set in rapid rotation and is placed on a frictionless horizontal plane with its axis inclined at an angle θ_0 to the vertical, and is constrained by two smooth planes parallel to the angle θ, so that its axis must remain in that plane. Prove that the top must fall.

No action of the constraining planes can alter the energy of rotation, or the angular speed $\dot{\theta}$. If $\dot{\theta}=0$ when $\theta=\theta_0$, and A be the M.I. of the top about a horizontal axis through its centroid, we have
$$\tfrac{1}{2}\{A\dot{\theta}^2 + wh^2\sin^2\theta\cdot\dot{\theta}^2\} = wgl(\cos\theta_0 - \cos\theta).$$

The left-hand side is positive, so θ must be greater than θ_0.

[It is important to remember that any constraints may impair the stability of a top or gyrostat. Conclusions, for instance, derived from the behaviour of a top mounted on a tray as in § 283, where a certain diameter of the flywheel is constrained to remain horizontal, cannot be regarded as necessarily holding for a top perfectly free to precess—*e.g.* a planet rotating in free space.]

3. A gyrostat is suspended from a fixed point by a string of length a fastened to a point P in the axis of rotation, and is in steady motion with the axis horizontal. Prove that if α be the angle which the string makes with the vertical, n the angular speed of the flywheel, h the distance of the point from the centre of gravity of the gyrostat, M the mass of the gyrostat, and C the moment of inertia of the wheel about its axis,
$$\tan\alpha = g\frac{M^2h^2}{C^2n^2}(h + a\sin\alpha).$$

[The string applies horizontal force $M\mu^2(h+a\sin\alpha)$, and the gravity couple is Mgh. Thus $\mu^2 = M^2g^2h^2/C^2n^2$, and so horizontal force
$$= M^3g^2h^2(h+a\sin\alpha)/C^2n^2.$$

By equating this to the horizontal component of the pull exerted by the string and the gravity of the top to the vertical component, the reader will obtain the required result.]

546   A TREATISE ON DYNAMICS.   [CH.

4. A simple conical pendulum is inclined at an angle α to the vertical, and its length is l. Find the period of a small oscillation about the steady motion.

5. A ring of wire, of radius c, rests on the top of a smooth fixed sphere of radius a, and is set rotating about the vertical diameter of the sphere with an angular speed n. Prove that the motion is unstable if $n^2 c^4 < 2g(2a^2 - c^2)\sqrt{a^2 - c^2}$. [Math. Tripos, 1885.]

Since the ring moves on the surface of the sphere it may be regarded as a top turning about the centre of the sphere.

6. Show that a gyrostat, balanced and free to turn about an axis AB through the c.g. at right angles to the axis of rotation, is in stable or unstable equilibrium with the axis of rotation vertical according as the rotation of the wheel is with or against the earth's rotation. Show also that if the gyrostat be placed with its axis of rotation horizontal in the meridian, and the axis AB vertical, it will be in stable or unstable equilibrium according as the direction of rotation of the wheel is from west to east or from east to west.

Show that the periods of oscillation about the positions of stable equilibrium are $2\pi\sqrt{A/Cn\omega\sin\lambda}$, $2\pi\sqrt{A/Cn\omega\cos\lambda}$, where n is the angular speed of the flywheel, ω that of the earth about its axis, and λ the latitude of the place.

7. Two intersecting rods are at right angles to one another. One is placed vertical, the other can turn in a horizontal plane about the lower end of the first. The ends of the axis of a gyrostat slide freely on these rods, and the axis (of length $2a$) is initially inclined at an angle θ_0 to the vertical, when also the horizontal rod is turning with angular speed $\dot{\psi}_0$. If at time t the inclination of the axis to the vertical is θ, and the azimuthal speed $\dot{\psi}$, prove that

$$(Ma^2 + A)(\dot{\psi}\sin^2\theta - \dot{\psi}_0\sin^2\theta_0) + Cn(\cos\theta - \cos\theta_0) = 0,$$
$$(Ma^2 + A)\ddot{\theta} + \{Cn - (Ma^2 + A)\dot{\psi}\cos\theta\}\dot{\psi}\sin\theta + Mga\sin\theta = 0,$$

where M is the mass of the gyrostat and C and A are its principal moments of inertia. [The M.I. of the case about the axis of symmetry is neglected. Take axes at the centroid and apply the method of § 26.]

8. Four rods, each of length $2a$, are freely jointed together so as to form a rhombus. At the centre of each rod is a gyrostat of mass M, the axis of which is along the rod. The rhombus is hung with one diagonal vertical, and the hinges at top and bottom are attached to rods which swivel in hooks, so that the frame can turn freely in azimuth, while a weight that does not turn is hung at the lowest point.

The gyrostats are all equal and are set spinning with the same angular speed n, in the same direction in each case to an eye looking downward along the rod. A weight W is hung at the lowest point: prove that if the angle at the lowest point be 2α, the arrangement will turn with steady azimuthal angular speed μ given by

$$\{Cn - (A + Ma^2)\mu\cos\alpha\}\mu + (2M + W)ga = 0.$$

[Discuss each of the two gyrostats on either side, as in Ex. 7.]

Find the period of oscillation about this state of steady motion.

[It was stated by Lord Kelvin in his lecture on "A Kinetic Theory of Matter" [*Popular Lectures and Addresses*, vol. i. p. 238] that this arrangement forms a spring balance which is drawn out a vertical distance proportional to any addition of weight made to W, and vibrates vertically when disturbed just as a spring balance does, that in fact, if the rotating and precessing masses were enclosed in a case leaving only the hooks accessible, it could not be distinguished from a spring balance. The reader may endeavour to verify these statements.]

9. Considering the earth as a rotating body with its centroid at rest in space, find the equations of motion of a particle with reference to axes Ox, Oy, Oz drawn from the centroid parallel to the horizontally southward, the eastward, and the vertically downward directions at a point P_0 on the surface.

The coordinates of P_0 are thus 0, 0, a, where a is the vertical distance of P_0 from O, approximately the earth's radius at the point. Let the direction of the gravitational force G on unit mass at P_0 make, as in Fig. 39, a small angle θ with the vertical. The components of gravity at P_0 are $G\cos(\tfrac{1}{2}\pi + \theta)$ along Ox, zero along Oy, and $G\cos\theta$ along Oz. The angular speeds (clockwise) are $n\cos\lambda$, 0, and $n\sin\lambda$, if n be the angular speed of the earth's rotation and λ the geographical latitude (see Fig. 39). The coordinates of any other point P with reference to these axes are x, y, z, and the components of force there are

$$X + G\cos(\tfrac{1}{2}\pi + \theta), \quad Y, \quad Z + G\cos\theta$$

due to gravity, with components X', Y', Z' due to any other applied forces. The equations of motion are therefore

$$\ddot{x} - 2\dot{y}n\sin\lambda + n^2\sin\lambda(z\cos\lambda - x\sin\lambda) = X + X' - G\sin\theta,$$

$$\ddot{y} + 2\dot{x}n\sin\lambda - 2\dot{z}n\cos\lambda - n^2 y = Y + Y',$$

$$\ddot{z} + 2\dot{y}n\cos\lambda - n^2\cos\lambda(z\cos\lambda - x\sin\lambda) = Z + Z' + G\cos\theta.$$

If, as is generally convenient, the axes be taken in the directions specified, but from P_0 as origin, it is only necessary to substitute $z + a$ for z in these equations, and to add, on the right, force-components equal and opposite to those required to give the acceleration $n^2 a\cos\lambda$, of a particle at P_0 towards the earth's axis of rotation.

10. Apply the equations of last example to a simple pendulum suspended from P_0 and executing small vibrations under gravity.

Change the origin to P_0, as explained in Ex. 9, and neglect terms in $n^2 x$, $n^2 y$, $n^2 z$ after this is done. If F be the pull per unit mass applied by the thread to the bob, $X = -Fx/l$, $Y = -Fy/l$, $Z = -Fz/l = -F$. These are the only applied forces besides those due to gravity.

Verify that the third equation gives $F = G\cos\theta = g$, nearly, where g is the apparent force of gravity on unit mass.

Verify also that the first two equations of motion are, if ω be written for $n \sin \lambda$, and $G \sin \theta$ be neglected,

$$\ddot{x} - 2\omega\dot{y} + \frac{g}{l}x = 0, \quad \ddot{y} + 2\omega\dot{x} + \frac{g}{l}y = 0,$$

and that these equations are satisfied to terms involving ω^2 by

$$x = a \cos mt \cos \omega t, \quad y = -a \cos mt \sin \omega t,$$

where $m^2 = g/l$. Hence when $t = 0$, $x = a$, $y = 0$, and at time t,

$$r = \sqrt{x^2 + y^2} = a \cos mt, \quad \tan^{-1}(y/x) = -\omega t.$$

The plane of vibration therefore turns round relatively to the axes Ox, Oy in the direction opposed to the earth's rotation with angular speed $\omega = n \sin \lambda$, an effect which is due to the turning of the earth with angular speed $n \sin \lambda$ under the pendulum.

This is the theory of Foucault's celebrated pendulum experiment for demonstrating the earth's rotation experimentally. After some preliminary trials it was carried out on a large scale at the Panthéon in Paris in 1851. The pendulum there consisted of a ball of lead weighing about 28 kilogrammes, carried by a steel wire 67 metres long. Underneath the pendulum, with centre vertically under the point of support, was a circle of wood 6 metres in diameter divided to fourths of a degree. Round part of this was placed a thin ridge of sand which was cut through by the pendulum, and gave a register of the turning of the plane of vibration relatively to the earth. A smaller concentric circle enabled the turning to be traced for a longer time, about 5 or 6 hours in all.

The period of turning at the latitude of the Panthéon is theoretically 31 h. 47 m. 14·6 s., and the pendulum appears to have shown a period of about 32 hours. The experiment was repeated immediately and successfully in the cathedrals of Reims and Amiens, and at other places. Extreme care is necessary to make the suspension perfectly symmetrical. [See *Travaux Scientifiques de Foucault*, Paris, 1878.]

11. Writing the equations of motion of the pendulum, referred to in Ex. 12, in the completer form (origin at P_0)

$$\ddot{x} - 2\omega\dot{y} + \left(\frac{g}{l} - \omega^2\right)x = 0, \quad \ddot{y} + 2\omega\dot{x} + \left(\frac{g}{l} - \omega^2\right)y = 0,$$

prove that they are satisfied by $x = a \cos mt$, $y = a \sin mt$, where m is a root of the equation

$$m^2 + 2\omega m - \frac{g}{l} + \omega^2 = 0.$$

Show that the motion of the bob is in a horizontal circle, in one case in the direction of the earth's rotation in period $2\pi/\sqrt{g/l - \omega}$, in the other in the opposite direction in period $2\pi/\sqrt{g/l + \omega}$.

[These two periods are perfectly analogous to the two periods of circular vibration of an electron moving in a plane at right angles to the direction of a magnetic field.]

12. Show that if a body be let fall from rest at a point at distance h above the origin of coordinates, the equations of motion are approximately
$$\ddot{x} - 2\dot{y}n\sin\lambda = 0, \quad \ddot{y} + 2\dot{x}n\sin\lambda - 2\dot{z}n\cos\lambda = 0, \quad \ddot{z} + 2\dot{y}n\cos\lambda = g,$$
and that after time t by the initial conditions
$$\dot{x} - 2yn\sin\lambda = 0, \quad \dot{y} + 2xn\sin\lambda - 2zn\cos\lambda = -2hn\cos\lambda, \quad \dot{z} + 2yn\cos\lambda = gt.$$
Hence show that $\quad x = (\tfrac{1}{2}gt^2 - h - z)\tan\lambda.$
But very approximately $h - (-z) = \tfrac{1}{2}gt^2$, and so $x = 0$ practically. There is therefore no southerly deviation of a falling body from the vertical.

Using this result in the second equation, prove that when the height h has been fallen through,
$$y = \tfrac{1}{3}gt^3 n\cos\lambda,$$

13. Apply the equations of Ex. 11 to find the deviations of a projectile fired from the origin with speed v at a small elevation α in a plane inclined at an angle ϕ to the plane of the meridian.

The first integrals obtained are
$$\dot{x} - 2yn\sin\lambda = v\cos\alpha\cos\phi, \quad \dot{y} + 2xn\sin\lambda - 2zn\cos\lambda = v\cos\alpha\sin\phi,$$
$$\dot{z} + 2yn\cos\lambda = gt - v\sin\alpha.$$

Find values of x and z by neglecting the terms in n in the first and third, substitute in the second and find y. Substitute that value in the first and third and so find a second approximation to x and y. Verify that
$$x = vt\cos\alpha\cos\phi + vt^2 n\sin\lambda\cos\alpha\sin\phi,$$
$$y = vt\cos\alpha\sin\phi - vt^2 n(\sin\lambda\cos\alpha\cos\phi + \cos\lambda\sin\alpha) - \tfrac{1}{3}ngt^3\cos\lambda,$$
$$z = -vt\sin\alpha + \tfrac{1}{2}gt^2 - vt^2 n\cos\lambda\cos\alpha\sin\phi.$$
The terms in n are the deviations.

Work out for $v = 2400 f/s$, $\alpha = 4°$, $\lambda = 56°$N, $\phi = 0$, $\phi = 45°$.

14. The resultant angular momentum of a body movable about a fixed point is H, and the body is acted on by a couple of moment λH about the axis of H, where λ is a constant. Find the equations of motion, and show that they can be reduced to those for the body acted on by no forces.

[Use Euler's equations, § 251, and the substitutions $\lambda t' = e^{\lambda t} - 1$, $p' = e^{-\lambda t} p, \ldots$]

15. A body which can turn freely about a fixed point at which two of the principal moments are equal and less than the third, is set in rotation about an axis inclined to that of maximum moment of inertia. It is acted on by a retarding couple proportional to the angular speed whose axis is that of rotation at the instant. Show that the axis of rotation will tend continually to coincidence with the axis of unequal moment.

[Thus near coincidence of the axis of figure and axis of rotation of the earth, does not prove that such coincidence has always existed. *Astron. Notices*, March 8, 1867.]

CHAPTER X.

GENERAL DYNAMICAL METHODS.

299. Dynamics of a Connected System of Particles. Work due to Constraints. Section IV. of the Second Part of the *Mécanique Analytique* of Lagrange contains an exposition of a general method for the solution of all the problems of a system of particles moving under any prescribed conditions. It is proposed to explain that method here, with the modifications necessary to enable it to be applied to a class of problems, such, for example, as the rolling of a disk or hoop on a horizontal plane, for which the method in the original form fails to give the equations of motion.

We suppose for the present that friction is excluded, and that the conditions under which a system of n particles moves are expressed by the m equations $(m<3n)$ which connect the coordinates $x_1, y_1, z_1, x_2, y_2, z_2, \ldots, x_n, y_n, z_n$ of the particles at time t with one another, and also, it may be, with t:

$$\left.\begin{array}{l} f_1(x_1, y_1, z_1, x_2, y_2, z_2, \ldots, x_n, y_n, z_n, t)=0, \\ f_2(x_1, y_1, z_1, x_2, y_2, z_2, \ldots, x_n, y_n, z_n, t)=0, \\ \ldots\ldots\ldots\ldots\ldots\ldots\ldots\ldots\ldots\ldots\ldots\ldots\ldots\ldots\ldots, \\ f_m(x_1, y_1, z_1, x_2, y_2, z_2, \ldots, x_n, y_n, z_n, t)=0. \end{array}\right\} \ldots(1)$$

These are the *equations of constraint* or simply *the constraints*. According as t appears or not in these equations, the constraints are said to be variable or invariable. Fixed guides along which some of the particles move are an example of invariable constraints; if the

§ 299]   DYNAMICS OF CONNECTED SYSTEM.   551

guides are themselves in motion, the motion will be recognised by the explicit appearance of t in the equations of constraint, which are then variable.

If the components of active force (§ 63) on a specimen particle of mass m be X, Y, Z, and δx, δy, δz be any variations of the coordinates of the particle which are possible acccording to the conditions which exist at time t, we have, summing for all the particles,

$$\Sigma\{m(\ddot{x}\delta x + \ddot{y}\delta y + \ddot{z}\delta z)\} = \Sigma(X\delta x + Y\delta y + Z\delta z). \quad \ldots\ldots(2)$$

We cannot, however, equate coefficients of δx, δy, δz on each side, since the forces X, Y, Z are not necessarily the only forces which act on the specimen particle; a sum $\Sigma(X\delta x + Y\delta y + Z\delta z)$, due to inactive forces, which is zero, is left out on the right-hand side. But if we replace (1) by

$$\left.\begin{array}{l} \dfrac{\partial f_1}{\partial x_1}\delta x_1 + \dfrac{\partial f_1}{\partial x_2}\delta x_2 + \ldots + \dfrac{\partial f_1}{\partial y_1}\delta y_1 + \ldots = 0, \\[4pt] \dfrac{\partial f_2}{\partial x_1}\delta x_1 + \dfrac{\partial f_2}{\partial x_2}\delta x_2 + \ldots + \dfrac{\partial f_2}{\partial y_1}\delta y_2 + \ldots = 0, \\[2pt] \ldots\ldots\ldots\ldots\ldots\ldots\ldots\ldots\ldots\ldots\ldots\ldots\ldots\ldots\ldots, \\[2pt] \dfrac{\partial f_m}{\partial x_1}\delta x_1 + \ldots\ldots\ldots\ldots\ldots\ldots\ldots = 0, \end{array}\right\} \ldots\ldots\ldots (3)$$

we have a set of equations connecting δx, δy, δz for each particle which coexist with (2). Now let the first of (3) be multiplied by λ_1, the second by λ_2, and so on, and let the sum of the products be added to (2). We get

$$\left.\begin{array}{l} \Sigma\{m(\ddot{x}\,\delta x + \ddot{y}\,\delta y + \ddot{z}\,\delta z)\} \\[2pt] = \Sigma(X\,\delta x + Y\,\delta y + Z\,\delta z) + \left(\lambda_1\dfrac{\partial f_1}{\partial x_1} + \lambda_2\dfrac{\partial f_2}{\partial x_1} + \ldots\right)\delta x_1 \\[4pt] \qquad + \left(\lambda_1\dfrac{\partial f_1}{\partial x_2} + \lambda_2\dfrac{\partial f_2}{\partial x_2} + \ldots\right)\delta x_2 + \ldots. \end{array}\right\} \ldots(4)$$

It is possible, as we shall see, to choose $\lambda_1, \lambda_2, \ldots, \lambda_m$ of such magnitudes that the coefficient of each δx, δy, or δz shall be zero in (4), and of course the multipliers can be taken of such dimensions that every product of the form

$\lambda \partial f/\partial x . \delta x$ shall have the dimensions of work. Thus we get the equations, $3n$ in number,

$$\left.\begin{aligned} m_1 \ddot{x}_1 &= X_1 + \lambda_1 \frac{\partial f_1}{\partial x_1} + \lambda_2 \frac{\partial f_2}{\partial x_1} + \ldots + \lambda_m \frac{\partial f_m}{\partial x_1}, \\ m_2 \ddot{x}_2 &= X_2 + \lambda_1 \frac{\partial f_1}{\partial x_2} + \lambda_2 \frac{\partial f_2}{\partial x_2} + \ldots + \lambda_m \frac{\partial f_m}{\partial x_2}, \\ &\ldots\ldots\ldots\ldots\ldots\ldots\ldots\ldots\ldots\ldots\ldots\ldots\ldots\ldots \end{aligned}\right\} \ldots\ldots(5)$$

That $\lambda_1, \lambda_2, \ldots$ can be thus chosen is clear from the fact that we have $3n$ coordinates and m multipliers $\lambda_1, \lambda_2, \ldots, \lambda_m$, $3n+m$ in all, and that the $3n$ equations of (5) and the m equations of (1) give $3n+m$ equations wherewith to determine them.

The equation (4) of virtual work (so called because $\delta x, \delta y, \ldots$ are virtual displacements, that is any arbitrary small displacements possible under the conditions of the system, *as they exist at the instant t*) only holds for the conditions of the system at time t. If we consider actual displacements $dx, dy, \ldots$, effected in an interval of time dt, we have to replace (3) by

$$\left.\begin{aligned} \frac{\partial f_1}{\partial x_1} dx_1 + \frac{\partial f_1}{\partial x_2} dx_2 + \ldots + \frac{\partial f_1}{\partial y_1} dy_1 + \ldots + \frac{\partial f_1}{\partial t} dt &= 0, \\ \frac{\partial f_2}{\partial x_1} dx_1 + \frac{\partial f_2}{\partial x_2} dx_2 + \ldots + \frac{\partial f_2}{\partial y_1} dy_1 + \ldots + \frac{\partial f_2}{\partial t} dt &= 0, \\ \ldots\ldots\ldots\ldots\ldots\ldots\ldots\ldots\ldots\ldots\ldots\ldots\ldots\ldots \\ \frac{\partial f_m}{\partial x_1} dx_1 + \ldots\ldots\ldots\ldots\ldots\ldots\ldots\ldots\ldots &= 0. \end{aligned}\right\} \ldots(6)$$

If we multiply these respectively by $\lambda_1, \lambda_2, \ldots \lambda_m$ and add, we get

$$\left.\begin{aligned} \left(\lambda_1 \frac{\partial f_1}{\partial x_1} + \lambda_2 \frac{\partial f_2}{\partial x_1} + \ldots\right) dx_1 + \left(\lambda_1 \frac{\partial f_1}{\partial x_2} + \lambda_2 \frac{\partial f_2}{\partial x_2} + \ldots\right) dx_2 + \ldots \\ + \ldots \left(\lambda_1 \frac{\partial f_1}{\partial t} + \lambda_2 \frac{\partial f_2}{\partial t} + \ldots\right) dt = 0, \end{aligned}\right\} \quad (7)$$

§§ 299, 300] INDEPENDENT COORDINATES. 553

and so the whole work done in an actual displacement of the system in consequence of the fulfilment of the m equations of condition (1) is

$$-\left(\lambda_1\frac{\partial f_1}{\partial t}+\lambda_2\frac{\partial f_2}{\partial t}+\ldots+\lambda_m\frac{\partial f_m}{dt}\right)dt.$$

If we multiply (4), the first by $\dot{x}_1$, the second by $\dot{x}_2$, ... and add, we get by the result just obtained, since

$$dT/dt = \Sigma\{m(\ddot{x}\dot{x}+\ddot{y}\dot{y}+\ddot{z}\dot{z})\},$$

$$\frac{dT}{dt}=\Sigma(X\dot{x}+Y\dot{y}+Z\dot{z})+\lambda_1\frac{\partial f_1}{\partial t}+\lambda_2\frac{\partial f_2}{\partial t}+\ldots+\lambda_m\frac{\partial f_m}{\partial t}\ldots(8)$$

The interpretation of this result is that the time-rate of increase of the kinetic energy is equal to the rate at which work is done by the forces $X_1, Y_1, Z_1, \ldots$ *plus* the activity

$$A=\lambda_1\frac{\partial f_1}{\partial t}+\lambda_2\frac{\partial f_2}{\partial t}+\ldots+\lambda_m\frac{\partial f_m}{\partial t},\ldots\ldots\ldots\ldots(9)$$

due to the forces brought into play by the varying of the kinematical conditions (1), § 299. Hence when

$$\partial f_1/\partial t,\quad \partial f_2/\partial t,\ldots$$

are all zero, the fulfilment of the kinematical relations has no effect on the energy of the system. Thus if the forces $X, Y, Z, \ldots$ are conservative, that is, are derived from a function V of the coordinates only, the sum of the kinetic and potential energies remains constant during the motion, provided t does not appear explicitly in (1).

300. Reduction to Independent Coordinates. From (1) of § 299 any m of the $3n$ coordinates can be determined in terms of the other $3n-m$, or k, coordinates. Thus, by elimination by means of (1) of any chosen m coordinates, say the first m, the discussion of any problem may be reduced to one regarding a system characterised by k *independent* coordinates. Instead of using the k coordinates left, we may substitute k parameters $q_1, q_2, \ldots, q_k$, which are known functions of the coordinates. These are connected with the x, y, z coordinates by definite relations such that the x, y, z for each particle can be expressed in terms of the parameters, either by finite equations

$$x = \phi(q_1, q_2, \ldots, q_k), \quad y = \chi(q_1, q_2, \ldots, q_k), \quad z = \psi(q_1, q_2, \ldots, q_k) \quad (1)$$

or by differential relations

$$\left.\begin{aligned}\delta x &= a_1 \delta q_1 + a_2 \delta q_2 + \ldots + a_k \delta q_k, \\ \delta y &= b_1 \delta q_1 + b_2 \delta q_2 + \ldots + b_k \delta q_k, \\ \delta z &= c_1 \delta q_1 + c_2 \delta q_2 + \ldots + c_k \delta q_k.\end{aligned}\right\} \quad \ldots\ldots\ldots\ldots(2)$$

Of these equations there must be as many sets as there are particles, and they take full account of course of the connections or constraints of the system, as expressed in (1). The displacements typified by δx, δy, δz are arbitrary, but must be such as can take place under the conditions of the system (1), *as they exist at the instant t*. If t appear explicitly in (1), the *actual* displacements which take place in dt in pursuance of the motion are given by

$$\left.\begin{aligned}dx &= a_1 dq_1 + a_2 dq_2 + \ldots + a_k dq_k + a\, dt, \\ dy &= b_1 dq_1 + b_2 dq_2 + \ldots + b_k dq_k + b\, dt, \\ dz &= c_1 dq_1 + c_2 dq_2 + \ldots + c_k dq_k + c\, dt,\end{aligned}\right\} \quad \ldots\ldots\ldots(3)$$

where $dq_1, dq_2, \ldots, dq_k$ are the actual variations of the parameters in dt. The coefficients a, b, c are zero if t does not appear explicitly in the conditional equations (1), § 299, when the displacement specified by $\delta q_1, \delta q_2, \ldots, \delta q_k$ is one that is consistent with the conditions of constraint as they exist both at time t and at time $t + dt$. We have, in the general case,

$$\left.\begin{aligned}\dot{x} &= a_1 \dot{q}_1 + a_2 \dot{q}_2 + \ldots + a_k \dot{q}_k + a, \\ \dot{y} &= b_1 \dot{q}_1 + b_2 \dot{q}_2 + \ldots + b_k \dot{q}_k + b, \\ &\ldots\ldots\ldots\ldots\ldots\ldots\ldots\ldots\ldots\ldots\end{aligned}\right\} \quad \ldots\ldots\ldots\ldots(4)$$

301. Generalised Coordinates. The parameters $q_1, q_2, \ldots, q_k$ are called the *generalised coordinates*: they are supposed to be such as suffice to express the configuration of the system at any instant. It may be remarked here that there are cases in which the motion can be expressed in terms of velocities (for example in the motion of a rigid body, the angular speeds of a body about its principal axes which are fixed in the body), unrelated to coordinates which fulfil this condition.

It is important to observe that the differential relations (3) may or may not be equivalent to a set of finite equations like (1). If they are, $a_1, a_2, \ldots, b_1, b_2, \ldots, c_1, c_2, \ldots$ must be partial differential coefficients

$\partial \phi/\partial q_1, \partial \phi/\partial q_2, \ldots, \partial \chi/\partial q_1, \partial \chi/\partial q_2, \ldots, \partial \psi/\partial q_1, \partial \psi/\partial q_2, \ldots$

of equations (1), § 301, and one set of conditions for this is

$$\left.\begin{aligned}\frac{\partial a_1}{\partial q_2}&=\frac{\partial a_2}{\partial q_1},\quad \frac{\partial a_1}{\partial q_3}=\frac{\partial a_3}{\partial q_1},\ldots,\\ \frac{\partial b_1}{\partial q_2}&=\frac{\partial b_2}{\partial q_1},\quad \frac{\partial b_1}{\partial q_3}=\frac{\partial b_3}{\partial q_1},\ldots,\\ &\ldots\ldots\ldots\ldots\ldots\ldots\ldots\ldots\end{aligned}\right\}\ldots\ldots\ldots\ldots\ldots(1)$$

The finite equations (1) and the differential relations (2) of § 299, then, express exactly the same thing—one can be derived from the other.

But if (1) and all the similar equations are not fulfilled by the coefficients $a_1, a_2, \ldots, b_1, b_2, \ldots$, a complete set of finite equations does not exist, and the conditions (2) of § 299 are not integrable, as a whole at least.

302. Holonomous and Not Holonomous Systems. Derivation of Lagrange's Equations. Lagrange's equations were given for the case of finite equations of condition, and that these exist has been tacitly assumed in most of the expositions of the subject since his time. That they "fail" for the case of non-integrable relations has been pointed out by several writers, and systems are now called *holonomous or not holonomous*, according as the constraints are or are not defined by finite equations.

We shall now derive the equations of Lagrange from the equations of motion of a system of free particles; as this mode of derivation shows very clearly where the assumption that the system is holonomous is introduced, and where, therefore, the process should be corrected if the system is not holonomous.

556   A TREATISE ON DYNAMICS.   [CH. X.

The equations of motion of a system of particles are of the type
$$m\ddot{x} = X, \quad m\ddot{y} = Y, \quad m\ddot{z} = Z, \quad \ldots\ldots\ldots\ldots(1)$$
and, of course, these are the equations of a particle of a connected system, when the forces due to the connections are included in X, Y, Z.

Now, from (4), § 299, find the values of $\ddot{x}$, $\ddot{y}$, $\ddot{z}$. They are
$$\ddot{x} = a_1\ddot{q}_1 + a_2\ddot{q}_2 + \ldots + a_k\ddot{q}_k + \dot{a}_1\dot{q}_1 + \dot{a}_2\dot{q}_2 + \ldots + \dot{a}_k\dot{q}_k + \dot{a}, \ldots(2)$$
with similar equations for $\ddot{y}$, $\ddot{z}$. Thus we get
$$\left.\begin{array}{l}\Sigma\{m(a_1\ddot{x}+b_1\ddot{y}+c_1\ddot{z})\} = \Sigma(a_1X+b_1Y+c_1Z),\\ \Sigma\{m(a_2\ddot{x}+b_2\ddot{y}+c_2\ddot{z})\} = \Sigma(a_2X+b_2Y+c_2Z),\\ \ldots\ldots\ldots\ldots\ldots\ldots\ldots\ldots\ldots\ldots\ldots\ldots\ldots\ldots\ldots\end{array}\right\} \ldots(3)$$

The quantities on the right-hand side are called the *generalised forces* of the Lagrangian system, and will be denoted in what follows by Q_1, Q_2, ...

It will be observed that, by (3), § 300,
$$\left.\begin{array}{l}\Sigma(X\,\delta x + Y\,\delta y + Z\,\delta z)\\ = \Sigma(a_1X+b_1Y+c_1Z)\delta q_1 + \Sigma(a_2X+b_2Y+c_2Z)\delta q_2\\ \quad + \ldots + \Sigma(a_kX+b_kY+c_kZ)\delta q_k\\ = Q_1\delta q_1 + Q_2\delta q_2 + \ldots + Q_k\delta q_k.\end{array}\right\} \ldots(4)$$

Thus any Q is the coefficient of δq in the expression $Q\,\delta q$ for the work done in a possible variation of the parameter q, and is not necessarily a force in the true dynamical sense; *e.g.* if δq is an angular displacement Q is a moment of dynamical force or a couple. Q does not depend on any of the *inactive* forces, that is, forces such as those due to guides and constraints which are invariable. Thus the results obtained from a system of free particles hold for a constrained system.

Now, by (2),
$$\left.\begin{array}{l}a_1\ddot{x}+b_1\ddot{y}+c_1\ddot{z} = (a_1^2+b_1^2+c_1^2)\ddot{q}_1 + (a_1a_2+b_1b_2+c_1c_2)\ddot{q}_2 + \ldots\\ \quad + a_1(\dot{a}_1\dot{q}_1+\dot{a}_2\dot{q}_2+\ldots) + b_1(\dot{b}_1\dot{q}_1+\dot{b}_2\dot{q}_2+\ldots)\\ \quad + \ldots + a_1\dot{a} + b_1\dot{b} + c_1\dot{c}.\end{array}\right\} (5)$$

303. K.E. in terms of Generalised Coordinates. The expression of the right-hand side of this equation, by means of the kinetic energy transformed to generalised coordinates, is the characteristic feature of the **Lagrangian** equations. To effect this transformation we substitute on the right-hand side of the equation

$$T = \tfrac{1}{2}\Sigma\{m(\dot{x}^2 + \dot{y}^2 + \dot{z}^2)\} \quad \ldots\ldots\ldots\ldots\ldots\ldots(1)$$

the values of $\dot{x}, \dot{y}, \dot{z}$ given by (4), §299. Thus we obtain

$$T = \tfrac{1}{2}\{A_{11}\dot{q}_1^2 + 2A_{12}\dot{q}_1\dot{q}_2 + 2A_{13}\dot{q}_1\dot{q}_3 + \ldots$$
$$+ A_{22}\dot{q}_2^2 + 2A_{23}\dot{q}_2\dot{q}_3 + \ldots + A_1\dot{q}_1 + A_2\dot{q}_2 + \ldots + A_k\dot{q}_k + A_0\}, \ldots(2)$$

where $A_{11}, A_{12}, \ldots, A_{22}, A_{23}, \ldots$ are functions of the coordinates $q_1, q_2, \ldots, q_k$. The expression thus consists of a homogeneous quadratic function of the speeds $\dot{q}_1, \dot{q}_2, \ldots, \dot{q}_k$, a linear part, $A_1\dot{q}_1 + A_2\dot{q}_2 + \ldots + A_k\dot{q}_k$, and a term A_0 which is a function of the *coordinates* only. These will be referred to below as T_2, T_1, T_0.

304. Generalised Components of Momentum. We notice in the first place that from (2), §303, we have

$$\left.\begin{aligned}
\frac{\partial T}{\partial \dot{q}_1} &= A_{11}\dot{q}_1 + A_{12}\dot{q}_2 + \ldots + A_{1k}\dot{q}_k + A_1, \\
\frac{\partial T}{\partial \dot{q}_2} &= A_{12}\dot{q}_1 + A_{22}\dot{q}_2 + \ldots + A_{2k}\dot{q}_k + A_2, \\
&\ldots\ldots\ldots\ldots\ldots\ldots\ldots\ldots\ldots\ldots\ldots\ldots \\
\frac{\partial T}{\partial \dot{q}_k} &= A_{1k}\dot{q}_1 + A_{2k}\dot{q}_2 + \ldots + A_{kk}\dot{q}_k + A_k.
\end{aligned}\right\} \ldots\ldots\ldots(1)$$

The expressions on the right-hand side are called the *generalised components of momentum*, and will be denoted in what follows by $p_1, p_2, \ldots, p_k$. Equations (1) enable the speeds $\dot{q}_1, \dot{q}_2, \ldots, \dot{q}_k$ to be expressed in terms of $p_1, p_2, \ldots, p_k$ and the coefficients $A_{11}, A_{12}, \ldots$ (which are functions of the coordinates $q_1, q_2, \ldots$), and therefore also the kinetic energy to be expressed in terms of $p_1, p_2, \ldots, p_k$ and functions of the coordinates. It is to be observed that the determinant $(A_{11}, A_{22}, \ldots, A_{kk})$ of equations (1) cannot vanish, since if it did the values of $\dot{q}_1, \dot{q}_2, \ldots, \dot{q}_k$ given by these equations would be zero, and T would be zero.

305. Equations for Holonomous System. Modified Equations for Not Holonomous System. Now we have, taking first the coefficients a_1, b_1, c_1,

$$a_1\ddot{x} + b_1\ddot{y} + c_1\ddot{z} = \frac{d}{dt}(a_1\dot{x} + b_1\dot{y} + c_1\dot{z}) - (\dot{a}_1\dot{x} + \dot{b}_1\dot{y} + \dot{c}_1\dot{z}),$$

and therefore

$$\Sigma\{m(a_1\ddot{x} + b_1\ddot{y} + c_1\ddot{z})\} = \frac{d}{dt}[\{\Sigma m(a_1\dot{x} + b_1\dot{y} + c_1\dot{z})\}] \\ - \Sigma\{m(\dot{a}_1\dot{x} + \dot{b}_1\dot{y} + \dot{c}_1\dot{z})\}. \quad \ldots(1)$$

But if we form $\frac{1}{2}\Sigma\{m(\dot{x}^2 + \dot{y}^2 + \dot{z}^2)\}$, or T, from the values of $\dot{x}$, $\dot{y}$, $\dot{z}$ given in (4), §300, we get

$$\Sigma\{m(a_1\dot{x} + b_1\dot{y} + c_1\dot{z})\} = \frac{\partial T}{\partial \dot{q}}, \quad \ldots\ldots\ldots\ldots(2)$$

and therefore obtain

$$\Sigma\{m(a_1\ddot{x} + b_1\ddot{y} + c_1\ddot{z})\} = \frac{d}{dt}\frac{\partial T}{\partial \dot{q}} - \Sigma\{m(\dot{a}_1\dot{x} + \dot{b}_1\dot{y} + \dot{c}_1\dot{z})\}. \quad (3)$$

Again, by the value of T thus formed

$$\Sigma\{m(\dot{a}_1\dot{x} + \dot{b}_1\dot{y} + \dot{c}_1z)\} \\ = \Sigma\left(\frac{\partial T}{\partial \dot{x}}\frac{d}{dt}\frac{\partial x}{\partial q_1} + \frac{\partial T}{\partial \dot{y}}\frac{d}{dt}\frac{\partial y}{\partial q_1} + \frac{\partial T}{\partial \dot{z}}\frac{d}{dt}\frac{\partial z}{\partial q_1}\right), \quad \ldots\ldots(4)$$

provided the relations (1), § 300, *are derivable from a set of k finite equations*, for then a_1, b_1, c_1 are partial differential coefficients $\partial x/\partial q_1, \ldots$ of x_1, y_1, z_1 expressed as there shown. Now

$$\frac{d}{dt}\frac{\partial x}{\partial q} = \frac{\partial}{\partial q_1}\frac{\partial x}{\partial q}\dot{q}_1 + \frac{\partial}{\partial q_2}\frac{\partial x}{\partial q}\dot{q}_2 + \ldots + \frac{\partial}{\partial q_k}\frac{\partial x}{\partial q}\dot{q}_k + \frac{\partial}{\partial t}\frac{\partial x}{\partial q}\ldots(5)$$

Hence, since $\partial x/\partial q$ is supposed to be the partial derivative with respect to q of an explicit function of $q_1, q_2, \ldots, q_k$, we get

$$\frac{\partial}{\partial q_1}\frac{\partial x}{\partial q} = \frac{\partial}{\partial q}\frac{\partial x}{\partial q_1}, \quad \frac{\partial}{\partial q_2}\frac{\partial x}{\partial q} = \frac{\partial}{\partial q}\frac{\partial x}{\partial q_2}, \ldots, \frac{\partial}{\partial t}\frac{\partial x}{\partial q} = \frac{\partial}{\partial q}\frac{\partial x}{\partial t},$$

and therefore

$$\frac{d}{dt}\frac{\partial x}{\partial q} = \frac{\partial}{\partial q}\left(\frac{\partial x}{\partial q_1}\dot{q}_1 + \frac{\partial x}{\partial q_2}\dot{q}_2 + \ldots + \frac{\partial x}{\partial q_k}\dot{q}_k + \frac{\partial x}{\partial t}\right), \quad \ldots\ldots(6)$$

and similarly for $\dfrac{d}{dt}\dfrac{\partial y}{\partial q}$, $\dfrac{d}{dt}\dfrac{\partial z}{\partial q}$.

LAGRANGE'S EQUATIONS.

Thus we get

$$\frac{d}{dt}\frac{\partial x}{\partial q_1}=\frac{\partial \dot{x}}{\partial q_1},\quad \frac{d}{dt}\frac{\partial y}{\partial q_1}=\frac{\partial \dot{y}}{\partial q_1},\quad \frac{d}{dt}\frac{dz}{\partial q_1}=\frac{\partial \dot{z}}{\partial q_1},\quad\ldots\ldots\ldots(7)$$

and therefore

$$\Sigma\{m(\dot{a}_1\dot{x}+\dot{b}_1\dot{y}+\dot{c}_1\dot{z})\}=\frac{\partial T}{\partial \dot{x}}\frac{\partial \dot{x}}{\partial q_1}+\frac{\partial T}{\partial \dot{y}}\frac{\partial \dot{y}}{\partial q_1}+\frac{\partial T}{\partial \dot{z}}\frac{\partial \dot{z}}{\partial q_1}=\frac{\partial T}{\partial q_1}.\quad(8)$$

Therefore, finally, (4) can be written, on the supposition italicised above, in the form

$$\frac{d}{dt}\frac{\partial T}{\partial \dot{q}_1}-\frac{\partial T}{\partial q_1}=Q_1.\quad\ldots\ldots\ldots\ldots\ldots(9)$$

Similar equations are obtained for the other coordinates such as

$$\frac{d}{dt}\frac{\partial T}{\partial \dot{q}_2}-\frac{\partial T}{\partial q_2}=Q_2,\quad\ldots\ldots\ldots\ldots\ldots(10)$$

and so on. These are Lagrange's equations. The kinetic energy T is supposed expressed as a function of the generalised coordinates $q_1, q_2, \ldots$, and of the speeds of these coordinates $\dot{q}_1, \dot{q}_2, \ldots$; and is, as stated above, in the most general case the sum of a homogeneous quadratic function and a linear function of these speeds, with a function of the coordinates only added.

The forces X, Y, Z are in many cases derivable, in part at least, from a function V of the coordinates which we call the potential energy, and which may also contain the time explicitly. We have then, if Q_1' be the part of the force independent of V,

$$\left.\begin{aligned}\Sigma(a_1X+b_1Y+c_1Z_1)-Q_1'&=-\Sigma\left(a_1\frac{\partial V}{\partial x}+b_1\frac{\partial V}{\partial y}+c_1\frac{\partial V}{\partial z}\right)\\ &=-\Sigma\left(\frac{\partial x}{\partial q_1}\frac{\partial V}{\partial x}+\frac{\partial y}{\partial q_1}\frac{\partial V}{\partial y}+\frac{\partial z}{\partial q_1}\frac{\partial V}{\partial z}\right)=-\frac{\partial V}{\partial q_1},\end{aligned}\right\}\quad(11)$$

provided, as before, that $a_1=\partial x/\partial q_1, \ldots$. If this proviso is not fulfilled, the part of the force which depends on V cannot be written in the form $-\partial V/\partial q_1$.

We get thus the equations of motion of a holonomous system

$$\left.\begin{array}{l}\dfrac{d}{dt}\dfrac{\partial T}{\partial \dot{q}_1}-\dfrac{\partial T}{\partial q_1}+\dfrac{\partial V}{\partial q_1}=Q'_1,\\[6pt]\dfrac{d}{dt}\dfrac{\partial T}{\partial \dot{q}_2}-\dfrac{\partial T}{\partial q_2}+\dfrac{\partial V}{\partial q_2}=Q'_2,\\[2pt]\dotfill\end{array}\right\}\quad\ldots\ldots\ldots\ldots(12)$$

If the system is not holonomous, we have, by (3), § 305,

$$\left.\begin{array}{l}\dfrac{d}{dt}\dfrac{\partial T}{\partial \dot{q}_1}-\Sigma\{m(\dot{a}_1\dot{x}+\dot{b}_1\dot{y}+\dot{c}_1\dot{z})\}=Q_1,\\[6pt]\dfrac{d}{dt}\dfrac{\partial T}{\partial \dot{q}_2}-\Sigma\{m(\dot{a}_2\dot{x}+\dot{b}_2\dot{y}+\dot{c}_2\dot{z})\}=Q_2,\\[2pt]\dotfill\end{array}\right\}\quad\ldots\ldots(13)$$

where the summations are taken for all the particles of the system. These equations are applicable in all cases.

In the very common case in which besides the finite equations of condition certain non-integrable relations also hold (as in the problem of the hoop discussed in the preceding chapter) the generalised coordinates can be reduced in number by taking account of the latter relations by the method of multipliers, as used in § 299 above. The equations of motion are then found by expressing the kinetic energy in terms of the remaining coordinates and proceeding in the usual manner.

306. The Lagrangian Function or Kinetic Potential. If we write $T-V=L$, we can, since V does not contain any of the speeds $\dot{q}_1, \dot{q}_2, \ldots$, put equations (12), § 305, in the form

$$\left.\begin{array}{l}\dfrac{d}{dt}\dfrac{\partial L}{\partial \dot{q}_1}-\dfrac{\partial L}{\partial q_1}=Q'_1,\\[6pt]\dfrac{d}{dt}\dfrac{\partial L}{\partial \dot{q}_2}-\dfrac{\partial L}{\partial q_2}=Q'_2,\\[2pt]\dotfill\end{array}\right\}\quad\ldots\ldots\ldots\ldots(1)$$

so that the system may be regarded as having only *kinetic* energy of amount $T-V$, that is the potential energy, V, *with its sign changed* may be regarded as a part of the kinetic energy of the system, destitute of terms involving the $\dot{q}$ s. Thus, for aught we know, the energy of configuration of a system may be really kinetic energy of changing (but unobserved and uncontrollable) coordinates of a system linked with that of which the motion and configuration are being considered.

L is called the Lagrangian function and sometimes the *kinetic potential*. It is interesting to consider its value for a system which may be divided into two parts for which the coordinates are $q_1, q_2, \ldots, q_i$ and $s_1, s_2, \ldots, s_j$ respectively, and which are such that the T contains no product of the form $\dot{q}\dot{s}$. The kinetic energy may therefore be divided into two parts T', T'', one which contains only squares and products of the $\dot{q}$ s and another which contains only squares and products of the $\dot{s}$ s. For a q-equation of motion we have

$$\frac{d}{dt}\frac{\partial T'}{\partial \dot{q}} - \frac{\partial(T'+T'')}{\partial q} + \frac{\partial V}{\partial q} = Q', \quad \ldots\ldots\ldots\ldots(2)$$

or, if $U = V - T''$, as

$$\frac{d}{dt}\frac{\partial T'}{\partial \dot{q}} - \frac{\partial T'}{\partial q} + \frac{\partial U}{\partial q} = Q'. \quad \ldots\ldots\ldots\ldots(3)$$

Now, so far as the motion depending on the q s is concerned, the part T'' with its sign changed may be classed with the potential energy V. Thus, as Sir J. J. Thomson has suggested, the potential energy of a system may be kinetic energy depending on speeds of coordinates distinct from the q s, and incapable of direct observation, but involving the q-coordinates, so that the potential energy is a function of the configuration of the parts of the system the motion of which can be traced.

In this case the value of L is $T' - U$; that is, of course, $T' + T'' - V$, or $T - V$ as before.

Ex. To illustrate what precedes, we take the motion of a particle of mass m in a plane curve. If at time t the radius-vector drawn from a fixed point be of length r, and make an angle θ with an axis of x drawn from the same origin, the coordinates of the particle are $x = r\cos\theta$, $y = r\sin\theta$, and therefore

$$\dot{x} = \dot{r}\cos\theta - r\dot{\theta}\sin\theta, \quad \dot{y} = \dot{r}\sin\theta + r\dot{\theta}\cos\theta.$$

Hence, for the kinetic energy T, we have

$$2T = m\{(\dot{r}\cos\theta - r\dot{\theta}\sin\theta)^2 + (\dot{r}\sin\theta + r\dot{\theta}\cos\theta)^2\}$$

or $\qquad 2T = m\{\dot{r}^2 + r^2\dot{\theta}^2\}.\qquad\qquad\qquad\ldots\ldots\ldots(4)$

If we apply (13), § 305, to the problem of finding the r, θ equations of motion of the particle, we have to take the first expression for the kinetic energy. We obtain

$$\frac{d}{dt}\frac{\partial T}{\partial \dot{r}} = m\ddot{r}.$$

We have to subtract from this the quantity (derived from (4)),

$$m(\dot{r}\cos\theta - r\dot{\theta}\sin\theta)\frac{d}{dt}(\cos\theta) + m(\dot{r}\sin\theta + r\dot{\theta}\cos\theta)\frac{d}{dt}(\sin\theta)\,;$$

that is, $mr\dot{\theta}^2$, which could, of course, be obtained at once by writing down $\partial T/\partial r$. Hence the r-equation of motion is

$$m(\ddot{r} - r\dot{\theta}^2) = R\,;$$

where R is the applied force in the outward direction along r.

For the θ-equation we have

$$\frac{d}{dt}\frac{\partial T}{\partial \dot{\theta}} = m(r^2\ddot{\theta} + 2r\dot{r}\dot{\theta}).$$

By (13), § 305, we have to subtract from this

$$-m(\dot{r}\cos\theta - r\dot{\theta}\sin\theta)\frac{d}{dt}(r\sin\theta) + m(\dot{r}\sin\theta + r\dot{\theta}\cos\theta)\frac{d}{dt}(r\cos\theta)$$

or zero. Thus the θ-equation of motion is

$$m(r^2\ddot{\theta} + 2r\dot{r}\dot{\theta}) = \Theta\,;$$

where Θ is the generalised force perpendicular to the radius-vector.

But $\partial T/\partial\theta = 0$, and so the ordinary form of Lagrange's equations gives the same result.

This example illustrates the important point that the form of the equations of motion given in (13), § 305, cannot be applied to the kinetic energy as given in the equation

$$T = \tfrac{1}{2}m(\dot{r}^2 + r^2\dot{\theta}^2).$$

The operations indicated in the second terms on the left of the form,

$$\Sigma\{m(\dot{a}_1\dot{x} + \dot{b}_1\dot{y} + \dot{c}_1\dot{z})\},$$

must be performed with reference to the fundamental equations from which the expression here written for the kinetic energy has been derived, that is, *the equations which embody the conditions to which the system is subject*. The axes of reference along which the speed components $\dot{r}$, $r\dot{\theta}$ are taken are specialised in such a way that in the formation of T the quantities $\sin\theta$, $\cos\theta$, which appear in the values of $\dot{x}$, $\dot{y}$ with respect to unspecialised axes, have been replaced by 0 and 1; and unless we go back to the fundamental expressions $\dot{r}\cos\theta - r\dot{\theta}\sin\theta$, $\dot{r}\sin\theta + r\dot{\theta}\cos\theta$, the process of equations (13), § 305, cannot be carried out.

It will be observed that in this example we have

$$\frac{\partial}{\partial \theta}(\cos\theta) = -\frac{\partial}{\partial r}(r\sin\theta), \quad \frac{\partial}{\partial \theta}(\sin\theta) = \frac{\partial}{\partial r}(r\cos\theta),$$

so that the conditions [(1), § 301] of integrability are fulfilled, and therefore it is impossible to proceed in the ordinary way by calculating $\partial T/\partial r$, and subtracting it from $m\ddot{r}$. The functions of r and θ involved in $\tfrac{1}{2}m\{(\dot{r}\cos\theta - r\dot{\theta}\sin\theta)^2 + (\dot{r}\sin\theta + r\dot{\theta}\cos\theta)^2\}$ and in $\tfrac{1}{2}m(\dot{r}^2 + r^2\,^2)$ are the same, and so in the latter case the ordinary process remains applicable, though then, *apparently*, the integrability conditions are unfulfilled. This explains why in many cases, as in the example first given and in others, the ordinary form of Lagrange's equations is applicable and the form in (13) is not. The latter can only be applied when the expressions for the speed components, whatever they may be, are those which arise from the kinematic conditions of the system. Different modes of breaking up the kinetic energy into a sum of squares correspond in general to different sets of conditions and involve different sets of forces; for two entirely different cases of motion may correspond to the same expressions for T and V, if one be holonomous and the other not.

307. Examples on the Lagrangian Equations.

Ex. 1. By the equations of the type

$$\dot{a}_i = \frac{\partial a_i}{\partial q_1}\dot{q}_1 + \frac{\partial a_i}{\partial q_2}\dot{q}_2 + \ldots, \quad \frac{\partial T}{\partial q_i} = \Sigma\left\{m\left(\dot{x}\frac{\partial \dot{x}}{\partial q_i} + \dot{y}\frac{\partial \dot{y}}{\partial q_i} + \dot{z}\frac{\partial \dot{z}}{\partial q_i}\right)\right\},$$

prove that equations (13), § 305, can be put in the form

$$\frac{d}{dt}\frac{\partial T}{\partial \dot{q}_i} - \frac{\partial T}{\partial q_i} - \Sigma\left[(m\ddot{x})\left\{\dot{q}_1\left(\frac{\partial a_i}{\partial q_1} - \frac{\partial a_1}{\partial q_i}\right) + \dot{q}_2\left(\frac{\partial a_i}{\partial q_2} - \frac{\partial a_2}{\partial q_i}\right) + \ldots\right\}\right]$$
$$- \Sigma\left[(m\ddot{y})\left\{\dot{q}_1\left(\frac{\partial b_i}{\partial q_1} - \frac{\partial b_1}{\partial q_i}\right) + \dot{q}_2\left(\frac{\partial b_i}{\partial q_2} - \frac{\partial b_2}{\partial q_i}\right) + \ldots\right\}\right]$$
$$- \Sigma\left[(m\ddot{z})\left\{\dot{q}_1\left(\frac{\partial c_i}{\partial q_1} - \frac{\partial c_1}{\partial q_i}\right) + \dot{q}_2\left(\frac{\partial c_i}{\partial q_2} - \frac{\partial c_2}{\partial q_i}\right) + \ldots\right\}\right] = 0,$$

which reduces to the ordinary form when the integrability conditions are fulfilled.

Ex. 2. A simple pendulum is hung from a fixed point and is of constantly varying length. Find the equations of motion.

Let r be the length, θ the inclination of the thread to the vertical, and ψ the inclination of the vertical plane containing the thread to a fixed vertical plane, all at time t. The components of speed are $\dot{r}$, $r\dot{\theta}$, $r\dot{\psi}\sin\theta$, and the kinetic and potential energies are given by

$$T = \tfrac{1}{2}m(\dot{r}^2 + r^2\dot{\theta}^2 + r^2\dot{\psi}^2\sin^2\theta), \quad V = -mgr\cos\theta.$$

Hence, since the system is holonomous, we find

$$\partial T/\partial \dot{r} = m\dot{r}, \qquad \partial T/\partial \dot{\theta} = mr^2\dot{\theta}, \qquad \partial T/\partial \dot{\psi} = mr^2\dot{\psi}\sin^2\theta,$$
$$\partial T/\partial \psi = 0, \qquad \partial T/\partial r = r\dot{\theta}^2, \qquad \partial V/\partial r = -mg\cos\theta,$$
$$\partial T/\partial \theta = r^2\dot{\psi}^2\sin\theta\cos\theta, \quad \partial V/\partial\theta = mgr\sin\theta,$$

and the equations of motion are

$$\ddot{r} - r\dot{\theta}^2 = g\cos\theta,$$
$$r\ddot{\theta} + 2\dot{r}\dot{\theta} + r\dot{\psi}^2\sin\theta\cos\theta = -g\sin\theta,$$
$$r\ddot{\psi}\sin\theta + 2\dot{r}\dot{\psi}\sin\theta + 2r\dot{\psi}\dot{\theta}\cos\theta = 0.$$

If the motion is in one plane $\dot{\psi} = 0$, and the equations are

$$\ddot{r} - r\dot{\theta}^2 = g\cos\theta,$$
$$r\ddot{\theta} + 2\dot{r}\dot{\theta} = -g\sin\theta,$$

and if $\dot{r}$ be constantly zero, we obtain the equation of the ordinary simple pendulum

$$\ddot{\theta} + \frac{g}{r}\sin\theta = 0.$$

Ex. 3. A particle moves without friction on a straight line which turns uniformly about a given vertical straight line: to find the motion.

Let the turning line be inclined at the angle α to the vertical, and r be the distance of the position of the particle at time t from the point of intersection of the turning line with the plane drawn so as to contain the fixed vertical and be perpendicular to the horizontal projection of the turning line, a the distance of that projection from the fixed vertical. Then we have for the kinetic and potential energies

$$\dot{r}^2 + (a^2 + r^2\sin^2\alpha)\omega^2,$$

and $\quad T = \tfrac{1}{2}m\{\dot{r}^2 - 2\omega a\dot{r}\sin\alpha + (a^2 + r^2\sin^2\alpha)\omega^2\}, \quad V = -mgr\cos\alpha.$
Hence

$$\frac{\partial T}{\partial \dot{r}} = m\dot{r} - m\omega a\sin\alpha, \quad \frac{\partial T}{\partial r} = mr\omega^2\sin^2\alpha, \quad \frac{\partial V}{\partial r} = -mg\cos\alpha.$$

The equation of motion is therefore

$$\ddot{r} - r\omega^2\sin^2\alpha = g\cos\alpha.$$

The particle moves as it would if the turning line were fixed and a repulsion $m\omega^2 r\sin^2\alpha$ were applied.

§ 307]   EXAMPLES.   565

Ex. 4. A particle moves without friction on a right circular cylinder with axis vertical, the radius of which (initially a) increases uniformly with the time : to find the motion.

At time t the radius r is $a(1+kt)$, where k is a constant. Taking coordinates from an origin on the axis of the cylinder (x, y horizontal, and z downward), we get $x = a(1+kt)\cos\theta$, $y = a(1+kt)\sin\theta$, and therefore

$$\dot{x} = -a(1+kt)\sin\theta \cdot \dot\theta + ak\cos\theta, \quad \dot{y} = a(1+kt)\dot\theta\cos\theta + ak\sin\theta,$$

so that $T = \tfrac{1}{2}ma^2\{(1+kt)^2\dot\theta^2 + k^2\} + \dot{z}^2, \quad V = mg(z_0 - z),$

if $z = z_0$, initially. Hence $\partial T/\partial\dot\theta = ma^2(1+kt)^2\dot\theta$, and the equations of motion are

$$\frac{d}{dt}\{a^2(1+kt)^2\dot\theta\} = 0, \quad \ddot{z} = g.$$

Thus $a^2(1+kt)^2\dot\theta = a^2\theta_0, \quad z = \tfrac{1}{2}gt^2 + bt + c.$

This is an example of constraint varying with t.

Ex. 5. A rigid body is suspended from a fixed support by means of a piece of steel wire attached at a point in a principal axis, OC, of the body through the centroid, and so short that it may be taken as untwistable, while yielding freely to bending forces in all vertical planes containing the wire. It is required to find the equations of motion with reference to OC, and two other axes, one OD at right angles to the vertical plane through OC, and a third OE perpendicular to these.

Take fixed axes $Oxyz$ through the point of support coinciding with the positions of the principal axes OA, OB, OC at time t, and denote the angular speeds and moments of inertia about them by p, q, r, A, B, C. Then, if $\dot{x}$, $\dot{y}$, $\dot{z}$ be the component speeds of a particle at x, y, z, we have for $\dot{x}$, $\dot{y}$, $\dot{z}$,

$$\dot{x} = qz - ry, \quad \dot{y} = rx - pz, \quad \dot{z} = py - qx,$$

and $T = \tfrac{1}{2}\Sigma[m\{(qz-ry)^2 + (rx-pz)^2 + (py-qx)^2\}],$

which do not depend on the special conditions of suspension.

From this we obtain

$$\frac{\partial T}{\partial p} = \Sigma[m\{-(rx-pz)z + (py-qx)y\}],$$

and therefore, since the axes of reference are principal axes,

$$\frac{d}{dt}\frac{\partial T}{\partial p} = \Sigma[m\{-\dot{z}(rx-pz) - z(-\dot{p}z + r\dot{x} - p\dot{z})\}]$$
$$+ \Sigma[m\{\dot{y}(py-qx) + y(\dot{p}y + p\dot{y} - q\dot{x})\}].$$

If now we subtract from this, according to (13), § 305, the expression $\Sigma[m\{-\dot{z}(rx-pz) + \dot{y}(py-qx)\}]$, and take account of

$$\dot{y} = rx - pz, \quad \dot{z} = py - qx, \quad Aq = \Sigma\{m(\dot{x}z - \dot{z}x)\}, \quad Cr = \Sigma\{m(\dot{y}x - \dot{x}y)\},$$

we get $A\dot{p} - (B-C)qr$, which is to be equated to the moment L of external forces about the axis for which the angular speed is p and the M.I. is A. Thus
$$A\dot{p} - (B-C)qr = L,$$
one of Euler's equations (§ 170). The other two equations can of course be obtained in the same manner, and may be inferred from this.

Now, taking account of the suspension, we see that the body must, if the wire do not twist, change the inclination θ to the vertical of the principal axis, to which the suspension is fixed, by turning about a horizontal axis, OD say, at right angles to OC, and that the angular speed about OC is $\dot{\psi}(\cos\theta - 1)$. Let the axis OA (angular speed p) make an angle ψ with OD, then ψ will change with angular speed $\dot{\psi}$. We get thus for the angular speeds about OA, OB, OC,

$p = \dot{\theta}\cos\psi + \dot{\psi}\sin\theta\sin\psi$, $q = -\dot{\theta}\sin\psi + \dot{\psi}\sin\theta\cos\psi$, $r = \dot{\psi}(\cos\theta - 1)$;

and if at the instant $\psi = 0$, $p = \dot{\theta}$, $q = \dot{\psi}\sin\theta$, $r = \dot{\psi}\cos\theta$.

The p-equation of motion is therefore
$$A(\ddot{\theta} + \dot{\psi}^2\sin\theta) + (B-C)\dot{\psi}^2\sin\theta(1-\cos\theta) = -mgh\sin\theta.$$

The q-equation is, since $rp = \dot{\psi}\dot{\theta}(\cos\theta - 1)$,
$$B\{\ddot{\psi}\sin\theta - \dot{\theta}\dot{\psi}(1-\cos\theta)\} + (C-A)\dot{\theta}\dot{\psi}(1-\cos\theta) = 0.$$

The third equation of motion is
$$C\{\ddot{\psi}(1-\cos\theta) + \dot{\theta}\dot{\psi}\sin\theta\} + (A-B)\dot{\theta}\dot{\psi}\sin\theta = 0.$$

If the axis OC be one of symmetry, the first two equations become
$$A\dot{\theta} + \{2A - C - (A-C)\cos\theta\}\dot{\psi}^2\sin\theta = mgh\sin\theta,$$
$$A\ddot{\psi}\sin\theta + (C-2A)\dot{\theta}\dot{\psi}(1-\cos\theta) = 0.$$

[For the discussion of the motion of this body when a fly-wheel with its axis of rotation along the axis of symmetry is contained within the bob of a pendulum, see a paper on Lagrange's equations, by A. Gray, in *Proc. R.S.E.* vol. xxix. 1909. See also §§ 284, 287.]

Ex. 6. Find the equations of a rigid body turning about a fixed point O under gravity. [Equations of an unsymmetrical top.]

Here the body is left free from restriction imposed by its mode of support. Let α, β, γ be the direction cosines of the downward vertical with reference to the principal axes through O in their positions at time t, and ξ, η, ζ be the coordinates of the centroid with the same axes. Then the vertical force mg gives components $mg(\alpha, \beta, \gamma)$ along the axes, and the moments of these forces about the axes are $mg(\gamma\eta - \beta\zeta)$, $mg(\alpha\zeta - \gamma\xi)$, $mg(\beta\xi - \alpha\eta)$, and therefore the equations of motion are

$$A\dot{p} - (B-C)qr = mg(\gamma\eta - \beta\zeta),$$
$$B\dot{q} - (C-A)rp = mg(\alpha\zeta - \gamma\xi),$$
$$C\dot{r} - (A-B)pq = mg(\beta\xi - \alpha\eta).$$

But α, β, γ are also functions of the time; the axes are carried with the body, and hence, by § 15, we have, since a point on the vertical through O remains at rest,

$$\dot{\alpha} - \gamma q + \beta r = 0, \quad \dot{\beta} - \alpha r + \gamma p = 0, \quad \dot{\gamma} - \beta p + \alpha q = 0,$$

with, of course, the condition $\alpha^2 + \beta^2 + \gamma^2 = 1$.

308. Appell's Dynamical Equations. A new system of dynamical equations has been given by M. Appell (*Méc. Ration.* t. ii.) which are applicable to both holonomous and not holonomous systems. If we square equations (2), § 302, and form the sum

$$S = \tfrac{1}{2}\Sigma\{m(\ddot{x}^2 + \ddot{y}^2 + \ddot{z}^2)\}, \quad \ldots\ldots\ldots\ldots\ldots\ldots(1)$$

the "kinetic energy of the accelerations," as it has been called by analogy, for the whole system, we express the function S in terms of the generalised accelerations and speeds, and of the quantities $a_1, \dot{a}_1, a_2, \dot{a}_2, \ldots, b_1, \dot{b}_1, \ldots$, and clearly

$$\frac{\partial S}{\partial \ddot{q}_i} = \Sigma\{m(a_i\ddot{x} + b_i\ddot{y} + c_i\ddot{z})\}.$$

Hence we get

$$\frac{\partial S}{\partial \ddot{q}_1} = Q_1, \quad \frac{\partial S}{\partial \ddot{q}_2} = Q_2, \quad \ldots, \quad \frac{\partial S}{\partial \ddot{q}_k} = Q_k. \quad \ldots\ldots\ldots\ldots(2)$$

The partial differential coefficients are most conveniently formed in practice by multiplying, say for $\partial S/\partial q_i$, the first of (2), § 302, by ma_i, the second by mb_i, and the third by mc_i, and similarly for all the particles; the sum of these products is $\partial S/\partial q_i$.

These are Appell's equations. They are as a rule much more convenient than the modified Lagrangian equations (13) of § 305, for the solution of problems regarding not holonomous systems.

As an example we take again the motion of a particle in a plane dealt with in §305. Here, calculating $\ddot{x}$, $\ddot{y}$ and squaring, we get

$$S = \tfrac{1}{2}m(\ddot{r}^2 - 2\ddot{r}r\dot{\theta}^2 + r^2\dot{\theta}^4 + r^2\ddot{\theta}^2 + 4r\dot{r}\dot{\theta}\ddot{\theta} + 4\dot{r}^2\dot{\theta}^2),$$

and therefore

$$\frac{\partial S}{\partial \ddot{r}} = m(\ddot{r} - r\dot{\theta}^2), \quad \frac{\partial S}{\partial \ddot{\theta}} = m(r^2\ddot{\theta} + 2r\dot{r}\dot{\theta}) = m\frac{d}{dt}(r^2\dot{\theta}),$$

so that we get the same equations of motion as before.

309. Hamilton's Transformation of Lagrange's Equations. Lagrange's equations admit of a remarkable transformation due to Sir William Rowan Hamilton. Let equations (1), §304, be solved for $\dot{q}_1, \dot{q}_2, \ldots, \dot{q}_k$, in terms of the components of generalised momentum, and the values be substituted in the expression for T, which then becomes a function of the p s, made up, if the untransformed expression was, of a homogeneous quadratic part and a linear part in terms of the p s and a function of the coordinates.

The transformation of the equations of motion can be investigated by the following method, given by Jacobi (*Vorlesungen über Dynamik*). Consider the function K defined by the equation

$$K = \Sigma \dot{q}p - T_s, \quad \ldots\ldots\ldots\ldots\ldots\ldots\ldots(1)$$

where T_s is T supposed expressed in terms of the $\dot{q}$ s. [For clearness we shall denote T when expressed in terms of the speeds, the $\dot{q}$ s, by T_s, and when expressed in terms of the p s, the momenta, by T_m.]

Now, let the coordinates be subjected to slight variations $\delta q_1, \delta q_2, \ldots, q_k$, and the speeds to slight variations $\delta \dot{q}_1, \delta \dot{q}_2, \ldots, \delta \dot{q}_k$, which are all consistent with the conditions of the system as they exist at time t. Then, if K become in consequence $K + \delta K$, and T become $T + \delta T$, we have

$$\delta K = \Sigma(p \delta \dot{q} + \dot{q}\delta p) - \delta T_s, \quad \ldots\ldots\ldots\ldots\ldots(2)$$

where δp is the variation of p due to the changes $\delta \dot{q}$ and δq But

$$\delta T_s = \Sigma\left(\frac{\partial T_s}{\partial \dot{q}}\delta \dot{q} + \frac{\partial T_s}{\partial q}\delta q\right) = \Sigma(p\delta \dot{q}) + \Sigma\left(\frac{\partial T_s}{\partial q}\delta q\right),$$

and therefore, by (2),

$$\delta K = \Sigma(\dot{q}\delta p) - \Sigma\left(\frac{\partial T}{\partial q}\delta q\right). \quad\ldots\ldots\ldots\ldots\ldots\ldots(3)$$

So far, each δp has been taken as depending on the related δq and $\delta \dot{q}$, regarded as independent variations. But if we please, we may take the q s and p s as independent variables, that is the δq s and δp s may be arbitrarily assigned, and the change $\delta \dot{q}$ deduced from them. The expression for δK holds in this sense.

But now, if K be expressed in terms of the variables p and q, we have

$$\delta K = \Sigma \frac{\partial K_m}{\partial p}\delta p + \Sigma \frac{\partial K_m}{\partial q}\delta q, \quad\ldots\ldots\ldots\ldots\ldots\ldots(4)$$

and, since in each case the variations δp and δq are arbitrary, we may identify (4) with (3), and obtain the typical equations

$$\frac{\partial K}{\partial p} = \dot{q}, \quad \frac{\partial K_m}{\partial q} = -\frac{\partial T_s}{\partial q}, \quad \ldots \quad\ldots\ldots\ldots\ldots\ldots(5)$$

which are of great importance. They enable the typical Lagrangian equation $\dfrac{d}{dt}\dfrac{\partial T}{\partial \dot{q}} - \dfrac{\partial T}{\partial q} = Q$

to be transformed to Hamilton's form, which, written along with its companion equation, gives

$$\frac{dp}{dt} + \frac{\partial K}{\partial p} = Q, \quad \frac{\partial K}{\partial p} = \dot{q}, \quad\ldots\ldots\ldots\ldots\ldots\ldots\ldots(6)$$

where it is to be remembered that K is a function of the q s and the p s.

It will be noticed that if T_s is a homogeneous quadratic function of the $\dot{q}$ s, that is, if the equations which express x, y, z in terms of the q s do not involve the time explicitly, $K = 2T$, and that then (5) become

$$\frac{\partial T_m}{\partial p} = \dot{q}, \quad \frac{\partial T_m}{\partial q} = -\frac{\partial T_s}{\partial q}, \quad\ldots\ldots\ldots\ldots\ldots\ldots\ldots(7)$$

and Hamilton's equations are of the form

$$\frac{dp}{dt} + \frac{\partial T_m}{\partial q} = Q, \quad \frac{\partial T_m}{\partial p} = \dot{q}. \quad\ldots\ldots\ldots\ldots\ldots\ldots(8)$$

If we now suppose that each Q is derivable from a function V of the coordinates (and it may be also explicitly of t) by the relation $-\partial V/\partial q = Q$, and write H for $K+V$, where K is supposed expressed in terms of the ps, then, since V does not contain any p, we can write the two equations (8) in the form

$$\frac{dp}{dt} = -\frac{\partial H}{\partial q}, \quad \frac{dq}{dt} = \frac{\partial H}{\partial p}, \quad \ldots\ldots\ldots\ldots\ldots(9)$$

which typify Hamilton's so-called *canonical equations of motion* of a connected system. There are as many pairs of such equations as there are variables. It will be observed that the system is supposed to be holonomous. The function H is called *Hamilton's reciprocal function*.

Ex. 1. Verify the relations

$$\frac{\partial K}{\partial q} = -\frac{\partial T_s}{\partial q}, \quad \dot{q} = \frac{\partial K}{\partial p}$$

by direct differentiation.

On the left K is supposed to be a function of the ps and the qs. If the ps were replaced by their values given in (1), § 304, so that K is expressed in terms of the qs and the $\dot{q}$s, that is, becomes K_s, we should have

$$\frac{\partial K_s}{\partial q} = \Sigma \left(\frac{\partial K}{\partial p} \frac{\partial p}{\partial q} \right) + \frac{\partial K}{\partial q}.$$

But we have also by the definition of K,

$$\frac{\partial K_s}{\partial q} = \Sigma \left(\dot{q} \frac{\partial p}{\partial q} \right) - \frac{\partial T}{\partial q},$$

so that
$$\dot{q} = \frac{\partial K}{\partial p}, \quad \frac{\partial K}{\partial q} = -\frac{\partial T}{\partial q}.$$

Ex. 2. A particle moves in a plane and its positions are referred to axes Ox, Oy which turn with constant angular speed n about O. If the forces on the particle are derivable from a function V of x and y, it is required to find the equations of motion in the canonical form.

The equations of motion are, by § 14,

$$m(\ddot{x} - 2n\dot{y} - n^2 x) = -\frac{\partial V}{\partial x}, \quad m(\ddot{y} + 2n\dot{x} - n^2 y) = -\frac{\partial V}{\partial y}.$$

From these we can deduce, by multiplying the first equation by $\dot{x}$, the second by $\dot{y}$, and integrating, the equation

$$\frac{m}{2}(\dot{x}^2 + \dot{y}^2) + V - m\frac{n^2}{2}(x^2 + y^2) = \text{const.},$$

which is the equation of energy.

Now write $q_1 = x$, $q_2 = y$, $m(\dot{x} - ny) = p_1$, $m(\dot{y} + nx) = p_2$, and substitute in the energy equation. The result is

$$\frac{1}{2m}(p_1 + mnq_2)^2 + \frac{1}{2m}(p_2 - mnq_1)^2 + V - \tfrac{1}{2}mn^2(q_1^2 + q_2^2) = \text{const.}$$

The expression on the left is the function H for this case, and the canonical equations are

$$\dot{p}_1 = -\frac{\partial H}{\partial q_1}, \quad \dot{q}_1 = \frac{\partial H}{\partial p_1},$$
$$\dot{p}^2 = -\frac{\partial H}{\partial q_2}, \quad \dot{q}_2 = \frac{\partial H}{\partial p_2},$$

where q_1, q_2, p_1, p_2, H have the values specified. The reader may verify that the insertion of these values leads back to the equations of motion in terms of x, y.

Ex. 3. Find H for the motion of a particle under the action of a central force which is a function V of the distance. Find also the equations of motion.

We have here $T = \tfrac{1}{2}m(\dot{r}^2 + r^2\dot{\theta}^2)$. Write $m\dot{r} = p_1$, $mr^2\dot{\theta} = p_2$, so that the coordinates q_1, q_2 are r and θ, and p_2 is the A.M. about the centre of force. We obtain $T = (p_1^2 + p_2^2/r^2)/2m$, and therefore

$$H = \frac{1}{2m}\left(p_1^2 + \frac{1}{r^2}p_2^2\right) + V.$$

The equations of motion are

$$\dot{p}_1 = -\partial H/\partial q_1, \quad p_2 = -\partial H/\partial q_2,$$

that is, $\quad m(\ddot{r} - r\dot{\theta}^2) = -\dfrac{\partial V}{\partial r}, \quad m\dfrac{d}{dt}(r^2\dot{\theta}) = 0,$

since the coordinate θ does not appear in H.

310. Variation of H with the Time. We now calculate the *total* rate of variation of H with the time. We have

$$\frac{dH}{dt} = \Sigma\left(\frac{\partial H}{\partial q}\dot{q}\right) + \Sigma\left(\frac{\partial H}{\partial p}\dot{p}\right) + \frac{\partial H}{\partial t},$$

which, by the canonical equations, becomes

$$\frac{dH}{dt} = \frac{\partial H}{\partial t}, \quad\quad\quad\quad\quad\quad\quad\quad\quad(1)$$

that is, the total time-rate of variation of H is equal to the partial differential coefficient of H with respect to t explicitly appearing in the expression of the function.

572   A TREATISE ON DYNAMICS.   [CH. X.

But since $H = K + V$, this result may be written
$$\frac{dH}{dt} = \frac{\partial K}{\partial t} + \frac{\partial V}{\partial t} = -\frac{\partial T}{\partial t} + \frac{\partial V}{\partial t}, \quad \ldots\ldots\ldots\ldots(2)$$
by the definition of K, (1) § 309.

Thus if H is not an explicit function of t, it is a constant, h say, that is, $h = T + V$, or there is conservation of energy in the system. This is also the case, it may be noticed, if
$$\frac{\partial T}{\partial t} = \frac{\partial V}{\partial t}, \quad \ldots\ldots\ldots\ldots\ldots\ldots(3)$$
that is, we have then $K + V = h$.

Now, by the definition of K, we have
$$K = 2T_2 + T_1 - T = T_2 - T_0$$
and so, when $K + V = h$,
$$\left.\begin{array}{c} T_2 - T_0 + V = h \\ T - T_1 - 2T_0 + V = h. \end{array}\right\} \quad \ldots\ldots\ldots\ldots(4)$$
or

Ex. Prove that, if t do not appear in the equations of condition, and D be the discriminant of the function T_2,
$$2(H-V)D = \begin{vmatrix} 0, & p_1, & p_2, & \ldots, & p_k, \\ p_1, & A_{11}, & A_{12}, & \ldots, & A_{1k}, \\ p_2, & A_{21}, & A_{22}, & \ldots, & A_{2k}, \\ \ldots\ldots\ldots\ldots\ldots\ldots\ldots\ldots \\ p_k, & A_{k1}, & A_{k2}, & \ldots, & A_{kk}, \end{vmatrix}$$
where $A_{ij} = A_{ji}$.

We have in this case $T_m = H - V$, and
$$2T_m = p_1\dot{q}_1 + p_2\dot{q}_2 + \ldots + p_k\dot{q}_k,$$
$$p_1 = A_{11}\dot{q}_1 + A_{12}\dot{q}_2 + \ldots + A_{1k}\dot{q}_k,$$
$$\ldots\ldots\ldots\ldots\ldots\ldots\ldots\ldots\ldots\ldots\ldots$$
$$p_k = A_{1k}\dot{q}_1 + A_{2k}\dot{q}_2 + \ldots + A_{kk}\dot{q}_k.$$
Hence, eliminating $\dot{q}_1, \dot{q}_2, \ldots, \dot{q}_k$, we get the result to be established.

311. Lagrange's Equations found by Variation of Lagrangian Function. The Lagrangian equations may be derived for a conservative holonomous system by the following process depending on the Calculus of Variations.

Let the system be carried from an initial to a final configuration, and consider the time-integral $\int L\, dt$ of L for the passage from one

§§ 310, 311, 312]   IGNORATION OF COORDINATES.   573

to the other. Let us suppose variations δq, $\delta \dot{q}$ to be made in each coordinate q and the corresponding speed $\dot{q}$, that is, let the mode of passage or "path" from one configuration to the other be slightly changed without any variation of the terminal values of t. The variation of L is

$$\delta L = \Sigma\left(\frac{\partial L}{\partial q}\delta q\right) + \Sigma\left(\frac{\partial L}{\partial \dot{q}}\delta \dot{q}\right),$$

so that, if $t_1 - t_0$ be the time of passage,

$$\delta\int_{t_0}^{t_1} L\, dt = \int_{t_0}^{t_1}\left\{\Sigma\left(\frac{\partial L}{\partial q}\delta q\right)\right\} dt + \int_{t_0}^{t_1}\left\{\Sigma\left(\frac{\partial L}{\partial \dot{q}}\delta \dot{q}\right)\right\} dt. \ldots\ldots\ldots(1)$$

But
$$\int \frac{\partial L}{\partial \dot{q}}\delta \dot{q}\, dt = \frac{\partial L}{\partial \dot{q}}\delta q - \int \frac{d}{dt}\frac{\partial L}{\partial \dot{q}}\delta q\, dt,$$

and thus we get

$$\delta\int_{t_0}^{t_1} L\, dt = \Sigma\left(\frac{\partial L}{\partial \dot{q}}\delta q\right)_1 - \Sigma\left(\frac{\partial L}{\partial \dot{q}}\delta q\right)_0 + \int_{t_0}^{t_1}\Sigma\left(\frac{\partial L}{\partial q} - \frac{d}{dt}\frac{\partial L}{\partial \dot{q}}\right)\delta q\, dt, \ \ldots(2)$$

where the integrated terms for the final and initial configurations are distinguished by the suffixes 1 and 0.

If now we assume as a new dynamical principle that the variation of the time integral of L is to vanish for the passage, the integrated terms and the terms under the integral sign must vanish separately. If, for example, the initial and final configurations be the same for different adjacent paths of transition, the integrated terms are zero at each limit. We get therefore the typical Lagrangian equation

$$\frac{d}{dt}\frac{\partial L}{\partial \dot{q}} - \frac{\partial L}{\partial q} = 0 \ \ldots\ldots\ldots\ldots\ldots\ldots\ldots\ldots\ldots\ldots\ldots(3)$$

for a system, the forces on which are derivable from a potential function V.

So far no variation of t has been imposed, that is, the time of passage has been supposed the same for all the transitions.

312. Ignoration of Coordinates. Let certain coordinates

$$q_{i+1}, \quad q_{i+2}, \ \ldots, \ q_k$$

be absent from the equations of condition of a holonomous system, while the speeds $\dot{q}_{i+1}, \ldots, \dot{q}_k$ appear, then it is possible so to modify the function L that the equations of motion for the coordinates $q_1, q_2, \ldots, q_i$ may be formed as if the speeds $\dot{q}_{i+1}, \ldots, \dot{q}_k$ did not exist.

Taking the unmodified L, we have

$$\frac{\partial L}{\partial q_{i+1}} = 0, \quad \frac{\partial L}{\partial q_{i+2}} = 0, \ \ldots, \ \frac{\partial L}{\partial q_k} = 0 \ \ldots\ldots\ldots\ldots\ldots\ldots(1)$$

and
$$\frac{\partial L}{\partial \dot{q}_{i+1}} = c_{i+1}, \ \ldots, \ \frac{\partial L}{\partial \dot{q}_k} = c_k, \ \ldots\ldots\ldots\ldots\ldots\ldots(2)$$

where $c_{i+1}, \ldots, c_k$ are constants. Hence if L_1 denote the function L as modified by the elimination of $\dot{q}_{i+1}, \ldots, \dot{q}_k$ by means of equations (2), we have

$$\frac{\partial L_1}{\partial q} = \frac{\partial L}{\partial q_1} + \frac{\partial L}{\partial \dot{q}_{i+1}} \cdot \frac{\partial \dot{q}_{i+1}}{\partial q} + \frac{\partial L}{\partial \dot{q}_{i+2}} \frac{\partial \dot{q}_{i+2}}{\partial q} + \ldots$$
$$= \frac{\partial L}{\partial q} + c_{i+1} \frac{\partial \dot{q}_{i+1}}{\partial q} + c_{i+2} \frac{\partial \dot{q}_{i+2}}{\partial q} + \ldots, \quad \ldots\ldots(3)$$

and in the same way

$$\frac{\partial L_1}{\partial \dot{q}} = \frac{\partial L}{\partial \dot{q}} + c_{i+1} \frac{\partial \dot{q}_{i+1}}{\partial \dot{q}} + c_{i+2} \frac{\partial \dot{q}_{i+2}}{\partial \dot{q}} + \ldots, \quad \ldots\ldots\ldots\ldots\ldots(4)$$

where q is any of the coordinates $q_1, \ldots, q_i$.

Thus we get

$$\frac{d}{dt} \frac{\partial L_1}{\partial \dot{q}} - \frac{\partial L_1}{\partial q} = \frac{d}{dt} \frac{\partial L}{\partial \dot{q}} - \frac{\partial L}{\partial q} + c_{i+1} \left(\frac{d}{dt} \frac{\partial \dot{q}_{i+1}}{\partial \dot{q}} - \frac{\partial \dot{q}_{i+1}}{\partial q} \right) + \ldots \quad \ldots(5)$$

But
$$\frac{d}{dt} \frac{\partial L}{\partial \dot{q}} - \frac{\partial L}{\partial q} = 0,$$

and therefore we get from (5),

$$\frac{d}{dt} \frac{\partial L_1}{\partial \dot{q}} - \frac{\partial L_1}{\partial q} - c_{i+1} \left(\frac{d}{dt} \frac{\partial \dot{q}_{i+1}}{\partial \dot{q}} - \frac{\partial \dot{q}_{i+1}}{\partial q} \right) - \ldots = 0. \quad \ldots\ldots\ldots(6)$$

But this is precisely what we should obtain if we constructed the function
$$L' = L - c_{i+1} \dot{q}_{i+1} - c_{i+2} \dot{q}_{i+2} \ldots - c_k \dot{q}_k, \quad \ldots\ldots\ldots\ldots\ldots(7)$$
substituted for $\dot{q}_{i+1}, \ldots$ everywhere their values as given by (2), and then with L' *as thus expressed* wrote

$$\frac{d}{dt} \frac{\partial L'}{\partial \dot{q}} - \frac{\partial L'}{\partial q} = 0 \quad \ldots\ldots\ldots\ldots\ldots\ldots\ldots\ldots\ldots\ldots(8)$$

for any coordinate in the series $q_1, q_2, \ldots, q_i$.

This theorem is due to Dr. E. J. Routh (see *Stability of Motion*, p. 61). It is proved in a paper on Lagrange's equations, by A. Gray (*Proc. R.S.E.* 1909), that for a not holonomous system equations (13), § 305, require no modification in order that coordinates represented only by their speeds may be ignored, except the elimination of these speeds by (2).

Ex. We take for comparison the problem of Ex. 2, § 307. Here the coordinate ψ does not appear while $\dot{\psi}$ does. Now we have

$$L = \tfrac{1}{2} m (\dot{r}^2 + r^2 \dot{\theta}^2 + r^2 \dot{\psi}^2 \sin^2 \theta) + mgr \cos \theta.$$

But $\qquad \partial L/\partial \dot{\psi} = m r^2 \dot{\psi} \sin^2 \theta = c.$

Hence the modified function is

$$L' = \tfrac{1}{2} m (\dot{r}^2 + r^2 \dot{\theta}^2) + mgr \cos \theta,$$

from which $\dot{\psi}$ has been eliminated as directed. Thus we get

$$\partial L'/\partial \dot{r} = m\dot{r}, \quad \partial L'/\partial r = mr\dot{\theta}^2 + mg \cos \theta.$$

The equation of motion is therefore

$$\ddot{r} - r\dot{\theta}^2 + g\cos\theta = 0.$$

Similarly, the θ-equation can be found.

313. Meaning of Integration of Equations of Motion. Hamilton's Differential Equation. Now let us reverse the process of §311 and begin by assuming the Lagrangian equations which have been otherwise established. Thus we get, from (2), §311,

$$\delta\int_{t_0}^{t_1} L\,dt = \Sigma\left(\frac{\partial L}{\partial \dot{q}}\delta q\right)_1 - \Sigma\left(\frac{\partial L}{\partial \dot{q}}\delta q\right)_0. \quad\ldots\ldots\ldots\ldots\ldots(1)$$

Thus, if we write $S = \int_{t_0}^{t_1} L\,dt$, we have

$$\delta S = \Sigma(p\,\delta q)_1 - \Sigma(p\,\delta q)_0, \quad\ldots\ldots\ldots\ldots\ldots\ldots(2)$$

to which must be added $\partial S/\partial t . \delta t$, if t is not taken as independent variable, and is therefore made to vary. The function S was called by Hamilton the Principal Function.

This expression is very important in connection with the integration of the equations of motion (9) of §309 above. Such integration means the expression of L, or H, as a function of t, and of $2k$ constants of integration (there are k independent coordinates), so that S is obtained by integration in terms of these $2k+1$ quantities, which may be the time t and the $2k$ initial values of the ps and qs, typified, we suppose, by (p_0, q_0). Thus, in (p_0, q_0) and (p, q) with t we have $4k+1$ quantities connected by the k equations of motion or their integrals, and the k equations $\dot{q} = dq/dt$. Thus any $2k$ of these can be found in terms of the other $2k+1$. If the $2k$ chosen to be found in terms of the remaining $2k+1$ be (p, p_0), and these be substituted in S already expressed as above, we obtain S as a function of t and (q, q_0).

The variation of S when thus expressed is

$$\delta S = \Sigma\left(\frac{\partial S}{\partial q}\delta q\right)_1 + \Sigma\left(\frac{\partial S}{\partial q}\delta q\right)_0. \quad\ldots\ldots\ldots\ldots\ldots(3)$$

If we compare this with (2), we see that

$$\frac{\partial S}{\partial q} = p, \quad \frac{\partial S}{\partial q_0} = -p_0. \quad\ldots\ldots\ldots\ldots\ldots\ldots(4)$$

But
$$\frac{dS}{dt} = L = \frac{\partial S}{\partial t} + \Sigma\left(\frac{\partial S}{\partial q}\dot{q}\right), \quad\ldots\ldots\ldots\ldots\ldots(5)$$

since in the most general case t is explicitly contained in S, and implicitly in the qs. But by (4), this is

$$L = \frac{\partial S}{\partial t} + \Sigma(p\dot{q})$$

or
$$\frac{\partial S}{\partial t} + \Sigma(p\dot{q}) - T + V = 0,$$

that is with $\Sigma(p\dot{q}) - T$ replaced by its value in terms of $(\partial S/\partial q, q)$,

$$\frac{\partial S}{\partial t} + H\left(\frac{\partial S}{\partial q_1}, \frac{\partial S}{\partial q_2}, \ldots, \frac{\partial S}{\partial q_k}, q_1, q_2, \ldots, q_k, t\right) = 0 \ldots \ldots (6)$$

This is the Hamiltonian differential equation. A second differential equation was given by Hamilton, but we shall not discuss it here.

314. Jacobi's Theorem. It was shown by Jacobi that if a complete integral of (6) is known, that is an integral which contains k constants, $a_1, a_2, \ldots, a_k$, besides the additive constant, the canonical equations can be integrated. For let the integral S be expressed in terms of $q_1, q_2, \ldots, q_k$, and $a_1, a_2, \ldots, a_k$, then if $b_1, b_2, \ldots, b_k$ be k other constants such that

$$\frac{\partial S}{\partial a_1} = b_1, \quad \frac{\partial S}{\partial a_2} = b_2, \quad \ldots, \quad \frac{\partial S}{\partial a_k} = b_k, \ldots \ldots \ldots \ldots \ldots (1)$$

these equations, together with

$$\frac{\partial S}{\partial q_1} = p_1, \quad \frac{\partial S}{\partial q_2} = p_2, \quad \ldots, \quad \frac{\partial S}{\partial q_k} = p_k, \ldots \ldots \ldots \ldots \ldots (2)$$

are the integrals of the canonical equations of the type

$$\frac{dq}{dt} = \frac{\partial H}{\partial p}, \quad \frac{dp}{dt} = -\frac{\partial H}{\partial q}. \ldots \ldots \ldots \ldots \ldots (3)$$

This proposition is proved indirectly as follows. If a known integral of the equation (6) is substituted in that equation, the left side identically vanishes. Differentiate then any equation $\partial S/\partial a = b_i$ with respect to t, which can be done, since S is supposed known in terms of $q_1, q_2, \ldots, q_k, t$. We get

$$\frac{\partial^2 S}{\partial t \partial a_i} + \frac{\partial^2 S}{\partial q_1 \partial a_i} \dot{q} + \ldots + \frac{\partial^2 S}{\partial q_k \partial a_i} \dot{q}_k = 0. \ldots \ldots \ldots \ldots (4)$$

But by the first set of canonical equations this becomes

$$\frac{\partial^2 S}{\partial t \partial a_i} + \frac{\partial^2 S}{\partial q_1 \partial a_i} \frac{\partial H}{\partial p_1} + \ldots + \frac{\partial^2 S}{\partial q_k \partial a_i} \frac{\partial H}{\partial p_k} = 0. \ldots \ldots \ldots \ldots (5)$$

But the differential equation (6) of § 313, differentiated with respect to a_i, gives

$$\frac{\partial^2 S}{\partial a_i \partial t} + \frac{\partial H}{\partial p_1} \frac{\partial p_1}{\partial a_i} + \ldots + \frac{\partial H}{\partial p_k} \frac{\partial p_k}{\partial a_i} = 0 \ ; \ldots \ldots \ldots \ldots (6)$$

for, since S in (6) is a function of $q_1, q_2, \ldots, q_k$ and the constants $a_1, a_2, \ldots, a_k$, these constants must be contained in the $p_1, p_2, \ldots, p_k$ of the function H, from which as it stands in (6) the constants are supposed to have been eliminated.

Now substitute in the last equation obtained the values indicated by $p_j = \partial S/\partial q_j$, and we get $\partial p_j/\partial a_i = \partial^2 S/\partial a_i \partial q_j$. Thus equation (6) becomes

$$\frac{\partial^2 S}{\partial a_i \partial t} + \frac{\partial^2 S}{\partial a_i \partial q_1} \frac{\partial H}{\partial p_1} + \ldots + \frac{\partial^2 S}{\partial a_i \partial q_k} \frac{\partial H}{\partial p_k} = 0, \quad \ldots \ldots \ldots \ldots (7)$$

which agrees with (5). The first set of canonical equations are thus verified.

The second set can be verified in a similar way. Begin by differentiating $p_i = \partial S/\partial q_i$ with respect to t, and substitute for the $\dot{q}$s and for $\dot{p}_i$ from the canonical equations. This gives, since $\dot{p}_i = \partial H/\partial q_i$,

$$\frac{\partial H}{\partial q_i} + \frac{\partial^2 S}{\partial t\, \partial q_i} + \frac{\partial^2 S}{\partial q_1 \partial q_i} \frac{\partial H}{\partial p_1} + \ldots + \frac{\partial^2 S}{\partial q_k \partial q_i} \frac{\partial H}{\partial p_k} = 0. \quad \ldots \ldots \ldots \ldots (8)$$

But (6), § 313, gives

$$\frac{\partial^2 S}{\partial q_i \partial t} + \frac{\partial H}{\partial q_i} + \frac{\partial H}{\partial \frac{\partial S}{\partial q_1}} \frac{\partial^2 S}{\partial q_i \partial q_1} + \ldots + \frac{\partial H}{\partial \frac{\partial S}{\partial q_k}} \frac{\partial^2 S}{\partial q_i q_k} = 0, \quad \ldots \ldots (9)$$

and if the values of $p_1, p_2, \ldots, p_k$ be inserted in this from the equations (2), we obtain (8). Thus again there is verification.

315. Case in which H does not contain t. If the function does not depend on t as an explicit variable, (6) of § 312 becomes

$$\frac{\partial S}{\partial t} + h = 0, \quad \ldots \ldots \ldots \ldots \ldots \ldots \ldots \ldots (1)$$

where h is put for the constant value which, as we have seen, H now possesses. Integrating from $t_0(=0)$ to t, we obtain

$$S = -ht + W(q_1, q_2, \ldots, q_k, a_1, a_2, \ldots, a_{k-1}, h). \ldots \ldots \ldots (2)$$

The function W is the value of Hamilton's *Characteristic Function* $[S + Ht - H_0 t_0]$ when H does not contain t. It is a complete integral of (1) for each value of h; that is, it is possible to choose the constants $a_1, \ldots, a_{k-1}$ so as to give for any chosen value of h arbitrary values of $\partial W/\partial q_1, \ldots, \partial W/\partial q_{k-1}$; and, conversely, if these constants can be so assigned, W is a complete integral of (1). For if we desire that $\partial W/\partial q_1, \ldots, \partial W/\partial q_{k-1}$ shall have certain arbitrary values

$$(p_1)_0, (p_2)_0, \ldots, (p_k)_0,$$

for t_0, $(q_1)_0, (q_2)_0, \ldots, (q_k)_0$, we put $h = h_0$, the corresponding value of h, and then the value of $\partial W/\partial q_k$ is that given by the value h_0 of H.

The equations

$$\frac{\partial W}{\partial a_1} = b_1, \quad \ldots, \quad \frac{\partial W}{\partial a_{k-1}} = b_{k-1}, \quad \frac{\partial W}{\partial h} = t_1 - t_0 \ldots \ldots \ldots \ldots (3)$$

give the "path" by the first $k-1$, and the time of passage is given by the last.

316. Examples on Jacobi's Theorem.

Ex. 1. Prove that the path of a particle the position of which is defined by three coordinates q_1, q_2, q_3 cuts the surfaces $W = C$ at right angles.

Let $\dot{x}$, $\dot{y}$, $\dot{z}$ be the component speeds of the particle at x, y, z and δx, δy, δz the components of a step perpendicular to the direction of motion. Then the condition of orthogonality is

$$\dot{x}\,\delta x + \dot{y}\,\delta y + \dot{z}\,\delta z = 0.$$

Now, from the equations

$$x = \phi(q_1, q_2, q_3), \quad y = \chi(q_1, q_2, q_3), \quad z = \psi(q_1, q_2, q_3),$$

find $\dot{x}$, $\dot{y}$, $\dot{z}$, δx, δy, δz and T. Then it will be found that the condition of orthogonality is

$$\frac{\partial T}{\partial \dot{q}_1}\delta q_1 + \frac{\partial T}{\partial \dot{q}_2}\delta q_2 + \frac{\partial T}{\partial \dot{q}_3}\delta q_3 = 0.$$

But since $p_1 = \partial T/\partial \dot{q}_1 = \partial W/\partial q_1, \ldots$, this is

$$\frac{\partial W}{\partial q_1}\delta q_1 + \frac{\partial W}{\partial q_2}\delta q_2 + \frac{\partial W}{\partial q_2}\delta q_2 = 0,$$

which proves the proposition.

Ex. 2. If any coordinate, q_1 say, be absent from H, so that H has the form $H(p_1, p_2, \ldots p_k, q_2, q_3, \ldots, q_k, t)$, show that, with α_1 a constant,

$$S = \alpha_1 q_1 + U(t, q_2, q_3, \ldots q_k).$$

Ex. 3. Prove that if coordinates $q_1, q_2, \ldots, q_i$ be absent from H,

$$S = \alpha_1 q_1 + \alpha_2 q_2 + \ldots + \alpha_i q_i + U(t, q_{i+1}, q_k).$$

Ex. 4. Find the function W for the motion of a particle under the action of a central force which is a function $-\partial V/\partial r$ of the distance of the particle from a force centre.

By Ex. 3, § 309, we get

$$H = \frac{1}{2m}\left(p_1^2 + \frac{1}{r^2}p_2^2\right) + V(r),$$

and therefore the differential equation (1), § 315, is

$$-h + \frac{1}{2m}\left\{\left(\frac{\partial W}{\partial r}\right)^2 + \frac{1}{r^2}\left(\frac{\partial W}{\partial \theta}\right)^2\right\} + V(r) = 0,$$

into which θ does not enter explicitly. Hence, we can write

$$W = \alpha\theta + R,$$

where R is a function of r only. Hence, the differential equation becomes

$$-h + \frac{1}{2m}\left\{\left(\frac{\partial R}{\partial r}\right)^2 + \frac{\alpha^2}{r^2}\right\} + V(r) = 0.$$

Thus
$$R = \int dr \sqrt{2m(h-V) - \frac{\alpha^2}{r^2}},$$

so that
$$W = \alpha\theta + \int dr \sqrt{2m(h-V) - \frac{\alpha^2}{r^2}}.$$

The finite equations are therefore

$$\frac{\partial W}{\partial \alpha} = \theta - \alpha \int \frac{dr}{r^2 \sqrt{2m(h-V) - \frac{\alpha^2}{r^2}}} = \beta,$$

$$\frac{\partial W}{\partial h} = \int \frac{m\, dr}{\sqrt{2m(h-V) - \frac{\alpha^2}{r^2}}} = t_1 - t_0.$$

The former of these last equations gives the path, the latter the time of passage from any position to any other. [The student should work out for $V = -\tfrac{1}{2}\mu r^2$, $V = -\mu/r$.]

Ex. 5. Discuss the elliptic motion of a planet referred to three coordinates. [Jacobi, *Vorles. ü. Dynamik.*]

Let the mass of the planet be 1, and adopt, to begin with, Cartesian coordinates. Then,

$$H = \frac{1}{2}\left\{\left(\frac{\partial W}{\partial x}\right)^2 + \left(\frac{\partial W}{\partial y}\right)^2 + \left(\frac{\partial W}{\partial z}\right)^2\right\} - \frac{\mu}{r} = h.$$

Now, at time $t = t_0$, let the planet be at (x_0, y_0, z_0), and at time t be at (x, y, z). Then, if ρ be the distance between these two points, show that

$$2\left(h + \frac{\mu}{r}\right) = \left(\frac{\partial W}{\partial r^2}\right)^2 + \frac{\rho^2 + r^2 - r_0^2}{r\rho} \frac{\partial W}{\partial \rho} \frac{\partial W}{\partial r} + \left(\frac{\partial W}{\partial \rho}\right)^2.$$

Next, putting $\sigma = r + r_0 + \rho$, $\sigma' = r + r_0 - \rho$, show that

$$\frac{\partial W}{\partial r} = \frac{\partial W}{\partial \sigma} + \frac{\partial W}{\partial \sigma'}, \quad \frac{\partial W}{\partial \rho} = \frac{\partial W}{\partial \sigma} - \frac{\partial W}{\partial \sigma'},$$

so that

$$2\left(h + \frac{\mu}{r}\right) = \frac{2\mu}{r} - \frac{\mu}{a} = \frac{1}{r\rho}\left\{\sigma(\sigma - 2r_0)\left(\frac{\partial W}{\partial \sigma}\right)^2 - \sigma'(\sigma' - 2r_0)\left(\frac{\partial W}{\partial \sigma'}\right)^2\right\},$$

and the differential equation is

$$\sigma(\sigma - 2r_0)\left(\frac{\partial W}{\partial \sigma}\right)^2 + \sigma'(\sigma' - 2r_0)\left(\frac{\partial W}{\partial \sigma'}\right)^2$$
$$= \mu(\sigma - \sigma') - \frac{\mu}{4a}(\sigma^2 - \sigma'^2) + \frac{\mu}{2a}(\sigma - \sigma')r_0.$$

Show that this can be integrated by splitting it into the two,

$$\sigma^2\left(\frac{\partial W}{\partial \sigma}\right)^2 + \sigma'^2\left(\frac{\partial W}{\partial \sigma'}\right)^2 = \frac{\mu}{4a}(\sigma - \sigma')(4a - \sigma - \sigma'),$$

$$\sigma\left(\frac{\partial W}{\partial \sigma}\right)^2 + \sigma'\left(\frac{\partial W}{\partial \sigma'}\right)^2 = -\frac{\mu}{4a}(\sigma - \sigma'),$$

so that $\quad \dfrac{\partial W}{\partial \sigma} = \pm\sqrt{\mu}\sqrt{\dfrac{4a-\sigma}{4a\sigma}}, \quad \dfrac{\partial W}{\partial \sigma'} = \pm\sqrt{\mu}\sqrt{\dfrac{4a-\sigma'}{4a\sigma'}}.$

Giving the $+$ sign to the first and the $-$ sign to the second, and putting $\frac{1}{2}\sqrt{u/a} = \sin\phi$, show that

$$W = \sqrt{\mu}\int_{\sigma'}^{\sigma}\sqrt{\frac{4a-u}{4au}}\,du = 4\sqrt{a\mu}\int_{\phi'}^{\phi}\cos^2\phi\,d\phi,$$

so that $\quad W = \sqrt{a\mu}(\sin 2\phi + 2\phi - \sin 2\phi' - 2\phi').$

Ex. 6. By giving the same sign to $\partial W/\partial \sigma$ and $\partial W/\partial \sigma'$, show that a second ellipse is obtained through the same initial point and having the same centre of force, and the same length of major axis.

Ex. 7. Show that in Ex. 5, $\partial W/\partial h = (2a^2/\mu)\partial W/\partial a$, and hence find $t - t_0$, proving Lambert's theorem [§ 146 above].

Ex. 8. By calculating $\partial W/\partial r_0$, find the equation of the path.
Write $s = \sigma - r_0$, $s' = \sigma' - r_0$, so that $s = r + \rho$, $s' = r - \rho$, and show that

$$W = \frac{1}{2}\sqrt{\frac{\mu}{a}}\int_{\sigma'}^{\sigma}\sqrt{\frac{4a-u}{u}}\,du = \frac{1}{2}\sqrt{\frac{\mu}{a}}\int_{s'}^{s}\sqrt{\frac{4a-w-r_0}{w+r_0}}\,dw.$$

Hence noticing that

$$\frac{\partial s}{\partial r_0} = \frac{r_0 - r\cos\theta}{\rho}, \quad \frac{\partial s'}{\partial r_0} = -\frac{r_0 - r\cos\theta}{\rho},$$

calculate $\partial W/\partial r_0$, and show that the path has the equation

$$\left(1 + \frac{r_0 - r\cos\theta}{\rho}\right)\sqrt{\frac{4a-\sigma}{\sigma}} - \left(1 - \frac{r_0 - r\cos\theta}{\rho}\right)\sqrt{\frac{4a-\sigma'}{\sigma'}} = C,$$

where C is a constant.

317. Lagrange's Equations for Impulsive Forces. The equations of Lagrange may be modified in the following manner for the case of impulsive forces. We have only to integrate each over the infinitesimal time τ, during which the impulsive forces act. The integral of any finite quantity, such as $\partial L/\partial q$, over that interval is zero. Thus we get, putting I for the time integral of the impulsive force Q, $p-p_0 = I$. The equations are therefore

$$p_1 - (p_1) = I_1, \quad p_2 - (p_2) = I_2, \quad \ldots, \quad p - (p_k) = I_k, \quad \ldots (1)$$

where the brackets denote values of the quantities enclosed for the beginning of the interval τ.

If T_s be a homogeneous quadratic function of the speeds $\dot{q}_1, \dot{q}_2, \ldots$, we have

$$T_s - (T_s) = \tfrac{1}{2}\Sigma\{p\dot{q} - (p\dot{q})\},$$

that is,

$$T_s - (T_s) = \tfrac{1}{2}\Sigma[\{p-(p)\}\{q+(\dot{q})\} - p(\dot{q}) + (p)\dot{q}]. \quad \ldots(2)$$

But if the terms in $\Sigma\{p(\dot{q}) - (p)\dot{q}\}$ be written out in full, it will be found that the sum is identically zero, so that (2) becomes

$$T_s - (T_s) = \tfrac{1}{2}\Sigma[\{p-(p)\}\{\dot{q}+(\dot{q})\}] = \tfrac{1}{2}\Sigma[I\{\dot{q}+(\dot{q})\}]. \quad (3)$$

Thus if W be the work done by the impulses in time dt we have, since there is practically no displacement of the system effected in time τ, and therefore no work done except that represented in the change of kinetic energy,

$$W = \tfrac{1}{2}\Sigma[\{p-(p)\}\{\dot{q}+(\dot{q})\}] = \tfrac{1}{2}\Sigma[I\{\dot{q}+(\dot{q})\}]. \quad \ldots\ldots(4)$$

318. Reciprocal Relation between Two States of Motion. The theorem

$$\Sigma\{p(\dot{q})\} = \Sigma\{(p)\dot{q}\} \quad \ldots\ldots\ldots\ldots\ldots(1)$$

proved above is very important. It shows that if p, $\dot{q}$, p', $\dot{q}'$ typify the momenta and velocities for two possible motions of the system, we have

$$p_1\dot{q}_1' + p_2\dot{q}_2' + \ldots + p_k\dot{q}_k' = p_1'\dot{q}_1 + p_2'\dot{q}_2 + \ldots + p_k'\dot{q}_k, \quad \ldots\ldots(2)$$

for one motion can be produced from the other by a properly chosen system of applied impulses. It has analogies in different parts of physics, the explanation of which is afforded by general dynamical theory.

319. Motion Started from Rest by Impulses. Theorems of Bertrand and Lord Kelvin. If the system be started from rest by the impulses, we have

$$W = \tfrac{1}{2}(p_1\dot{q}_1 + p_2\dot{q}_2 + \ldots + p_k\dot{q}_k) = \tfrac{1}{2}(I_1\dot{q}_1 + I_2\dot{q}_2 + \ldots + I_k\dot{q}_k). \quad \ldots(1)$$

We can now prove two important theorems due to M. J. Bertrand and Lord Kelvin respectively. They may be stated as follows:

Bertrand's Theorem. A material system is set into motion by definite impulses applied to certain points, while the rest of the system is constrained to move by the internal connections: the kinetic energy taken by the system is greater than that for any motion which could be brought about by the applied impulses together with any system of impulses which do no work on the whole.

Kelvin's Theorem. A material system is set into motion by impulses applied to certain selected points, such that these points are given assigned velocities, while the rest of the system takes the motion to which it is constrained by the connections: the kinetic energy taken by the system is less than that for any other motion (produced by another set of impulses), for which the selected points have the same velocities.

We shall prove the two theorems together. First divide the generalised coordinates which specify the configuration of the system into two groups $q_1, q_2, \ldots, q_i, q'_1, q'_2, \ldots, q'_j$, and let $p_1, p_2, \ldots, p_i, p'_1, p'_2, \ldots, p'_j$ be the momenta which measure the impulses applied. We have for the kinetic energy
$$2T = \Sigma(p\dot{q}) + \Sigma(p'\dot{q}'). \quad \ldots\ldots\ldots\ldots\ldots\ldots(2)$$

For another system of impulses $p + \delta p$, $p' + \delta p'$, for which the velocities are $\dot{q} + \delta\dot{q}$, $\dot{q}' + \delta\dot{q}'$, we have

$$2(T + \delta T) = \Sigma\{(p + \delta p)(\dot{q} + \delta\dot{q})\} + \Sigma\{(p' + \delta p')(\dot{q}' + \delta\dot{q}')\}, \ldots(3)$$

and therefore

$$2\delta T = \Sigma(\dot{q}\delta p + p\delta\dot{q} + \delta p\delta\dot{q}) + \Sigma(\dot{q}'\delta p' + p'\delta\dot{q}' + \delta p'\delta\dot{q}'). \ldots(4)$$

Now let the impulses $p'_1, p'_2, \ldots$ be all zero, so that the two systems of impulses the effects of which are to be compared are $p_1, p_2, \ldots, p_i$, and $p_1, p_2, \ldots, p_i, \delta p'_1, \delta p'_2, \ldots, \delta p'_j$, and take the first set as those applied at the specified points; then by the conditions of Bertrand's theorem, we have
$$\Sigma\{\delta p'(\dot{q}' + \delta\dot{q}')\} = 0. \quad \ldots\ldots\ldots\ldots\ldots\ldots(5)$$
But since $\delta p = 0$, $2\delta T = \Sigma(p\delta\dot{q} + \dot{q}'\delta p' + \delta p'\delta\dot{q}'). \quad\ldots\ldots\ldots\ldots(6)$

§ 319] THEOREMS OF BERTRAND AND KELVIN. 583

Now $(p, \dot{q}, 0, \dot{q}')$ and $(p, \dot{q}+\delta\dot{q}, \delta p', \dot{q}'+\delta\dot{q}')$ define two states of motion of the same system, and therefore, by the theorem of (2), § 318, we get

$$\Sigma\{p(\dot{q}+\delta\dot{q})\} = \Sigma(p\dot{q}+\dot{q}'\delta p),$$

that is, $\quad \Sigma(p\,\delta\dot{q}) = \Sigma(\dot{q}'\delta p') = -\Sigma(\delta p'.\delta\dot{q}'),$

by (5). Hence $\quad 2\delta T = -\Sigma(\delta p'\delta\dot{q}').$ ....(7)

Thus the motion produced by the second set of impulses has less kinetic energy than that produced by the first set by the amount $\Sigma(\delta p'\delta\dot{q}')$.

For Lord Kelvin's theorem we have, since the speeds of the first set of points are the same for both sets of impulses, $\delta\dot{q}_1, \delta\dot{q}_2, \ldots, \delta\dot{q}_i$ all zero, with, as before,

$$p_1' = p_2' = \ldots = p_j' = 0.$$

Then $\quad 2\delta T = \Sigma(\dot{q}\,\delta p + \dot{q}'\delta p' + \delta p'\delta\dot{q}'),$ ....(7)

and in the same manner as before the theorem of (2), § 318, gives

$$\Sigma(\dot{q}\,\delta p + \dot{q}'\delta p') = 0.$$

Thus we have $\quad 2\delta T = \Sigma(\delta p'\delta\dot{q}'),$

or the kinetic energy of the first motion is smaller than that of any other motion with the same velocities $\dot{q}_1, \dot{q}_2, \ldots, \dot{q}_i$ by $\Sigma(\delta p'\delta\dot{q}')$, that is, the kinetic energy of the motion which combined with the first motion would give the second.

As Lord Rayleigh has remarked (*Theory of Sound*, vol. i. § 79), both theorems are consequences of the fact that the imposition of any constraint on the system increases the effective inertia of the system. [Thus, if there were only a single coordinate, the inertia might be regarded as measured by the ratio $p/\dot{q}$.] If then the $\dot{q}$s be fixed, any constraint, for example that required to make the velocities of $\dot{q}_1, \dot{q}_2, \ldots, \dot{q}_k$ the same as before for the second set of impulses, will increase the value of p and therefore the kinetic energy; and on the other hand, if the ps be fixed, the constraint will diminish the $\dot{q}$s, and diminish the kinetic energy.

Of these theorems, § 218 and the examples there given are illustrations.

EXERCISES X.

1. A heavy particle moves without friction along a vertical guiding circle which turns with uniform angular speed about a vertical axis in its own plane. Write down expressions for the kinetic and potential energies of the particle, and find the equation of motion relatively to the circle.

Find the positions in which the particle can rest in equilibrium on the circle.

2. A particle is constrained to remain on a plane which turns about a horizontal axis in the plane with uniform angular speed ω. The particle is otherwise free, and moves without friction.

Show that if r be given by the equations $y = r \sin \omega t$, $z = r \cos \omega t$ (z vertical), the equations of motion are

$$\ddot{x} = 0, \quad \ddot{r} - \omega^2 r + g \cos \omega t = 0.$$

Integrate these equations completely.

Show that if at time t the particle be at rest on the plane at distance a from the axis of rotation, the distance r at time t is given by

$$r = \frac{1}{2} a(e^{\omega t} + e^{-\omega t}) - \frac{g}{4\omega^2}(e^{\omega t} - e^{-\omega t}) + \frac{g}{2\omega^2} \sin \omega t.$$

3. Discuss the motion of a falling ladder the ends of which bear against a horizontal floor and a vertical wall. [Take the ladder as a uniform beam of length l, and the coefficients of friction at its ends as both equal to unity.]

Show from the equations of motion that if θ be the inclination of the ladder to the horizontal at time t,

$$k^2 \ddot{\theta} - l^2 \dot{\theta}^2 + gl \sin \theta = 0,$$

and putting $\dot{\theta} = \phi$, integrate this equation.

4. A vertical shaft is hollow and has a hollow projecting horizontal arm in which slides, without friction, a particle of mass m. To that particle is attached a string which passes inwards along the arm, over a pulley at the junction of the arm and the shaft, and then down along the inside of the vertical shaft to a second particle of mass m', which it carries at the lower end. The masses of the string and pulley are negligible. The vertical shaft is set rotating about its axis with angular speed ω by external forces. Find the energy of the system, and the equations of motion.

If T be the kinetic energy of *revolution* of the particle m, and dW the work done in time dt in driving the system of two particles, and r be the distance of m from the vertical axis, prove that

$$\frac{dW}{T} = \frac{d}{dt}\{\log(r^4 \omega^2)\} dt.$$

5. A particle is moving in a tube in the form of a plane curve, which is rotating in its plane with angular speed ω, about an axis rigidly connected with it. Show that if there be no friction the tangential and normal accelerations are, with the usual notation,

$$v\frac{dv}{ds} - \omega^2 r\frac{dr}{ds} + \dot\omega p, \quad \frac{v^2}{\rho} + 2\omega v + \omega^2 p + \dot\omega r\frac{dr}{ds}.$$

6. Prove that a self-contained system is in stable equilibrium in a configuration for which its potential energy is a minimum.

For all configurations near that of minimum potential energy the potential energy V is greater than the minimum value V_0 in question. Consider the neighbouring configurations in which the potential energy is greater than V_0 by the amount e where e is any small positive quantity that is assigned. If in any configuration whatever in the neighbourhood of the given one the energies be T and V, we have $T + V = T_0 + V_0$, where T_0 is the kinetic energy which corresponds to V_0. Now by hypothesis $V > V_0$, and so $T < T_0$. If now, as we suppose, T_0 be small, we have $V(= T_0 + V_0 - T)$ less than $T_0 + V_0$. By taking $T_0 < e$, we see that V can never reach the value $V_0 + e$, that is none of the neighbouring configurations for which $V = V_0 + e$ can be reached by the system. Further, since $T < T_0$, the speeds must all remain below an assigned limit.

7. The particles of a system execute small vibrations about a configuration of equilibrium. Show that the kinetic energy and the potential energy are quadratic functions of the coordinates relative to the equilibrium configuration.

Let $c_1, c_2, \ldots$ be the equilibrium coordinates, and $c_1 + q_1, c_2 + q_2, \ldots$ the coordinates at time t. We suppose that second and higher powers of $q_1, q_2, \ldots$ may be neglected in comparison with $q_1, q_2, \ldots$ themselves. By (1) § 300, we have

$$x = \phi(c_1, c_2, \ldots) + q_1\frac{\partial\phi}{\partial c_1} + q_2\frac{\partial\phi}{\partial c_2} + \ldots, \quad \ldots, \quad \dot x = \dot q_1\frac{\partial\phi}{\partial c_1} + \dot q_2\frac{\partial\phi}{\partial c_2} + \ldots, \quad \ldots$$

Hence, forming the expression $T = \tfrac{1}{2}\Sigma\{m(\dot x^2 + \dot y^2 + \dot z^2)\}$, we get

$$T = \tfrac{1}{2}(a_{11}\dot q_1^2 + 2a_{12}\dot q_1\dot q_2 + \ldots + a_{22}\dot q_2^2 + 2a_{23}\dot q_2\dot q_3 + \ldots),$$

where $a_{11}, a_{12}, \ldots a_{22}, \ldots$ are constants.

Again, for the potential energy, we have

$$V = V_0 + \tfrac{1}{2}\left(q_1^2\frac{\partial^2 V_0}{\partial c_1^2} + 2q_1 q_2\frac{\partial^2 V_0}{\partial c_1 \partial c_2} + \ldots\right)$$

since $\partial V_0/\partial c_1, \partial V_0/\partial c_2, \ldots$ are all zero for a configuration of equilibrium, that is to say

$$V = V_0 + \tfrac{1}{2}(b_{11}q_1^2 + 2b_{12}q_1 q_2 + \ldots + b_{22}q_2^2 + 2b_{23}q_2 q_3 + \ldots).$$

8. Prove that the Lagrangian equations of motion derived from the kinetic and potential energies set forth in last example are

$$a_{11}\ddot q_1 + a_{12}\ddot q_2 + \ldots + a_{1k}\ddot q_k + b_{11}q_1 + b_{12}q_2 + \ldots + b_{1k}q_k = 0,$$
$$a_{21}\ddot q_1 + a_{22}\ddot q_2 + \ldots + a_{2k}\ddot q_k + b_{21}q_1 + b_{22}q_2 + \ldots + b_{2k}q_k = 0,$$
$$\ldots\ldots\ldots\ldots\ldots\ldots\ldots\ldots\ldots\ldots\ldots\ldots\ldots\ldots\ldots\ldots\ldots\ldots$$

Show that if we write $q_1 = A_1 e^{int}$, $q_2 = A_2 e^{int}$, ... where $i = \sqrt{-1}$, we get the determinantal equation for n,

$$\begin{vmatrix} b_{11} - a_{11}n^2, & b_{12} - a_{12}n^2, & \ldots, & b_{1k} - a_{1k}n^2 \\ b_{21} - a_{21}n^2, & b_{22} - a_{22}n^2, & \ldots, & b_{2k} - a_{2k}n^2 \\ \ldots\ldots\ldots\ldots\ldots\ldots\ldots\ldots\ldots\ldots\ldots\ldots\ldots\ldots\ldots\ldots\ldots \\ b_{k1} - a_{k1}n^2, & b_{k2} - a_{k2}n^2, & \ldots, & b_{kk} - a_{kk}n^2 \end{vmatrix} = 0.$$

If we write λ for n^2 in this equation, we get an equation of the kth degree in λ. The student may prove that all the roots of the equation in λ are real, and may also show that if the function $V - V_0$ of Ex. 7 can be reduced to a sum of k squares, multiplied by positive coefficients, these values of λ are all positive, and therefore the periods of vibration all real. This condition amounts to the statement that the potential energy V_0 is a minimum for the equilibrium configuration. [See Routh, *Elementary Dynamics*, chap. ix.]

9. Prove that when the expression of $V - V_0$ thus obtained is written in the form

$$\lambda_1 \xi_1^2 + \lambda_2 \xi_2^2 + \ldots + \lambda_k \xi_k^2,$$

where $\lambda_1, \lambda_2, \ldots, \lambda_k$ are the roots of the determinantal equation, we can write also

$$2T = \dot{\xi}_1^2 + \dot{\xi}_2^2 + \ldots + \dot{\xi}_k^2.$$

The coordinates $\xi_1, \xi_2, \ldots, \xi_k$, which have thus taken the place of $q_1, q_2, \ldots, q_k$ are called the *principal coordinates*.

The equations for the x, y, z of any particle are now, by Ex. 7 and equations (1) of § 300,

$$x = x_0 + \alpha_1 \xi_1 + \alpha_2 \xi_2 + \ldots + \alpha_k \xi_k,$$
$$y = y_0 + \beta_1 \xi_1 + \beta_2 \xi_2 + \ldots + \beta_k \xi_k,$$
$$z = z_0 + \gamma_1 \xi_1 + \gamma_2 \xi_2 + \ldots + \gamma_k \xi_k,$$

where $\alpha_1, \beta_1, \gamma_1, \alpha_2, \ldots$, are constants. Thus the motion of any particle in the mode determined by the coordinate ξ, say, in period $2\pi/\sqrt{\lambda_1}$ is determined by the values of $\alpha_1, \beta_1, \gamma_1$ for that particle, with all the other coordinates put equal to zero.

The existence of equal roots of the determinantal equation does not involve instability. The equations obtained in Ex. 8 by substituting $q_1 = A_1 e^{int}$, ... enable $n - 1$ of the coefficients $A_1, A_2, \ldots, A_k$ to be obtained in terms of the assumed value of any one. If two roots are equal, then two of the coefficients are to be arbitrarily assumed and the remaining $n - 2$ determined, and so on. [See Routh, *loc. cit.*]

10. By means of Bertrand's theorem (§ 582) prove that if a circular disk, radius a, receive an impulse in its plane along a line distant p from the centre, it will begin to turn about a point on the diameter perpendicular to the impulse and distant $(a^2 + 2p^2)/2p$ from it.

CHAPTER XI.

STATICS.

320. Equilibrium of a Particle. A particle is in equilibrium under the action of a system of forces, when it is at rest or in uniform motion: hence the forces must have a zero resultant. If there are two forces acting, they must be equal in magnitude and opposed to one another; if the number of forces is three, any one of them must be equal and opposite to the resultant of the other two; and if there are n forces acting, any one of them must be equal and opposite to the resultant of the remaining $n-1$ forces. In other words, the graphical representation of the forces must result in a closed polygon.

Analytically, we proceed as follows. The forces are referred to rectangular axes passing through the particle. Each force is resolved into components in the directions of the axes. Denoting the components of a specimen force by X, Y, Z, we see that the resultant force R acting on the particle is given by

$$R = \sqrt{(\Sigma X)^2 + (\Sigma Y)^2 + (\Sigma Z)^2}. \quad \ldots\ldots\ldots\ldots\ldots(1)$$

Its direction-cosines are $\Sigma X/R$, $\Sigma Y/R$, $\Sigma Z/R$. If the particle is in equilibrium, $R=0$, and consequently $\Sigma X = 0$, $\Sigma Y = 0$, and $\Sigma Z = 0$.

321. Particle in Equilibrium in a Smooth Tube. As an example, we may consider the case of a particle maintained in equilibrium in a smooth tube. We refer the particle to axes of reference $Oxyz$. Let the forces acting on the particle (leaving out of account the action of the tube) in the directions of the axes be X, Y, Z. If the length of the tube from a fixed point up to the point occupied by the particle be s, the direction-cosines of the tube at the point (x, y, z) are dx/ds, dy/ds, dz/ds. The force acting on the particle along the tube is

$$X\,dx/ds + Y\,dy/ds + Z\,dz/ds,$$

and there is no component of force along the tube due to the action between it and the particle. Consequently, the condition that there should be no acceleration of the particle along the tube is

$$X\frac{dx}{ds} + Y\frac{dy}{ds} + Z\frac{dz}{ds} = 0.$$

322. Flexible String in Equilibrium. The consideration that three forces meeting at a point are in equilibrium, provided that they can be represented graphically by the sides of a triangle taken in order, suffices to solve the problem of a string suspended from two fixed points, and subjected to forces applied at points distributed along its length. We suppose the string perfectly flexible, inextensible, and of negligible mass. In Fig. 142 it is shown attached to fixed points S_1, S_2: at points A, B, C, D forces are applied to the string in the directions indicated by the arrows. The relation that must exist among the weights may be determined graphically as follows. Selecting any point 0, draw a line 01 parallel to S_1A, and from any point 1 in it, draw 12 parallel to the direction of F_1; from 0 draw 02 parallel to AB. Now, the three forces T_1, F_1, and T_2 are in equilibrium, and hence are proportional to the sides 01, 12, 20 of the triangle 012. Again, from 2 draw 23 parallel to F_2, and from 0 draw 03 parallel to BC: the three forces T_2, F_2, and T_3 are evidently proportional to the sides 02, 23, 30 of the triangle 023. Proceeding similarly for the points C and

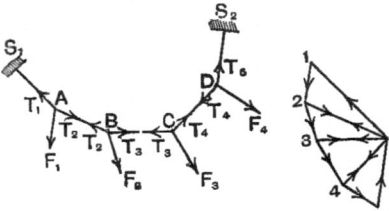

Fig. 142.

§§ 321, 322]   EQUILIBRIUM OF STRING.   589

D, we obtain the diagram 0123450. Such a diagram is called a force-diagram or force-polygon: the polygon S_1ABCDS_2 assumed by the string is called a funicular polygon.

The relation which must hold among the forces is evident. Provided that they are proportional to the sides 12, 23, 34, 45 of the force-polygon, the funicular polygon will be that of the figure. The student will see that if the forces are given in magnitude and direction, and likewise the stretching force in, and the direction of, any one side of the funicular polygon, the stretching forces in, and the directions of, the remaining sides can be determined.

We now consider the case where the forces are due to weights attached to points in the string. The applied forces are all vertical, and if the force-polygon is constructed, the lines 12, 23, etc., will lie in a vertical straight line.

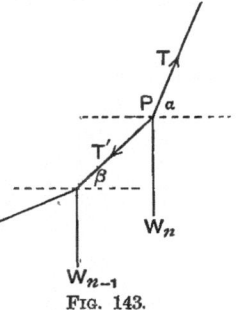
Fig. 143.

To solve the problem analytically, let P (Fig. 143) be one of the vertices of the funicular polygon. The three forces T, T', and W_n meet in a point, and are in equilibrium. Resolving vertically and horizontally, we obtain

$$T \sin \alpha - T' \sin \beta = W_n, \quad \ldots\ldots\ldots\ldots\ldots\ldots(1)$$
$$T \cos \alpha = T' \cos \beta. \quad \ldots\ldots\ldots\ldots\ldots\ldots\ldots(2)$$

Equation (2) shows that the horizontal component of the stretching force is constant throughout the string. Denoting it by H, we have

$$\tan \alpha - \tan \beta = \frac{W_n}{H}. \quad \ldots\ldots\ldots\ldots\ldots\ldots(3)$$

Equation (3) shows that when all the weights, together with the inclination of any one side and the stretching force in that side, are given, the inclinations and stretching forces for the other sides can be determined. This is evident from consideration of the force-polygon, as has already been pointed out.

Now suppose that the suspended weights are equal. Further, let the lowest portion of the string be horizontal, as shown in Fig. 144. Denoting the inclinations of the

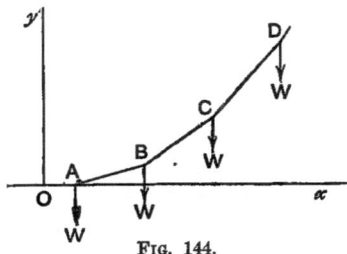

Fig. 144.

succeeding portions of the string to the horizontal by θ_1, θ_2, etc., we obtain

$$\tan \theta_1 = W/H; \quad \tan \theta_2 = \tan \theta_1 + W/H = 2W/H;$$
$$\tan \theta_3 = \tan \theta_2 + W/H = 3W/H; \quad \ldots;$$
$$\tan \theta_n = \tan \theta_{n-1} + W/H = nW/H. \quad \ldots\ldots\ldots\ldots(4)$$

323. Horizontal Projections of Sides of Funicular Polygon equal. If the horizontal projections of the sides of the funicular polygon are equal, it is easy to prove that the vertices lie on a parabola. Taking horizontal and vertical axes in the plane of the string and passing through the mid-point of the lowest side, we obtain $\frac{1}{2}a$, 0 as the co-ordinates of A, a being the length of the lowest side; those of B are $\frac{3}{2}a$, c, where c is the vertical distance apart of B and A; those of C are $\frac{5}{2}a$, $c+2c$; those of D are $\frac{7}{2}a$, $c+2c+3c$; and if x and y are the coordinates of the nth vertex counted from A, we have

$$x = \frac{2n+1}{2}a, \quad y = \frac{n(n+1)}{2}c. \quad \ldots\ldots\ldots\ldots\ldots(1)$$

Eliminating n between these two equations, we obtain

$$x^2 = \frac{2a^2}{c}y + \frac{a^2}{4} \quad \ldots\ldots\ldots\ldots\ldots\ldots(2)$$

as the equation to the curve passing through the vertices. Hence the vertices lie on a parabola whose axis is Oy and whose vertex is at a distance $c/8$ below the origin.

324. Chain of Suspension Bridge. If the number of vertices be very great and the suspended weights all equal, the parabola on which the vertices lie coincides with the string. An example is furnished by the chain of a suspension bridge (Fig. 145). The vertical bars carry the weight of the flooring, and are equally spaced throughout the span. The vertices of the funicular polygon formed by the chain thus lie on a parabola, and if the number of bars be great the polygon will coincide with the curve.

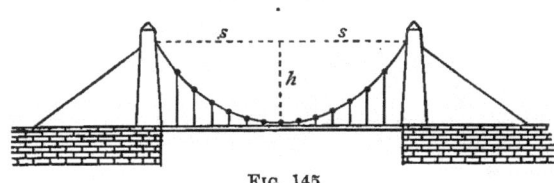

Fig. 145.

We refer the chain to axes of reference in its plane, with the origin at the lowest point. The curve in which the chain lies is represented by the equation

$$x^2 = 4ay,$$

where a has not the same meaning as in § 323. Differentiating, we obtain $dy/dx = x/2a = 2y/x$.

Hence, if $2s$ is the span of the bridge, and h is the height, the tangent of the angle α, made by the chain at the highest point with the horizontal, is $2h/s$. If T is the stretching force in the chain at the point of attachment, and W the total weight carried, we have $T \sin \alpha = W/2$, or

$$T = W \frac{\sqrt{4h^2 + s^2}}{4h}; \quad \ldots\ldots\ldots\ldots\ldots\ldots(1)$$

and if H denote the stretching force in the chain at the lowest point,

$$H = T \cos \alpha = \frac{1}{4} W \frac{s}{h}. \quad \ldots\ldots\ldots\ldots\ldots\ldots(2)$$

These results may be obtained more directly as follows. Let OPB (Fig. 146) represent a portion of the chain, and T denote the stretching force in the chain at the point

(x, y). Then, taking axes of reference as shown, denoting by w the load per unit of the span, and resolving horizontally and vertically, we have

$$T\frac{dx}{ds}=H, \quad T\frac{dy}{ds}=wx.$$

Hence $\dfrac{dy}{dx}=\dfrac{wx}{H}$,

which gives on integration

$$y=\frac{1}{2}\frac{w}{H}x^2,$$

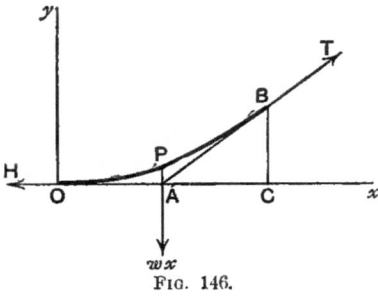
Fig. 146.

the constant of integration being zero, since $y=0$ when $x=0$.

Again, we may suppose the load carried by the portion OPB of the chain to act in the vertical line PA, where A is the mid-point of OC. We have at B $dy/dx = \tan \angle BAC$. Now the forces H, wx, and T are parallel to the sides of the triangle BAC. Consequently

$$\frac{T}{wx}=\frac{AB}{BC}, \quad \frac{H}{wx}=\frac{AC}{BC},$$

from which the expressions for the stretching force at the highest point may easily be determined in terms of the total load, the height, and the span.

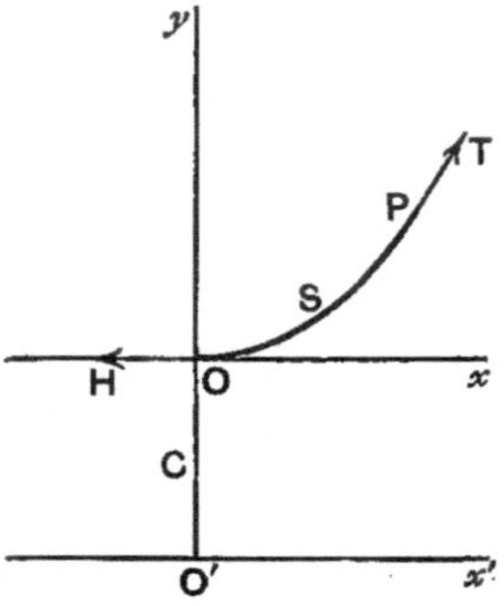

325. Catenary. The form of the curve (called the *catenary*), assumed by a perfectly flexible, homogeneous, inextensible cord when suspended from two fixed points, and acted on solely by its weight, and the forces applied by the supports, can be found as follows. Since the cord is perfectly flexible, the action of one part of the cord on a neighbouring part will be everywhere along the cord. Let the weight of unit length of the cord be

Fig. 147.

w, and take axes as shown in Fig. 147, with the origin at the lowest point. If T be the stretching force at a point P, at a distance s from O measured along the cord we have, resolving vertically and horizontally,

$$T\frac{dy}{ds}=ws, \quad T\frac{dx}{ds}=H, \quad \ldots\ldots\ldots\ldots\ldots(1)$$

where H is the stretching force in the cord at the lowest point. Hence
$$\frac{dy}{dx}=\frac{ws}{H}=\frac{s}{c}, \quad \ldots\ldots\ldots\ldots\ldots\ldots(2)$$
where $c=H/w$.

Now, if ds denote an element of the cord at P, we have $ds^2=dx^2+dy^2$. From (2), we obtain

$$\frac{dy^2}{dy^2+dx^2}=\frac{s^2}{s^2+c^2}, \quad \frac{dx^2}{dx^2+dy^2}=\frac{c^2}{s^2+c^2};$$

or, taking the square roots and rejecting the negative signs, since x and y both increase as s increases,

$$\frac{dy}{ds}=\frac{s}{\sqrt{s^2+c^2}}; \quad \frac{dx}{ds}=\frac{c}{\sqrt{s^2+c^2}}. \quad \ldots\ldots\ldots(3)$$

The first equation of (3) gives on integration

$$y=\sqrt{s^2+c^2}+\text{const.}; \quad \ldots\ldots\ldots\ldots\ldots(4)$$

and when $s=0$, $y=0$, and hence the value of the const. is $-c$. The equation is thus

$$y+c=\sqrt{s^2+c^2}. \quad \ldots\ldots\ldots\ldots\ldots\ldots(5)$$

The second equation of (3) yields on integration,

$$x=c\log\{s+\sqrt{s^2+c^2}\}+\text{const.} \quad \ldots\ldots\ldots\ldots(6)$$

Since the value of the constant is $-c\log c$, (6) can be written in the form

$$e^{\frac{x}{c}}=\frac{s+\sqrt{s^2+c^2}}{c}, \quad \ldots\ldots\ldots\ldots\ldots(7)$$

where e is the base of the Naperian system of logarithms. Multiplying the numerator and denominator of the right-hand side of (7) by $-s+\sqrt{s^2+c^2}$ and taking the reciprocal, we obtain

$$e^{-\frac{x}{c}} = \frac{-s+\sqrt{s^2+c^2}}{c}, \quad\quad\quad\quad\quad (8)$$

and subtracting (8) from (7),

$$s = \frac{c}{2}\left(e^{\frac{x}{c}} - e^{-\frac{x}{c}}\right), \quad\quad\quad\quad\quad (9)$$

the equation of the catenary in terms of x and s. The x, y equation may easily be obtained from it by (5). Or we may proceed thus: we have $dy/dx = s/c$, and therefore

$$\frac{dy}{dx} = \frac{1}{2}\left(e^{\frac{x}{c}} - e^{-\frac{x}{c}}\right). \quad\quad\quad\quad\quad (10)$$

Therefore $\quad\quad y = \frac{c}{2}\left(e^{\frac{x}{c}} + e^{-\frac{x}{c}}\right) + \text{const.}$

The value of the constant is $-c$, and hence

$$y + c = \frac{c}{2}\left(e^{\frac{x}{c}} + e^{-\frac{x}{c}}\right). \quad\quad\quad\quad\quad (11)$$

If we transfer the origin to a point at a distance c vertically below the lowest point of the cord, equation (11) takes the simpler form

$$y = \frac{c}{2}\left(e^{\frac{x}{c}} + e^{-\frac{x}{c}}\right). \quad\quad\quad\quad\quad (12)$$

Equation (5) becomes $\quad y = \sqrt{c^2 + s^2}, \quad\quad\quad\quad\quad (13)$

so that (3) may be written in the form

$$\frac{dy}{ds} = \frac{s}{y}; \quad \frac{dx}{ds} = \frac{c}{y}. \quad\quad\quad\quad\quad (14)$$

The stretching force at any point in the cord may easily be obtained. We have $T\,dy/ds = ws$, and substituting the value of dy/ds given by the first equation of (14), we get

$$T = wy. \quad\quad\quad\quad\quad (15)$$

The stretching force at any point in the cord thus equals the weight of a part of the cord whose length is equal to the ordinate of the point. It is to be remembered that the origin is now at a distance c below the lowest point of the cord.

§§ 325, 326] CATENARY. 595

326. Geometrical Properties of Catenary. We may here establish some geometrical properties of the curve. If θ denote the angle made with the horizontal by the tangent at a point P, we have $\tan\theta = s/c$, and therefore

$$\sec^2\theta \, d\theta/ds = 1/c,$$

that is, $(1 + s^2/c^2) d\theta/ds = 1/c.$

Hence, if R is the radius of curvature at P, (13) gives

$$R = \frac{ds}{d\theta} = \frac{y^2}{c}. \quad\quad\quad\quad\quad\quad\quad\quad (1)$$

In Fig. 148 a point P is taken on the curve, and a perpendicular is let fall from P upon the axis of x, meeting the axis in N. On PN as diameter a circle, centre O, is constructed; NT is a chord of the circle of length c; TM is a perpendicular let fall from T upon PN. Joining T to P, we have the angle MTP equal to the angle PNT. Again,

$\cos \angle TNP = c/y,$

by construction; hence

$\cos \angle MTP = c/y.$

But by equations (15) above, $dx/ds = c/y$.

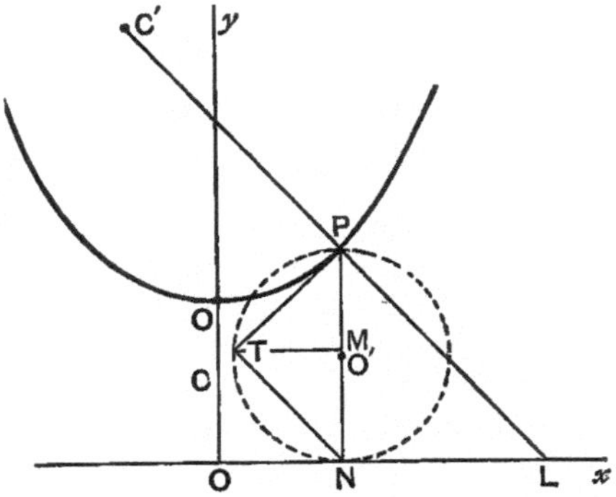

FIG. 148.

Hence PT is a tangent to the curve at P. A line drawn through P perpendicular to TP is the normal at the point P. If $C'P = y^2/c$, then C' is the centre of curvature of the curve at the point P.

Now, let the normal PC' be produced backwards to meet the axis of x in L. It is easy to see that the triangles PNL and PTN are similar, and hence $PN/NT = PL/PN$, that is, $PL = y^2/c$. Hence PL is the length of the radius of curvature. This suggests a geometrical method of constructing the curve if the lowest point A, and the value of

c are given. From the value of c we find the origin O. From O, Fig. 149, we draw OA and produce it to A' making

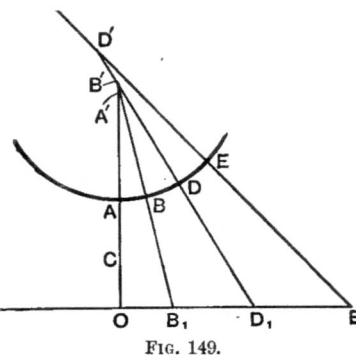

Fig. 149.

$AA' = OA$; with A' as centre, and $A'A$ as radius, we draw a short circular arc AB; A' is now joined to B, and $A'B$ produced to meet the axis of x in B_1. BB_1 is the radius of curvature of the curve at the point B. We now produce BA' backwards to B' making $BB' = BB_1$; B' is the new centre of curvature. With B' as centre and $B'B$ as radius, we draw a short circular arc BD.
Repeating this process, the complete curve may be built up.

327. Flexible Chain under Great Stretching Force. The radius of curvature for the lowest point of the curve is c. Consequently, if the curve is flat, the value of c is great. This will be the case if the sag is small in comparison with the distance between the points of attachment. If the span $2x$ and the sag d are given, we have $y = c + d$, and hence $(c+d)^2 = c^2 + s^2$, or $d^2 + 2dc = s^2$.

If the cord is very tightly stretched, c is great, and we get as an approximation from (9) of § 325, by expansion, $s = x + \frac{1}{6}x^3/c^2$, which leads to $c = x^2/\sqrt{3}d$.

328. Transmission of Power by Belt. Power is often transmitted by means of a belt passing over two wheels or pulleys, and tightly stretched to prevent slipping. In Fig. 150, let W_1 be the driving wheel and W_2 the driven wheel. When the motion is uniform, let the stretching forces in the parts AB, CD of the belt be T_1 and T_2 respectively. To find the relation which holds between T_1 and T_2 when slipping is about to occur, let PQ (Fig. 151) represent a small portion of the belt. The forces acting on PQ are (1) the force T at P, (2) the force $T + dT$ at Q, (3) the reaction dR of the pulley. Since these three forces are in equilibrium, they must meet in a point, and since slipping is on the point of taking place, dR must make with the radius C_1P of the wheel an angle ϕ, where

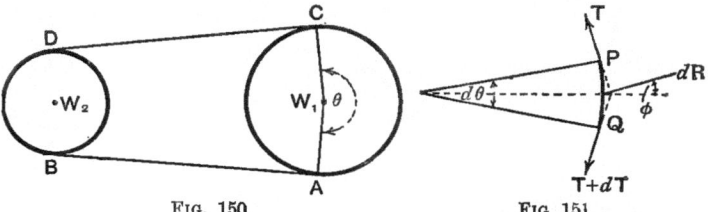

FIG. 150.   FIG. 151.

$\tan\phi$ is the coefficient of friction between the belt and rim of the wheel. Resolving along and at right angles to the belt at P, we obtain

$$(T+dT)\cos d\theta = T + dR\sin\phi, \quad (T+dT)\sin d\theta = dR\cos\phi.$$

These equations give, since $\tan\phi = \mu$, and $d\theta$ is small,

$$\frac{dT}{T} = \mu\, d\theta. \quad \text{...........................(1)}$$

Hence, integrating over the part of the rim embraced by the belt, we obtain
$$T_1 = e^{\mu\theta} T_2, \quad \text{...........................(2)}$$
where e is the base of the Naperian system of logarithms.

Let r be the radius of the driving wheel in feet, n the number of revolutions made by it per minute, T_1 and T_2 the stretching forces in the tight and slack sides of the belt expressed in Pounds. Then if H is the rate in horse-power at which work is being transmitted,

$$H = \frac{2\pi r n (T_1 - T_2)}{33000}. \quad \text{.....................(3)}$$

Now, from (2) above, we have

$$T_1 - T_2 = T_1(1 - e^{-\mu\theta}), \quad \text{....................(4)}$$

and hence
$$H = \frac{2\pi r n T_1}{33000}(1 - e^{-\mu\theta}). \quad \text{.................(5)}$$

Equation (5) may be used to determine the width of belt of a given thickness necessary to transmit a required horse-power. If p be the maximum safe stress for the material of the belt expressed in Pounds per square inch of the section, t the thickness and b the breadth of the belt, in inches, we have $T_1 = btp$. Introducing this value of T_1 in (5), we obtain an equation which determines b.

329. Equations of Equilibrium of Flexible Unstretchable String in Field of Force. Let PQ denote an element of the string, s the distance, measured along the curve, of P from a fixed point in the string, ds the length of the element PQ. Let the string be situated in a field of force, in virtue of which there is exerted on the element (mass μ), situated at the point (x, y, z) say, forces μX, μY and μZ in the directions of the axes. Let T be the pull on the element at the end P; then we have $T\,dx/ds$, $T\,dy/ds$, $T\,dz/ds$ for the components of T in the directions of the axes. The components of the pull at the end Q are

$$T\frac{dx}{ds}+\frac{d}{ds}\left(T\frac{dx}{ds}\right)ds,\quad T\frac{dy}{ds}+\frac{d}{ds}\left(T\frac{dy}{ds}\right)ds,\quad T\frac{dz}{ds}+\frac{d}{ds}\left(T\frac{dz}{ds}\right)ds.$$

Hence, for the equilibrium of the portion PQ of the string, we have
$$T\frac{dx}{ds}+\frac{d}{ds}\left(T\frac{dx}{ds}\right)ds+\mu X - T\frac{dx}{ds}=0,$$

with two similar equations. If σ be the mass per unit length of the string at P, $\mu = \sigma\,\partial s$, and the equations become

$$\left.\begin{aligned}\frac{d}{ds}\left(T\frac{dx}{ds}\right)+\sigma X &= 0,\\ \frac{d}{ds}\left(T\frac{dy}{ds}\right)+\sigma Y &= 0,\\ \frac{d}{ds}\left(T\frac{dz}{ds}\right)+\sigma Z &= 0.\end{aligned}\right\} \quad\ldots\ldots\ldots\ldots\ldots\ldots(1)$$

If the forces X, Y, Z are derivable from a potential, they take the form
$$\frac{d}{ds}\left(T\frac{dx}{ds}\right)-\sigma\frac{\partial V}{\partial s}=0,\text{ etc. }\ldots\ldots\ldots\ldots\ldots(2)$$

If the string is not in equilibrium we have to equate the

forces on the left of (1) to $\sigma\ddot{x}$, $\sigma\ddot{y}$, $\sigma\ddot{z}$ respectively, and the equations of motion

$$\sigma\ddot{x} = \frac{d}{ds}\left(T\frac{dx}{ds}\right) + \sigma X, \text{ etc.} \quad \ldots\ldots\ldots\ldots\ldots(3)$$

are obtained.

Resolving along the string we get, since

$$(dx/ds)^2 + (dy/ds)^2 + (dz/ds)^2 = 1,$$

$$\sigma\left(\ddot{x}\frac{dx}{ds} + \ddot{y}\frac{dy}{ds} + \ddot{z}\frac{dz}{ds}\right) = \frac{dT}{ds} + \sigma\left(X\frac{dx}{ds} + Y\frac{dy}{ds} + Z\frac{dz}{ds}\right). \quad (4)$$

On the left is the acceleration of the element along the string, on the right is the rate of variation dT/ds of the stretching force, and the tangential component of applied force along the string.

If now as in Ex. 5, p. 95, the only sensible forces applied to the string be due to the normal action of the peg, the second term on the right is zero. Thus we get for an element of length ds,

$$\sigma\, ds\left(\ddot{x}\frac{dx}{ds} + \ddot{y}\frac{dy}{ds} + \ddot{z}\frac{dz}{ds}\right) = \frac{dT}{ds}\, ds. \ldots\ldots\ldots\ldots(5)$$

The integral of this is small if the part s integrated over is small. This is the justification of the assumption of the equality of T_1 and T_2 made in the Example referred to.

330. Application of General Equations to Catenary. As a first example, we may apply equations (1) of § 329 to the case of a uniform flexible string suspended from two points and hanging under the action of gravity. For axes of reference in the plane of the string, the equations become, since $X = 0$, $Y = -g$,

$$\frac{d}{ds}\left(T\frac{dx}{ds}\right) = 0, \quad \frac{d}{ds}\left(T\frac{dy}{ds}\right) = \sigma g. \quad \ldots\ldots\ldots\ldots(1)$$

Integrating the first of these equations we obtain

$$T\frac{dx}{ds} = H, \quad \ldots\ldots\ldots\ldots\ldots\ldots\ldots(2)$$

where H is a constant. This equation shows that the

horizontal component of the stretching force is constant throughout the string. Integrating (2), we obtain

$$T\frac{dy}{ds} = \sigma gs + c',$$

where c' is a constant. If the origin be taken at the lowest point of the curve and the weight of unit length of the string be denoted by w, the last equation becomes

$$T\frac{dy}{ds} = ws. \quad \ldots\ldots\ldots\ldots\ldots\ldots\ldots\ldots(3)$$

Equations (2) and (3) agree with (1) of § 325, from which the equations of the catenary were derived.

331. Equation of Catenary of Uniform Strength. Again we may apply the equations to find the form assumed by a flexible string hanging under gravity, when its cross-section at any point is proportional to the stretching force there existing. Here T varies as σ, so that we may write $T = \lambda\sigma$, where λ is a constant. We have

$$T\,dx/ds = H.$$

Introducing this value of T in the second of (1), § 330, we obtain

$$H\frac{d^2y}{dx^2}\frac{dx}{ds} = \sigma g;$$

and since $H = T\,dx/ds$ and $T = \lambda\sigma$, the equation just obtained may be written

$$\frac{d^2y}{dx^2}\left(\frac{dx}{ds}\right)^2 = \frac{1}{c}, \quad \ldots\ldots\ldots\ldots\ldots\ldots(1)$$

where c is written for λ/g. Writing $1/\{1 + (dy/dx)^2\}$ for $(dx/ds)^2$ and integrating, we get

$$\tan^{-1}\frac{dy}{dx} = \frac{x}{c} + \text{const.} \quad \ldots\ldots\ldots\ldots\ldots(2)$$

If the origin is taken at the lowest point of the curve, the constant is zero, and we have $dy/dx = \tan(x/c)$, which gives

$$y = c\log\sec\frac{x}{c}. \quad \ldots\ldots\ldots\ldots\ldots\ldots(3)$$

For the reason that the stretching force per unit area is constant throughout the string, the curve determined by (3) is called the catenary of equal strength.

332. Rigid Body acted upon by Forces. The equilibrium of a rigid body is best regarded as the limiting case of the conditions set forth in Chaps. II. and IV., in which the accelerations are zero. But it is sometimes useful to consider the subject separately, and therefore the following outline of the statics of a rigid system is given. The effect produced by a given force upon a body depends on (1) the magnitude of the force, (2) its direction, (3) its line of action. It is easy to see that the force may be supposed to act at any point in its line of action. Thus, let F act at the point A in the line BA (Fig. 152). At B apply two

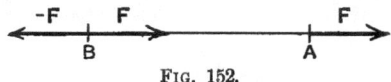

FIG. 152.

equal and opposite forces of magnitude F, one along BA and the other along AB. Provided that the point A is rigidly connected to the point B, it is evident that the three forces specified are together equivalent to the force F at A. But the force F at A and the force $-F$ at B are in the same line, and hence have a zero resultant. Thus the force F at A is equivalent to the force F at B. Hence we may suppose a force applied to a body to act at any point in its line of action, provided that the point be rigidly connected to the body.

If a rigid body is acted upon by a system of forces which are concurrent, the conditions of equilibrium are easily established. Each force may be supposed to act at the point of intersection of the forces, and the conditions of equilibrium are identical with those found above for the case of a particle.

333. Resultant of Two Parallel Forces. Before dealing with the general case of a rigid body in equilibrium under the action of forces, it is necessary that we should discuss the properties of parallel forces. A force P

(Fig. 153) is applied at A and a force Q in the same direction at B. Join AB and apply at A a force F in the direction BA, and at B a force F in the direction AB. Evidently these two forces together produce no effect upon the equilibrium of the body. The forces P and F

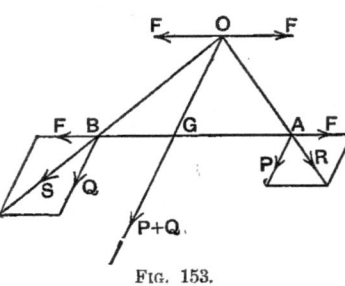

Fig. 153.

acting at A are equivalent to a force R acting in the line OA. Similarly, the forces Q and F acting at B are equivalent to a force S acting in the line OB. At O, where the lines of action of R and S intersect, we resolve R into the components F parallel to BA and P along OG, which is parallel to the directions of the forces P and Q. Treating the force S in a similar manner, we obtain a force F at O parallel to AB, and a force Q along OG. The two equal and opposite forces at O may be removed, and we are left with a force of amount $P+Q$ acting in the line OG. Thus the two parallel forces P and Q acting at the points A and B are equivalent to a force of amount $P+Q$ acting in the line OG.

Now the sides OG, GA, OA of the triangle OGA are parallel to the forces P, F and R. Hence

$$OG/GA = P/F.$$

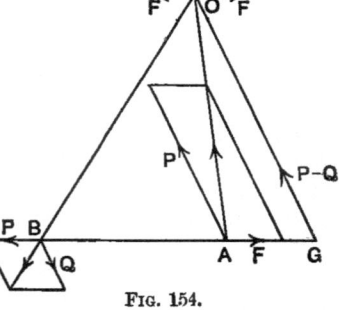

Fig. 154.

Similarly, from the triangle OGB, we obtain $OG/GB = Q/F$.

These two equations give $P \cdot GA = Q \cdot GB$, which determines the position of G.

The case in which the parallel forces are in opposite directions is dealt with in an exactly similar manner. The procedure is illustrated in Fig. 154. The student will have no difficulty in proving that the two forces P and Q applied at the points A and B are equivalent to a single force of amount $P-Q$ acting in the line OG, which is parallel to the lines of action of P and Q. The position of G is again given by $P \cdot AG = Q \cdot BG$.

334. Centre of System of Parallel Forces. Obviously where the number of parallel forces is greater than two, the magnitude and line of action of the resultant may be found by repeated application of this method. Let the forces be F_1, F_2, F_3, ..., F_n, and let them be applied at points whose coordinates are

$$(x_1, y_1, z_1),\ (x_2, y_2, z_2),\ (x_3, y_3, z_3),\ \ldots,\ (x_n, y_n, z_n).$$

If we denote the coordinates of the point of application of the resultant of F_1 and F_2 by (x', y', z'), those of the point of application of the resultant of F_1, F_2, and F_3 by (x'', y'', z''), etc., we have at once, by the previous paragraphs,

$$F_1(x' - x_1) = F_2(x_2 - x')$$
or
$$(F_1 + F_2)x' = F_1 x_1 + F_2 x_2, \ldots\ldots\ldots\ldots\ldots(1)$$

with similar equations for y' and z'. Proceeding a step further, we obtain,

$$(F_1 + F_2)(x'' - x') = F_3(x_3 - x'')$$
or
$$(F_1 + F_2 + F_3)x'' = F_1 x_1 + F_2 x_2 + F_3 x_3, \ldots\ldots\ldots(2)$$

with similar equations for y'' and z''. Dealing with all the forces in turn, we obtain finally for the coordinates $(\bar{x}, \bar{y}, \bar{z})$ of the point of application of the resultant,

$$(F_1 + F_2 + F_3 + \ldots + F_n)\bar{x} = F_1 x_1 + F_2 x_2 + F_3 x_3 + \ldots + F_n x_n, \quad (3)$$

with similar equations for $\bar{y}$ and $\bar{z}$. Hence we have

$$\bar{x} = \frac{\Sigma Fx}{\Sigma F},\ \ \bar{y} = \frac{\Sigma Fy}{\Sigma F},\ \ \bar{z} = \frac{\Sigma Fz}{\Sigma F}\ldots\ldots\ldots\ldots(4)$$

It is to be noted that the expressions for $\bar{x}$, $\bar{y}$, and $\bar{z}$ do not depend on the direction of the parallel forces. It follows that the position of this point is not changed by turning all the forces about their points of application, provided that they remain parallel. For this reason the point $(\bar{x}, \bar{y}, \bar{z})$ is called the centre of the parallel forces.

335. Centre of Gravity of Body. A body situated at the surface of the earth is acted on by a system of very nearly parallel gravity forces, since the body may be supposed built up of a system of particles rigidly connected together. Supposing the body divided up into such particles of masses m_1, m_2, m_3, etc., we have $F_1 = m_1 g$, $F_2 = m_2 g$, etc. Hence

$$\bar{x} = \frac{\Sigma mgx}{\Sigma mg}, \quad \bar{y} = \frac{\Sigma mgy}{\Sigma mg}, \quad \bar{z} = \frac{\Sigma mgz}{\Sigma mg};$$

that is

$$\bar{x} = \frac{\Sigma mx}{\Sigma m}, \quad \bar{y} = \frac{\Sigma my}{\Sigma m}, \quad \bar{z} = \frac{\Sigma mz}{\Sigma m}. \quad \ldots\ldots\ldots\ldots(1)$$

The point ($\bar{x}$, $\bar{y}$, $\bar{z}$) is called the centre of gravity of the body. It coincides with the C.I. as found in § 59. In strictness a C.G. does not exist except for bodies belonging to a limited class called *centrobaric bodies*. But the discussion of centrobaric conditions belongs to the subject of Attractions, which is not dealt with in this book.

336. Graphical Method for Parallel Forces. The line of action of the resultant of a system of parallel forces applied to a rigid body may be found by a graphical process. We take as an example the case of a bridge carrying a series of loads as shown in Fig. 155. The load W_1 may be supposed to act at any point A' in its line of action, the line being supposed rigidly connected to A. The force W_1 at A' may now be resolved into two components, one (arbitrary) in the line I, and the other in line II, it being of course understood that the lines I and II are rigidly connected to A'. The line II is produced backwards to meet the vertical through B in B'. Let now a force equal and opposite to that acting at A' in the line II act at B'. Combining this with the force W_2 acting in the line BB', we obtain a force in the line III.

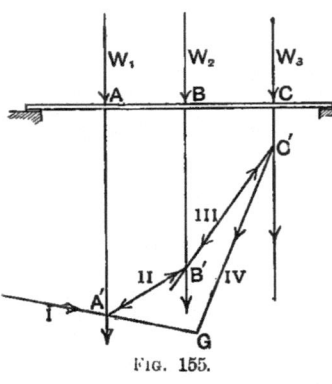

Fig. 155.

§§ 335, 336, 337]   GRAPHICAL STATICS.   605

A force equal to this reversed must now be supposed to act at the point C', the point of intersection of the line III and the vertical through C. Combining it with W_3 acting in the line CC', we obtain a force acting in the line IV. This force together with the force acting in the line I are equivalent to the forces W_1, W_2, and W_3 acting at the points A, B and C. Producing the lines I and IV until they meet, we obtain a point G in the line of action of the resultant.

337. Application to Loaded Bridge. The method of carrying out the graphical construction is shown in Fig. 156 for a bridge carrying loads W_1, W_2, W_3, W_4, and W_5. On a vertical line set off parts 12, 23, 34, 45, and 56 to represent

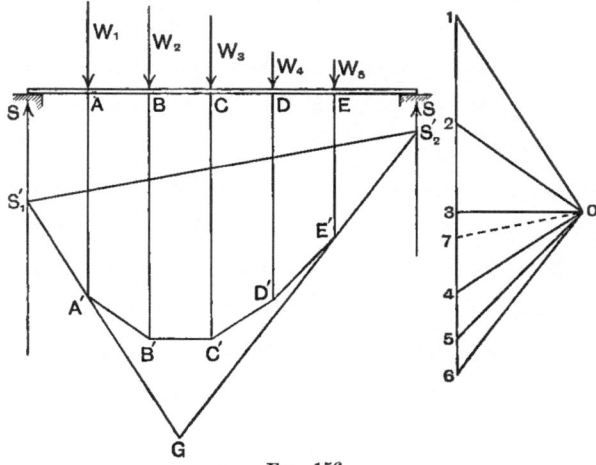

FIG. 156.

the loads. Then, selecting any point O as pole, join 01, 02, 03, 04, 05, and 06 as shown. Starting at any point S_1', in the vertical through the left-hand point of support of the bridge, draw a line $S_1'A'$ parallel to 01, meeting the vertical through A in A'; from A' draw $A'B'$ parallel to 02, meeting the vertical through B in B'; and from B' draw $B'C'$ parallel to 03, meeting the vertical through C in C'. The process is continued until finally we arrive at the point S_2''

in the vertical through the right-hand point of support of the bridge. The diagram on the right is called the force-polygon; the polygon

$$S_1'A'B'C'D'E'S_2'$$

is called the funicular polygon.

From the force-polygon we see that the force represented by 12 is equivalent to the forces represented by 10 and 02; the force represented by 23 is equivalent to the forces represented by 20 and 03; and similarly for the remaining vertical forces. If, now, we suppose the weights to act at the points A', B', etc., we see that we may replace W_1 by the forces represented by 10, 02 acting in the lines $S_1''A'$, $A'B'$; similarly we may replace W_2 by the forces represented by 20, 03 acting in the lines $A'B'$ and $B'C'$; and similarly for the other weights. We observe that we have two equal and opposite forces acting in each of the lines $A'B'$, $B'C'$, $C'D'$, $D'E'$. Consequently the forces W_1, W_2, W_3, W_4, and W_5, acting at the points A, B, C, D, E, are equivalent to the forces represented by 10, 06 acting in the lines $S_1'A'$, $S_2'E'$; producing these lines until they meet, we obtain a point G in the line of action of the resultant.

The vertical thrusts exerted at the points of support S_1 and S_2 are readily deduced from the diagram. If from 0 we draw 07 parallel to the line $S_1'S_2'$, it is easy to see that 17 represents the force applied to the left-hand support and 76 the force applied to the right-hand support. The force represented by 10 is equivalent to the forces represented by 17 and 70, and the force represented by 06 to the forces represented by 07 and 76. Consequently, if the force along $S_1'A'$ be resolved into a vertical component and a component along $S_1'S_2'$, and likewise the force along $S_2'E_1'$ into a vertical component and a component along $S_2'S_1'$, the two component forces in the line $S_1'S_2'$ are equal and opposite. Consequently the vertical thrusts applied to the supports are represented by 07 and 76.

338. Theory of Couples. The methods described above for the finding of the resultant of a pair of parallel forces break down in the case where the two forces are equal in amount, parallel, and opposite in sign. Such a system of forces is termed a couple. The subject of couples has already been touched upon in §79. We give here some further explanation. Referring to Fig. 153, we have for the point G, $P.GA = Q.GB$. If we put $P = Q$ in this equation, we have $GA = GB$, which is true only when G is at infinity. The resultant force is $P - Q$, and hence in the case of a couple the resultant force is zero, and its line of action is a line parallel to the forces, and at an infinite distance from them.

The perpendicular distance apart of the lines of action of the two forces is called the arm of the couple. In Fig. 157 let the arm be represented by AB. The product of either force into the arm is called the moment of the couple. Thus, in the case of the couple shown in the diagram, the moment is $F \times AB$. This moment evidently measures the moment of the forces about any point in their plane. Thus, if we produce AB to O and take moments about O, we have

Moment of forces about $O = F.OA - F.OB = F.AB.$

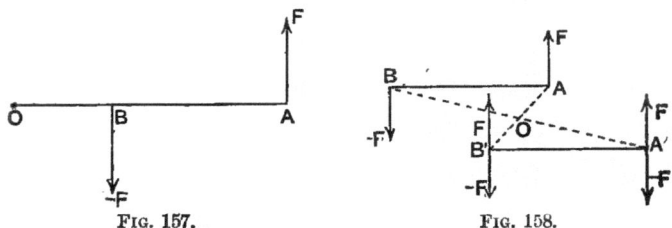

FIG. 157.   FIG. 158.

The same result is obtained if O lies between A and B; in this case the moments of the forces are of the same sign.

Certain theorems hold for couples acting on a rigid body. In the first place, we shall prove that the effect of a couple is not changed by translating it in its own plane or to any parallel plane. In Fig. 158 let AB be the arm of the couple in its initial position, and $A'B'$ the arm of the couple after the translation. Let the magnitude of each of the forces of the couple be F. Now introduce at A' and B' two equal and opposite forces, each equal and parallel to the forces at A and B; obviously the system is in no way altered. Now the force $+F$ at A and the force $+F$ at B' combine to give a force $+2F$ at O; likewise the force $-F$ at B and the force $-F$ at A' combine to give a force $-2F$ at O. These two resultant forces being equal and opposite have a zero effect upon the system. We are left with the force $+F$ at A' and the force $-F$ at B', which proves the proposition.

The effect of a couple is not changed if it is rotated in its own plane. To prove this proposition, let AB be the arm of the couple in its initial position, and $A'B'$ the arm turned about O through an angle. At A' and at B' let two equal and opposite forces each of amount F be introduced, each force being at right angles to $A'B'$. The force $-F$ at A' and the force $+F$ at A combine to give a resultant along ED; and the force $-F$ at B and the force $+F$ at B' combine to give a resultant along DE. These two resultants are equal and opposite, and we are left with the force $+F$ at A' and the force $-F$ at B', which constitute a couple equal to the original couple in all respects.

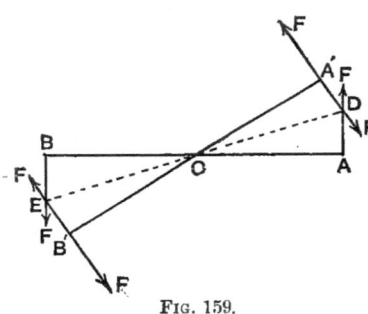

Fig. 159.

The effect of a couple is not changed if the magnitude of each of its forces and its arm are changed, provided that the moment of the couple remains unaltered. Let $AB=p$ be the original arm of the couple, and let $A'B'=p'$ be the new arm. At A' and B' introduce two equal and opposite forces, each of amount $F'=Fp/p'$, in directions parallel to the original forces. The force $-F'$ at A' and the force $-F$ at B combine to give a resultant $-(F+F')$ at O; likewise the force F at A and the force F' at B' combine to give a resultant $(F+F')$ at O. We are left with the force F' at A' and a force $-F'$ at B'.

It thus appears that the effect produced by a couple upon the equilibrium of a rigid body depends on (*a*) the moment of the couple, (b) the direction in which the couple tends to produce rotation, (c) the normal to the plane in which it is situated.

339. Graphical Representation of a Couple. It follows from the preceding section that a couple may be represented completely by a straight line. The line is drawn at right angles to the plane of the couple; its length represents the moment of the couple, and the direction in which it is drawn indicates the direction in which the couple tends to produce rotation. The convention adopted in drawing the line is as follows: if the couple, as viewed from one side, tends to produce counter-clockwise rotation, the line is drawn towards the observer; if it tends to produce clockwise rotation, the line is drawn away from the observer. In Fig. 160 the couple shown in the plane *abcd* tends to produce counter-clockwise rotation as viewed from above; we therefore represent it by a line OA drawn upwards at right angles to the plane. The student will see that if the couple is viewed from below it will tend to produce clockwise rotation, and hence the line OA must be drawn upwards as before.

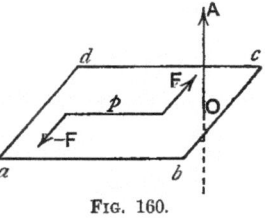

FIG. 160.

Since the effect of a couple is not altered by translating it in its own plane or to a parallel plane, it is immaterial where the initial point O of the line OA is taken. The line OA is called the axis of the couple.

340. Composition and Resolution of Couples. Now let two couples in planes inclined to one another act on a rigid body. It is easy to show that the two couples are equivalent to a single couple, the axis of which is obtained by compounding the axes of the two couples according to the parallelogram law. Let the couples act in planes perpendicular to the paper (Fig. 161); let OA be the trace of one plane, and OB the trace of the other. The two planes intersect in a line, which is represented in plan by O in the figure. We may represent the couple in the plane OA

by its axis Oa, drawn for convenience from O, and the couple in the plane OB by its axis Ob, as shown. In the figure the couples are both supposed to be counter-clockwise, as seen by an eye placed at C. The axis of the resultant couple is obtained by completing the parallelogram and taking the diagonal passing through O.

For let the arm of each couple be so changed that each of the forces become unity; the magnitudes of the couples will then be represented by their arms. Now let the couple in the plane OA be translated until one of its forces passes through O towards the reader; and let the couple in the plane OB be translated until that one of its forces which is from the reader passes through O. The two forces at O being equal and opposite, we are left with a force of unit amount at A at right angles to the paper and away from the reader, and a force of unit amount at B at right angles to the paper and towards the reader; that is, we have a couple in the plane of which AB is the trace, whose magnitude is represented by AB.

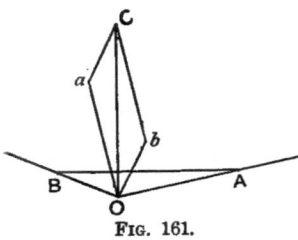

Fig. 161.

The student will have no difficulty in proving that the triangle oaC is equal to the triangle AOB, and that the line OC is perpendicular to the line AB; that is, that the two couples in the planes OA and OB are equivalent to the couple whose axis is OC.

When a number of couples act on a rigid body, their resultant is found by adding their axes geometrically. We resolve each axis into components along three rectangular lines of reference Ox, Oy, Oz. The axes which lie along Ox are added, and likewise those along Oy and Oz. If L, M, N are the sums of the axes in these directions, we have for the magnitude G of the resultant couple, and its direction-cosines l, m, n,

$$G = \sqrt{L^2 + M^2 + N^2}; \quad \dots \dots \dots \dots \dots \dots (1)$$
$$l = \frac{L}{G}; \; m = \frac{M}{G}; \; n = \frac{N}{G}. \quad \dots \dots \dots \dots \dots \dots (2)$$

FORCE AND COUPLE.

It is easy to see that a couple G and a force F in the same plane are equivalent to a force of equal amount, and in the same direction, acting in a line at a distance G/F from the line of action of F. To prove that this is the case, we merely have to rotate and translate the couple in its plane until that one of its forces which is opposite in sign to the force F lies in the same line. Keeping the line of action of this force fixed, we transform the couple so that each of its forces is of magnitude F. The two equal and opposite forces annul one another, and we are left with a single force of amount F acting in the line specified.

Conversely, a single force F applied at a point P in a rigid body can be replaced by an equal and parallel force F applied at any other point Q of the same body, together with a couple formed by F at P and $-F$ at Q.

341. Reduction of System of Forces to Force and Couple. Let forces $F_1, F_2, \ldots, F_n$, having components $X_1, Y_1, Z_1, X_2, Y_2, Z_2, \ldots, X_n, Y_n, Z_n$, be applied to a rigid body at points $(x_1, y_1, z_1), (x_2, y_2, z_2), \ldots, (x_n, y_n, z_n)$. Let X, Y, Z be the components of a representative force F applied at the point $P(x, y, z)$. We drop a perpendicular from P (Fig. 162) upon the plane yx meeting it in m, and from m we draw a line mn parallel to Oy meeting the plane xz in n. The force Z may be supposed applied at the point n. At each of the points n and O we introduce two equal and opposite forces, each of amount Z. The force Z at P and the force $-Z$ at n form a couple $+Zy$ with axis Ox; likewise the force Z at n and the force $-Z$ at O form a couple $-Zx$ with axis Oy. Hence the force Z at P is equivalent to the force Z at O together with the two couples specified. Dealing with the forces X and Y in like manner, we arrive at the result that

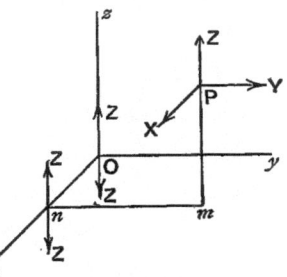

FIG. 162.

the force F' at (x, y, z) is equivalent to the force F at O together with a couple $Zy - Yz$ with axis Ox, a couple $Xz - Zx$ with axis Oy, and a couple $Yx - Xy$ with axis Oz. We thus see that the system of forces F_1, F_2, etc., applied at the points (x_1, y_1, z_1), etc., are equivalent to a system of equal and parallel forces applied at the origin O together with a couple $\Sigma(Zy - Yz)$ with axis Ox, a couple $\Sigma(Xz - Zx)$ with axis Oy, and a couple $\Sigma(Yx - Xy)$ with axis Oz. If F is the resultant force, we have

$$F = \sqrt{(\Sigma X)^2 + (\Sigma Y)^2 + (\Sigma Z)^2}; \quad \ldots\ldots\ldots\ldots\ldots(1)$$

its direction-cosines are

$$(\Sigma X)/R, \quad (\Sigma Y)/R, \quad (\Sigma Z)/R. \quad \ldots\ldots\ldots\ldots(2)$$

If G is the axis of the resultant couple, and L, M, N are its components, we have

$$L = \Sigma(Zy - Yz), \quad M = \Sigma(Xz - Zx), \quad N = \Sigma(Yx - Xy); \quad \ldots(3)$$
$$G = \sqrt{L^2 + M^2 + N^2}; \quad \ldots\ldots\ldots\ldots\ldots\ldots\ldots(4)$$

the direction-cosines of G are L/G, M/G, N/G.

342. Conditions of Equilibrium. To obtain the acceleration of the centroid of a body, we suppose all the forces transferred to the centroid without change. Hence the centroid will be without acceleration if

$$\Sigma X = 0, \quad \Sigma Y = 0, \quad \Sigma Z = 0. \quad \ldots\ldots\ldots\ldots\ldots(1)$$

Further, the rate of change of moment of momentum of the body about all axes will be zero if

$$\Sigma(Zy - Yz) = 0, \quad \Sigma(Xz - Zx) = 0, \quad \Sigma(Yx - Xy) = 0. \ldots(2)$$

When a rigid body is without linear acceleration of its centroid and angular acceleration about any axis, it is said to be in equilibrium. The equations (1) and (2) are called the equations of equilibrium. (See § 75 above.)

343. Poinsot's Central Axis, Wrench. We have seen that any system of forces acting on a rigid body is equivalent to a single resultant force F, acting at an arbitrary origin O, and a resultant couple G. In Fig. 163 let O be the origin, F the resultant force, and G the axis of the couple, drawn for convenience from O. We resolve G into two components Om and On along and perpendicular to F. The component Om represents a couple in any plane perpendicular to F, and On represents a couple in any plane perpendicular to On. This latter couple and the force F are equivalent to a force of amount F acting in a line $O'T$, whose distance from O is On/F, that is, $G \sin \theta/F$, where θ is the angle between F and G. The line OO', it will be observed, is perpendicular to the plane containing F and G. The force F at O and the couple G are thus equivalent to a force F in $O'T$ together with a couple in a plane perpendicular to $O'T$. The line $O'T$ is called Poinsot's central axis.

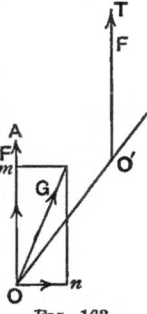

Fig. 163.

The combination of a force acting in a straight line and a couple whose axis coincides with the line is termed a *wrench*. The ratio G/F, which evidently represents a length, is termed the *pitch* of the wrench.

Let X, Y, Z be the components of the force F at O, and L, M, N those of the couple G. The component couples about any point of coordinates x, y, z are

$$L - Zy + Yz, \quad M - Xz + Zx, \quad N - Yx + Xy.$$

Now the central axis is a line in the direction of the force F, such that the force system reduces to the parallel force F along that line, and a couple about that line. Hence the axis of the couple must have direction-cosines proportional to X, Y, Z. They are also proportional to the component couples written above. The equations of the central axis are therefore

$$\frac{L - Zy + Yz}{X} = \frac{M - Xz - Zx}{Y} = \frac{N - Yx + Xy}{Z}. \quad \ldots\ldots(3)$$

This as the reader may verify can be transformed to

$$\frac{x-a}{X} = \frac{y-b}{Y} = \frac{z-c}{Z}, \quad \ldots\ldots\ldots\ldots\ldots\ldots\ldots(4)$$

where $a, b, c = (NY - MZ, LZ - NX, MX - LY)/F, \ldots\ldots(5)$

so that a, b, c are the coordinates of a point through which the central axis passes. [Compare the discussion of the *Central Axis of the Motion of a Body*, § 247.]

We conclude the chapter with some examples, worked and unworked.

EXERCISES XI.

1. A man walking at the rate of 5·5 feet per second drags behind him 19 feet of flexible rope weighing five pounds per foot. If he holds the end of the rope 5 feet above the ground, show that he works at the rate of ·12 H.P. in dragging the rope (coefficient of kinetic friction between rope and ground = 0·2).

Let l feet be the length of the rope dragged along the ground; the remaining $19-l$ feet will hang in a catenary. Denoting the weight of one foot of the rope by w and the coefficient of friction by μ, we see that the stretching force in the catenary at the lowest point is $\mu w l$. Hence $c = \mu l$. The value of y at the highest point is $5 + c$, and the length of the catenary is $19 - l$, so that

$$(5 + \mu l)^2 = \mu^2 l^2 + (19 - l)^2.$$

Introducing the value of μ and reducing, we get

$$l^2 - 40l + 336 = 0,$$

which gives $l = 20 \pm 8$.

Hence the length of rope dragged along the ground is 12 feet. The horizontal force applied is therefore 12 Pounds, and the rate of working in horse-power is $12 \times 5·5/550 = 0·12$.

2. A heavy uniform chain 110 feet long is stretched between two points in the same level 108 feet apart. Find the stretching force in the chain at either of the points of attachment.

If l denotes the length of the chain and d the span, we have

$$l = c \left(e^{\frac{d}{2c}} - e^{-\frac{d}{2c}} \right).$$

Expanding the right-hand side of this equation and remembering that c is great, we obtain

$$c^2 = d^3/24(l - d) = 108^3/48,$$

from which $c = 162$. If h is the droop in the centre, we have very approximately, by § 327, $h = \sqrt{\tfrac{3}{8} l (l-d)} = 9·08$. Hence if T be the stretching force in the chain at one of the points of support,

$$T = wy = w(c + h) = 171·08 w.$$

The maximum stretching force which the chain is called upon to bear is 1·55 times its own weight.

XI.]   EXERCISES.   615

3. Two uniform rods connected at one extremity by a smooth hinge rest on two smooth pegs on the same level and distant d from one another. If each rod be of length l and be inclined to the horizontal at an angle θ, show that $\theta = \cos^{-1} \sqrt[3]{d/l}$.

Let w be the weight of either rod, F the force applied by each of the pegs to the rod resting upon it. Taking moments about the hinge, we have
$$w \frac{l}{2} \cos \theta = F \frac{d}{2 \cos \theta}.$$

Resolving vertically, we obtain
$$F \cos \theta = w.$$

From these two equations, we have, finally,
$$\cos^3 \theta = \frac{d}{l}.$$

4. Three rods OA, OB, OC, of equal length l and weight w, are freely jointed at O, and their other ends are connected by threads AB, BC, CA, each of length k. The system is placed on a smooth horizontal plane on which A, B, C rest, the threads being tight. Show that the stretching force in each thread is $wk/6\sqrt{l^2 - \frac{1}{3}k^2}$.

Let fall a perpendicular from O upon the horizontal plane meeting it in O'. Since the ends A, B, C of the rods form an equilateral triangle, we have $O'A = k/\sqrt{3}$, and hence $OO' = \sqrt{l^2 - \frac{1}{3}k^2}$. Obviously the reaction of the plane on each of the ends of the rods is w. The forces acting on the rod OA are (1) the weight w of the rod acting at its centre of gravity, (2) the reaction w applied by the plane at A, (3) the stretching forces, each of amount T in the strings adjacent to A, (4) the force applied to the rod OA at the hinge. Taking moments about O, we have

$$2T \cos 30° \sqrt{l^2 - \frac{1}{3}k^2} + \frac{wk}{2\sqrt{3}} = \frac{wk}{\sqrt{3}};$$

that is
$$T = wk/6 \sqrt{l^2 - \frac{1}{3}k^2}.$$

5. Twelve equal forces act along the edges of a cube, the parallel forces acting in the same direction. Find the central axis of the system.

Let a be the length of an edge of the cube, P the magnitude of each force. Consider first the forces parallel to the axis Ox (Fig. 164). We have

(1) The force along OA, which is P along Ox.
(2) The force along BF; this force can be replaced by P along Ox together with a couple $-Pa$, whose axis is along Oz.
(3) The force along CD; this force can be replaced by P along Ox together with a couple $+Pa$, whose axis is along Oy.

(4) The force along EG; this force is equivalent to P along Ox, together with a couple $Pa\sqrt{2}$, whose axis is perpendicular to the plane containing OA and EG; this last couple may obviously be resolved into a couple $+Pa$ whose axis is along Oy, and a couple $-Pa$ whose axis lies along Oz. Thus the four forces parallel to Ox may be replaced by a force of amount $4P$ along Ox, a couple $+2Pa$ whose axis lies along Oy, and a couple $-2Pa$ whose axis lies along Oz.

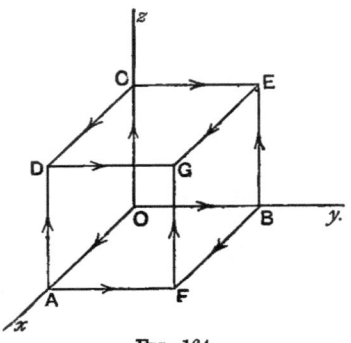

Fig. 164.

The forces parallel to Oy yield similarly a force $4P$ along Oy, a couple $+2Pa$ whose axis lies along Oz, and a couple $-2Pa$ whose axis lies along Ox. The forces parallel to Oz are equivalent to a force $4P$ along Oz, a couple $2Pa$ whose axis is along Ox, and a couple $-2Pa$ whose axis lies along Oy.

It will be seen that the couples destroy one another in pairs. The twelve original forces are thus equivalent to the three forces $4P$ along Ox, $4P$ along Oy, and $4P$ along Oz. The Poinsot couple is zero; the system reduces to a force $4P\sqrt{3}$ along the diagonal OG, which is the central axis.

6. A is the lowest point of a uniform flexible chain hanging from two fixed points B and C. If a and b are the heights of A and B above the directrix of the catenary in which the chain hangs, show that the length of chain between A and B is $\sqrt{(b^2-a^2)}$.

One end of a uniform chain of length 13 feet is fastened to a fixed point at a height 3 feet above a *rough* horizontal plane (coefficient of friction $\frac{1}{3}$). Part of the chain rests on the horizontal plane, and the whole chain is in one vertical plane. Show that the greatest length of chain which can hang between the point and the plane is five feet.

7. Show that a uniform heavy flexible inextensible string supported from two points A, B hangs in the form of the curve $c\sec^2\psi = \rho$, where ρ is the radius of curvature at any point and ψ the inclination to the horizontal of the tangent at that point.

Assuming that the force exerted by the wind on a flexible ribbon is at each point entirely normal to the ribbon and proportional to the square of the normal component of the wind's velocity, show that a ribbon attached to two points P, Q will assume the form of a catenary. [Take PQ perpendicular to the direction of the wind and neglect the weight of the ribbon.]

8. Two equal pulleys on the same level and 260 feet apart are connected by a long wire cable, and it is found that when the pulleys are in motion the maximum sag in the cable is 4 feet for the driving side and 8 feet for the slack side. Find approximately (in Pounds per square inch) the stress in the cable at the pulleys for both the slack and the driving sides, the weight of the cable being taken as 0·3 pounds per cubic inch. If the cable be just on the point of slipping on a pulley, find approximately the coefficient of friction.

9. A belt laps the driving wheel of a steam engine, the angle subtended at the centre of the wheel by the arc of contact being 150°. The wheel is of diameter 3 feet, makes 110 revolutions per minute, and transmits 20 horse-power. Show that if the coefficient of friction between the wheel and belt is 0·36, and slipping is about to take place, the maximum pull in the belt is about 1042 Pounds.

10. Two equal beams, AB, AC, hinged freely at A, stand in a vertical plane with the ends B and C resting on a smooth horizontal plane. The rods are kept from falling by two strings connecting B and C with the middle points of the opposite beams. Show that if T is the stretching force in either string and W the weight of either beam,
$$\frac{T}{W} = \frac{1}{4}\sqrt{9\cot^2\theta + 1},$$
where θ is the inclination of either beam to the horizontal.

11. A heavy uniform rod of length $2l$ rests partly within and partly without a smooth fixed hemispherical bowl of radius r. Show that the rod is in equilibrium when the inclination to the horizontal is given by
$$\cos\theta = \frac{l + \sqrt{l^2 + 32r^2}}{8r}.$$
Consider the question of stability of equilibrium.

12. A smooth rod, length $2l$, has one end resting on a plane inclined at an angle α to the horizon, and is supported by a horizontal rail which is parallel to the plane and distant d from it. Show that the angle θ between the rod and plane is given by the equation
$$d\sin\alpha = l\sin^2\theta\cos(\theta - \alpha).$$

13. A heavy uniform rod AB can turn freely about the fixed end A while B rests against a rough vertical wall, coefficient of friction μ.

If B is just on the point of slipping, specify, with the aid of a careful sketch, the forces maintaining equilibrium; and show that if N is the foot of the perpendicular from A on the wall, θ the inclination of NB to the vertical and ϕ the angle NAB, then

$$\tan\theta\tan\phi = \mu.$$

14. A square drawer, of length l, is pulled out by a handle to one side, at a distance d from the edge of the drawer. Show that the drawer will jam unless the coefficient of friction is less than $l/(l-2d)$.

15. A bicycle is driven by two pedals, each of length $2a$ and mass m, attached to the ends of two cranks, of length $2b$ and mass m_2, at distance $2c$ apart. If the pedals are rotating with angular velocity ω and a vertical force F is applied to one pedal while the cranks are horizontal, find the resultant action on the bearing of the pedal axle. (Neglect the friction in the bearing and regard the pedals and cranks as uniform rods.)

16. Equal forces F act along the sides AB, CD of a regular tetrahedron $ABCD$; determine the equivalent wrench.

17. A right circular cylinder of radius r is acted on by a force P along, and a couple G round, its axis, and also by a force Q tangential to the circumference and perpendicular to the axis. Prove that the system is equivalent to a force $R=\sqrt{P^2+Q^2}$ and a couple of moment

$$(P.G + P.Q.r)/R,$$

the axis of the couple coinciding with the direction of R.

18. Forces la, mb, nc act in three non-intersecting edges of a rectangular parallelepiped, where a, b, c are the lengths of these edges. If the directions of the forces be taken in cyclic order and the system be reduced to a wrench, show that the product of the force and couple of that wrench has the numerical value

$$(lm + mn + nl)V,$$

where V is the volume of the parallelepiped.

19. Two forces P and P' act along lines whose shortest distance apart is c; show that the central axis of the two forces intersects the shortest distance between the lines in a point at distance

$$\frac{P'(P' + P\cos\theta)c}{R^2}$$

from the force P, R being the force along the central axis and θ the angle between the two forces P and P'.

20. Four equal heavy uniform bars, freely jointed at their ends, form a square $ABCD$; the joint A is fixed, while the joints B and D are connected by a string, and the whole system rests in a vertical plane, the string being horizontal. Show that the stretching force in the string is $2W$, where W is the weight of a rod. Prove also that the reaction at C is horizontal and of amount $\frac{1}{2}W$; that the force on BC at B is $W\sqrt{5}/2$ in a direction inclined at $\tan^{-1}1/2$ to the vertical; that the force on AB at B is $W\sqrt{13}/2$ inclined at $\tan^{-1}3/2$ to the vertical; and that the reaction on AB at A is $5W/2$, and intersects BD at a distance $\frac{1}{5}BD$ from B.

21. Three forces P, Q, R act along the non-intersecting edges of a rectangular parallelepiped, whose edges corresponding to the forces are a, b, c. Prove that the forces have a single resultant if

$$a/P + b/Q + c/R = 0.$$

22. Two forces P and Q, acting in directions making an angle α with one another, have c for the shortest distance between their lines of action. Prove that when they are reduced to their central axis the couple is $PQ\sin\alpha \cdot c/R$, where R is the resultant force.

INDEX.

The references are to pages.

Acceleration, 16.
  examples of, 22.
  components of, 30.
  in direction of motion, applications, 339 *et seq.*
  of point of rotating body, 443, 456.
Action and reaction, 98.
  Newton's law of, 98.
Active and inactive forces, 105.
Activities, equal and opposite, 103.
  Newton's law of, 103.
Angular displacements, signs of, 446.
  composition of, 447.
  components of, 449.
Angular velocity,
  components of, 449.
Angular momentum, 114.
  components of, 116.
  about parallel axes, 117.
  rate of change of, 119.
    with effective inertia different in different directions, 120.
    when body gains or loses mass, 121.
    equal to moment of force, 122.
    examples of, 127.
  of rigid body, 305, 457.
    rate of change of, 458.
    relation of axes of, and instantaneous axis, 461.
APPELL, dynamical equations, 567.
Apsides, theory of, 279.
ATWOOD, machine of, 138, 436.
Axes, of coordinates, 13.
  moving, 17, 30, 33.
  principal, of moments of inertia, 312.

Ball-bearings, theory of, 436.
Bell and clapper, 409, 412.
BERTRAND, theorem of impulsive motion, 582.
Bicycle, on banked track, 350.
Bifilar suspension, theory of, 421.
BINET, theorem of, 333.
Body-point, acceleration of, 443.
  curvature of path of, 444.
BONNET, theorem of central forces, 293.
Brachistochrone, 179.
  in conservative field, 180.
  under gravity, 182.
  variational method of investigating, 184.
  in any field of force, 185.
Brakes, efficiency of, 344.
BRENNAN, monorail car, 528.
Buffers, proper height of, 363.
  action of, 437.

Canonical equations of motion, 570.
  integration of by Jacobi's method, 576.
Carriage, passage of, over obstacle, 359.
  extra work on causeway, 361.
  effect of springs, 361.
  proper height of buffers of railway carriage, 363.
Catenary, 594 *et seq.*
  geometrical properties of, 597.
  application of general equations to, 601.
  of uniform strength, 600.

INDEX. 621

Central axis, of motion of rigid body, 452.
  examples on, 453.
  of forces on rigid body, 612.
Central forces, 220...306.
  differential equation of path of particle, 221.
  transverse force, 221.
  inverse square of distance law, 230 et seq., 245 et seq.
  inverse cube of distance law, 281 et seq.
  from different centres for same orbit, 287.
  Hamilton's theorem, 288.
  Halphen and Darboux, theorem, 293.
  Bonnet's theorem, 293.
  Curtis' theorems, 294.
  examples of multiple centres of force, 295.
  earth-moon system disturbed by sun, 297.
    stability of, Hill's theorem, 298.
  exercises on, 300.
Centre of mass, or centroid, 100.
  properties of, 101.
Centrodes, space and body, 441.
Chain, of suspension bridge, 591.
  flexible under great force, 596.
  equations of equilibrium, 598.
Components of Velocity and Acceleration, 30.
Compound Pendulum, 379.
  theory of, 380.
  suspension and oscillation axes, 382.
  experimental, 385.
  Kater's, 385.
  buoyancy and airdrag of, 386.
  examples on, 388 et seq.
  reactions of, on axis, 391.
  double, theory of, 405.
  ballistic, 429.
Constraints, work due to, 550.
  equations expressing, 551.
Couples, 134.
  equivalence of, 134.
  theory of, 606.
  graphical representation of, 611.
  composition and resolution of, 611.

CURTIS, theorems of orbital motion, 237.
  theorems of central forces, 294.
Curvature of Path, in three dimensional space, 36.

DARBOUX, theorem of central forces, 293.
Directed quantity, 17.
  rate of growth of, 17.
Displacement, 1 et seq.
  of rigid body parallel to fixed plane, equivalent to rotation, 439.
  of rigid body equivalent to that of nut on screw, 440.
Double compound pendulum, theory of, 405.
  examples of, 407.
  small vibrations of, 408.
  bell and clapper, 409, 412.
  driving and driven pendulums, 411.
  theory of seismographs, 411.

Elliptic functions, 161.
Energy, kinetic, 86.
  potential, 87.
  kinetic, of translation and rotation, 132.
Equations of motion, 90.
  for systems of varying mass, 91.
    examples, 92.
  for rigid body, 125.
  Euler's, for rigid body, 320.
  for impulsive motion, 400.
  of rigid body with reference to rotating axes, 456.
  integration of, 575.
Equilibrium, of particle, 587.
  in smooth tube, 587.
  of flexible string, 588.
  conditions of, for rigid body, 612.
Equimomental cone, 332.
  Binet's theorem, 333.
EULER, theorem as to brachistochrones, 181.
  of time in orbit, 264.
  equations of motion of rigid body, 320, 459.
  motion of top deduced from, 502.
Exponential motion, 77, 78.

INDEX.

Force, 85.
  units of, 96.
  as space-derivative of potential energy, 111.
  frictional or dissipative, 113.
  polygon of, 588.
  reduction of force-system to force and couple, 611.
FOUCAULT, gyrostatic indicator of earth's rotation, 526.
  pendulum showing rotation of earth, 549.
Free axis, 317.
Friction, laws of, 369 et seq.
  rollers, theory of, 436.

General dynamical methods, 550...588.
Generalised coordinates, 553.
  Lagrange's equations in, 555.
  kinetic energy in terms of, 556.
  Hamilton's equations, 568, 572.
Generalised momenta, 557.
  Hamilton's equations, 568, 572.
GILBERT, barygyroscope, 526.
Gravitation, universal, 257.
  experimental illustration, 261.
Gravity, apparent and true, 169.
GRAY, A., method of forming equations of motion of rotating body, 9, 475.
  on Lagrange's equations, 574.
GRAY, Thomas, seismographs, 411.
  vertical motion seismograph, 420.
GREENHILL, Sir George, reaction of compound pendulum, 391.
Gyration, radii of, 330.
  ellipsoid of, 330.
  Binet's theorem, 333.
Gyrostat, 504...536.
  motion of, 504.
  stability of, 506.
  elementary explanation of precession of, 509.
  experiments with, 510.
  on trunnions, 511.
  equations of motion of, 512.
  steady motion of, 513.
    oscillations about, 513.
  on gimbals, 515.
  in pendulum bob, 516.
    analogy to motion of electron, 519.

Gyrostat, Bessemer's gyrostatically supported cabin, 519.
  virtual increase of M.I. produced by, 521.
  theory of vibrator containing, 523.
Gyrostatic, action, 509 et seq.
    of rotating bodies on their bearings, 520.
  increase of M.I. due to, 521.
  controller of rolling of ship, 524.
  of turbines in steamers, 531.
  on locomotive or carriage, 535.
  controller of torpedo, 538.

HALPHEN, theorem of central forces, 293.
HAMILTON, theorem of central forces, 288.
  equations of motion in generalised coordinates, 568, 572.
  canonical equations, 570.
  "reciprocal function," 570.
  partial differential equation, 575.
  "principal function," 575, 577.
  "characteristic function," 577.
Herpolhode, 465.
  form of, 467.
Holonomous and not holonomous systems, 555.
Hoop or disk, rolling on horizontal plane, 544.
  vibrations of, about steady motion, 543.
  condition of upright rolling, 544.
Horizontal plane, rolling and sliding of solid of revolution on, 376.

Ice-boat, motion of, 432.
Ignoration of coordinates, 573.
Impact, 396 et seq.
  duration of, 399.
Impulses, theory of, 395.
  inelastic bodies, impact of, 396.
  theory of pile-driver, 396.
  equations of motion for system under, 400.
  applied to compound pendulum, 402.
  applied to rod on smooth table, 403.
  examples of, 404.

INDEX.   623

Inclined plane,
  rolling of solid on, 368.
  sliding of body on, 369.
  railway carriage at rest on, 372.
    in motion on, 374.
Inelastic bodies,
  impact of, 396.
  energy changes in, 398.
Inertia, effective, different in different directions, 136.
  moments of, 125, 309.
  products of, 311, 313.
  foci of, 329.
  rotary, 362.
  effective of wheeled vehicle or of train of wheelwork, 366.
Integration of equations of motion, meaning of, 575.
Invariable line, 463.

JACOBI, dynamical theorem of, 576.
  examples on, 578.
  elliptic motion of planet, 579.

KATER, determination of gravity, 385.
KELVIN, Lord, tide predicter, 68.
  influence of suspension on rate of chronometer, 421.
  theorem of impulsive motion, 582.
Kinematics of moving point, 1.
Kinetic potential, 560.

LAGRANGE, equations of motion, 555.
  examples on, 563.
  equations for impulsive forces, 580.
Lagrangian function, 560.
LAMBERT, theorem of time in an orbit, 263.
LAPLACE, tautochronic motion, 178.
Laws of motion, 88.
  first law of motion, 88.
  second law of motion, 89.
  third law of motion, 97.
Locomotive, on super-elevated rail, 350.
  gyrostatic action of, 535.

Mass, effect of change of, 84.
Momental ellipsoid, 310.
  principal axes of, 312.

Moments of inertia, 125, 309, 310.
  in different cases, 320.
  of a lamina, 321.
  of triangular plate, 321.
  about axes at any point parallel to principal axes at centroid, 324,
  examples of, 325.
  condition that an ellipsoid may be momental ellipsoid, 328.
  radii of gyration, 330.
  ellipsoid of gyration, 330.
  equimomental cone, 332.
  Binet's theorem, 333.
Motion, varying, 4.
  graphical representation of, 11.
  curvilinear, 25.
    radial and transverse components of, 26.
  in three dimensional space, 35.
  uniplanar, 30.
  of particle along moving guide, 38.
  of projectile in uniform field of force, 42.
    properties of path, 43.
  under acceleration towards fixed point and varying inversely as square of distance, 54.
    equations of, 55.
    equation of hodograph for, 56.
    path of particle for, 57.
  simple harmonic, 61:
    velocity and acceleration in, 62.
    equation of, 62.
    amplitude, period and phase, 63.
    uniform circular motion derived from, 64.
  exponential, 77.
  first law of, 88.
  second law of, 89.
  third law of, 97.
  equations of, 90, 320, 456.
  non-rotational, 91.
  rotational, 114, 438.
  translational and rotational, 122.
  resisted, 144 *et seq.*
  of a simple pendulum, 159, 160.
  of particle in vertical circle, 161.
  cycloidal, 172.
  tautochronous, 174.
  Lagrange's equations of, 555.

624   INDEX.

Motor-bus, time of running, 348.
Motor-car, on convex road, 168.
  turning corner on level, 349.

NEWTON, laws of motion, 88 ... 97.
  revolving orbit, 236.
  dynamical deductions from Kepler's laws, 251.
    correction of Kepler's third law, 254.
    theory of universal gravitation, 257.
  theorem of different centres for same orbit, 287.

Orbital motion, 220.
  differential equation of path, 220.
  force transverse to radius-vector, 221.
  speed from infinity, 225.
  exhaustion of potential energy, 225, 242.
  force varying as distance, 227.
  laws of force in different cases, 229.
  solutions of differential equation in various cases, 230.
  discrimination of orbit, 232.
  period of particle in orbit, 233.
  determination of orbit, 234.
  Newton's revolving orbit, 236.
  law of force for inverse of given orbit, 237.
  relation of orbit and brachistochrone, 241.
  acceleration in terms of tangential and radial forces, 244.
  hodograph, 245.
  velocity resolved into two constant components, 246.
  laws of force deduced from form of orbit, 247.
  Kepler's laws, 248.
    verification, 249.
    Newton's dynamical deductions, 251.
  effect of mass of planet, 252.
  experimental illustration of, 261.
  elements of an orbit, 262.
  time in an orbit, 263.
    Lambert and Euler's theorems, 264.

Orbital motion, disturbed orbits, 266 ... 271.
  examples of, 271 et seq.
  disturbed circular orbit, 276.
  under forces from different centres, 287.
  Bonnet's theorem, 293.
  Curtis' theorems, 294.
  examples, 295.
  stability of earth-moon system, Hill's theorem, 298.
  exercises, 300.

Parabolic motion, 42 et seq.
Parallel forces, centre of system, 605.
  graphical method for, 606.
  application to loaded bridge, 607.
Pendulum, simple, 159, 160.
  cycloidal, 172.
  conical, 188.
  double, 189, 191.
    physical analogues of, 194.
  spherical, 197 et seq.
  compound, 379.
    suspension and oscillation axes, 382.
  on vibrating supports, 414, 425.
  gyrostatic, 516.
Periodic variation of speed of vehicle,
  (1) time periodic, (2) space periodic, effect of on activity, 354.
Pile-driver, theory of, 396.
  how far a pile should be driven, 399.
Planetary motion, 54.
  hodograph for, 55.
  equation of path, 57.
  resolution of velocity into two parts of constant amount, 59.
Plummet, equilibrium of, 168.
  in railway carriage, 170.
POINSOT, momental-ellipsoid, 310.
  method of representing motion of rigid body under no forces, 462.
  central axis, 615.
Polar coordinates, 27.
Polhodes, and herpolhodes, 465.
  projections of, 466.

INDEX. 625

Polygons, funicular, 586.
  with equal horizontal projections of sides, 590.
Power, transmission of by belt, 596.
Precession, of symmetrical top, 476.
  effect of accelerating or impeding, causing top to rise or fall, 492.
  astronomical, 497.
  of equinoxes, 498.
Principal coordinates, 586.
Projectile, in uniform field, 42.
  properties of path of, 43.
  horizontal range of, 44.
  range of, through fixed point, 44.
  envelope of coplanar paths of, 46.
  examples of motion of, 48.
  time of flight of, 49.
  drift of in air, 536.
  stability of, 537.

Rate of change of momentum, in curvilinear motion, 85.
  effect of change of mass on, 84.
RAYLEIGH, Lord, on effect of constraints, 583.
Reactions of rigid body, 315.
Rectilinear Motion in resisting medium, 144.
  limiting speed in resisting medium, 145.
Relative motion, 11.
  of parts of ship, effect of, on activity, 356.
Resistance to shot, 217.
Resisted motion, 144.
  when resistance varies as v^n, 149.
  when resistance varies as v, 153, as v^2, 153, as v^3, 154.
  in vertical line, 155.
  examples of under gravity, 156.
  curvilinear in uniform field, 206.
    resistance, kv, 210.
    trajectory for, 211.
    resistance, kv^n, 213.
    hodograph, 214.
    intrinsic equation, 214.
    flat trajectory, 216.
  exercises, 218.
Revolution of particle in vertical circle, 164.
  examples on, 165.

Rifle bullet, speed of in air, 353.
  drift of, 536.
  stability of, 537.
Rigid body, translatory motion of, 122.
  rotation of, 125.
  moments of inertia of, 125.
  rolling motion of, 125.
  equations of rotational motion of, 317.
  Euler's equations for, 320.
  examples on central axis and rotation of, 453.
  motion of, under no forces, 462.
  stability of motion of, under no forces, 466.
  examples on motion of, 468.
  equilibrium of, 601.
Road surface, effect of on vehicular traffic, 343.
Rolling, of solid on inclined plane, 368.
  of M.E. on invariable plane, 463.
  of body cone on space-cone in motion of top, 500.
  of solid of revolution on horizontal plane, 539.
  of hoop or disk, on horizontal plane, 543.
  oscillations of, 543.
Rotation, 114, 122, 438 *et seq.*
  of tops and gyrostats, 475...544.
ROUTH, *Stability of Motion*, 574.
  Elementary Dynamics, 586.

Salisbury, railway accident at, 351, 352.
SCHLICK, gyrostatic controller of rolling of ship, 524.
Screw-motion, theory of, 440.
  cylindroid, exercises, 472.
Seismographs, 411.
  for vertical motion, 420.
Simple harmonic motion, 61.
  velocity and acceleration in, 62.
  equation of, 62.
  amplitude, period, and phase, 63.
  uniform circular motion derived from, 64.
  composition, 66, 67, 68, 69.
  resisted, 75.
  differential equation, 77.

INDEX.

Solid of revolution, rolling of on horizontal plane, 539...544.
Speed, 1.
  varying, 5, 9.
  curve of, 6.
  distance traversed at varying, 7.
Spiral of Archimedes, motion in, 31.
Spiral springs, connected, 195, 196.
Stability, of earth-moon system, 298.
  of motion of rigid body under no forces, 466.
  of top, 489.
  of gyrostat, 506.
  of projectile, 537.
Statics, 586...619.
Steamship comparison, law of, 147.
  examples, 148.
Suspension bridge, chain of, 591.

TAIT, elliptic orbit and brachistochrone, 241.
Tautochronous motion, 174.
  examples of, 175.
Tops and gyrostats, 475...544.
Top, symmetrical motion of, 475.
  spherical, 478.
  path of point on axis of top, 479.
  rise and fall of top, 479.
  started with rapid rotation, 482.
  vibrations of rapidly rotating, 483, 489.
  reaction of on support, 484.
  examples on motion of, 486.
  steady motion of, 488.
  graphical representation of condition of stability of, 489.
  effect of forcing precession above free value, 492.
  reaction of ring-guide or spacecone on, 494.
  explanation of clinging of axle of, to curved guide, 495.
  rising and falling of ordinary, 510.
Torpedo, gyrostatic controller of, 538.
Trains, problems, regarding, 341, 344 et seq., 433.
  time from station to station, 344.
Turbines, steam, gyrostatic action of, 531.

Vehicle, self-propelled, dynamics of, 346.
  dynamics of on curve, 348, 350.
  time of starting and stopping, 348.
  effect of periodic variation of speed of, 354.
  wheeled, inertia of, 366.
    motion of on inclined plane, 366.
    at rest on incline, 372.
Velocity, 1.
  graphical representation of, 11.
  relative, 15.
  curve of, 15.
  angular, 17, 449.
  components of, 30.
  linear, of point in turning body, 450.
Vibrations, theory of, 61 et seq.
  of simple pendulum, 159.
  of double compound pendulum, 408.
  of simple pendulum with vibrating support, 414.
  resonance, 416.
    examples of, 417.
  examples of forced, 418.
  examples of mutually influencing, 420 et seq.
  of balance and case of watch, 193, 420.
  of watch hung by bifilar suspension, 421.
  of carriage on springs, 424.
    steadiness of, 425.
  retarded by friction, 426.
    tidal example, 427.
  general theory of, 585.

Watch, influence of suspension on rate of, 193.
  as double compound pendulum, 420.
Weather helm, why a ship carries, 137.
Work, 104.
  units of work, 105.
  variational equation of, 108.
  done in starting and stopping trains, 341.
  due to constraints of system, 550.

By Prof. Andrew Gray

The Theory and Practice of Absolute Measurements in Electricity and Magnetism. Two volumes. Crown 8vo. Vol. I. 12s. 6d. Vol. II. 2 Parts. 25s.

Absolute Measurements in Electricity and Magnetism. Fcap. 8vo. 5s. 6d.

A Treatise on Magnetism and Electricity. Part I. 8vo. 14s. net.

By Prof. Andrew Gray and Prof. G. B. Mathews

A Treatise on Bessel Functions and their Applications to Physics. 8vo. 14s. net.

LONDON: MACMILLAN AND CO., LTD.

APPLIED MECHANICS

Elementary Applied Mechanics. By T. Alexander, M.A.I., and A. W. Thomson, D.Sc. Second edition. 8vo. 21s.

Experimental Mechanics. A Course of Lectures delivered at the Royal College of Science, Dublin. By Sir R. S. Ball, F.R.S. Second edition. Crown 8vo. 6s.

Applied Mechanics. An Elementary General Introduction to the Theory of Structure and Machines. By Professor J. H. Cotterill, F.R.S. Sixth edition. Revised and Enlarged. 8vo. 18s.

Lessons in Applied Mechanics. By Professor J. H. Cotterill, F.R.S., and J. H. Slade. Fcap. 8vo. Vol. I. containing Parts I. and III. 3s. Vol. II. containing Part II. 3s. Complete 5s. 6d.

Applied Mechanics for Beginners. By J. Duncan. Globe 8vo. 2s. 6d.

Treatise on Hydrostatics. By Sir A. G. Greenhill, F.R.S. Crown 8vo. 7s. 6d.

Elements of Graphic Statics. By L. M. Hoskins. 8vo. 10s. net.

The Mechanics of Machinery. By Sir A. W. B. Kennedy, F.R.S. Crown 8vo. 8s. 6d.

Steam, Gas, and Oil Engines. By Professor John Perry, F.R.S. New edition, with additions. 8vo. 7s. 6d. net.

Application of Dynamics to Physics and Chemistry. By Sir J. J. Thomson, F.R.S. Crown 8vo. 7s. 6d.

Graphical Methods in Applied Mathematics. By G. C. Turner, B.Sc. Crown 8vo. 6s.

LONDON: MACMILLAN AND CO., LTD.

Milton Keynes UK
Ingram Content Group UK Ltd.
UKHW040808120324
439192UK00005B/372